I'LL TELL YOU A STORY ...

PHILOSOPHY FOR CHILDREN

I'll Tell You A Story ...

Philosophy for Children

Vasyl Sukhomlynsky

Compiled by Olha Sukhomlynska

Translated by

Nataliya Bezsalova, Alan Cockerill and Berta Karaim

EJR Publishing

A catalogue record for this book is available
from the National Library of Australia

ISBN: 978-0-6455154-1-1 (hardback)

First published in 2024 by EJR Language Service Pty Ltd
Trading as EJR Publishing
9 Taralye Place, Chapel Hill, QLD 4069 Australia
https://www.ejr.com.au

Contents

Acknowledgements

The publication of this translation is the result of years of work involving many people, including the original compiler.

I would like to acknowledge the generous help and advice I have received from Sukhomlynsky's daughter, Professor Olha Sukhomlynska, who has supported my efforts to popularise her father's work over the past thirty years. This book is a translation of one of her publications: *Ya rozpovim vam kazku ... Filosofiia dlia ditei* [I'll tell you a story ... Philosophy for children]. It is she who conducted the labour of love that has brought all the stories in the book together, interspersed with Sukhomlynsky's reflections on values education.

I would especially like to thank my co-translators, Nataliya Bezsalova and Berta Karaim, each of whom approached me and selflessly offered to assist in bringing Sukhomlynsky's legacy to an English-speaking audience. I have relied on their knowledge of the Ukrainian language in preparing this work for publication.

Berta Karaim approached me in 2018. During that year she translated the reflections on values education that introduce each section of the book and also translated some of the stories.

Nataliya Bezsalova approached me at the beginning of 2021 and has translated a large proportion of the stories. She has also checked translations that I had made from Russian language versions of the stories, recommending modifications where required. Without her sustained help over the past four years the project would not have been completed.

Finally I would like to thank my wife Hiroko and son Christopher for their support and encouragement.

Alan Cockerill
Project Coordinator

From the translators

This book is a translation from Ukrainian of the 2016 publication *Ya rozpovim vam kazku … Filosofiia dlia ditei*[i] [I'll tell you a story … Philosophy for children], a collection of Vasyl Sukhomlynsky's stories for children and his reflections on values education, compiled by his daughter, Professor Olha Sukhomlynska. Three people have worked on the translation: Nataliya Bezsalova, Alan Cockerill and Berta Karaim.

Stories and fables have been used for millennia to illustrate ethical principles and to pass on wisdom. Stories are especially suited to teaching values to children, but adults also appreciate them. Stories engage us at an emotional level in a way that a purely intellectual explanation cannot.

The stories in this collection were written to support the values education program at a combined primary and secondary school in the village of Pavlysh, in central Ukraine, where Sukhomlynsky served as the principal from 1948 until his death in 1970. The stories also served as models for the children's own writing. The stories in this book are organised in sections, with each section having a theme and being introduced by reflections on values education relating to that theme. This is further explained in the introduction written by the compiler of the book, Olha Sukhomlynska. (See pp. xiii–xxiv.)

The inculcation of values was at the heart of Sukhomlynsky's holistic approach to education. He considered the development of humane qualities to be even more important than the development of intellectual or vocational skills. In one of the reflections in this book Sukhomlynsky writes:

> Children meet each other every day at school, in the corridors, in the classrooms. They look each other in the eye, share secrets, argue, enjoy each other's company, get upset, sometimes fight, nursing injuries great and small. Sometimes in our daily work we lose sight of the subtleties of these human relationships. Dear educators, do

---

i Sukhomlynsky, Vasyl. *Ya rozpovim vam kazku … Filosofiia dlia ditei* [I'll tell you a story … Philosophy for children]. Kharkiv: Shkola, 2016, compiled by Sukhomlynska, O.V.

> not forget that understanding these human relationships is your first responsibility. How each of your pupils views other human beings, what they discover in them, what they impart to others, and what remains in their hearts from others—this is a hundred times more important than whether or not they have completed today's homework.

Sukhomlynsky believed that whatever vocation his students chose, their happiness would be determined to a large extent by their ability to harness their energies to creative ends and develop positive relationships with others. He also considered the development of strong character to be an area in which anyone could excel, regardless of their physical, intellectual or artistic abilities. In the moral sphere there were limitless opportunities for every individual to shine.

The values education program at Pavlysh Secondary School involved informal discussions of ethical issues, the telling of stories to illustrate ethical principles, and many opportunities to put ethical principles into practice at home, at school, and in the community. Discussions and storytelling often took place outdoors in natural settings, and opportunities to put principles into practice often arose during extracurricular activities that were conducted in the afternoons after formal lessons. Readers who are interested will find detailed descriptions of Sukhomlynsky's approach to education in his books *My Heart I Give to Children* and *Our School in Pavlysh*, both of which have been translated into English.[ii]

There are over 800 little stories in this book, covering a broad range of themes and oriented towards varying ages, from preschoolers to young adults. The stories for very young children often feature animals, while those for senior students and adults may examine parenting issues and the development of positive relationships between teachers and students. [iii]

---

ii Sukhomlynsky, Vasyl, *My Heart I Give to Children*. Brisbane: EJR Language Service Pty. Ltd. 2016; Sukhomlynsky, Vasyl, *Our School in Pavlysh*. Brisbane: EJR Publishing, 2021.

iii See, for example, 'Who takes who home?' (p. 193), 'Mathematics is an interesting subject!' (p. 394).

The stories cover a wide range of themes that include developing an appreciation of beauty, the development of empathy and love for others, respect for elders, developing a sense of duty, the nature of maturity, the role of parents, the development of a conscience, self-discipline and the modification of desires, hard work, generosity, kindness and cruelty, curiosity and the quest for knowledge, the role of teachers, the development of talent, acceptance of diversity, the role of tact and good manners, and patriotism and self-sacrifice.

The compiler of the book, Professor Olha Sukhomlynska, suggests that it may be read by teachers, parents and children. Most of the stories are written for children, but the reflections that introduce each section of the book are primarily addressed to adults. Given the range of ages the stories are oriented to, from preschool to young adult, the prime function of the book is as a source of stories to be selected by adults to share with children according to their stage of development and the issues that are facing them.

The translators have supplied endnotes to explain the cultural context of some of the stories. Endnotes are denoted by an Arabic numeral, while footnotes (which appear only in the translator's and compiler's notes) are denoted by a Roman numeral.

Sukhomlynsky wrote his reflections and stories during the 1950s and 1960s, at a time when the Soviet Union was recovering from the devastation of World War II. Readers may not agree with all of the statements that Sukhomlynsky makes in his reflections and will find some of the stories more relevant than others.[iv] It is very likely though, that they will be stimulated to think deeply about their own values and attitudes and will find stories that move them and that they wish to share with the children in their lives.

---

iv Two wartime stories from the final section of the 2016 publication have been omitted. In other respects, this translation reflects the content of the original. Occasionally the title of a story has been modified, if a literal translation seemed awkward or obscure.

The hidden effect of Sukhomlynsky's stories

'They ask for more stories; they wait for them. When they are listening to the stories, their faces change, they become more relaxed, calm. It seems at that moment they forget where they are.' The captain sounded exhausted.

'And they forget for a moment that every minute could be their last,' quietly added my friend, who had been recording Sukhomlynsky's stories and sending them to the front line to provide moral support after the full-scale Russian invasion of Ukraine in 2022.

For four months these soldiers had been listening to the stories, and for four months the stories had brought them hope and joy. At the end of those four months, 92 out of a 100 were killed in a single battle ...

Vasyl Sukhomlynsky did not intend his stories for people on the battlefield. His primary audience was supposed to be educators and children, especially those who suffered from post-traumatic stress as a result of World War II. Their fathers, who returned from war, or their mothers, widows left without support, were full of grief and anxiety that was detrimental for the children's hearts and minds. The beauty, observed and described by Sukhomlynsky, together with the virtues that he discussed and demonstrated, were supposed to provide a healing effect. The stories achieved their goal. Unfortunately, eighty years later, these stories are again needed to soothe fear and alleviate tremendous stress, including that experienced by the soldiers. Who knows, maybe, after the war ends, Sukhomlynsky's stories will again help to heal the shattered hearts and souls of Ukrainians.

Dear reader, you can ask why am I providing this example, including some details that could be disturbing? The reason is to emphasize that in addition to helping people become better human beings, Sukhomlynsky's stories have a curative, healing effect for everyone. I can attest to this based on personal experience. I translated some of these stories when I was working full-time in an extremely demanding, fast-paced field. I felt absolutely exhausted returning home after work. Then, when I began working on the translations, my exhaustion would immediately leave me, and I would feel invigorated.

I can give another example of the impact of Sukhomlynsky's stories on peoples' lives. In the past, some of his stories were part of the school curriculum. Forty years later, I still vividly remember half of our class crying while reading the story 'Lily of the valley for Natalia'. (In this book it appears on page 460 as 'The lily of the valley by the window'.) Throughout my life I have remembered the stern voice of a mother in another story, telling her daughter, who showed no empathy for their elderly neighbour, 'The floor will be clean ... but what about your soul?' These recollections are carved in my memory and in the memories of many other people. The stories became beacons that showed us what is right and what is wrong.

Today, many parents are concerned about their children's upbringing. For many of them, the goal of raising thoughtful, compassionate children is paramount. Some of my friends were looking for good stories to read to their children, so I gave them some of Sukhomlynsky's stories. Their feedback was that it was exactly what they were looking for. Simple reading and discussion of the stories, combined with observation of the beauty of nature, would be one way to achieve the goal of raising a harmoniously developed and kind child. A compassionate child would never become a bully, would never deliberately harm others.

So, immerse yourself in these extraordinary stories, explore the didactic advice provided at the beginning of each chapter, and feel the beauty of the stories and their healing effect on many levels.

Nataliya Bezsalova

A reflection

Sukhomlynsky's work is an embodiment of the deep commitment to living well that has not only existed in Eastern Europe for generations, but largely transcends religious and other boundaries. The stories and the reflections in this book illustrate that while ideologies may come and go and metamorphose, there are principles of a life well-lived that have stood the test of time and have survived in spite of societal and political upheavals. It is an honour to have contributed to bringing these words of wisdom to readers who may otherwise not have had the opportunity to experience them.

Berta Karaim

From the compiler

> The eminent authority on educational science Vasyl Sukhomlynsky was also an author of wonderful stories for young children. His refined sensitivity to the poetry of childhood and deep understanding of a child's psychology combined to reveal a genuine literary talent. The educator and scholar became a fine children's author. And this was a natural result of the creative development of this gifted and sensitive soul.
>
> Vasyl Vitka, children's author

ABOUT THIS BOOK

Dear reader, this book is the fruit of the inspired work, reflection and convictions of Vasyl Oleksandrovych Sukhomlynsky, the Ukrainian educator, publicist and children's author, whose name is among the treasures of our Ukrainian cultural heritage and has become known in many countries of the world. All his life he worked in a village school, as a principal, a teacher and educator, living with his family on the school grounds, conducting lessons every day, frequently communicating with children outside lessons, during walks or while working together.

He explained his views on education[v] in many books, articles and essays. He built his system of education on a foundation of faith in the uniqueness of each child and love and respect for them, developing the creative abilities of each young person on the basis of ethical and aesthetic values, interests and needs, in a climate of friendship and cooperation between adults and children. His books enjoyed widespread popularity, including *Sertse viddaiu ditiam* [My Heart I Give to Children], *Narodzhennia gromadianyna* [The Birth of a Citizen], *Lysty do*

---

v Translator's note: The word education has been used here to translate two separate words: *osvita* (which refers to formal education and appears in expressions like 'Ministry of Education') and *vykhovannia* (which is often translated as 'upbringing' and encompasses the development of character and inculcation of values). Throughout the translation of this introduction, the word *vykhovannia* has been translated as 'education' rather than 'upbringing', but the reader should at all times understand education to involve the development of character and inculcation of values, and not just instruction in the school curriculum.

syna [Letters to My Son], *Sto porad uchytelevi* [100 Pieces of Advice for Teachers] and others. By the beginning of the 21st century, 65 of his educational works had been published in print runs totalling many millions, and translations had appeared in 59 languages.

Sukhomlynsky's books have a particular style of exposition—simple, natural, emotional—a conversational style. In his texts he includes many examples from his long years of work in the field. These include accounts of his students' lives, family histories, scenes from children's everyday lives and from school life in all its variety. Interspersed through the fabric of his works are stories, fairy tales, fables and legends—vignettes that he composed himself. These were most frequently encountered in *Yak vykhovaty spravzhniu liudynu* [How to Educate a True Human Being], first published in 1975, after the author's death. Subsequently this book was reprinted several times.

How to Educate a True Human Being contains advice for educators about the moral development of students and about educational ethics, a field in which Sukhomlynsky was the founding figure in the Soviet Union. The book consists of 59 discussions on moral themes that Sukhomlynsky considered it was necessary to discuss with children, in order to answer the questions that youngsters, adolescents and young men and women expected adults, and especially parents and teachers, to provide answers to, as they embarked upon the complex, contradictory, and beautiful process of life. These discussions examine the nature of beauty and how to preserve it; joy, grief, and human suffering; family relationships, love for parents, respect and understanding for grandparents; honour, having a conscience, modesty and selflessness; the significance of schools and teachers, books and knowledge; moral freedom and responsibility; love for one's native land. These discussions may rightfully be referred to as philosophy for children. They encompass a whole range of questions of 'good' and 'evil' in a way that is accessible for children, with digressions, stories and vignettes that serve as affirmations, convincing arguments and illustrations of various moral axioms, rules and laws.

To supplement this manual on moral education Sukhomlynsky created *Khrestomatiia z etyky* [An Ethics Anthology] which, on the one hand, could stand alone, and on the other hand, was an integral component of his holistic approach to the entire education process, and especially to moral education. He writes:

> In the educational work of our school over a period of many years we have developed a system of ethical discussions with our students, and an ethics anthology to be read by students of various ages at school and in their families. We have created a special ethics anthology containing two thousand stories and fairy tales of a didactic nature. They contain rich and diverse ethical content.[vi]

Sukhomlynsky himself composed around 1500 stories, fairy tales and novellas, and retold fables, legends and anecdotes for the anthology. If one considers the stories scattered throughout his educational works, there are even more, and nearly all of them should be considered part of his artistic output.

We can thus see that Sukhomlynsky himself saw his stories and fairy tales primarily as an artistic and illustrative component of values education. They were used extensively at Pavlysh Secondary School, where he worked. The anthology of stories and vignettes 'was divided into five sections (for preschool, for grades 1–2, 3–4, 5–7, 8–10). The content of the stories and fairy tales takes into account the age of the children, their perceptions of the world and their interests.' The miniature stories written by Sukhomlynsky served as models of how to support children's development so that they could reflect on their actions and behavior, exercise their imaginations, and compose their own stories and fairy tales. And the stories were also useful for teachers.

Sukhomlynsky referred to his system of values education as 'Conversations on moral and ethical themes' or 'Ethical conversations with students'. But if we consider the stories in the context of Sukhomlynsky's educational work as a whole, we can see that they extend far beyond ethical discussions and embrace the whole of a child's life and are aimed at the development by young people of a holistic perception of the world and emotional engagement with it.

Although Sukhomlynsky created his system of education many years

---

vi Sukhomlyns'kyi, V.O. *Problemy vikhovannia vsebichno rozvynenoi osobistosti. Vybrani tvory u 5 t.* [Issues in the Education of a Fully Developed Personality. Selected Works in 5 volumes], Radianska shkola, 1976, Vol. 1, p. 123.

ago, an approach like his is now in demand among educators. Over the past two decades, the idea of imparting knowledge with the aid of artistic illustration, followed by open discussion and dialogue, often involving spontaneous reflections of a subjective and evaluative nature, arising from children's state of mind, their view of the world, and their level of intellectual and language development, has spread around the world in the practice of teaching philosophy for children. N.S. Yulina, one of the popularisers of this approach in the post-Soviet space, describes this pedagogical approach as follows:

> As soon as a child begins to talk and to become aware of themselves and the world around them ... as if from the horn of plenty, questions rain down upon their parents: 'Why does tomorrow not come today? Where was I before mum and dad were born? Where did grandma go when she died? Why are people good and bad?' Such questions are essentially philosophical and metaphysical questions about the nature of time, existence, the relationship between people and nature, good and evil, and so on.[vii]

The questions listed here echo those posed and addressed by Sukhomlynsky.

Philosophy for children may thus be described as the posing of fundamental philosophical questions (both epistemological and ontological) by professional educators in fictional and informational texts, supplemented by appropriate educational and methodological literature developed by those educators. There are currently quite a few methods and technologies available in this field of education, notably those based on the ideas of the American philosopher and educator Matthew Lipman, who is considered the founder of philosophy for children.

Today, philosophy for children is a popular educational approach that involves schools and preschools, research scientists and teachers. It is aimed at the formation of reflective, creative and critical thinking, the conscious adoption of ethical norms and models of spiritual culture, the

vii Yulina, N.S. Filosofiia dlia detei [Philosophy for children]. *Voprosy filosofii* [Issues in philosophy]. 1993, No. 9, p. 151.

ability to listen sympathetically to others and communicate with them, and the development of oral language.

All of the above can be found in Sukhomlynsky's educational works. And one does not have to look very hard. The pages of his works are full of observations on these topics, especially those related to children's moral education.

In addition to developing values education at his school, Sukhomlynsky dreamed of publishing a book of his miniature stories and vignettes separately through a children's publishing house. He rightly believed that his children's stories had sufficient artistic and educational potential, characteristic of children's literature, to justify publication. The educator sent his stories to children's magazines. He selected several dozen stories and offered them to the 'Veselka' [Rainbow] children's publishing house. However, he received negative editorial reviews. He experienced setbacks but it was not in his nature to give up. Sukhomlynsky began sending his stories to educational magazines, and in 1969 the magazine *Doshkolnoe vospitanie* [Preschool Education] (Moscow) was the first publisher to accept them. The stories were published in four issues, presenting three or four in each issue. From early 1970, Sukhomlynsky's stories and fairy tales began to appear in the Belarusian children's magazine *Vyaselka* [Rainbow] (Minsk), translated from Ukrainian by Vasyl Vitka, who was a children's author, the editor-in-chief of the magazine, and a great admirer of Sukhomlynsky who valued his artistic creativity very highly from the outset. Sukhomlynsky had the satisfaction of seeing his stories published in this Belarusian journal several times. In his letters to the editor-in-chief, Sukhomlynsky wrote:

> I would be very grateful if you could add a note to tell your readers that these stories are from an 'Ethics Anthology' that the author is working on. I also request that these seven flowers not be torn apart. Let them be presented in a single bouquet. And if you would like to give them an overall title, it could be 'Blue cranes'.[viii]

Subsequently, Vasyl Vitka created a small book of stories and fairy

---

viii From a letter to Vasyl Vitka dated 16.10.1969. (From a personal archive.)

tales, and did indeed use the title *Blue Cranes*, but Sukhomlynsky did not live to see it, though he was very much looking forward to it. It was published in 1971.

As was the Soviet custom, recognition of Sukhomlynsky as a children's author and moralist came after his death. Moscow publishers were the first to pay attention to his stories and vignettes. In 1974, the 'Malysh' [Youngster] publishing house published the book *Poyushchee peryshko* [The singing feather], and in 1977, *Pust' budet i solovei i zhuk* [May there be both the nightingale and the beetle].

In Ukraine, the first collection of Sukhomlynsky's stories, *Hariacha kvitka* [The hot flower] was published in 1974 by the 'Veselka' publishing house. It included 107 stories and fairy tales. Everything happened just as Sukhomlynsky had sadly written in a letter to one of his Ukrainian correspondents:

> I would like my fairy tales and stories to be published in Ukrainian. It would be a sad state of affairs if they had to be translated from Ukrainian to Russian, and then from Russian to Ukrainian, in order to be published in Ukraine.[ix]

Over the years, Sukhomlynsky's stories occupied an increasingly prominent place in our children's literature, especially after Ukraine's declaration of independence. Collections of stories included *Kazky shkoly pid blakytnym nebom* [Tales from a school under the blue sky] (1991), *Chysta krynytsia* [The pure well] (1993), *Vichna topolia* [The Eternal Poplar] (2003), *Vognegryvyj konyk* [The horse with a fiery mane] (2008), *Kvitka sontsia* [The sunflower] (2009), and *Vsi dobri liudy—odna simia* [All good people are one family] (2014).

So, with the passage of time, Sukhomlynsky's dream of becoming a children's author was realised. The philosophical and cultural content of his miniature stories is of interest to today's readers. Collections of his fairy tales now occupy a prominent place in children's and school libraries, as well as in home libraries, where they are used by parents or read by the children themselves. Sukhomlynsky's stories are included

---

ix Zavoloka, S.P. (ed.) *Spohady pro Sukhomlynskoho* [Recollections of Sukhomlynsky]. Kyiv, 1990, p. 198.

in textbooks on Ukrainian children's literature that are used to prepare future preschool workers and teachers.[x] Sukhomlynsky's fairy tales and stories are also included in textbooks and reading books for students in grades one to four, for students in special schools, and in manuals on secular and Christian ethics.

And today, when there has been a particular growth of interest in moral and ethical issues among teachers and parents, and in society as a whole, it is time to implement Sukhomlynsky's idea of combining his manual on values education (*How to educate a true human being*) with its artistic and aesthetic companion (*An ethics anthology*), and to present it as a philosophy for children. This idea was partially realized 25 years ago. In 1989, the book *How to educate a true human being* was published in Moscow by the 'Pedagogika' publishing house, following the author's manuscript, which differs significantly from the edited and distorted text published in 1975. And in 1990, the same publishing house also published *An ethics anthology.* Both were intended for teachers, as practical guides offering advice to teachers on values education. Unfortunately, the publication of these books did not have a tangible educational effect, partly because they were published a year apart, and partly because one era was ending and another beginning, leading to the development of new projects of varying scale and significance.[xi]

As the compiler of these two books, as a daughter who grew up under the influence of my father's artistic vision of the world, and as one of the first readers of Sukhomlynsky's fiction—he instructed me to sort out typed copies of his tales and was interested in my impressions—for a long time I dreamed of the successful implementation of this project.

The prospect of realising this dream began to materialise when the 'Shkola' publishing house in Kharkiv, which specializes in children's books and educational and methodological literature, and had recently

---

x See, for example, *Ridne slovo: Ukrainska dytiacha literatura. Khrestomatiia: u 2 kn.* [Our native language: Ukrainian children's literature. An anthology in 2 volumes]. Kyiv, 1999. Vol. 2, pp. 387-396.

xi Translator's note: Professor Sukhomlynska is referring here to the dissolution of the Soviet Union in December of 1991, and the gaining of independence by Ukraine. This led to conscious attempts by Ukrainians to cut ties with their Soviet past and to emphasise their Ukrainian cultural identity.

published two collections of Sukhomlynsky's stories (*The sunflower* and *All good people are one family*) expressed an interest in treating readers to a collection of Sukhomlynsky's stories in a book for parents and teachers. The publishing house supported the idea of combining two earlier books: *How to educate a true human being* and *An ethics anthology*. This new edition provides a fresh view of the material, which may already be familiar to readers, but now needs to be read anew.

So now, as a result of extensive textual work and a balanced and methodically measured approach, a new book, *Ya rozpovim vam kazku … Filosofiia dlia ditei* [I'll tell you a story ... Philosophy for children], has emerged, which combines the two earlier works into one, and incorporates Sukhomlynsky's reflections on values education, together with an actual demonstration of the values through stories.

This new approach provides teachers and parents with a tool that, in an accessible form, explains moral issues that arise (or will eventually arise) in children's lives. These issues are perennial, eternal, confronting every generation of teachers and parents, who strive to educate a good person and ensure that, in Sukhomlynsky's words, 'each one shines like a star' and each child becomes 'a true human being, not a human-like animal, whose behaviour is governed by the blind forces of instinct.'[xii] Every teacher and every parent consciously or unconsciously tries to find the right words, reasoning and images to reach a child's heart. And they can find them in this book.

Sukhomlynsky addresses teachers, parents and children in simple and comprehensible, and at the same time figurative and symbolic language. His writing reflects his deep erudition, his knowledge of the traditions and culture of the Ukrainian people, of everyday school life, and of child psychology. The author is distinguished by his keen observation of nature and of the entire world surrounding the child. Sukhomlynsky's artistic world is amazingly fluid, expressive, and at the same time laconic.

The author populates his fairy tales, stories, parables, and anecdotes with characters and events that are easily understood by a child and accommodated by a child's perception of the world. A story often

xii Sukhomlynsky, V. *Narozhdennia gromadianyna* [The birth of a citizen], p. 73.

presents a situation in which a moral choice must be made between good and evil, responsibility and irresponsibility, compassion and indifference, tenderness and rudeness, respect and contempt. Sukhomlynsky merely poses the question. The purely didactic nature of some works is softened by the lyrical intonation and poetic description. Quite often, Sukhomlynsky leaves the reader in a situation of moral choice, which the child must resolve independently.

From an educational point of view, each story may present several educational opportunities that the teacher must unpack creatively in each specific situation, taking into account the moral and emotional development of the children and their level of awareness.

This book is intended for both adults (teachers and parents) and children, because it is primarily addressed to a child's soul, mind and emotions. The structure of the book was influenced by the central ideas of philosophy for children and, most importantly, by Sukhomlynsky's creative legacy. His stories provide the foundation and are the dominant feature of the book. They are arranged in sections by topic. The first section introduces the reader to Sukhomlynsky's thoughts about the formation of a child's ethical worldview and does not contain any artistic or illustrative material. Sukhomlynsky's thoughts on the role of a school, the importance of language in education, the importance of moral education and, most importantly, about the role of fairy tales in a child's development, are included here. The statement about the role and significance of fairy tales, unlike the remainder of the book, is taken from Sukhomlynsky's books *My heart I give to children* and *Metodyka vykhovannia kolektyvu* [A methodology for educating a collective]. It is in these two books that we found the most vivid, figurative, aphoristic statements about the importance of fairy tales in children's education.

Each of the subsequent sections has a governing theme, presented in a heading taken from the manual *How to educate a true human being*. The headings of the sections include: 'Beauty is the joy of our life', 'The child in the world and the world in the child', 'Parents and children: The harmony of love and will', and so on.

The stories in each section are preceded by Sukhomlynsky's thoughts, reflections, and methodical advice in the form of individual thoughts or quotations relating to the questions and issues that are addressed in the stories and fairy tales. These fragments are not always arranged in the sequence in which they appear in the book *How to educate a true human being* but are focused on the themes of the stories in that section. The compiler has arranged Sukhomlynsky's reflections in such a way as to introduce the stories through the prism his thoughts. The thematic fragmentation of Sukhomlynsky's reflections and advice is compensated for by their educational refinement and their frequently aphoristic quality.

In each section, several leading themes are highlighted as subtopics with their own content. These are presented with varying degrees of detail, depending on the completeness of Sukhomlynsky's understanding of the topic, as well as the extent to which that topic is reflected in the stories. These subtopics, as a rule, begin with the preposition 'On' (e.g. 'On Curiosity', 'On levels of expectation').

Sukhomlynsky's reflections sometimes refer the reader to this or that story, fairy tale, or anecdote, located in that section. As for the titles of the individual fairy tales and stories, over the years of their repeated publication in children's and educational literature, many of them changed their original title and acquired more expressive, attractive ones, at the instigation of the publishers (compilers, editors, translators). And so it happens that the same story may exist under different names, in various translations and under various editors. The current edition is fully based on the author's reading, according to the preserved author's texts.

Sukhomlynsky's statements about morals and morality, together with with his stories, presuppose the existence of communication, dialogue, and involvement in a child's spiritual world. Their aim is not to artificially accelerate a child's intellectual development, nor to fill a child's head with dubious abstractions and competences, but to contribute to the imaginative, holistic, emotional and sensual enrichment of a child's spiritual world through the joint efforts of adults and children, in a patient and balanced way.

The selection of stories, and their arrangement in sections, should not limit the creativity of an adult using them. Each story can be read in its own way, and each reader can interpret them in their own way, finding things to delight or concern them.

The logic governing the arrangement of the book's sections is based on the logic of a child's education and development, from growing awareness of one's place in the world, to enchantment with its beauty, from the parental and family circle and the laws and rules prevailing in a child's environment, to self-knowledge and the development of character and an expanding worldview, to seeing schools as cradles of the nation and wellsprings of living thought, and finally to the highest manifestation of morality, to patriotism. Some sections end with unfinished stories or fairy tales, which Sukhomlynsky has left for the reader or listener to complete. There are not many of them, and they are marked with an asterisk "*".

It should be noted that the content of some stories reflects features of everyday life typical of the time when Sukhomlynsky lived and worked. Teachers and parents should prepare children in advance for the reception of such texts.

I would like to make special mention of those stories in which Sukhomlynsky touches upon the issues of human birth and especially death. These are special areas of moral education, which, as Sukhomlynsky himself noted, should be approached with caution. Not constrained by generally accepted stereotypes, and departing from the narrowness of Soviet educational thinking, Sukhomlynsky tried to understand the innermost, secret corners of a child's inner world. He considered the issues of life and death to be important moral issues, because they concern everyone: children, teenagers, young men and women. But they are largely ignored by educational science, an almost unexplored field of education, and Sukhomlynsky himself only touched on them. Therefore, conversations and stories about them require thoughtful and careful handling of the material and should be based on a sympathetic understanding of a child's state of mind, their character and their emotional development. Teachers and parents who do not feel inclined to reflect on these issues should simply bypass them in the process of their work.

Sukhomlynsky himself liked to conduct conversations on moral issues and to tell and compose fairy tales and stories in natural settings, as exemplified in his 'Lessons of thought in nature', his 'Journeys around the globe', his 'Fairy Tale Room', his 'Island of Wonders', and his 'Nook of Dreams', and he referred to such informal communication with children as the 'School of Joy' or the 'School under the blue sky'.

We may not be able to recreate the romantic settings that Sukhomlynsky created for his students, but we can always foster open communication with children in an atmosphere of attention, kindness, respect and love. As adults, and as children and grandchildren, let us enter the magical world that Vasyl Sukhomlynsky reveals to us.

Olha Sukhomlynska

On the significance of schooling

A school does not only teach how to read, write, think, and get to know the surrounding world and the riches of science and art. **In school we learn how to live.** A school is the spiritual cradle of a nation. Without schools a nation has no future. The more wisdom there is, the brighter is a nation's future. School students are not just children gathered in one place. They constitute a society of children, living according to their own harmonious laws, in a way that develops humanity and makes it wiser, and at the same time enhances adult society and is a source of pride. The laws by which a school lives are an expression of a nation's ethos, of a nation's life. The centuries old culture of a nation lives in a school. You are not just a traveller, come to drink at that wellspring; you are a bee, enriching the hive of national culture. Your duty is to make a contribution to the hive, to enrich the spiritual heritage of your nation.

The *attitude towards itself* that a school is able to inspire determines its influence on the sensitive, impressionable younger generation, and on the fate of the nation. A school is the cradle of a nation in the sense that it is the main sculptor of a nation's soul. A school leaves an indelible impression on the cultural predispositions of its former students. A school worthy of the name takes pride in the fact that adults are proud to call themselves its students.

I consider it to be exceptionally important to educate amongst our youth a view of school as the most important cradle of the spiritual life of a nation. A school must preserve the spiritual values of a nation, both human values and values that transcend the human. As soon as a school is built, and the first student crosses its threshold, as soon as the heart and mind of a teacher makes subtle contact with the heart and mind of a student (and that is the point at which a school really begins), from that moment an eternal book takes its place in the school library. I am not referring to an ordinary library that lends books for reading. I mean the school library in the sense of a depository of the spiritual life of a nation. The school will live for three hundred, five hundred or a thousand years, and that book should live on through all those years. The foundation stone, the bricks and mortar, may have turned to dust in a thousand years, but that book must never turn to dust. The school as the cradle of a nation, as the cradle of a nation's spiritual life, lives first and foremost in that book. How important it is that this is understood not only by the teachers, but by the school's students. Every school should have its own unique face, its own customs, traditions and anniversaries.

On the significance of words

I believe in the limitless power of an educator's words. Words are the most subtle and at the same time the sharpest instrument that we as teachers can use to touch the hearts of our pupils. Educating through our words is the most complex and difficult part of pedagogy and of school life. It is completely absurd to say that verbal education is a vice that afflicts many of our schools. What we should be talking about is the primitive nature of verbal education, about the inability of some teachers to educate through their words.

I consider a teacher's words to be a most essential and most subtle form of contact between a person who is convinced of the value of their own philosophy of life, and the heart of a young person *thirsting to be good*. Note that we are speaking of contact between conviction and a *thirst to be good*, to be better today than we were yesterday. Only when these two things meet does true education take place. Consequently, education through words is only possible when you are dealing with an *educable* person. The creation of human *educability* is the foundation of ethical education.

The things that make a child educable are joy, happiness and an optimistic outlook. A truly humane pedagogy protects the joy and happiness that is every child's right. An incident from my own practice is described in the story 'Blue cranes' (p. 467).

There are some children's questions that are painful to hear, and terribly difficult to answer. Education does not have such magical power that it can make a person happy independently of their circumstances, but education is obliged to protect children's incomparable spiritual inheritance, the joy and happiness that reside within their little hearts. And if a child's soul does encounter grief, we must remember that we are dealing with a person who needs peace of mind, who needs to have their suffering, confusion and disappointment lifted, and then to be given joy, the joy without which a crane will never appear blue. If your child sees the world with optimism, if they perceive the beauty and fragility in everything that surrounds them, they will be easier to educate. They will listen eagerly to your every word.

Beauty makes a person educable, more precisely, a spiritual life in the world of the beautiful. My ideal is that literally every child should perceive beauty, stand before it in wonder, and make the beautiful a part of their spiritual life, feeling the beauty of words and images. The world of beauty that surrounds us is inexhaustible and limitless. Find a way to reveal this world in such a way that words resonate in a child's soul like music, so that the quest to find the right word brings incomparable joy to a child. Once the music of words begins to resonate in a child's soul, they will become receptive to your educational influence. Your words, your ethical guidance, will reach the hidden recesses of their soul and awaken a desire to be good.

Human actions may take the form of words or even just a glance. Words are a delicate way to touch someone's heart. They can be like a tender kiss, like the scent of a flower, like refreshing water, restoring faith in goodness; or they may be like a sharp knife, stabbing the sensitive fabric of the soul, like a bucket of cold water, or like lumps of sticky mud. Human words can be all of these things. Words can turn out to be actions in unanticipated ways, even when they are absent and take the form of silence.

Every word spoken within a school's walls must be premeditated, wise, purposeful, sound, and, most importantly, addressed to the conscience of the living, concrete person with whom we are dealing. Everything in a school should be planned and carried out in such a way that words are not devalued, that there is no verbal inflation, but on the contrary, the value of words constantly increases. Childish things should not be given pompous names, as if often the case, giving rise to a frivolous attitude to words and to empty words. (For example, a children's after school group is for some reason given the name 'Little Academy of Sciences'; or an adult literacy class is set up, with great difficulty, and called a 'university'.) We should not pressure children to make loud promises that are in essence impossible to keep. (e.g. 'We will study so well that all our marks are either 'excellent' or 'good'!) We should not praise children for work in which they have invested no serious effort. If someone tries to avoid serious effort by making an empty promise, I advise the group, and the person who has opened their mouth, not to promise anything yet. Let us first reflect on it. The main thing is that we must *learn to make an effort.*

An educator's ethical guidance will only be accepted if they have the moral authority to guide. You do not have to be an angel to have the moral right to educate a true human being, but you do need to be genuine, to live a good life, to love people, to guard your integrity as a patriot, a citizen, and a toiler. If your words of ethical guidance resonate with your inner spiritual world and are inspired by your convictions, they will act like a magnet, attracting those who have begun to lose faith in humanity, and you will be a support to them, and a light showing the way.

On Moral Education

A person's moral character depends to a great extent on what brings them joy and happiness in childhood. If we were to try and express the essence of education in an aphorism, it would not be a distortion of the truth to say that the virtues and vices that take root in the soul of *a child who is being educated* are *fed* by joys and sorrows, happiness and misfortune, disappointments and delights, depression and inspiration.[1] I have deliberately juxtaposed and italicised the words 'a child who is being educated' [*pitomets* in the original Russian text] and 'fed' [*pitayutsya* in the original]. The wise word *pitomets* [a child who is being educated] is linked by many threads to the word *pitat'* [to feed or nourish]. Children are nourished not only by their mothers' milk and their daily bread, but by food for the spirit. To learn to nourish children with joys and sorrows—that is the art of education. A person's nobility of spirit depends ultimately on what elicited delight or tears in childhood. Generosity and unselfishness are totally dependent on the nobility of our sources of delight and disappointment, joys and sorrows. I am not exaggerating in the slightest when I assure my dearest readers—young teachers—that the joy that comes from generosity is the noblest of spiritual impulses, capable of awakening in young hearts feelings of wonder at human refinement, and pride from a consciousness of their own participation in that refinement.

A characteristic of the art of education is that the whole process involves an intervention in the life of the human spirit—in all that is so complex and at times hard to capture in the way a person expresses themselves. I am firmly convinced that all the actions and deeds that we motivate our students to undertake should be part of the life of the human spirit. Only then will our everyday lives and relationships constitute an education, without the need for any specially invented forms of activity. If I give a spade to a child and ask them to plant a tree, that means that the future work that forms the essence of my intention, the tree itself, the earth and water that will feed its life—all of these things will express spiritual impulses and relationships. One of the most unacceptable failings in education is the fact that children's work—sometimes very significant work—appears to be divorced from the life of the spirit, does not inspire children or develop conviction, does not awaken thought, feelings or the exercise of the will.

In order to see themselves as others see them, little people must learn to see life. They must learn to see another person, to understand and feel the beauty in them, to be inspired with feelings of admiration, to compare themselves with what they have seen and understood, and to measure their own worth against those whom they consider to be models. I consider it very important to tell adolescents and young men and women about how others have lived their lives, about what they have achieved, and how they have fulfilled their duty to future generations, who in their turn will accept the baton from them, continuing their creativity and constructive efforts. I have tried to do this in the story 'The happiest person in the world' (p. 544).

Children meet each other every day at school, in the corridors, in the classrooms. They look each other in the eye, share secrets, argue, enjoy each other's company, get upset, and sometimes fight, nursing injuries great and small. Sometimes in our daily work we lose sight of the subtleties of these human relationships. Dear educators, do not forget that understanding these human relationships is your first responsibility. How each of your pupils *views* other human beings, what they discover in them, what they impart to others, and what remains in their hearts from others—this is a hundred times more important than whether or not they have completed today's homework. In essence, education is a lengthy process, taking many years, that prepares young people to realise the essential truth that human beings are of supreme value. This is a realisation not as a consumer, not in a selfish sense, but in an altruistic sense, with a concern for others. One of the most subtle aspects of educational skill is the ability to foster in our pupils a need to relate to other human beings in this way.

In this connection we need to reflect on one very important aspect of the extremely complex process of education. In education two things are in sharp contrast: affirmation and negation. We are always trying to affirm something or to negate, to overcome something. The wisdom of our educational approach depends on the interrelationship between these two things. When affirmation predominates, creative work and mutual trust reign. Teachers and parents breathe easily, and the children being educated obey their educators. When our relationships with children consist mostly of negation, as we strive to overcome their vices, school life becomes a burden, and it is unbearably hard for teachers and parents.

Less flowery talk about love for humanity in general, and more concrete deeds and heartfelt participation in life, in the creation of joy—this should be the rule in moral education. It is very dangerous when good deeds are done for show, when a child helps a friend in order to win approval and praise.

The ideal of education is when the gift of our inner resources to others remains in our hearts as something precious and untouchable. The need to relate to others is one of the most private of feelings. Leo Tolstoy considered even feelings of patriotism to be of this nature.

In childhood an exceptionally important role is played by self-education, self-discovery, the development of resilience, of an ability to make demands of oneself and exercise self-control. The spirit and psyche are inseparable from the body, and strength of spirit is manifested in an ability to harness our physical energy, in an ability to combine physical resilience with sensitive and tender feelings. I have always been astonished that children's physical education, in both theory and practice, is divorced from the spiritual and psychological development of the personality. This separation is unacceptable. Physical effort must always incorporate the spiritual and psychological realm and awaken a person's awareness of their strength of spirit. Only then will people acquire the ability to educate themselves.

I would like to emphasise once again the importance of developing spiritual and psychological resilience in the early years. If you miss the early years, you miss everything. It is completely unacceptable to encourage grade one students to think that they are still little, that they are not yet strong enough and things are too hard for them. Children do not want to think and feel that they are weak, defenceless and small. That they are small and need to be defended by you, that they must be protected from misfortune and danger, should be thought but not expressed. In children's hearts and minds you should implant the thought: 'I am strong and courageous. I do not need defending. I should defend others. The world is full of creatures who are much weaker than me, and I should defend them.'

Fairy tales in the life of a child

Childhood is an important stage in life, not a preparation for a future life but a genuine, bright, unique, unrepeatable stage in life. And how that childhood is spent, who leads children by the hand during their early years, what enters their hearts and minds from the surrounding world, determines what sort of people today's infants will become. During the preschool and early school years, a person's character, way of thinking, and speech are formed. Perhaps everything that enters the minds and hearts of children from a book, from a textbook or a lesson, only enters because alongside the book is the surrounding world: nature, fields and meadows, the blue sky and the misty haze on the horizon, the song of the lark and rustling at night, the howling of a cold winter wind and the strange ice patterns on the window panes, the opening petals of a snowdrop and the scent of new leaf awakening; and because little children observe good and evil in the world that surrounds them. It is in this real world that they take their first difficult steps on the long road from birth to the day when they can open a book and read it independently.

Why do fairy tales develop speech and thought more powerfully than any other means? It is because the images in fairy tales are so laden with emotional colouring. The words from a fairy tale live in a child's consciousness. Children's hearts miss a beat when they hear or pronounce words that create a world of fantasy. I cannot imagine school instruction that does not include making up and listening to fairy tales.

There was once an incident at our school. A teacher took the first graders to the forest. The children sat on the grass. The trees in the forest rustled quietly in the wind and somewhere a wild pigeon sang, 'Coo … coo … ' They could clearly hear the sound of running water in a brook nearby.

The teacher opened a book and read a fairy tale. The fairy tale told that in a land far, far away, on a very high mountain, beneath a blue stone, a Little White Cloud was born, tiny and delicate, like a baby bird. In the morning, a light breeze began to blow, touching the wings of the Little White Cloud, and it flew off into the sky …

The children sat completely still, listening with bated breath; the sparks of a daydream could be seen in the children's eyes. Once he finished reading, the teacher spoke:

'This is a fairy tale. In reality, nothing like this could happen. A cloud is not a bird—it does not have wings. The wind cannot caress a cloud, as the fairy tale suggested. A cloud is made of drops of water. Like the morning mist—you know? Grey, unpleasant … '

The light in the children's eyes was extinguished.

My little daughter Olia came home crying.

'Why are you crying, Olia? Has someone hurt you?'

Olia explained her misfortune. How joyful it was to believe that a little cloud is a fairytale bird with tiny wings, but it turned out that there was no mountain, no magical blue stone, no wings, no loving wind, only cold grey fog.

'I want the Little Cloud to have wings', said Olia quietly. Then I understood what the matter was. I told Olia my own fairy tale about the faraway mountain, the magical blue stone, and a girl named Olia.

'Is it true?' asked Olia with a mixture of joy and anxiety.

'Yes, it is true, Olia … '

Joy bloomed in the child's eyes like a wildflower.

I bring up this incident because it illustrates the subtle influence we can have on a group of children. We live in the age of knowledge. Every object, every phenomenon has an origin and a cause. Everything is becoming understandable, knowable, subject to natural laws. But we must not forget that alongside the unbreakable natural laws of the surrounding world there exists the world of childhood. Children discover the world and their peers, their teachers and their parents, in their own way. Their thoughts are directed to the world of reality on the wings of a fairy tale. And so, when a white cloud becomes just a cluster of grey drops of moisture, the world of childhood is dimmed, and a child's thinking is crippled. When we impoverish the world of childhood, we close children's eyes to people, making their entry into society more difficult.

As soon as children cross the school threshold, they are drawn towards school and their peers, because they want to collectively experience the incomparable emotions that a fairy tale evokes. They are drawn towards their teachers because it from them that they hear fairy tales, listening with bated breath. Teachers are remembered for the rest of a child's life when they enter the child's life spiritual life primarily as storytellers. Heartfelt memories of their class take root in children's emotional memories when they gather in the classroom on a quiet evening, sitting close to each other, listening to a fairy tale, while outside the window the winter dusk descends, or a quiet summer night reigns.

Fairy tales, games, imagination—these are life-giving wellsprings of children's thinking, of noble feelings and emotions. … Language, with all its subtle nuances, enters a child's consciousness through fairytale imagery, becoming a part of a child's spiritual life and a way of expressing their thoughts and feelings. Without fairy tales—tales that are bright and alive, tales that capture a child's thoughts and feelings—it is impossible to imagine children's thinking and children's speech as the first step in developing human thinking and speech.

Fairy tales are inseparable from beauty, and foster the development of aesthetic sensibilities, without which, in turn, nobility of soul, as well as empathy, are impossible. Through fairy tales, children discover the world not only with their reason, but also with their hearts. And not only discover, but also respond to the events and phenomena of the surrounding world, developing their own notions of good and evil. From fairy tales children develop their first conceptions of justice and injustice.

Dear friend and educator! Do not deprive children of seeing the world reflected in the magical mirror of fairy tales. If you wish your students to become rational, curious and intelligent, if your aim is to educate them to be sensitive to the subtlest variations in other people's thoughts and emotions—educate, awaken and inspire their minds with the beauty of words and thoughts, the beauty of their native language, whose magical power is revealed first and foremost in fairy tales. Fairy tales are the cradle of thought. Structure children's education in such a way that they treasure heartfelt memories of this cradle for the rest of their lives. The beauty of our native language, with its emotional colouring and shades of meaning, reaches children, exciting them, giving rise to a sense of their own worth, when one heart connects with another, when one mind connects with another. The poetic sounds of our native language become music to a child when children take the instrument into their own hands, create music themselves, and see and feel how their music influences other people. Underneath a guelder rose[2] we told the same tale hundreds of times, just to feel the magic of the words *gusy-lebedi* [geese and swans], *lis-pralis* [the forest, the primordial forest], *zoria-zorianytsia* [a star, the morning star].[3] As a singer longs to test his strength with a new song, we longed to sing these words.

Learn to expose children to some single phenomenon in the natural world, but in such a way that this little part of the world comes to life with all the colours of the rainbow. Always leave something unsaid, so that children want to return again and again to what they have learnt.

Whenever I am asked how I compose fairy tales with children, I am reminded of my Grandma Mariia. When I think of my childhood, I see her black eyes and feel the magic of her fairy tales. At the time, it appeared to me that Grandma was witnessing the fairy tale unfold: her gaze was directed into the faraway steppe or the dense leaves of the orchard, into the evening twilight or a white blizzard. I used to dream that one day I would finally catch a glimpse of that place where Grandma watched the tale unfold and would learn myself to see things that were miraculous, fairytale, extraordinary.

Fairy tales are the gracious well from which love for one's homeland, which cannot be replaced by anything else, can be nurtured. The patriotic ideas in a fairy tale are found in the depth of its content. The fairytale images created by our people, images that have lived for thousands of years, convey to a child's heart and mind the industrious spirit of our working nation, our nation's world view, ideals and dreams. Fairy tales nurture love for our homeland for the simple reason that they are a creation of the people. Fairy tales seem to be constructed around 'everyday' scenarios: Grandpa and Grandma planted a beetroot, or Grandpa decided to fool the wolf by making a straw calf. But every word in these fairy tales is like a fine stroke on an immortal mural. In every word, in every image, the creative power of the national spirit is at play. Fairy tales are a spiritual treasure of our national culture and, in discovering them, children sense in their hearts the life of the nation.

It is a warm summer evening. The first star appears in the blue sky. Today the children are coming to see me: pre-schoolers, first-graders and second-graders. We sit beneath a hundred-year-old oak tree. The village falls silent. The steppe begins to slumber. Mysterious sounds drift to us from the orchard. The lake is asleep. The whole world around us is sleeping, except for a star shining in the sky and a cricket chirping in the field.

This is our School Beneath the Blue Sky. Children enter a fairytale world. On these beautiful summer evenings, we become poets—we compose fairy tales. Everything that we see appears to us in these magical hours as if part of a fairy tale. Our School Beneath the Blue Sky is a wellspring of living thought and speech, to which I lead the children each day, so that they can become people with big hearts, and intelligent, compassionate, and wise thinkers.

For thirty-five years I have touched their hearts with words. Decades of work—not easy, but joyful—have convinced me that fairy tales and art are the most sensitive and the gentlest way of connecting with a child. Fairy tales are the childhood of thought. They make the world of childhood bright and interesting.

We wrote thousands of tales. Who is the author? That magical Ukrainian night, several generations of little children and I: we were all creators of those tales of the School Beneath the Blue Sky.

I tell you tales. They are created spontaneously. Every one of us—the children and I—becomes a poet in these magical hours. If I cannot find the sparkling word I need, the children help me. We have composed thousands of fairy tales. Our creativity is not something unique or extraordinary. It is accessible to every teacher and every student, because all children are poets if their teacher will but lead them into the world of creativity.

BEAUTY IS THE JOY OF OUR LIFE

On developing a sense of beauty

Beauty is the joy of our life. People became human because they saw the depth of the blue sky, the twinkling of the stars, the rosy glow of sunset, the transparent haze of the vast steppe, the crimson sunrise before a windy day, the shimmering of a mirage on the horizon, the blue shadows on March snowdrifts, a flock of cranes in the blue sky, the reflection of the sun's rays in myriad drops of morning dew, the grey threads of rain on an overcast day, the purple cloud on a lilac bush, the tender stalk and the blue bell of a squill.[4] They saw all this and, in awe, went forth into the world, creating new beauty. The joy of life revealed itself to humanity because people heard the whisper of leaves and the song of a grasshopper, the babbling of a spring stream, the modulating silver bells of a lark's song in the scorching summer sky, the whispering fall of snowflakes and the moaning of a blizzard, the gentle lapping of waves and the majestic silence of night. Humanity heard all these things and, with bated breath, has been listening to the wonderful music of life for hundreds and thousands of years.

We repeat these words in those happy moments when children discover some new facet of beauty in the surrounding world, awakening emotions of joy, excitement and wonder. We speak of the silver bells of a lark's song on a hot summer day, when, after a day's work or after a hike, children rest in the shade of an oak grove and gaze upon that quivering little ball of life … Words about the beautiful only reach the ears of children when they themselves can feel beauty. Seeing and hearing, feeling with the heart what has been perceived—these are the first windows into the world of beauty.

To ensure that young people, during their childhood years, come to treasure beauty in all of its forms, that they are inspired by the beautiful, that they strive to create, to preserve, and to affirm the beauty around them and within them, is a very subtle and complex educational objective.

I have a number of stories intended to teach children to be inspired. I consider the story 'Beauty, Inspiration, Joy and the Mystery' (p. 16) to be of great educational significance.

I strive to ensure that each and every one of the children in my care will, by the time they reach the transition from childhood to adolescence, be enthralled by the thought of the eternal nature of beauty and of the beauty of a life filled with work, creating and caring for the beautiful.

I lead the children in my care to sources of beauty a thousand times during the years when they are studying in primary school. These are lessons in experiencing a vision of the beautiful. The children learn to see, to admire, and to listen to the music of the world around them, and thus to understand it.

Beauty refines us

Beauty is one of the streams that feeds kindness, warmth and love. The wonder we feel when we see a dog-rose bush, blazing with red berries and orange leaves; a little maple tree, or a shapely apple tree, on which only a few yellow leaves linger; a tomato bush, burnt by the breath of the first night frost: all these things awaken in children's hearts a tender, benevolent and caring attitude towards the living and the beautiful. A child feels sympathy for plants that are preparing for the winter. For children, plants are living creatures who will feel the cold of the penetrating winds. Children want to protect plants from the cold. When we cover roses and grape vines for the winter, the children carefully, tenderly bend each little branch to the earth, trying not to break or damage them. In winter the children talk anxiously about young trees, wondering if they feel the cold. And when we collect snow to supply more moisture to the trees, the children see this work as an expression of their heartfelt concern for beauty, and not just as a fulfilment of an obligation.

I see great educational significance in a child witnessing, understanding, feeling, experiencing, and ultimately realising the great mystery that is the *awakening of life* in nature. The first spring blooms and opening buds, the first tender blades of grass, the first butterfly, the first croak of a frog, the first swallow, the first thunder, the first trill of a sparrow: all these things I show to children as expressions of the beauty of eternal life. And the more deeply they are inspired by this beauty, the more strenuously they strive to create beauty. For the children, a blossoming orchard is a real occasion for celebration. Early in the morning the children come to the orchard and admire the waves of white, pink, violet and orange blossoms, which appear to float over the orchard, and listen to the chorus of the bees. You must not sleep in on these days, I teach the children; you must get up at dawn, or you will sleep through this beauty! And the children get up before sunrise, so as not to miss those magic moments when the first rays of the sun light up the flowers, laden with dew. They witness an amazing display of many shades of colour, and if children admire this beauty with bated breath, they will never become insensitive, indifferent, heartless people. The spiritual wealth that is acquired through the contemplation of beauty is developed and further enriched in work aimed at creating joy for others.

People pass through a lengthy school of refining their feelings, before ascending to such a lofty and selfless perception of beauty. This school begins with contemplation of the beauty in nature, with the ability to see and hear beauty. It includes wise lessons in understanding human loyalty, devotion, affection, duty and responsibility. It is not possible to be selflessly in love with beauty if one has never suffered, if one has failed to comprehend the beauty of a mother's soul, as she silently bends over her son's grave.

Teach how to perceive beauty

I consider it very important to teach little children to see beauty and at the same time to think of the beauty of human refinement. Thought, understanding and reflection play an exceptionally important role in refining feelings. The children and I walk to greet the dawn on the bank of a lake, and there I tell them the story of 'The ox and the chickadee' (p. 33).

I have a whole collection of stories about beauty for little children. The most important thing in these stories is to stimulate reflection on beauty, and to establish attitudes and convictions about the beauty of nature, and of human beings and their actions. The story 'The ox and the chickadee' makes children reflect on the fact that beauty is only revealed to the wise and the thoughtful.

We also have a story about the first dandelion. It tells about how, amid some green grass, there burst forth a dandelion, as bright as the sun. All the green blades of grass turned towards it. What was it? Where did such amazing beauty come from? The dandelion became vain and thought, 'I am the most beautiful. I am the only one like me in the world.' But then tens and hundreds of other bright little suns burst forth, and everyone forgot about the first dandelion. The blades of grass now admired the flowers that were closest to them. Listening to this story and inwardly experiencing it, the children reflect that true beauty is inseparable from modesty and dignity.

When dealing with children's concepts of beauty, one must be very thoughtful and careful. There is possibly no other occasion when superficiality can do as much harm as when discussing beauty. A careless word can do great harm.

Beauty opens our eyes to the world. Over the passage of time, the evil, the ugly and the nondescript gradually become intolerable in the light of beauty. One of the laws of education is that evil and ugliness should gradually be displaced by beauty. If you place a beautiful sprig of flowering willow on a table in the middle of the classroom, children will notice the spider's web in the corner. If you plant an evergreen fir tree at the entrance to the school, each of your pupils, as they pass by it, will feel in the depths of their soul a vague desire to do something good. Help each one to realise this desire.

STORIES AND VIGNETTES

Beauty, Inspiration, Joy and Mystery

A little boy set off for a walk in the forest. He met an old man coming out of the forest. The old man looked tired but was smiling with joy.

'Why are you smiling, Grandpa?' asked the boy. 'Is there something wonderful in the forest?'

'Yes, my boy, in the forest there is Beauty, Inspiration, Joy and Mystery. I saw these things, and now I feel like living for many more years.'

The boy ran into the forest.

He looked around. Everything was beautiful: the mighty oak, the elegant fir tree, the weeping willow and the silver birch. But the boy thought the most beautiful of all was a violet. It raised its deep blue head and violet eye from the grass and looked with wonder at the boy.

'This is Beauty,' whispered the boy to himself.

The boy listened and heard far off in the distance the quiet cooing of a wild pigeon: 'Coo … coo … ' And in that instant the boy remembered something kind and loving. He remembered his mother's hands. He wanted to make up song about his mother.

'This is Inspiration,' he whispered to himself.

The boy concentrated even harder on his surroundings. The sun was shining brightly, birds were flying high up in the blue sky, and waves of green forest stretched as far as the eye could see.

'How good it is, that I can see and feel all of this,' thought the boy. 'The world is made of Joy and to live is a Joy.'

But where was the Mystery? For a very long time the boy looked and listened, but he could not find it.

The boy went back to the forest the next day. Again, he met the old man, coming out of the forest. The boy told him how he had encountered Beauty, Inspiration and Joy, but how he had been unable to find the Mystery.

'Grandpa, where is the Mystery?'

The old man smiled mysteriously and answered, 'When you have grey hair like me, you will see the Mystery.'

Many years passed. The boy grew up and became an adult. He

married, raised a family, and his children grew up. He became a grey-haired old man.

One day he went to the forest. Many years had passed since, as a little boy, he had heard about Beauty, Inspiration, Joy and Mystery. And now he recalled the words of the old man. The first thing that caught his eye in the forest was an amazingly beautiful violet in the midst of the green grass.

'That is the same flower I saw so many years ago,' thought the old man. 'Does it live forever?'

The old man listened. The grass was whispering in just the same way, and the leaves were rustling. He raised his head and saw white clouds floating, and a flock of cranes flying in the blue sky.

'So that is the Mystery,' realised the old man. 'Beauty is eternal.'

A drop of dew

Early one morning, a drop of dew woke up on a rose. 'How did I get here?' wondered the dew drop. 'Last night I was high in the sky. How did I end up on the earth?'

It wanted to climb back up into the sky.

The sun warmed it, and it evaporated, rising up and up into the blue sky, till it reached the sun. There were thousands of other drops there. They gathered to make a dark cloud and covered the sun.

The sun was angry. 'Why are you hiding me from the people?' it boomed and sent a fiery arrow flying at the cloud. Lightning flashed and thunder rumbled. The dark cloud was frightened and sprinkled water everywhere. It started raining. The drop of water fell back to the earth.

'Thank you for coming back,' said the earth. 'I really missed you.'

The horse and the rider

In a little house, there lived a sculptor. From a piece of wood, he could carve people, animals, fairytale birds and even flowers with transparent petals.

Next door to the sculptor lived a little boy and his mother. The mother burnt wood to produce charcoal, which she sold at the market. That was their livelihood.

The little boy would come into the sculptor's workshop, sit on the bench, and watch how life and beauty are born out of wood.

One day, a large log was brought to the sculptor from the forest. It was cut into two parts. One half was brought into the sculptor's workshop, while the other half was thrown onto a pile of rubbish in the yard, near the house where the little boy lived with his mother.

The sculptor worked for many days. The little boy watched how a horse was born out of the wood. It was as if the horse were real. The horse wanted to charge forward, but an invisible rider was holding him back. 'But where is the rider?' asked the little boy.

'The rider is in the other half of the log,' answered the sculptor.

The sculptor's hands began to shake. He was old and his body was weak. The daily work exhausted him.

The little boy ran to his mother. He wanted to ask her, 'Mum, please bring the other half of the log into the sculptor's workshop—the rider is in it.'

However, the other half of the log had disappeared. The little boy's mother had chopped it up and burnt it to produce charcoal.

'Mum, why did you burn the rider?' asked the disappointed little boy.

The mother stared at her son in bewilderment.

A fire in the field

It is a quiet autumn day. The sun is shining, but it no longer gives out warmth. Silver spider webs are floating in the air. Cows are grazing in a meadow by the pond.

Mum and I are in the field. Mum is working, and I am beside her. In the evening, we sit near a big pile of potatoes. A small campfire is burning, and we are baking potatoes.

How nice it is to sit by the campfire, stirring the coals with a stick and waiting for the baked potatoes!

At last, they are baked. As we sit enjoying the delicious potatoes, a flock of cranes sails across the sky. The sun sets behind the forest, the field darkens, and a wave of cold can be felt coming from the valley.

Whenever I remember that day, my heart becomes so light …

An apple at dawn

Little Myshko often went to the orchard to visit Grandpa Kornii, who would treat his grandson to delicious apples, pears and honey.

Myshko couldn't take his eyes off one enormous, white apple that glistened at the very top of a particular apple tree.

'Grandpa, can I please climb that apple tree and pick that apple?'

'No,' answered his grandfather, 'That apple is for someone who comes to the orchard at dawn and does an hour's work, bringing water for the bees and pruning dead branches.'

Myshko planned to come to the orchard at dawn so many times, but he could not overcome his laziness.

Finally, Myshko made a big effort, opened his eyes when it was still dark, threw aside his pillow and ran to his grandfather's orchard. Myshko brought water for the bees and pruned the dead branches.

Dawn broke. Myshko went over to the tree with the precious apple, and the sight took his breath away. Now the enormous apple at the top of the tree was not white, but pink, the colour of the dawn sky.

'What are you waiting for? Now the apple is yours. Climb up and pick it,' said Myshko's grandfather.

'No, Grandpa … I would rather wait till tomorrow,' said Myshko.

'Why?' asked his grandfather.

'I want to see the dawn again,' said the boy.

How many mornings have I slept through?

Tomorrow the summer holidays will begin.

Vasylko, who is in grade three, asks his father, 'What will I do this summer?'

'You can have a rest,' answers his father. 'And if you want, tomorrow you can come into the field with me.'

This makes Vasylko very happy. Vasylko's father is an agronomist. He wakes up before sunrise and spends the whole day in the field.

In the morning, when Vasylko is still deep asleep, he feels someone touching his shoulder, shaking him, waking him up. He really does not want to get up! But he remembers that today he is going into the field with his father. Vasylko jumps out of bed and looks around. It is still dark outside. The stars are shining in the sky, and a pink glow is beginning to appear in the east.

Vasylko washes and has breakfast with his father.

When they are outside, Vasylko points to the pink sky and asks, 'Dad, is there a fire over there?'

Vasylko's father smiles. 'Have you never seen how the sun rises?' he asks.

'No,' answers Vasylko.

They stop on the outskirts of the village.

The wheat field that stretches in front of them gradually turns yellow in the rays of the rising sun. Drops of dew sparkle in the light. A lark sings in the blue sky above them.

'It's so beautiful!' says Vasylko quietly. 'Does every day begin like this? How many mornings have I slept through!'

What a musician!

In a field of tall, green millet, lives a cricket. During the day, he hides from the sun. As soon as the sun goes down, the cricket climbs onto the tallest stalk and sits on a green leaf. The millet stretches in front of him like a forest. He sits and tunes his violin, for the cricket is an incredible musician! He has a little violin that sings. The cricket runs his bow over the strings of his violin, and divine, enchanting music rings out. The trees and the flowers listen to his music. Little hares and mice listen. The whole steppe listens.

The gentle breeze and the cold wind

In a deep ravine, in a dark forest, two winds were sleeping: a gentle wind (a young lad with blue eyes), and a cold wind (an old man with a prickly beard).

Winter came. The sun no longer rose high in the sky. The fields were covered with white snow. The treetops whispered anxiously to each other. In the deep ravine, the old man woke. He rose and strode out of the forest. A blizzard began to blow. The cold wind stalked the earth, rivers froze, and the blizzard howled.

At long last the sun began to rise higher in the sky. The old man's back began to ache. He dragged his feet back to the deep ravine and fell asleep.

The gentle breeze woke up and danced out of the forest. The sun smiled, streams of water broke free from their icy prison, flowers began to bloom, and the grass whispered of the spring.

The rainbow in the icicle

During the day, snow started melting and water dripped from the roofs, but during the night it froze again.

Yurko came out and saw a huge frozen icicle hanging from the roof. The sun rose and the icicle sparkled in many different shades of blue, pink, red, turquoise, and yellow. Yurko stood there, holding his breath in awe. The icicle was so beautiful, like a rainbow!

On the roof, beside the icicle, sparrows were chirping. They were admiring the icicle too.

How snowflakes ring

It was a dark winter evening. The sun was hiding below the horizon, lending a rosy glow to the carpet of snow. Stillness was in the air, and only the stars were twinkling in the sky.

Suddenly, a black cloud appeared in the north and floated above. The carpet of snow turned dark. Snowflakes fell to the ground. They quietly covered the field, forest, and road. I listened to the quiet snowfall and heard a gentle ringing. It was as if somebody far, far away was touching a crystal bowl with a tiny silver hammer.

What was that ringing? I walked toward the sound, listening attentively. The ringing was coming from a little fir tree that was growing in the school yard. I was stunned: the tiny snowflakes were ringing! They were hanging on the branches of the little fir tree, touching each other and ringing, ringing like little silver bells. Even the moon was listening.

The boy and the snowflake

A snowflake fell from the sky. It was fluffy, soft, light, crystal clear, and as beautiful as a star.

A boy was standing on the ground. He was watching the snowflake fall and was thinking to himself, 'It is going to fall under somebody's feet and will be trampled.'

No, it must not fall to the ground! It must not be trampled underfoot!

The boy raised his hand. He wanted to caress the snowflake. But it fell onto his gentle, warm palm and melted. Almost crying, the boy gazed at his palm, and the drop of water sparkled like a teardrop.

The acacia and the bee

Early in the morning, a bee flew out of her beehive. She remembered that yesterday she had gathered nectar from the buckwheat. The field of buckwheat was far away. What if started raining? She might fly to the buckwheat to get a drop of nectar and get soaked in the rain. The bee buzzed as she thought about this, and she came to a decision.

'I'll ask the acacia. She will know what to do. When it is going to rain, she has lots of nectar. When it is going to be dry, she has none.'

The bee flew to the acacia and asked, 'Is it going to rain today?'

'Take a look in my little nectar cups and you will see,' said the acacia.

The bee looked inside the little nectar cups and they were full, so it was going to rain.

She should not fly far from home. And she had no reason to fly further afield, when the acacia was treating her to so much sweet nectar!

The green apple and the rosy apple

A young apple tree grew in a garden. Two flowers bloomed on it: one at the top of the tree and the other on the lowest branch, very close to the ground. Two little apples formed: one at the top of the tree and the other at the bottom. Both apples were tiny, green, and covered with a silky coating. A little boy ran by the tree. He looked at the apples and screwed up his face. 'You look sour,' he said.

The summer days were hot. The bottom apple was comfortable in the cool shade. The top apple was exposed to the heat of the sun. The bottom apple was happy, and told the top one, 'I'm glad I am down here. The sun does not burn me. How can you live so close to the sun?'

The top apple did not reply.

The summer came to an end. One day, early in the morning, the bottom apple looked up and saw that the top apple was golden and rosy. The bottom apple looked at itself. It was still green and covered with a silky coating, almost the same as it had been in springtime.

The bottom apple was stunned.

'Why are you so rosy?' it asked the top apple. 'And why am I so green?'

'I spent all day in the sun and was not afraid of its rays, but you hid in the shade,' replied the rosy apple.

The snowflake and the sun

High in the sky, in a white cloud, a little snowflake was born. It was beautiful and sparkled like silver lace. Quietly, it descended onto the branch of a fir tree and looked around. It saw a field carpeted with snow, the green branches of the fir trees, and the sun, round and blindingly bright, in the blue sky.

The snowflake boasted, 'What is so beautiful about you, sun? You are round like a plate, but I am like lace carved from fine silver. Each of my needles sparkles. If I want, I can shine more brightly than you.'

The sun smiled but said nothing. The next day, it rose early in the morning. Instantly, it became very hot.

'I can't breathe, it's so humid,' groaned the snowflake and started crying. Tiny teardrops fell from its fine needles onto the snow-covered field.

The snowflake disappeared, but the sun still shone and sparkled. The forest woke from its winter dream, welcoming spring with joyful song. Streams began to flow. The snowflake turned into a little drop of water, but the everlasting sun remained the same. The sun will always be there.

The bumblebee and the lilac flowers

A lilac bush was flowering in a garden. One cluster of violet flowers stood out amongst all the others. Its flowers were soft and fragrant. Every morning, that cluster of violet flowers waited for the sunrise. It knew that once the sun rose, a bumblebee would fly to it. It liked the buzzing of the bumblebee. It liked the way the bumblebee landed on its flowers and gently caressed them with its abdomen. Those were the happiest moments of its life. The sun shone in the blue sky, birds twittered in the trees, butterflies flitted past, an old oak rustled its leaves, and the wind mysteriously whispered some tender message. And all of this was just for it, a cluster of lilac flowers.

One morning, it woke up and could not believe its eyes. There was no longer any bush or oak tree beside it. Most surprising of all, it was standing in a crystal vase by an open window. The sun rose, and its rays were reflected in the crystal in thousands of rainbows. The lilac cluster held its breath in wonder. It had never seen anything so beautiful in all its life. 'And all of this is for me,' it thought.

At that moment, it heard the buzzing of the bumblebee. It thought that the bumblebee was going to caress its flowers as usual but, buzzing anxiously, the bumblebee circled its flowers and disappeared through the open window.

'Whatever has happened to that bumblebee?' wondered the cluster of lilac flowers. 'It's a strange one. Can't it see how beautiful this crystal vase is?'

A piece of the sea

A boy used to live by the shore of a great sea. For hours, he would sit and watch its mighty waves, as they heaved up and down, rumbling angrily or gently whispering.

The sea was never silent. The boy understood its ferocity and tenderness, its rage and kindness. Going to bed, the boy would always say, 'Good night, sea!' And the sea would respond with the everlasting sound of its waves.

But the boy's parents decided to move far away from the sea, into the steppe. Sad and full of longing, the boy went to the sea to bid it farewell. The sea rumbled quietly, but the boy could tell that its feelings were hurt. The sea cast a spiral shell onto the shore. The boy understood that the sea was giving him a small gift. He took the shell and brought it home.

At his new home, surrounded by the quiet steppe, the boy put the shell to his ear … and heard the gentle sound of waves caressing the sandy shore.

Deeply moved, the boy pressed the shell to his chest. What could be dearer to him than a piece of the sea?

The water lily and the fish

A little fish lived in a pond. He noticed that as soon as the sun set, a white water lily descended and hid underwater, and that early in the morning it rose up and showed off its beauty all day.

The fish wondered why the water lily behaved that way, so he asked it, 'Why do you hide underwater at night, and then come out of the water during the day?'

The water lily answered, 'I want people to admire me. They look at me in the daytime and say, "What a beautiful flower the water lily is!" But who will see me at night? At night, everything is black.'

The main entrance

A bright and spacious new school was built in a small town.

The school had two doors: a large one facing the road, that was called the main entrance, and another, a bit smaller, that opened onto the school yard.

As soon as the new school opened, the main door was locked, and only the back door was used.

Years passed. Teachers and principals came and went. Everybody who studied and worked at the school completely forgot that there used to be two entrances. It never entered anyone's head that they could enter the school through the front entrance, without using the back door.

One spring morning, a couple of little first-graders, who usually come to school earlier than everybody else, approached the back door and froze in astonishment. A blue violet was blooming in front of the porch. Green shoots had pushed their way up between the paving stones, and a tender flower shone among the green leaves.

Boys and girls circled the flower. They did not want it to be trampled underfoot. And children kept arriving. Finally, all the students and all the teachers were standing there. The whole yard was filled with boys and girls. The principal was standing next to the flower and wondering what to do.

'What should we do?' wondered a thousand children.

'There is another door to the school.' Little Dmytryk from grade one broke the silence.

'What door?' asked the principal.

'The main entrance door,' said Dmytryk. 'We play hide and seek there.'

The principal recalled the door, and so did the other teachers. The students also remembered that every day they walked past the locked door.

'Let's open the main entrance door!' joyfully announced the principal.

They opened the main entrance door. Everybody started entering the school through the big front door, and the back door was closed while the violet flowered on its threshold.

How a bee found a lily of the valley

A bee flew out of her beehive and circled above the apiary. She caught the sound of bells jingling in the distance and flew towards the music of the bells. She reached the forest and found lilies of the valley in a meadow. Each flower was a tiny silver bell with an exquisite golden hammer inside. The hammer struck the silver, and it rang. This sound could be heard everywhere, in the steppe and in the apiary. That was how the lily of the valley summoned the bee.

The bee settled on a flower and collected its nectar. 'Thank you,' she said to the lily of the valley.

The flower did not respond. It could not speak. It only humbly bowed its head. The bee understood that that was how the lily of the valley acknowledged her gratitude.

The bee carried the nectar to her babies.

The music of the bees

The music of the bees resounds in the bee garden from morning to evening. You close your eyes and hear a sound like a string humming. Where is that string? Perhaps in the hives? Perhaps the little bees are sitting there and playing on some unusual instrument? But the music is ringing everywhere, near the hives, in the garden, in the flowering buckwheat. The whole world is singing. Even the blue sky and the sun—everything is singing. Perhaps there are fine strings in the flowers? Perhaps the sun has stretched strings between the petals? Perhaps each bee flies up to a flower, sits between the petals and plays on those little strings with its little legs.

Soon the sun will rise

I wake at dawn, venture outside, and am instantly enveloped in the cool of the morning. The sky to the east is a pale blue. The grass and leaves are covered with cold morning dew.

Somewhere, high in the sky, a lark sings. The lark is golden and seems to be sailing on a sea of pink. But what is making the lark golden? It is the sun, gently caressing the lark in its tender embrace.

The edge of the sky turns red. A starling wakes in his nesting box. Welcoming the sun, he sings joyfully and flies somewhere. He soon returns, bringing something in his beak for his chicks.

The dawn is ablaze. Bands of gold spread across the sky. A mist rises from the pond in the valley. Soon the sun will rise.

Morning breeze

It was a quiet summer night. Everything was asleep. Even the breeze was asleep, lying under a willow bush.

But then the morning dawn began to glow. The breeze woke up and ran out from under its bush. It ran along the bank of the pond, waking up the reeds. The reeds rustled and swayed. A butterfly was sleeping on the reeds, and it, too, woke up. It flew towards the village, while the dawn blazed ever brighter. Soon the sun would rise. The butterfly flitted over to a rose blossom and settled on it. The rose woke up and looked around. The sun was already shining.

A morning at the apiary

One sunny spring day, a bee flew out of her beehive. She circled above the apiary and rose into the air. From above, she noticed something white down below. The bee flew down to have a look. It was an apple tree in flower! The bee found its most fragrant flower, settled on its petals, and drank its sweet nectar.

She soon had enough for herself and for her children. But on her way back, she spotted a bright island of yellow flowers amid a sea of green grass: the dandelions were in bloom. Their flowers were large and very fragrant. The bee found the most fragrant flower, landed on its petals, and collected lots and lots of honey.

When the bee returned to her apiary, she met a friend. She told her friend all about the apple tree and the dandelions. Together, the bees brought the honey home, put it into small bowls, and set off again.

The sun lit up the whole world. It gave its warmth to the apple tree, to the meadow, and to the pond. And the bees sang joyfully because the sun was shining.

The blade of grass and last year's leaf

The autumn frosts hit hard. A green blade of grass wilted and lay on the ground. To make things worse, a leaf fell on it. The blade of grass lay under the leaf. A blizzard blew and covered the ground with snow. The blade of grass was warm under the snow.

The blade of grass slept for a long time. In a dream it heard something singing above it. Something was ringing out all over the forest. The blade of grass wanted to stand up, but it could not. The dry leaf would not let it. The blade of grass gathered all its strength, rose up and poked its sharp tip through last year's leaf. It looked around and trembled with joy. Birds were singing in the trees, spring waters were thundering in the gully, and in the blue sky the cranes were calling. 'It's spring!' rejoiced the blade of grass, and it raised itself even higher.

The red butterfly

A red butterfly flitted above the green grass. He was bright and beautiful. He settled on the green grass for a few minutes and set off again. A sparrow spotted the butterfly and started chasing him. The sparrow drew closer and closer. At any moment he would catch the butterfly.

The butterfly was scared. He did not know how to escape. He flitted over to a red rose bush and settled on a flower. The sparrow was confused: where did the butterfly go? The sparrow looked for the butterfly everywhere. He stopped near the red rose and looked around, but the butterfly froze, and he could not see it.

Empty handed, the sparrow returned to his nest, while the butterfly sat safely on the flower.

By the pond

A hot July day is drawing to a close. The sun is setting. We are sitting on the bank of a pond. The water is as still and motionless as a mirror, and the blue dome of the sky is reflected in it. Looking at the water, we can observe every movement of the sun. We see the moment when it touches the pond, and in an instant the water ignites and becomes a river of fire. The flaming disk of the sun descends lower and lower into the depths of the water. The pond is all ablaze. Finally, the sun sets, hiding below the horizon, and suddenly the river of fire is extinguished. The mirror-like surface turns a soft, pale blue.

In the twilight, the stars start twinkling in the sky. The water in the pond turns a deeper blue, and now the stars are twinkling in its depths.

An old willow leans over the pond. Not a single leaf rustles, not a single branch stirs. The willow looks at its reflection in the water, sad that summer is coming to an end, that soon all its leaves will be gone, and dark clouds will cover the sky.

Don't be sad, dear willow! Soon the pond will freeze over, snow will cover you with its warm blanket, and you will look forward to the spring.

The purple flower

In the middle of the night, a rose bud opened and straightened its gentle purple petals. A new flower was born. It was not beautiful yet: its petals had still not fully straightened, and one petal was a bit wrinkled.

The rose looked at the stars twinkling in the sky, quietly shivered, and whispered, 'The dawn is breaking. I need to introduce myself to the sun in all my beauty. The whole world will be looking at me and my purple petals.'

The petals roused themselves. The wrinkled petal straightened up. A drop of dew fell onto its purple surface, trembled, and also turned purple.

The flower stood tall, its petals quivered, the drop of dew shuddered and shone with many shades of purple.

'Look,' the flower told its petals, 'Even the sky in the east has turned purple. It is because of our beauty. The whole world will be purple!'

Having made this pronouncement, the flower froze in anticipation.

But the purple sky turned pale, then scarlet, and then a rosy blue.

Surprised, the rose looked around. Suddenly, it saw a green tree with a white candle on it.

'Who are you?' asked the flower.

'I am a chestnut. A chestnut flower.'

'Why are you not purple? Why are you white? Why is the sky blue? And why are the trees green?'

'If everything looked alike, there would not be any beauty in the world,' answered the chestnut flower.

The chamomile and the broom

A man came to a pond to gather willow twigs to make a broom. He cut a lot of twigs, but together with the twigs, he accidently cut a chamomile flower on a tall stem. The man made a good broom. He swept the yard and made it clean. But the meadow felt sad without the chamomile flower.

A drawing of a rose

Pavlo drew a rose. It seemed alive, with its pink petals, golden anthers, and tiny drops of dew on its petals.

Pavlo put the drawing of the rose on a windowsill. A wasp was flying by. It saw the rose and settled on its petals, thinking, 'I'll take my fill of honey and bring some to my babies.' But the rose was as hard as stone. 'Why is there no honey in it?' wondered the wasp, and it flew away.

You lucky children!

Today, a class of little children came to school for the first time in their lives. Tomorrow, they would be sitting at their desks, but today, their parents brought them to be introduced to their teacher. The mothers went home, but the children stayed with their teacher in a glade under a tall lime-tree.

Today, the old teacher, Ivan Pylypovych, was meeting his tenth generation of students. He would be their classroom teacher until grade four. By that time, he would have been working at the school for forty years. His gentle, welcoming eyes looked into the black, blue, grey, and light blue eyes of his little students. The children smiled back.

'Children, have you ever seen how the sky changes colour long before the sun rises?' asked Ivan Pylypovych, and his gentle smile was mirrored by dozens of children's warm smiles.

'No, we've never seen that,' answered the students.

'Have you ever seen how a nightingale drinks the dew?'

'No … '

'Have you ever seen how a bumblebee cleans its wings before it takes off from the flower where it slept during the night?'

'No … '

'Have you seen how a sleepy ladybug looks out from the bark of the tree where it was hiding during the winter, to check whether spring has arrived?'

No … '

'You lucky children,' said Ivan Pylypovich. 'You're lucky, because you have so much to see. Lucky, because you will see many beautiful and wonderful things. I'll take you to the pond, and you will see how the sky changes colour before the sun rises. We shall hide behind a bush, as quiet as mice, and we shall see how the nightingale drinks a drop of morning dew. At sunrise, we shall come to a big pumpkin flower and find a lazy bumblebee who slept there during the night, and watch it wake up and clean its wings. Early in spring, we shall find a tree trunk, warmed up by the sun, and shall see how a ladybug peeps out from the bark and is surprised to see all the snow. She will wonder how it is possible that it is too hot for her to continue sleeping under the bark, when there so much snow on the ground. You are so lucky, children, because you will see all these things … '

There is only one sun

Sashko was sitting at a table in a green garden and doing his homework. Today, the teacher had given them an unusual assignment. The children had to look around and evaluate every object close to them and then compare it with another object.

Sashko thought hard. Above, the wind played with the leaves of an aspen. The leaves trembled and whispered as if sharing secrets, just like first-grade girls sharing secrets during the break between classes.

The boy looked down at the ground and saw two green leaves with white flowers between them. It was a lily of the valley. Its flowers were just like tiny crystal bells! It seemed you only had to touch them, and they would ring.

He heard a bee buzzing, and then the deep drone of a bumblebee.

Sashko closed his eyes and imagined two strings, one thin and one thick. A musician was sitting and playing on both strings. That was what the buzz of the bee and the drone of the bumblebee could be compared to.

A mosquito's high-pitched sound was really hard to compare. Maybe, Sashko thought, it could be compared to a reedpipe made from a dandelion's stem.

The sun was setting. The sky in the west turned red and was like a huge poppy field with thousands of red flowers in bloom. If you could find a field like that, wouldn't it be beautiful!

The sun touched the horizon. The sun was a huge crimson orb … What could it be compared to? Sashko thought for a long time, but he could not think of anything, because there is nothing else like it. There really is only one sun.

The most beautiful and the most ugly

At school, a boy was asked to write an essay about what he thought was most beautiful and what was most ugly. The boy thought hard, but he could not come up with an answer. It seemed to him that a flowering lilac would be the most beautiful thing in the world, and a toad would be the ugliest. However, he was not sure, so he asked his grandfather whether he was right. The grandfather said that the boy was wrong.

'The most beautiful thing,' said his grandfather, 'Is human work. And the ugliest, the most despicable thing, is when human work is cast to the wind. Go and spend a couple of days observing what is going on around you, and you will see those two opposites.'

The boy went walking through a wheat field. The wheat was almost ready to harvest, its golden ears heavy with grain.

'This is what is most beautiful,' thought the boy, 'This is human work.'

The boy continued observing. He went to school. The students were running around, playing and laughing. One girl was eating bread and butter, but without finishing it, she threw her piece of bread to the ground and rushed to her friends.

'And that is most ugly,' concluded the boy. 'She is casting human work to the wind.'

The ox and the chickadee

During the night, the pond was covered with a thin layer of the most delicate ice (just like you can see here now). When the sun rose, the ice shone with all the colours of the rainbow. (Can you see, children, how the dawn colours are flowing into each other?) First the ice turned pink, then red, then violet. Then it blazed like a sea of fire. When the sun rose above horizon, the ice turned crimson.

Sitting on a willow, a little chickadee enjoyed this symphony of dawn colours on the ice. He sang a simple song about this delicate, fragile beauty. His song was both joyful and melancholy, because at any moment the sun would rise and melt the ice, and all this magic would disappear.

'I am tiny,' the chickadee was singing to the world, 'And my claws are soft as down, but even I cannot land on this magic mirror. Yes, this is a mirror in which the whole world is reflected. Look at this beauty! How can anyone sleep at a time like this?'

On the bank of the pond, an ox was standing and listening with wonder to the chickadee's song. If he were not an ox, he would have shed tears of joy. But he was an ox. He wanted to get closer to the beauty of which the bird sang. He walked onto the ice, breaking it, and the magic mirror was shattered. Clouds of sediment rose to the surface of the pond.

'Where is the beauty?' mooed the ox, and, after drinking his fill, he waded to the other side of the pond.

Sunset

The sun descends below the horizon. Where does it go? What does it do during the night? The blazing orb touches the horizon and disappears, but the sky is still aflame. Why? Because the sun has a garden where it rests during the night. There is a large lake in this garden, but instead of water, the lake is full of molten gold, because the sun itself is made of molten gold. The sun lies down to rest in this blazing lake, spreading its mighty shoulders and stirring up the molten gold. Flecks of fire are sent flying, pouring down like golden rain. The blue sky turns crimson, and this crimson evening sky lasts until the sun settles down.

The swans are leaving

It is a quiet autumn evening. The sun goes to sleep and the purplish red sky on the horizon warns of a windy day to come. But for now, the air is still and motionless.

Suddenly, from beyond the forest, an anxious cry resounds: 'Oh-OH, oh-OH … ' A flock of swans is flying high in the sky. Why do they cry out so anxiously?

They seem to be taking something with them from their native land. It reminds me of a fairy tale my grandmother told me. She said that when the swans are flying away, their wings sow sadness over the earth. I gaze at the passing flock. The swan's fine wings are tinged with purple from the rays of the setting sun. But sadness cannot be purple! It should be azure or lilac, like the tall, distant burial mounds in the steppes.

'And when the swans return, what do their wings sow then?' I asked my grandmother.

'Joy!' she whispered.

The fields are bare

In late autumn, there is nothing in the fields: no ears of grain, no stubble, no straw. Everything has been harvested and stored in silos or barns. Young winter crops form patches of green in the dark ploughed fields. A cold autumn wind sings in the bare trees. Heavy grey clouds float low above the earth. They bring constant drizzle, day after day. The sun is nowhere to be seen. If you come to the fields, you cannot tell what time of day it is, morning, afternoon, or twilight. The birds have fallen silent.

Two men are crossing a field. One is wearing city clothes. He is visiting for just a few days. Looking at the bare, ploughed fields, he remarks, 'It is so empty and unwelcoming in the fields now. It makes me feel sad. It was quite different in summer when the ears of grain were whispering in the wind.'

The other man is an agronomist. He has been working in these fields for many years. He looks at the bare, ploughed fields with joy in his eyes and replies, 'These fields are beautiful now! They are beautiful precisely because they are bare.'

The girl and the chamomile flower

One bright, sunny day, a little girl was playing in a clearing in the forest. Suddenly, she heard somebody crying. She listened more attentively and realized that the cry was coming from under a stone on the other side of the clearing. The stone was not large, but very hard. The girl leaned over the stone and asked, 'Who is that crying under the stone?'

'It is me, a chamomile flower,' replied a soft, weak voice from under the stone. 'Please free me, little girl, I can't breathe under this stone.'

The girl cast the stone aside and saw a delicate chamomile flower.

'Thank you, little girl,' said the chamomile, breathing a deep sigh of relief. 'You have freed me from my stone prison.'

'How did you end up under the stone?' asked the girl.

'The stone tricked me,' said the chamomile flower. 'In autumn, when I was just a little seed, I was seeking a warm place to shelter from the winter cold. The stone gave me shelter, promising to protect me from the cold and heat. However, when I told it that I wanted to see the sun, it nearly crushed me. Little girl, I want to be yours! Let's be friends!'

'Sure, I'll be your friend,' the girl agreed.

The girl and the chamomile flower became friends. Every morning, the girl would come to visit the chamomile flower and they would greet the sun together.

'It is so nice to be yours!' the chamomile liked to say.

'But what if you grew in the forest or by the road? What if you didn't belong to anybody?' asked the girl.

'I would die from grief,' replied the chamomile softly. 'But I know that there are no flowers that do not belong to anybody. They are always somebody's. Can you see that bell-shaped poppy flower? It is friends with the sun. The tiny, blue forget-me-not is a friend of the spring breeze. No, a flower cannot live without belonging to somebody.'

How the shepherd sheared his sheep

I asked my grandma why there were so many white clouds in the blue sky, and she told me this story.

Far, far away, beyond blue seas and dark forests, there were some high mountains. Between those mountains there were green valleys. In one of those valleys a shepherd pastured his sheep. The sheep were as white as snow … One day, the shepherd drove his sheep to a valley high up in the mountains. There he sheared them and made a huge pile of white wool. Suddenly, a swirl of wind snatched up the wool and scattered it across the sky. In the blink of an eye, the wool turned into the white clouds that you can see.

The multi-coloured milkmaid's yoke

Beyond the pond there is a blue cloud, with a rainbow shining right through it—a mixture of yellow, green, blue and red. It is as if a multi-coloured milkmaid's yoke is hanging over the river. Beyond the forest, high in the mountains, lives a mighty giant named Thunderstorm. He takes this wondrous milkmaid's yoke and draws a bucket of water from the pond. Then he pours the water into the cloud, so that rain can fall from it.

A 'grandma's summer'

A 'grandma's summer' is what we call those warm autumn days when the sun still shines gently and silver gossamer threads float in the air.[5] An old grandmother sits on a bench, warming herself in the sun. Her shoulders are covered with a warm shawl. She gazes at a field and her eyes are sad because there is nothing left there. The field is empty and quiet. But then the old grandmother smiles, because she sees a tiny chamomile flower by the road.

The sun sets during a frost

It was a frosty January day, but the sun was shining so brightly that the snow started melting under an oak tree. A ladybug crawled from under its bark and began to warm herself in the sun. A stream of water sparkled under an apple tree, and a sparrow rushed to get a fresh sip of water. He drank and bathed himself, but the water made him cold, so he flew to the nearest branch and warmed himself in the sun. By the time he had dried himself, the sun was already setting. It grew huge and red, as if just forged by a blacksmith. The sky, too, turned red, as if a fire was burning beyond the horizon. Even after the sun set, that fire still burnt, and the snow on the roofs turned red. Anxiously cawing, some crows flew westwards.

There would be a frost tomorrow. The sparrow hid in his warm nest under the eaves and dreamt of the warm summer. The ladybug crawled back under the bark of the oak tree and went to sleep.

It is quiet in the forest in winter

It is a quiet winter's day in the forest. Mighty trees wrapped in snowy hats and coats stand motionless, and only the sound of a woodpecker breaks the silence. He is tapping at the bark of an oak tree, looking for bugs. What is that whispering sound?

A hare runs by, stops, sits under the oak, and looks around. He raises his paw and touches his ear. Somewhere the icy surface of a pond cracks, and something rings out like the note of a song. It is a snowflake falling onto a rosehip bush.

The bullfinch carver

Where do such beautiful snowflakes come from?

I will tell you where they come from.

Once upon a time, two bears rolled a huge block of clear, transparent ice to the top of a high mountain. A wonderful master craftsman lives there, the bullfinch carver. Using tiny knives and mallets, he carves beautiful white snowflakes from the ice and sprinkles them around. They fall to the ground and sparkle in the sunlight like tiny stars. And when the bullfinch carver gets tired, it stops snowing.

A green field

One sunny autumn day we walked to a field. The green field stretched as far as the eye could see. All the way to the horizon you could see nothing but green, while in the dark blue sky a flock of birds could be seen, flying to warmer lands.

It was so quiet in the field. You could not hear birdsong or the sound of a tractor. At that moment, the whole wide world stretched boundless before me.

The first frost

In the evening, the sky cleared, and the stars shone brightly. During the night it turned cold. I woke at the break of dawn and went outside. How everything had changed during the night! The green blades of grass had all turned white. I looked closely at them: each blade was covered in tiny white needles.

That night, while everyone was asleep, Grandpa Frost had woken up in a deep ravine and decided to stretch his old bones. He had stridden across the fields, looking into every yard, and wherever he had breathed, tiny needles of ice had appeared.

I approached a little red rose. Yesterday it was the only one left, still smiling at the sun. Now it was all covered with white needles and looked like a tiny porcupine.

The sun rose. As soon as its rays touched the rose's icy dress, the needles turned into tiny drops of water, covering the flower with morning dew that glittered in the sunlight. Why are you so sad, dear rose? Why don't you raise your head? Your petals have wilted. Sun, dear sun, can't you help this poor red rose?

A cherry tree in bloom

It flowered in spring next to our simple village house. Bees hummed in its flowers, the sun shone, and birds sang joyfully in its branches.

I could not take my eyes off that cherry tree in bloom.

Now, when I look back on that distant time, it seems as if that cherry tree bloomed all through my childhood.

That cherry tree still blooms to this day, the bees still hum, the sun still shines, and the birds sing just as joyfully. And it seems to me that there is no place like home, and that our native land is the most beautiful in the world. For we were born here, and it has given us life and strength.[6]

Frost and the chamomile flower

One moonlit night, Autumn Frost paid a visit. He approached a rose bush and breathed onto it. Its pink petals fell to the ground and its green leaves wilted.

Frost strode across the meadow, and wherever he breathed and whatever he touched—whether it was the grass or the green leaves of the maple tree—everything turned yellow and wilted. He stopped to rest under a rowan-tree, and its leaves turned crimson, like the sky at sunset on a windy day.

Frost roamed wide through gardens and fields, but he missed a little chamomile flower. It still stood by the road, stretching its white petals to the sun. It looked at the poplar tree and was surprised. Why had its leaves turned yellow?

The sun rose, its warm rays gently caressing the chamomile flower, and the flower smiled joyfully back.

A pond shrouded in mist

We come to the pond at dawn, but we cannot see the water at all. We just hear the lap of its waves. Perhaps it is not a pond at all, but the boundless sea? Perhaps that is not a willow over there, but a mysterious ship exploring the wide ocean, its crew seeking to discover new lands?

We listen closely to the lapping of the waves. Somewhere in the mist, the sun rises. Now the white wall of mist begins to disperse. Something appears in its depths, something wonderful and mysterious, as if from a fairy tale. A high, rocky crag, and on it a crystal palace. Who lives there? If only the fog would disperse more quickly, so we could see the boundless sea and the fairytale palace.

A light breeze blows the white clouds of mist to the shore. The fairy-tale palace shimmers and shrinks. Its high towers turn into a green wall of reeds, among which ducks are swimming. It was their splashing that we took for the sound of waves lapping at the hull of a ship.

A lily of the valley

Petryk went into the garden in the morning and a saw a lily of the valley. The boy gazed at it for a long time, enchanted by its beauty.

'I'll pick it and put it in a vase on the table,' thought Petryk. 'It will look beautiful inside.'

He reached out to pick the flower but was suddenly struck by an image of what the garden would look like without it. He covered the flower with his hands, and instantly the garden turned sad and unwelcoming, the green leaves were wrapped in shadow, and the birds stopped singing. Petryk took his hands away from the flower, and straight away the green leaves started whispering joyfully and the birds began singing.

'I did not realise how wonderful you are!' thought Petryk. 'How could I pick you and take you inside?'

When the birds return

When I look back on my childhood, I think of a warm, sunny day. The melting snows filled the air with the sound of running water, and mist rose from the earth. Some patches of white snow remained, but a flock of migratory birds could be seen crossing the blue sky.

'That is geese returning from warmer lands,' my mother explained. 'They are bringing the spring on their wings.'

I was amazed. Where was the spring, and how could they carry it on their wings?

Why the magpie has white sides

A magpie came to old Crow the Tailor and said, 'Sew me some new clothes and make them as beautiful as you can.'

The crow took his big scissors and cut the clothes from dark grey fabric.

'I want you to add some white fabric, so that I have white on each side,' instructed the magpie.

The crow sewed a dark grey garment with white sides. Ever since, the magpie has boasted about her clothes, and we have called her *soroka-biloboka*—Magpie-Whitesides.

Why did Grandpa chuckle?

An old sycamore tree grew beside the yard. Mykola asked his father how old the tree was. His father answered, 'I don't know, it seemed this old when I was a little boy.'

Mykola asked his grandfather how old the sycamore tree was. His grandfather answered, 'I don't know, it seemed this old when I was a little boy.'

Every spring, buds sprouted on the tree's branches, and it was covered in green leaves that whispered in the breeze. But one spring, the buds did not sprout. The little birds that used to nest in its branches circled the tree, chirping anxiously, and flew away. The sycamore stood motionless and bare.

Mykola's father said to his grandfather, 'I suppose we need to cut it down. It has died.'

'Let's wait until next spring,' his grandfather replied.

The buds did not sprout next spring either. Mykola's father and grandfather took a big saw and cut the tree down. The mighty sycamore fell to the ground.

The spring ended and summer began. One day, Mykola was walking past the stump of the old tree when he froze in awe: strong, new, green shoots with big leaves were growing from the old tree's roots. Mykola rushed to tell his grandfather about the green shoots. His grandfather came to look at the stump and chuckled.

Mykola wanted so much to know why his grandpa chuckled.

The flower and the snow

It was wintertime.

Vira, a grade one student, was tobogganing. On the way home she found a broken twig next to a lilac bush.

Vira picked up the twig and brought it home. She poured some water into a jug and placed the twig in it.

A few days later some buds opened, and green leaves appeared.

One day Vira looked at her green twig and clapped her hands with joy. Between the leaves a violet-coloured flower had bloomed.

The girl placed the jug with the green twig on her windowsill.

It seemed to her that the twig was looking at the carpet of snow with fear.

Vira looked very attentively at the flower, and then at the snow, and became sad.

A stick from an elder tree

During the summer, Grandpa Ivan and his grandson Ivasyk were grazing a herd of cows.

Ivasyk found a stick from an elder tree lying on the grass, and said to his grandfather, 'I can tie a rope to it and make a whip for herding the cows.'

His grandfather took the little branch in his hands, examined it carefully, and said, 'We can make something better than that with it.'

'What?' asked Ivasyk.

'Something that will stir your soul,' said his grandfather.

And with that stick from an elder tree, Grandpa Ivan made a beautiful sounding folk pipe.

Why the rooster has a comb

Our rooster has a red comb. At night, as soon as the hens settle on their roost, he takes his comb and brushes his colourful tail. That is why his tail is so magnificent. He brushes his tail and puts his comb back on his head. Then, during the day, he walks around, proudly showing off his tail.

Little Rain and Thunder

Little Rain was sleeping on a warm cloud. (He is a little bird, like a cockerel.) Little Rain was sleeping quietly.

Thunder crept up to him. (Thunder is a wild animal, with shaggy hair.) Thunder crept up to Little Rain and rumbled loudly. Little Rain was frightened, woke up and started crying. Many tears fell pitter-patter to the earth.

And people said it was raining. The fields and meadows were washed clean. The wheat and the cabbages were washed clean.

Little Rain finished crying, and the rain stopped.

Autumn has brought golden ribbons

Two birch trees, tall and slim, with white bark, grow by a pond. Their long green hair hangs down. The wind blows and combs their hair. The birch tree leaves whisper quietly, talking about something.

One night it turns cold. White crystals of ice shine on the grass. Autumn comes to the birch trees, bringing them golden ribbons. The birch trees plait the ribbons in their green hair.

The sun rises, melting the crystals of ice. He looks at the birch trees and does not recognise them, with the golden ribbons in their hair. The sun laughs, but the birch trees are sad.

How an ant crossed a stream

A little ant was running along a forest path. She was looking for food, as she had little children at home.

Suddenly the path was cut by a trickle of water. On the other side of the water lay some sweet-scented grains. How could she reach them? The ant saw a tall blade of ryegrass growing by the water. The ant cut down the blade of grass with her teeth, which were as sharp as knives. The blade of grass fell across the water. The ant crossed over to the other side and gathered the sweet-scented grains. 'I'm coming, children,' she called. 'I'm bringing you some food!'

When the poppy opens its petals

In the evening, a poppy flower closes its petals. The poppy sleeps all through the night. The day begins, the sun rises, but the poppy keeps on sleeping, without opening its petals.

Suddenly, a hairy bumblebee flies out of an apple tree. It buzzes as it flies.

The flower hears the bumblebee approaching and opens its petals. The bumblebee flies up and lands between the petals. The poppy flower is happy. Now it will have a full boll of poppy seeds. That is why the poppy flower waited so long before opening its petals. It was waiting for the bumblebee.

How the hamster prepares for winter

A grey hamster lives in a burrow deep under the earth. His fur coat is soft and fluffy.

The hamster toils from morning to evening, preparing for the winter. He runs from his burrow into the field, looking for ears of wheat, shaking the grain from them and collecting it in his mouth. He has little sacks for grain in his cheeks. He brings the grain to his burrow and empties it from his little sacks. Then he runs back to the field. People have not left many ears of grain in the fields, and it is difficult for the hamster to gather enough food.

Eventually the hamster fills his pantry with grain. Now he need not fear the winter.

The corncrake and the swallow

Autumn came. Clouds of milky mist swirled over the cold earth. The water turned chill. Even the blue sky seemed cold. A swallow was flying to warmer lands. It had fallen behind its flock and was trying to catch up. It landed in a meadow to have a short rest. The swallow noticed a corncrake walking across the meadow. It did not seem to be in a hurry.

The swallow asked, 'Where are you going, corncrake?'

'To warmer lands,' answered the bird.

The swallow did not believe this was possible. It flew on to warmer lands. A week later the corncrake arrived.

'Don't look so surprised, swallow,' said the corncrake. 'I walked day and night.'

Serhii and Matvii

Two young men, Serhii and Matvii, came to a flowering meadow.

'What beauty!' whispered Serhii. 'Look! It is as if someone has woven pink, red, white, and blue flowers into a green carpet.'

'The grass really is lush here,' said Matvii. 'If we bring our cow here, we'll have two buckets of milk by evening.'

'And the sound of the bees is like a harp,' whispered Serhii, uplifted by the enchanting music.

'We should bring the beehives here as well. Think how much honey they would give us!' said Matvii with excitement.

'And there are some people who cannot see this beauty,' whispered Serhii.

'I'll go and drive the cow here. And I'll bring the beehives,' said Matvii, and he headed back to the village.

The lone willow

A lone willow grew on the bank of a pond. It shed its leaves. Three thin, bare branches reached into the water. The willow looked into the mirror-like surface of the pond and wondered what those three thin sticks were.

'What are you bare twigs doing here?' asked the willow. 'Why are you sticking into the water?'

'That's you, willow. You're looking at your reflection,' said the pond.

'Oh, what beautiful branches!' said the willow. 'I didn't know I was so beautiful.'

The lark is helping the sun

In the dense forest and in the deep gullies, cold snow still covered the ground. The squills were still sleeping under last years' leaves. The blue sky was reflected in a thin layer of ice that still covered the pond.

Only on the hillsides had the snow melted, causing streams to flow. Steam was rising from the earth, and the sun was shining brightly in the sky.

A little girl named Marynka came out of her house and saw a grey bird in the sky. The bird sang, and it was as if a silver bell was ascending into the sky on wings and ringing continuously.

'Mum, what sort of bird is that, singing?' Marynka asked her mother.

'It's a lark,' her mother replied.

'Why has it come so early? Why is it singing so joyfully? There is still snow on the ground,' said Marynka.

'The lark is helping the sun,' her mother answered.

'How can it help the sun?' asked Marynka in surprise.

'When a lark flies up into the blue sky, it gets warmer,' replied her mother.

How a stream watered a chamomile flower in a meadow

A chamomile flower grew up in a meadow. A yellow flower bloomed on its tall stem, like a tiny sun. The hot summer arrived. The soil dried and cracked. The chamomile flower's head drooped. 'How will I survive in this dry soil?' it cried.

Not far away, a stream was babbling. It heard the flower sobbing and felt pity for it. The stream came to the flower, playing and singing. It watered the soil, and the flower raised its golden head. The chamomile flower smiled at the stream. 'Thank you!' it said. 'Now I need not fear the blazing sun.'

They cut down the willow

The willow grew by a pond. On quiet summer mornings, it gazed into the water. Its leaves neither stirred nor whispered. But when birds landed on the willow, its leaves trembled. That was because it was surprised. 'What bird has landed on me?' it wondered.

One day a man came to the pond with an axe. He went up to the willow, took aim, and struck. Wood chips flew. The willow shook and even groaned, and its leaves anxiously asked each other, 'What is that man doing?'

The hewn willow fell. The pond fell silent. The reeds were still, and a bird called anxiously. A grey cloud covered the sun, and everything around became sad.

The hewn willow lay stretched out, and its leaves whispered to each other, asking, 'Why are we lying on the ground?'

Where the axe had cut through it, the willow began to weep. Pure, transparent tears fell on the earth.

It was only beautiful when it was alive

A magnificent butterfly—a swallowtail—settled on a red canna flower and fluttered its wings.

A boy crept up to the butterfly and caught it. The butterfly struggled, but it could not escape. The boy attached it to a sheet of paper with a big pin. The butterfly's wings drooped.

'Why have you stopped fluttering your wings, butterfly?' asked the boy.

The butterfly was silent. The boy placed the sheet of paper with the dead butterfly on the windowsill. When he looked at it a few days later, its wings had dried out and fallen off, and ants were crawling over its body.

'No, it was only beautiful when it was alive,' said the boy despondently, 'When its wings were fluttering on the canna flower. Not stuck to a sheet of paper.'

The violet and the bee

At the green edge of the forest grew a violet. It gazed at the world with its violet eye and smiled at the sun each morning.

In a forest clearing, not far from the edge of the forest, a bee lived in a hive.

The bee and the violet became friends. The bee flew to the violet many times each day to collect pollen and nectar. The violet waited impatiently for its friend.

But one day the bee noticed that the violet was sad, and its petals had faded.

'Why are you sad, violet, and why are your petals so pale? Why don't you have any pollen or nectar?'

'I am dying,' whispered the violet.

'What do that mean, "I am dying"?' asked the bee in surprise.

'It means I will no longer be able to see the sun and the sky.'

'Where will the sun and the sky be?' asked the bee, even more surprised.

'They will still be here, but I won't be,' said the violet.

Although the bee could not understand why the violet would not be there anymore, she became very sad.

The water lily and the moth

On the quiet surface of a pond grew a water lily, a beautiful white flower. All day its petals warmed themselves in the sun.

Evening approached, and the sun set. The sky turned red, and everything around took on a rosy hue.

Suddenly a moth settled on one of the water lily's delicate petals.

'Kindly permit me to spend the night on your petal,' requested the moth.

'Dear moth, I would gladly give you a place to sleep, but I cannot. Every night I sink under the water,' replied the water lily.

'Why?' asked the moth in surprise.

'I have a soft bed there,' answered the water lily, 'But tomorrow, as soon as the sun rises, I will rise. Fly to me then, moth.'

The white lily folded its petals and quietly sank beneath the surface, and the moth flew to the bank of the pond.

In the morning, as soon as the sun rose, the water lily rose from its bed and unfolded its petals. It waited for the moth, but he did not come. It waited all day, but the moth was nowhere to be seen. He only came flying in the evening, when the sun was setting, and the whole world took on a rosy hue once more. Through its tears the water lily said, 'I waited for you all day, but now I have to sink under the water.'

The moth fluttered his wings and flew once again to the bank of the pond. The water lily looked for a long time at the darkening sky, and its heart ached.

The scent of apples

It is a quiet autumn day. The apple orchard hums with the sound of bumblebees. They have swarmed to an apple that has fallen from a tree and is lying on the ground. Sweet sap is oozing from the apple, and it is covered with bumblebees.

The sun sets, but the scent of apples warmed by the sun still lingers. Somewhere a cricket starts singing. Suddenly an apple falls to the ground with a thump … The cricket falls silent, and a frightened bird flits by. Beyond the forest, a star appears in the evening sky. The cricket starts singing again.

Now the moon is drifting across the sky, but the apples still smell of the hot sun.

Sunflowers during a storm

Heavy, black storm clouds cover the sun. It grows dark and gloomy in the field. The forest stands beside the field, black and silent, as if watchful and expecting something. The yellow field of wheat turns grey. An anxious lark drops from the sky into a meadow and falls silent.

Only the field of flowering sunflowers is aflame with colour. It seems to radiate light and to reduce the gloom above the earth. A lustrous fire blazes in its flowers, reminding us of the sun above the clouds. Soon lightning will tear the clouds apart, and the blue sky will peep through. Once again, the field will laugh with joy.

A lilac grove in a ravine

In the middle of the steppe is an old ravine. The slopes of the ravine are overgrown with grass. But what is that blue colour at the bottom of the ravine? We look from a distance and see a sky-blue stream winding through the bottom of the ravine. How clear the water seems, just like the sky! We want to reach it as quickly as we can.

We descend to the bottom of the ravine, and what do we see? It is not a stream after all, but lilac bushes. Someone has planted lilac bushes all along the bottom of the ravine. They have taken root and flourished. The lilac is in bloom, and from a distance it looks just like a stream.

The shepherd oak

On the edge of the forest stands a solitary oak, strong and thickset, like an old shepherd. It has probably grown on the edge of the forest so it can keep watch over its brothers.

One summer day, a thunderstorm rumbles over the forest. The oak is struck by a fiery flash of lightning. Its branches shake, and the top of the tree bursts into flame. The rain pours down, but the oak keeps burning, and the top is completely burnt out. The forest is sad. Who will be its shepherd now?

But the oak does not die. A year later, its burnt branches are covered in green shoots. The old oak is covered in curly, green leaves, but its topmost branches remain dry and bare. Some storks arrive from warmer lands. They see the bare branches at the top of the tree, settle there, and build a nest. The old oak is overjoyed. Now it will not be alone.

As the sun sinks beyond the horizon, a stork stands on one leg in its nest, and gazes far into the distance, towards the setting sun. He is keeping a lookout for any thunderstorm. The stork stands quietly, and the oak breathes easily. It rustles its green leaves and falls asleep.

The dawn

One by one, the stars in the sky go out. The dark blue sky in the east grows lighter, and a pink band rises from the horizon and spreads over the whole sky. Then everything turns pink: the water in the pond and the drops of dew on the grass. Even the mist spreading through the valley is pink. A lark soars high into the sky and sings its heart out. Already the sun's rays are shining on its little wings, and they turn pink. At any moment the sun will rise from the horizon, and the lark is singing, 'I can see the sun already!'

The maple sighed

A maple tree slept all through the winter. As it dozed, it could faintly hear the howling of the blizzards and the anxious cries of a black raven. The cold winds shook its trunk and bent its branches towards the earth.

Then, one sunny morning the maple felt the caress of something warm and tender. It was a spring breeze. 'You have slept long enough,' whispered the warm spring breeze. 'Wake up, spring is nearly here.'

'What spring?' asked the maple. 'I can't see any spring.'

'I have blown from the distant shores of a southern sea,' replied the breeze. 'Beautiful spring is making its way through the fields, covering the earth with flowers. And the swallows are bearing many-coloured ribbons on their wings.'

That is what the spring breeze told the maple tree.

The maple sighed, stretched its shoulders, opened its green buds and waited for the beautiful spring to arrive.

The autumn oak

On the edge of the forest stands an ancient oak. It can see the spreading linden trees, the thickset elms and the singing maples. It can see an open field and a tractor ploughing.

All the trees have already shed their leaves. Only the oak stands at the edge of the forest, still clothed in its many-coloured garment. It is proud of its crimson, yellow and scarlet leaves. A woodpecker settles on a branch of the oak tree and asks, 'Dear oak, why have you still not shed your leaves? Winter is almost upon us, and it will soon be snowing.'

The oak answers, 'I do not wish to part with my beautiful clothes. I would like winter to see me dressed in my finest.'

Soon winter comes from beyond the mountains and spreads a white carpet of snow over the earth. The oak still stands in its festive attire. At first, even winter is surprised, but then it just admires the oak's luxurious coat of many colours.

Dewdrops on a flower

A red poppy was in flower. During the night, dew fell. The flower woke in the morning and saw dewdrops on its petals.

'Who are you?' it asked.

The dewdrops answered, 'We are born from the warm night winds. We are dewdrops.'

The flower was surprised. It watched to see what the dewdrops would do. They just sat on its petals. The sun rose, and a little sun appeared in each dew drop.

As the sun rose above the earth, the dewdrops grew smaller. Then they began to disappear one after the other.

'Where are you going?' asked the disappointed flower.

'To the sun, to the sun!' answered the dewdrops.

Go and graze under the poplar

Early in the morning, as soon as the sun rose, Hryts and his mother set off for the fields. They crossed a dew-soaked meadow. Every blade of grass in the meadow was covered with dewdrops that sparkled and gleamed in the sunlight. Hryts stopped, fascinated by the dew.

'Mum, look at all the crystal beads!' he said.

His mother stopped too. It was very quiet in the meadow. All that could be heard was the song of a nightingale.

A grey calf emerged from under a poplar. It started munching on the grass, and the crystal beads began to tremble and disappear. It seemed to Hryts that they were tinkling plaintively. Quietly, so as not to spook the nightingale, Hryts approached the calf. Then he scolded it, shouting, 'Go and graze under the poplar!'

The calf ambled over to the poplar. There were no crystal beads there.

The lark descends from the sun

It was a clear summer morning. My father and I were crossing a field in a small cart. The sun rose. A golden wall of wheat surrounded our cart. I lay on the sweet-scented, freshly cut grass in the cart, and gazed at the sky. I saw a little bird. Now folding, now spreading its wings, its little body trembled as it sang.

'What bird is that?' I asked my father.

'It's a lark,' my father answered, and stopped the cart.

We stood there for a long time, listening to the lark's song. I seem to hear it even now. It was as if a bee were playing on a stringed instrument. I asked my father where the lark had come from, and he told me a story about how this enchanting bird descends from the sun.

I will never forget that morning, that song, and that story about the lark descending from the sun.

In the middle of the steppe in July

Endless fields. A light breeze stirs up waves in a sea of golden wheat. I stand on top of an ancient burial mound, gazing at my home village, the steppe, and a blue band of forest on the horizon that looks like an enchanted river.

The song of a lark rings out in the blue sky. It is hovering above its nest, singing to its chicks. 'Look, I am very close to the sun,' it sings. 'Very soon, you too will fly as high as me, and the sun will bathe you in its rays.'

Blue cornflowers are all around. From the top of the burial mound, I can smell the bitter scent of wormwood. Somewhere in some grove, or in a green meadow, a turtledove coos. A poplar is growing beside the road. Next to it is a little wild rose bush, covered in white flowers. Above one of the flowers, a bee is buzzing, and it seems to me that the flowers are singing, that the whole field is singing, and that the sun is playing on a violin.

When the trees wake

Little Varochka went outside for a walk. She had been sick for a long time, so she was especially curious about everything around her.

It was a sunny February day. The little girl walked into the garden. Everything around her was silent. It seemed to her that the motionless trees were listening to something very remote.

Varochka looked at the snow under the trees and caught her breath: the shadows of the trees were as blue as the winter sky! Then Varochka noticed that the trees' branches were trembling slightly. It seemed to her that the trees were looking closely at their shadows so that they could admire their own beauty on that warm winter's day.

Many years later, the girl realised that at that moment one of life's greatest mysteries had unfolded before her very eyes: the trees were waking from their winter slumber. Spring was still far away, but the trees were already waking up and admiring their beauty.

The fir tree and the linden tree

Autumn arrived. The leaves turned yellow and withered. The linden tree was sad, because it was about to shed its bright leafy gown and sleep till spring. An evergreen fir tree grew just beside the linden tree. The linden tree knew that the fir tree would remain green throughout the winter, so it asked its neighbour, 'Please, dear fir tree, when spring comes, tell me what the winter was like. I'll be asleep and will not see it … The woodpecker told me that winter is beautiful and the colour of silver. Is it really so beautiful?'

Winter came. The linden tree slept, but the fir tree admired winter's evening stars and its white blanket of snow.

Spring arrived. The snow melted, and springs, streams and brooks filled the air with the sound of running water. A lark trilled high in the sky. The linden tree woke up and asked the fir tree, 'Dear fir tree, tell me all about the winter.'

The fir tree was silent for a while, then it sighed and quietly said, 'Can you hear the sound of the babbling streams?'

'Yes, I can,' answered the linden tree.

'Their song is a recollection of winter.'

The river and the pond

A small, swift-flowing river runs through the steppe. In spring, it bursts its banks, spreading across meadows and visiting people's gardens. Once it even visited the dairy farm, reaching the door of the cowshed, peeping inside, and returning to the meadow.

In summer, the river narrows, but it never dries out. One day, I walked along the riverbank until I found a quiet place where the river seemed to hide between two hills. The hills were covered with bushes, and I could see water gleaming deep down in the gully below. I clambered down to the river and discovered clear water streaming from the ground. It was a spring. So that was what was feeding the river!

In the village, the river flows into a wide pond. All its banks are lined with weeping willows that lean over the water's edge, touching it with their long branches. The water is still, undisturbed by waves or ripples. The pond is like one huge mirror, and everything surrounding it—the sun, the willows, and the village—is reflected in it.

A sunny winter's day

The sun rises and reveals an amazing scene: the trees are covered with white hoarfrost, as if overnight they had grown leaves made of fluffy bird's down. I approach a willow and touch its branches. I am instantly covered with light silver flakes. 'No,' I think to myself, 'I won't touch you again, willow. May everyone see your enchanting attire.'

A chickadee flies over to me, chirps a greeting, and lands on the willow's branch. How did it manage to settle there without disturbing the tree's fluffy garment?

'Chickadee,' I ask, 'Can you make this beauty last forever? Can you stop the wind from blowing and disturbing this soft down?'

The chickadee replies, 'If this beauty were to last forever, you would never see beauty again. You would miss the beauty of the sky in spring, the beauty of dawn, and the song of a nightingale.

I return home, sit by the window, take a pencil, and record all this beauty on a large piece of paper: the willow's white gown, the blue sky, the bright sun, and the kind chickadee.

The quail's song

It is a warm summer evening. The sun has set. The crimson glow in the west has faded. Stars sparkle in the dark blue sky. We sit on an ancient burial mound and gaze at the village with its white huts and green gardens.

Tall poplars grow on the outskirts of the village, watching the road as it disappears into the distance. They seem to be wondering where the road ends. They watch day after day, but they still do not know.

From a deep ravine, the evening darkness spreads out like a river. Its waves have covered the steppe and the village. In this sea of darkness, everything seems strange. Tall haycocks resemble enchanted fairytale ships. In the dusk, the forest looks like a gigantic wave that has come rolling in and then suddenly frozen.

Far away, in a field, a quail starts singing. A nocturnal bird flaps nearby. A fish splashes in the pond. Its ripples murmur and then fall silent.

Everything in the forest sings

In spring we went for a walk in the forest.

The sun rose, a light breeze sprang up, and all the trees in the forest began to sing. Each one sang its own song.

The birch tree sang a tender song. Hearing it, we felt like going over to the white-barked beauty and embracing it.

The oak sang a song of courage. When we heard the song of the oak, we wanted to be strong and brave.

The willow, drooping over the pond, sang a thoughtful song. When we listened to its song, we reflected that autumn would come, and all the leaves would fall from the trees.

The rowan tree sang an anxious song. This song brought on thoughts of a dark night and a furious storm, forcing the slender rowan tree to bend over and seek the earth's shelter.

Those are the songs we heard in the forest.

The autumn maple

We went to the forest to admire the trees' autumn attire. We stopped by a tall maple tree and sat on the ground. How beautiful it was! The maple stood there dressed in its gorgeous attire, and not a single leaf stirred or made a sound.

'Look, children,' said the teacher. 'The maple is asleep. It is dreaming of all the things it saw from spring to autumn. Look at that yellow leaf, the colour of a dandelion. In spring the maple was enchanted by the beauty of a dandelion, and it remembered that beauty. It went to sleep recalling the beauty of the dandelion, and that leaf turned yellow.

And over there you can see a leaf the colour of the morning dawn, a tender pink. And that one is like the crimson evening sky on the eve of a windy day.

And look over there at that branch. That leaf is as bright and beautiful as the wing of an oriole. Probably an oriole once settled on that branch, and now the maple is dreaming of its wing.'

We all admired the beauty with bated breath. Everyone was silent, as if afraid of disturbing the maple's magic sleep.

The willow is like a golden-haired maiden

A weeping willow droops over a pond. Its green leaves hang down as it gazes into the water. A breeze blows, and its branches sway like a maiden's hair.

A little bird has weaved a nest right next to its trunk. Whenever the bird flies out of her warm little nest, the willow's green hair stirs. That is the willow listening to the bird's song.

Autumn arrives. The cold wind turns the willow's branches to gold. The maiden is now golden haired. But the bird has disappeared. Where has she gone? She has gone to warmer lands, far away beyond the sea. In spring she will return, and the willow will no longer grieve for her. Its hair will turn green again, and early every morning the maiden will wake up happy.

The little bird will also be happy, because she is back home in her native land. Our homeland is our dearest treasure. Nothing is dearer to us than our homeland.

But for now, the golden-haired maiden is sad. It is quiet by the pond. A golden leaf drops into the water and floats far, far away. The willow sighs.

The oak and the willow

An oak and a willow have grown side by side on a riverbank. The willow is the first to wake in the spring. You rise at dawn, walk to the river, and see the willow's branches wrapped in a clear, green mist. The willow buds are sprouting. As they sprout, they fill the air with their scent. A starling comes to the willow, lands on its branches, feasts on a green bud, and trills its joyful song.

When the willow is already covered with rustling leaves, the oak is still dark and leafless. It sleeps and does not want to wake. People say that an oak will not wake until it hears the rumble of the first thunderstorm. Finally, thunder rumbles, and the oak's buds start sprouting. The first sticky leaves emerge, and each day they grow larger and larger, till by summer they are thick, sinewy, and strong.

In autumn, when the cold winds blow, the willow's leaves turn golden, but the oak is still green. It does not want to prepare for winter, even when the willow's golden gown has been shed into the river. The oak remains as green as a field of wheat. Only frost can make the oak reconsider its stubbornness: the oak's leaves change colour and whither, but they are not shed. Yellow, golden, brown, cherry-coloured, the leaves remain on the tree throughout the winter, a coat of many colours.

Spring rain

It was a warm spring day. A mother ant ran out of her anthill and hurried along her path to a tall poplar. She ran to the poplar and crawled up its trunk. On the leaves of the poplar were sweet little drops of sap. The mother ant crawled out onto a leaf, took a sweet drop between her legs and put it on her back. She was about to head home when she suddenly heard a clap of thunder. Large drops of warm spring rain began to fall. The mother ant took fright. 'What if the rain washes away the sweet food that I am taking to my babies. What will I feed them?' she thought. The ant hid under the bark of the poplar and sat and listened. The rain thundered down.

Finally, the rain stopped. The mother ant looked out and saw the sun was shining. She crept out from her cosy shelter and crawled down the tree. She found her path and returned home. There her baby ants were waiting for her. She shared out the sweet drop of poplar sap to all her children, and there was even some left over for herself.

A little bit of summer

Five-year-old Larysa got up early, at dawn, and went to the orchard. Her mother had told her that it was time to say good-bye to autumn. Soon snow would cover the earth, and blizzards would swirl. At night Grandpa Frost would come and breathe on their windows with his icy breath, and the glass would be covered in icy patterns.

The orchard was empty and quiet. All the leaves had long fallen from the trees. Their bare branches rocked in the wind.

Under the trees a carpet of dry leaves quietly rustled underfoot.

Suddenly, among the grey leaves, Larysa saw a large pink apple. It must have fallen recently because it was whole and fresh.

The girl was overjoyed. She picked up the apple, looked around her, and felt that the orchard had become brighter and more sheltered. Perhaps Larysa only imagined it, or perhaps it was real, but she thought she heard a bumblebee droning.

Larysa took the apple home. She put the pink apple on the table and said to her mother, 'This is a little bit of summer. Let's leave it here until spring.'

Her mother smiled.

From that day on, the apple lay on the table: large, pink and fresh, as if it had just fallen from the tree.

Outside there was frost, and a blizzard howled, but it still lay on the table. Whoever came into the house would see the apple and smile.

The oak in the way

People were constructing a road between two large towns, from north to south. They wanted to make a road that was straight and wide, strong and beautiful.

They began construction. They made a high earth embankment, with stone retaining walls, and surfaced it with asphalt. The road passed through meadows and steppes, and along the banks of rivers.

One day the road builders came to a field where small bushes were growing. The engineer indicated where the future road was to be built, and the workers hammered pegs into the ground.

Suddenly the workers stopped and put down their pegs. A mighty oak tree, tall and strong, with a wide trunk, stood in their path, like a sentry guarding the steppe. The engineer came over to the workers. He stood silently, not saying a word. The workers also fell silent.

The engineer looked at his road plans for a long time, then looked at the oak tree and sighed. The workers also sighed heavily.

'We can't change the plan,' said the engineer.

'We can't cut the oak tree down either,' said the workers.

The engineer pulled out a peg, walked a hundred metres from the oak tree and hammered it into the ground.

'Now no-one will judge us,' he said.

Several years passed. A wide asphalt road was laid from north to south, as straight as an arrow. But in one place it was bent like a horse-shoe. People driving past in a bus smiled joyfully and said, 'The people who built this road had noble hearts.'

Good-bye, Sun!

In the evening a little girl was saying good-bye to the sun. It was setting on the horizon.

'Good-bye, Sun,' said the little girl.

'Good-bye, little girl,' answered the sun. 'Go to sleep. I will also rest. Early in the morning I will wake up and tenderly greet you. Wait for me by that window.'

The girl went to sleep. She dreamt of a blue sky.

At last, the sun rose. Its gentle rays touched the little girl's face. She woke up and said, 'Good day, Sun! How glad I am to see you!'

That's the sun!

It was a clear summer's day. A teacher led some little children into the forest.

The forest was vast and silent. The trees stood straight and tall, like giant candles. The dense foliage hid the sun, and the children walked in semi-darkness.

The children walked and walked, and it seemed there would be no end to the forest. Something rustled overhead.

'What is that sound?' asked the children.

'That is the treetops whispering to each other,' said the teacher. 'They are happy because they can see the sun.'

Suddenly the children stopped. On the broad trunk of a hundred-year oak, they saw something bright and shining.

'What is that?' asked the surprised children.

'That's the sun!' answered their teacher. 'Look from here. See how bright it is?'

One by one, the children stood by the trunk of the hundred-year oak and admired the sun.

Beautiful and ugly

Mariia Ivanivna said, 'Children, I would like you to think about what seems most beautiful to you, and what seems most ugly. Think about it, and then write about it.'

I thought for a long time about what is most beautiful. It seemed to me that the most beautiful thing of all is the little white flowers of a lily of the valley, the colour of marble. They are so soft and tender. The very sight of them makes me happy. They make me feel like doing something good. I want people to say that I am a good, obedient girl and a kind daughter to my mother and father.

The most beautiful thing is when people are kind to each other. For instance, one day an old man was sitting on a bench under a tall tree. He had been travelling on the bus when he began to feel ill. He had got off the bus and sat down to rest on the bench. My mother invited him into our home, gave him some medicine and fed him. The old man had a rest and then went home.

And I'll tell you what the ugliest thing is. A boy's grandmother died. She was really old: ninety years old. And he did not go to the funeral. And when his grandmother was ill, he did not visit her. How could he feel no pain? The ugliest thing is when people are heartless and mean.

The hot flower

There was an early spring that year. Orchards flowered in the middle of April. Then May arrived.

One clear spring morning a little girl named Olia went to the orchard and saw a large red rose in bloom. She ran to her mother and joyfully told her, 'Mum, a red rose has flowered!'

Her mother came to the orchard, looked at the red flower, and smiled. Then she looked at the sky, and her face became anxious.

A black cloud was bearing down from the north. The wind picked up, the cloud covered the sun, and it became cold.

Olia and her mother sat inside and anxiously looked out the window. Snow began to fall, like white butterflies. Everything became white. The wind died down. Snowflakes fell softly to the ground for a while, and then stopped.

Olia and her mother went to the orchard. The green leaves were wearing little hats of snow. The ground was covered with a snow-white carpet. Only the rose was red, like a glowing coal. Drops of dew sparkled on it.

'It's hot. It's not afraid,' said Olia, and she smiled joyfully.

If I were invisible

If I were invisible, I would see so many interesting things! I would visit meadows and riverbanks, creeping up to a nightingale and listening to his song. I would sit beside him, listening to the way he sings and looking into his eyes! What do they look like? What does he see when he is singing his mesmerizing song?

I would also like to see another wonder. A cricket lives in our garden. Every evening, he starts chirping his song. It is more like the sound of a violin than a song. I think that he takes his tiny violin just before sunset, runs his bow over the strings, and enchanting music rings out. If I were invisible, I would get to see his violin and bow. Otherwise, whenever I come close to the cricket, he sees me and falls silent.

In the evening, a red rose closes its petals, but in the morning, it shows off its beauty, its petals now open and charming. My mother says that a rose wakes at dawn but is very shy and will never open its petals if somebody is watching it. If I were invisible, I could watch and see how the rose washes its petals in the morning dew and opens them. Though I would not dare to spy on it like that. That would be impolite. Modesty is a beautiful quality, and beauty should be preserved.

Dusk

When the sun sets, dusk begins. Everything around us begins to live a wonderful, fairytale life.

Far away in the steppe stands an ancient burial mound. As soon as the steppe is wrapped in dusk, it ceases to be a burial mound. It becomes a little island, standing in the middle of an ocean. Waves of wheat caress the shores of this little island.

On the edge of the village stand three haystacks. In the dusk, they are no longer haystacks, but large ships with violet sails. They have sailed across the boundless ocean and arrived at our village.

And the green forest is no longer a forest, but waves, frozen in time. Green ocean waves. They just look like trees.

The dusk has crawled out from a deep ravine and has spread across the steppe, throughout our village, and all over the world.

The sunflower

A large flower with golden petals sits atop a tall stem. It looks like the sun. That is why it is called a sunflower. At night, the sunflower sleeps, and its golden petals droop. But when the sky begins to grow light, the sunflower's petals quiver. That is because the sunflower is looking forward to the sunrise. At last, the sun appears from beyond the horizon. The sunflower turns its golden head towards it, and gazes at the fiery red ball. The sunflower smiles with joy and greets the sun, saying, 'Good morning, dear sun! I have waited for you all through the long night.'

The sun rises higher and higher, and sails across the sky. The sunflower turns its golden head, following its path. Now the sun is sinking below the horizon, and the sunflower smiles one last time at its golden rays. The sun sets.

The sunflower turns towards where the sun will rise the next day. The golden flower sleeps and dreams of the dawn.

The sun and the ladybird

In autumn, a ladybird crawled under the bark of a tree to rest. The little bug slept through the winter, unafraid of the severe frosts and the burning winds. She slept and dreamt of a warm, sunny day, a fluffy cloud in a blue sky, and a brightly coloured rainbow.

In the middle of winter there was a warm, sunny day. It was quiet in the forest, with not a breath of wind. The sun warmed up the dark bark, and the ladybird grew hot. She woke up, yawned luxuriously, and peeped out from under the bark. She wanted to spread her wings and fly, but the sun warned her, 'Don't venture out, ladybird! Hide away in your warm bed. It is too early for you to fly out. You will perish. My rays are warm, but the frost is treacherous and will kill you. There are blizzards and freezing winds and hard frosts still to come.'

The ladybird heeded this good advice. She took a deep breath of fresh air and crawled back into her warm bed.

How autumn begins

Autumn is Grandpa Frost's elder daughter. He also has a younger daughter named Spring. Autumn's hair is decorated with ears of wheat and the red berries of the guelder-rose. Autumn likes to wander through the meadows and along the banks of rivers and ponds. Wherever she breathes, the air grows cold. Autumn loves to spend her nights sitting on the bank of a pond. In the morning, a grey mist rises from the pond and lingers for a long time. That is how autumn begins.

Birds are frightened of Autumn. As soon as the swallows see her, they flock together and whisper anxiously. The cranes rise high into the sky and cry out anxiously.

Autumn likes to go into orchards. Whenever she touches an apple tree, the apples turn yellow.

But the woodpeckers are very happy when they meet Autumn. They cry out loudly and fly from one place to another, looking for things to eat on the trees.

Today is a warm, sunny day. The sun is low in the sky. It is shining, but not giving much warmth. Grandpa Frost's elder daughter sits leaning against a haystack, unplaits her hair, and warms herself. She sings a song about silver spider webs.

The butterfly and the flower

Someone threw a red flower into the pond. A white butterfly flew over the pond and saw the red flower. It landed on it and sat there, and gently waved with its wings. The flower sailed along, and the butterfly sailed with it.

A swallow swept down over the water and was amazed. How strange! How did that butterfly learn to swim?

The swallow touched the water with its wing, sending a ripple over its surface. The flower rocked, and the butterfly swayed.

It was having fun sailing on the pond!

There are so many folk pipes here!

Twelve-year-old Mykola was grazing a cow. It was a hot summer's day, and everything around was trying to hide from the sun. Mykola sat down under a willow tree. He noticed a thin branch from an elder tree lying on the green grass.

'I could make a folk pipe from that,' thought the boy.

He evened off the ends of the stick, carved out the soft core, and dried it in the hot wind. A quiet melody soon rang out. It was a song about a sunny summer's day, the blue sky, and the song of the lark.

Mykola looked around, and it seemed that everything had become more beautiful: the willow drooping over the pond, the green meadow, and a solitary chamomile flower.

The afternoon drew to a close, and Mykola drove his cow home. By the pond he saw a tall elder bush. Its slender, flexible, spreading branches swayed in the soft evening breeze.

'There are so many folk pipes here!' thought Mykola. He stepped up to the elder bush and reached up to touch a smooth, flexible branch. He thought he could hear the branch begin to sing and make music.

The boy stood by the pond and listened to that magical music.

The noisy stream and the silent river

A deep, wide river flows through a green valley. Its water flows slowly. Ships and rafts wend their way along it. The river is quiet, silent.

Meanwhile, a small stream flows between the mountains. Swift and noisy, it is always in a hurry, gushing over the pebbles and always babbling about something, explaining how it was born from melting snow high in the mountains. Then the noisy stream meets the silent river. Enchanted by the majesty of the river, the stream falls silent. It is suddenly ashamed to chatter, when the river is so silent.

How the hare warmed himself in the moonlight

The hare was cold in winter, especially at night. He ran to the edge of the forest. The frost was crackling, the snow was shining in the moonlight, and a cold wind blew from the gully. The hare sat under a bush, reached his paws out to the moon and begged, 'Dear Moon, please warm me with your rays. It is a long time till sunrise.'

The moon was sorry for the hare, and said to him, 'Keep hopping through the field, and I will light your way. Head straight for that big haystack.'

The hare made his way to the haystack, buried himself in the hay, looked out, and smiled at the moon.

'Thank you, dear Moon,' he said. 'Now your rays are warm as can be.'

How the bee became golden

A bee was buzzing here and there when she saw a pumpkin flower. And a pumpkin flower is huge. The bee crawled into the flower and collected some sweet nectar. She had collected enough, and it was time for her to move on, but she wanted to inspect the flower. She spent a long time wandering between the flower's petals, and her wings were covered in yellow powder. She became golden all over. The bee flew back to her hive, but the bee guarding the hive would not let her in.

'You're not one of ours,' said the guard. 'Look at you. You're all yellow.'
'But look how much honey I have brought,' said the bee.
'Now I recognise you,' said the guard, joyfully. 'You **are** one of ours. You're a golden girl.'

The tree stump and the oak

A young, curly, green oak grew in the forest. Underneath the oak was a stout, grey, rotting tree stump.

'Once, I was a young, green oak just like you,' murmured the stump. 'But now, look at me, I am just a stump!'

'Will I really become a stump like you?' protested the young oak tree.

'Yes, just like me.'

'I don't like that idea at all,' said the oak tree. 'I would rather be struck by lightning and burnt to a crisp.'

There was a peal of thunder, and a flash of lightning struck the crown of the young oak. The oak was set ablaze and burned like a candle. Then rain poured down and quenched the fire. Just one green branch remained. From it the oak regrew, spreading its branches, until it finally became as green and curly as it was before the thunderstorm.

As for the stump, when the lighting struck, it was so frightened that it collapsed in a heap.

How did it grow on the road?

There was once a green meadow. In spring, flowers bloomed there, butterflies flitted about, and bees hummed. The meadow smelled of honey, like a giant slab of honeycomb.

Beyond the meadow was a forest. To reach the forest, you had to travel around the meadow.

Somebody thought, 'Why should people travel so far around the meadow? Why not make a road through it?'

And they built a road. It was wide, compacted, and dusty. No trace of grass or flower remained on that wide band of grey.

One warm spring day, when a lark was singing in the azure sky above that dreamy meadow, two travellers were walking along the road. Heat rose from its dusty surface. One of the travellers, an old man, suddenly stopped in surprise. There, in the middle of the road, was a flower. The other traveller, a little boy, also stopped. They could not take their eyes off that flower. It was a little island of fairytale magic in the midst of the dust.

'How did it grow on the road?' whispered the boy.

'How did it survive?' whispered the grandfather.

The green hair and the red pantry

A grandmother planted some carrot seeds in the ground. Warm spring rains fell, and the seeds began to grow. A red root burrowed down into the earth, and a green shoot reached for the sun. Both the root and the shoot grew and grew.

Rain fell, and the earth drank up the water. The green shoot turned into a curly head of hair, and the root grew fatter and fatter. Soon it was as fat as the stalk, and then like a little barrel, red and round. No matter how much it rained, it was never enough for the red root. One day the curly green hair asked, 'What are you, down there in the ground underneath me? No matter how much it rains, you can't get enough to drink.'

From the earth the root replied, 'I am a red pantry. I am storing lots and lots of sugar.'

'Really?' said the green hair. 'So that is why children admire my green head of hair so much. If they pull on my hair, they will reach the sweet pantry.'

The luckiest leaf

At night, the leaves of an aspen tree sleep, but when the sun rises, they tremble as if they are alive.

I once witnessed how aspen leaves greet the sun. I woke just before dawn, walked to a tall aspen tree, and sat under it, waiting for the sun to rise. The sky to the east was crimson red and at any moment the sun's blazing disc would appear on the horizon. I could not yet see it, but the aspen leaf at the top of the tree could. It turned red and rustled joyfully, greeting the sun, while its brothers lower down were still dozing.

'I am the luckiest one and the happiest,' sang the leaf at the top of the aspen tree. 'I see the sun before everyone else and bathe the longest in its rays. I am the last one to bid it goodnight.'

I want to be as fortunate as that leaf up on high.

The bristly beetle

A bristly beetle climbs to the top of a clover stalk. He has two long moustaches that look like radio antennas. He raises them towards the sky. The antennas start waving. Do you know why he raises them? He is sending a signal, a telegram, to his friend in the garden, saying, 'Come over, my friend! I've found a sweet clover leaf. Let's eat it together and drink from a drop of dew.'

I am interested to see what happens next. I see another bristly beetle fly over to the clover. He must have flown over from the orchard. The two sit together and wave their moustaches.

Why do they not eat the clover leaf? Perhaps the bristly beetle from the garden has not understood the telegram from the bristly beetle on the clover. Or perhaps they will have a chat first and then eat the clover leaf.

The field and the meadow

The field and the meadow have lived side by side for a long time. People come to the field from early spring to late autumn. They plough the earth, sow seeds, pull out weeds, gather in the harvest, and plough again. They are full of joy when the field gives a rich harvest of wheat.

Grass grows in the meadow. In spring, flowers bloom and bees hover over them. From spring to late autumn, cows and sheep graze there. The meadow is green from spring to autumn.

One day, the field asks the meadow, 'Tell me, meadow, how is it that you are green from spring to autumn, though nobody ploughs you or sows you with seeds?'

'I am fed by spring waters,' says the meadow. 'They give me strength.' The field replies, 'I am green because I am fed by human labour.'

Blue eyes

The green stem of a squill, as sharp as an arrow, poked through last year's carpet of dry leaves. It spread its leaves, and between them trembled two blue eyes—two little flowers. The flowers looked all around, and what did they see? A big, red circle, like a ball of fire.

'What is that?' asked the little blue eyes.

'That is the sun,' answered a bumblebee.

Then the little blue eyes saw tall trees, the blue sky, and a flock of cranes in the sky.

The sun rose higher and higher, until it was in the middle of the sky. Then it began to descend towards the earth and changed its colour.

'Why has the sun turned red?' asked the little blue eyes.

'That is its way of saying goodbye to the earth,' said a wasp.

The sun hid itself. It grew dark.

'Why has it grown dark?' asked the little blue eyes, with fear in their voices. 'We're scared.'

'Don't be afraid,' said a little mosquito. 'That is just the day ending. Go to sleep. The night will pass, and a new day will begin.'

How a grain grew into an ear of wheat

All day long they sowed a field with wheat. The tractor driver drove the tractor, and the tractor pulled a huge seed drill. Evening came, and it was time to go home. The tractor driver towed the seed drill on to the road. He was about to go home when he noticed a grain of wheat lying in the box of the seed drill. He picked up the grain of wheat, put it into the ploughed earth and covered it with some damp soil. 'Grow, little grain, and produce an ear of wheat,' he said.

The grain of wheat sent a root down into the earth, and a green shoot up into the air, which grew into a blade of grass. In winter it kept warm under the snow, and in spring it grew into a tall stalk and produced a big ear of wheat. There were a hundred grains of wheat in that ear. The ear of wheat looked around and saw a whole sea of ears just like itself. It felt so happy it started singing.

The tractor driver came walking through the field. The ear of wheat recognised him and bowed low in greeting.

The beautiful song of the lark

A man was walking through a field of wheat. Suddenly a lark burst from under his feet. It rose high in the air above the man and began to sing its wonderful song. As the man listened to the song, he felt he was listening to a fairy tale about silver strings stretching from the sun to the earth. The song told him of the golden sun, which went to rest each evening in a magic garden, and about a rainbow—a golden bridge over which giant blacksmiths came down to earth to find iron and coal …

The man listened to the lark's song, and followed it further and further, towards the forest. Finally, when the lark saw that the man had reached the edge of the forest, it flew quickly back and hid once again in the wheat.

That was where its nest was. It reached its nest, where its babies had been waiting anxiously for their mother. They asked, 'Mum, what were you singing about in your song?'

'I was singing about that man,' said their mother. 'I asked him to go far away from my nest and leave my chicks in peace.'

'And did the man like your song?' asked the chicks.

'He liked it very much,' their mother replied. 'He followed me all the way to the edge of the forest.'

Yasenets—the first thin ice

Yesterday evening, waves still lapped at the edge of the pond, but today there is a frost. The pond is covered with the first thin layer of ice, which in Ukrainian we call *yasenets.*

A little crucian carp lives in the pond. He is swimming around and wants to take a look at the shore, but the ice will not let him. The fish is surprised. 'What is that?' he wonders.

The rainbow in the sky

A rainbow is shining high up in the clouds above the pond. It is a colourful bridge linking the sun to the earth. The sun uses it to drink water from the pond. It built the rainbow, and now it is tired and thirsty.

The snowflake and the drop of water

Little Olenka is running over the ice. Snowflakes are falling, floating in the air. One snowflake settles on little Olenka's sleeve. She looks at the fluffy snowflake. It is a six-pointed star, so beautiful and shiny, that a fairytale master might have cut it from a plate of silver.

Little Olenka bends her face to the snowflake, studying it, admiring it. Suddenly a miracle happens. The snowflake turns into a drop of water.

UNFINISHED STORY

* The curious seed

A large green tomato grew in a vegetable bed. It had a lot of seeds inside. One of them was very curious. It wanted to know everything. It peered at the world through the green skin of the tomato and wondered, 'Why is the whole world green? The sun is green and so are the trees, the earth and the sky. Even those birds flying by are green.' Then, over time, everything around started turning red. The curious seed was even more surprised. 'Why is everything turning red—the sun, the trees, the earth, and even the birds?' It asked the other seeds, 'What is going on?' But other seeds had not even noticed how everything was turning from green to red.

By chance a little girl came over and exclaimed, 'What a beautiful red tomato!'

The seed was even more puzzled.

'Am I really red?' it whispered quietly …

THE CHILD IN THE WORLD AND THE WORLD IN THE CHILD

On the happiness of being

The extent to which a small child becomes a thinker who understands and experiences the great human right to life, happiness, joy, personal freedom and safety, largely depends on us—the mothers, fathers, and educators, who at every step come into contact with the sensitive, open heart of that child. This sphere of inner life requires great tact and deep respect for the human right to happiness. Everyone who is involved in the upbringing of a child must wisely lead the child by the hand into the world of human society, without closing the child's eyes to either joy or suffering. (See 'How the Sun Sets', p. 82.)

How can I find a way to the wellspring of a child's thoughts, from which new questions stream so freely—that is what I think about each time my soul is troubled by the question of how to nurture that subtle human life skill: the ability to appreciate the joy of being.

Teach children to observe, to think, to discover and to wonder. Let the child in your care understand the eternal truth that a person is born, grows, develops, matures, ages and that every day of this life lived well enriches the person with wisdom, adding another precious grain to the incomparable value of a human being. (See 'And Where did that little boy go?', p. 82.)

The earlier children ask the question 'Where do little children disappear to?', the more they will treasure human values and the happiness to be found in living and working, thinking and experiencing. We should not protect children from the things they will inevitably encounter in life, which should awaken within them thoughts about their own existence.

On our perception of our surroundings

One of the responsibilities of an educator is to teach children to perceive the consequences of each of their actions . And in order to perceive the consequences, one has to think about them. Thought gives the conscience eyes. When educating, we teach children to reflect on that which surrounds them and that which is within them, to put themselves in another's shoes. When leading the children in their care into the complex world of human society, a true educator takes care to develop the keen sight of that which I refer to as 'the eyes of conscience'.

You are returning from the forest. It is a hot July day. You are nearing a well under a tall oak tree. Everyone is thirsty. The nearer the well, the more unbearable the thirst becomes. From the other direction, an old man is approaching the well. He has come from afar and is clearly exhausted. He too is thirsty. The children see the old man, but they do not think about him. The eyes see, but not the mind or the heart. Both the children and the old man reach the well almost simultaneously. At the edge of the well stands a bucket of cold water. In a moment, the children reach the well, encircle the bucket and, overwhelmed by a single desire—to quench their thirst—they push aside the old man. No-one even remembers he is there.

A human being is a frightening and ugly creature, when instinct overpowers the feelings of human worth that have been carefully nurtured through reason and thought. Learn to prevent this from happening! Do not give rein to instinct. Awaken noble human thoughts in the children in your care. Do not miss this valuable opportunity for the children to critically reflect on their intentions.

With a quiet but firm and decisive word—'Stop!'—you compel the children to look around. Now they see the old man, grey, exhausted by the heat, his eyes inflamed. His face wears a guilty smile. The thought of quenching their thirst no longer blazes in the children's minds like a house on fire; it burns weakly somewhere in a corner. Their minds are now engulfed by a new thought: the old man approached the well at the same time as we did, from the opposite direction. We saw him. Why did we not think about him? How did this happen?

'Sit down, dear children, let's rest,' you tell the children quietly. The children sit next to you beneath the oak.

'Please forgive us, Grandpa,' you say, turning to the old man, 'we nearly took over the bucket. Please, drink, and we will drink after you.'

'Please forgive us, Grandpa,' repeat the children one by one.

They look at the old man, whose hands and feet are trembling with exhaustion. They become embarrassed and the word 'forgive' becomes something more than a mere formality on their lips; it becomes a sincere expression of emotion. At this moment, a new image arises in the children's mind: what if they had drunk the entire bucket? There would not have been a drop left in the bucket, and—heaven forbid!—the old man would have had to lift a bucket of water from the deep well.

'Don't worry about me, dear children,' replies the old man. 'I should not be drinking at all ... It is hot, I will sweat, and my heart is weak. I only wanted to wash my eyes and rinse my mouth ... '

The shocked children watch: the old man, having rinsed his mouth and washed his eyes, sets off again on his journey. They feel sorry that the old man cannot sit down and rest. 'If I sit down and rest,' he explains, 'It will be difficult to get back up again.' When the old man leaves, the children stand up and wish him good health.

A wonderful vision of human life is revealed to the children. Your responsibility, as their educator, is to ensure that this vision is ingrained in their minds and hearts for the rest of their lives. The old man has left, but none of the children run to the bucket of water. You help the children in your care to clearly understand something that is still in a formative stage in their consciousness. You are awakening thought, which is one of the most complex elements of education. In the light of thought, emotions are deepened: compassion for the elderly, guilt from the knowledge that you have wronged them. (See 'A Drop of Water', p. 91.)

On a sense of duty

It is difficult to overestimate the importance of this pedagogical and human wisdom: the ability to talk with children about duty. It is important to talk about duty often; a teacher's words are indispensable here. To nurture a sense of duty means first of all to teach children how to observe life, how to observe people, how to observe everything that surrounds them, and to understand that everything around them, in one way or another, relates to them. And not only to understand that, but to feel it in their hearts, and to reject indifference, insensitivity and coarseness.

Whether the little children and I are walking in the school orchard, walking down the main street of the village, or catching a train to the warmth of the seaside, always and everywhere we find ourselves in a world of human relationships, and always and everywhere, I see my educational mission in conversing with the children about what it means to be dutiful, in teaching little people how to behave dutifully.

In the orchard we see the broken branch of an apple tree. The wind has damaged the tree. No-one is to blame, but we cannot simply ignore it. It is especially important to feel responsibility when it seems that everything is happening of its own accord. The children could have seen the broken branch and walked on—that would have been a lesson in indifference, and the more lessons like that a child witnesses during childhood, the greater the risk of egotism. We stop and tie the branch, and the children experience both joy and concern—not everything that they will meet in the world will be good. And that is a lesson in responsibility. And it is like this at every step.

We walk down the main street in the village and see an old lady crying near the shop. To walk past her would be a lesson in indifference. We stop and ask her what the matter is, and we help her. (The grandmother has lost her wallet. She came to buy bread, but she has no money.) We have 10 kopiika[7] *each – we were going to go to the cinema. We hand the money over to the grandmother and she kisses the children.*

It is difficult to find a human happiness greater than the happiness of a duty fulfilled. The children experience great happiness, and it is not the happiness of consumerism.

With every generation of schoolchildren, we embark on a hike into a particular neglected corner of the steppe. On the banks of a dry creek bed the schoolchildren see a stunted shrub, behind the shrub a few oaks, and a little further on, a field. The dry creek bed peters out in a barren field scorched by the sun, beyond which there is a village. It is here that I narrate a true story from the past. (See 'Do not forget the source', p. 106.)

There is nothing more terrible than egotism. There is nothing more destructive than justifying one's laziness by saying, 'Why should I do more than others? It's none of my business.'[8] The roots of egotism have lived in human consciousness for centuries.

On attitudes towards elders

Many years of educational experience have convinced me that respect for elders is strongest in those students who have come to understand and to feel that some behaviour is unacceptable: behaviour that has its roots in a lack of refinement or emotional maturity. In our system of ethical education, we have formulated ten restraints or prohibitions. In our community, observance of these prohibitions is considered to be a matter of honour and integrity, while breaking them is considered shameful and an indicator of moral ignorance. These are our ten prohibitions:

Do not be idle while everyone around you works;

Do not laugh at old age or at elderly people;

Do not enter into arguments with respected adults, especially the elderly;

Do not express discontent that you lack some material object;

Do not permit your mother to give you something that she denies herself;

Do not do what your elders condemn, either in their sight or behind their back;

Do not leave an elderly relative to live alone; in the life of every person there comes a time when they are unable to experience any joy other than the joy of human company;

Do not leave on a journey without requesting your elder's permission and advice;

Do not sit down to a meal without having invited your elders;

Do not sit while an elderly person stands, especially a woman; do not wait for an elderly person to greet you—you should be the first to extend greetings, and to wish good health upon parting.

The implementation of these ten prohibitions requires a very high degree of attention to the harmonious integration of the whole educational process. Our own behaviour, our way of thinking, our attitudes to one another and to the moral values of the community—these are, figuratively speaking, a tuning fork that sets the tone of our children's convictions. Whether each of our words carries genuine weight for our children depends on the actions that they observe behind our words. If our actions contradict our words, we are raising hypocrites and presenting the whole older generation in a bad light.

Our teaching staff are very concerned that the relationships between children and the older generations should be heartfelt, and conducted at an individual level, and that they should not in any circumstances take on the character of a routine campaign or activity. Under no circumstances allow a students' meeting with a respected elder to become an exhibition, or the care of the elderly to become a chore. Interactions with the elderly should always be heartfelt. A child's behaviour towards the elderly is a sure indicator of what kind of a citizen they will grow up to be.

To nurture humane qualities is a most complex and difficult task. It means to instil in a young child the need for a friend, who is dearer than anyone else in the world. One of the greatest joys of childhood should be the simple joy of communicating with others: I have come to see you because I cannot live without you.

We teach and advise children: share your joys with your grandmother and grandfather, spend time with them during the holidays. Many years of experience have shown that a child's ability to relate well to elderly people develops noble qualities of soul. The kindness of a child who respects old age, with all of its wisdom and weakness, becomes a great strength of the soul. It is of utmost importance that this kindness is strong, determined, steadfast and sustained.

Without a doubt, the most reliable remedies for the many weaknesses that come with inevitable aging are devotion, sincerity and trust. Elderly people are especially sensitive to the heartfelt feelings of others. They reward kindness with a huge internal effort to overcome their own weaknesses. Any child's impatience with the weaknesses of the elderly, the weak, the lonely, and the sick, should be regarded as a great evil. Such impatience is a toxic fruit born of the flowers of egotism and narcissism. An inability to accept an elderly person, just because they have some minor weaknesses, is most likely to arise when adults attempt to create a sterile, 'enhanced' environment, shielding children from anything that a caring adult may consider too much for a child's soul to bear. It is outrageous that some parents try to protect children from the elderly and the elderly from children. Attempts to shield a child from human weakness cripple the soul.

On the ability to love

A child cannot live, cannot enjoy proper moral development, cannot subsequently enter the wide world of civic life as a responsible citizen, if they do not know how to love. I wrote the story 'Little Hunchback and Shimmering Star' (p. 118) so that the children listening to it and digesting its content can discover an important truth of human life: a person only becomes truly human when they love.

The fantasy images in this story have an earthly, human character. Even the youngest children are led to think that real beauty is to be found in devotion, in the urge to bring joy to another person. My story teaches children to value human devotion and love. To feel and understand that others hold you dear is of great human value.

The following touching scene took place recently near the school in our village.

Seven children from up and down the street gathered on the green grass: three boys and four girls. The next day was to be a joyful holiday. And on this day, the eve of that joyful holiday, it had long been a tradition that adults give gifts to children. The children began to boast about the presents they were to receive from their parents and grandparents. Mykola, the eldest, knew that his parents had bought him a bicycle three days earlier. His mother and father thought that he knew nothing about the bike. They had hidden it in a spare room, but it was impossible to hide anything from that boy. He had already tried riding the bike, unscrewed a bolt, and changed the bulb in the headlight. A small toy gun had been purchased for little Mykhas, dolls for Tetiana and Lida, a teddy bear for Olia, and coloured pencils for Zina.

'And my grandmother picked me up and gave me a kiss', said eight-year-old Serhiiko, a first-grader, and such happiness shone in his eyes that all the other children were jealous. The bicycle, the gun, the dolls, the teddy bear, the coloured pencils—all seemed pale and insignificant in comparison to what Serhiiko felt … The presents had only just been purchased, had not yet been presented, but already the children had begun exchanging them—the doll for a gun, the teddy bear for a doll, the pencils for a bike ride … Only Serhiiko sat proud and independent: his treasure could not be bought, could not be exchanged for anything else. It was love, which is worth more than any other treasure.

If only all adults understood how much children treasure the love of their mothers and fathers, grandmothers and grandfathers! Not the blind, unthinking love that is willing to turn a blind eye to anything reprehensible and see only goodness, even when there is no goodness to be seen, but wise, demanding love, restrained or generous according to human need. What can you do, mothers and fathers, grandfathers and grandmothers, so that your child treasures your love? Here one elusive thing is supremely important: a child must always feel that they have not yet become the person that their loved ones would like to see and that they love. This is a pure, noble urge to be loved. Serhii values his grandmother's affection because she does not kiss him every day. With an aching heart she explains to him the kind of person he should be, but, unfortunately, has not yet become. He needs to keep trying, and he will become a true human being. The son of wise parents always feels that there are more beautiful, morally better, more worthy people than him. One has to strive to become like those people. I love you not so much for what you are now, as for the person I believe you will become. This, essentially, is the foundation of parental love and filial devotion.

However, in life no two people are completely identical. The Little Hunchback suffers because no one wants her devotion, while the Shimmering Star generously gives its love to her. We love those who love us. There is always an element of protection in human love: with one being stronger and one being less strong, or weaker. The weaker one does not feel unfortunate. They are only weak in a relative sense, when compared with the great inner strength of the one who is capable not only of loving equally, but of defending, saving, shielding from unhappiness. Faith, trust and devotion depend on this lack of human uniformity, on the fact that there is always one who is stronger and one who is less strong, or weaker.

How important it is that in our daily human contacts within the walls of a school, this lack of uniformity in will, thought and feeling is understood, protected and nurtured. How important it is that one individual does not come in conflict with another, but harmoniously aligns themselves with the other's unique, inimitable characteristics. I believe it is crucial that in the relationships between children, and especially between adolescents and between young men and young women, devotion, faith and trust are developed, so as to affirm the nobility, generosity, and sincerity of the stronger ones and the inner strength of those who are less strong or weaker. As each generation of students crosses the threshold between childhood and adulthood, I tell them a story about faith and devotion: 'Vania Senior and Vania Junior' (p. 119). It shows how a person becomes invincible when they feel that they are responsible for someone else's life. Similarly, a person becomes invincible when they feel that someone else is responsible for their life. Do not fear being 'Senior'. Neither should you fear being 'Junior'. I use that word with the same respect as the word 'Senior' and write both words with a capital letter. The main thing is that you love, believe and trust. True love educates people who are strong in spirit, because love is the gift of our inner strength, of our worry, care and concern.

The art of education and upbringing lies in ensuring that each child feels themselves to be Senior in relation to one person, and Junior in relation to another, that everyone is both the Strong one and the Weak one, protecting someone and being protected by another. Such a harmony of human relationships in the community is our ideal. For us, as teachers, it is the greatest joy to see this ideal come to life in deeds and interactions.

If you ever witness a miraculous scene like the one described in 'Joy in a Child's Eyes' (p. 120), then know that you are a fortunate person.

How to comfort a child

To understand a person on an emotional level means first of all to understand the motives behind their actions. Many children's actions that we, as adults, perceive as inappropriate, originate from noble impulses, and if you have not understood these good intentions, you can extinguish a tiny flickering flame of human refinement.

Keep some joy in reserve for your child for those situations when their heart will be breaking with pain. We not only advise this, we explain how to do so with a concrete example. (See 'The Oriole', p. 128.)

Educators and parents are aware that if pain lingers in a child's heart without consolation, it hardens the soul, eventually making it indifferent, especially if the child observes that pain also lingers in the hearts of others without any consolation. It can happen that the pain takes root deep in a child's heart, estranging the child from adults and breeding mistrust.

If adults respond to each of a child's impulses reasonably, sensibly and in a disciplined way, then the child themselves will become reasonable, sensible and disciplined.

It is not possible to imagine a proper moral upbringing that does not nurture an appropriate attitude towards death. To fully clarify my philosophical and pedagogical stance, I reiterate—understanding the ethical aspects of death is a fundamental precondition for true optimism, joyfulness and the capacity to cherish and protect life. Many years of pedagogical work have convinced me that a child who, in the company of adults, comprehends death as an irreversible tragedy, absorbs from those adults an optimistic faith in the invincible power of life.

I have been convinced thousands of times that when the death of a loved one touches a child's heart, the sense of loss gives rise not only to an enhanced appreciation of the joy of living, and a thirst for life, but a new outlook on life in general. The young person discovers with wonder the true value of being alive, of feeling, of seeing the world, savouring the joy of living and learning. In becoming aware of death, a person does not make peace with it, but takes a stand against it, denies it, striving to affirm the joy of being with their love of life. And, most importantly, understanding death as an irreversible tragedy teaches a child to cherish another human being, to protect their life, to spare their feelings.

When children do encounter death, a teacher with highly developed educational skills is able to direct the intellectual and emotional energies of the children to discovering the greatness of life.

The children in grade two were having a drawing lesson. Somebody knocked at the door. The teacher opened the door and saw a woman who had been crying. It was the mother of little blonde-haired, blue-eyed Natalka.

'Please let Natalka come home,' the mother asked the teacher. 'Her grandma has died.'

The teacher returned to his desk and quietly said, 'Children there has been a great misfortune. Natalka's grandma has died.'

Natalka left with her mother, and the teacher spent the remaining two lessons telling the children all about the life of the lady who had died. The children learnt of a history of human courage and endurance that was known to only a few people in the village.[9]

The children felt deep pain. Someone had died who deserved to be remembered beyond their immediate family circle. I believe it is crucial to hold classroom discussions about the lives of children's grandfathers and grandmothers when they die. As the sun is reflected in a drop of dew, the fate of the nation is reflected in the fate of each individual.

On adulthood

Learn to think about your own growth to adulthood …

Is it necessary to talk to a child about this? Many years of experience have convinced me that a common weakness of upbringing in schools, and especially in families, is the treatment of a child as an eternal infant. Forgetting the reality that today's child is tomorrow's adult often leads to unpleasant surprises. The education of maturity is an important issue in values education, in which the intellectual, moral and creative development of a human being intersect. I have in mind the exceptional importance of the early years for the education of creative abilities, so that a divine spark can be discovered in everyone. This is not just a question of psychology. An individual's personal happiness, and consequently the happiness of the community as a whole, ultimately depends on what abilities are developed in each individual, what facets of their personality are developed and continue to shine throughout their life. It is impossible to imagine a harmonious society if children transition from childhood to adolescence and adulthood without ever experiencing success or discovering aptitude for anything. And issues often begin in early childhood when children are preparing to go to school and are studying in the early grades. The issue of nurturing and developing children's abilities is a broad ethical issue. I have been convinced by many years of experience that the foundations of our abilities are laid in childhood. It is important to teach young people to think about their path to adulthood, if they are to develop *maturity of thought* and *maturity of spirit.*

STORIES AND VIGNETTES

How the sun sets

A teacher and a little boy liked to watch the sunset. Every night they would go to the edge of the village. From the top of an ancient burial mound, they would watch the sun disappear below the horizon.

For three days in a row—the day before yesterday, yesterday and today—the boy had observed the same thing: a fluffy little cloud floating in the blue sky above the fiery disk of the sun.

'Teacher,' the boy asked, 'Is that little cloud the same one we saw yesterday and the day before yesterday?'

'No, it's not the same one,' replied his teacher. 'Yesterday it was not the same one as the day before, and today it is not the same one as yesterday.'

The little boy became thoughtful. The fiery disk of the sun sank below the horizon. First it was reduced to a narrow band of crimson, then just a little spark and finally even the spark disappeared.

'Teacher,' the little boy asked, 'Where did yesterday go, and the day before yesterday?'

The teacher gave the boy a hug and gently stroked his head.

Where did that little boy go?

Once little Petryk and his grandfather went to the pond to fish. They sat on the bank and cast their fishing lines. Petryk's grandfather told him, 'When I was a little boy, like you, the pond was very, very deep here. There were carp as big as this … '

'Grandpa, were you really a little boy?' little Petryk asked incredulously.

'Yes, I was. I swam here, fished here,' said his grandfather.

'Where did that little boy go?' wondered little Petryk.

A handful of wheat

An old farmer named Grandpa Karpo brought a sack of wheat to the mill. Soon his turn came. He carried his sack over to the basket used to feed grain into the millstone, opened his sack, and began to pour the heavy grains from one hand to another. Joy shone in his eyes. Then, with a heavy sigh, he fed the grain into the millstone. He felt as if he were parting with a dear friend.

When there was only a little wheat left in the basket, Grandpa Karpo took a handful of grain and put it into his pocket.

At home he dug a seedbed, took the grain from his pocket, and planted the wheat. 'You can live happily here,' he said.

The chick

A hen settled on an egg. She sat there for a long, long time. The egg grew so warm that a chick developed in it.

At first, the chick slept. Then he woke up and saw that everything around him was yellow. The chick thought that the whole world must be yellow. The chick became cramped in his yellow world, so he started pecking at the yellow wall. He pecked for a long time and managed to make a hole in the eggshell.

Through this hole, the chick could see a whole new world, with a pale blue sky, green trees, and a dark blue river. The chick was delighted that the world was so beautiful. He spread his wings, broke open his yellow home, and burst out, cheeping, 'Cheep, cheep, cheep.' That was him saying, 'What a wonderful world of blue and green!'

The storks have arrived

'The storks have arrived,' says my mother. 'They bring a key from the sun. With that key, they open huge golden gates, and the sun rises higher and higher in the sky. The sun wakes Mighty Thunder from its slumber in the gullies. Mighty Thunder wakes up and rumbles in the clouds, casting flashes of lightning here and there. That is what the storks bring in the spring. They live in pairs and build nests on the roofs of homes and barns.'

'Wherever there are storks, there is happiness,' says my grandmother, 'Because they are birds of the sun. They greet the sun early in the morning and bid it good night in the evening. At dawn, the storks take off from their nests and fly high in the sky. They screech and croak, joyfully welcoming the sun. In the evening, they stand in their nests and gaze westwards.'

'That is them wondering how many more days the sun will keep rising higher in the sky,' says my mother, 'And when its path will begin to get lower. In the autumn, the storks will fly away. Then they will circle above their nests for a long time, saying goodbye to their home, to Ukraine. They always promise to return in the spring.'

The stillness of the evening

We are in the school yard. The sun has set. A starling flies out from his nesting box, flits off somewhere, and returns almost immediately. His chicks are quiet. Doves are sitting on the roof of their dovecote. One dove starts cooing and then falls silent. A little bee is running late. She hurries home after a long day foraging for honey for her little ones. Somewhere under the eaves, a sparrow, half asleep, breaks the silence with a short cheep.

Everything is still. Stars twinkle in the sky. We walk from the village to a field, so we can listen to the evening music of the steppe. The field is still. The quiet song of a quail breaks the silence. The little bird bids good night to the sun. Or perhaps it wants to hasten the sunrise?

Far away, a girl's voice sings, '*The wind is blowing in the field*,' and this makes the field seem even more still and quiet. It seems that everything is listening to her pensive song: the wheat, the forest, the lofty ancient burial mound in the steppe, and the village.

The old man and the swallow

Every morning, when a baby boy woke in his cradle, he could see a swallow's nest just above his window. The swallow was always busy taking care of her chicks, flying back and forth, bringing food to her little ones and cheeping tenderly.

The first word the boy spoke was 'mamma', and the second word was 'swallow'. The boy stood up on his two feet, learnt to walk, and then to run. The years passed by. Every autumn, the swallow would fly south for the winter, and then return in the spring.

The boy went to the city to study. His busy life meant that he did not visit his home village for many years. He married, had children, and then grandchildren.

His grandchildren had their own children. The boy became an old, old man …

One day, this old, old man felt a sudden desire to go and visit his home village. Why he felt this sudden impulse, he could not say. As he travelled to his village, he told himself, 'There is probably no trace of that swallow's nest.'

He arrived in the village, entered his front yard, and could not believe his eyes: in the very same place, above the very same window, was the same nest. And busily going about her business was the same swallow, with a grey stripe on her wing.

The old, old man was deeply moved. His hands began to tremble, and tears glistened in his eyes.

At least I saw the dear sun again!

It was wintertime. The sun was shining, but it was frosty and bitterly cold. A boy came to the greenhouse, where chrysanthemums were in bloom: white, blue, pink, azure and violet. The boy took a sky-blue chrysanthemum and hid it in his pocket. He was burning with shame for what he was doing, but he so much wanted to bring a sky-blue flower to his mother.

The boy walked home. On the way, the flower began to suffocate, and begged the boy, 'Please take me out of your pocket. I cannot breathe!'

The boy was surprised. 'But it is freezing outside,' he said. 'You will die!'

'Take me out anyway,' the flower replied.

The boy took the flower from his pocket. But the flower was not done. 'Put me on the ground, please,' it asked.

The boy lay the flower on the snow. It stretched out, straightened its petals, sighed, and whispered, with a faint smile, 'At least I saw the dear sun again!'

How a butterfly sheltered from the rain

Dark clouds covered the sky, blocking the sun. Thunder rumbled and it began to rain. When the first drops of rain began to fall, a little butterfly was flying among the trees. One of the raindrops fell right on him. 'Oh, no!' thought the butterfly, 'What should I do? Where can I shelter from the rain?' And he flew to a beetroot and hid under its broad leaf. The rain poured down, but the butterfly was no longer afraid, because he was safe and dry under the leaf. He even dozed off. When he woke, it was already dark, and the rain had stopped.

Autumn in the melon plantation

Early in the morning, my father and I went to the melon plantation. Our horses ambled slowly, as if they too were listening to the morning stillness. The east turned red, and a nightingale trilled in the meadow. We passed a tall, spreading poplar. Some bird that lived in it had woken up, perhaps disturbed by the sound of our cart. She was sitting on a branch and cleaning her beak.

In the melon plantation, everything was drenched in a heavy dew: vines, watermelons and rockmelons. Bathed in dew, the watermelons looked like silver balls. Grandpa Panas sat hunched over near his hut. He was gazing to the east, waiting for the sun to rise.

I noticed something near a huge watermelon. What was it? It was a hare! He was sitting and drinking dew from a vine. I did not want to disturb him. He looked over at me and waved his paw, and it seemed to me that he was smiling. What a happy morning it was!

The boy and the chickadee

A boy set up a bird feeder in his garden. A little chickadee flew over to him. She was not afraid of the boy. She bravely took food from his hands, so the boy asked her, 'Would you like to be my chickadee?'

'All right,' replied the chickadee. 'I'll be yours, and you can protect me.'

One day, the boy fell ill. He asked his mother to open the window a little. His mother opened it, and the chickadee flew in and sat on the table near the boy's bed.

'Please get well soon!' she said. 'The frosts and blizzards are coming, and who else will protect me?'

Tetianka is smiling

Tymko in grade three is very happy. He has a new sister named Tetianka.

His mother is constantly by Tetianka's cradle, smiling at her, but Tetianka just sleeps or cries. When Tetianka starts to cry, her mother picks her up and holds her.

Tymko wants Tetianka to look at him. He bends over Tetianka and shows her a teddy bear, but Tetianka does not seem to see anything.

'Why doesn't she want to look at me?' Tymko asks his mother, feeling hurt.

'She is still too small,' answers his mother. 'When she starts smiling, she will look at you and at your teddy bear.'

Every morning Tymko goes to Tetianka's cradle and waits to see if his sister will smile at him today.

And then one day she does smile. Tymko calls out joyfully, 'Mum! Tetianka is smiling!'

His mother comes running and bends over Tetianka, and the baby smiles at her too. 'Run to the field, Tymko, and tell your father that Tetianka is smiling,' she says.

Tymko runs to the field where his father is sowing wheat. He runs up waving his arms. His father stops the seed drill and waits for Tymko with anxious eyes.

'Dad, Tetianka is smiling!' shouts Tymko.

His father's eyes light up with joy. He smiles and hugs his son and kisses him.

And all the other people working in the field with his father smile as well.

The moon in the trough

My mother poured some water into our trough. The sun sank below the horizon, and the moon rose. When it climbed high in the sky, I could see the moon in the water, looking just the same as in the sky, round and white. I wanted to take a closer look at something that looked like a small cloud on the moon's surface. I leaned over the trough, but the moon was far, far away. I thought that when morning came, I would be able to see what was on the moon's surface more clearly.

But in the morning, there was no moon in the sky or in the trough.

The playful sunbeam

Little Tymko wakes up very early in summer. He has so much work to do, feeding the pigeons, watering the flowers, reading his book, and drawing a picture to illustrate a fairy tale. When he wakes up, he watches a playful, pink sunbeam creep towards his bed. As soon as it touches his pillow, Tymko quickly gets up and does his exercises.

But today Tymko does not feel like getting up. He could not say why he feels that way. The sunbeam touches his pillow and jumps right up onto it. 'What will happen next?' wonders Tymko, and he just keeps lying there in bed.

But then the sunbeam creeps all the way across his pillow and touches Tymko's face. It burns him, like a hot coal. Tymko feels ashamed that the sunbeam has caught him napping. He jumps out of bed and does his exercises.

Many years pass, and Tymko becomes an adult, with children of his own. But he never forgets the shame he felt when that burning sunbeam caught him napping.

A New Year's tree for the sparrows

In three days, it would be New Year's Eve, but Vitia was sick in bed. His mother put a New Year's fir tree[10] at the foot of Vitia's bed, and decorated it with toys, sweets and apples. In the evening it was lit up by coloured lights.

The morning of New Year's Eve arrived. Vitia looked out the window and saw three little sparrows. They were hopping from foot to foot, looking for food. Vitia felt sorry for the little birds.

'Mum,' said Vitia, 'Let's make a New Year's tree for the sparrows.'

'How?' asked his mother in surprise.

'I'll show you,' said Vitia.

He stuck a twig from the fir tree into a sweet box, and scattered grain and crumbs all over it. His mother took the little New Year's tree and put it in the garden. The sparrows saw it and flew over to the grains, feasting on them and chirping joyfully.

Vitia had a very happy New Year!

Because it is night

Yulia asks her mother for a large sheet of paper.

'What do you need paper for?' asks her mother.

'I want to draw everything that lives in my room,' she replies.

Yulia's mother gives her a large sheet of paper, and the little girl sits down to draw.

Half an hour later, she shows her picture to her mother. The paper is not white anymore, but black all over.

'Look what I have drawn, Mum,' Yulia exclaims joyfully. 'Here is my bed, and this is me, sleeping in the bed. Here on the carpet under my bed is my horse with a fiery mane. My dolly Melanka is right beside me. The fish in the aquarium is sleeping, and so is the cat, and there is a blizzard outside.'

'But why can't I see any of those things?', asks her mother. 'Where is the bed? Where is the horse with the fiery mane? Where are the doll and the cat?'

'You can't see them because it's night-time,' Yulia answers, and thinks to herself, 'Why doesn't Mummy understand?'

The old tree stump

A large tree with wide spreading branches grew in the forest. In spring it was covered with green leaves and white flowers that attracted the bees and the bumblebees. Songbirds built their nests in the tree's branches. Every year in spring they returned from warmer lands, found their tree, and merrily chirped, 'Happy Spring to you, dear tree. We have come to visit you again.' The tree lived very happily because it had so many friends.

Many years passed. The tree grew old and withered. Some people came to the forest and cut down the dry old tree and took it away.

All that was left of the tree was a stump. Lonely and sad, it was gradually covered in a layer of grey dust. It was painful for it to remember how the bees and bumblebees used to visit it, and how the songbirds built their nests in its branches …

The songbirds did arrive in spring, circled above the stump, cheeped anxiously, and flew away. The lonely stump wept. It so much wanted someone's friendship.

Autumn came. One day a hedgehog came running up to the tree stump. It dug a hole next to the stump and brought sweet smelling dry leaves and moss to make a winter bed for itself. The old tree stump was overjoyed, and tenderly embraced the hedgehog. And the hedgehog was kind to the tree stump. They made friends and told each other about their lives. The tree stump even began to look younger and was covered with beautiful green moss. Now it had a friend.

The piglet who wanted to be green

A little white piglet trotted into the meadow. Everything there was green. The grass was green, the bushes were green, the reeds in the water were green and their rustling leaves were green. A green frog sat near the pond while a green fly circled above it. The little piglet looked at this green world and wanted to be green himself. But how? By the pond he spotted a puddle full of very green water. The piglet jumped into the puddle and came out looking as green as could be. He returned to the meadow, but everybody just laughed at him saying, 'Just look at this huge green frog!'

The grass laughed, the bushes laughed, the reeds laughed, the frog laughed, and the fly laughed. Even the sun laughed.

The fly and the cat

Our cat is sitting on the windowsill, enjoying the warmth of the sun. He closes his eyes and dozes off. He dozes so sweetly that he starts purring in delight. Suddenly, a fly comes buzzing by, lands right on the cat's nose and bites him! The cat wakes up and whips his head around, but the fly is already hiding outside.

The cat closes his eyes. Once more he dozes and purrs with delight. And once again the fly comes buzzing and bites him on the nose! Angrily, the cat jumps down from the window and crawls under the bed.

When the fly returns, the cat is nowhere to be found.

The hare and the rowan tree

Winter set in. The earth was covered in snow. It was hard for the hare to find food.

One day he saw some red berries on the rowan tree. The hare leapt up all around the tree, but the berries were too high.

The hare begged the rowan tree, 'Dear rowan tree, please give me some berries.'

The rowan tree replied, 'Ask the wind. It will help you.'

The hare asked the wind for help. The wind blew. It rocked and shook the rowan tree. A bunch of red berries broke off and fell in the snow. The hare was overjoyed to have the berries.

'Thank you, wind,' he said.

Two butterflies

Two butterflies flutter over a green meadow. One butterfly is white, the other is red. They meet, land on a green leaf, and start boasting to each other.

'My wings are more beautiful than yours,' says the white butterfly. 'I am like a white cloud.'

'No,' objects the red butterfly. 'My wings are more beautiful. I am like the sun.'

The sun sets, and it gets dark. Now both butterflies are grey.

The lark and the sun

A clod of grey soil lay in a field, covered with snow. The sun shone down, and the snow melted. A cloud drifted over the field, sprinkling raindrops. One drop of rain, heated by the sun, fell onto the grey clod of soil, and it turned into a grey bird—a lark.

The lark soared high into the sky. He tried to sing but it sounded terrible, so he flew up to the sun and asked, 'Dear sun, dear golden sun, teach me to sing beautifully.'

The sun replied, 'Take this ball of golden thread and stretch it all the way to the earth.'

The lark took the ball of golden thread and flew right down to the earth. The finest of golden threads stretched behind him, and an enchanting song filled the air.

Since that day, every morning at dawn, the lark flies up to the sun, and the sun gives him a golden ball of thread. The lark stretches the thread over the fields and brings divine song to the people below. The blue sky sings, the golden wheat sings, the whole world sings. It is beautiful!

A drop of water

It was a hot July day. A group of schoolchildren was approaching a well beneath a tall oak tree. They were returning from a hike. The children were very thirsty, and the closer they drew to the well, the faster they walked.

An old lady was approaching from the other side of the well. She had been walking for a long time and was very tired. The old lady and the schoolchildren arrived at the well at the same time.

At the edge of the well stood a bucket of cold water. The children took it and drank from it one by one. They pushed the old lady aside. She stepped back and leaned sadly against the oak tree.

When the schoolchildren had quenched their thirst and had set off again, the old lady followed them with her gaze and shook her head thoughtfully.

The oriole's nest

An oriole has beautiful, multi-coloured feathers. When you look at an oriole, you are reminded of a rainbow. Its coat is made up of red, orange, yellow and blue-grey feathers.

An oriole built her nest in a thicket, in a blackthorn bush. She raised some chicks. Then she flew to warmer lands for the winter.

It was a cold winter, and somebody cut down the blackthorn bush for fuel.

In spring, the oriole returned from warmer lands, but the blackthorn bush was gone. The oriole flew all around where the bush had been. There had been a thicket there, but now there were only weeds. The oriole was sad. She sat on a dry twig that was all that remained of the blackthorn bush and sang a sad song. That was her way of crying.

Where would the oriole build her nest now?

The willow by the pond

Little Oksanka was walking by a pond. She picked up a willow twig on the bank of the pond and stuck it into the damp earth. And then she went home. Soon Oksanka's parents moved to the city, and Oksanka went to school there.

Ten years passed. Oksanka returned to her native village. Now she was a tall girl with long black hair. Oksanka visited the bank of the pond again. She saw a tall, spreading willow, leaning over the pond. Oksanka was surprised.

'Willow, where did you come from?' she asked.

'You planted me when I was just a little twig,' answered the willow.

'How big you have grown,' said Oksanka. 'I did not recognise you.'

'But I recognised you,' whispered the willow gratefully.

The snail

A little snail lives under a raspberry bush. He is an amazing traveller. He lives in a little bony house, squeezes out through a tiny little window, sticks out his soft little horns, and looks around with his tiny little eyes. If there are no magpies or horny bugs around, the snail slowly crawls under the raspberry bush, taking his house with him. He climbs up onto a leaf, finds a sweet berry, and eats it. But if he senses danger, he hides in his house and waits. As long as he is in his safe little house, he is not afraid.

A tree for our unknown friend

Spring arrived. The children in grade one were learning how to read and write. Their teacher said to them, 'Let's plant some trees so we will always remember our childhood. There are thirty students in our class, and each one of you can plant your own tree.'

The children happily set to work. They dug holes, poured some water into them, and brought compost. Then some fir tree saplings were delivered. The teacher dug a hole for herself. But why did she dig an extra, thirty-second hole?

'This is for a boy or girl that may come to our school from far away,' explained the teacher. 'We will plant an extra tree for our unknown friend.'

The children planted thirty-two fir trees and took care of them, watering them during the summer and covering them with snow to keep them warm during the winter. The trees grew magnificently, with spreading branches.

Time passed. The children completed grade two, then grade three. They were already in grade four, but their unknown friend had still not appeared. Not a single new student had come to the village. Even when the students were in their final year of high school, there was still no sign of a new student.

The fir trees were now graceful, with spreading branches. Just before their graduation, the young people visited their fir tree alley. They came to muse about their unknown friend. 'It cannot be that we will never meet our unknown friend,' they thought. 'Surely the thirty-second tree will not remain alone forever.'

Somewhere in the meadow

Somewhere in the meadow, a bird calls anxiously. Why is its call so sad? I look up at the sky and see a flock of cranes. Perhaps, somewhere in the meadow, a crane with an injured wing has been left behind. He cannot fly south with his brothers, and is desperately crying out, 'Why are you leaving me behind?'

By a solitary pond, a little flower shows off its bright colours. It is a wild chamomile. A bee flies over to the flower. She lands on it, settles there for a while, then takes off and circles above it, buzzing anxiously. She also misses the summer.

Where are the swallows flying?

In the autumn, swallows gather in long lines on the local telegraph wires and quietly chirp to each other. They are discussing something. They keep looking first at the green meadow and then at the horizon.

Gradually, the grass in the meadow turns yellow and the nights become longer. The sun rises later and sets earlier. Silver gossamer threads float in the air. From beyond the forest, from beyond the primeval forest, Grandma Winter comes with her white blizzards, followed by Grandpa Frost. It is time to fly to warmer lands.

The swallows end their discussions and fly far away to warmer lands, to warm lakes with green banks. Huge, bright flowers bloom there, like our sunflowers. The swallows fly above the banks of a warm lake, but they are sad. Why? Because it is not their native land.

A wasp is tapping at the window

It was the beginning of the school year. It was hot and stuffy in the classroom. The deep blue sky of an Indian summer could be seen through the windows.

The young teacher was talking about wasps, and how they float out from their nest and fly from one flower to another, collecting honey.

Little, dark-eyed Fedko was sitting near the window. He wanted to listen to the teacher and follow what she was saying, but it was more than he could do. He looked out the window. The teacher's words droned on, like the wind in the ash trees that grew in the school yard.

Suddenly, something tapped on the windowpane. Startled, Fedko looked and caught his breath. Near the window, was a wasps' nest. Wasps were crawling into it, one after another. But one wasp was tapping at the window, buzzing, as if crying.

'Fedko, why aren't you listening?' the teacher asked.

Deeply moved, Fedko excitedly told his teacher, 'Look, there's a wasps' nest outside, just above the window. And this wasp … It's buzzing and buzzing, tapping at the window … '

The class fell silent. All that could be heard was the wasp's buzzing.

'You're right. The wasp is tapping at the window,' whispered the teacher. 'Open it for her, Fedko.'

Sunray and Winterbell

At the bottom of a deep well lived a tiny girl made of ice named Winterbell, the daughter of Mother Winter and cold Father Wind. She was born on the first bitterly cold day of winter. Mother Winter and Father Wind lowered her into the well and said, 'Make sure the water is cold even in summer.' Winterbell spent her entire life sitting in the water and keeping it cold.

One hot summer day, Sunray came dancing by the well. He jumped playfully into the water and met Winterbell, who opened her eyes wide in amazement. 'Who are you? You are so bright and beautiful!'

'I am Sunray,' he answered. 'A ray of sunshine! Why are you sitting down here? Come and see the sun!'

So, they went out to look at the sun. For the first time in her life, Winterbell could see the blue sky and the flowering orchards. She looked, then started crying and … melted. She turned into a tiny puddle. But she did not regret it because she saw the sun and the blue sky.

The first bee

The spring sun was growing warmer and warmer. The bees grew restless in their hive. It seemed the time was ripe to fly out and begin their work, and one bee said, 'I'll fly out and see if there are any flowers yet.'

The bee flew out. The field was grey with patches of snow here and there. On the edge of the forest, the bee spotted a blue flower. It was a squill, one of the first spring flowers. The bee flew over to the flower and sampled its juicy nectar. However, a cold draft was still blowing from the forest. The bee returned to the hive and told her sisters, 'Let's wait a little longer and let the sun warm the earth a little more.'

Why was Brisk worried?

Little Nadiika had a true friend, a dog named Brisk.

One hot June day, Nadiika and Brisk went swimming in the river. As soon as Nadiika entered the water, Brisk jumped in after her. He swam around her, whining anxiously. Then he swam up to her and pushed her with his paw, as if trying to tell her, 'You shouldn't be swimming!'

Surprised, Nadiika stopped swimming, got out of the water, and sat on the riverbank. Still barking anxiously, the dog disappeared. In the blink of an eye, he was back with Nadiika's mother.

Now, Brisk splashed into the water. Playing, swimming, even being a bit naughty, he swam over to where Nadiika was sitting, as if inviting her to join him for a frolic in the water.

The brave gosling, the hawk and the tadpole

A gosling was making his first splashes in the water. He had just hatched and looked like a fluffy yellow ball.

High in the sky, a hawk was searching for prey. He spotted the gosling and plummeted down. Fearing that his short life was coming to an end, the terrified gosling dived down into the water. The hawk crashed into the water and died instantly. The gosling rose to the surface and could not believe his eyes: the hawk was dead.

A tadpole was swimming nearby. He saw how the gosling escaped and thought that he had dived on purpose to kill the hawk. 'How brave you are, gosling!' exclaimed the tadpole.

The brave gosling swam proudly round the pond, quacking loudly. It was saying, 'I'm not even afraid of an eagle now!' But the tadpole thought, 'It is wiser to hide in the murky water.' And that is what he did.

The bullfinch's song

After a dreary, rainy autumn, winter arrived. Snow covered the ground with a white blanket, and snowdrifts were piled up everywhere. Rivers and streams froze over. Miraculously, one tiny lake remained unfrozen amidst the white snowdrifts. Somehow Grandpa Frost missed it.

A bullfinch flew over to the lake, sipped some water and started singing joyfully. He was happy because at last winter had arrived, children could ride their sleds, and woodpeckers could peck on the frozen trunks of pine trees.

Grandpa Frost heard the bullfinch's song. He crept up and leaned over the lake. As the bullfinch sang, the lake froze over. The bullfinch's song also froze, and the bullfinch flew away. Grandpa Frost returned to the forest, and everything fell silent.

A little girl came to the frozen lake. She found a frozen icicle and brought it home. The icicle melted, and the girl heard a joyful song. The bullfinch's song was frozen no more!

How the squill woke

A mighty old oak lived in the forest. Its spreading branches were covered with snow caps that covered its withered leaves, for the oak refused to surrender its leaves until the spring arrived.

At night, it was still frosty. In the morning, the sun rose, and the snow started melting. One little icicle that hung from a snow cap also started melting.

A drop of water fell onto a snowdrift below, then a second and a third. It was as if the droplets were chasing one another, creating a narrow hole in the snow. The droplets reached the ground and the grass under the snow. In this grass, a squill, one of the first spring flowers, was sleeping. It sensed something unusual and thought, 'Spring has come!'

It raised its head, washing its petals with the drops of water that were falling from the oak, climbed up a blade of grass, looked up out of the hole and saw blue sky above. 'It's spring, it's spring!' the squill exclaimed happily.

Its slender stalk rose high above the blanket of snow. Its tiny blue head looked all around and fell silent in fear. 'Oh, no!' it thought. 'What will happen now? It is still winter! There is snow everywhere, and I have woken up!'

But the water kept on dripping. The squill was frightened and happy at the same time. As it watched on, the snowdrifts grew smaller and smaller. The soil drank the water, winter retreated into the ground, and the spring woke all the other squills.

The swallows say goodbye to their homeland

For many years swallows lived under the eaves of a house. In spring they came from warmer lands and raised their chicks, but in autumn they flew away again to where it was warm.

In the house lived a mother and father and a little girl named Olenka. She would wait impatiently for the warm spring day when the swallows would arrive. That was a very special day for Olenka. In summer she liked to watch how the swallows fed their chicks and then went to sleep.

In autumn, when the swallows flew away, Olenka was sad. She felt like she was parting with dear friends.

For several days before they flew away, the swallows would gather in a flock, settle on the telegraph wires near their yard, and sit there for a long time. It seemed to Olenka that they were sad about something. She listened to their anxious twittering, and wondered, 'Why do they sit there for so long?'

She asked her mother, 'Mum, why do the swallows gather on the telegraph wires and stay there for so long before they fly away?'

'They are saying goodbye to their homeland. It is a long and dangerous route they must fly to get to warmer lands,' said her mother.

Olenka stood under the telegraph wires where the swallows were gathered. She wanted them to say goodbye to her as well.

The starling has returned

It was a quiet spring morning. The sun had not yet risen, but the sky in the east was turning pink. A starling began to sing loudly from the bare branch of a maple tree. He had just returned from a distant, warmer land. He had found his nesting box, had perched next to it, and was joyfully announcing, 'I have returned! Spring has arrived!'

In his warm nest, a sparrow heard the starling singing. He was sleeping comfortably and did not want to get up early, but when he heard the starling, he became alarmed. He woke up his sparrow wife and said, 'The starling has returned! From now on we will have to get up earlier. Otherwise, it will be hard to find food. The starling always manages to get there first.'

His sparrow wife sighed and answered, 'Thank goodness for the starling. He will wake you up, you lazybones.'

Chicks

A hen was sitting on her eggs. It was not much fun sitting for such a long time. Finally, her chicks began to hatch. One by one their shells started cracking, tiny yellow heads peeped out from the holes in the shells, and the chicks came out cheeping, 'Cheep! Cheep!'

'Cluck, cluck,' called the mother hen, 'Follow me!'

She led them to the backyard. The chicks ran after her, looking for all the world like rolling yellow balls. The chicks looked all around in wonder. 'Oh! How big the world is!'

'You think this is the whole world?' said the mother hen. 'No, there is also the vegetable garden, where there is some millet growing, and beyond that there is some burdock, and beyond the burdock there is a huge field of wheat.'

How the cat tried to catch a fish

A cat was sitting by a pond. 'I think I'll catch a fish,' he thought. He watched the fish, but they were all swimming far away from the water's edge and would not come closer.

'Why don't you swim closer to the water's edge?' the cat asked the fish.

'We'll come closer when you go home,' answered the fish.

A boy was passing by. He asked the cat, 'Are you fishing?'

'Not at all,' answered the cat. 'I'm just warming myself in the sun.'

The petal and the flower

A pretty dahlia was blooming in the garden. It was as white as marble and very fragrant. Bees and bumblebees were flying over to it to collect its nectar.

There were forty-two petals on this flower, and one of them started boasting, 'I am the most beautiful of all petals. Without me, the flower would not be a flower! I am the most important! Without me, the flower could not survive!'

So saying, the petal pulled itself from the flower and jumped to the ground. At first, she sat under a wild rose bush, watching to see what the flower would do without her. But the flower was oblivious to the loss. It was smiling at the sun and still attracting bees and bumblebees.

The petal set off by herself. She met an ant.

'Who are you?' asked the ant.

'I am the most beautiful petal, the most beautiful and the most important. Without me, the flower is not a flower.'

'A petal?' The ant was puzzled. 'I have seen petals on a flower, but I have never seen a petal with two little legs.'

The petal walked and walked, and by evening it had wilted. But the flower was still blooming.

And that is the end of the story. A flower without one of its petals is still a flower, but a petal without a flower is nothing.

A blizzard

Our home stands on the edge of the village. One winter morning, snow began to fall, and then the wind picked up. The field was covered in a cloud of snow. It swirled, like a white waterfall. Wherever you looked, there were white waves, sweeping quickly and irresistibly over the land.

I opened the door and looked outside. Suddenly I saw a little grey bird swept through the air towards a haystack in the field nearby. It seemed not to be flying of its own accord, but to be carried along on a white wave. The bird fell to the ground next to the haystack. What should I do? The bird would be covered with snow and freeze to death.

I put on my sheepskin coat and trudged over to the haystack. I found the bird already half covered with snow. I picked it up, put it inside my shirt, and took it home. I put it on the table, and it was hardly breathing. When it had warmed up a bit, it lifted its head. I could see blood on one of its wings. It must have been injured by a predator.

The little bird lived in our hut for a few weeks. Its wing healed, and when I released it, it flew away. In the evening it came and perched by my half-open window and chirped. I suppose it was saying, 'I am grateful to you. I love you, but it is still better for me to be free.'

The one and only rainbow stone

Vitia was playing in the sand on a riverbank. He was building a fairytale castle with a tall tower.

Suddenly, something sparkled in the sand, and Vitia spotted a little stone. It was small, the size of a sparrow's egg, but it was quite unique.

It was full of different crystals, so it sparkled with all the colours of the rainbow.

Fascinated by the stone, Vitia forgot about his fairytale sandcastle. He took the stone and went home.

He met some of his friends in a clearing in the forest. Vitia showed them his little stone. The boys were surprised to see its gleaming rainbow colours. They all started offering Vitia something in exchange for the stone. One boy offered his four-bladed pocketknife, another boy offered him a ball, a third boy offered a fishing rod, and a fourth boy his electrical flashlight.

But Vitia did not want to trade. 'Why don't you want to swap?' asked the boy with the flashlight. 'Because this little stone is the only one like it in the whole wide world,' answered Vitia. 'There is no other stone like this.'

The apple tree is coming back to life

Myshko in grade one was running through the school yard when he accidently broke a young apple tree.

'Myshko broke the apple tree! Myshko broke the apple tree!' shouted the children, and they ran to the teacher and told her all about it.

'Why don't you look where you are running?' asked the teacher reproachfully. 'What will we do now? The apple tree is dead. We'll just leave its broken stem there.'

Myshko became quiet and thoughtful. He would come to school each day, long before lessons began, and look at the row of young green apple trees. The broken tree still stood there, withered and misshapen. It was hard for Myshko to look at it.

One day the teacher took the whole class into the school orchard. 'Children,' she said, 'Let's count how many apple trees, pear trees and cherry trees we have in our young orchard.' Myshko walked along the row of apple trees. He knew very well that there were thirteen living apple trees and one dead one. It was painful for him to look at the withered stem. He walked up to the dead apple tree and nearly screamed—a green branch was growing from the dry stem.

'The apple tree is coming back to life!' he told his teacher with excitement. The teacher came over to the dried out little tree.

'Yes, the apple tree is coming back to life,' she said with joy. 'This can be your apple tree, all right Myshko?'

'Great!' said Myshko, and his eyes shone. He ran towards the well.

'Where are you going?' asked his teacher.

'I'm going to water my apple tree,' he shouted.

The most difficult lesson

When the children in grade three learnt that their friend Olia was moving away forever to the distant island of Sakhalin, they asked their teacher, 'Where is that island?'

Their teacher explained that a swallow would have to fly for many days to reach the island of Sakhalin.[11] The children were surprised. 'So, it's a long way away!' they said.

Then their teacher said, 'Children, Olia is going away forever. That means you will never, ever see your friend again. The years will pass. Decades will pass, and you will all be grown up, and grow old, but you will never see Olia again.'

The children were sad. They asked, 'Can we go to the station to see Olia off?'

The teacher answered, 'She is leaving tomorrow. We will go as a class to see her off. Here is an album. I would like each of you to draw a picture in it to express your wishes for Olia.'

The children stayed after school and each one drew what they wished for Olia. They drew the sun, which stood for happiness. They drew a sunflower, which stood for joy. They drew two storks, which stood for friendship. They drew a bee, which stood for a love of work. And one boy drew a multicoloured butterfly. When they asked him what it stood for, he answered, 'Beauty'.

Early the next day, the whole class walked to the station, instead of going to school. They saw Olia off. They could not forget that they would never see her again. Tears shone in the children's eyes. By the time they came back it was already midday. Someone asked the teacher, 'Will we have any lessons today?'

'Today we have already had the most difficult and the most essential lesson,' answered their teacher.

The most important thing is to make yourself feel

Genka was studying in grade four. Whatever questions the teacher asked, Genka immediately gave a full and correct answer and got full marks. Genka wrote better than everyone else and solved problems faster.

But his classmates did not like Genka. He showed off his intelligence too much. He would answer the teacher's question and look around the class as if to say, 'I'm the cleverest.'

In spring, the class was getting ready for a hike. The children were happy. What fun it would be to hike and spend the night in the forest!

They thought about what things to take, how to cook dinner, how to build a shelter for the night. They decided to take just one blanket and one bowl to share between two children. They quickly sorted themselves into pairs. But nobody wanted to share a blanket and bowl with Genka.

Genka started crying. He went to the teacher and said, 'I've never said a rude word to anyone ... Why don't they like me?'

The teacher answered, 'It's not easy to make yourself speak up. It's even harder to make yourself keep silent. And harder still to make yourself think. But the hardest of all is to make yourself feel.'

'How do I make myself feel?' asked Genka.

'You need to see people with different eyes. You're pleased that you're cleverer than everyone else. But you should be sad that there is no-one cleverer than you. Because anyone who thinks he is better than everyone else ends up lonely.'

'Thanks for the lesson,' said Genka. 'So, should I go hiking with my classmates?

'Yes, go. Take your own blanket and bowl and begin your new life. Open your eyes and learn to see people differently.'

The wonderful icicle

It was warm during the day but became frosty in the evening. Water dripping from the melting snow on the roofs froze and formed icicles. That is how one very long icicle was born. It hung above the window like a crystal wand.

When the sun rose, a rainbow shimmered in the icicle. The icicle had never seen the sun before, because it was born that night and had only seen the stars in the sky. But now the warm sun was shining brightly. Overwhelmed by emotion, the icicle burst into tears. But nobody realised the icicle was crying. Everybody thought that it was melting. But no, it was not melting, it was crying, and its hot tears were falling on the frozen ground.

Who the rowan tree was waiting for

The rowan tree shed its leaves. Only bunches of red berries remained. They hung like beads, beautiful, but bitter and tart. Whenever birds came and tried the berries, they found them bitter and flew on.

Then, one morning, a beautiful song rang out above the rowan tree, as if silver strings were being played. Some wonderful, crested birds had arrived. They were waxwings. They had flown from the far north. They were the ones the rowan tree had been waiting for! Joyfully it welcomed its guests with its red berries. None of the other birds knew the rowan tree's berries had become sweet.

People say frost makes the berries sweet, but it was not the frost. It was grief. The rowan tree had waited so long for its dear guests, feeling sad, grieving, worrying that they would not come. And its grief made the berries sweet.

How snow changes colour

When the sun rises, white snowdrifts turn pink. The sun paints them with its rays. As the sun rises higher and higher, the sky becomes strikingly blue, and the snow becomes dazzlingly white. You look out over the steppe, and against the white blanket of snow you can see a little bird, and a hare darting here and there.

Just before the sunset, the snow turns a deep blue, as if reflecting the sky like a mirror, and in the shade, the snow is even violet.

Then the sun sets. The sky in the west turns crimson red—tomorrow will be a windy day. The snowdrifts now reflect this crimson glow, as if the sun has splashed them with crimson paint. The evening glow fades, and so does the crimson reflection on the snowdrifts. The stars twinkle in the sky. The snow turns grey. The bird hides in her nest. The hare sits under a bush.

The forest in spring

The forest wakes from its long winter sleep. Buds open on the hazelnut trees and the elms, on the maples and the linden trees. Small, bright green leaves reach towards the warm sun. These springtime leaves are fragrant and sticky. A drop of dew falls on a tiny leaf, and it quivers in surprise.

The leaves are not rustling, but quietly whispering. The branches are swaying, and one leaf stretches out to touch another, but cannot reach. The branches make a sound like a magic wooden flute.

Somewhere a woodpecker is tapping on a tree trunk, and an oriole is singing.

But what is that sound in the depths of the forest? We walk towards a quiet ringing sound. In a deep ravine we find a stream. That is where the sound was coming from.

We come to the edge of the forest and see a wide field stretching before us. Above the field and the forest, a solitary white cloud floats in the deep blue sky.

Only the oak tree is still asleep. What are you waiting for, oak? Probably you are waiting for the first thunderstorm. That will wake you from your sleep.

How our cat washes himself

Our grey cat wakes up early in the morning. He crawls out of his bed near the woodstove, arches his back, and stretches. Then he sits down, half closes his eyes and starts washing himself. Washing is a ritual for him. It begins with poking out his tongue, raising his paw, and wetting it with saliva to brush his whiskers. Then, wetting his paw again, he cleans his face and eyebrows.

After he is done with his morning hygiene, he goes out into the yard. Some sparrows immediately take off from the ground and settle in a tree's branches, chirping loudly and warning each other, 'Fly to safety! A fierce beast is on the prowl!'

The cat seems not to take any notice of the sparrows. He moves slowly around the yard, threading his way through the bushes, while the sparrows chatter incessantly.

We need both the nightingale and the beetle

A nightingale sang in the garden. Its song was beautiful. It knew that everyone loved its singing, and it looked around with pride at the flowering orchard, the bright blue sky, and a little girl who was sitting in the orchard and listening to its song.

Not far from the nightingale flew a large horned beetle. It made a loud buzzing sound as it flew. The nightingale stopped singing and said to the beetle with irritation, 'Stop your buzzing. You're spoiling my singing. No-one needs your buzzing. In fact, it would be better, beetle, if you did not exist at all.'

The beetle answered with dignity, 'No, nightingale, the world needs me, just as it needs you.'

'You are a wise one!' laughed the nightingale. 'Do you really believe people need you. Let's ask that little girl. She will tell us who people need and who they do not need.'

The nightingale and the beetle flew over to the little girl and asked her, 'Tell us little, girl, who should we keep in this world, the nightingale or the beetle?'

'We should keep both the nightingale and the beetle,' answered the little girl. She thought a little more and added, 'How could we have a world without beetles?'

The hedgehog and the foxfire

A hedgehog was walking through the forest, carrying an apple on his spines, when he spotted a glowing tree stump, something we call 'foxfire'. It was dark at home in the hedgehog's hut, and he decided to take a piece of the stump home with him, to bring light to his little children, so they would not be afraid of the dark. The hedgehog took a piece of the glowing wood and brought it home. Their little house was now lit up. The hedgehog's children were thrilled. 'It's nice to have some light!' they said. 'Now, we can look at the pictures in our books.'

Do not forget the source

The teacher asks, 'Do you see this bare wasteland, scorched by the sun?'

'Yes,' answer the children.

'Then listen to this true story. Many, many years ago, here, where this bare wasteland now is, there used to be a deep, deep pond. Many carp swam in the pond, and willows grew on its banks. It was possible to row a boat from the village to those shady oaks you see over there. There were many of those oaks back then. There were squirrels in the forest. What happened? Why did the pond disappear?

This used to be an ancient Cossack settlement. The Zaporizhzhian Cossacks dug a pond here after the Battle of Zhovti Vody[12] and settled on its banks. But they noticed that the pond was becoming clogged with silt. The villagers called a meeting and decided that everyone who swam in the pond, or even came to its banks to simply enjoy its beauty, must take a bucket of silt, carry it to the other side of the gully, and empty the bucket into the field.

People followed this arrangement. Wooden buckets hung on willow stakes by the bank of the pond. For grown men there were large buckets, almost half the size of today's barrels, for women and teenagers the buckets were a little smaller, and for children there were little ones. Only those who were still babes in arms did not pay with their work for the joy of being here.

With each passing year, the pond became clearer and deeper, until a new family moved into the village—a mother, father, four sons and two daughters. They settled on the edge of the village, not far from the pond. Both the adults and the children from that family swam in the pond, but they never used the buckets. At first, the villagers did not pay much attention. However, soon the villagers noticed that more and more teenagers were doing the same—they swam in the pond but did not remove any silt.

The elders began to reprimand the young ones, saying, 'What are you doing?'

But the teenagers answered, 'If they don't have to, then we don't have to, either.'

The bad example prevailed. Many teenagers, and later even adults, began to come and swim in the lake after dusk, so that no one would see them …

The elders were concerned, but there was nothing they could do. The wooden buckets that hung on the branches of the willow first fell apart and then disappeared completely.

The ancient tradition was forgotten.

Everyone thought, 'There is enough for my lifetime.'

The pond was neglected. Soon it turned into a swamp and became overgrown with weeds.

There came a time when water could only be found here during the spring. Then even that water failed to appear.

The pond disappeared. Only the memory of it remained.

The ants and the pumpkin seed

Some ants found a pumpkin seed in a vegetable garden. It was fragrant and tasty, but very heavy. They needed to carry the seed to their anthill. Such a treasure was too good to leave behind. But their anthill was far away in the forest, beyond high mountains and wide valleys. One ant just managed to lift the pumpkin seed onto his back. All his friends followed him, the whole tribe of ants. As soon as the ant was too tired to go on, and put the seed down, another ant immediately picked it up.

In this way the ants carried the pumpkin seed, one after another, over high mountains and across wide valleys. When the sun was nearly setting, they brought the seed to their anthill. They delivered it and headed back to the vegetable garden. Perhaps there would be another seed there, just as good?

The Old Year and the New Year

On New Year's Eve, two years met: the Old Year, a grey-haired old man, and the New Year, a youth. The Old Year handed his keys over to the New Year and said, 'This big key is to earthly riches. Hand it over to the people straight away. May they mine much coal, ore and oil. May they make many machines.

This middle key is to the grain fields. You can give it to the people immediately as well. May they grow much wheat, rice and sugar beet. May they have much milk, meat and butter.

And this is the smallest key. It is to the armoury. Protect this key more than your own eye. As soon as you notice that an enemy is planning to attack our land, give this key to the people and tell them to quickly arm themselves. Do not sleep either day or night.'

Those are the instructions the Old Year gave to the New.

The rainbow

Little Mykhailyk fell seriously ill. He was an old farmer's only son, and his mother and father loved him dearly. Their hearts were breaking at the thought that he might die. What would they do then? They could not have another son, because they were already old, and their two older sons were killed during the war.[13] Little Mykhailyk was their only consolation.

The boy lay by the window, breathing heavily. The doctor whispered, 'He has a weak heart. My medicines cannot help him.'

Mykhailyk opened his eyes and looked out the window at the grey winter sky. Everything was still covered with a white blanket of snow.

'How I wish I could see a rainbow,' whispered Mikhailyk softly.

His mother and father leaned over him in despair. Suddenly, the father stood up and started putting on his coat.

'Where are you going?' asked the mother.

'To get a rainbow,' the father answered quietly. 'Mykhailyk, please keep looking out the window. You will soon see a rainbow.'

The father went to see the blacksmith. He told him all about his grief. The blacksmith took his forge and all his tools and brought them to the farmer's front yard. He set up his equipment right near the window, fired up his forge, and placed a plough share into the fire. When the iron was glowing red like the sun, the blacksmith took the plough share out of the fire, put it on his anvil and began to strike it with his heavy hammer. At the first stroke, the iron plough share sent up a shower of sparks, all the colours of the rainbow. The sparks flew everywhere, onto the ground and onto the snow-covered branches of the trees, as if it were raining fire.

Mesmerized, the boy could not take his eyes off the wonderful rainbow. He lifted his head from his pillow, and his pale cheeks turned red. His heart started beating more steadily and evenly.

'Mum, what is going to come out of this fire?' he asked, pointing at the rainbow.

'A plough share,' answered his mother.

'Oh, how I want to plough the earth!' he exclaimed, and he sat up in his bed.

'Now he will live,' said the doctor quietly.

How the hedgehog built a stove

A hedgehog had a nest. One day, his wife asked him to build a woodstove so that their babies would not be cold during the winter.

The hedgehog made some little bricks and built a stove. His wife brought some wood and made a fire. Now it was warm in the hedgehog's nest.

The baby hedgehogs started playing happily and jumping around. Then they crawled closer to the woodstove and told stories until they fell asleep, warm and cozy.

Meanwhile, outside, a blizzard was howling, the frost was crackling, and trees were moaning in the wind. On the pond, a bird wept by a hole in the ice.

Petryk and Mariika

Petryk is studying in grade one. His sister Mariika does not go to school yet. She will start school next year. Petryk has one big problem. He is lazy. He knows that if he is going to learn to read, he has to pick up a book, open it, and read aloud for half an hour every day. But Petryk does not want to pick up a book. He does not want to read. It is more fun to play outside. Petryk comes home each day, drops his school bag, eats, and runs outside to play. In autumn he plays ball, in winter he skates. And his books just lie there.

Half a year passes. All the other children can read well, but Petryk can hardly sound out a single word. One day his teacher comes to speak to Petryk's mother and says, 'If Petryk does not read every day, he will have to repeat grade one.'

Petryk sits listening to his teacher's words and feels very ashamed. But Mariika is delighted. 'That would be wonderful! If you keep Petryk in grade one, I will be able to go to school with him and study in the same class!'

Petryk's face turns red, and tears glisten in his eyes. Then Mariika continues, 'I can already read.' And she takes a book from the table and begins to read.

'You read as well as my best students!' says the teacher.

The teacher goes home, but Petryk sits at the table, thinking to himself, 'I don't want to be weaker than Mariika! I'll make myself study.'

Petryk opens his book and begins to read. Outside the snow is sparkling, the sun is shining, the sparrows are chirping, and his skates are lying under the bench … Petryk so much wants to go out and play! But the thought of studying in the same class as Mariika is terrifying, and he reads and reads …

Now, every day, when Petryk comes home from school, has a meal, and grabs his fur hat to go outside, little Mariika asks, 'Petryk, are we still going to be studying in the same class?'

As soon as he hears these words, Petryk throws aside his fur hat and sits down to read.

How Mykolka became brave

Grade three student Mykolka came to school very early today. Two girls were sitting on a bench under a poplar tree. They were looking up into the tree and in their eyes Mykolka noticed an expression of concern.

Suddenly a bird rose up from a large branch of the tree and chirped anxiously. At the same time, a little chick fell to the ground near the bench. Mykolka understood that the chick had fallen out of its nest, and that its mother was in despair.

One of the girls picked up the chick and said, 'If there was a brave person at school, they would climb up the tree and put the chick back in its nest.'

Mykolka was a very fearful boy. As soon as it got dark, he was too frightened to leave the house. Once his mother had sent him to the vegetable patch to pick a head of cabbage, and he had seen a mouse and come running back to his mother.

But the girl's words cut him to the quick. Did she really think he was a coward?

'I'll climb the tree,' said Mykolka.

'You?' asked the girls and looked at the boy in surprise.

Mykolka tucked the chick inside his shirt and climbed up into the tree. His arms and legs were shaking with fear, but he kept climbing higher and higher. The boy placed the chick carefully in its nest and climbed back down.

The girls looked at him with admiration. He picked up his school bag and went to meet his classmates.

Don't forget the screw!

Yurko was sitting at home doing his grammar homework. First, he copied out several sentences. He was supposed to underline all the nouns, but Yurko was in a hurry and did not do that. He quickly closed his exercise book and ran outside to play ball with the other boys.

That evening Yurko's father checked his homework. He saw that Yurko had not finished the exercise. 'Why didn't you finish your work?' asked Yurko's father. Yurko hung his head and did not reply.

'I'll tell you a story,' said his father. 'A large passenger aeroplane was being built at a factory. Many workers laboured to make sure everything was done properly. They just had to screw in one small screw under the wing. They gave the task to one of the workers, telling him, "Take this screw and screw it in under the wing." But the worker forgot to do it. And they delivered the aeroplane to the aerodrome just as it was.

The aeroplane flew its first flight. Fifty passengers boarded the plane. But it was missing a screw … The aeroplane broke up and crashed. The people on board died.

That is what can happen when someone forgets a small screw. Don't forget the screw, my boy!'

Why did the pigeons fly to Oleh?

In a little village school, in the middle of the schoolyard, stood a beautiful little wooden house on a tall post. It had windows and doors, just like a real house. Pigeons lived in it.

Every day children brought food for the pigeons. Some brought wheat, some bread, some buckwheat. They took it in turns to feed the pigeons. The child whose turn it was to feed the pigeons called them, saying, 'Gul-gul, gul-gul.' The pigeons took the food, but they were too frightened to come close to the children. 'Why are they frightened of us? Why won't they settle on our arms?' wondered the children.

On the last day of school, the teacher asked the children to keep coming in turn during the holidays to feed the pigeons. The summer holidays flew by, and the first day of school arrived. Each student, as they got ready for school, thought, 'I wonder how the pigeons are?' Each one took a pocket full of feed.

When they were all in the schoolyard, the teacher suggested, 'Children,

I would like you to spread out all over the schoolyard, standing by yourselves. I want to see who has been feeding the pigeons over the summer.'

The children ran and spread out all over the schoolyard, standing by themselves. Each one began to say, 'Gul-gul, gul-gul' and to scatter feed on the ground. The pigeons took off from their little house and they all flew to Oleh. They pecked at the ground right next to him. One pigeon even landed on his shoulder, and another landed on his arm. But they did not seem to notice the other children.

Why does Grandpa Maksym wake up so early?

For forty-two years Grandpa Maksym worked as an engineer on a steam engine. For forty-two years his working day began very early. He rose at five o'clock, travelled to the railway station, climbed into the steam engine and hauled a train to a distant city. He did not return home until five o'clock in the evening.

Now Grandpa Maksym has retired. In the morning, he does not have to hurry anywhere. His grandson Roman, who is in grade five, envies his grandfather. He says, 'Gee, you're lucky Grandpa! You can sit on your bench all day. You don't have to go to school or learn lessons.'

'You think I'm lucky?' snorts Grandpa Maksym. 'Wait till you get to my age, and then see how lucky you feel.'

It is five o'clock in the morning. Grandpa cannot sleep. He gets up. Very quietly, so as not to disturb anyone, he gets dressed, goes outside, and sits on his bench. The train that he always used to catch to the station pulls up. It toots, as if calling Grandpa Maksym. The old man sighs and for a long time he watches the line of green carriages disappearing into the distance.

Grandpa Maksym sits motionless on the bench for an hour or two.

Roman, meanwhile, really does not want to get out of bed and go to school …

Think correctly about work

The grade five students planted a large number of young rowan trees. One day they would grow into a flourishing grove, but for now, they needed to be watered and taken care of. The rowan trees were allocated to the students. Each student had four little trees to water. Mariika and

Olia sat next to each other, and their rowan trees were next to each other as well. The girls arranged to come at the same time and water their trees together.

Mariika found watering the first little rowan tree was easy, the second a little more difficult, the third was difficult, and she barely had enough strength left to water the fourth. But then one day Olia fell ill, and the teacher asked Mariika, 'Could you water Olia's trees? You are good friends with her.'

Mariika gave a deep sigh, took her bucket, and walked to the rowan trees. She kept thinking that now she had to water eight trees. She would have to carry eight buckets of water from the well.

The girl set to work. She watered one tree, a second tree, a third tree … And then she noticed something strange. The work seemed easy. When she got to the sixth tree it became harder. The seventh tree was really difficult, and she barely had enough strength left to water the eighth tree.

'I get it,' thought Mariika, as she finished her work. 'Now I know how to make the work easier. I need to think that I have to water twelve trees. Then it will be quite easy to water eight trees.'

And that is what she did the next day. As she was preparing to do her watering, she kept thinking, 'I have to water twelve trees. I have to draw twelve buckets of water from the well and carry them to the rowan trees.'

While she was watering, she kept thinking the same thing: 'I have to water twelve trees.' She watered eight trees and did not feel any tiredness. Then Mariika remembered some words her teacher had said: 'The most difficult thing is to teach yourself to think correctly about work.'

A shack for Grandpa

Yurko's grandfather fell ill. He lay in bed and coughed. Yurko's mother and father said nothing about it.

One day, Yurko came home from the kindergarten and noticed that his father was putting up posts near their house.

'What are you doing, Dad?' asked Yurko.

'I'm building a shack for Grandpa to live in.'

Yurko took his little shovel, walked over to the vegetable garden, and started digging a hole in the middle of the potato patch.

'What are you doing, Yurko?' asked his father.

'I am making a dugout. said Yurko.

'What do you need a dugout for?' asked his father.

'It's for you and Mum to live in when you get older,' said Yurko.

The voice that told me fairy tales

I remember as if it were today. It is getting dark. Evening descends quietly over the earth. I am listening to a fairy tale about Baba Yaga[14] and her bony leg. I feel as if I can see the dark forest with its mighty oaks, a mysterious ravine, and the hut on chicken's legs. A grey wolf roams the forest …

I can hear my grandmother's voice. She is the one telling me the story.

Everything is so familiar and dear to me in these memories, and at the same time so remote, extraordinary, and magical. When I was little, I sincerely believed that somewhere in the dark and mysterious forest there was a hut on chicken's legs, and that somewhere, far, far away, Little Red Riding Hood had lost her way and was wandering through the forest, crying …

I still believe it even now, and I can still hear my grandmother's soft voice.

An apple tree for Grandma

I told my grandmother, 'I'm going to plant an apple tree, and it will be just for you. We'll call it "Grandma's apple tree". When the apples are ripe, I'll bring them to you!'

My grandmother smiled and said, 'Go ahead and plant it, but you must plant it over there, next to that old apple tree.'

And she pointed to a very old apple tree. We walked over to it. Grandma fell silent, and I noticed that tears were rolling down her cheeks.

'Why are you crying, Grandma?' I asked.

'I planted this apple tree when I was a little girl, just like you. I planted it for my mother.'

I felt so sorry for Grandma that I started crying as well. She is so old. Her hands shake. Every evening, she sits on a bench, watching the evening sunset. What does she think about? I love you so, so much, Grandma!

Grandma is coming tonight

In the morning, Dmytryk went to visit his grandmother. She treated him to fried walnuts and told him the fairy tale about the little straw bull with tar on its back.

Dmytryk came home at noon. The sun was shining, and the snow was sparkling like an endless white tablecloth.

The boy entered the house, but he did not close the doors. The door to the front porch and the door into the house were both left open.

He took a fried walnut out of his pocket and gave it to his mother.

'Try this, Mum,' he said. 'Grandma treated me to walnuts like this.'

'Why did you leave the doors open?' his mother asked. 'It's cold outside!'

'But Grandma is coming tonight,' said Dmytrik. 'What's the point of closing the doors?'

Grandpa and Andriiko

Andriiko cannot resist the dark berries. He climbs the mulberry tree and eats to his heart's content, but then it starts raining.

Andriiko sits out the rain in the thick branches of the tree. When he is ready to climb down, he notices that Grandpa Petro is now sitting under the mulberry tree. He has come out into the garden after the rain in his white shirt. His hair, too, is as white as snow.

'What can I do?' wonders Andriiko in alarm. 'If I climb down from the mulberry tree, I will shake water on to Grandpa. He will get soaked and fall ill.'

Andriiko sits there, hugging a branch and afraid to move. He waits for his grandfather to go inside, but his grandfather is in no hurry.

At last, his grandfather gets up heavily from the bench. He looks up and sees Andriiko. He is surprised and asks, 'What are you sitting up there in that tree for, my boy?'

'I don't want to shake water on to you,' says Andriiko.'

Grandpa moves away and Andriiko climbs down from the mulberry tree.

Grandpa Petro hugs his grandson and gives him a kiss.

'Why is Grandpa so kind today?' wonders Andriiko.

The floor will be clean … but what about your soul?

Mariika in grade one came home from school and noticed that all the floors were sparkling clean.

'It's just like in our classroom after school,' said Mariika.

'What do you mean "after school"?' asked her mother in surprise. 'What about during school?'

'We wash the floor after lessons,' said Mariika. 'The inspection team comes after school and gives us a mark for cleanliness. Why wash the floor during lessons?'

'You have a strange way of doing things,' chuckled her mother.

Just then, someone knocked on the door. Mariika's mother went to greet them. Their elderly neighbour, Grandma Khrystyna, walked into the house. She was ninety-nine years old. She had seven sons, three daughters, forty grandchildren and a hundred and three great-grandchildren. Mariika's mother bowed low to the old lady, took her by the arm, and led her into the living room.

Mariika was horrified. It was raining outside, the old lady's shoes were muddy, and puddles of water appeared where she had walked through.

Grandma Khrystyna sat for a long time at the table, and Mariika's mother gave her tea. When the old lady had left, Mariika said, 'We would not have let someone into our classroom with such dirty shoes … The floor has to be kept clean.'

'The floor will be clean, dear … But what about your soul?' said her mother quietly.

A scarf for Grandma Mariia

Grandma Mariia worked at our school for forty years. She knew all the students, and all their parents too, because she had watched the mothers and fathers grow up. Long ago, when they first enrolled in the school as little children, she had led them to their various classes, and now they would soon be grandparents.

After lessons all the students came to a meeting. The school principal said, 'I would like you to think about what gifts we can present to Grandma Mariia. On Saturday we will have a gathering of the whole school community to see her off.'

The grade five students returned to their classroom after the meeting and began to discuss what they could give Grandma Mariia. Some thought they should give her a picture album. Others proposed buying a book, and some suggested a little alarm clock.

Maksym said, 'My father told me that a long time ago a little grade one student cut his leg with a piece of glass. Grandma Mariia—she was a young woman back then—took a white scarf from her head and bandaged the wound with it. There was a lily of the valley embroidered in the corner of the scarf. The whole scarf was covered in blood.'

'We'll buy Grandma Mariia a white silk scarf!' the children decided.

They collected scrap metal and received money for it. They went to the shop, but there were no scarves there. Someone told them there were silk scarves in the city. They travelled to the city, but there were no white silk scarves there either. They bought some white silk, and the girls embroidered a lily of the valley in the corner.

When they presented the white silk scarf to Grandma Mariia, she looked Maksym in the eyes and said, 'That is just like the scarf I bandaged your father's leg with … He had eyes just like you … Thank you, children.'

Little Hunchback and Shimmering Star

In a large building in a city lived many boys and girls. One of them was a young girl called Little Hunchback. She was, indeed, little, and she did, indeed, have a hunched back. Just like the other boys and girls, she often went outside to play. Three other beautiful girls used to go outside to play: Blue-eyed Beauty, Azure-eyed Beauty and Black-eyed Beauty. Each one of these girls was convinced that she was the most beautiful of all, and that she was the only one worthy of admiration.

Little Hunchback could not take her eyes off these beautiful girls. Oh, how she wanted to give her love to one of them! She approached them in turn, and tried to play with them, but none of them paid the slightest attention to her. It was as if she did not exist.

And so Little Hunchback began to love faraway Shimmering Star. Little Hunchback saw Shimmering Star one starry night and whispered warm words of love to it. 'I want to be yours, Shimmering Star! I love you and I want to be loved in return!' she said.

Shimmering Star was unimaginably far away and appeared to be no more than a tiny spark, but the strength of Little Hunchback's love was so great that—just imagine!—Shimmering Star replied, 'So be it, Little Hunchback, you will now be mine.'

A deep happiness appeared in the eyes of the little girl. She looked into the eyes of Blue-eyed Beauty, Azure-eyed Beauty and Black-eyed Beauty and was overwhelmed by a feeling of compassion for them. Little Hunchback whispered, 'How unfortunate these girls are.'

Vania Senior and Vania Junior

This happened in Belarus during the darkest days of the war.[15] The fascists burned down the village of Ivanivka, murdering many innocent old people, women and children, for no reason other than that they sympathised with the partisans.

Miraculously, two nine-year-old boys escaped death—two Vanias. Both were very small, and both were very much like each other. The only way to tell them apart was by their eyes—one Vania had blue eyes, the other had black eyes.

The boys sat near the smoking ruins for a long time, crying, and then decided, 'We will cross the frontline to our side and join our own soldiers. We will fight alongside them against the fascists to avenge the blood of our mothers.'

But the frontline was two hundred kilometres away. The boys began to think, 'Who will be senior on this difficult march?' One of them had to be in charge.

The black-eyed Vanya said, 'I will be Senior.'

And the blue-eyed Vanya replied, 'OK, I will be Junior.'

And they set off on their difficult journey. They walked hand-in-hand. The moment anything dangerous appeared on the horizon, Vania Senior went in front and Vania Junior walked behind him. Their injured feet bled, their eyes burned from the wind, but the boys kept walking ahead and endured all the difficulties of their journey. At every step, death threatened them, but they did not pay attention to it, and consequently it could not trap them with its iron claws.

They became courageous and daring.

Vania Senior became courageous and daring because he felt that he was responsible for the life of the Vania Junior, while Vania Junior became courageous and daring because he felt that Vania Senior had taken on the responsibility of caring for him.

A person becomes invincible when they feel that they are responsible for someone else's life. A person also becomes invincible when they feel that someone else is responsible for their life. Do not be afraid of being Senior, and do not fear being Junior. The most important thing is to be human.

Joy in a child's eyes

It was a warm, sunny day, and everything seemed to be joyfully welcoming the spring. The orchards were flowering, and birds were twittering. A flock of cranes flew across the azure sky. Somewhere a spring brook was babbling happily.

However, underneath a tall poplar, a little boy was standing and crying. He did not see the orchards in flower. He did not hear the twittering of the birds. To him the sky seemed black, not blue. The flock of cranes seemed a thread of tears.

People walked past the little boy and did not notice him crying.

Only one old man saw the crying boy, walked up to him, and put his hand on his head. The old man spent a long time talking to the boy, asking him about something. Through his tears, the boy told the old man all about what was troubling him.

They talked like that for about an hour. Their conversation ended with the boy smiling. He noticed that the orchards were in flower. He heard the birds twittering. He saw a flock of cranes shimmering in the blue sky and thought, 'Spring has come!'

The most beautiful thing is when one person dries another's tears and awakens a smile.

The abandoned kitten

A little grey kitten had been chased out of the house. It was sitting by the road, miaowing. It wanted to go home to its mother. People walking past looked at the kitten. Some shook their heads sadly, others laughed. Some were sorry for the poor kitten but did nothing to help it.

Evening came. The little kitten was frightened. It snuggled up to a bush and sat there, shivering.

A little girl named Natalochka was walking home from school. She heard the kitten miaowing. Without saying a word, she picked up the kitten and took it home. The kitten snuggled up to the little girl and purred. It was as happy as could be.

How Vasylko was born

'Children, today is your friend's birthday—Vasylko's birthday. Today, Vasylko, you are eight years old. Happy birthday! Let me tell you, children, how Vasylko was born.

Before Vasylko was born, his father worked as a tractor driver and his mother worked in the silk production team.

The tractor driver's young wife was about to become a mother. Her young husband was planning on taking his wife to the maternity hospital the next day.

During the night, a blizzard developed, spreading snow everywhere and blocking the roads with deep snowdrifts. It was impossible to drive a car anywhere, but the trip could not possibly be postponed. The young wife could feel that her baby was on its way. Her husband went to get the tractor, and while he was gone, his wife began to feel terrible labour pains.

The husband hitched a large sled to the tractor, lay his wife in it, and set off. It was seven kilometres to the maternity hospital. The blizzard still raged, the steppe was covered in a shroud of snow, his wife was groaning, and the tractor struggled to make its way through the snowdrifts.

Halfway there, it became impossible to drive any further. The tractor plunged into the snow and its motor died. The young husband lifted his wife from the sled, wrapped her in a blanket, and carried her in his arms, barely struggling from one snowdrift to the next.

The blizzard howled, the snow blinded his eyes, the husband was bathed in sweat, and his heart was hammering in his chest. It seemed as if every step would be his last, but he knew that if he stopped to rest for even one minute they would perish.

After a few dozen metres he stopped for an instant to throw off his coat and continued in just his shirt.

His wife was groaning in his arms and the wind was howling over the steppe, but all the husband could think of at that time was the tiny living creature who was about to be born and for whom he, the young tractor driver Stepan, must answer to his wife, to his father and mother, to his grandfather and grandmother, to all of humanity, and to his conscience.

For several hours the young father trudged for four terrible kilometres. It was evening when he knocked on the door of the maternity hospital, handed his wife wrapped in a blanket to the nursing staff, and collapsed unconscious on the floor.

When the doctors unwrapped the blanket, they could not believe their eyes. Next to the wife lay a baby, alive and well. He had just been born, and the mother immediately began to feed her son right there in the corridor.

Doctors now surrounded the husband's bed. For ten days Stepan hovered between life and death. The doctors saved his life.

That is how Vasylko was born.'

Farewelling a horse

Grandpa Mykola worked in the stables for many years, but the time came for him to retire. On his last day at work, Grandpa Mykola rose at dawn and went to the stables to say farewell to the horses. The young horses stood in a straight line along their trough. Grandpa Mykola stroked each one on the neck. And in the corner of the stable stood an old horse named Wind. He had once been as swift and hot-tempered as a summer wind in the steppe, but now his legs were as thick as tree stumps and his mane was thinning.

Wind immediately recognised the old stableman. He stretched his neck towards him and placed his head on the old man's shoulder. Grandpa Mykola stood for a long time by the old horse. Then he gave a deep sigh and walked home. A young stableman came to take charge of the stables.

The next day, Grandpa Mykola rose at dawn. He came out of his home and stopped in amazement. Standing there by his door was his faithful friend Wind.

Silver hairs

For two weeks, little Olesia was very ill. It was feared she could die any minute. Her mother spent days and sleepless nights by her daughter's side, not leaving her even for a minute.

When the worst of the illness had passed, and Olesia began to get better, her mother lay down beside her and fell asleep. When she woke up, Olesia asked her, 'Mum, why do you have so many silver hairs?'

'My grief turned them silver,' answered her mother.

'Mummy,' Olesia went on, 'How much joy do I need to bring you for these silver hairs to disappear?'

The kitten and the baby hedgehog

A hunter found a little hedgehog in the forest. He wrapped him in his handkerchief, brought him home, and placed him gently on the floor.

In the corner sat a little kitten. 'What is that little grey ball?' he wondered. He hopped over to the hedgehog and stretched out his paw to touch him, pricking himself on the hedgehog's sharp quills. The kitten meowed in pain and the hedgehog took fright and hid his tiny head.

The hunter poured some milk into a saucer and placed it on the floor. The kitten started lapping up the milk, but the hedgehog was too afraid to approach. After some time, however, he plucked up the courage to come over to the plate and start lapping up the milk with the kitten.

They became friends. They slept together, and in the evening, they went for a walk in the forest together.

One day, the hedgehog went into the forest and never came back.

The kitten waited for his friend for days, meowing pitifully … When the hunter poured some milk for him, he would always leave some for his lost friend, still hoping that the hedgehog would return.

But the hedgehog was not coming back.

The ant's home

In the anthill there are many babies. Here is an ant, hurrying home. She is carrying a tiny piece of sweet watermelon. The mother ant enters her home, where her baby is lying in its cradle. The mother ant chews on the sweet watermelon, producing a sweet juice in her mouth, and feeds it to her baby. The baby ant savours his meal. The juice is delicious. When he is full, he falls asleep, but the mother ant dashes back to the forest again. She needs to gather as much food as possible for the winter.

The fearless squirrel

This happened deep in a dark forest. In a warm hollow, at the top of a tall linden tree, lived a squirrel. She had two newborn babies. Tiny, fluffy, still blind, they clung to their mother and sucked her milk.

One day, the squirrel hopped far away through the trees, looking for nuts. She tried to find some nearby, but there were none to be found, so she roamed further and further away from her nest. While she was hopping from tree to tree, dark clouds gathered, thunder rumbled, and a bolt of lightning flashed and hit the linden tree, setting it ablaze.

The flames soon reached the squirrel's nest where the baby squirrels were sheltering. The poor things started crying out, calling for their mother. The squirrel heard their cries and leapt from tree to tree to rescue them.

The whole linden tree was aflame when the squirrel reached it. Fearlessly, she leapt into the fire to save her babies …

A nightingale flew to a neighbouring tree that was still green and began to sing. He sang of the wonder of life.

How a squirrel fried some nuts

A squirrel gathered a big pile of nuts for the winter, enough to fill her hollow in a tree. Now she had enough for her babies to eat. Winter arrived. The squirrel gave nuts to her babies, and they happily ate them, but one spoilt little squirrel said, 'Mummy, I want fried nuts.'

'All right,' replied the squirrel, 'You shall have fried nuts.'

She put some nuts into a frying pan, took it into the forest, placed it on a glow-worm's nest, and fried the nuts.

'Yum! Now they're delicious!' said the spoilt little squirrel.

How a bee spent the night on a flower

A bee flew far, far way into a meadow, looking for honey, though the sun was already setting. It took quite some time for her to find a patch of clover flowers, but they had lots of nectar. The bee flew from one clover flower to another, collecting nectar, and did not notice the time fly by. When she raised her head to fly home, night had fallen, and it was pitch dark.

The bee was frightened. What was she to do? She hid under the petals of a clover flower and fell asleep. In the morning, she woke up and hurried home, bringing lots of nectar for her babies.

How a mother hedgehog comforted her babies

A mother hedgehog had two babies, as round as balls, with little quills. One day the baby hedgehogs rolled like balls to look for food. They rolled through the orchard, then rolled through the vegetable garden, where they met a hare. It was eating a sweet carrot. The baby hedgehogs also wanted to try some carrot, but as soon as they poked their little heads out, the hare shouted at them, 'Go away, you nasty, prickly things!'

The baby hedgehogs rolled home to their mother, crying.

'Why are you crying, my dears?' asked their mother.

'The hare said that we are nasty and prickly,' sobbed the baby hedgehogs.

The mother hedgehog hugged her little children and comforted them. 'My dear children, you're not prickly!' she said. 'Your hair is as soft as flax. You are round and fluffy, like little balls.'

The fox and the mouse

A mother fox had five babies. She loved her little fox cubs very much. Every day she went hunting and brought them something tasty to eat: a bird, a baby hare, a mouse, or sometimes a frog or a beetle.

One day the mother fox noticed a mouse's burrow not far from her den. The mother mouse and her babies only just had time to hide in their burrow before the fox reached it. She sat by the entrance to the burrow and said, 'You will have to come out of your burrow some time, or your babies will, and then I will catch you.'

The fox waited by the burrow for a long time. The mouse and her babies were getting very hungry, but the fox just sat there waiting for them to come out. The mouse tried to think of a way to scare off the fox. She called out from her burrow, 'Run away, fox. A wolf is coming from the forest to get you.' But the fox just laughed.

Then the mouse called out, 'Run away, fox. A hunter is coming with his gun.' But the fox did not stir.

Then the mouse called out, 'Fox, a wolf has just crawled into your den to get your babies!' And the fox ran to save her babies.

How the magpie made some porridge

A magpie had seven chicks. When she came home, they all called out at once, 'We're hungry!'

'Just wait a minute, my dears,' she said, 'And I'll make you some porridge.'

And the magpie cooked some buckwheat porridge. The porridge smelt so good, it made her babies' mouths water.

The mother magpie dished up the porridge into seven little plates, gave her children spoons, and watched them gobble it up in silence. She sat by the table without dishing up any for herself. She gave all the porridge to her children.

'Let them eat it all, so they won't be hungry,' she thought to herself, 'And I'll fly around and find something else for myself to eat.'

Visiting a sick child

Mariika has been sick for a long time. She cannot get out of bed. Sometimes her friends come to visit her. Today Oksana and Valia have come to visit her. They have brought her two books. They talk about what has been happening at school, and then they sit in silence by her bed. Mariika also sits in silence and feels very uncomfortable.

During this moment of tense silence, the sun comes out from behind a cloud, and sunlight fills the room. Oksana and Valia are delighted. 'At last, the sun is warming up,' twitters Oksana. 'As soon as it is a little warmer, we can go for a walk in the forest and to the river.'

'Perhaps we can even go for a swim,' says Valia happily.

'And we can pick some flowers and go out in the boat,' Oksana chatters away happily.

Mariika looks at them in silence and tears fall from her eyes onto her pillow. Oksana and Valia see that Mariika is crying and are surprised. 'Why are you crying, Mariika?, they ask. 'Is something hurting? Perhaps we should bring you another book? Why don't we go to the shop and buy you some sweets?'

'I don't need books or sweets,' whispers Mariika.

Love and cruelty

A baby sparrow fell out of its nest. Its little wings were not yet strong enough to fly. It flopped about in the grass, while its mother hovered over it and cheeped anxiously.

A hawk spotted the chick and flew towards it. It thought it could grab the chick and eat it. It landed near the chick and moved towards it. All the birds in the trees froze with fear. What would happen now? They were amazed to see that the mother sparrow did not retreat in fear but dived towards the hawk. She puffed herself up, landed on the hawk, pecked it in the eyes and sunk her claws into its head. The hawk took fright and flew away.

All the birds were astonished. What a brave mother sparrow! How could she defeat the hawk?

'I'll tell you how,' said the owl. 'The mother sparrow loves her chick. But the hawk feels no love. It only knows cruelty. And cruelty has never defeated love.'

All good people are one family

The children in grade two were having a drawing lesson. They were drawing a swallow.

Someone knocked at the door, and the teacher opened it. A woman was standing there, and the teacher could see that she had been crying. It was the mother of little blonde-haired, blue-eyed Natalka.

'Please let Natalka come home,' the mother asked the teacher. 'Her grandma has died.'

The teacher returned to his desk and quietly said, 'Children there has been a great misfortune. Natalka's grandma has died.'

Natalka turned pale. Her eyes filled with tears. She lay her head on the desk and cried quietly.

'Natalka, you can go home. Your mother has come for you.'

While the girl gathered her things to go home, the teacher said, 'We will not have any lessons today either. Our family has suffered a great misfortune.'

'Isn't it just Natalka's family?' asked Mykola.

'No, it is our human family,' explained the teacher. 'All good people are one family. And if someone in our family has died that is a loss for all of us.'

The oriole

In the evening, Oleh, the youngest in the family, a first grader, told his grandmother, 'Tomorrow is our last day of classes. The best students will be receiving books as a reward.'

'And will you receive one?' asked his grandmother.

'If Mariia Ivanivna gives me an "excellent" in maths, then I will. This year, I have received both "excellent" and "good" in maths.'

The next day, Oleh's grandmother waited impatiently for her grandson to come home. As soon as he opened the door and laid his schoolbag on the bench, she could see that there was no joy in his eyes.

'The teacher did not give him an "excellent",' she thought. She put away her knitting, walked over to Oleh and told him very quietly, 'You'll never guess what I am about to show you ... '

'What?' asked Oleh, and the life-affirming joy that had always comforted his grandmother returned to his eyes.

Oleh's grandmother took him by the hand and led him into the orchard. They came to a thicket of wild grapes. Oleh's grandmother parted the branches and pointed to a nest. In the nest, Oleh saw an extraordinary bird—an oriole.

Oleh's grandmother had never seen him so joyful.

She had been saving this joy for him for many days.

Sew a patch for me

Nine-year-old Mykolka went to his mother with his head hanging low. 'Mum,' he said quietly, 'I've ripped my shirt.' His mother looked at his torn sleeve and replied, 'All right. I'll patch it. Take off your shirt.'

Mykolka took off his shirt, stood next to his mother, and watched her sew a small patch on to his shirt sleeve. Three-year-old Katrusia sat next to her mother. She thought the patch on the shirt sleeve looked very nice. 'Mum, can you sew a patch for me as well?' she asked. 'All right,' answered her mother. 'Take off your cardigan.'

Katrusia took off her cardigan, and a few minutes later she came out, beaming with joy, to show everyone her sleeve. 'Mum sewed a patch on my cardigan for me! Look how beautiful I am!' she exclaimed.

The children looked at Katrusia's cardigan with disbelief.

The wheaten hedgehog

My mother made some *pyrizhky*[16] and had some leftover dough.

'Mum, could you make me a wheaten hedgehog?' I asked her.

And she made a hedgehog: small and round, with quills. But where was his head?

'Mum, why is he hiding his head,' I asked.

'Just wait until we bake him in the oven,' replied my mother. 'Then his head will pop up.'

The hedgehog sat in the oven for quite some time. When fully baked, he turned golden brown. We took him out of the oven and put him on the table. The hedgehog had spread his quills and arched his back, and it seemed that any moment he would show his head.

The stepdaughter's present

A man had three daughters of his own and one who was his stepdaughter. One day, he went to the city and bought presents for all his daughters. The girls sat in front of him, breathlessly waiting for the presents to be unveiled.

'This is for you,' said the father, taking out a comb and giving it to his first daughter.

'And this is for you,' he went on, handing a bead necklace to his second daughter.

'These are for you,' he said, giving his third daughter three ribbons for braiding her hair.

'And this one is for you,' he said, presenting a bright silk dress to his stepdaughter.

The stepdaughter was delighted to receive the dress, and held it against her body, while her father kissed each of his own three daughters and asked after their health.

The stepdaughter saw him kissing her sisters and put down the dress, waiting for her father to come over to kiss her and ask after her health.

She waited and waited, but she waited in vain.

The happy leaf

Little Olesia and her grandmother were sitting on the riverbank. The autumn sun warmed them with its gentle rays. A willow that drooped over the river had already cast off its golden attire, and only a single leaf remained. Suddenly, that leaf fell into the water and was instantly sucked into a whirlpool. The leaf started swirling round very quickly. Olesia watched it spinning round and round and felt a thrill of joy. But her grandmother gave a quiet sigh.

'Grandma, why are you sighing like that? Are you sad?' asked Olesia. 'Look how happy that leaf is!'

Olesia's grandmother reached out with her trembling hand, stroked Olesia's head and gave her a gentle smile.

New trousers

Vitia, who was in grade three, was getting ready to go to school. It was the first day of a new school year, and Vitia's mother had bought him some new trousers. The boy put them on for the first time. It was nice to have something new.

Vitia waited for Andrii to come to his house. They always walked to school together. The day before, they had sat for a long time on the Warm Stone by the river and promised to be faithful friends forever. They would graduate from school together, do their military service together, and if they had to fight, they would defend each other with their lives.

Andrii arrived, and he was wearing old trousers. 'Mum,' said Vitia, 'Can you give me the old trousers that I wore during the summer?'

'But you've got new ones,' said his mother in surprise. 'You've already put them on.'

'They're too tight,' said Vitia quietly. 'I can't walk in them.'

His mother looked at her son in amazement. Then she saw Andrii's old trousers and understood everything. 'You're right,' she said. 'They are tight. Put on the old ones.'

Vitia put on his old trousers, and the friends walked to school as happy as could be. On the way they agreed to meet again that evening on the Warm Stone by the river.

Why everyone was happy

Our whole class went for a walk in the forest. It was a warm, spring day. The sun was shining brightly, and birds were singing. We had fun in the forest. We played at being 'partisans' and admired the beautiful flowers and butterflies.

Towards evening we arrived at a green clearing and sat down to rest. Once we were refreshed, we stood up to go home. Someone suddenly called out, 'Galia can't find her scarf.' Galia was standing under an oak tree, looking upset and confused. The teacher said, 'Perhaps you lost it in the forest.'

'No, I had it just now. I just took it off and put it down on the grass.'

We walked around the clearing, looking for the scarf in the grass. There was no scarf to be found. We all felt awkward. Everyone was quiet. We could not look each other in the eye. We walked out of the forest and set off for home in silence.

Suddenly someone called out, 'Look, there's a scarf hanging in that oak tree!'

Everyone turned around and saw Galia's white scarf hanging in an oak tree.

'I hung it there and forgot,' said Galia quietly.

Everyone was suddenly happy. Now nobody was silent. We all talked about how much fun we had had in the forest.

Grandma's borshch

A grandmother had two granddaughters. The granddaughters lived in a big city and came to visit their grandmother during the summer holidays. The grandmother was delighted to see them. She treated them to sweet cherries, fresh honey, and *varenyky*.[17] But the girls' mother had told them that their grandmother made the most delicious borshch[18], and that is what they wanted to try most of all.

The grandmother made them borshch, with fresh tomatoes, fresh cabbage, fresh beets and potatoes, and homemade sour cream. But unfortunately she was becoming forgetful, and she salted the borshch twice. She served two plates of borshch and invited the girls to try it. 'I'm getting old and forgetful,' she said. 'I can't remember whether I added salt or not. Here is some salt, anyway. Please add it to suit your own taste.'

The girls had a spoonful of borshch each, and it was so salty! They looked at each other and smiled quietly so that their grandmother would not notice. Spoon by spoon, they ate it all up and even asked for more, thanking their grandmother all the time. Their grandmother was delighted.

'So did I put salt into the borshch or not?' she asked.

'We didn't notice,' answered Nina. 'It was so delicious; we did not think about the salt.'

'Then I must have added salt,' said their grandma with relief. 'Tomorrow, I'll delegate that task to you, girls. I'm afraid I will forget the salt.'

'We would love that, Grandma!' replied the girls. And they quietly exchanged glances again. And quietly smiled.

Fiery Mane

Yurko's father carved him a horse out of wood. It was high-spirited and hot-tempered. It struck the earth with its hoofs, and its fiery mane blew about in the air.

Yurko called his horse 'Fiery Mane'. He would not part with it. He put it on the table and sat watching it. It seemed to Yurko that at any moment the horse would start galloping.

When it was time to sleep, Yurko put his horse on the floor by his bed. He was dozing off when suddenly he saw Fiery Mane lift his head, shake himself, and start galloping round the room.

Yurko jumped out of bed and wanted to chase after Fiery Mane, but it was already standing by his bed again. Yurko bent down to the horse and stroked its head. Fiery Mane calmed down. Only its legs still shook a little, and its fiery mane was still warm.

How the sparrows waited for the sun

A mother sparrow was sitting in her nest with her chicks. The sun rose, slowly ascending from below the horizon, large and red. The chicks asked, 'What is that, Mum?'

'That is the sun,' answered their mother. 'When it rises, the day begins, and insects come out of hiding.'

'How wonderful the sun is,' cheeped the chicks.

The mother sparrow flew from her nest and brought some worms. Her children ate them and then asked, 'Please fly and get some more worms. The sun is still shining.'

The mother sparrow flew off again to look for food. She brought some insects, which the chicks ate, and then they asked for more. All day long, while the sun shone, the mother sparrow flew here and there looking for food.

Night fell, and the chicks went to sleep. They woke before dawn and asked their mother to go looking for food. But their mother answered, 'The sun has not risen yet.'

The chicks waited a long time for the sun to rise. At last, it appeared above the horizon, and their mother flew off to look for worms.

Taking a sword to face a wolf

Andriiko's father was a forest ranger. During the day, Andriiko played in the forest, and he was not afraid of its dense thickets or of the rain, because he could shelter from the rain under the trees.

The only thing that Andriiko was afraid of was a deep and dark ravine. He did not know what was in that ravine. He would have gone to explore it by now, to find out what was there, but his mother would not let him. As soon as the sun drew close to the horizon, his mother would call him inside.

Andriiko would reluctantly come home. His mother told him about a wolf that lived in the ravine, and that came out and roamed the forest as soon as it grew dark.

'Don't go into the forest at night,' warned his mother. 'A wolf is a fierce beast.'

'And how can you beat a wolf?' asked Andriiko.

'Maybe, with a sword,' said his mother.

These words made a great impression on Andriiko. The next day, he went to the work shed and spent the whole day working on something. Whatever it was he made, he hid it under his bed.

In the evening, his mother went to bed, and Andriiko was left to himself. His father was away in the city. Andriiko pretended to go to bed as well.

Then he got out of bed. He could see clearly in the moonlight. He put on his clothes, took something from under his bed, and tied it to his waist with a rope.

'Where do you think you're going?' asked his mother quietly, laying a hand on his shoulder.

Andriiko was neither frightened nor surprised. He was not going to lie about where he was going. If his mother had not woken up, he would have gone quietly to her bed, woken her up himself, and told her everything. But his mother had heard him getting ready, and now she was asking, 'Why?' So he answered, 'I am going to find the wolf… Look, I made a sword.'

How the children celebrated, and the fir tree cried

The New Year was approaching. A family went to the forest and cut down the finest fir tree they could find. They placed it in the middle of a large, well-lit room and decorated it with sweets and pretty balls. The children ran around the New Year's tree, admiring it and joyfully singing songs.[19] But the New Year's tree was frightened and sad. She missed her dear, dark forest, the grey hare, the blue sky, and the bright moon. Instead of being surrounded by a blanket of snow, she was surrounded by bits of coloured paper.

In despair, she started crying, but nobody noticed the bitter tears that ran down her branches and dripped onto the floor. Only one blue-eyed girl noticed. She sighed quietly, and whispered, 'The tree is crying.'

The celebrations came to an end. The children ate the sweets and put away the New Year decorations. The fir tree was thrown on a rubbish heap in the backyard. And only the girl with blue eyes stood by the tree to comfort it.

Joy and grief

A narow bridge passed over a stream. Actually, it was not so much a bridge as a wooden pathway, a single plank in width. Only one person could cross it at a time, and it was quite impossible for two people to pass each other.

One day, a man in a white shirt started to cross the wooden pathway from one side of the stream, singing merrily.

A man in a black shirt began to cross from the other side, his head hanging sadly, deep in thought.

The two travellers met in the middle of the bridge. The man in the black shirt said, 'Let me through, I am in a great hurry. Go back to the other side and cross after me.'

'Where are you going in such a hurry?' asked the man in the white shirt.

'I have to get home. My son has died,' replied the other man

'I'm also in a hurry,' said the man in the white shirt.

'Where are you going?' asked the man in the black shirt.

'I also have to get home. My wife has given birth to a son.'

The two men stood silently facing each other, looking into each other's eyes. Then the man in the white shirt said, 'You need to get home sooner.'

The man in the white shirt turned and went back, giving way to the man in the black shirt, because joy must always give way to grief.

Yurko's flower

'Each of you will be making a paper flower today,' said the teacher during the handicrafts lesson.

All the children set about their work. They cut narrow strips of coloured paper, then pasted them and wove them. Everyone wanted to make the most beautiful flower.

Yurko was the only one who did not want to work. He just pasted a few paper strips together any old how. The result was something weird, more like a potato than a flower.

The teacher said, 'Now put your flowers on the windowsill.'

Everyone placed their flowers in a row. So did Yurko. Then every student came out and described their flower.

'My flower has pink petals … '

'Mine has white ones … '

'My rose has tiny anthers … '

One by one, the children proudly presented their flowers. And only Yurko sat quietly at his desk, hanging his head.

The rag doll

For many years, a mother collected leftover fabric and tiny pieces of cloth in a corner of the wardrobe. Sometimes, one of her little daughter's worn-out dresses would end up there.

That pile of old rags lay there for goodness knows how long—long enough for the little daughter to grow up and became a mother herself, and for the mother to become a grandmother.

One day, the grandmother remembered the old pieces of cloth and decided to use them to make a rag doll for her granddaughter. The doll turned out to be a real beauty. It had a white face, black eyebrows, blue eyes, slender legs, and a plait of blonde hair.

The grandmother put the doll on her granddaughter's bed. The doll sighed heavily and started sobbing. The grandmother understood why the doll was crying. It wanted to say something, but it was unable to do so it because it did not have a tongue in its mouth.

The grandmother opened the doll's mouth and inserted a tongue made of the finest pink fabric. The doll clapped her hands and asked the grandmother in a ringing voice, 'Where is the mirror?'

The grandmother picked up the doll to take her to the mirror, but the doll threw a tantrum and demanded, 'Bring the mirror here!'

The grandmother placed the mirror in front of the doll, who looked at herself and became even more angry, dissatisfied with her appearance. It seemed to her that her face was too yellow, her eyes were too sad, her cheeks were not rosy enough, and her hair was too thin.

'I don't care what you have to do,' demanded the doll, 'But make me beautiful!'

'As you wish,' agreed the grandmother quietly, and with a heavy sigh, she untied, unpicked, and unglued the pieces of old fabric from which the doll was made. Once more the doll became just a pile of pretty rags.

'How beautiful!' exclaimed the granddaughter when she saw the rags, and she happily began to play with them.

It is hard to be a human being

Some children were returning from the forest, where they had spent the whole day. The path home led through a small hamlet in a valley a few kilometres from their village. The tired children just managed to reach this cluster of little houses. They called into the first house to ask for water.

A woman came out of the house, followed by a little boy. The woman drew water from her well, placed the bucket on a table in the middle of the yard, and went back inside. Having drunk their fill, the children rested on the grass and got their strength back.

When they had walked on a further kilometre from the hamlet, Mariika suddenly remembered something. 'We forgot to thank the woman for that water,' she said, and her eyes expressed concern.

The children stopped. They had indeed forgotten to thank her.

'Well, so what?' said Roman. 'It's not a big deal. The woman has probably already forgotten all about it. Is it really worth going back over such a small thing?'

'Yes, it is,' said Mariika. 'Aren't you ashamed of yourself, Roman?'

Roman sniggered. He was clearly not ashamed.

'Well, you do what you like,' said Mariika, 'But I am going back to thank the woman.'

'Why? Tell me, why do we have to do that?' asked Roman. 'We are all so tired.'

'Because we are human beings,' said Mariika.

She turned and set off back towards the huts. Everyone else followed her.

Roman stood for a moment on the path, sighed, and then followed the others.

'It's hard to be a human being,' he thought.

The boy with a heart of stone

A woman gave birth to a son. He was the apple of her eye. She was worried that a speck of dust would land on him, or that he would be exposed to a draught. She took special care to make sure her son did not take other people's pain and suffering to heart.

When the boy's grandfather was near death, she took her son to stay with her sister in a neighbouring village. She only brought her son home when the grandfather had been buried. Her son asked, 'Where's Grandpa?' She replied, 'He's gone to visit relatives.'

One day the boy saw the girl next door cut her finger. The mother immediately took him by the hand and led him home. In winter, the son brought home a woodpecker with an injured wing and asked how he could help the bird. The mother took the bird somewhere and told her son that the bird had been cured, was alive and well, and had flown away.

The boy grew older, but his mother continued to protect him from life's problems. He did not know the meaning of grief, suffering, pain, hurt or disappointment. He grew tall and was approaching manhood.

One day his mother fell ill and was confined to bed. She sent her son to the pharmacist to buy some medicine. The son went to the pharmacist and handed him a note that his mother had written.

'The medicine will be ready in five minutes,' said the pharmacist.

'While you are getting the medicine ready, I'll go and play soccer with my friends,' answered the son.

'You have a heart of stone,' whispered the astonished pharmacist.

Without a scarf

Today the grade six students went on an excursion into the forest. When everyone returned home, it somehow happened that Nadiika and Vitia fell behind their friends and walked back together. They walked along the forest path. The forest was just beginning to wake up from its winter slumber. Squills were flowering in the clearings and clumps of snow still lay under the trees, like giant mushrooms.

Vitia was telling Nadiika an interesting story about a journey into the depths of space. He had read it recently and wanted to share his thoughts and feelings about it.

They came to the edge of the forest. Their path now lay through a field, where a strong, gusty wind was blowing. The wind caught Nadiika's light head scarf and carried it far into the forest. Vitia started to chase after it, but Nadiika stopped him, saying, 'You'll never find it. It's not worth looking for it.'

Vitia took off his scarf and offered it to Nadiika, saying, 'Put it on. Cover your head. It's cold and you'll catch a chill.'

But the girl would not hear of it. She said the wind was not cold at all. 'The wind smells of spring,' she added.

'But it's still a winter wind,' objected Vitia. 'You'll catch a chill and get ill.'

Nadiika just laughed.

Then Vitia looked at Nadiika and said, 'You don't look as nice without a headscarf.'

Nadiika blushed, and said, 'You're right, the wind is cold. Let me borrow your scarf, and I'll bring it to school tomorrow.'

Why do people say 'thank you'?

Two people were walking along a forest road—an old man and his grandson. It was hot, and they were thirsty.

The travellers came to a stream. The cool water murmured quietly. They bent down and drank.

'Thank you, stream,' said the grandfather.

The boy laughed.

'Why did you say thank you to the stream?' he asked his grandfather. 'The stream is not alive. It won't hear your words and won't understand your gratitude.'

'That's true,' said his grandfather. 'If a wolf had drunk, he wouldn't have said "thank you". But we're not wolves, we're people. Do you know why people say "thank you"? Think about who needs that word.'

The boy started thinking. He had plenty of time. They had a long way to go …

How the butterfly drank birch sap

Snow still lay under trees in the shade, but a little butterfly, woken by the warm spring sun, flew out from his winter home. He felt dizzy from weakness and hunger. He had not eaten anything throughout his long winter sleep.

'I know,' thought the butterfly, 'I'll find a sweet-smelling flower and drink its sweet nectar. Then my head will stop spinning.'

But there were still no flowers, except for a single blue squill peeping out from the earth. The butterfly was overjoyed to see it, but when he settled on the flower it had no sweet nectar. It felt cold.

The butterfly flew on. His strength was failing him, and he was about to fold his wings and fall to the earth, when suddenly he heard a sweet, kind voice, calling, 'Fly over to me! Over here, to the silver birch tree. I'll give you a drop of sap to drink.'

The butterfly flew over to the birch tree and saw a drop of a sap seeping from a crack in the bark. The butterfly drank his fill and happily flapped his wings. 'Thank you!' said the butterfly. 'You saved my life. Without your help, I would have starved to death.'

The mole and the lark

A lark built her nest amidst a sea of wheat. She found a small hole in the ground, brought some soft grass and feathers, and soon her home was ready. She soared into the blue sky and sang joyfully, 'I have a home! I have a home!'

Just beside the lark's nest, a mole had dug a deep burrow. He came out of it very rarely, in the evening or just before sunrise. Once, the kind mole told the lark, 'I feel sorry for you, my friend! You do not have a real home. Let me make a burrow for you, so you can have a warm and cozy place to live.'

The lark just laughed at him. She rose into the sky and sang, 'I have little chicks at home! I have little chicks at home!'

Listening to the lark's song, the mole once more felt so painfully sorry for the lark, that all he could say was, 'Oh, that poor lark!'

A flower or a wolf's jaw?

Two boys, Serhiiko and Mykola, were walking home from school. Serhiiko was happy. He had been called out to the blackboard by the teacher three times today and had received 'excellent' marks on all three occasions.

Mykola was sad and deep in thought. He had been called to the blackboard twice today and had not performed well, so the teacher had written 'unsatisfactory' in his diary. She had even said, 'When I see your mother, I will have to talk to her about your work.'

It was a warm, spring day. The sun was shining brightly. A fluffy white cloud floated across the blue sky.

Serhiiko looked at it and exclaimed, 'Mykola, look at that beautiful cloud! It looks just like a white rose. Can you see? It is opening its petals! They are soft and delicate, trembling in the wind.'

Mykolka looked at the cloud for a long time. Then he said quietly, 'Where are the petals? Where is the flower? That cloud looks like a wolf.

Look, his head is on that side. The fierce beast has opened his jaws and is about to attack.'

The boys looked at the cloud for a long time, and each one saw it in their own way.

The fiery stallion

My mother told me this story …

In our village, there was a stallion, a fiery stallion. He was completely untamed and would not obey anyone. Even the most experienced and strongest men were afraid of approaching him. When they tried to saddle him, he would strike the ground with his hooves, biting and snorting.

Finally, one brave boy, Yurko, managed to saddle the restive creature. However, the stallion reared up, whinnied, jumped onto the road, and threw Yurko off. Then he galloped through the village and stopped on its outskirts. Two small children were playing right in the middle of the road. I know from my mother that it was me and my twin sister Olena. We were only eighteen months old. We ran to the stallion, sat down under him, and hugged his front legs. My mother's heart sank in fear. She thought that the stallion would kill us or maim us. But he stood quietly. Occasionally, he would slowly lift his leg and then stand quietly again, looking at us as if afraid. Meanwhile, we continued to play, oblivious to any danger.

Eventually, cautiously, the fiery stallion stepped away from us and trotted back to the village, where they barely managed to herd him into his stable.

My mother sometimes asks me whether I remember us playing under that horse, but I cannot recall it. All I remember is that, from my earliest years, my favourite toy was a stallion. I am eleven now, and I still play with my fiery stallion.

The owl and the maple leaf

The owl did not sleep during the night. She hunted mice, looking for food. When the sun rose, the owl flew to the forest, settled in a maple tree, and hid under a broad leaf. She slept all day, and then in the evening she took off to hunt. It continued like that for several weeks. The maple leaf grew accustomed to greeting the owl. When the sky turned red, just before sunrise, the leaf became expectant, anticipating the arrival of the owl. The owl, in turn, became accustomed to the maple leaf. She was very gentle as she settled under it, trying not harm it.

One morning, the owl did not come. The sun rose, the lark sang, but the owl did not arrive. Another night passed and morning came again, but there was still no sign of the owl.

The maple leaf grew sad and hung its head. Nothing was dear to it now, not even the sun and the life-giving rain. The leaf turned yellow, withered, and died.

Will we really never see each other again?

This little incident took place at a railway station in a big city. The trains leaving that station travel to distant places all over our nation.

One warm June day, in a green garden next to the station, two little children, Olia and Serhiiko, made friends. They were still too young to go to school. The boy and the girl were both travelling home with their mothers, and both had to change trains at this station. Olia lived in a city in the far north, on the shore of the Arctic Ocean. Serhiiko lived in a city far to the south, in the middle of a sandy desert.

They had two hours to wait until their trains departed. Children make friends very quickly. Olia and Serhiiko played and told each other about the cities where they lived, about the wonderful northern lights, about birds that made nests of stones, about the ships of the desert, camels, and about the mysterious ruins of ancient cities covered in sand dunes.

Suddenly the girl noticed a sweet lying on the grass, melting in the sun. A many-coloured butterfly had landed on it, and was beating its wings, trying to escape from the sweet's sticky surface. Olia rescued the butterfly and handed it to Serhiiko. They spent a long time admiring its beautiful wings. Then Serhiiko raised his hand, and the butterfly took off, its many-coloured wings fluttering in the warm summer air. The excited children joyfully held each other's hands and watched the butterfly flit about.

The children's mothers came up to them. Olia's mother said, 'Children, our trains are leaving. Let's go. We need to get into our carriages.'

'Say farewell to each other, children,' said Serhiiko's mother. 'Say farewell, because you will never see each other again.'

The children did not know what 'farewell' meant, but they felt the pain of parting forever. Their hearts ached.

'Will we really never see each other again?' asked Olia, her voice shaking.

Serhiiko was silent. He looked at Olia and thought to himself… What that boy was thinking about, nobody will ever know, because nobody can express in words what a five-year-old boy is thinking when he is in pain.

What causes heartache?

Five-year-old Vitia was playing in the garden. He fell on a prickle, and it stuck into his hand. Vitia pulled the prickle out straight away, but the wound began to bleed, and he cried from the pain.

Vitia wanted some sympathy, so he ran to find his mother, who was working in the fields.

'Mum! Mum!' his mother heard, and she saw the little scratch on her son's hand and the blood.

When Vitia's mother saw the blood on his hand, her face went pale and her eyes filled with tears.

'Mum … Mum,' whispered the boy. 'Why are you crying? What is hurting?'

'My heart is hurting,' said his mother, hugging him.

'Then why aren't you bleeding?' asked the boy. 'Where are you hurt?'

'Don't you know, child, what wounds the heart?' asked his mother. 'Don't you know what makes the heart ache?'

His mother's eyes became anxious and stern.

'You have been a child for too long, my boy,' said his mother. 'If a person still behaves like a baby when they are five years old, it will be hard for them to become a real human being.'

The laziest cat in the world

A cat was lying on the table. A little girl put two saucers on the table, one with milk and one with sour cream. The cat thought, 'The little girl has brought me a treat, but which is better, sour cream or milk?' The cat was about to consider which was better, but he could not be bothered to think about it, he was so lazy.

Suddenly a sparrow flew in at the open window. It landed on the table and began to peck at some crumbs. Now the cat had three tasty things to choose from: the milk, the sour cream, and the sparrow. But it was not easy to decide which of the three was the tastiest. The cat was about to consider which was the tastiest, but it seemed too much like hard work, so he closed his eyes and went to sleep.

He was the laziest cat in the world.

Indifference

In our village lived an old lady named Grandma Oryna. She was so old that nobody knew her age. The old lady had two neighbours, both tractor drivers. One had a daughter name Galia, in grade seven, and the other had a daughter named Nina, in grade three.

One day, Nina asked the old lady, 'Grandma, when is your birthday?'

'Tomorrow, dear,' answered the old lady.

Nina waited till the next morning, picked some flowers, and took them to the old lady. Galia asked her, 'Where are you taking those flowers?'

'To Grandma Oryna,' said Nina. 'It's her birthday today.'

Galia laughed and said, 'She isn't your grandma, is she? Why are you congratulating a stranger on her birthday?'

Nina was shocked by Galia's words. 'How can a grandma be a stranger?' she asked in surprise.

The seagulls and the crayfish

A crayfish was hiding under a submerged log in the murky water of a river and chewing on a green leaf that had fallen from a willow. He noticed two seagulls settle on the water above him and begin talking. One asked the other, 'What do you think is the best thing in the world?'

The other answered, 'Being high up in the sky is the best thing in the world. The sun shines down, and the blue sky is never-ending.'

The crayfish listened to their conversation and decided to take a look and see for himself what this blue sky was like. He crawled out onto the riverbank, gazed up at the sky and became frightened: in all that blue sky, there was no silt, no submerged log, no murky water, and no swamp.

'No,' he thought, 'The best thing in the world is a quiet little burrow in the riverbed.'

How could they all be here without me?

Yarynka was seven years old. Tomorrow she would start school.

Her mother opened the wardrobe and spread out Yarynka's dresses, going through them and wondering which one would look the smartest.

Then, amongst her dresses, Yarynka spotted a tiny smock, a little bigger than her mother's hand, and a little smaller than her father's.

'That was your first smock,' explained her mother.

Yarynka clapped her hands.

'Was I that small for long?' she asked.

'No, only for about a week.'

'And before that?'

'Before that you weren't here at all.

The little girl looked at her mother in amazement.

'What do you mean, I wasn't here at all? But the trees and the flowers and the doves and the cat—were they all here?'

'They were all here.'

'How could they all be here without me?' asked Yarynka.

The hand withheld

A mother took her five-year-old son, Mytko, to the park. For a long time, they walked along the narrow, stony paths, and then sat down to rest on a bench.

Suddenly a cat appeared out of nowhere. It sat next to Mytko and purred, looking up at him. Mytko smiled, and his hand reached out to stroke the cat, but his mother pulled his hand away. The cat got up, came over to Mytko, rubbed its side against him, and purred even more loudly.

Mytko raised his arm again, and nearly stroked the cat, but his mother slapped his hand and said, 'Don't touch the filthy thing.'

Mytko's eyes shone with tears.

A few days later Mytko and his mother went to the park again. This time there were lots of children playing there. One little boy, about three years old, accidentally stood on Mytko's foot. Mytko looked at the boy angrily and pushed him in the back. The little boy cried.

'Why did you hurt that little boy?' asked his mother in amazement.

'What was he doing standing on my foot? The filthy thing.'

Unhappy Andrii

Andrii did not study hard at school. If he passed, that was good; if he failed sometimes, that did not really bother him. His parents were often summoned to the school and asked to make him study harder, but they could not do anything with their son. Andrii just did not want to study.

Andrii barely managed to complete his schooling. He began to work in a tractor brigade, but he did not want to work either. Andrii especially hated getting up early, and he had to get up very early and be in the field before sunrise.

Andrii would walk to the field in the morning and curse his life. 'Why am I alive? Why do I have to suffer so much?' he thought. And the whole world seemed gloomy and without joy.

Andrii is an unhappy man. He does not like work. But everything in the world that is beautiful and great is created by work. Work is the most beautiful thing.

The crucian carp in the aquarium

Petryk has a small aquarium at home. Goldfish live in it. Petryk feeds them.

One day Petryk went to the pond and caught a little crucian carp in a bowl. He brought it home and put it in his aquarium. He thought the little fish would like it there.

Petryk gave the fish some food. The goldfish ate it, but the crucian carp did not. He squashed himself into a corner on the very bottom of the aquarium and stayed there.

'Why aren't you eating?' asked Petryk.

'Put me back in the pond,' said the fish. 'If you keep me here, I will die.'

Petryk put the crucian carp back in the pond.

How can the bumblebee escape?

A bumblebee flew into the classroom. It was yellow and furry. It flew around the classroom for a long time, and then flew over to the window. It beat against the glass and cried, but it could not get out.

When the children arrived at school, the bumblebee was quietly crawling across the windowpane. Sometimes it tried to fly, but it had no strength left.

The bumblebee crawled over the glass. Nobody took any notice of the poor bumblebee, except for Nina, the smallest girl in the class, who stared at it all the time.

Nina wanted so much to go up to the bumblebee, take it in the palm of her hand, lift it up to the open ventilation window, and let it out.

Nina could not wait for the break.

If only the time would go faster.

If only the bell could ring sooner.

The paper boat

A boy made a paper boat. But to him, it was not just a paper boat; it was a mighty vessel with huge sails. The boy took his white paper boat to a puddle, though to him it was not a puddle, but the wide blue sea. Somewhere, far, far away, beyond that sea, there were azure mountains full of unknown beasts and birds. His ship traversed the wide blue sea. Now it was approaching the shore. Birds circled above the ship, and people greeted it.

A hare in a blizzard

It was a cold winter. In the morning, the sun shone, but later, heavy clouds covered the sky. A wind blew up, and it started snowing. The light snow turned into a blizzard. I went out to watch the falling snow and caught some snowflakes in my hand. As I studied them, I wondered who had crafted such beauty? Then I saw a little grey hare crossing the field and a large bird circling above it. The hare hurried to a haystack and hid in it. The bird circled above the haystack for a while and then flew away.

In the meantime, the blizzard worsened: the wind whistled and howled, and the snowdrifts grew higher and higher. I trudged over to the haystack. The hare was there, buried in the hay and covered with snow, so all I could see was his shining eyes. He looked at me as if begging, 'Please don't touch me, boy. I want so much to live. I want to run in a green meadow and to munch on sweet cabbage.'

I felt pity for the hare and walked back home.

The blizzard howled the whole night long. In the morning, I woke up and looked out the window. The sun was shining once again. I made my way over to the haystack, struggling through the deep snowdrifts. The hare was no longer there. He had left his hiding place and hopped back to the forest. I could see his tracks in the snow. Run free, dear hare! Enjoy your forest! But if you ever need to escape from danger, come running to me.

A nest in a hat

When I was a little, I had a hat. As I grew bigger, I did not need that hat anymore. It was worn out anyway, so I told my mother that I wanted to give it away to a bird.

'What use would it be to a bird?' my mother asked in surprise.

'They could make a nest in it,' I answered.

I hung my hat on a bush. Very soon, I observed that a bird was making a nest in it. The bird looked at me and said, 'Thank you, little girl, for such a lovely warm hat!'

The squirrel and the kind person

A kind person was walking through the forest. He gazed at the grass and the flowers with tender eyes. He did not tread on the flowers, because he noticed them.

The kind person approached a tall pine tree and saw a squirrel. The squirrel was leaping from branch to branch, and a red-haired animal was chasing her. The kind person saw that it was a marten, a squirrel's worst enemy. At any moment the marten would catch up to the squirrel and tear her to pieces with his sharp claws.

The kind person watched the poor creature, and his heart ached with pity. The squirrel noticed the kind person's eyes, jumped from the tree, and landed on his shoulder. The wicked marten ran away into the dark forest. The kind person stroked the squirrel and said, 'Now you can take shelter in your hole in the tree.'

The squirrel gazed into the kind person's eyes with gratitude, and quickly jumped into her hole in the tree.

Her babies had long been waiting for her. She told them about the kind person.

A soap bubble

A boy was sitting by an open window and blowing bubbles. They were light and beautiful. The rays of the sun played on the bubbles with all the colours of the rainbow: yellow, blue, green, orange and violet. A light breeze lifted the bubbles, and they flew over the flower bed and above some lilac bushes. They wanted to rise higher than the trees, but as they brushed against their leaves they burst.

However, one large soap bubble, lifted by the wind, flew up into the blue sky. A swallow saw the soap bubble, fluttered over to it, and flew alongside in amazement.

'How beautifully dressed you are!' cheeped the swallow. 'What a beautiful bird you are! You are wonderful!'

'Yes, I am a wonderful bird,' said the bubble, swelling with pride. 'Look at how all the colours of the rainbow play on my coat.'

The swallow reached over to touch its coat, and the bubble burst.

UNFINISHED STORIES

* Olenka's sparrow

Little Olenka dreamed of catching a sparrow, but she could not lay hands on one, so she decided to create a sparrow herself out of grey feathers. She cut a small hole in a pillow and removed some feathers. Then she moulded a featherless sparrow from some dough. She covered it with cherry glue and a layer of grey feathers. Lo and behold, she had a sparrow. It was grey, with a tiny beak and black eyes like poppy seeds. Olenka put her sparrow on the windowsill, sprinkled some millet for it and gave it some water. But the sparrow was silent. Olenka gave it some breadcrumbs, but the sparrow did not utter a sound. Suddenly, somewhere nearby, a mother-sparrow started chirping to her chicks. Olenka's sparrow raised its head, turned to the window, and spread its wings …

* A little girl's grief

A mother bought her daughter a doll. Dressed in a light blue silk gown and pink stockings, the beautiful doll smiled at her. Before going to bed, the little girl said to her doll, 'Good night, my dear daughter. I do not want to part with you, but I have no choice; it is time to sleep. My mum will worry if I don't go to sleep, but I'll see you in my dreams. Will you see me as well?'

'No, I cannot see anything when I am asleep.'

'Why?' asked the little girl in surprise.

'Because I never sleep.'

The girl was stunned. 'Do you really never sleep? Then how do you count the days: one, two, three days, a week?'

The doll did not respond. She just smiled quietly.

One day, the little girl dropped her doll on the floor. Now there was a crack in its back, and some sawdust trickled out of it. The girl was very upset. 'So that is why she does not sleep,' she thought. 'She has sawdust inside. So, why does she look so real?'

PARENTS AND CHILDREN: THE HARMONY OF LOVE AND WILL

On the secret of birth

Parents and teachers are often troubled by the question of how to explain to children the secret of their own birth. Some believe that it is best to tell the story of the stork; some are convinced that it would be better to tell the child the truth (or at least most of the truth); and some are certain that the most suitable answer is 'You're young; when you grow up, then you'll find out.' All things considered, the tale of the stork is the most suitable option from a moral standpoint, because it is an artistic image that captures folk wisdom and poetry, as well as expressing sensitivity to our intimate and private lives and to a child's impressionable soul. Tell a child the story of the beautiful and kind stork and the child will understand it as a fairy tale and believe in it the same way that children believe in fairy tales.

Some things must be left unsaid when talking of things that are private and inviolable, otherwise a person will simply stop being human. There must be room for poetic thinking, otherwise we will descend into vulgarity and primitivism. When a child finds joy in a new addition to the family, let them find satisfaction for their curiosity in a pure, romantic tale. There is no danger in that. In fact, it is the only way to encourage chastity. I invented a story about the birth of a person especially for young children—for preschoolers and those in the early years. The story is as follows:

'Dear Olia, you ask me where your little brother has come from, how he came to us, why your mum became his mum too, why you became his sister, and he became your brother? Listen carefully, dear children, I am about to tell you the most truthful of all the stories in this world. Look over there at the red sky in the east. Soon the sun will rise. Over there, far, far away, where the dear sun rests at night, is a wonderful poppy field. The sun is now nearing its poppy field. Red poppies bloom there eternally, and a clear stream babbles in a valley. To every mother, including yours, dear Olia, the sun gives a poppy plant in that poppy field. When a mother longs for a son or a daughter, she dreams of the kind of a child she will have. And, just as she has dreamed, a son or a daughter is born under her poppy plant. A new person is born from

the mother's longing and the sun's golden rays. The little child lies on the poppy petals, stretching out its hands, drawn to his mother's breast. At that moment, the stork swoops down into the poppy field. The stork is a beautiful bird with silver wings and emerald eyes. The stork takes the child and carries it to its mother. It is her own dear child, the one she had longed for in her dream. The dear sun created you Olia, just as your mother dreamed. And that wonderful bird, the stork with the silver wings, flies back to the poppy field, because there are many mothers in the world, each with her own dream.'

I have written another story on this topic: 'The stork and the little girl' (p. 159).

On the heart's memory

To every generation of my students, once they can appreciate human values, I narrate the tale 'You have to be human to understand' (p. 159). With each retelling of the story, my aim is that the children may understand a great moral truth: a person affirms themselves in this world not only as a creature who thinks and feels, but also as a living link in the eternal chain of generations, a link that connects past generations with future generations. Those who treasure their memories of their parents, grandparents and great-grandparents are more likely to feel the weight of their responsibility for the future. We have a homeland due to the fact that each person sees the roots of their existence, their honour and their worth in their parents, grandparents and great-grandparents.

We discuss honouring and respecting older generations with our students' mothers and fathers. During the sessions in our school for parents, we narrate cautionary tales about mothers and fathers who have not had the wisdom to nurture respect for elders, and who have harvested the bitter fruits of their moral ineptitude. One mother's fate is lucidly illustrated in the tale 'Little Petryk and little Pavlyk' (p. 160).

The way to discover the spirit of our nation, of our people's understanding of morality and of pure human relationships, is through experiencing a sense of wonder at the selflessness of others. When faced with a child's open heart, be selfless, and let this selflessness be expressed in your attitude towards our homeland, our nation, and your family. These words occupy a very significant place in our system of pedagogical education for parents and future parents.

When educators, mothers and fathers strive to develop a child's moral sensitivity and receptiveness to words of guidance from their elders, they need particular wisdom when nurturing something that we call 'the heart's memory'. We need to develop and deepen this refined human trait in our children.

I strive to ensure that, throughout their years of schooling, each student refines the subtle and complex art of observing themselves. Each student, while still an adolescent, should reflect on what they are capable of leaving behind in other people, in their work, in things that live and flower. Will I at least contribute some little drop to the eternal ocean of human existence? What is necessary for this? How can we lead our students in this direction?

There is a folk tale about a man whose life bore no fruit, like a barren flower.[20]

A man loved to sing and to have a good time, but he could not stay for any length of time in one place. He kept travelling from green field to flowering meadow, from flowering meadow to shady grove. And then a son was born to him. This idle man hung his son's cradle on the branch of an oak tree and sat and sang to him. And his son grew not by the day but by the hour. He jumped out of his cradle, walked up to his father, and spoke.

'Father, show me something you have made with your own hands.'

The father was amazed that his son should speak such wise words and smiled. He thought about what he could show his son. His son waited for an answer, but his father just stood there in silence. He stopped singing. The son looked at the tall oak tree and asked, 'Perhaps you planted this oak tree?'

The father bent his head in silence.

The son took his father to a field and looked at the heavy ears of wheat. 'Perhaps you grew this fine crop of wheat?'

His father's head hung even lower, and he remained silent.

The father and son came to a deep pond. The son looked at the reflection of the blue sky in the water and said, 'Father, give me some wise words of advice.'

But the father was not just incapable of doing anything with his hands, he was unable to utter words of wisdom. Struck dumb, he hung his head even lower … and turned into the barren flowering grass that in Ukrainian is called 'pustotsvit'. This grass flowers from spring to autumn, but never produces any fruit or seeds.

'What trace should a person leave upon the earth?' (p. 161) is a similar tale.

'May', 'may not' and 'must'

Moral upbringing involves setting wise limits. A child has to understand that there are three concepts: 'may', 'may not' and 'must'. Mothers and fathers who, figuratively speaking, do not know how to alternate these three courses of a balanced meal—may, may not, and must—make a huge, sometimes fatal, mistake. Until the age of 12, sometimes until the age of 13 or 14, and even until the age of 15 or 16, they offer only one meal: 'You may.' The child, and later the teenager, is allowed to do anything. The child gets the impression that they are basically the centre of the universe, that everything revolves around them. Later, when it turns out that the child is riding on the parents' backs, the mother and father suddenly realise they have an emergency on their hands and change the food to 'You may not!' Suddenly an absolutely new dimension of the world is revealed to the little person: this is forbidden, this is not allowed. The little person is offended. They have a distorted conception of good and evil, of what is fair and unfair. Until this time, they felt in every cell of their being that they were giving their parents joy; it did not matter what they did, the mother and father praised them. Even if the child shook their little fist at their grandmother, they still praised them, saying, 'Look how independent our son is!' And suddenly the child realises that they are not bringing joy to their parents, but only problems and disappointment. Now, they are no longer a 'treasure' and the 'apple of their parents' eye' but God's retribution. Instead of soothing words there is a clip over the head or even a belting. The child develops an unhealthy sense of hurt pride. Every sharp word of criticism from the parents is like salt sprinkled on the bleeding wounds of hurt pride. Self-pity is a mental state that I consider to be an inexhaustible source of egotism. Do not let your children fall into self-pity—this mental state will give rise to bitterness. Let a child feel sorry for themselves only to the extent that they are kind and feel sorry for others.

I am certain that the first school of civic responsibility begins with a child thinking, 'What will my mother and father think and say about my behaviour?' I consider that developing a child's sensitivity to their parents' worries, thoughts and feelings, and to their spiritual world in general, is an extremely important child-rearing aim. As far as possible we should refrain from inviting parents to school for 'talks' about their children's moral failings, from threatening sons with their 'father's strong hand' and warning about the dangers that lie ahead, saying, 'If things continue like this … ' Instead, we should facilitate the kind of relationships between children and parents that give joy to mothers and fathers. This is an important principle we uphold in developing relationships between mothers and fathers on the one hand, and children on the other. We consider it to be very important that a child feels humbled in front of their mother and father (as, by the way, the parents should feel humbled in front of their children, but that is a different topic), that a child knows from a very early age what a joy it is to bring their parents happiness, satisfaction, and a sense of fulfilment. When you raise children, make sure they experience the kind of joy that brings joy to their mothers and fathers. Everything that is in the child's thoughts, mind, soul, exercise book or diary—all of it we consider from the point of view of the relationships between children and parents.

It is absolutely unacceptable for a child to bring his parents nothing but grief—this is bad child-rearing. Pay attention and make sure that during the primary school years there are no bad children, that a mother's heart does not harden, and that a child does not lose the urge to be good. Relationships between children and parents should be built on a child's urge to be good, to bring joy to their family. This is a special, unexplored side of school education. The essence of it is that all of the instruction you give a child in class forms an integral part of their character development. In everything you say, explain, or ask, you are touching their hearts; you are shining a light that ultimately is reflected on to the parents.

We often invite mothers and fathers to our school. We invite them to Mothers' Day and Fathers' Day, to Book Day and Creative Work Day. On these occasions—and this is our intention—mothers and fathers come in contact with their children's intelligence, abilities and talents. Parents see the intellectual work and progress of their sons and daughters. Each mother, each father, comes with the secret hope that today their son's or daughter's progress will bring them joy. These hopes may not always be realised today, but not one mother or father has hopes that are never realised. Without this, it would be impossible to imagine educating children correctly.

I find it strange, unusual, incomprehensible, that the majority of schools ignore the most important stimulus that encourages children to study and to be a good human being: their desire to bring joy, happiness, peace and contentment to their family. This wish is the most delicate and at the same time the strongest thread that binds school and family. When there is no such thread, or it is broken, talk of passing on pedagogical knowledge to parents is just hollow words, and the school's requests for support from families will be fruitless. Schools and parents can only work together when a child wants to bring joy to their family and is successful in doing so.

I will never agree with objections of those who say, 'What can we do if a child does not study well? Where is his joy to come from?' The whole point is that no child should feel or think, 'I am a failure, I can't do anything, I won't achieve anything.' The moment a child has these thoughts, that child is no longer being educated by you, and their family—the mother and father—have fallen out of the sphere of your educational influence. The humanitarian mission of a teacher is to make sure that even the weakest student experiences the joy of success: only then are they being educated by you. And for their family, their small joys become a huge spiritual force that reinforces the relationship between their mother and father. The mother and father will be able to help you a thousand times more when their son brings home joy from school, than when they are trying to force their child to be good. You can force someone to *do* something, but you cannot force anyone to *be* what they do not want to *be*. In the urge to be good the most important component is the child's goodwill. The child's goodwill gives rise to their sense of duty and is the precondition that ensures that the sensitive regions of a child's heart will never harden.

Remember, not all of your students will become engineers and doctors, scientists and artists; but all of them will become fathers and mothers, husbands and wives. If you prioritise your school's responsibilities correctly, educating a good human being, husband or wife, father or mother takes pride of place, and educating a future engineer or doctor is of secondary concern.

On love for parents

The problem of parents and children is one of the most complex issues in education. There are as many sides to this issue as there are living, unique children in front of you. At the very beginning it is necessary to be aware that any attempt to influence a child will be in vain if the father and mother are not the ones children turn to for moral guidance and when seeking to experience life fully. Only if the father and mother have a moral right to give direction (and parental upbringing is, in essence, the father's and mother's will multiplied by their love for their children and the children's love for them), will their moral guidance reach their children's hearts, generate appropriate feelings in response, and awaken the urge to be good. The parents' right to give direction, together with their love, protect and shield the child. They understand their parents' expectations and strictness, and know that they will not tolerate misbehaviour. Expectations without love turn a child's life into torture. There is another correlation: the gentler and more generous parents' love, the wiser and more experienced their will has to be. Love without the ability to direct, to manage a child's desires, and especially to place limits on their desires, turns a child into a capricious, wilful being, who, as the parents will soon learn, will become unmanageable. Disobedience, in most cases, is the result of an imbalance between love and the ability to assert the parent's will.

That is why we teach parents and future parents to both love and give direction, and to vigilantly ensure that the harmony of these two is not disturbed.

As well as educating parents, we conduct the ethical education of children, adolescents, and our senior boys and girls. How, in practical terms, do we teach young people how to relate to their parents?

We consider a school culture of respect for mothers to be extremely important. Teacher, your mission is to develop in each child the sense of caring for their mother as the most precious person in the world.

In my talks with students, especially with those transitioning from childhood to adolescence, I consider it very important to make sure a child clearly understands that their mother's peace, happiness and well-being depend on the child. A mother's happiness is created by the child, adolescent, or young man or woman.

Ideological upbringing begins when a child says the word *'Mummy'*. What will become of someone who is born of a human being, and in the image of a human being, depends to a huge extent on how this person relates to their mother and father, and what feelings they experience when they say the words '*mum*' and '*dad*'. A son's sense of duty towards their parents is a measure of their humanity. The old Ukrainian tale 'A legend about a mother's Love' (p. 176) examines this issue.

Children enjoy listening to tales and stories about mothers from my ethics anthology. Every generation of my students memorises 'The tale of a mother goose' (p. 177) when they are at a tender and impressionable age.

There are several stories and tales about a mother's heart in my ethics anthology, including 'The apple of his mother's eye' (p. 178), 'The grey hair' (p. 178), 'Why a mother ran from the field' (p. 179).

One story in my anthology is a legend about seven daughters (p. 179). When I tell this story I try to awaken grown up thoughts in the minds of little sons and daughters. Why do I need a mother? Why is she dear to me? A poppy flower needs the sun's rays; dry soil needs a drop of water; a helpless nestling needs a caring mother bird; a bee needs a flower; a rose needs the morning dew; a cherry orchard needs a nightingale's song. All of these are needed to make my life better, less difficult, more pleasant, more beautiful. It is very important to develop in a child's soul a sense that a mother is precious not just as a source of personal joy and comforts, but as a living, loving human being with their own world of feelings and thoughts!

STORIES AND VIGNETTES

The stork and the little girl

Little Natalka asked her mother and father, 'Where did I come from?'

'You were born,' answered her mother.

'What do you mean, I was born,' asked the little girl in surprise.

'Early one morning the stork brought you,' said her mother. 'He carried you here, tapped at the window, and Dad and I went out and took you from the stork.'

'And where did the stork get me from?' asked Natalka, even more surprised.

'Go and ask him,' said her mother.

Natalka went out into the meadow. She saw the stork standing there in its red shoes, one foot on the ground, and the other tucked under it. Natalka looked at its red shoes. She had some exactly the same colour. 'So, the stork really did bring me to Mum and Dad,' thought the little girl, and she forgot to ask the stork where he got her from. She ran quickly home and again asked her mother, 'Mum, did the stork bring me with my red shoes?'

'No, without shoes,' said her mother.

'That's strange. He has exactly the same red shoes as me.'

'We gave him the same red shoes that we gave you, to thank him for bringing us such a nice present,' said her mother.

You have to be human to understand

A man walked to the cemetery to visit his father's grave. He pulled out some weeds, then dug a little hole and planted a rose bush.

A dragonfly was sitting nearby on a blade of grass. She carefully observed the man's work and wondered, 'What is he doing? Why is he pulling out grass, and why is he planting a rose bush? This is not a vegetable bed or a flower bed.'

Several days passed. The man returned to the cemetery, pulled out some weeds and watered the rose bush. He smiled when he saw the first flower on the rose bush.

'Man,' asked the dragonfly, 'What are you doing? Why are you planting flowers on this little mound? Why are you pulling out weeds and watering the grass? What is underneath this mound?'

'My father is here,' answered the man. 'This is his grave.'

'What is a father?' asked the dragonfly, 'And what is a grave?'

The man tried to explain, but the dragonfly could not understand a word he said. She asked, 'Man, please tell me what I need to do to understand what you are talking about.'

'You have to be human to understand,' answered the man.

Little Petryk and little Pavlyk

A mother and father were sitting at the table. The mother was sewing; the father was reading the newspaper. Five-year-old Petryk was playing on the sofa, saddling his horse, preparing for a long journey, dreaming of a voyage beyond the deep blue sea.

Petryk's mother looked out the window and said to his father, 'The devil's brought us Grandma Marfa.'

Petryk quickly dismounted from his horse and ran to the window to see this wonder of wonders, but he was too late. Grandma Marfa was already knocking at the door.

His mother said, 'Please come in.'

When Grandma Marfa came into the room, Petryk's mother spoke to her affectionately and asked her to sit down. The old lady sat down, sighed deeply, and murmured, 'I barely managed to walk here. My legs are so sore, so sore.'

Petryk looked with amazement at Grandma Marfa. He asked, 'Grandma Marfa, did you really walk here all by yourself?'

'Yes, my dear, I walked. I was not given a lift,' answered Grandma Marfa, and she smiled and gave Petryk a sweet shortcake to eat.

'Mum, you said the devil brought Grandma Marfa,' said Petryk reproachfully.

His mother's face flushed and then turned pale. She looked down at her sewing. His father hid behind his newspaper. Grandma Marfa got up and quietly left. An oppressive silence came over the house.

Many years passed. Petryk grew into an adult. He had a wife and a five-year-old son named Pavlyk. His father died, and his mother lived by herself in their old home.

One day the elderly mother visited her son. She spent the afternoon there, and evening was approaching. The old mother said, as if thinking aloud, 'Should I walk home, or spend the night here? It is getting dark, and it's a long way.'

'You should go home, Mum,' said her son.

Meanwhile, five-year-old Pavlyk was playing on the sofa, saddling his horse, preparing for a long journey, dreaming of a voyage beyond the deep blue sea.

When he heard his father saying good-bye to his grandmother, Pavlyk said, 'You can have my horse, Grandma. You can sit on it and ride home.'

His grandmother put on her coat, and tears fell from her eyes.

What trace should a person leave upon the earth?

An old master builder constructed a stone house. He stood to one side and admired the building. 'Tomorrow, people will move in,' thought the builder with pride.

At that time, a seven-year-old boy was playing nearby. He hopped onto one of the steps and left a footprint on a part of the cement that had not yet hardened.

'Why are you spoiling my work?' lamented the builder. The boy looked at his footprint, laughed, and ran away.

Many years passed. The little boy grew up. His life unfolded in such a way that he kept moving on, never settling in one place, and never really applying himself to anything, physically or mentally.

Old age came upon him. The old man remembered the village on the banks of the Dnipro where he had grown up. He felt an urge to visit the place, and he travelled back to his home. He met people and introduced himself, but they simply shrugged their shoulders. No one remembered any such person.

'What trace did you leave here of yourself?' an elderly local asked him. 'Do you have a son or a daughter?'

'I don't have any son or daughter,' replied the old man.

'Perhaps you planted an oak tree?'

'No, I didn't plant an oak.'

'Perhaps you cared for a field?'

'I didn't care for a field.'

'You have probably written a song?'

'No, I didn't write any songs.'

'So, who are you? What did you do with your life?' asked the puzzled local.

The old man could not answer. He remembered the moment when he left a footprint on one of the steps of a stone house. He walked to the place. The house was still there as if built only yesterday, and on the lowest step was his tiny little footprint.

'And that is all that will be left of me on this earth,' thought the old man bitterly. 'But it is not enough, not nearly enough. I should have lived differently.'

Even in his sleep, he could smell his mother's hands

A mother ant was in a hurry, scurrying home to her ant nest with a tiny little piece of sweet watermelon. She opened the door and went in. Inside the ant nest were lots and lots of little beds, and in each bed was a baby ant.

The mother ant found her baby in his bed. She sat at the head of the bed and hugged and kissed her baby. The baby ant was happy and said in his own ant language, 'I knew it was you, Mum. Your hands smell so sweet.'

The mother fed her baby with the sweet watermelon. The baby ant ate his fill, smiled, and went to sleep. Very quietly, so as not to wake her baby, the mother ant got up. She took what was left of the watermelon and put it in a jar for the winter.

The mother ant ran off into the forest to look for more food, while the baby ant lay in his bed and smiled. Even in his sleep, he could smell his mother's hands.

Grandpa's belt

For more than a month little Sashko had been counting down the days until he would start school. At last, the happy day arrived. The next day was the first of September, the first day of the school year.

Sashko woke up at dawn. He put on his new trousers and jacket and checked to make sure he had packed everything in his school bag.

Quietly, so his mother and father would not hear him, Sashko opened the cupboard. There hung his grandfather's belt. Sashko's grandfather was killed on the frontline.[21] His friend, when he returned, had brought Grandpa's belt, a wide one, with a big buckle.

Sashko took down the belt and put in on under his shirt. He would show the other boys what sort of belt his grandfather had worn. He would tell them how his grandfather was a hero.

His mother woke up in the room next door.

'I'm ready for school,' said Sashko.

A letter to a grandson

This happened during World War II. Our troops were engaged in heavy fighting. The fascists[22] were advancing with tanks and machine guns, and our soldiers were outnumbered.

On a tall, ancient burial mound in the steppe, one of our soldiers, Ivan Krasnoshapka, set up his machine gun. He cut down many fascists with his machine gun fire, but the enemy kept advancing. Then he ran out of bullets.

He took out a small piece of paper and wrote, 'I, Private Ivan Krasnoshapka, fought to my last bullet. I still have a grenade. Some fascists are approaching. I will throw my grenade, kill a few more enemy soldiers, and die. I will not surrender alive.

Mykola, my son! You were ten years old when I left home to fight. If you find this letter, you will learn how your father fought the enemy and died. If you do not find it, your son, my grandson, will find it. You will grow up to be true sons of our homeland.'

Ivan Krasnoshapka put the letter into a cartridge case, sealed it, and buried it in the earth …

Twenty-five years passed. Myshko Krasnoshapka, a ten-year-old boy, came to that burial mound in the steppe. He saw the cartridge case, opened it and read the letter aloud. His friends listened to every word with bated breath.

'I swear, Grandpa,' said Myshko quietly, 'I will be a true son of our homeland. I will plant an oak tree on your grave. It will be an eternal monument to your heroism.'

He will come

An elderly mother lives in our village. During the first month of the war against the fascists, she received an official notice signed by the commander of her son's unit. In it appeared the words 'Your son died the death of a hero.' His comrades in arms had added a note: 'A shell exploded, leaving no trace of your son. We filled in the crater, and having honoured it as a war grave, we went into battle with the enemy.'

The old mother wept, and placed the notice under her icon, but she did not believe that her son was dead. Throughout the war, she kept expecting a letter from him, but no letter came.

And when the war ended, the old mother waited expectantly for her son's return. She believed that her son was alive and that he would return.

As soon as the sun began to sink towards the horizon, she would go to the edge of the village, stand by an ancient burial mound, and gaze along the road. All those who came by bowed low to the mother. They all knew that she was waiting for her son. Each one wanted to say a kind word of support to her. 'If he doesn't come today, he is sure to come tomorrow,' a traveller would sometimes say, when they met the old mother, and she would reply, 'Yes, he probably won't come today. The sun is setting … I'd better be off home. He'll come tomorrow.'

Every day, for twenty-seven years, the elderly mother went out to meet her son. She was fifty-three years old when she received the official notification of her son's death, and now she was already eighty. Her hair had turned grey, her hands were wrinkled, and her eyes were watery … The ancient cossack burial mound stood with her by the road, like an eternal sentry, the only companion for the old mother, with her grief and her eternal hope.

'My dear boy,' the mother would whisper, on her way home after sunset, 'I would have died long ago … But who … Who will greet you when you return?'

The everlasting flowers

Eleven-year-old Vitia had never seen his father. He was only three months old when his father, a fighter pilot, had died in an air battle above Berlin on one of the last days of the war.

On the table where Vitia and his mother worked in the evenings there was a portrait of his father. Each year, on the anniversary of his father's death, Vitia's mother placed some everlasting flowers by the portrait. On other days, a vase with a red rose always stood there.

For several weeks, Ivan Vasylovych, an engineer, had been visiting them in the evenings. He worked at the same factory as Vitia's mother. Vitia understood that his mother was going to marry Ivan Vasylovych. It pained him greatly to think that his mother would forget about his father.

On the day when Vitia's mother told him that Ivan Vasylovych was going to ask her to marry him, Vitia could think of nothing but his father. He thought, 'I will come home from school today, and Mum will have put Dad's portrait somewhere else.' As he walked home from school, his heart ached. 'If it was not winter,' he thought, 'I would go into the field, find some everlasting flowers, and place them by Dad's portrait.'

When he arrived home and opened the door, he saw his mother sitting by the table in a new dress. And in the vase by his father's portrait, instead of a red rose, he saw everlasting flowers.

'Mum,' whispered Vitia, 'You'll never forget Dad, will you?'

'Never,' whispered his mother, and she burst into tears.

Why Andrii was sad

One hot summer's day, some black clouds suddenly appeared, and thunder rumbled across the sky. A tall and slender poplar was growing near the tractor depot. Lightning struck it and split the poplar from its crown right down to its roots.

Two young tractor drivers, Stepan and Andrii, came out of the tractor depot and went over to inspect the damaged poplar. Stepan laughed. He thought the poplar looked funny split in two. But Andrii looked sad. 'Why are you so sad?' asked Stepan. 'There are lots more poplars.'

'I planted that poplar,' said Andrii. 'It was tiny then, as small as this twig.'

Let him believe …

There was a student in our class named Petro Rybalka. His faithful dog Som came to school with him every day for three years. Som did not just keep Petro company, he carried a drawstring bag with the sneakers that Petro needed for the physical education class in the gym.

As the winter break approached, Petro's parents made plans to move somewhere far away, and they did not want to take Som with them. No matter how much Petro begged his parents not to leave the dog behind, they would not listen. 'You know what?' Petro said to us before leaving, 'I'll leave my bag and my sneakers with you, and I want you, Mykola, to have Som and take care of him.'

So, I adopted Som and moved his doghouse to my front yard. Som became very sad, but he did not completely give up hope. Every morning, as I left for school, I would give Som the bag with Petro's sneakers in it, and he would cheer up right away, nuzzling up to me and wagging his tail. I would walk to school, and he would trot along beside me carrying the bag.

Near the school entrance, I would take the bag from him, and he would look at me as if to say, 'Where is Petro?' Then Som would wait by the school entrance until the end of classes. When I went home, I would give him the bag with the sneakers again, and again he would cock his head sideways and look at me with a puzzled expression. My friends and I walked home together, looking at Som from time to time, and we all felt bad.

'Why are we fooling him?' asked Stepan. 'Leave the bag at home, Mykola. Hide it, and forget about it! Som needs to know the truth!'

So, we decided to ask our teacher, Ivan Petrovych, whether we should hide the bag from Som.

'No, boys, I wouldn't do that,' said Ivan Petrovych. 'Let him believe. That way it will be easier for him to keep going.'

After a pause, the teacher added, 'People could learn a lot from a good dog.'

Why? Why?

Early one Sunday morning, Andriiko went with his mother to the cemetery. A year earlier they had buried his grandmother. They often went to her grave and watered the flowers there.

It was quiet at the cemetery. Andriiko and his mother sat on a bench by his grandmother's grave. The sun rose, and birds began to sing.

Not far from the grandmother's grave was a new grave. On it lay dried out wreaths, flowers that were now no more than rubbish.

'Mum, why is there rubbish on that grave?' asked Andriiko.

'People have forgotten about it,' said his mother.

'Why have they forgotten about it?'

'Because they have forgotten about the person who is buried there.'

'Why have they forgotten about that person?' persisted Andriiko. 'Why did they bring wreathes here and lay flowers?'

His mother shook her head and said nothing.

And the boy sat and thought.

Sorry for himself

Six-year-old Hryts stepped on a little prickle while running in the yard. The prickle stuck into his foot, and it hurt. The boy sat on a bench, rested one leg on the other, and began to take the prickle out.

The mother saw her son. What was Hryts doing? She threw up her hands, ran to her son, hugged him, kissed him, and cried, 'My poor little boy! Does it hurt?'

At that moment Hryts felt a stabbing pain in his heel. His mother washed his foot and bandaged it.

'You sit still, now, son, and don't run,' she said to Hryts, wiping her tears away.

But Hryts did not want to sit still, and he ran off to play.

An hour passed. Running in the yard, Hryts stood on a sharp little stone. He remembered how his mother had cried over the prickle, and he felt pain. He ran to the house and sat on the bench. He lifted up his foot and saw a red mark from the stone. When he saw the red mark, his foot hurt even more.

'Mum,' he snivelled, 'Come quickly, my foot is hurting.'

His mother saw him, threw up her hands, ran to her son, hugged him and kissed him. Tears fell from Hryts's eyes. He felt sorry for himself …

Several years passed. Hryts became a school student. When there were hard frosts, he stayed at home. When the weather was foul, the boy did not want to go to school, and his mother said it would not matter if he missed one day. She told him to stay at home.

Hryts became a teenager. His teachers now called him by his full name, Hryhorii. Now he stayed at home whenever his class went to work in the fields. Sometimes he had a stomach-ache, and sometimes his foot was sore.

Hryhorii turned eighteen. He was a tall, handsome young man. He was called up for compulsory military service.[23] In the middle of the night a battle alarm sounded out. In three minutes, the soldiers dressed and lined up. They set off on a long march. Everyone was marching quickly and energetically, and only Hryhorii was hanging his head and dragging his feet along.

'Why are you so slow?' the commanding officer asked Hryhorii.

'I can't keep up … It's hard,' he answered.

'Did you think serving in the army would be easy?' asked the officer.

Hryhorii had nothing to say.

Father and son

A mother and father had a son. When the son was only three years old, the father left his son and his wife. He left them and went away, without telling them where he was going or why.

The mother and son remained alone. The little son often asked his mother, 'Why do all the other children have a father, but not me? Why did my father leave us?'

His mother answered, 'He did not love us, and so he left us.'

'Does he love himself?' asked the son.

'He loves himself even less than he loves us. He not only does not love himself; he does not respect himself,' said the mother.

'What does it mean to respect yourself?' asked the son.

'It means to leave something of yourself in your son. If a man cannot leave something of himself in his son, he does not want to be a man.'

'But doesn't Dad understand that?' asked the puzzled son.

'He will only understand it in his old age. He will understand it when he is old and weak.'

The years passed. The son became an adult. He married and had a son. His elderly mother died.

And then, one day, his elderly father came to see him.

'Take me in, son,' he asked. 'I am old and all alone. I am your father, and you should respect your father.'

The son looked at his father, and his heart ached with pity.

'All right, I will take you in,' answered the son. 'But I cannot respect you. The only thing I respect in you is your old age and your loneliness.'

I asked Grandma

Pavlyk is a lively and mischievous grade four student. His grandfather died fighting on the frontline. At home, his grandmother keeps his grandfather's medals and awards in an old chest.

Not long ago, a portrait of Pavlyk's grandfather was painted and hung on the classroom wall next to Pavlyk's desk. Pavlyk's eyes shone with pride when he saw his grandfather, as if still alive, his chest covered in medals.

But his joy soon turned to bitterness, as people began to use the painting to reproach him. If he did not complete an assignment, his teacher would say, 'You should be ashamed of yourself. Your grandfather was a hero, and you are sitting next to his portrait.'

One day Pavlyk brought a piece of old mirror to school and began to reflect sunbeams onto his desk. Olenka, who sat next to him, whispered, 'How can you behave like that during a lesson? Do you think your grandfather would have played with sunbeams?'

Pavlyk felt bitter and depressed.

One Saturday, the teacher said, 'We are going for a walk in the forest today. Run home with your books and quickly bring some food to eat.'

Pavlyk went over to the open window, jumped out, and was about to run home when he saw his teacher walking towards him. How she had managed to get there so quickly he could not imagine.

She reproached him, saying, 'Is that how students are supposed to behave? Ask your grandmother if your grandfather ever jumped out the window.'

The next day, Pavlyk raised his hand and said, 'I asked Grandma.'

'What about?' asked the teacher, who had forgotten what she had said.

'I asked if Grandpa ever jumped out the window.'

'And what did your grandmother say?' asked the teacher.

'Once, when Grandpa had to stay back after school, he climbed out through the chimney.'

A summer storm

One Sunday, a family went for a walk in the forest: the father, the mother, grade five student Tolia and four-year-old Sashko. They really enjoyed being surrounded by the beauty of the forest. The parents showed their children a clearing where lilies of the valley were growing. Next to the clearing a dog rose bush was growing. It had just produced its first flower—pink and sweet-scented. The whole family sat in the shade of the dog rose bush. The father read from an interesting book.

Suddenly they heard a clap of thunder. A few heavy drops of rain fell, and then drenching rain poured down. The father gave his coat to the mother, and she was not afraid of the rain. The mother gave her coat to Tolia, and he was not afraid of the rain. Tolia gave his coat to Sashko, and he was not afraid of the rain. Sashko asked, 'Mum, why did you all do that? Why did Dad put his coat on you, then you put your coat on Tolia, and Tolia put his coat on me? Why didn't you all just put your own coats on?'

'Because we should always protect someone who is weaker,' answered his mother.

'And why aren't I protecting anyone?' asked Sashko. 'Does that mean that I am the weakest?'

'If you are not protecting anyone, you are the weakest,' answered his mother with a smile.

'But I don't want to be the weakest!' said Sashko with determination.

And he walked over to the dog rose bush, stretched out his coat, and protected its pink flower. The rain had already torn off two petals, and the flower was drooping, weak and defenceless.

'I'm not the weakest now, am I, Mum?' asked Sashko.

'No, now you are strong and brave,' answered his mother.

The persistent ant

A little black ant was hurrying home. She was carrying a poppy seed for her babies. Suddenly she spotted a big pumpkin seed right in front of her, and it was sweet and smelt so good! The ant put the tiny poppy seed aside and tried to pick up the pumpkin seed. She managed to heave it on to her back, but it slipped off and fell back to the ground. Again, the ant tried to lift the seed onto her back, but again it slipped off. Again and again, she tried to lift the seed onto her back, but again and again it fell to the ground.

Then the ant noticed that somebody was quietly laughing nearby. She turned around and saw a dragonfly. 'You have lifted that seed a thousand times,' said the dragonfly. 'Why don't you just give up? It's hopeless. You can't succeed. Why don't you just leave the seed where it is?'

'You can't succeed if you count your failures,' replied the ant, and she made one more attempt to pick up the seed. This time, the seed did not fall off her back, and she happily carried it home.

What a persistent ant that was!

The lion and the sparrow

When the lion was young and brave, all the other animals were afraid of him. A fox would often come to his den. She would bow down to him and offer him a fried chicken.

Time passed, and the lion grew old. He lost his teeth and some of his fur. One day, blind and helpless as a kitten, the lion was lying near his den, when he noticed somebody approaching furtively. He recognized the fox. Memories of fried chicken made his mouth water.

'Good afternoon, dearest King of the Beasts,' the fox greeted him in a sweet voice. 'Everybody else has forgotten you, and I alone have thought of you. I have brought you a treat: some soft pickled cucumbers. They are delicious. I pickled them myself.'

The lion was so thin and hungry that he was glad even to see some pickles. He ate them up, but almost immediately felt so thirsty he could not bear it. He felt like running to the brook to drink some water, but he did not have enough strength to move. As he lay by his den, his tongue swollen with thirst, the lion bitterly recalled past times when all the other animals trembled in fear before him.

Meanwhile, a sparrow had been sitting in a tree nearby, and had observed the lions' torment. The sparrow settled on a branch above the lion and shook it. Cold drops of dew fell onto the lion's swollen tongue.

'Thank you, sparrow,' said the lion.

The sparrow continued hopping from branch to branch in this way, shaking them, so that refreshing dew drops fell onto the lion's tongue. When the lion had slaked his thirst, he asked the sparrow, 'Tell me, please, sparrow, why did you take pity on me? All the other animals hate me.'

The sparrow did not answer. He just chirped joyfully, because the sun was shining, and his little chicks were waiting for him in his nest.

The inquisitive woodpecker

In a mother woodpecker's nest there were four chicks. One of them could not keep still. He kept looking out of the nest and wanted to know about everything.

'What is there outside our nest?' he asked.

'When you grow up and learn to fly, you will see what is outside the nest,' replied his mother.

But the restless baby woodpecker did not follow his mother's advice. He kept stretching his neck out of the nest until he fell onto the ground. He sat in the grass and cried. The mother flew to her chick. 'How am I going to rescue you, you disobedient son?' she said. 'Sit on my back, take my feathers in your beak, and hold on tight.'

The baby woodpecker sat on his mother's back and gripped her feathers with his beak. His mother flew back to the nest, carrying her son, and asked, 'Now, will you stop stretching out of the nest?'

'Yes, Mum,' said the baby woodpecker, crying. But almost immediately he raised his little head and stretched his neck to look out of the nest.

One drop at a time

Mykyta, a student in grade four, was very lazy. He did not want to work hard, so he failed grammar and was given extra homework to do over the summer holidays. With a heavy sigh, he put his grammar textbooks on his desk. He needed to complete two hundred exercises, and, to him, it seemed an impossible task.

A day passed, then a second and a third, and before he knew it a week had passed, and all he had done was look at the textbooks each day with a heavy sigh. His idleness made him tired. One day, he sat looking out the window, and noticed how water was dripping from a downpipe into an empty bucket. Instead of working, Mykyta spent the whole day watching the water drip into the bucket. In the evening, he stepped outside and was surprised to see the bucket was half-full. By the morning, the bucket was full.

Mykyta was amazed: so, you could fill a whole bucket one drop at a time!

With a heavy sigh, Mykyta opened his textbook and turned a fresh page in his exercise book.

Pavlo and the sun

One day a teacher came into a class and said, 'Children, there are a hundred tonnes of wheat lying in the yard at the collective farm, and we are expecting rain. The wheat needs to be moved into the grain storage area. Let's all go together and help the collective farm workers.

After school the children happily went to help the farm workers. Pavlo was the only student not to come and help. Everyone else worked, but he stayed at home. The next day the other children asked Pavlo, 'Why didn't you come and help yesterday?'

Pavlo answered, 'My mum is sick … I had to help my mum.'

The children believed their friend. Of course, he had to help his mother.

But then, during the lunch break, Pavlo's mother came to school. The teacher was standing in the yard, and the students were playing nearby. Pavlo was playing ball with them. Pavlo's mother went over to the teacher and said, 'I wonder if you can help me. My son does not want to do any work at home. He won't fetch water or sweep the floor.'

When they heard these words, the children surrounded Pavlo and looked at him in surprise. Pavlo lowered his head … It became very quiet in the school yard.

The sun hid behind a cloud …

'Even the sun is ashamed,' said Katia.

The rubbish heap

At the end of the school yard, by the fence, there was a rubbish heap. At first it was only a small rubbish heap, and then it grew into a bigger rubbish heap, and finally it grew into a giant rubbish heap.

Then it did not get any bigger, but it was already huge. People threw wastepaper there, and dry leaves they had raked up.

Everyone saw the rubbish heap, but no-one paid any attention to it. Everyone thought that you had to throw rubbish somewhere, and since there was rubbish, you probably needed a heap for it.

Then, one day in spring, a group of chattering children ran out of their classroom, dug a hole, planted a rose bush, and watered it. Every day they came to the rose bush to water it and were overjoyed to see that it developed buds and little green leaves. At last, one warm spring day, a big red flower opened up on the rose bush. It was so beautiful that all the students and teachers came to admire it. While they were admiring how beautiful the rose was, they suddenly noticed the rubbish heap. Everyone felt ashamed. How could they have a rubbish heap here?

Everyone thought, 'This is my fault. If I had paid attention to the rubbish heap earlier, it would have been removed long ago.'

They brought a big cart. The students and teachers shovelled all the rubbish into the cart and took it far away to a distant ravine.

Grandpa's watermelons

During the summer, Fedko and Myshko spent a whole month with their grandfather Ostap at the watermelon plantation. That summer was full of joy and happiness: the boys ate many delicious watermelons and rock-melons and saw many picturesque sunrises!

Grandpa Ostap selected the best watermelon seeds and put them in a little bag made of fabric. He asked the boys to put aside the largest seeds for the next spring planting, but Fedko and Myshko were lazy and did not bother.

In winter, Grandpa Ostap became very ill. He summoned his grandsons and told them, 'Take this little bag of seeds and plant them on the watermelon plantation!'

Grandpa Ostap passed away. The boys planted his watermelon seeds in a separate section of the plantation. Huge watermelons grew there.

Every morning Fedko and Myshko would come to the plantation and stand there in awkward silence. As they gazed over the plantation and the enormous watermelons, they felt that in some way they had let Grandpa Ostap down.

The apple at the top of the tree

Every week, grade one student Myshko visits Grandpa Ivan. His grandfather lives on the edge of the village and does not work anymore.

Today is Sunday, and the grandson is visiting his grandfather.

'Let's go into the garden,' says Grandpa. 'The apples are ripe.'

In Grandpa's garden there is a big apple tree. On it are tasty, red apples. Myshko walks up to the apple tree and sees many juicy, sweet-smelling apples on the ground under the tree.

'When they fall, that means they're ripe,' says Grandpa.

As soon as Grandpa says these words, a big, red apple falls at Myshko's feet.

'Take which ever one is looking at you,' invites his grandfather.

But Myshko does not want to take an apple from the ground. He lifts his head, and his grandfather sees excitement in his eyes. The boy dearly wants to climb that tree. He has taken a fancy to an apple that stands out at the top of the tree.

Myshko stands, admiring the apple, but he feels uncomfortable asking his grandfather for permission to climb the tree.

'That apple at the top of the tree,' he says, 'Do you think it will fall down soon?'

His grandfather answers, smiling, 'No, I think it will be quite a while … You climb up, Myshko, and pick it for yourself.'

Joyfully, the boy climbs the tree.

Why does Stepan's mother praise Mykola?

A mother had a son named Stepan. He graduated from school and became a tractor driver. His mother thought Stepan would help her in her old age, but his work in the tractor brigade was not up to scratch. He did not want to get up early and he arrived late for work. People said that Stepan was a lazybones.

Another mother lived next door with a son named Mykola. He was also a tractor driver, and everyone was full of praise for him. He was hard working and conscientious.

As soon as Stepan came home from work each day, his mother would give him his dinner and say, 'That Mykola is a hard worker … He gets up before sunrise and hurries to the field.'

Stepan would sit by the table with his head bowed.

The next day his mother would say, 'Everyone is saying what a good job Mykola is doing. They say he ploughs the ground and sows seed better than anyone.'

Stepan would just sit there silently with his head bowed.

Every day Stepan's mother would say something good about Mykola.

Why does Stepan's mother praise Mykola?

A legend about a mother's love

A mother had an only son. He married a young woman of unearthly beauty, but her heart was black and evil.

The son brought his young wife home. The daughter-in-law took a dislike to her mother-in-law and told her husband, 'I don't want your mother to come into our home. She can live in the porch.'

The son moved his mother into the porch and forbad her to come into the house … but even that was not enough to satisfy his wife. She told her husband, 'I don't want to see her face around our home.'

The son moved his mother into the barn. She only came out to get a breath of fresh air at night. One evening the young beauty was resting under a flowering apple tree when she saw the mother come out of the barn.

The wife flew into a rage and ran to her husband. 'If you want me to live with you, kill your mother, rip out her heart, and bring it to me.' The son's heart did not waver. He was bewitched by his wife's unearthly beauty. He said to his mother, 'Let's go and bathe in the river.' As they were walking along the stony path to the river, his mother tripped on a rock. Her son was angry. 'Watch where you're going, or it will take us till evening to reach the river.'

They came to the river, undressed, and bathed. The son killed his mother, tore her heart from her chest, lay it on a maple leaf, and set off for home with it. The mother's heart was still beating.

The son tripped on a rock and fell and hurt himself. His mother's heart fell on a sharp rock and started bleeding, but still it beat and whispered, 'Have you hurt your knee, my dear? Sit down and rest and rub the part that hurts.'

The son burst into tears, took his mother's heart in his hands, pressed it to his chest, and returned to the river. He placed the heart back in his mother's wounded chest and watered it with his bitter tears. He understood that nobody had ever loved him, or would ever love him, as devotedly and selflessly as his own mother.

So powerful was the mother's love, and so deep and overwhelming her desire to see her son happy, that her heart sprang to life, the wounded chest healed, and the mother rose and hugged her son's head to her chest. After that the son could not return to his wife. He now found her repulsive. The mother did not return home either. They walked together into the steppe and became two burial mounds. Every morning the tops of those two mounds are the first things to be lit up by the rising sun.

The tale of a mother goose

One hot summer day, a mother goose took her little yellow goslings for a walk. She showed her children the wide world. The world was green and full of joy—a huge meadow stretching as far as the goslings could see. The mother goose taught her children how to nibble the tender blades of grass. The stalks were sweet, the sun was warm and comforting, the grass was soft, and the green world sang with the many voices of beetles, butterflies and moths. The goslings were happy.

Suddenly dark clouds covered the sky and the first drops of rain fell on the ground. Then hailstones, as large as sparrows' eggs, began to fall. The goslings ran to their mother, who lifted her wings and covered her children with them. Under her wings it was warm and cosy. As if from a distance, the goslings could hear the claps of thunder, the howling of the wind and the hammering hailstones. They even enjoyed it: beyond their mother's wings something terrible was happening, but they were warm and comfortable.

Then everything fell quiet. The goslings wanted to return to the meadow as soon as possible, but their mother did not lift her wings. The goslings cheeped insistently, 'Let us out, Mum!'

Their mother quietly lifted her wings, and the goslings ran out onto the grass. They saw that their mother's wings were injured, and that she had lost many feathers. She was breathing heavily. But the world around was so full of joy, the sun shone so brightly and gently, the beetles, bees and bumblebees sang so beautifully, that for some reason the goslings did not think to ask, 'Mum, what's the matter?' And when one of them, the smallest and weakest gosling, waddled up to his mother and asked, 'Why are your wings hurt?', she quietly answered, 'It's alright, my son.'

The yellow goslings ran hither and thither through the grass, and their mother was happy.

The apple of his mother's eye

A mother had an only son. He was the apple of her eye, her beloved son. She let him sit at the table, while she sat by the door and ate the leftovers from her son's meal.

One day, the mother cooked some fish in cream sauce. The son loved the meal so much that he demanded it every day. 'I want some fish,' he insisted. 'If there is no fish, I won't eat anything.'

How could the mother go against the will of her beloved son? Every day she went to the pond, cast a fishing net, and caught some fish. Then one day in late autumn, the mother entered the icy water, caught cold, and fell ill.

The mother lay in bed. She could not get up even to have a drink of water, but her son just sat at the table, sulking and silent. There was not even a boiled potato on the table, let alone fish.

The mother moaned, not because of her illness, but because of the grief she felt as a mother—she had raised a son who was tall and strong, but heartless. The mother asked, 'My son, what is the most precious thing in your life?'

The son was silent. He was silent because he had nothing to say: there was nothing precious in his life.

The mother's heart could bear it no longer. She died from grief and disappointment.

The grey hair

Little Mykhailyk saw three grey hairs in his mother's plait.

'Mum, you've got three grey hairs in your plait,' said Mykhailyk.

His mother smiled but did not say anything.

A few days later Mykhailyk saw there were four grey hairs in his mother's plait.

'Mum,' said Mykhailyk in surprise, 'Now you've got four grey hairs in your plait. Before there were only three … Why have you got one more grey hair?'

'From pain,' answered his mother. 'When my heart aches I get a grey hair.'

'But why did your heart ache?' asked Mykhailyk.

'Do you remember when you climbed that really tall tree?' asked his mother. 'I looked out the window and saw you on a thin little branch. My heart ached, and I got a grey hair.'

Mykhailyk sat for a long time, silent and thoughtful. Then he went up to his mother, hugged her, and asked, 'Mum, if I sit on a thick branch, will that stop your hair going grey?'

Why a mother ran from the field

A mother was preparing to work in the fields. Her two little children were staying at home.[24] The mother told the older one, 'Katia, look after little Tania. Make sure she doesn't go out on the road—there are cars there. And make sure she doesn't go to the well.'

The mother worked in a field for half a day, but her soul was restless. She suddenly remembered that when she was leaving for work, she left a needle on the table. 'What will happen if Tania sees the needle?' she thought. 'She has a habit of putting everything she lays her hands on in her mouth.'

The mother left her work and ran home.

People were surprised to see the woman running and asked, 'Why are you running? Is the village on fire?'

'Even worse,' the woman answered.

She arrived home. Tania was playing on the floor with her dolls, and there was a little needle on the table.

No one else would have noticed that needle. The mother would not have noticed it either, if not for her mother's heart.

The seventh daughter

A mother had seven daughters. One day she went to visit her son, who lived far, far away. She returned home a month later. When she entered the hut, her daughters began in turn to tell her how much they had missed her.

‘I longed for you, as a poppy flower longs for the sunlight,’ said the first daughter.

‘I looked forward to seeing you, as the parched earth looks forward to the rain,’ murmured the second daughter.

‘I cried for you, as a baby bird cries for the mother bird,’ cooed the third daughter.

‘It was hard for me without you. I felt like a bee without a flower,’ said the fourth daughter, caressing her mother and gazing into her eyes.

‘I saw you in my dreams, as a rose dreams of the morning dew,’ twittered the fifth daughter.

‘I watched for you, as a cherry orchard watches for a nightingale,’ whispered the sixth daughter.

The seventh daughter did not say anything, though she had much to say. She took off her mother’s shoes and brought some water in a tub to wash her feet.

If I had a magic carpet …

Far, far away, on the other side of the sea, in the mountains, grows a wonderful flower. It blooms in early spring and flowers all through the summer until late autumn. This flower has a wonderful property: it cleanses the air. Whoever breathes the air near this flower never falls ill.

If I had a magic carpet, I would fly across the sea, land in the mountains, and find that wonderful flower. I would collect its seeds and bring them home.

I would give every person one seed, so they could all grow that wonderful flower, so that there would not be a single sick person. So that people could live till they were very old without getting ill.

My grandmother is often ill. I would take her to that wonderful flower. She would breathe its healing air and get better for ever.

My mum smells of bread

One day two new boys came to the kindergarten—Tolia and Mykolka. Their mothers brought them.

The boys got to know each other.

Tolia asked Mykolka, ‘Where does your mum work?’

'Can't you guess?' asked Mykolka. 'She smells of medicines. My mum is a doctor. If someone gets sick, Mum helps them get better. People can't live without doctors. Where does your mum work?'

'Haven't you worked it out?' said Tolia. 'She smells of bread. My mum is a baker. She feeds people. No-one can live without bread.'

'Not even a doctor?' asked Mykolka in surprise.

'Not even a doctor', said Tolia with pride.

My mother's eyes

I close my eyes and see my mother's eyes. Wherever I am, whatever I think of, I see them everywhere. In her eyes I see kindness, affection, and love.

I am happy when my mother has joyful, kind, smiling eyes. When I come home from school, Mum looks me in the eye to see how I am, and she sees everything: how I am feeling, whether everything is all right.

But sometimes in my mother's eyes I see sadness, anxiety, confusion. Sometimes I see reproach, hurt feelings ... I would surrender all my happiness, just to see peace in my mother's eyes, so that she would not feel sadness and would not suffer.

My mother's eyes were the first thing I became aware of in the world. They were the first ray of happiness and the first ray of thought. Our homeland begins with a mother's eyes.

Who is going to make our bread?

Five-year-old Andriiko's father works as a tractor driver. Every day he goes to work very early. He has to be in the field before sunrise.

When Andriiko wakes up, his father has already left the house. He asks his mother, 'Mum, where's Dad?'

'He's gone to work,' she says.

'What work does he do?' asks Andriiko.

'Dad works in the field so we can have bread,' says his mother.

Every day, Andriiko's mother goes to the shop and brings home a big loaf of white bread. She also buys two small bread rolls.

'Is that the bread that Dad makes?' asks Andriiko.

'Yes, that's the bread that Dad makes,' answers his mother.

One day Andriiko wakes up and sees his dad lying in bed.

'Shush … ' whispers his mother. 'Dad is sick.'

Andriiko washes, gets dressed, and sits by the window, sad and thoughtful.

'Mum,' says Andriiko, 'Who's going to make our bread now?'

She forgot

Olenka has only her mother: no father, no grandmother, no brother or sister.

Her mother's birthday is on the first of May. How could she possibly forget that day?[25]

Long before her mother's birthday, Olenka would prepare a present for her. She would draw something nice in a little exercise book—a flower, a bird or an ear of wheat—and she would write, 'Happy Birthday, Mum!'

But this year things went terribly wrong.

Olenka's teacher asked her to learn a poem by heart and recite it at the May Day celebration.

Olenka was so focused on the poem that she did not notice her mother's birthday creeping up.

She suddenly remembered it on the evening before her mother's birthday and blushed with shame. She looked over at her mother. Her mother was sitting at the table, quiet and thoughtful, looking out the window.

Olenka took her drawing album and coloured pencils and went to school. There was no-one there, just the caretaker sitting in the corridor.

Olenka sat at her desk and began to draw. She spent a long time drawing a blue sky above a wide field. In the sky a lark was singing, and the sun was shining.

The girl finished her drawing and went home. Her mother was still sitting at the table.

Olenka showed her mother her album with the drawing, and said, 'Happy Birthday, Mum!'

And she kissed her mother.

Her mother smiled with joy.

Dad came home

In one happy family, two little girls, Zina and Zoia, lived and grew. They were both two years old. Every day they would wait impatiently for their father to come home from work. They would run to meet him at the gate, and their father would lift them into his arms, holding Zina in his right arm and Zoia in his left. That was how he entered the house, with his daughters in his arms, and their happy mother welcomed them as they came in.

But then a great misfortune visited our land: fascist troops invaded. The girls' father went to the frontline.

For three years he fought the invaders. Letters often arrived, in which he asked their mother to kiss Zina and Zoia, and their mother cried as she kissed them. 'Mum, don't cry,' the little girls said. 'Dad will come home.'

Then there were no letters for several months. Suddenly, a letter came from their father's friend on the frontline. He wrote to Zina, Zoia, and their mother, that their father and husband had been wounded, and would soon be coming home.

One sunny morning in early spring, Zina and Zoia were playing in the garden. They were now five years old. They were standing next to a melting snowman and wondering how they could get it to survive for just one more day. Their mother was standing by the house.

'Dad is coming!' she shouted.

Zina and Zoia saw a tall, well-built soldier approaching, with a bag over his shoulder. Joyfully screaming 'Dad!', the girls ran to meet him. They stretched out their arms, expecting that he would lift them into his arms as he always did, Zina in his right arm, and Zoia in his left.

But their father was silent and did not lift them up. The children wanted to take his hands in their little hands, so that he would lift them up, but they suddenly saw that he did not have any arms. The sleeves of his great coat were hanging limp.

The girls lifted their heads and looked fearfully into their father's eyes.

He bent over them, and tears fell from his eyes onto the white snow. Zina and Zoia hugged their father, resting their cheeks on his empty sleeves, and wept.

'Don't worry Dad, you don't need to lift us in your arms. We're not little anymore,' whispered Zina.

'We're five already,' added Zoia.

Mum, put that letter in the drawer

This happened in the spring of 1945[26] in a large village near the Dnipro River. All the local men were still on the frontline, but by then they were fighting in Europe, far away from Ukraine.

Every day, the postman, Grandpa Yukhym, would deliver several blue envelopes to women in the village. As soon as the envelopes were opened, the air was filled with moaning and wailing, because those blue envelopes were notices about the death of their loved ones: husbands and fathers. Everyone—adults and children—knew what those blue envelopes meant.

One mother had four little children. Early in the morning, when the children had eaten breakfast and she was getting ready for work, Grandpa Yukhym came. He took a blue envelope from his bag and handed it to the mother. Her heart sank with grief. The children stared at the envelope, eyes wide with fear.

The oldest daughter, Mariia, approached her mother, took the envelope from her hands, held it tightly to her chest, and stiffened like an adult.

'Mum, please, don't open that letter!' she pleaded. 'Put it in the drawer, right down the bottom!'

The other three children also started crying. They hugged their mother and begged through their tears, 'Please, put the blue letter in the drawer!'

Grandma's hands

Grandma knits stockings. Her old, overworked hands move rapidly. Now the right and left hands come together, one helping the other. Now they have stopped and seem to be consulting each other. They consult each other, and then get back to work. They begin to knit even more quickly. And in the evening, the fingers of one hand squeeze the fingers of the other hand. They are thanking each other for their cheerful work.

But then Grandma falls ill. She lies in bed, overcome by her ailment. Mum says, 'It is the years that have laid her low.'

Grandma's hands are motionless. They lie next to each other on her chest. Her fingers move slightly, as if her hands want to be with each other. But the years do not allow it. The right hand creeps over to the left, and her fingers grip each other, and are still. Her hands are complaining of the pain.

Gradually Grandma gets better. Her hands come to life. She still does not get out of bed, but her hands cannot live without each other, and they knit some stockings. But why do they consult each other more and more often? Can they really have forgotten how to knit?

A hurtful word

A son once lost his temper and, in his anger, he spoke some rude, hurtful words to his mother. His mother burst into tears. The son realised he was in the wrong and felt sorry for his mother. His conscience gave him no peace, and he could not sleep at night. He had insulted his mother.

The years passed. The schoolboy son became a grown adult. The time came for him to travel to a distant region. The son bowed down to his mother and said, 'Forgive me, mother for the hurtful words I said.'

'I forgive you,' said his mother, and sighed.

'Please forget, mother, that I ever said those words.'

The mother became thoughtful and sad, and tears appeared in her eyes. She said to her son, 'I want to forget it, my son, but I cannot. The wound from a splinter heals, and not trace of it remains. The wound from a hurtful word also heals, but the mark it leaves is deep.'

The wooden stork

In a village lived a family: a husband and wife and their little son Serhiiko. Serhiiko's grandfather also lived with them, but not in the house. He lived in a tiny room allocated to him by his son, Serhiiko's father.

Serhiiko's birthday was approaching. He was turning five. The young parents decided to celebrate the birthday of their only son. They invited many guests to the party—the chairman of the village council and other leaders, as well as some neighbours.

The only person they forgot to invite was Serhiiko's grandfather. For many days he had been making a present for Serhiiko—a stork that he had carved from wood.

In the evening, when all the guests arrived with presents, celebrations began under the apple trees. But Serhiiko's grandfather was left sitting in his tiny room. The wooden stork stood on a little table in front of him. The bird raised its head and looked out the window, as if listening to the music that carried from the garden.

The green saucepan

Every evening, Tolia crawls onto his grandma's bed, and she tells him stories. When his eyes grow heavy with sleep, she carries her grandson in her arms and puts him to bed. These are the happiest moments in the boy's life.

Grandma is often sad. Tolia asks her, 'Why are your eyes sad, Grandma?' But she does not tell him.

One day, Tolia wakes up very early and sees his grandmother washing a green saucepan and crying. The boy knows that his mother only uses the green saucepan to cook soup for his grandmother.

When it is time to have dinner, Tolia's mother pours some soup for grandma from the green saucepan and puts her bowl on a little table near the door. That is where Grandma eats.

Tolia feels very sorry for his grandma, and says, 'Mum, I want some soup from the green saucepan.'

His mother looks at Tolia in amazement and whispers angrily, 'Don't be smart!'

Tolia starts crying. 'No, Mum, I'm not being smart. I just want to eat with Grandma.'

He leaves the dining table, sits down at Grandma's table, and begins to eat soup from her bowl. The room falls deathly silent.

The father and mother put spoons on the dining table.

Tolia's grandmother cries.

My mother

Perhaps I dreamt this, or perhaps it happened during my early childhood. I was sleeping, and I dreamt of a sunlit meadow and many,

many butterflies … I felt my mother's warm, tender hands touching me. I recognised them as my mother's hands. The warmth and tenderness of a mother's hands is unique. Mum picked me up, held me close, and carried me somewhere, and it was as if I was floating. And I felt so much joy and pleasure … I wanted that moment to last forever.

I suppose our sense of our homeland begins with the tender touch of a mother's hands.

Missing a father's words

Sashko and Oleksii went skating till late at night and did not do their algebra homework. The mathematics teacher, Ivan Petrovych, wrote the same comment in both of the grade six boys' homework diaries: 'You should only play when your work is done. Someone who plays without first doing their work is an idler.'[27]

On the way home, Oleksii called in to Sashko's house to collect a book. Sashko's father had just come home. He said to Sashko, 'Show me your diary. Let me see how you are going with your work.'

Sashko handed over his diary. His father read the comment and began to tell his son some home truths. He told Sashko, 'School is your workplace. When you go to school, you are going to work. You have no right to study any old how, let alone badly.'

Sashko listened to his father with his head bowed.

When the father had finished speaking with his son, Oleksii took the book, and went home.

Oleksii did not have a father.

He took his diary out of his schoolbag and put it on the table.

His mother pushed the diary aside and put dinner on the table.

Oleksii leant on his elbows at the table and sat silently for a long time.

'Why aren't you eating?' asked his mother.

Oleksii could not answer. He felt ill at heart.

A mother's grey hairs

Every evening, seven-year-old Tarasyk greeted his father as he came home from work. Those were happy moments. His father opened the door, Tarasyk ran to meet him, and his father lifted him into his arms. His mother smiled as she prepared their dinner.

One day Tarasyk came home from school and saw his mother sitting by the window, thoughtful and sad.

'Why are you sad, Mum?' asked Tarasyk anxiously.

'Dad won't be coming home anymore,' said his mother quietly.

'What do you mean, he won't be coming home?' asked the boy in astonishment. 'Where will he go?'

The boy could not get his head around the idea of his father not coming home.

His mother said, 'He won't be living with us anymore … He … He came today and took his things. He's gone to live with another woman.'

'Why?' shouted Tarasyk. 'Why has he gone to live with another woman?'

His mother did not know what to say. She feverishly thought of something to say to her son. Then she said the first thing that came into her head: 'Because I have some grey hairs … and that woman doesn't have any grey hair.'

Tarasyk burst into tears, hugged his mother, lifted his little hand, and stroked her black hair, flecked with a few, shining grey hairs. Then he quietly said, 'But it's your hair, Mum … Your hair is the most beautiful hair in the world … Doesn't Dad understand that?'

'He doesn't understand, Tarasyk,' said his mother.

A gentle hand

Andriiko's grandfather died. For a week the boy did not come to school. When he did come to school, it was with a heavy heart. He could not forget for a minute that his grandfather would never again tell him a story and would never again caress him.

Andriiko sat silent and sad. Andrii Yukhymovych came into the classroom, put his diary and a pile of exercise books on his desk, and began to check the homework. When the teacher reached Andriiko, the boy quietly said, 'I haven't done my homework today.'

Andrii Yukhymovych put his hand on the boy's head—a gentle, tender, kind hand.

'But I will do it all tomorrow, Andrii Yukhymovych,' said Andriiko.

'That's fine,' said the teacher softly.

Why is the bread stale today?

Serhiiko is in grade one. His father is a baker. For ten years Serhiiko's father has been working in the village bakery. He gets up very early, before sunrise, and goes to work. At midday they bring fresh bread to the shop. They bring it to the school dining room as well.

Today Serhiiko's father is sick. For the first time in ten years, he does not go to work. Serhiiko's mother sits by his father's bed.

'Serhiiko, tell the students that the bread will be stale today,' whispers his father.

At midday the students go to the school dining room. On the table are pieces of stale bread. The children ask, 'Why is the bread stale today?'

Serhiiko says, 'My dad is sick. He is the baker … Today the bread will be stale, and maybe tomorrow as well.'

The children take the pieces of bread and try not to drop a single crumb on the floor.

Daddy's eyes

Little Olenka's daddy became very ill and was taken to the hospital. One day, Olenka woke up in the middle of the night and heard her mother crying. The little girl started crying as well: it was so hard without her daddy.

Olenka's mother visited the father at the hospital every day. One day, she came home very happy. In a week, the father would be released from the hospital.

The week passed, and Olenka's mother went to the hospital to bring the father home. Olenka stayed at home. She could not wait to see her daddy. At last, she heard her mother opening the door. A man with a black beard walked into the room. He seemed strange and familiar at the same time. Olenka's mother followed him in, smiling.

The man also smiled, picked up a towel, and covered his beard. Olenka clapped her hands, 'Daddy, it's you! I've missed you so much!'

She hugged and kissed him. The towel fell off, and Daddy once more became a man with a black beard.

'You're not afraid of the beard, are you, Olenka?' asked her mother.

'No, I'm not afraid of it. Daddy isn't the beard; he's the eyes!'

Why is Mum praising me?

A mother went to work and left her six-year-old daughter Liuda at home by herself.[28] Liuda was not old enough to go to school yet.[29] The mother told her to feed the chickens and water the flowers. The girl did what her mother told her, and then she thought, 'I'll make some borshch.[30] Mum will be very tired when she comes home from work. If I cook, she can have a rest.'

Liuda made some borshch and tried it. It did not taste very nice. She was worried that her mother would scold her for making borshch like that.

Liuda's mother came home. She was surprised that her little daughter had made the main course from scratch all by herself. She served herself some borshch, took a mouthful, and exclaimed, 'Oh, what delicious borshch you have made, Liuda!'

Liuda was embarrassed to hear such praise, because she had tried the borshch herself and knew that it was not very nice. 'Why is Mum praising me?' she wondered.

Grandma's felt boots

Vira was already studying in grade one. In winter, when it was bitterly cold, her feet would be freezing by the time she walked home from school. So, when she came home, Vira would take off her shoes and put on her grandmother's felt boots. They were large and warm, and her feet would warm up as quickly as if she was toasting them by their big brick oven.

Vira would wear Grandma's felt boots while she ate her dinner and told her grandma all about her day at school. In the evening, she would quickly undress, jump into her grandma's bed and snuggle up to her. Her grandma's blanket and pillow were as warm as her gentle hands. Then her grandma would lean over her and tell her the story about the grey wolf and the little straw bull.

Vira was afraid of the grey wolf, but she knew that all her fears would melt away if her grandma was with her.

In the morning, Vira would wake up in her own bed, but she would dive straight back into her grandma's warm felt boots.

But then, something terrible happened. Her dear old grandma became very ill and died. They took her to the cemetery and buried her.

But when Vira came home from school, her grandma's felt boots were still waiting for her. Now the little girl almost never took them off.

Then, one day, Vira came from school, and could not find the felt boots anywhere.

'Where are Grandma's felt boots?' she asked her mother.

'I took them to the farmers' market and sold them,' her mother replied. 'What use are they to us? I bought you some nice new warm shoes.'

Vira burst into tears. Her heart was pounding, and she felt empty inside.

'Why … Why have you sold them?' she asked her mother quietly. 'I could still feel the warmth of Grandma's feet when I wore them.'

The mother tried to console Vira, but in vain. The little girl was inconsolable.

The grandmother and the chrysanthemum

A little girl's grandmother fell ill. She fought the illness for a long time, but it was stronger, and, one gloomy autumn day, she passed away.

The little girl grieved for her grandmother. She could not imagine life without her, so, in the spring, she walked to her grandmother's grave and said, 'Dear Grandma, in your memory, I will plant a chrysanthemum on your grave.' While she was speaking, a lark started singing high in the blue sky, and a cuckoo started cooing in the oak grove.

'That must be Grandma telling me to go ahead and plant the chrysanthemum,' thought the little girl.

She brought a chrysanthemum bush and planted it in the shade of an oak tree. In autumn, its pink buds opened, and the chrysanthemum flowered.

On the first anniversary of her grandmother's death, the girl went to visit her grave again. Among the many pink flowers, a single large white chrysanthemum had opened up. The girl smiled, and then she saw a dove settle on the grave's cross and start cooing.

'That must be Grandma telling me that she wants me to have a soul as bright and pure as this beautiful white flower,' she thought.

My mum is the most beautiful

A mother owl had a baby owl. He was quite big, with grey wings. He had big eyes and a big mouth.

Owls only fly at night. They avoid bright sunlight. The mother owl taught her son, 'Don't leave our nest during the day. The sunlight will blind you, and you won't be able to find your way home.'

But the owl was disobedient. He crawled out of their nest, screwed up his eyes, and flew to the meadow. There he opened his eyes, looked at the sun, and was blinded. He sat in the grass and cried. A heron approached him.

'Who are you?' asked the heron.

'I'm a baby owl,' answered the bird. 'My mum is an owl. I can't see anything. Could you take me to my mum?'

'What does your mother look like?' asked the heron.

'My mum is the most beautiful in the world,' answered the baby owl. 'She has the kindest, gentlest, most tender eyes. No-one else has eyes like that. Only my mother.'

'Ha! Ha! Ha!' laughed a nightingale, a woodpecker and a thrush. 'But you are really ugly. Your mother must be just as ugly as you.'

'That's not true!' cried the baby owl. 'My mother is the most beautiful in the world.'

The owl heard her baby's cry, flew down quietly, took him in her claws, and carried him to their nest.

The baby owl looked carefully at his mother. She really was the most beautiful bird in the world.

A letter to her father

Three-year-old Zina's father fell ill. He was taken to hospital. The little girl was sad.

There was a bitter January frost. Zina's mother was getting ready to go to the hospital to see Zina's father. Zina also wanted to see her father, but her mother would not let her. It was too cold.

'You can write a letter to Dad,' said her mother, 'And I will give it to him.'

Zina could not write, but she could draw, so she drew her father a letter.

She drew herself in bed with eyes wide open. That meant, 'Dad, I can't sleep at night, because I keep thinking about you.'

Then she drew a picture of herself and her father in the forest. There were trees all around, and they were picking flowers. That meant, 'Dad, come home soon, so we can go together to the forest and pick flowers.

Then she wanted to write, 'Dad, I love you very, very much.' Zina thought about how to draw that for a long time. Then she drew the sun. That meant, 'I love you very, very much.'

Grandpa's spoon

Every day before dinner, Natalochka used to take the spoons from the buffet and put them on the table—Mum's, Dad's, Grandpa's and her own.

In winter, Natalochka's grandpa died. The girl wept and grieved. She loved her grandpa very much.

From then on, at dinner time, Grandpa's spoon stayed in the buffet. Each time Natalochka laid the table, she reached for it, took it in her hand and then put it back on the shelf.

The years passed. Natalochka grew up, became a young woman, and completed high school. On the day that Natalia[31] graduated from school, she put Grandpa's spoon on the table.

Grandpa's spoon sat next to Natalia's plate. Her mother and father were silent. Natalia was silent too. The silence was solemn and beautiful.

Who takes who home?

At the kindergarten, there were two five-year-old boys—Vasylko and Tolia. Their mothers worked at the animal breeding farm. At six o'clock in the evening, the women would come to the kindergarten for their children.

Vasylko's mother would put his coat on, take him by the hand, and lead him, saying, 'Let's go home, Vasylko.'

But Tolia would put his own coat on, take his mother by the hand, and lead her, saying, 'Let's go home, Mum.'

The road would be covered in snow, through which there was just a narrow path.

Vasylko's mother would walk in the snow, while her son would take the path. After all, she was taking him home.

Tolia would walk in the snow, while his mother would take the path. After all, he was taking her home.

Twelve years passed. Vasylko and Tolia were now both strong, well-built, handsome young men.

During the winter, when the roads were covered with thick snow drifts, Vasylko's mother fell seriously ill.

On the same day, Tolia's mother also fell ill.

The doctor lived in a neighbouring village, five kilometres away.

Vasylko went out on to the street, looked at the snow, and said, 'How can anyone walk through snow like that?' He stood there for a while and went back inside.

But Tolia trudged through the deep snow to the neighbouring village and came back with the doctor.

On Grandma's bed

Little Svitlanka's very best friend was her grandmother. Nobody knew how to understand and feel sorry for the little girl like her grandmother.

Mum and Dad loved Svitlanka, but sometimes they did not let her have things that she really wanted. Sometimes Svitlanka would do something wrong, and her mum would not get angry, but she would get sad. It was painful for the little girl to see how she had made her mother sad, and then she would go and get into bed with Grandma. She would snuggle up to Grandma's cheek, and Grandma would stroke her head, and her heart would feel so warm and calm that she wanted to go up to her mother and say, 'Mum, I will never do it again.'

But now, Svitlanka did not have a grandmother. Her grandmother had died. Only Grandma's bed remained, with its dark blue blanket and snow-white pillow. Svetlanka's mother said, 'Let's keep Grandma's bed forever.' From time to time, she hung Grandma's bedding out in the sun and washed and ironed her sheets and pillowslips.

One day Svitlanka went into the garden and picked some green apples and ate them. Mum saw her, and did not say anything, but shook her head and became sad. For a whole day she was sad and silent. And Svitlanka thought, 'It would be better if you got angry with me, Mum, instead of getting sad.' She wanted someone to feel sorry for her. She lay on Grandma's bed and snuggled her face up to the pillow. And it seemed to her that the pillow was still warm and had kept the warmth of Grandma's cheek.

Svitlanka felt more at ease. 'Mum,' she thought, 'I will never do anything to make you feel sad again.'

A cardigan for Nastusia

Grandma Olena was knitting her granddaughter a cardigan. Nastusia was two years old, so the cardigan had to be small.

The back was already complete, as were the sleeves, and on the front, there was a golden autumn-coloured maple leaf.

Grandma was old and could not knit quickly. She often became tired and had to rest. Nastusia helped her grandmother, holding the ball of wool in her hands.

But one day Grandma fell ill. She did not get out of bed for several days. The ball of wool lay on the table, cold and motionless, and next to it lay the unfinished cardigan.

Grandma died. Nastusia did not understand what had happened to her, why she was lying there and not getting up. When the coffin was carried out of their house the little girl cried.

'Where have they taken Grandma?' she asked.

Her mother said, 'They have taken her to the hospital. When she gets better, she will come home.'

'What if she does not get better?' asked Nastya searchingly.

Her mother was silent. She took the unfinished cardigan and began to unravel it, winding the wool back on to the ball. The cardigan got smaller and smaller, and the ball got bigger and bigger.

'Why are you undoing the cardigan, Mum?' asked Nastusia. 'Grandma knitted it for me.'

'Never mind, Nastusia, we will buy you a cardigan,' said her mother.

'I don't want you to buy me a cardigan!' shouted Nastusia and she began to cry bitterly. 'I don't want a cardigan. Let's buy a grandma instead!'

The gentlest hands

A little girl went with her mother to a big city. They went to a market. The mother held her little daughter's hand. The little girl saw something interesting, clapped her hands with joy, and became lost in the crowd. She realised she was lost and burst into tears.

'Mum!' she cried. 'Where's my mum?'

People gathered around the girl and asked her, 'What's your name, dear?'

'Olia.'

'And what is your mother's name? Tell us, and we'll find her straight away.'

'Mum's name is … Mum … Mummy.'

The people smiled, calmed the girl, and again asked, 'Well, tell us, what your mother's eyes are like. Are they black, dark blue, light blue, grey?'

'Her eyes are … the kindest.'

'And her hair? Is your mum's hair dark or blonde?'

'Her hair … is the most beautiful.'

Again, the people smiled and asked, 'Well what are her hands like … Perhaps she has a birthmark on her hand … Try and remember.'

'Her hands are … the gentlest.'

So, they announced over the loudspeaker, 'A little girl is lost. Her mother has the kindest eyes, the most beautiful hair, and the gentlest hands in the world.'

And Mum came straight away.

I want to be like Dad

Three-year-old Sofiika is very much like her mother. Every feature is just like her mother's: dark blue eyes, black eyebrows, a blonde plait, a straight little nose, pink lips, long eyelashes. She even has a little black birthmark under her left ear, just like her mother. Sofiika even smiles like her mother, screwing up her eyes and lifting her eyebrows very high, as if surprised.

Everyone who comes to visit her father says, 'Your daughter is so much like her mother!'

Sofiika is surprised. Why is she not like her father? She asks her mother, who says, 'When you grow up a bit more, you will be like Dad as well.'

But Sofiika does not want to wait.

Each evening, when Sofiika's father returns from work, he washes, changes his clothes, and sits at the table. Sofiika and her mother wait for him, and they all have supper together.

Today, as usual, Sofiika's father comes home, and washes himself in the yard near the well. Sofiika goes over to the washbasin and begins to wash herself as well.

'Why are you washing, Sofiika?' asks her mother in surprise.

'I want to be like Dad,' she says.

What was Nina meant to do?

Nina's mother went to work in the fields very early, when seven-year-old Nina was still asleep. The mother needed to tell her daughter what work to do that day[32], but she did not want to wake her. So, she decided to show the little girl what to do from morning to evening. When Nina woke up, she understood perfectly.

Next to her bed she saw a pan of water and a rag. That meant, 'Wash the floors.' On a stool she saw a handful of grain and a stick. That meant, 'Feed the hens, and in the evening drive the brood-hen into the barn.' She saw a tomato stalk and a weed pulled out by the roots. That meant, 'Weed the tomatoes.' Nina really enjoyed her work that day.

Mum's watermelon

Kostyk is seven years old. During the summer, his mother leaves him at home by himself, while she goes to work all day. She says, 'Stay at home. Feed the chickens, and water the cabbages in the vegetable garden when the heat dies down.'

Today Kostyk had a day that was both happy and difficult. It was happy because in the morning, as soon as his mother had left for work, Grandpa Matvii came and brought two watermelons. Kostyk knew very well that the watermelons at the plantation had not yet ripened. He asked Grandpa Matvii many times where he had managed to get these two watermelons from, but the old man just smiled and would not say.

'This one is for you,' said Grandpa Matvii, pointing to the smaller of the two watermelons. 'And the other one is for your mother.'

Of course, it could not be any other way. Kostyk's mother was bigger than him, so she had to have the bigger watermelon.

'Shall I cut up your watermelon for you now, or will you cut it up yourself?' asked Grandpa Matvii.

'Now, Grandpa, now,' requested Kostyk impatiently.

The old man cut up the watermelon. It was red inside and smelt sweet.

Kostyk smacked his lips and ate slowly, trying to make his pleasure last as long as possible, while his grandfather sat silently and sometimes gave a little laugh. It was a strange sort of laugh that did not express happiness.

Kostyk's grandfather left, and Kostyk finished eating the watermelon. Then he gnawed on the discarded pieces of watermelon rind. He went out to play and then came back inside. He wanted to chew on the watermelon rind again, but there was nothing left to chew.

His mother's watermelon lay on the table. Kostyk tried not to look at it, but from time to time it was as if someone turned his head towards the watermelon. So as not to look at the watermelon, Kostyk went outside. He gave the chickens some barley and drew a bucket of water from the well. Some irresistible force still drew him to the house. He opened the door, sat by the table, and reached out to touch the watermelon.

'What if I ate half?' he wondered.

But at this thought Kostyk suddenly felt ashamed. He remembered his grandfather's disapproving laugh. He had been unhappy because Kostyk had not offered his grandfather any of the watermelon—not a single piece. Kostyk was so ashamed, he left the house. He went outside and sat under a mulberry tree. He sat there for a long time, watching white clouds float across the blue sky, until he fell asleep.

Kostyk woke up in the evening. The sun was setting on the horizon.

'Soon Mum will come home,' Kostyk thought.

As his mother approached the house, Kostyk went out to meet her, carrying her watermelon.

'This is for you, Mum,' Kostyk said joyfully.

His mother cut up the watermelon and invited him to have some. 'Eat up, Kostyk.'

'No, that is for you, Mum,' answered Kostyk. 'You eat it, Mum.'

Kostyk's mother had never known him to be so attentive. She looked with amazement at her son's joyful eyes and took a piece of the watermelon.

An apple in autumn

In late autumn, two little sisters named Olia and Nina were walking in the apple orchard. It was a quiet, sunny day. Nearly all the leaves had fallen from the apple trees, and they rustled underfoot. Only a few yellow leaves remained on the trees, scattered here and there.

The girls walked up to a big apple tree. Next to a yellow leaf they saw a big, red apple.

Olia and Nina squealed with joy.

'How did it last so long?' asked Olia in amazement.

'Let's pick it', said Nina.

The girls picked the apple. Olia wanted to keep it, but she restrained herself and said, 'You can have the apple, Nina'. Nina also wanted the apple, but she said, 'You can have the apple, Olia'.

The apple passed from one to the other, but then they suddenly had the same thought.

'Let's give the apple to Mum.'

They ran to their mother, joyful and excited, and gave her the apple.

Joy shone in the mother's eyes. She cut up the apple and gave the girls half each.

Sleep, Mummy, sleep

Serhiiko fell seriously ill. He tossed feverishly from side to side, and sometimes lost consciousness. Whenever he regained consciousness, he would see his mother's exhausted face. His mother would be telling him a story.

It is believed that when a severe illness begins to retreat in its battle with the vital forces of the human body and soul, the climax of the illness occurs. If the mysterious forces of the human organism defeat the illness, the climax passes, and the sick person will breathe a sigh of relief and fall into a deep and healthy sleep.

Serhiiko had just such a victory in his battle with the illness, and health triumphed. Still weak, and covered in perspiration, the boy fell asleep. Completely drained after several sleepless nights, his mother dozed off as well. She allowed herself to fall asleep when she saw that the little spark of life that barely glowed in her son's body was not in danger anymore.

The son woke up first. He saw his mother sitting on the sofa and sleeping. He got out of bed, crept over to his mother, gently placed a pillow under her head, tucked her legs up onto the sofa and covered her with a warm blanket. Then he crept back to his bed.

When his mother woke, the first thing she saw was her son's eyes, shining with joy. 'Sleep, Mummy, sleep,' he whispered to her gently.

'Am I dreaming, or is this real?' the mother thought. 'If it is a dream, then I would like to sleep a little longer.'

Afraid of waking fully, she held her breath and then asked quietly, 'What did you say? Please say it again.'

'Sleep, Mummy, sleep,' whispered Serhiiko.

Important news

On the north side of a pond was a small hut. An old woman lived there. On the opposite, southern side of the pond, there was a large and spacious house. The old lady's grandson Sashko lived there. He was already going to school.

In summer, Sashko rarely visited his grandmother, because the pond was wide and, to reach his grandmother's hut, he needed to walk around it, which was a long way. In winter, he visited his grandmother every day, because it was very easy to cross the pond when it was frozen and covered with ice.

The grandmother would sit by the window waiting for her grandson. He would come in the evening and tell her all about his adventures and discoveries.

Spring arrived. A warm south wind was blowing, and the sun was shining brightly. In the morning, the pond was still covered with ice, but by the afternoon its surface was covered with water.

Sashko's grandmother sat by the window and sadly thought to herself, 'Sashko won't come today.'

The grandmother spent the whole day waiting for her grandson. In the evening, she saw him running along the bank of the pond. She recognized him immediately and rushed to hug him. 'Grandma!' exclaimed Sashko joyfully, 'Look, the ice is gone! I came to tell you that the ice is all gone. Spring has arrived!'

Grandma is resting

Little Galynka came home from school. She opened the door happily and wanted to say something to her mother. But her mother shook her finger at her and whispered, 'Quiet, Galynka dear, Grandma is resting. She couldn't sleep all night because her heart was hurting.'

Galynka very quietly put her schoolbag on the table. She had some dinner and sat down to do her homework. She did not read her book aloud, because she didn't want to wake her grandmother.

The door opened and Galynka's friend Olia came in. She said loudly, 'Galynka, guess what … '

Little Galynka shook her finger at her, just like her mother, and whispered, 'Quiet, Olia, Grandma is resting. She couldn't sleep all night because her heart was hurting.'

The girls sat at the table together and looked at some pictures. Two tears trickled from Grandma's closed eyes. When Grandma got up, Galynka asked her, 'Grandma, why were you crying in your sleep?'

Grandma smiled and caressed little Galynka. Joy shone in her eyes.

I will always look after you!

Little Katrusia's mother was always busy. She had to wash and iron their clothes and prepare their dinner early so she would be in time for work.

Katrusia's mother rarely smiled. Katrusia was afraid to ask what was grieving her but could see that she was often sad.

Then one Sunday, when they had some free time, her mother said, 'Katrusia, let's go into the fields.'

'Do you have to work today?' asked Katrusia.

'No, let's just go and have a break,' her mother replied.

Katrusia could hardly believe her ears. Were they really going to the fields just to have a break?

Katrusia flew, as if on wings. She picked some wildflowers and gave them to her mother. She stopped when she heard the song of a lark, and her mother stopped as well.

Katrusia and her mother sat down on a narrow path in the middle of a field of wheat. The wide steppe stretched out before them.

Katrusia's mother began to softly sing:

In the field the wind is playing,
Yellow rye is softly swaying,
A Cossack loves a maiden dearly,
But dare not say so out aloud ...

Katrusia listened to the song with bated breath. When her mother fell silent and turned and smiled at her daughter, Katrusia said, 'Mum, I didn't know you could sing like that. You are so beautiful, Mum ... I will always look after you.'

And the little girl burst into tears.

'Why are you crying, dear?' asked her mother.

'Because I haven't looked after you,' said Katrusia.

The baby crow and the nightingale

A crow had just one chick, a baby crow. The mother crow loved her baby and fed it tasty worms.

But one day, the crow went looking for food and disappeared. The sun rose higher than the tree where the crows lived, and still the mother had not appeared. The baby crow began to cry. It cried so much that its tears poured in a stream onto the ground. Many birds living in the forest fell silent because they were sorry for the poor chick.

A nightingale heard the baby crow's cries. Its heart was moved with pity. The nightingale left its nest and flew to the baby crow's nest, settled beside it, and began to sing its wonderful song. Even the wind settled down and listened.

But the baby crow seemed not to hear the nightingale's song. It kept wailing and choking on its tears.

Then suddenly the baby crow heard its mother's voice in the distance: 'Caw! Caw!' The baby crow stopped crying instantly and said to the nightingale, 'Can you hear, that's my mother singing. Be quiet, please, and stop cheeping.'

'Caw! Caw-caw!' sounded out quite close, and the nightingale fell silent. It flew to a neighbouring tree and fell to thinking ... That night the forest did not hear the nightingale's song.

What is happiness?

My mother asked me, 'What is happiness?'

I answered, 'Happiness is when none of us kids are crying.'

But happiness is also when nobody locks little songbirds in a cage, because is it impossible to be happy in a cage. When my mum does not cry and is not sad—that is also happiness. Because when my mum is sad, I also have tears in my eyes.

Why was Mum crying?

Olesia in grade one had an older brother named Mykola. He was a tractor driver.

The time came for Mykola to serve in the army.

Seeing her son off, the mother burst into tears. Olesia understood why her mother was crying. Her brother would serve for two years. For two years her mother would not see him. That is why she was crying. Olesia started crying too …

Two years passed. The joyful news arrived—Mykola was returning from the army.

Olesia and her mother went to the station to meet her brother.

Mykola stepped out of the carriage and smiled. His mother ran to him, hugged him, and burst into tears.

Olesia was puzzled. Why was her mother crying now?

Why was Dad upset?

Pavlyk began a new exercise book because he had completely filled his old one. He decided, 'I will write so well that I get "excellent" on every assignment.' Pavlyk's father was a truck driver who travelled great distances. He would not be home for a long time. When he returned, he would say, 'Let me have a look at your exercise book, so I can see how you are studying.' And by that time the exercise book would be full of excellent marks.

That was what Pavlyk wanted, but that was not how it turned out. On the first page he wrote badly, and the teacher did not give him any mark. She just wrote, 'You need to improve.' Pavlyk was upset. 'Surely I can make myself work better,' he thought to himself. And he did try much harder and received 'excellent' for all his other work.

At last his exercise book was full, and his father was due home the following day. Pavlyk thought, 'I am ashamed to show Dad that first page. What could I do so I will not feel so ashamed?' And Pavlyk had the idea of rearranging the pages in his exercise book so that the worst page would appear at the very end. His father would probably not read all the way to the last page.

Pavlyk's father arrived home. He turned the pages of his son's exercise book, carefully examining his work. On every page he had full marks. Joy shone in the father's eyes. The closer he came to the end of the book, the louder Pavlyk's heart beat.

Then he reached the final page, and Pavlyk saw sorrow in his father's eyes. 'If this page had been at the beginning of the book, that would not have been so bad,' he said. 'But at the end … Why did you let yourself down my boy?'

Three apples

When Mariika turned seven, she planted an apple tree. Three years later the apple tree flowered, and three apples appeared.

Each day Mariika went into the garden to see how the apples were growing. With each day they grew bigger and juicier. Mariika could not wait for them to ripen. She had planted this apple tree for her mother and named it 'Mum's apple tree'. She dreamt of the day when the apples would ripen, and she would come into the garden, pick them, and take them to her mother.

At last, the day arrived. The apples became rosy and sweet-smelling. On a clear summer morning, Mariika went into the garden, picked the apples, put them on a plate, and took them into the house. Her face was flushed with emotion.

'Mum, please accept this present from me,' said Mariika quietly. 'They're from your apple tree.'

The mother gave her daughter a hug and kissed her. She took the plate with the three rosy apples and placed it on the windowsill.

A day passed, then a second and a third. Each day Mariika reminded her mother, 'Mum, you should eat your apples.'

But her mother just smiled and said, 'Let them sit there a little longer.'

A baby brother is born

Olenka's mother gave birth to a baby boy. Olenka was happy. 'Now I have a baby brother,' she thought.

Olenka woke up in the middle of the night and saw her mother leaning over her brother's cot and singing a lullaby to him. Suddenly Olenka felt jealous. She thought, 'Now Mum won't love me as much as she did before. Now she has to love Petryk as well.'

'Mum,' said Olenka the next morning, 'I love you so much … '

'Why are you saying that?' asked her mother, with concern.

'Because I want you to love me just as much as Petryk … '

Her mother sighed with relief and said, 'Go outside, Olenka, and ask the sun how it shares its warmth between all the people.'

Olenka went outside and asked, and the sun answered, 'Every person gets all my warmth. Every little bit of it.'

A boy and his sick mother

A little boy's mother fell ill. The boy was sad. He wondered what he could do to cheer his mother up. He sat on the end of her bed and said, 'Mum, if you like, I can draw the garden for you. It will make you feel better. You can pretend that you are going for a walk in our real garden.'

'All right, dear. Draw the garden for me,' said his mother.

The boy took a large sheet of paper and drew a cherry tree with ripe, red cherries, and an apple tree with pink apples. He drew a beehive and bees, and the deep blue sky. He began to draw the sun, but he could not draw it the way he wanted.

'Mum, why should I draw the sun?' he said. 'I can just open the window and you can see how bright it is today.'

The boy opened the window, and his mother saw the bright sun shining in the sky. She saw it and smiled.

Dreaming of a father

Natalka did not have a father. She only had a mother. Before Natalka started going to school, she sometimes asked her mother where her father was, but her mother never answered. When the little girl started going to school, she stopped asking.

Natalka had a friend, Nastusia, who had a mother and a father. Her father was a diesel locomotive driver. Nastusia sometimes visited Natalka. One day she asked her, 'Where is your daddy?'

Natalka was embarrassed to confess that she did not have a father, so she answered, 'My daddy's a pilot. He's always flying all over the place. He even flies over the sea. He's hardly ever at home.'

Every day, Natalka would save a little bit of the lunch money that her mother gave her. After a few months, she was able to buy a pilot's hat at a shop. When Nastusia came to Natalka's house, she noticed the hat and asked, 'Is your daddy at home today?'

'Yes,' said Natalka. 'We have to be quiet because he is resting.'

The girls talked in a whisper.

Who painted the rooster?

Grandma Mariia had two grandsons in grade one: Mykolka and Yurko. One day the two boys visited their grandmother. They saw a wooden rooster high up on their grandmother's roof. The rooster was standing on top of a steep spire and raising its head.

Mykolka took some paint, climbed up onto the roof, scrambled up the steep spire to reach the rooster, and painted it. The rooster came to life, with a brightly coloured tail and a red comb.

Yurko sat on the grass and watched. He was afraid that at any moment Mykolka would fall … Wouldn't Grandma be cross then! Mykolka would be in terrible trouble!

At last, Mykolka climbed down from the roof. Grandma came out. She saw the painted rooster and asked, 'Who climbed on the roof? Who painted the rooster?'

'Not me, Grandma,' answered Yurko.

Mykolka stood there, hanging his head.

'So, it wasn't you?' Grandma said to Yurko, and she shook her head.

A heart of stone

A family suffered a great misfortune—the father died. His son followed his coffin to the cemetery, and they buried the father.

The young man returned home, and almost immediately his friends came to see him and said, 'Today our soccer team is playing the team from the next village. You are our best player, and we need you to come and play.'

'All right, I'll come,' said the young man. And he went and played soccer as if nothing had happened at home, as if his father had not died, as if there had been no funeral.

He had a heart of stone. How could he have grown into such a frightful, soulless, heartless person? It was because this young man had only lived to satisfy his own desires. He had never done anything kind for another human being. That was how he grew to have a heart of stone.

How a nightingale gives her chicks a drink

A mother nightingale has three chicks in her nest. All day long she brings them food: little bugs, flies and spiders. The baby nightingales eat their fill and fall asleep. Early the next morning, before the sun rises, they start begging for a drink. The nightingale flies to a nearby grove. On the leaves of the trees are drops of dew, clear and pure. The nightingale finds the clearest drop of dew, takes it in her beak, and flies to her nest, bringing her babies a drink. She carefully places the drop of dew on a leaf, and the baby nightingales drink the water. Just then, the sun rises, and the nightingale flies off again to look for bugs.

Mariika has two aunts

Petryk's grandmother gave birth to a boy. Petryk asked his mother, 'Is he really your new brother, Mum?'

'Yes, he's my brother.'

'Is he my brother, too?'

'No, he's your uncle. When he grows up a bit, you can take him to kindergarten.'

Petryk's jaw dropped. He already had two uncles—his father's brothers—but those uncles cuddled him when they visited during the holidays. But this was something amazing: now he would be able to pick up his uncle and cuddle him. Petryk was happy: now he had something to boast about. Nobody else in his first-grade class had a baby uncle.

Petryk was so keen to tell all his friends that he ran all the way to school. But when he came home, he looked miserable.

'What happened at school today?' asked his mother, looking worried.

'Mariika's got two twin aunts that she takes to kindergarten,' said Petryk, 'And I've only got one baby uncle.'

Who is the grandfather related to?

At the edge of the village lived a grandfather and a grandmother. During World War II, the grandfather had served in the army and bravely fought the fascists. His portrait was hanging on a wall in the house. In the portrait, his whole chest was covered in medals.

The grandfather passed away, and within in a year, so did the grandmother. A relative of the grandmother came from far away—the house now belonged to him. He sold everything—the furniture, the crockery, and the house itself.

New owners moved into the house: a father, a mother and a daughter. The house was entirely empty except for the grandfather's portrait. The grandmother's relative apologised and said, 'I'll take the portrait down and put it in the attic.'

'No, no, let it hang there,' answered the mother. 'The portrait can stay there for as long as the house stands.'

'Is he one of your relatives?' asked the man who had just sold the house.

'He is a relative of all honourable people,' answered the mother. 'He's just not your relative.'

My dad bakes bread

Two boys in grade one, Ivanko and Andriiko, sat together in the front row. From their first days at school, they became inseparable friends. They would go out together to play during the break, they were together when they looked at the colourful illustrations in the interesting books in the corridor, and they would run to the school dining room together.

One day, they were sitting together drinking tea and each munching on a bun. The buns were delicious.

'My dad baked this bun,' said Ivanko with pride. 'He works at the bakery and bakes bread. Where does your dad work?'

'He oversees all the bakeries in the region,' replied Andriiko.

'What do you mean "oversees"?' asked Ivanko, not understanding. 'What does he do?'

'Well, he oversees,' saidAndriiko.

'Interesting … My dad bakes bread. You can take a loaf of bread in your hands, and it smells delicious,' said Ivanko. 'What about your dad? What does he make that you can take in your hands?'

Andriiko fell silent. He simply did not know whether he could take something that his father made in his hands.

In the evening, when his father came home, Andriiko asked him, 'Dad, what do you make when you're at work?'

'What do you mean, what do I make?' asked his father in surprise. 'I oversee all the bakeries.'

'Can you take what you make in your hands?' asked Andriiko.

The father was even more surprised. He did not know what to say to his son.

'Dad, please bake a loaf of bread,' said Andriiko. 'Even just one loaf … but it must smell delicious. Like the ones that Ivanko's dad bakes, so you can take it in your hands.'

Andriiko's father sat at the table deep in thought.

Mum does not like fried mushrooms

One Sunday, Dmytryk went with his mother to the forest.

It was early autumn, and it was quiet in the forest. Somewhere in a thicket a woodpecker was tapping. The first yellow leaves were falling from the maples.

There were many mushrooms in the forest. Dmytryk's mother had brought a basket from home, and from time to time she bent to pick an aromatic white mushroom. Dmytryk also wanted to help, but for some reason he rarely spotted a mushroom.

They returned home at midday. Dmytryk's mother cleaned and washed the mushrooms and began to fry them in a frying pan. It smelt so good in the room that Dmytryk began to salivate. He waited impatiently for the mushrooms to fry.

At last, they were ready. Dmytryk's mother dished up the mushrooms on a plate. Dmytryk began to eat.

'Oh, they're so good!' he said, 'But why aren't you eating, Mum?'

'I don't like fried mushrooms,' she said quietly.

'So, what mushrooms do you like?' asked Dmytryk.

'Ones in the forest,' said his mother.

A week later Dmytryk's Uncle Petro—his mother's brother—came to visit from a distant town. He brought many tasty things: fish, caviar, salami. His mother spread everything out on the table. Dmytryk had never eaten anything so tasty.

'Don't you like salami either, Mum?' he asked.

'No, I don't,' answered his mother quietly.

The willow switch

Mytko really struggled with mathematics. Today the teacher was giving them a test, and Mytko was given a very difficult problem to solve. He sat thinking about it for a long time but could not make any sense of it. Discouraged, he began to draw on his piece of paper. He was upset that the other children were able to solve their problems, but he could not. Could it be that he really was dumb, as his father had said the night before?

The teacher saw that he was drawing. He went over to him and wrote in his school diary, 'Your son is idle again. Why are you not taking any action?'

Mytko's hands and feet went cold. His father was strict and would hit him again.

Mytko walked home sad and depressed. 'All right, since I'm good for nothing, hit me, hit me,' thought the boy, and a hot wave of anger filled his heart and flowed out in tears. Mytko broke a switch off a willow tree and tucked it into his diary.

That was how he handed his diary to his father, with the willow switch tucked into it.

His father opened the diary, read the comment, and looked at the switch. His face flushed red with shame. He sat deep into the night with the open diary and the switch in his hand.

Mytko went up to his father and touched his hand. His father reached out and hugged his son to his chest.

Mum comes home

It is a winter's evening. Outside, a blizzard is howling . Little Zoia is listening, waiting for her mother to come home from work. It seems to

Zoia as if a huge and terrible beast is crashing around outside. Now he has crept right up to the window. Now he is knocking on the glass. Zoia screws her eyes up tight.

Suddenly her mother comes silently into the room, goes up to her daughter, and gives her a hug and a kiss.

'You weren't frightened by yourself?' asks her mother.

'No, I wasn't frightened,' says Zoia happily.

Outside the blizzard has fallen silent. The wind is now just a sound in the distance.

Zoia goes up to the window. Snowflakes are swirling merrily in the air.

How the swallow escaped

A swallow was flying high in the sky. A predatory kite saw her and chased after her, wanting to eat her. At any moment he would catch her. The swallow cheeped plaintively. She was crying from grief. Then she remembered her little chicks, naked and helpless. They were waiting for their mother.

'Who will feed you, my little ones, if I perish?' she thought. 'No, the cruel kite will not catch me!'

The swallow flew like an arrow and hid in her nest. The chicks were so pleased to see her, they chirped with joy.

Let's make Grandpa's bed

Five-year-old Yurko has a father, a mother, and Grandpa Mykola.

In the morning Dad goes to work, Grandpa sets off on his morning walk, and Mum says to Yurko, 'Let's go and make Grandpa's bed.'

The two of them go and take the feather quilt from Grandpa's bed, beat it in the fresh air, and put it back on the bed.

Yurko really likes this job: now Grandpa will sleep comfortably on his bed and smile in his sleep.

One day Yurko and his father travelled to a distant island on the Dnipro River. They left at dawn, walked around the island all day, and returned home late in the evening.

They had supper and went to bed. In the middle of the night Yurko's mother heard Yurko crying and found him sitting up in bed.

'What's the matter, Yurko?' asked his mother anxiously.

'We didn't make Grandpa's bed today,' said Yurko.

'No, we didn't, but it's only one day … It won't matter,' his mother consoled him.

'Grandpa will be uncomfortable,' said Yurko. 'You said he's got old bones, and he was wounded on the frontline.'

His mother had trouble reassuring him.

The next day they made Grandpa's bed twice—once in the morning and once in the afternoon.

Let me be yours, Grandma

Old Grandma Maryna lives on the edge of the village.

'She doesn't have a soul in the world,' Mariika's mother often says to her three-year-old daughter. Mariika and her mother live across the road from Grandma Maryna.

Mariika gets up in the morning and sees the old lady sitting on a chair in her yard, warming herself in the sun, and looking at her.

Mariika runs over to Grandma Maryna.

'Good morning, Grandma,' she says.

'Good morning, Mariika,' answers the old lady joyfully. 'Sit next to me, dear.'

Mariika sits next to her for a little while and listens to a story, but she cannot sit still for too long. The meadow is calling to her. There are so many butterflies fluttering there.

The creek is also calling to her. There is such clean sand on the bank of the creek, and such warm water.

Mariika gets ready to leave, and the old lady lets out a sigh.

'Why are you sighing, Grandma?' asks Mariika.

'Because I have no-one to talk to. I'm all by myself,' says the old lady.

'Let me be yours, Grandma,' whispers Mariika quietly, and kisses her wrinkled cheek.

'All right, dear, you can be mine,' smiles Grandma Maryna.

All day Mariika runs in the meadow, bathes, and admires the butterflies, but she does not forget Grandma Maryna. She runs around the meadow, then runs to the old lady's yard and whispers, 'I haven't forgotten that I'm yours, Grandma!'

Mum and Dad argued

Yesterday, Tina's mother and father argued. Her father said something to her mother, and her mother hung her head and sobbed. Then she walked out of the room, and her father walked anxiously from one corner of the room to the other.

Today, when her mother and father came home from work, they did not eat together at the dinner table as they always did, with little Tina sitting between them. First, her father had dinner, and then her mother did. They each separately asked Tina whether she would like to eat with them, but she did not feel like eating.

When Tina was left in the room all by herself, her mother and father came in one at a time and stroked her head and kissed her, but it seemed to Tina that they were doing this in secret.

In the evening, Tina's mother sat at the table and started reading a book. Her father settled on the sofa and opened his book. Tina sat between them. She took her mother's hand and put it on the sofa, right on top of her father's hand. At that moment, Tina felt both their hands start. Her mother seemed to want to remove her hand from her husband's, but Tina would not let her, and a mischievous smile sparkled in her eyes. Her father held her mother's hand tightly in his.

I won't do it again

During the spring, some grade five students were helping the collective farm workers sow watermelons and rockmelons. Two old men were in charge of the work—Grandpa Dmytro and Grandpa Dementii. They were both grey haired and both had faces covered in wrinkles. To the children they seemed about the same age. None of the children knew that Grandpa Dementii was Grandpa Dmytro's father. One was ninety years old and the other was about seventy.

And then Grandpa Dementii began complaining that his son had not properly prepared the watermelon seeds for planting. The children were amazed to hear Grandpa Dementii scolding Grandpa Dmytro.

'How could you be so careless, son, so thoughtless … I've been trying all your life to teach you some sense, but there's no end to it. You need to keep watermelon seeds warm, and what have you done? They're frozen. They will sit in the ground for a week without sprouting.'

Grandpa Dmytro stood in front of Grandpa Dementii like a seven-year-old boy, quietly shifting from leg to leg, his head bowed, and respectfully whispered, 'Dad, it won't happen again. I'm sorry, Dad.'

The children became thoughtful. Each of them was thinking of their own father.

How a little girl saw herself

One day little Sofiika threw a tantrum. She wanted to go out to play, but her mother said that she must have some breakfast first, and then she could go out. And at that she burst into tears.

She thought her mother would beg her, 'Dear Sofiika, please come and have some breakfast.' But her mother did no such thing. She said, 'All right, if you're not hungry, you can go out to play. But you will not be getting anything to eat until dinner time.' And with that, her mother left the room.

Sofiika started screaming even more. Suddenly, through her tears, she saw herself in a little mirror that was standing on the table. At first, she did not understand who that little girl in the mirror was. Why was her face all screwed up, and why were her eyes red? Why did she have tears all over her face? In her surprise Sofiika stopped crying, and then she realised it was her reflection in the mirror.

Sofiika was ashamed. Was that really her? She looked around to see if her mother could see how ugly she was when she was crying. Her mother was not there. Sofiika quickly wiped away her tears.

From that day she never threw a tantrum again. She sometimes wanted to. Sometimes her lips screwed up and her eyes filled with tears, but then she remembered the mirror and felt ashamed. That was how the mirror helped Sofiika to see herself.

My lark flew out the window

A mother had seven sons. The oldest was nine years old and the youngest was three.

The mother baked eight lark-shaped bread rolls—one for each son and one for herself. She took them out of the oven and put them on the table, and her boys sat in a row and could not take their eyes off them.

They were light and fluffy and golden brown. They sat and looked out the window as if they were about to fly away.

'You go outside and play for a few minutes while they cool down,' said the mother.

Six boys went out to play but the youngest—his mother called him her 'little finger'—remained behind. The larks smelt so good that he could not go outside. He sat down at the table and his hand reached for a lark all by itself. It took the hot bread and brought it to his mouth. The mouth opened, the teeth did their work, and the lark disappeared. The little boy was shocked at what he had done and ran outside and played with his brothers.

The mother called the boys in, sat the seven brothers at the table, and gave them each a lark. There was no lark left for her.

'Where is your lark?' asked the oldest brother, who was her best helper.

'My lark flew out the window,' answered the mother with a sigh, and she rested her elbows on the table and became thoughtful.

Tears fell from the youngest brother's eyes …

The clay sister

A father and a mother had a little boy. He wanted to have a sister, so he asked, 'Mum, why don't I have a sister?

'Because she hasn't been born yet,' said his mother.

'And how are children born?' asked the boy.

The mother smiled and said, 'From clay.'

The boy went out to the backyard, kneaded some clay, and made a little girl. The little clay girl dried out in the sun, and the boy brought her inside. He dressed her in a doll's gown, lay her in a toy bed, and started singing a lullaby. But the clay sister was silent. He took it to his father. 'Dad,' he said, 'Can you please say some kind words to my sister, so she comes to life?'

The father took the little boy's clay sister in his hands and spoke some kind words to her, but she did not respond. He kissed the doll, but she still remained silent. So, the boy took her to his mother. 'Mum,' he said, 'Can you please say some kind words to my sister, so she comes to life?'

The mother took the boy's clay sister in her hands and hugged her and kissed her. The mother's warm tears fell onto the clay doll's face. The clay girl shivered, sighed, stretched her little arms towards the mother, opened her mouth, and said, 'Ma-ma.'

What is a lily-of-the-valley like?

A woman had a blind daughter who had never seen the blue sky, or white clouds, or the bright sun, or a pink flower. All she had seen throughout her life was a dark black night.

One day, the mother and daughter went for a walk in the forest. They stopped to rest in a peaceful forest glade. The girl was struck by the wonderful scent of the flowers.

'What is that flower that smells so nice?' asked the girl.

'That is a lily-of-the-valley,' answered her mother.

They sat on the grass. The girl stretched out her delicate fingers and gently felt the flower's large leaves, and the little bell-shaped flowers nestled among them.

'Those little bells are the lily-of-the-valley's flowers,' explained her mother.

'Mum, can you tell me what a lily-of-the-valley is like?' asked the girl.

The mother leaned towards her daughter and kissed her gently on the forehead. 'A lily-of-the-valley is like my kiss, dear,' she said quietly.

What have you brought the cradle in for?

Olesia came home from school earlier than usual because her teacher was sick. She walked in and was surprised to find both her mother and her father at home. They were examining a cradle. Olesia had seen that cradle in the storage room. It had been covered by an old rug. But now it had been brought into the living room.

'Mum, what have you brought the cradle in for?' asked Olesia in surprise.

Her mother and father turned around, startled. They had not heard her entering the room. Olesia could sense that they felt awkward. A wave of excitement swept over her, and she started feeling awkward as well.

UNFINISHED STORY

* Grandma's wrinkles

Grandma's face was covered with tiny wrinkles. Her granddaughter studied her wrinkled face and asked, 'Why do you have so many wrinkles?'

'Because I have lived a long life,' answered her grandmother.

'But you don't have any wrinkles around your eyes,' noted the little girl. 'Don't people get wrinkles around their eyes?'

'Some people do,' replied her grandmother.

On developing a conscience and conscientiousness

I consider one seemingly simple but rather difficult thing to be supremely important: the memory of a reprehensible action committed in childhood should evoke feelings of regret and sadness in a young person. It is not easy to bring a person to such an emotional state. The most important thing is that a person be left in solitude with their conscience, and that their soul is illuminated with the idea of goodness. This thought will become clearer when I tell you about a particular lesson aimed at nurturing a conscience. This lesson occurred when the children and I were harvesting potatoes. (The incident is retold in the story 'How Fedko began to sense the human being within himself' on page 235.)

To discover the human being within oneself—that is the point to which each child must be brought. Here it is most important that the disapproval that the little person feels for their negative action comes not so much from their elders, as from the child themselves, that adults only kindle the spark from which the notion of goodness is born.

Even a person's glance may express kindness or malice. One should be kind towards others and strict with oneself, because kindness is a wealth that grows within you the more you give it away. The ability to *see the world through the lens of goodness* leads one to place high expectations on oneself and to be self-disciplined. The idea of goodness only establishes itself properly in one's heart when one learns to censure oneself.

An educator only becomes a sower of that which is wise, kind and eternal when they *can discriminate* between goodness and evil and are able to correctly evaluate the subtlest impulses of the soul: thoughts, intentions and aspirations. The correct perception of goodness and evil is the foundation of fairness, and education ceases to be education if a child feels that they have been treated unfairly.

Solitude

The nurturing of a conscience, of shame, conscientiousness, responsibility and a sense of duty, is one of the subtlest areas of spiritual and moral development and of self-development. The complexity of this work lies in the fact that it is must be entirely conscious; even the youngest first-graders should appreciate that 'evil knows no shame', in the words of a Ukrainian proverb.

At the same time, one must come to this awareness through one's own independent reflection. In this sphere of education, a person needs to reflect on their own behaviour. In order to not become a shameless egotist, one must learn to place strict demands on oneself.

Conscience in action requires that a person evaluates their own behaviour and character independently. If we were to carefully examine the origins and the foundations of a conscience, we would reach the following conclusion: the voice of the inner 'I' is only active if one has, from a young age, become accustomed to feeling that one is being watched. The nurturing of conscience and of shame involves a child experiencing the penetration of others' thoughts and emotions into their own inner world. It is crucial to nurture in a child the sense that they are being watched even when there seems to be no one around. It is not necessary to stand behind their back all the time and carefully watch their every move. Excessive attention numbs the conscience, making it feeble and helpless. The art of education involves giving little people time to themselves. That is the only way that self-awareness can be developed.

In nurturing a conscience, it is exceptionally important that physical effort is motivated by spiritual effort, that the prime source of self-awareness is strength of spirit, and that the testing of a child's strength of spirit is seen by others. A child experiences great joy from the knowledge that they are spiritually strong. The experience of this joy is essential for moral development, which is a sensitive area involving the subjective feelings and experiences of each child. It may be the case that, in order for a child to see themselves through the eyes of others, it is necessary not only to take advantage of suitable circumstances, but actually to create them. Just as each human being is unique, so are the conditions that are most favourable for the education of a conscience.

I wish to advise educators: in seeking out or creating the circumstances in which this complex inner work of educating a conscience can occur, recognise the right emotional moment.

It is necessary to begin with the seeds of morality. I believe it is crucial that a little child, in solitude, experiences pride, and that the desire to express themselves through their work brings them satisfaction and personal joy.

We should treasure these impulses of the soul, and not profane them with indifference. Look carefully at children's work and you will find many 'withered trees'. A young boy brought an acorn from school with the intention of planting it in his parent's garden and growing an oak tree. However, he soon forgot about the acorn, and it lay on the window-sill for several weeks, until the boy's mother threw it out. This, too, is a 'withered tree' and a withered dream. (See 'Five oak trees' on page 271 and 'Acorns for an oak grove' on page 272.) A young girl brought home a kitten, but her mother did not like it when the kitten made a mess on the first night, and they got rid of it. A girl ran to her father to ask him to help a dog, but her father ignored her concern ('The death of a dog', p. 273). This is even worse: not only a 'withered tree', but also a wounded heart and a crippled conscience.

When the Kremenchuk hydroelectric power station was being built, a settlement near the Dnepr River found itself in the area that was going to be flooded. The people moved to new places, leaving behind their family homes. One old man brought the entirety of the household's property with him. He even took apart his house and reconstructed it in the new settlement, brick-by-brick. Nothing was left in the old settlement. Then this old man, the head of a family with an ancient lineage, told all his relatives, 'Get ready! We're off to do the most important task!'

Everyone got into the back of a truck: the wife, the two sons, the daughters-in-law, the daughter and the grandchildren. They came back to their old homestead. Everyone wondered, 'What are we going to do here?' The old man had brought twelve brooms and he gave one to each family member. 'Sweep,' he instructed. Everyone began to sweep the old yard, not leaving behind even a single dry pine needle or a scrap of paper. The eldest son asked his father, 'Why are we doing this? This is all going to be at the bottom of a deep lake anyway … And we're loading our truck with rubbish.'

The old man became angry, signalled to everyone to stop what they were doing, and said, 'A person's conscience must be clean. That's why we are sweeping the old yard and taking away the waste. We are not making this effort for the fish, but for ourselves, so that we are not ashamed to look into our own conscience. When we die, we go to the earth, but we still keep a clean white shirt for the occasion. Remember that, my grandchildren.'

'Don't forget that we are human beings!' I say to the children, teaching them to be governed by their conscience and to cultivate self-discipline. (See 'Ashamed of what the nightingale will think', p. 279.)

We are resting in a forest clearing in the shade of a linden tree. We are having a feast: sweet watermelons. On the grass is a carefully constructed pile of rind. Some of the children are looking into the bushes for a place to throw the rind ... Stop and think about what you are about to do. No one will see us, and even if they did, there does not seem to be anything wrong with it, but ... your conscience! Wouldn't we be ashamed of ourselves? Will it be pleasant to remember that we left a pile of waste to rot beneath a flowering bush? We collect the scraps, walk to a field, dig a hole and leave the waste there: compost enriches the soil.

On shame

The ability to lead a child to the experience of shame is a great art. Essentially, it is the ability to address a person's consciousness via the subtlest and the most sensitive corners of the heart. Ultimately, a person is able to experience shame when they become aware of something. Figuratively speaking, shame is the ability to be surprised by one's conscience. When a person experiences shame, they take a step towards developing moral consciousness. Awakening a feeling of shame requires great tact from the teacher. The emotions that accompany shame are equivalent to those that one experiences when punished. The art of reaching a child's heart lies in replacing punishment, whenever possible, with what I would call the pangs of conscience, or shame. However, it is important to note that shame should not have anything in common with humiliation, offence or mockery. After experiencing shame, a person should be left feeling morally empowered, rather than weakened or humiliated. The great power of shame lies in the fact that it does not dehumanise a person, but rather refines their best qualities. Countless times I have been convinced that a person who has just experienced the feeling of shame appears purer, more beautiful, as if born again. There is nothing artificial or contrived about it. The one who is ashamed is drawn to you with all the strength of their soul; they experience an intense need for human fellowship.

Self-discipline is born when one is ashamed. A person is ashamed of their inappropriate behaviour, considers what others are thinking about them, and senses the ideal person in their soul. Shame is stronger than the most severe punishment by another person, because it is the punishment of one's conscience by one's conscience. The ability to make a person feel ashamed—that is the magic wand that each teacher needs. I am convinced that this magic wand is equally powerful in the hands of mothers and fathers. There are no recipes for making a person feel ashamed. In life, there are millions of connections between things and circumstances, but in each case, it is necessary to seek out the point of contact that will inevitably lead to feelings of shame. Most importantly, the little person must feel ashamed, and then they will be afraid of doing wrong. Figuratively speaking, shame is the wind beneath the wings of human responsibility. When a person feels responsibility, they also feel fear doing the wrong thing. This fear does not inhibit one's powers, but rather stimulates them, giving rise to moral steadfastness.

Putting someone in a position where they are laughed at and humiliated is entirely immoral. To expose human shame publicly is to strike at a person's very heart. If you are intending to shame someone, you must know how to spare them and have compassion for them, because the one who has been ashamed will inevitably be drawn to you, as long as you have not offended them.

To cause someone to experience shame is to give them the opportunity to reflect and come to a judgement about their own behaviour. Shame always requires secrecy. For that reason, a teacher must be very careful about group discussion of any behaviour whose examination may evoke shame.

On desires

To teach a developing person to express their true human nature is no easy task. The complexity of this task can be explained by fact that we are dealing with children's *desires*, which must be respected, treated with understanding and sensitivity, and even developed. The nurturing of moral freedom is inextricably linked with the refinement of desires, providing a foundation for the development of higher moral needs or imperatives. Not everything that a child desires is a genuine need—that much is clear. The wisdom, skill and art of a teacher's influence on the will of a student involves ensuring that a person's desires and inner urges become aligned with morally justified, community approved needs.

It is necessary for an educator to be deeply familiar with the logic of children's desires and aspirations, as well as their relationship to genuine needs and to a person's holistic development. We cannot ignore the fact that a child desires to do precisely that which is forbidden. The story 'A grandson's request' (p. 291) illustrates this point. Why is this? Why is a child, and especially an adolescent, drawn towards that which is forbidden?

It appears a child wishes to express their human nature, to test, to prove, and to assert their independence, exploring and affirming the strength of their personality. That which is permitted appears uninteresting; that which is forbidden appears far more attractive.

How should we resolve this sensitive issue? How can we nurture a child's ability to express their human essence and demonstrate their independence in the process, exploring and affirming their strength of character? What must we do to ensure that a spirit of self-control prevails within our school? That the application of the human will leads to the creation not only of objects and circumstances, but of human character? For that it is necessary to replace the forbidden with the difficult; even to make the forbidden permissible, but to reveal the difficult within it. The more difficulties are overcome, the fewer prohibitions there will be.

On goodwill

Goodwill is a feeling that is nurtured when the abilities of all students, without exception, are developed harmoniously. There is not and there should not be anyone who is 'good for nothing'. Success in studies should not be, metaphorically speaking, the only soil in which the human seed can grow. Where there is no other soil, some individual students will always feel weak and left behind. When there are people in the class who are, at best, the objects of constant pity, we cannot hope for the overall harmonious development of abilities, and consequently there will be no harmonious development of morality.

For the nurturing of moral refinement, I believe it is very important that each person, both in their individual and in their collective relationships, is connected to others by bonds of goodwill. At the same time as they take their first steps on the path to knowledge of the surrounding world, each child should also experience joyful excitement over another person's good fortune, or experience concern over their sorrow. Let their own experience convince them that their inner peace depends on how they view other people and how they relate to them. In the childhood years, it is impossible to imagine a complete, or even a minimally adequate education, unless each child, when they meet someone connected to them by the bonds of goodwill, is moved to enquire about their health and how they are feeling. This is one of the most subtle areas in the education of attitudes, convictions and ideals.

A small village school with thirty-two students. In the schoolyard there is a well. The villagers often come to the well. Everyday, at exactly the same time, Grandpa Oleksandr comes to the well with his bucket. The children know him well. He is a disabled war veteran: instead of his left leg, he has a prosthetic leg, but he still works hard, looking after bees and growing seedlings. Every time Grandpa Oleksandr comes for water, the children run to the well. They help Grandpa Oleksandr pull the bucket out of the well; he has also lost three fingers on his right hand.

'How is your health, Grandpa?' ask the children as soon as the old man enters the schoolyard.

'Thank you, children,' answers the old man, 'My health is good. The bees are buzzing. Come and visit me and I will give you some honey. The seedlings are growing ... And how are your studies going? Are you all reading well now?'

'No, Grandpa, not all of us. We are learning, but we still get some words wrong.'

The old man shakes his head with concern and promises the children that he will read them an interesting book next time they come to the apiary. The children are curious. 'What interesting book have you got, Grandpa?' they ask. Both the old man and the children are glad that they have met, talked, and felt the need for one another. They are connected by bonds of goodwill. This represents enormous spiritual wealth.

The words 'hello' and 'good day' express a subtle aspect of human relationships. (See 'Good health to you, Grandpa!', p. 296.) I organise special discussions with small children and teenagers, dedicated to these words and the emotions that the human race has gradually instilled in them over many centuries. To my mind, it is crucial that when a child speaks these words, they carry, metaphorically speaking, the subtle music of human emotions, impulses, desires and aspirations.

One quiet spring morning, when the school is drowning in the white blossoms of apple, pear, apricot and peach trees, my students and I walk to the most beautiful part of the orchard. One of my most cherished hopes is that the children, overwhelmed by the beauty that surrounds them, will feel the subtlest shades of meaning of that beautiful and wise word 'hello'.[33]

During our first meeting beneath the blossoming trees, I tell the children the story 'Say "hello" to people'. The word 'hello' has the miraculous ability to awaken feelings of mutual trust, to bring people closer together, to open souls to one another. To greet someone in this way is not simply to live, but to see the world around you and to relate to it in a certain way—that is what we teach the children. (See 'Say "hello" to people' on page 298 and 'Borrowing a spade' on page 297.)

The bonds of goodwill are invisible, but they are the most powerful of all spiritual impulses. In order to create a bond between a small child and another person, it is necessary to impart a specific orientation to their whole spiritual life—an orientation towards other people. All other values must be seen by the child in the light of what benefits other people.

Among the aspects of ethical culture that must be revealed to a developing soul, we highlight those relationships connected with the word 'please'. We take great care is to fill these relationships with the bonds of goodwill, heartfelt warmth and mutual trust.

On generosity

I strive to ensure that children want to be generous and selfless. For a child to feel happy when they give something away it is necessary to make generosity appealing. For the smallest schoolchildren, I have legends and fairy tales in which not only is generosity surrounded by a romantic halo, but it is also presented in a simple, accessible form. The educator shows children how to become generous and the children begin to understand that the opportunity to be generous awaits them at every step. These stories make a great impression on the children. They long to express generosity—but how? Here is necessary to act in line with the proverb 'Strike while the iron is hot.' We must not allow a child's inspiration to be extinguished without having burnt brighter. We must not allow it to be transformed into a blank shot. It is very important that small children, when they aspire to be generous, find an opportunity to do so.

On what is acceptable and what is unacceptable

One of the most important educational tasks, I believe, is to instil in each individual (I emphasise, human self-respect is a deeply individual sphere) a philosophy of life that expresses a view regarding what is acceptable and what is unacceptable.[34]

Such convictions provide a most precious moral immunity, which does not allow a person to debase themselves, to lose their human dignity, conscience, honour and moral courage.

During the many years of our school's educational work, we have developed moral guidelines around *Nine Unacceptable Things* that debase a human being. We affirm in the minds of the children the unacceptable nature of certain behaviour. This feeling for what is unacceptable must be based on thought and conviction. The confluence of thought and feeling establishes a valuable moral characteristic: an aversion to that which is unacceptable in one's own behaviour; an aspiration to behave in a way that is worthy of a human being and elevates a person; a readiness, no matter what, to act in accordance with one's convictions about what is acceptable and what is unacceptable.

The *Nine Unacceptable Things*, an understanding of which provides a foundation for the convictions and for the emotional world of a morally decent and spiritually beautiful person, are as follows:

It is unacceptable to seek one's own welfare, happiness, enjoyment and peace at the expense of another person's oppression, unsettledness, distress or anxiety. Do not allow yourself to be treated with disrespect but show no disrespect to others. In order to develop this conviction, we have a number of educational narratives and fairy tales, which lead children to reflect on harmony in human relationships. To each generation of schoolchildren, I narrate the story 'Blind love' (p. 332).

It is unacceptable to abandon a friend who is in trouble or in danger, or to indifferently walk past another's grief, distress and suffering. Moral deafness and blindness, a hardened heart—this is one of the most dangerous vices. To feel another's pain and to understand that it is unacceptable to be a passive bystander—that is one of the most important aims of all educational work. I have several vivid tales that are accessible to the minds and emotional worlds of children, in which the unacceptable nature of indifference to another's suffering is illustrated.

The nurturing of acceptable behaviour with regard to the suffering of others plays a significant role in school life, when we consider that a major cause of suffering in schools is the failure to master knowledge. It is very important that children view a classmate's lagging behind as a misfortune, that they empathise with their classmate, that they are not indifferent to the fact that some students in their class struggle to succeed.

It is unacceptable to appropriate the results of another person's work, to hide behind someone else's back. This is an area that concerns delicate interpersonal relationships connected with studies, and the whole way of life of the community and the individual. To be a worker is an honour; to be a freeloader is a disgrace. We believe that the nurturing of such an attitude provides a basis for the convictions that give rise to good citizenship. It is very important that a person experiences a sense of wonder when they discover that they can stand on their own two feet; that they think to themselves, 'I achieved this through my own efforts. I achieved this with my own intelligence.'

It is unacceptable to be timid and weak; it is shameful to display a lack of resolve, to retreat in the face of danger, to snivel.

Observance of this principle requires certain conditions that give rise to courageous action. To find these conditions in life or to create them is a very subtle process, as a teacher also bears responsibility for students' health and safety.

In courageous deeds there is always a risk, but without taking some wise risks parenting is not possible. It seems that the art of touching a young heart lies in being able to identify that one moment in a lifetime, when, inspired by the prospect of a courageous deed, little Vania or little Mykolka displays strength of spirit. Life is so rich and complex that there are many such moments; we just need to notice them and not shy away from a test of will.

It is unacceptable to give free rein to needs and desires, releasing them from the control of the human spirit.

When satisfying your needs, you should display refinement, restraint and fortitude. This is not just a question of modesty. This is something higher and more significant: in taking control of your needs and desires, you are refining your spiritual essence.

After a difficult trek in the scorching hot steppe, we enter a forest. We can hear a spring babbling. Everyone is thirsty. But the teacher is teaching the children restraint. The children sit down and rest. No one approaches the water. This is not just because everyone is sweating and so it would be ill-advised to drink icy cold water. The teacher explains, 'Imagine what will happen if we all rush to the water at once … We might even bump into each other's foreheads. That is not behaviour that becomes a human being. The water will not disappear anywhere. Let the girls drink first.' The girls drink some water, one after the other. Then the boys drink some water. But for some reason tall, grey-eyed Tolia does not get a drink of water. 'You're not thirsty?' asks the teacher. Tolia answers, 'Yes, but not very. I also want to be a real human being.' The teacher smiles. (See also 'One sip for the weakest', p. 332.)

In nurturing restraint, generosity and fortitude, a teacher consolidates in young souls a precious moral quality: intellectual refinement, self-discipline, refined relationships. The children learn to concede to one another.

It is unacceptable to be silent when your words will express honour, refinement and courage, and your silence is the result of faint-heartedness and meanness. It is not acceptable to speak when your silence expresses honour, refinement and courage, and your words would be the result of faintheartedness.

Amongst the most delicate issues in values education is educating a sense of responsibility to one's own conscience. I strive to ensure that someone who has committed a reprehensible action is punished by their own pangs of conscience, that their faint-heartedness weighs heavily on them, and that the removal of these pangs of conscience is experienced as great relief.

It is unacceptable for a genuine human being not only to lie, to be a hypocrite, to grovel, be subservient to someone else's will, but also to not have their own views, to lose their sense of self.

In order to nurture courage in speech and courage in silence, it is necessary for the teacher themselves to be noble and courageous. It is necessary to respect the independent views and convictions of young people, especially adolescents, even when not everything in their behaviour appears sensible or justified.

It is unacceptable to thoughtlessly throw words around, to make promises that cannot be fulfilled.

For this reason, it is necessary to nurture in young people something that I refer to as *refinement of will.* From a young age it is necessary to teach children to set themselves challenges, to direct them towards self-education and self-development. Let the initial goal be insignificant, but a person cannot live *in vain*; it is necessary for a person to be driven by *aspirations.* Let the attainment of a goal bring them joy and pride. One of the most subtle and most significant things in the difficult field of education is encouraging children's aspirations. Aspirations are not the same as wishes. Wishes arise even in a lazy soul; the more of a child's wishes that adults satisfy without the exertion of the child's spiritual efforts, the less refinement of will there will be in the life of the child. Aspirations involve a person having self-control, making commitments to themselves, making demands upon themselves. Recognising aspirations to be an expression of their own will, a person arrives at a most important truth: correct human speech is always *difficult* because it is impossible without the soul's labour.

Consider it your mission to bring children to an understanding of this truth. Only then will they value their words, understanding that to cast them to the wind is to break a promise they made to themselves.

It is unacceptable to have excessive pity for oneself, in the same way that a pitiless and indifferent attitude towards the suffering of others is also unacceptable. It is unacceptable to exaggerate one's own personal injuries, insults directed against oneself, misfortunes and suffering.

In a child's tears is a narrative without words, a recollection of the suffering they have just experienced. A child expects you to lovingly and gently touch their soul. Do not be indifferent towards this expectation, this hope; guard against indifference as you guard against major failures.

When I say that excessive self-pity is unacceptable, I am talking about a long-term process of developing endurance and perseverance. When a child approaches you, hoping that you will share their pain, it is necessary to share that pain and wisely comfort the child, but also to draw a lesson from the experience, so that self-pity does not consume the child's spiritual energies, does not transform the child into a cry-baby and a sissy. The tendency to pity oneself excessively should be wisely countered by redirecting that pity towards others.

When a person is crying, we are dealing with secrets of the individual spiritual world that have not yet been comprehended by science. I would consider myself to have not reached the depths, the innermost corners of a student's heart, if I have not once seen their tears in the ten years spent at school. Tears express an indivudual's spiritual struggle and subtle aspects of their perception of the world.

On the refinement of desires

The school of desires provides the most fertile ground for the formation of convictions, for faith or faithlessness, compassion or indifference, benevolence or malevolence and animosity.

The ABC of parental education begins with giving attention to the refinement of desires. Normal education and the nurturing of personal development within a school would be completely unthinkable if the children were not surrounded by an atmosphere of their elders' noble desires, and if those desires were not expressed in actions. We tell fathers and mothers how a sincere urge, a sincere desire, nurtures the capacity to love others; we give advice on how to express opposition to the smallest manifestations of egotism.

In telling children of the great power of noble desires, we convince them that a good desire, which inspires selfless action, is capable of saving a person, while an evil desire is capable of ruining them. We tell the miraculous story 'A kind word' (p. 352) to each generation of our students. Children are most receptive to the idea behind this story when they are approaching adolescence.

The most important educational task is to fill each child's heart with the desire to bring joy, happiness, well-being, kindness and peace to another person. To awaken a lofty desire, to inspire action—that is perhaps the most complex task in education and in parenting. We are talking here of moral schooling in a genuine love for another person, of educating a deep sensitivity towards another person's inner spiritual world.

It is necessary to establish in children's hearts not only joyful emotions, but also the ability to grieve and to feel longing. To teach a child to be joyful and to take pleasure in their happiness is not a difficult task. It is much more difficult to nurture sensitivity and to prepare someone psychologically to experience grief and compassion. Without this sensitivity, a person does not truly appreciate happiness.

A shining example of sublime, devoted love is essential if a young person, especially in adolescence and youth, is to have a noble, chaste conception of love. Many years of experience has convinced us that with adolescents and young men and women it is necessary to speak about love sincerely, openly, and, most importantly, intelligently. At the centre of an educator's discussion should be the advice on how thought, reason and consciousness may govern our emotions. When speaking of love, let wisdom and rationality prevail, rather than emotional enthusiasm.

A conscious, wise human attitude towards desires is the essence of those words about love that an educator should use when reaching out to that which is most delicate in a human being.

Over many years I have compiled a cycle of discussions about love. I instil the idea, even in young adolescents aged twelve or thirteen, that love is the predecessor of parenthood. To love is to feel a great sense of responsibility for another person, both for the one whom you love and the one whom you are creating. Love is only highly moral when it is intelligent, wise and considerate.

It is necessary to teach everything ahead of time. A person may only begin to work seriously from the age of eighteen, but they are taught to work from the time they take their first step. It is the same with preparation for continuing the human race. To teach how to raise one's children is to give knowledge about the most important thing in life. Is it not astonishing that an adolescent, a young man, is taught many things—to till the soil, to grow crops, to drive a tractor and to work on a lathe—but no one thinks to teach him about raising children. Yet that is the most important thing.

I emphasise once again that it is extraordinarily important that when the man or woman awakens in a person, they should be inspired by thoughts about the meaning of life and a person's mission, about beauty, refinement and virtue in one's desires and actions, and about the higher happiness afforded by communion with other human beings. The richer a boy's or girl's spiritual life during this period, the brighter and nobler the moral complexion of their emotions and experiences, the more they will feel a need to protect the privacy of their feelings, to preserve the secret of their awakening impulses.

Morality is expressed in action

The topic to be discussed here is the activity of moral consciousness. Moral truths, experienced by students as an expression of goodness, live in actions. Morality is expressed in relationships. If there are frequent discussions and verbal instruction about good deeds, but the good deeds themselves are absent, the psychological resources of the teaching staff will be spent battling misbehaviour … your will and reason will be consumed sorting out who did what, and who is to blame. Where morality does not live in noble actions, there will be many victims and it will be hard to find the perpetrators.

How can we ensure that moral consciousness and moral convictions are lived, expressed, strengthened and emboldened in action? The most important thing is that the life of the school community must always be a life of ideas. The mission of the educator lies in ensuring that the community always strives for refinement and moral beauty. We must sow seeds in the minds of children, adolescents and young people that will inspire action to overcome indifference, heartlessness, moral ignorance and egotism. The community will then be in a state of readiness to confront amoral behaviour, and the goodness implanted in each young heart will be able to immediately confront evil, so that evil will be perceived as entirely unacceptable. The teacher should be placed in the role of the creator of moral wealth, not in the role of a person continuously battling with the perpetrators of reprehensible actions and having to conduct investigations … The spiritual impulse of the community should drive it forward so irresistibly that actions that discredit its ideals are met with widespread condemnation.

Why do students misbehave, with one behaviour incident following another, while the better, more disciplined students are afraid to raise their voices against evil, despite knowing very well who is at fault? Why is it that impunity reigns in the school, teachers are in despair, and it it is all so unbearably difficult? It is because insolent evil dominates the field, while goodness has dug in and is defending itself. Essentially, under such circumstances there is no community, because there is no genuine independent action—action inspired by moral consciousness. There is no morality in action. The understanding of *may not*, which represents such an important element of independently motivated activity, has been transformed from a community ideal into an everyday tool that a teacher uses. *May not*, in the teacher's hands, has become a cane, with the aid of which the teacher is forced to pursue 'transgressors'.

Constant inspiration by the ideal, constant striving for the sublime and the beautiful—that is how the activity of moral consciousness begins. That is the beginning of the educator's active role. It is not necessary to organise any public condemnation if a community is inspired by a lofty ideal. The strongest disapproval is the attitude of peers towards a person who has crossed the line beyond which *may not* begins.

We were wary of the danger of raising over-protected people who were carefully sheltered from emotional storms and misfortune. Such an education, in essence, amounts to squandering our spiritual resources—the intelligence and will of the educator—ensuring that young people are spared any encounter with evil. The less often a person has to confront evil, the more helpless they will be when it is necessary to display strength of will and resilience.

Many years ago our teaching staff began to reflect on the fact that some students pass through childhood, adolescence and young adulthood without having had to take a single independent step that required strength of spirit. These students never break the rules and never give teachers cause for concern. But a year or two passes after such a conscientious student has completed school and it is hard to remember them: they are faceless. And such students struggle in life: they cannot cope with difficulty and are helpless when it is necessary to express independence. After examining such inert, passive students, we reached the following conclusion: they are beyond our educational influence.

We began to think about how to prompt each *unnoticeable*, 'harmless', faceless student to perform actions that would awaken strength of spirit. It sometimes happens that one such deed is enough for someone to be properly born, but without such a deed, they leave the walls of the school 'unborn'.

To prompt a courageous deed requires the exercise of an educator's reason and will, and an ability to discern some field of endeavour where it will be possible to awaken a student's strength of spirit.

STORIES AND VIGNETTES

How Fedko began to sense the human being within himself

Little Fedko went to a field with his mother to dig up potatoes.

'You are eight years old now,' said his mother. 'You need to work properly.'

Fedko's mother took four rows, and Fedko took one. His mother would dig up a potato plant, and Fedko would pull the potatoes from the ground and throw them in a bucket.

Fedko did not feel like working. He would pull out the potatoes on the surface but did not bother to dig down for the ones that were covered with soil. His mother noticed how he was working, pulled out some potatoes that Fedko had left behind, and said, 'Aren't you ashamed? Do you realise someone is watching and seeing everything you do?'

Fedko looked around in surprise. 'Who is watching? What can they see?' he asked.

'The human being within you is watching, Fedko. They see everything and notice everything, but you do not always listen to what they tell you. If you listen, you will hear the voice of the human being within you, and it will tell you how you are working.'

'Where is the human being within me?' asked Fedko, even more surprised.

'In your head and in your chest, in your heart,' his mother explained.

Fedko moved on to the next potato plant and pulled out the potatoes lying on the surface. He wanted to leave that plant and move on the next one … when suddenly he really did seem to hear a voice reproaching him: 'What are you doing Fedko? There is another potato there under the soil.' Fedko was surprised and looked around. There was no-one there, but it seemed as if someone was watching his work and making him feel ashamed.

'I suppose there is someone who can see my work,' thought Fedko, and he sighed, dug up the soil, and found several more large potatoes. Fedko felt better then and gave a sigh of relief. He even started singing.

The boy worked for an hour, and then for another, and felt more and more amazed. He thought to himself, 'Why dig so deep in the soil? There probably isn't any potato there.' But as soon as he had that thought, it was as if someone was reading his mind, and he felt ashamed. But he felt glad at the same time. He could not have explained why he felt glad, but he understood why he felt ashamed. He did not want to be a bad person.

'He's a good friend, this human being within,' thought Fedko.

What is tastier?

Some children set up a bird feeder on a tree in the garden. Every day they would bring sunflower seeds and wheat for the birds, and for the chickadees they would bring a small piece of lard. That day, as usual, they brought some lard and hung it on a thread.

Dmytryk came to the garden. He wanted to see for himself how a chickadee ate its breakfast. He sat near the window and watched. A chickadee settled next to the lard and started pecking at it. She took a bite and started singing joyfully. Then she took another bite and sang again.

'She is saying thank you for the lard,' decided Dmytryk.

He wanted to bring the chickadee something even more delicious. Since he loved *varenyky*[35] with cottage cheese, he brought some of those for the chickadee and placed them in the bird feeder. He did not realise that chickadees do not eat *varenyky*.

The man with one leg

At the bus stop, a man clambered on who only had one leg and walked on crutches. On his chest were several ribbon bars from the medals he had been awarded. He had lost a leg during World War II.

The bus was packed full. The war veteran stood next to a seat where a young man and an old woman were sitting. The young man had a transistor radio. He saw the handicapped war veteran, but quickly turned his eyes away and looked out the window.

The old woman stood and invited the war veteran to sit down.

'What an idea,' snorted the man with one leg. 'How can I take a seat from a lady? There are men sitting here.'

The young man heard these words but did not even turn his head.

They travelled on like this for several stops. The young man sat on a seat for two, while next to him stood a man with one leg and an old woman. An oppressive silence fell over the bus.

'Good for nothing,' muttered an old man sitting by the door. The young man appeared not to hear these words.

Two brothers

Two brothers, Maksym and Yukhym, lived in a large stone building. Both worked on a farm. Their elderly mother lived with Maksym's family, and their elderly father lived with Yukhym's family. Maksym had a son, a tractor driver, and Yukhym had a beautiful daughter who was to be married. She worked as a milkmaid.

For a week Yukhym had been preparing for a great family celebration—his daughter's wedding. It was to be held on Sunday.

In Yukhym's hut, they had been baking and boiling, frying and salting, from morning to night. There would be many guests at the wedding, and everyone had to be well fed.

On the Saturday morning the grandmother and grandfather came to congratulate their granddaughter on her marriage.

That same day in the evening, the grandmother went to bed early, complaining of a headache. She groaned, gave a quiet sigh, and died. All the relatives gathered round the dead woman's bed: the sons—Maksym and Yukhym—the grandson and granddaughter with her fiancé, and the dead woman's husband—Maksym's and Yukhym's father. It became very quiet in that large stone building where the two families lived.

'You need to postpone the wedding,' Maksym said to his brother. 'You can't have it tomorrow,' he said to his niece.

'What am I to do?' lamented Yukhym. 'How can we postpone it? We have done so much preparation!'

'What are you saying, Yukhym. Come to your senses!' said his father. 'And why don't you say something?' said the grandfather to his granddaughter.

'No, we won't put off the wedding!' said Yukhym.

The old father wept. A terrible silence fell over the house. The old father said, 'No-one will come to your wedding. Has that entered your head?'

The next day no-one came to Yukhym's home. Everyone went to Maksym's home for the mother's funeral. Maksym stood by his mother's body, his head bowed in grief.

Yukhym stood by his door. People avoided him. 'That's the one who wanted to celebrate a wedding by his mother's coffin,' they whispered.

Ivan's house is burning

Petro and Stepan were working in the field. Suddenly they noticed that there was a fire in the village. It seemed to them that the fire was burning where they lived.

'It looks like that is our houses burning,' said Petro.

'Let's go home straight away,' said Stepan, and he harnessed their horses to their cart.

Petro and Stepan drove their horses as hard as they could.

'Whose house is burning?' they asked, when they reached the edge of the village.

'Ivan's house is burning,' answered a neighbour.

Petro sighed with relief, stopped the horses and said, 'We don't need to go any further. Shall we turn the horses around and return to the field?'

'Why should we turn back?' asked Stepan in surprise.

'It's not our houses burning,' reasoned Petro. 'Why should we give up our time. We've got work to do in the field.'

Stepan looked at Petro in disbelief.

'Were you really only rushing to save your own house?' he asked.

Petro was silent. Stepan left him with the horses and ran to help put out the fire. Petro sat in the cart and did not know what to do—follow Stepan or ride to the field.

When you think about it, can anyone be considered a good person if they only run to put out a fire when it is their own house that is burning?

Didn't your heart tell you anything?

Andriiko came home from school and saw his mother had been crying. He put his bag down and sat at the table, waiting for his dinner.

'They've taken Dad to hospital,' said his mother. 'Your father is very sick.' She thought her son would be concerned and anxious. But the boy remained calm and unaffected. The mother looked with amazement at Andriiko.

'We have to go to the forest tomorrow', said Andriiko. 'Tomorrow is Sunday … The teacher told us all to come to school at seven in the morning.'

'Is that so. And where will you be going tomorrow?' asked his mother.

'To the forest … The teacher told us,' said Andriiko.

'And didn't your heart tell you anything?' asked his mother, and she burst into tears.

Why did Grandma leave?

Mariika's mother was helping her get ready for school. Mariika was in grade three.

Mariika's mother ironed her dress and helped her to put it on. Then she helped Mariika put on some red shoes.

Mariika did not like the red shoes. She said, 'I want the green shoes.'

Mum brought the green shoes and helped the girl to put them on.

But the girl did not like the green shoes either. She took them off and said to her mother, 'I want the black shoes.'

The girl's grandmother was sitting near the window. She was watching Mariika and shaking her head. When Mariika said she did not like the black shoes, the grandmother gave a deep sigh and walked out of the house.

Why did she leave?

Who ate the *pyrizhok*?

Three brothers—Ivan, Petro and Vasyl—were cutting hay in a meadow. At noon they decided to stop and rest. They lay down in the shade of a haystack and fell deep asleep.

While they were sleeping, their mother came and brought them some lunch: a bowl of porridge, some bread, and three large *pyrizhky* with poppy seeds.[36] The mother did not want to wake her sons. 'Let them sleep,' she thought. 'When they wake up, they will find the food and eat.' She covered the food with green burdock leaves and returned home.

Meanwhile a traveller passed that way—an old man with a walking stick. He was very tired and hungry. The old man approached the haystack and saw the three brothers sleeping. He also smelt the food. The traveller thought to himself, 'Would these boys give me something to eat if they were not sleeping? Of course, they would.' He did not want to disturb the brothers' sleep, so he ate one *pyrizhok*, thanked them in a whisper, and walked on.

The brothers woke up and sat down to eat. They saw that there were only two *pyrizhky* and knew that their mother always brought three. Each one thought, 'One of my brothers has woken up and quietly eaten one of the *pyrizhky*.' All three brothers felt ashamed, and all hung their heads, because each one thought one of his brothers was at fault. They ate the porridge and bread, but the *pyrizhky* lay there untouched. They silently went back to cutting the hay. They did not say a single word to each other until evening.

In the evening the traveller came back that way. He walked over to the brothers and was surprised to see them all standing grim and silent, with their heads down. Why were they not saying a word to each other?

'Good evening,' said the old man. 'Thank you for the *pyrizhok*. I did not want to wake you, so I ate one of your *pyrizhky* without asking you.'

The brothers were overjoyed. 'So, it was you who ate the *pyrizhok*,' said each of the brothers. 'That's wonderful. Come over here, Grandpa. We've left the other two *pyrizhky* for you as well. Come and eat them.'

The old man followed the brothers. Now they were walking happily and looking joyfully into each other's eyes.

The rissole that felt like a stone

This happened during the very difficult year that followed the war.[37] Grade three was going on an excursion into the forest. The teacher, Mariia Mykolaivna, asked everyone to assemble at the school. Everyone arrived before sunrise.

Each student had a little packet of food—a piece of bread, an onion, a boiled potato—and some children even had some lard. The children unpacked all their food, wrapped it up in a large piece of paper, and packed it into a haversack. The children had decided that they were all collectively one family, so why should each child keep their food to themselves?

Lonia also contributed his bread, some potatoes, and a pinch of salt to the communal haversack. But he kept a small packet containing a rissole in his pocket. His mother had wrapped it in paper and said, 'Eat it when no-one is looking.'

In the forest the children played, read a book, and told stories by a campfire. Then they spread out all their food on a large tablecloth and sat down to eat. Lonia was sitting next to Maiia, a thin, blonde-haired girl. Her father had been killed on the frontline on the last day of the war. Everyone had a small piece of lard. Maiia cut her piece of lard in two and gave half to Lonia. The rissole in the boy's pocket now felt like a stone.

When the children had finished eating, Mariia Mykolaivna said, 'Children, collect all the paper and burn it.' When all the paper had been collected and placed in a pile, Lyonia secretly threw his packet containing the rissole into the pile of rubbish.

Hurtful words

A little boy was playing loudly. His mother asked him not to make so much noise because his father was sick. Instead of listening to his mother, the boy lost his temper and said some rude, hurtful words to her.

Deeply wounded, the mother started crying. The boy felt ashamed and begged his mother, 'Please, Mum, forget those rude words I said. Forgive me!'

'I can forgive you, but I cannot forget your rude words,' his mother replied. 'It is easier to catch a swallow in the sky than to forget hurtful words.'

Lost coins

Stepanko found some coins in the schoolyard—twenty *kopiika*.[38]

'Somebody must have lost them,' thought the boy. 'I'll take them to Mariia Grygorivna.' And he took the money to his teacher.

Mariia Grygorivna praised him. 'You are a good, honest person, Stepanko,' she said.

It was during the lunch break. Stepanko was surprised to hear the school radio airing a story about what he had done. They were saying how Stepanko, a student from grade one, had found some money in the schoolyard and had not kept it to spend on candy and ice-cream, but instead had taken the money to his teacher.

The next day, Stepanko's photo was in the school bulletin. He managed to sound out the headline one syllable at a time: 'We should follow Stepanko's example'.

Several days later, during the lunch break, another grade one student, Semenko, approached the teacher and said, 'Mariia Grygorivna, I found thirty *kopiika* in the schoolyard. Somebody must have lost it.'

'Really?' asked the teacher in surprise. 'Two fifteen-*kopiika* coins?'

'No … Two ten-*kopiika* coins and two five-*kopiika* coins … '

Mariia Grygorivna smiled strangely and shook her head. 'All right. I expect we will find the owner,' she said.

One day passed, then a second, and a third. Semenko came to the teacher and asked her, 'Have you found the person who lost the money?'

'No, I haven't,' she said. 'But think hard, Semenko. Perhaps it was you who lost the money, and forgot that you lost it, and then found it again?'

Semenko's face turned a deep red …

Why was Mum upset?

One day, we had visitors—an elderly couple. They were not our relatives. They were good friends from a village nearby.

My mother invited our guests into the living room. She set up the dinner table, seated the guests, and served dinner. That day she had made borshch[39] with chicken. It was delicious. After the borshch, my mother served fried fish.

Our elderly guests did not eat much. They left borshch in their plates and only tried a little fish. My mother was concerned about it and kept urging them, 'Please eat up, dear guests.'

The old people assured her that they were not hungry. Only after the guests had left did my mother realise why they had not eaten much, and it made her very upset.

She had placed a loaf of white bread on the table but had only cut two small slices from it. She could not say why she had neglected to cut more. Perhaps she was just in a hurry. The old people ate their food with bread and had felt too uncomfortable to ask for more, and that must be why they had eaten so little.

My mother never forgot that visit, and whenever she recalled it, her face would turn red.

Fried chicken

This happened during the difficult year that followed the war.[40] Those were hard times for everyone, at home and at work. When people went to work in the fields, all they brought for lunch was a small piece of dark rye bread, a boiled potato and an onion.

One day, the farmers sat down in the middle of the field to eat, and everyone took out their lunches, but Karpo had fried chicken for lunch. He did not feel comfortable putting his delicious food out next to everyone else's rye bread and potatoes, so he went and hid behind some bushes and ate his lunch there.

Everybody else finished their food in a complete silence and felt rather awkward.

Eventually, everyone, including Karpo, finished their lunch. Once Karpo had eaten his chicken, he wrapped the bones in some newspaper, and put them in his pocket.

Karpo came out from behind the bushes and joined the other workers, but he could not look them in the eye.

Juicy red apples

Some children were heading home after a long hiking trip. They still had about seven kilometres to walk. They were passing through a large village. It was very hot.

The children stopped by a house. In the front yard, they could see a well and an apple tree. The children could not take their eyes of its juicy red apples.

'I wish I could have an apple,' said little Olesia.

'Let's go in and ask for a drink of water,' suggested Mykola. 'Maybe the owner will let us each have an apple. There she is, sitting by the well.'

The children knocked at the gates.

'What do you want?' asked the woman, approaching the fence.

'Could you please give us a drink of water?' asked Olesia.

The woman looked grimly at the children and said, 'I'll bring you some.'

A minute later she brought a bucket of water and put it down outside the gate.

'Help yourselves,' she said.

The children drank the water but kept looking over at the apples.

Betrayal

A woman's husband passed away. She buried him and planted a rose bush on his grave. However, after the funeral, the woman did not once visit the cemetery and never watered the rose, so it died.

The husband had a dog who was his faithful friend. As a matter of fact, the dog's name was 'Friend'. When the man was buried and everyone left the cemetery, Friend stayed by the grave. He lay down on the grass and whined mournfully. Then he fell silent and watched the rose as it slowly withered. When the rose finally died, Friend whined one last time, closed his eyes, and died.

People might say that if the woman had watered the rose, and it had flourished and bloomed, Friend would still be alive.

The dog had at least learnt to be faithful to a human being. But the woman … She forgot her husband so quickly that even the flowers on his grave did not have time to bloom.

Who is scarier, God or Grandpa Trokhym?

Yurko had a grandfather and a grandmother—Grandpa Trokhym and Grandma Paraska. The grandfather was a beekeeper. The grandmother was a housewife. Both were very religious. They believed in God and went to church.

Yurko was a grade two student. Grandma Paraska would tell him a lot about God, about how powerful he was, and how he knew everything. 'Do you see that icon on the wall? That is God's image,' his grandmother told him. 'God sees everything and knows everything. He sees everything that we do, and if we do something wrong, he punishes us.'

Over the summer, the beehives were always taken far away into the fields, and Grandpa Trokhym lived with the bees from spring to winter. He lived in a small, brightly lit hut that had been built for him. Each spring, Grandma Paraska would hang an icon on the wall in that hut in the steppes, so that Grandpa Trokhym would not forget God. She would take the icon home over winter.

During the summer, Grandma Paraska and Yurko would often visit Grandpa Trokhym. They would bring him clean linen and clothes, freshly cooked borshch[41] (the grandfather loved borshch!) and fried chicken.

In the hut there were some large tanks of honey. One day, Grandpa Trokhym stepped out for a moment, and Grandma Paraska quickly stepped over to one of the metal tanks, opened it, filled a jar with honey and hid it in her basket. Then she took out another empty jar. She was about to fill it as well, when she heard Grandpa Trokhym's heavy footsteps outside. She quickly hid the jar in her basket, sat down on a bench by the window, folded her arms, and looked intently at a beehive outside.

Yurko watched everything that his grandmother did. He saw that God was also carefully watching her from the icon on the wall.

'If Grandma isn't afraid of God,' thought Yurko. 'Why is she afraid of Grandpa Trokhym?'

That thought kept bothering Yurko. On their way home, he asked, 'Grandma, who is scarier, God or Grandpa Trokhym?'

'Why are you asking?' asked his grandmother in surprise.

'God saw you steal the honey, and you weren't afraid,' said Yurko. 'But as soon as you heard Grandpa Trohkym coming, you looked scared and hid the empty jar.'

Yurko's grandmother looked at him reproachfully and shook her head …

The girl in felt boots

It was a cold winter morning. The sky in the east was crimson-red, and the trees were covered with frost.

Three girls were making their way along a snow-covered path that led from a farm hidden in a deep ravine. They were hurrying to a New Year's party that was taking place at school. They still had to cover another five kilometres on foot.

Two of the girls, Tania and Galia, were wearing shoes, while the third girl, Olia, was wearing warm felt boots.

'My feet are freezing!' said Tania.

'So are mine!' replied Galia.

Olia was silent. Her feet were not cold. They were warm, but she felt uncomfortable. She felt guilty because she was wearing warm felt boots. 'Why did I put on these warm felt boots?' she thought.

'My feet are really freezing!' groaned Tania again.

'So are mine!' echoed Galia.

Olia remained silent.

Disapproval

A building was being constructed on a vacant lot. The workers excavated a trench for the foundation and a deep pit for the boiler room. A tree was growing in the middle of the construction site: a beautiful cherry tree covered in blossom.

Everybody understood that the tree was doomed and was living out its last days, because workers had already started laying bricks for the walls. The tree had to be cut down, but nobody would lift a hand to do it.

And then somebody suggested, 'Let's ask Fedko.'

This Fedko was a grim, silent, merciless fellow. Two years ago, he had left his wife and his three children, and he had not visited the children once.

Fedko heard his name mentioned and asked the supervisor, 'How much will you pay me to do it?'

When Fedko cut down the cherry tree, everyone left the construction site. They all suddenly had a job to do somewhere else, as long as it was nowhere near the walls of the building.

Later, everyone avoided Fedko and did not want to talk to him. 'Why are you treating me like this?' Fedko asked, 'Somebody had to cut the tree down.'

Yes, somebody had to. Everyone understood that to be true, but somehow, they still disapproved of what Fedko had done.

The wolf's teeth

Once upon a time there was a wolf, as wicked as could be. His jaws were fitted with terrible teeth like knives. He would seize a sheep and rip it to shreds. Everyone feared the wolf, but when it had eaten its full, the ram, passing by, bowed low to it. He wanted to flatter the wolf and said, 'Oh, mighty wolf, how strong and wise you are! I admire you.'

Several times the ram drove little lambs to the wolf for its supper.

But after some time, the wolf grew old. All his teeth fell out, and he could not even eat a chicken. The wolf began to hunt frogs. The ram realised that there was no need to fear the wolf anymore and came to him one day and laughed at him.

'Oh, mighty wolf, I do not fear you anymore. I hate you. You are a pitiful wreck,' he said.

The amazed wolf answered, 'So, it was not me you were praising, but my teeth.'

Why is the water in the well warm?

The tents at a children's camp were pitched under the spreading branches of an oak tree. There were five boys in each tent.

In one of the tents, the boys agreed that at midnight one of them would bring cold water from a nearby well. The well was in a dark ravine in the middle of the forest. It was frightening to walk through the forest at night, and even more frightening to climb down into the ravine, but the boys told each other they were not afraid of anything. Quietly, so as not to wake the others, they got up one at a time and went to get water.

Today was Andriiko's turn. When the sun set, he looked anxiously at the dark forest, and felt he did not have the courage to go down into the ravine in the middle of the night. Secretly, so the other boys would not see him, he took the bucket, ran for the water, and hid it in the bushes behind the tent.

At midnight he took the bucket from behind the bushes and put it on a little table in front of the tent.

It was a hot night, and everyone would be thirsty. Whoever woke up first would go straight to get a cup of water.

Andriiko could not sleep. He felt anxious. Would anyone notice that he had brought the water in the evening and not during the night?

In the morning, Mykola, Andriiko's friend, asked, 'Why is the water from the well warm?'

He asked and looked Andriiko straight in the eye. All the boys were looking at him.

'That's how it was,' he replied. 'The water in the well was warm.'

Andriiko could not look his friends in the eye.

Honey in his pocket

Dmytro, Vasyl and Yurko were getting ready for a walk in the forest. Their mothers gave them each of them a *pyrizhok*.[42] The friends wrapped their *pyrizhky* in paper and put them in their pockets.

Yurko's mother also gave him a little jar of honey. She said to her son, 'Don't tell the other boys you have honey. Find a place in the forest to sit and eat it by yourself.'

Yurko put the little jar of honey in his pocket. The friends walked into the forest and finally found a clearing where they could sit and rest. They were hungry and took out their *pyrizhky* and ate them.

Suddenly a bee flew up to Yurko, settled on his trousers and tried to crawl into his pocket. Then a second bee came, and a third. A host of bees came flying, and they all tried to crawl into Yurko's pocket.

Dmytro and Vasyl were amazed. 'What have you got there?' they asked.

And the bees just kept on coming.

Yurko took the jar of honey from his pocket and threw it into the grass. It was soon covered in bees.

Yurko lowered his head, and Vasyl and Dmytro laughed. 'So that's what you were hiding!' they said.

The lilac bush

A lilac bush grew near a pond. In spring it was covered with light blue flowers.

Whenever anyone came to the pond, they smiled as soon as they saw the lilac-coloured flowers. It was as if a piece of the blue sky had fallen to Earth. That is what the colour was like.

But one day a gloomy man came to the pond. He broke several branches off the lilac bush and took them somewhere.

Some young hikers were in the area. They came to the pond, washed themselves, and had a rest. As they left, they broke off many of the flowering branches.

There was no longer a flowering bush by the pond, and it seemed as if there was a little less of the blue sky.

People coming to the pond no longer smile. There are fewer smiles in the world.

Ingratitude

Grandpa Andrii invited his grandson Matvii to visit him.

Grandpa Andrii placed a big bowl of honey and some white bagels on the table.

'Help yourself to some honey, Matviiko,' he invited his guest.[43] 'If you want, you can eat it with a spoon; it you want, you can dip the bagels in it.'

Matvii ate the honey with a spoon, and then he dipped the bagels in it. He ate so much he could hardly breathe. He wiped the perspiration from his face, sighed, and asked, 'What sort of honey is that, Grandpa, linden tree or buckwheat?'

'Why?' asked Grandpa Andrii in amazement. 'I treated you to buckwheat honey.'

'I think linden tree honey is tastier,' said Matvii, and yawned. After eating so much he felt sleepy.

Grandpa Andrii felt a sharp pain in his heart. He said nothing, but his grandson continued, 'And the flour in the bagels—is that made from spring wheat or winter wheat?'

Grandpa Andrii turned pale. His heart felt unbearable pain, and he found it hard to breathe. He closed his eyes and groaned.

The rubbish heap

Zina is already in grade two. Her mother wants her to start helping and says, 'Zina, I would like you to sweep the house every day and take the dust out to the rubbish heap.'

Zina begins to sweep the house every day, but she does not want to take the dust out to the rubbish heap. It is quite a long way to walk, on the other side of the vegetable garden. She looks at the rubbish heap, which is surrounded by a little fence, and thinks, 'I could just sweep the dust under the wardrobe.'

Zina sweeps the house and puts the dust under her wardrobe, which is next to her bed.

One day Zina comes home from school and sees her mother and father sitting together. They take the wardrobe and move it. Where the wardrobe had been is a whole pile of dust.

Zina hangs her head, and her face turns red.

Her father brings the little fence from outside and puts it around the pile of dust.

'What are you doing, Dad?' asks Zina.

We need to put a fence around the rubbish heap. It's not out behind the vegetable garden anymore; it's in the house.

Dad puts the fence around the pile of dust and moves Zina's bed next to it.

Zina is embarrassed and begs, 'Oh, Dad! I'll take the dust outside! I don't want the rubbish heap to be in our house.'

Zina gets a bucket and takes the dust out to the rubbish heap behind the vegetable garden. Then she washes the floor.

The horse ran away

The mathematics teacher gave the grade four students a problem to solve independently. All of them leant over their exercise books and concentrated on their work.

Vitia was sitting in the back row. He had completed the problem. Suddenly a note fell on his desk.

'That's probably another note from Petryk,' thought Vitia. 'I bet he wants to borrow my skates again. Why should I always lend him my skates?'

'Ivan Petrovych,' said Vitia, raising his hand, 'Someone threw me a note … Are you allowed to write notes during the lesson?'

'You're not allowed write notes during the lesson,' said Ivan Petrovych. 'But if someone did write you a note, then it's not good to tell the teacher about it, Vitia. A note is a secret that should only be known to you and your friend. And you are exposing that secret. Take the note, hide it, and read it during the break.'

Vitia's face turned red. The class fell silent. From time to time some of the boys looked at Vitia, and in their eyes he saw surprise and indignation.

Vitia opened the note and read it. 'Vitia,' Petryk had written, 'I have drawn a horse with a fiery mane. If you want, I can give it to you.'

During the break Vitia went up to Petryk.

'Give me the horse,' said Vitia.

'The horse ran away,' answered Petryk quietly.

How Natalka bought a trick from the fox

A fox came to the market and brought a basket full of goods to sell. The basket was covered with a white cloth. It was wintertime, and the fox found a place, pulled her fur collar up around her neck, and placed her basket on a table. When she lifted her cloth, everyone saw that the basket was full of tricks.

A school student named Natalka was walking through the market and saw that the fox was selling tricks. She went over and chose one—a little wooden girl holding her hands to her head and pitifully wailing, 'Oh, my head is aching!'

Natalka bought the trick and took it home. She had to do some homework, but she did not feel like it. 'I have a headache,' Natalka complained to her mother. 'I can't do my homework.'

'All right, Natalka, dear, go and lie down,' said her mother.

Natalka lay down on her bed, but immediately forgot her headache, and said to her mother, 'Mum, I'm going to go out skating.'

'But you have a headache!' said her mother in amazement.

Natalka blushed with shame.

'I'll take the trick back to the market and return it to the fox. I don't need her cunning tricks,' decided Natalka. She went back to the market, but when she put her hand into her pocket to find the little wooden girl, it had disappeared.

'Where did it go?' wondered Natalka. She had no idea where the trick had gone. She told her mother all about it, and her mother said, 'You frightened the trick away. It's afraid of your conscience.'

'Where is my conscience? How did it know I had one?' asked Natalka.

'Because you were ashamed,' said her mother.

The hardest test

Two grade four students, Dmytryk and Sashko, are bending over their sheets of paper. Today they have their most difficult maths test. Galyna Grygorivna said that whatever mark they get on this test will be their mark for the year.

Dmytryk has already solved the problem and is copying his answer from his rough notes onto a clean sheet of paper. Dmytryk is the best maths student in the class.

Sashko has been given the seat next to Dmytryk to help him improve, because Sashko is lagging behind. But even though he is a slow thinker, he is a very proud boy. He will never copy someone else's work. Even now, Dmytryk has placed his rough notes where Sashko can see them, as if to say, 'Look, here is the solution to the problem.' But Sashko is frowning, fixing his eyes on his own sheet of paper, and will not look at Dmytryk's work.

Dmytryk feels sorry for Sashko. His heart aches with a feeling of foreboding. Once again it is going to be like it always is after a test. Dmytryk will have a top mark, and Sashko will just manage to scrape a pass. Perhaps Galyna Grygorivna will not even give Sashko a mark, saying that he has not yet earnt a mark and needs to do a bit more work. Dmytryk will be ashamed to look Sashko in the eyes. For two weeks Sashko will be silent and brooding. And when Dmytryk asks him to go somewhere (it is already warm enough to swim in the river), Sashko will say he does not have time, because he has to help his mother …

With a deep sigh, Dmytryk deliberately makes a mistake. He leaves out one line of his answer, so that he can get just a pass mark on this difficult test, the same as Sashko. A wave of joy pours over Dmytryk's heart, and it stops aching. He has passed the hardest test.

How two boys ate some honey

A mother sent her two seven-year-old twins, Oleh and Roman, to visit their grandfather in a neighbouring village. The brothers were delighted. They had not visited their grandfather for a long time. He had tasty apples growing in his garden. 'We'll get to eat some,' they thought.

The brought their grandfather a shirt that their mother had embroidered. Their grandfather thanked them and said, 'Go into the garden, boys, and pick yourselves some apples.'

Oleh and Roman ran into the garden. There were lots of apples and they were all tasty. The boys climbed into one apple tree and picked some apples. Then they climbed into another tree, and the apples were even more delicious. It was all so tempting.

When they had eaten their fill of apples, their grandfather put a jar of honey on the table. Oleh and Roman had one spoonful each, but they could not eat any more. As they got ready to return home, their grandfather gave them the jar of honey and said, 'Your mother should try the honey, too.'

The boys set off for home. It was a long way to walk, and after a while they were hungry. They sat under a willow tree and ate a little of the honey. They walked on, then stopped again and ate what seemed like just a little honey, but there was not much left in the jar. Then they stopped a third time and polished the honey off.

When they reached home, they sat under a maple tree and thought, 'What will Mum say?' Their mother came out of the house and saw her boys sitting under the maple tree, crying.

'What are you crying for, boys?' asked their mother in surprise.

When they told her how they had eaten all the honey, their mother seemed very happy and laughed.

The boys were surprised, and asked, 'What are you so happy about, Mum?'

'I'm happy that you are crying,' she said.

Mum sent me

Some boys were playing with a ball in the meadow. Ihor boasted, 'I can throw the straightest!'

The other boys laughed, 'Don't brag, Ihor.'

But Ihor wanted to prove he was the most accurate. He said, 'You see that white shirt hanging in that yard? I'll hit it with the ball.'

It was Grandma Yaryna's yard. She lived next door to Ihor. Ihor threw the ball and hit the shirt, leaving a black spot on it.

Grandma Yaryna saw who threw the ball and went to Ihor's mother to complain.

When Ihor came home, his mother already knew about his mischief. She told Ihor, 'Grandma Yaryna is old, and it is difficult for her to wash clothes. She washed her shirts and put them out to dry, and you dirtied one. Now she has to wash it again.'

Ihor stood hanging his head.

'Go to Grandma Yaryna and ask her forgiveness,' she said.

Ihor went next door to Grandma Yaryna's house, approached her, and stood sulking.

'What do you want to say, Ihor?' asked Grandma Yaryna.

'Mum sent me to ask your forgiveness,' he said.

Grandma Yaryna looked at the boy without saying anything. Then she sighed deeply and went inside.

From the willow to the poplar

A poplar grows at one end of a quiet, wide street, and a willow grows at the other end. The end of the street where the willow grows is slightly higher, and the end where the poplar grows is slightly lower, so it is downhill from the willow to the poplar and uphill from the poplar to the willow, though the slope is hardly noticeable.

In winter, boys like to skate on this street. Two brothers, Yurko and Pavlyk, came to ride their sled there. Yurko is in grade three and Pavlyk is in grade one. They did not have any skates, but they brought a light sled with iron runners. Yurko said, 'We can ride our sled here.'

'All right,' said Pavlyk. 'But how can we ride our sled here? There is no slope.'

'I will pull you from the willow to the poplar, and you can pull me from the poplar to the willow,' suggested Yurko.

'All right,' agreed his brother with delight.

Pavlyk sat in the sled and Yurko pulled him from the willow to the poplar. He galloped along and the sled raced over the snow. When they reached the poplar, Yurko sat in the sled and Pavlyk pulled him all the way back. The sled now moved slowly. 'Why can't I pull you as fast as you pulled me?' asked Pavlyk.

'Because you are small,' answered Yurko. 'You are still weak and not as strong as me.'

Pavlyk felt ashamed to be weak. He tried to pull Yurko faster. They pulled each other back and forth several times, Yurko pulling Pavlyk from the willow to the poplar, and Pavlyk pulling Yurko from the poplar to the willow.

Grandpa Karpo was sitting in the sun nearby, on a dry tree stump. Yurko boasted to him, 'Look, Grandpa, how strong I am. The sled is racing along … But Pavlyk is weak.'

'He might be weak, but he's honest,' answered the old man. 'And you might be strong, but you are tricking your weaker brother.'

Yurko stopped and hung his head. Pavlyk was surprised and asked the old man, 'Grandpa, why is Yurko dishonest?'

At Uncle Matvii's house

On Saturday, little Demko's mother told him, 'Tomorrow we're going to Krutoiarivka to visit Uncle Matvii. He has lots of apples. There will be a bowl of apples on the table. Your uncle will probably invite us to eat an apple. Make sure you behave properly, Demko. Only take the smallest apple, and make sure you say "thank you". And then, no matter how many times Uncle Matvii offers you an apple, say "no, thank you".'

Demko carefully remembered what his mother had taught him.

The next day they visited Uncle Matvii, who sat at the table, while Demko and his mother sat on the sofa. There was a bowl of apples on the table. Demko wanted to take a big red apple, but he knew he must not … He was planning on taking another apple that was not very big, but not the smallest either.

Uncle Matvii talked with his mother for a long time. They talked about the harvest and the weather, but Uncle Matvii did not mention the apples.

Demko asked his mother in a whisper, 'If Uncle Matvii does not offer us any apples, should I say "thank you" or "no, thank you"?' His whisper was so loud that as well as Uncle Matvii hearing it, Auntie Motria heard it as she washed the dishes in the next room.

The room became very quiet. The mother's face turned red with shame, but Uncle Matvii's face was not red at all.

The guilty hand

A mother sent her five-year-old son Petryk to the shops.

'Here are fifteen *kopiika*[44],' she said. 'Hold them in your right hand, so you don't forget that they are for you to buy a loaf of bread. And you can hold these fifteen *kopiika* in your left hand. They are for you to buy yourself an ice-cream.'

Petryk ran off to the shop. A few minutes later he came back, eating what was left of his ice-cream.

'Where's the bread,' asked his mother.

'I didn't buy it,' said Petryk.

'Why didn't you buy it?' asked his mother.

'I lost the money,' he said.

'You lost the money?' said his mother. 'Then you should have bought the bread and not the ice-cream.'

'But I lost the fifteen *kopiika* that were in my right hand,' said Petryk, 'And not the fifteen *kopiika* that were in my left hand.'

His mother just shook her head.

They sat down to have supper. Petryk's mother poured soup into the bowls, but there was no bread to eat with it.

'Mum, is there any bread?' asked Petryk.

'No, you lost the money, didn't you,' she said.

Petryk picked up his spoon in his left hand and began to eat his soup.

'Why are you eating with your left hand?' asked his mother in surprise.

'I want my right hand to know what happens when it loses money,' said Petryk.

The sound of an axe

One Sunday, nine-year-old Yashko was returning from a neighbouring village with his father. They had been to visit Yashko's grandmother. The path led through a forest.

It was a clear spring day. It was not yet hot, but the sun was already beating down. It was nice and cool in the shade of the trees. The boy's father said, 'Let's have a little rest.'

They sat on the grass. Suddenly they heard the chopping of an axe in the distance.

'Someone's cutting down a tree,' said Yashko's father with concern. 'How dare they? No-one is allowed to cut trees in this forest. Let's go quickly, Yashko, and catch the thief.'

They got up quickly and walked towards the sound of the axe. Soon they could see people. Two men were standing near a graceful oak tree. One was chopping while the other had a rest.

Yashko could see that his father was becoming more and more agitated.

'That is how you destroy a forest,' he said with indignation.

But when they drew close enough to recognise the men, Yashko's father suddenly lowered his head and fell silent. He seemed to be ashamed of something. He hid behind some bushes and took Yashko with him.

'It's Uncle Mykola chopping the tree,' mumbled Yashko's father with a sigh. 'Let's go home, son.'

Quietly, so as not to be seen, the father walked out of the forest, leading his son by the hand.

Yashko could not understand why his father's indignation had given way to awkwardness. 'Dad, they're still thieves, aren't they?' he asked.

His father did not answer.

Grandma and Petryk

One warm spring day, Petryk's grandmother decided to take him for a walk in the forest. As they prepared to leave, she gave Petryk a basket of food to eat and a flask of water. Petryk was a lazy boy, and he soon tired of carrying the basket. Then his grandmother carried the basket of food for him.

In the forest, they sat down by a bush to rest. Soon a little bird came flying to a tree nearby. She was carrying a hair in her beak. Petryk got up very quietly, so as not to frighten the bird, and in the tree he discovered a large nest made of hair.

The bird flew away and soon returned with another hair in its beak. Petryk's eyes opened wide with astonishment.

'Grandma,' he whispered, 'Has she really brought hairs one at a time and built such a big nest?'

'Yes, one hair at a time,' said his grandmother. 'That's a very hard working little bird.'

Petryk became thoughtful. A minute later he said, 'Grandma, can I carry the basket of food again? And I'll carry your coat. OK?'

The glass mouse

There was a little glass mouse on Olenka's windowsill.

One day she accidentally moved it too close to the edge of the windowsill, and it fell to the floor and broke into pieces. Little Olenka was frightened. What would her mother say? She had bought that glass mouse on the same day that Olenka had brought home a kitten from her neighbour's house. The kitten had grown into a big, grey cat, but the mouse had remained little.

'What can I do?' wondered little Olenka, as she picked up the pieces. She hid all the broken pieces of glass in their large brick oven. It was the beginning of summer, and they were not lighting a fire in it.

In the evening, Olenka's mother asked her, 'Where is your little mouse?'

'I don't know,' answered Olenka, pretending to be surprised. 'I wonder where it could have got to?'

Her mother made a bit of a fuss about it, but she went and bought a new mouse at the shop.

Autumn came, and Olenka's mother cleaned out the oven, preparing to light a fire there. She discovered the remains of the glass mouse.

'Who broke it?' asked Olenka's mother.

'Probably the cat,' said Olenka, lowering her head.

'What a clever cat we have,' said her mother with a smile. 'He broke the mouse, collected all the pieces, and hid them in the oven.'

Olenka's face turned bright red with shame. The little girl thought, 'How did Mummy know that it was me that broke the mouse and not the cat.' Her mother also knew that Olenka was thinking about how she had been dishonest, and that she was too ashamed to raise her head.

Little Olenka covered her face with her hands and closed her eyes tightly. She felt as if her mother could read her thoughts.

Three *pyrizhky*

Fedko and Mykolka went to visit their grandmother. She lived at the other end of the village, so they did not see her very often.

Their grandmother was overjoyed to see them. She sat them at the table and served up a bowl of honey and three large *pyrizhky* filled with sweet cottage cheese.[45] The boys each took a *pyrizhok* and started eating. They were delicious! And so was the honey! They dipped their *pyrizhky* in the honey and could not take their eyes off the third one.

Fedko thought, 'I wouldn't mind eating another *pyrizhok*, but it wouldn't be fair for me to eat two *pyrizhky* and for Mykolka to only eat one. What can I do?'

Mykolka thought, 'I wouldn't mind eating another *pyrizhok*, but it wouldn't be fair for me to eat two *pyrizhky* and for Fedko to only eat one. What can I do?'

The boys each ate up one *pyrizhok*, then sat looking at the third one, sitting on the plate.

Their grandmother came over and looked at her grandsons, sitting there silently with knitted brows. 'Why aren't you eating, boys?' she asked them. The boys just looked from under their brows at the remaining *pyrizhok*. Their grandmother picked it up, broke it in half, and offered it to them. 'Eat up boys,' she said.

The boys hung their heads even lower, from shame, but they took half each and ate in silence.

The doll in the rain

Zina was going to sleep, while outside a thunderstorm was raging. Dark clouds swept in from the Dnipro River, and thunder rumbled. Rain beat like a drum on the iron roof.

There was a flash of lightning, and for a moment everything could be seen as clear as day. Zina could see the rain pouring down, puddles of water in the yard, and—oh, what was that? Her doll Zoia was lying on a bench out in the rain!

She had forgotten Zoia and left her on the bench. How did that happen? Why didn't she remember Zoia as she was getting ready for bed? Why didn't she think of her when the thunderstorm began?

These thoughts made Zina very sad, and she began to cry. But the thing that really made her sad was that her Zoia was lying out there on a bench in the cold rain.

Zina got out of bed, quietly opened the door, and ran outside. The rain soaked her nightdress in an instant. The little girl ran to the bench, picked up Zoia, and hugged her to her chest.

When Zina opened the door into the house, her mother turned on the light and looked with fear at the empty bed. Then her mother saw her with her doll hugged to her chest, and she took a deep breath. She found a towel and wiped Zina dry, and helped her put on a dry nightdress. As she dried Zina, she said, 'You must dry Zoia as well. How could you leave her out on the bench?'

'It will never happen again, Mummy,' said Zina.

They helped themselves to apples

A big apple tree grew next to an old lady's house. It bore so many apples that its branches were hanging low. Autumn came, and the apples ripened.

Three young boys—Petro, Mykola and Ivan—were walking home from school, laughing. They saw the apples on the tree, red and sweet-smelling.

Petro said, 'Let's ask the old lady if we can have some apples.'

They asked her, and she invited them to help themselves. 'Go ahead, boys,' she said, 'Pick some apples and eat them.'

The boys picked a whole bucket of apples and sat down and ate them. They threw the apple cores on the ground near the lady's house. When they had eaten their fill, they got up and went home. They forgot to thank the old lady, and just left the apple cores where they had thrown them.

The old lady got up, sighed, and went to clean up the apple cores. She collected them and gave them to her goat.

To repay kindness with ingratitude is ugly.

Why Pylypko could not sleep

Pylypko found a ballpoint pen on his way to school. It had two colours: blue and red.[46] To change the colour, you just pressed a button.

Pylypko came to school and started writing with the pen he had found. During the break, Petryk approached Pylypko. He took a close look at the pen and said, 'I had a pen just like that, but I lost it.'

Pylypko felt a hot wave going through his body and he turned red. He could not look Petryk in the eyes and was relieved when Petryk finally left him alone.

After classes, Pylypko walked home, but he took a different route to his usual one. He walked along the riverbank and over the dam. As he crossed the dam bridge, he stopped and took the pen out of his pocket. He stood and peered down at the cascading waterfall and the dark whirlpool below. Then he threw the pen into the whirlpool and ran home.

The following morning, during the break, Petryk came up to Pylypko and asked, 'Where's your pen?'

'I lost mine, too,' answered Pylypko.

'That's strange,' whispered Petryk.

That night, Pylypko hardly slept at all.

Why didn't you look for my glasses yesterday?

Myshko came home from school very happy. As soon as he walked in the door he shouted, 'Grandma! Grandma! Come quickly and look at my school diary. We've been given our marks, and my marks are good!'

Myshko's grandmother took the diary in her hands and wanted to look at Myshko's marks, but she had mislaid her glasses, and without them she could not see properly. Myshko began to look for the glasses. He looked on the shelf and crawled under the table. Then he crawled under his grandmother's bed, and there, against the wall, he found the glasses. His grandmother had dropped them there without noticing.

'Why didn't you look for my glasses when I asked you yesterday?' said Myshko's grandmother reproachfully. Myshko didn't know what to say.

The birthday party

Nina has a big family: her mother, her father, two brothers, two sisters and her grandmother. Nina is the youngest—she is nine years old. Grandma is the oldest—she is eighty-two. When the family has a meal, Grandma's hand shakes. Everyone is used to this and tries not to pay any attention. If someone looks at Grandma's hand and wonders why it is shaking, it shakes even more. When Grandma uses a spoon, the spoon shakes, and food drips on the table.

Soon it will be Nina's birthday. Her mother has told her there will be a special meal for her birthday, and that she and Grandma will bake a big cake. Nina can invite her friends.

The guests arrive. Mum covers the table with a white tablecloth. Nina realises that her grandmother will soon sit down at the table and her hand will shake. Her friends will laugh and tell everyone at school.

Nina quietly says to her mother, 'Mum, is it all right if Grandma doesn't sit at the table with us?'

'Why?' asks her mother in surprise.

'Her hand shakes … and she drops food on the table,' says Nina.

Her mother turns pale. Without saying a word, she takes the white tablecloth from the table and puts it away in the cupboard. She sits silently for a long time, and then says, 'Grandma is sick today. There won't be any birthday party. Happy birthday, Nina. My wish for you is that you will become a fine human being.'

The glass man

A boy had a little friend—a glass man. He was completely transparent and had an amazing ability. He always knew what the boy was thinking and feeling. If the boy had not done his homework and wanted to go out to play, the glass man would become a little darker, so he was no longer completely transparent, and he would say, 'You should not think like that, my boy. First do your work, then go out to play.' The boy would feel ashamed and would sit down to do his homework, then go out to play. The little glass man would become transparent again and say nothing more.

One day the boy's best friend, who he sat next to at school, fell ill. A day passed, and then a second day, and the boy did not think of his friend at all. Then he noticed that the glass man had become as dark as a storm cloud.

'What have I done or thought that was wrong?' asked the boy anxiously.

'You haven't done anything wrong or thought anything wrong,' said the glass man, 'But you have forgotten all about your friend.'

The boy felt ashamed, and he went to see his sick friend. He took some flowers and a huge apple that his mother had given him.

In this way, the glass man taught the boy how to live. The glass man was his conscience.

The chair with a broken leg

This happened in a small eight-year school.[47] Half an hour before classes began each day, a rostered student would come to each classroom. They would wipe dust off the desks, wash the blackboards and water the plants.

One day the student on duty in grade eight went to move the teacher's chair, and one of its legs fell off. 'Why the heck did this have to happen to me?' thought the boy. 'I'll take the chair to grade seven and swap it for the chair there.' He quietly opened the door to grade seven, placed the chair with the broken leg by the teacher's desk, and took the good chair. The grade seven student on duty was watering some flowers and did not notice that someone had come into the classroom.

But when the grade seven student went to straighten the chair, its leg fell off, and he thought, 'I'll swap it for the chair in grade six.' He quietly opened the door into grade six, put the chair with the broken leg by the desk, and took the good chair. The grade six student on duty did not notice anything, as he was washing the blackboard. But then he touched the chair, and the leg fell off again.

The grade six student took the broken chair to grade five, the grade five student took it to grade four, the grade four student took it to grade three, the grade three student took it to grade two, and the grade two student took it to grade one.

The grade one student on duty touched the chair and the leg fell off. The little boy stood next to the chair and cried. The teacher entered the classroom and saw the boy standing there and crying.

'Why are you crying, Yurko?' asked the teacher.

'Because … I accidentally broke the chair,' said the boy.

'What good, honest children we have,' thought the teacher.

I put my nesting box up in the forest

The grade one students were preparing to greet the spring birds returning from warmer lands. It was agreed that each student would make a nesting box for starlings and hang it on a tree near the school.

A week passed. Every day children would bring their handmade wooden houses and hang them on the trees. The school yard was filled with children's joyful voices. One fine day, the teacher led her class out into the school yard. They gazed happily at their nesting boxes, where birds had settled into their new homes.

'Where is your nesting box?' the teacher asked Hryts, who was standing to one side.

'I put it up in the forest,' answered Hryts.

The teacher was surprised. After a moment's silence, she asked, 'Why did you take your nesting box to the forest?'

'Because starlings want to live there, too,' said Hryts. 'There are so many starlings there!'

The big bucket

Fourteen little children came to school in the evening to water some apple tree seedlings. Young apple trees need extra water in autumn, because the soil is dry after the summer heat. The teacher put fourteen buckets in the orchard: thirteen little buckets and one big bucket.

The children quickly grabbed all the little buckets, and only the big bucket was left. The only student left without a bucket was little blue-eyed Myshko. He was a very slow and thoughtful little boy.

'Never mind, Myshko,' said the teacher. 'Take the big bucket and carry it half full.'

The children began to water the young apple trees. All of them were carrying water in small buckets, except for Myshko, who was using the big bucket. And he was not carrying it half full. He was filling it up. Everyone carried their buckets easily, except for Myshko, who was finding it difficult.

One girl said, 'You need to wake up, Myshko. You should have quickly grabbed a small bucket.' Someone laughed.

When they finished watering, the teacher said, 'Now you can pick some apples to take home and give a treat to your mothers and grandmothers. You can fill up your buckets.'

Myshko's bicycle

Myshko's parents bought him a bicycle. He lives right next to the school. There is an orchard between his parents' house and the school yard, so there is no point in riding a bike to school. Myshko walked his bike to school, as if leading a horse by the reins.

The other boys surrounded Myshko. They felt the tyres, pedals, handles and light. They all liked the bike and were jealous of Myshko.

'Well, why don't you ride it?' said Fedko, stepping back from the bike as if he was not thinking of riding it.

'Do you think I really want to ride it?' said Myshko, as if he could not care less. 'You take it and try it out.'

A delighted Fedko took the handles, sat on the bike and rode around the school sports area. He kept riding until the bell went for lessons.

At the first break, Ivan rode the bike, at the second break—Stepan, at the third break—Serhii, and at the fourth break—Olia. The children stayed back to ride after school as well. The bike was passed from hand to hand. By four o'clock everyone had had a ride.

Myshko walked his bike home at half past four, as if leading a horse by the reins.

'Where have you been riding all this time?' asked his mother. 'What were you thinking?'

'I didn't ride it,' said Myshko.

'What do you mean, you didn't ride it?' asked his mother.

'The other boys rode it, and the girls,' said Myshko.

His mother gave a sigh of relief, and said, as if to herself, 'The only think I was afraid of was that you would ride it all by yourself.'

Repentance

Eight-year-old Kostia and ten-year-old Pavlo are brothers. On Sunday, their mother gave them a loaf of bread and said, 'Boys, I want you to visit Grandpa Yukhym at the beehives. Take him this loaf of bread and this clean shirt.'

The boys took the bread and the clean shirt and headed off into the forest. The beehives were taken from a farm into the forest over the summer, and that was where Grandpa Yukhym lived from spring through to autumn.

The old man was very pleased to see the boys. He told them about his work and showed them how the bees toiled away.

Then the old man sat down on a broad tree stump and told the boys, 'Pour some honey into this bowl, boys, and have something to eat.'

The boys quickly poured a full bowl of honey. They cut up the loaf of bread they had just brought and began to eat.

They sat at the table, silently dipping big chunks of bread in the honey and eating. The old man just sat on the tree stump and watched them. The apiary fell silent. The only sound was the buzzing of the bees.

The boys finished the honey. Only a small crust remained of the loaf of bread. Grandpa Yukhym asked, 'Would you like to eat some more?'

'No, thank you,' said the boys, and prepared to leave.

The old man still sat silently on the tree stump, sometimes chuckling, as if at his own thoughts.

The boys looked at the crust of bread—all that was left of the loaf they had brought—and hung their heads. They quietly said good-bye to the old man and headed off home.

At the edge of the forest, the boys sat down on the path. They were silent for a long time. They looked back at the forest, where Grandpa Yukhym lived from early spring to late autumn.

With a deep sigh, the boys got up and returned home.

How Pavlyk copied Zina's homework

Pavlyk came to school looking worried. He had spent a long time on a maths problem set for homework but had been unable solve it. Now he had only one thought: whose homework could he copy?

Zina arrived. She was good at solving maths problems. Pavlyk asked her, 'Zina, how many steps were there in the maths problem?'

'Three,' answered Zina. 'Couldn't you solve it?'

'No, I couldn't do it,' said Pavlyk. 'Can I copy yours, Zina?'

'Oh, Pavlyk, why don't you think for yourself?' said Zina, but she gave him her exercise book.

Pavlyk copied the first step, and then the second. When he came to the third step, he noticed that Zina had made a mistake. She had written 32 instead of 23. Pavlyk wrote the correct answer in his own exercise book, but he did not tell Zina about her mistake.

The teacher collected the exercise books to correct the homework. The next day she said, 'Pavlyk has full marks. Well done, Pavlyk. You worked well on that problem. Zina, I had to take a mark off you, because you made a mistake.'

Zina was surprised and looked over at Pavlyk. Pavlyk lowered his head, and his face turned red.

Petryk left his exercise book at home

Yesterday the children were sad when they came to school. They knew that the following day their teacher, Mariia Petrivna, would be travelling far, far away, to live by the deep blue sea. That is where her husband—a pilot—was living, and she was travelling with her son to join him.

During lessons everyone was quiet and gloomy. They could not forget that after the final bell, they would be saying goodbye to their teacher and would never see her again. Every student wanted to write and read and answer questions as well as possible, so as to earn Mariia Petrivna's praise.

During the arithmetic lesson the teacher said, 'I will not be asking anyone to come out to the board today. Open your exercise books, and I will check your homework.'

When the teacher reached Petryk's desk, he did not have an exercise book. Petryk blushed with shame and said, 'I left it at home.'

Mariia Petrivna did not say anything, and she also blushed. Petryk sat there wishing he could sink through the floor.

The next day Mariia Petrivna caught a bus to the station, which was about five kilometres from the village. She bought tickets and sat waiting for the train, which was due soon.

The sun rose, and Petryk approached Mariia Petrivna. He was puffing from walking quickly.

'Mariia Petrivna,' he said quietly. 'Here is my exercise book. I did solve the problem … I don't know how I could have left it at home yesterday!'

A dirty word

Myshko, who was in grade seven, went into the toilet. He picked up a piece of charcoal from the floor and wrote a dirty, offensive word on the wall.

'So, you've learnt to write?' Myshko heard a stern voice behind him and looked around fearfully. It was one of the teachers, Mykola Vasylovych.

'Well, let's see if you can read what you have written,' he said.

Myshko did not reply. He had written such a dirty word that he could not make his tongue say it. Mykola Vasylovych was also silent. Then he asked, 'Do you know who works as a cleaner in our school?'

'Auntie Mariia,' whispered Myshko.

'Let's go and find Auntie Mariia and ask her to paint over this sample of your literacy,' said the teacher.

Myshko was so ashamed his hands went cold.

'We don't need to get Auntie Mariia,' he said through his tears, and he wiped away the word with the sleeve of his white shirt. But there was still a black mark on the wall.

'I'll bring some clay and a brush,' begged Myshko. 'Please forgive me.'

'It is not for me to forgive you,' said Mykola Vasylovych sternly. 'With that dirty word you have insulted your mother. You have insulted Auntie Mariia. You have insulted all women. It is your mother you should ask for forgiveness.'

'I couldn't do that … I would be too ashamed,' said Myshko.

'If you are too ashamed to ask forgiveness today, ask for it in a year, or two years, or even ten years. But you should not dare to say the sacred words "I love you" to a girl until she has forgiven you for that dirty, offensive word,' said the teacher.

Myshko wept.

The years passed, and Myshko became a young man, but he could not forget what he had done as an adolescent. And then Myshko fell in love with a girl named Olesia. Olesia could not understand why Myshko was sometimes silent and melancholy.

One day Myshko said to Olesia, 'Forgive me, Olesia, for insulting you.' And he told her how he had once insulted all mothers and all women.

Olesia looked at him in disbelief and asked, 'Why didn't you just forget about it? It was so long ago … And why were you silent?'

'I could not carry the guilt any longer. I have judged myself for all these years. Now I would like you to either condemn me or forgive me.'

'I forgive you,' said Olesia quietly.

Who will fetch some firewood?

On the edge of the village lived a widow with her three sons. Two of her sons were already young men—tall, strong, and impressive to look at. The youngest son, Yurko, was still an adolescent, small and skinny as a rake. It was winter. The ground was deep in snow, a cold northerly wind was blowing, and frost was everywhere.

The mother quietly said, as if to herself, but so that her children could hear her, 'It's cold, but we have no firewood to light a fire. I wonder who could fetch some wood?'

The two older sons said nothing. They kept their heads down and looked at the floor.

'I'll go and get some wood, Mum,' said the youngest son.

'You're not afraid of the frost?' asked his mother, looking at the two older boys.

'No, I'm not afraid,' said Yurko, putting on his coat.

'All right, my boy, thank you,' said his mother with a sigh. And she kissed him goodbye.

Yurko left, and it became very quiet in the house. It was as if everyone was listening to see what would happen next. Even the wind outside fell silent.

The older brothers raised their heads, looked into their mother's eyes, and said, 'We'll go into the forest too, Mum.'

'Thank you, my boys,' whispered the mother, and gave a sigh of relief.

Collect her tears

Anatolii in grade seven was friends with a girl in his class named Olha. He was a year older than her, and good at mathematics, and he often helped her solve maths problems.

One day Anatolii and Olha came to school very early, before any teachers or students had arrived. Olha asked Anatolii to help her with some algebra. The two of them sat at a desk in their classroom. They were so involved in solving the problems that they did not notice their friends start arriving for their lessons, or their amused faces as they looked in at the window. They only noticed when their friends started joking about them being a bride and groom.

Anatolii was mortified by their jokes. He went up to Olha during the break and angrily told her, 'Don't come near me again. It's your fault they are laughing at me.'

Olha looked at Anatolii in surprise. 'What have I done wrong?' she asked, and added, 'Don't take any notice of their stupid jokes.'

Anatolii swore at the girl, using a dirty, hurtful word. Olha burst into tears. She cried for a long time and did not come to the next lesson.

Anatolii came to his senses. 'I insulted her,' he thought. 'What will she think of me now?'

The boy still felt bad when he arrived home. His conscience tormented him. He could not get the girl's words out of his head, or the sound of her shaking voice. He could still see her, all by herself, leaning against the window. That night he told his mother all about it.

'Mum,' he said, 'Tell me what I should do to make Olha forget the rude word I said to her.'

His mother thought about it for a long time. 'Will your conscience permit you to repeat that word to me?' she asked.

'No, Mum … I would rather die than say that word in front of you.'

'Well then … I'll tell you what to do,' she said. 'Collect her tears. Yes, collect every single tear she cried. Only then will the girl forget the word that you cannot say in front of your mother.'

Anatolii lowered his head in deep thought.

Borshch and fresh bread

A mother had two sons, a hard-working one and a lazy one. One day the hard-working son drove to the field to plough, while the lazy son went to the orchard to lie under a pear tree.

The mother wondered, 'What could I make for my sons' dinner that would be nice and tasty?'

She made some borshch[48] with fresh cabbage, sour cream, dill and beetroot. And to go with the borshch, she made some fresh, delicious-smelling bread.

The mother sat by the table and waited for her sons. The sun was already setting, but the hard-working brother had not yet returned home. His lazy brother was not lying under the pear tree any more, but he knew his mother would only serve dinner to the two of them together.

At last, the hard-working brother arrived. He washed, changed his clothes, and sat down to eat. The lazy brother sat down to eat with him.

Their mother poured borshch into two bowls and cut the bread into pieces. The whole house smelled of borshch and fresh bread.

The hard-working brother ate and thanked his mother. 'This borshch you have made is delicious!' he said. The hard-working brother ate up all his borshch and asked for a little more.

But the lazy brother ate one spoonful and frowned, ate a second spoonful and looked sad, and when he had had a third spoonful, he put his spoon down and asked his mother, 'Mum, why doesn't the borshch taste nice?'

'Go and work in the field tomorrow, dear,' answered his mother. 'Then the borshch will taste delicious, and the bread will smell lovely.'

The most delicate tree

Katrusia and her mother were watering apple trees in the garden. There were ten apple trees, and each one was given ten buckets of water from a colourful blue bucket, so they would flourish, bloom and produce fruit.

Katrusia was near the end of her first year at school, so she was good at counting. According to her count, they had already emptied the blue bucket ten times under each apple tree but, for some reason, her mother was now giving each tree an eleventh bucket of water.

'How many buckets do we need to bring for each apple tree?' asked Katrusia.

'Ten,' answered her mother.

'So why are you bringing eleven?' asked the girl.

'Because there is another, very delicate tree,' replied her mother with a smile. 'It also needs to be watered if it is to flourish.'

'What tree is that?' asked Katrusia.

'My conscience,' said her mother.

Five oak trees

Two schoolboys, Dmytryk and Serhiiko, went into the forest with their teacher. The teacher dug up three little oak seedlings for each of them and said, 'Take these oak seedlings home and plant them near your house.'

Dmytryk brought his oak seedlings home. He dug one hole and planted the first seedling. He looked at the second seedling and decided that the root was too weak. He threw it out on the road. He looked at the third seedling and decided the branches were too thin, so he threw it on the road as well.

Serhiiko planted his three oak seedlings, then came out onto the road and saw two seedlings lying in the dust. He picked them up and planted them next to his three seedlings. Serhiiko watered his seedlings, and they grew and produced new leaves. But Dmytryk forgot all about his seedling, and his little tree withered and died.

Many years passed. Dmytryk and Serhiiko grew up and became fathers. Now that they were older, people called Dmytryk 'Dmytro,' and they called Serhiiko 'Serhii.' Dmytro had a little son named Dmytryk, and Serhii had a little son named Serhiiko. One day Dmytryk asked his father, 'Dad, why are there five oak trees growing next to Serhiiko's house and none growing next to ours?'

His father did not reply.

Acorns for an oak grove

Mykola came home from school happy and excited. 'Mum!' he said enthusiastically, 'Today we were given an assignment. Each of us has to collect a hundred acorns in the forest and bring them to school. And guess what the acorns are for?'

'What are they for?' asked his mother.

'We are going to plant an oak grove!' said Mykola. 'Oak trees will grow from the acorns. A hundred years will pass, and two hundred, and three hundred, and the oak trees will still grow there and turn green each year. That's what the teacher told us … Oh, Mum, I'll run to the forest straight away.'

Two hours later Mykola returned from the forest. He had collected not one hundred, but three hundred acorns. 'So that we can have a bigger oak grove!' he said excitedly, and his eyes shone with joy.

At school, they put all the acorns in a big sack, and they put the sack in a storage area at the end of the corridor. A month passed, and winter came, and the sack was still sitting at the end of the corridor. Then the chair used by Auntie Mariia—the school nanny—broke, and Auntie Mariia started sitting on the sack of acorns instead of a chair.

Several times Mykola asked his teacher, 'Why are the acorns still sitting there? They should be put in sand over winter.'

'There's plenty of time,' said his teacher. 'By the way,' she added, 'Our school won the competition for collecting acorns. We are being awarded the challenge banner.'

The chair was mended, and the sack of acorns disappeared. Mykola was overjoyed. That meant they had finally buried the acorns in sand.

It was a long and cold winter. With all its cares, joys and excitement, Mykola forgot about the acorns. Spring came, and the blossom in the orchard came and went. Then the final day of the school year arrived. Mykola's teacher sent him on an errand to the groundsman. 'Go and ask for a sack,' she said. 'We are going to the forest to collect medicinal herbs.'

Mykola ran to see Uncle Fedir, the groundsman. He was standing next to a small table in the storeroom. When Mykola asked him for a sack, he looked in all the nooks and crannies, and then said, 'I'll just tip out these acorns, and then you can take this sack.'

He picked up the sack full of acorns and tipped them out in a corner and handed the sack to Mykola.

'What are you collecting this time?' asked Uncle Fedir.

Mykola looked at the acorns in stunned silence.

The death of a dog

Nina ran to her father and anxiously told him, 'Dad, a dog is dying … It was run over by a car.'

Her father was getting ready to go fishing.

'I don't have time right now,' her father said, waving his hand. 'You can see I'm in a hurry. There are many dogs running around outside.'

Nina began to cry.

'But this is Bilochka,' she said.

'What do you mean Bilochka?' asked her father in surprise.

'My Bilochka,' said Nina. 'She didn't belong to anybody. Someone threw her out when she was small, so she lived in our yard. I made a little house for her there.'

The father listened to Nina in silence, took his rods and went to the pond.

Nina went out onto the road, sobbing, and stood next to the dying dog. Bilochka looked up at Nina, and tears fell from her eyes.

The sun shone brightly in the sky, a nightingale sang in the blossoming orchard, and a swallow twittered over its nest. People walked along the road, talking about their own worries. No one knew that at that moment a dog named Bilochka was dying, and that little Nina's heart was breaking.

The hermit ant

The ants worked all through the summer, building a large storehouse and collecting food for the winter. They filled the little rooms in their storehouse with grain and tiny pieces of sweet grass.

One ant did not want to work with the others. He said, 'Why do I need such a big storehouse? An ant does not need much. A handful of grain is enough. I am a hermit ant. I do not need anybody, and nobody need concern themselves about me. I am a proud hermit ant.'

The ant built himself a little hut and sat in it and thought deep thoughts.

The ants from the large anthill built a brick factory and made bricks to strengthen the walls of their storehouse. They invited the hermit ant to join them, saying, 'Come and join us. It will be more fun with us.'

The hermit ant said, 'Don't disturb my thinking.'

'What are you thinking about, hermit ant?' they asked.

'I am thinking about the meaning of life,' he said.

Winter came. It was warm and cosy in the large anthill, but it was cold in the hermit ant's little hut, and hoar frost appeared on the walls. And he had nothing to eat. The hermit ant shivered from cold and hunger. Finally, he could stand it no longer and left his hut. He asked to be admitted to the large anthill.

'Why don't you just think your deep thoughts, hermit ant?' said the other ants. 'It's easier to think when you are by yourself.'

'It's all right to think when you have enough to eat,' replied the hermit ant, 'But when you are hungry, you cannot think any thoughts.'

It is not so good to be a hermit ant.

How Serhiiko learnt to feel compassion

Serhiiko was playing by the pond. He noticed a girl sitting on the bank.

When he approached her, she said, 'Please don't disturb me. I like listening to the sound of the splashing waves.'

Serhiiko was surprised. He threw a pebble into the pond.

The girl asked him, 'What did you throw into the pond?'

Serhiiko was even more surprised.

'Didn't you see?' he said. 'I threw a stone.'

'No, I couldn't see,' said the girl. 'I'm blind.'

Serhiiko stared at the girl for a long time. He could not imagine what it was like not to be able to see anything.

Night fell, and Serhiiko went to bed. In the middle of the night, he was woken by a noise outside. The wind was howling, and rain was beating against the windowpanes. It was pitch dark inside.

Serhiiko was frightened. He remembered the blind girl. Now, he no longer felt surprised, but his heart ached with compassion. 'How could that poor girl live in darkness all the time?' he thought.

Serhiiko waited impatiently for the sun to rise. He would go and see that blind girl and show her that he cared.

How Petryk became angry

Little Petryk is five years old. His father told him about the heroism of a young soldier during the war against the fascists. The young man was seriously wounded, but he did not abandon his weapon. Until his last breath he kept firing his machine gun and killing enemy soldiers.

Petryk went to the bank of the pond. He wanted to cut the slender branch of an elder tree to make a folk pipe. He cut his finger, and it hurt so much that tears began to flow from his eyes. His finger hurt and he felt sorry for himself, but then he suddenly remembered the heroism of the young soldier, and he felt ashamed of himself.

Petryk wanted his eyes to stop crying, but he could not make them. 'Am I really so faint-hearted?' thought the boy. And he became angry with himself. His anger made his eyes dry up, and his finger did not hurt anymore.

Green mittens

Today a new student named Zoia joined grade two. She is small, with dark blue eyes and blonde pigtails. He parents have come to our village from the far north.

It is winter now, with crackling frosts. Zoia arrived wearing green mittens. She left them in the corridor next to her coat.

The boys and girls gave Zoia a friendly reception. They gave her an interesting book with pictures.

After school, Zoia could not find her green mittens. She felt too ashamed to tell her new friends that her mittens had disappeared. Could it really be that someone had taken them?

Zoia walked home quiet and thoughtful. There was a frost outside, and by the time she reached home her hands were frozen. Her mother asked her, 'Where are your mittens, Zoia?'

'Oh, Mum,' said Zoia, 'I was crossing a bridge over a deep ravine … I took my mittens off for a second, and the wind caught them and carried them down into the ravine.'

'How careless you are,' said her mother reproachfully. 'It is just as well that you still have some other mittens—green, red and white. Which ones will you wear tomorrow?'

'The green ones, Mum,' said Zoia.

Fearful Lonia

A boy named Lonia studies in grade three at our school. He is so shy and fearful that even his mother once told him, as he headed off for school, 'If you are so fearful, even the chickens will peck you.'

Lonia had blushed when he heard those words. They reminded him of something that had happened during the winter. Lonia had been on his way to school, and a large rooster had been perched on his neighbour's gate. Lonia had walked around it, but the rooster had run after him, raising its head as if it wanted to jump on the boy. Lonia had run away from the rooster, and the other children had seen it. Since then, they had teased him.

In the spring, a new girl came to our school and joined grade three. She had blue eyes and blonde hair, and her name was Olia. They sat Olia next to Lonia. She asked him, 'Do you like to swim?'

Lonia mumbled something inaudible.

'Can you jump into the water?' she asked.

Lonia's face turned red, and he said nothing.

Summer arrived, and there were only a few days of school left. One day after lessons, Olia suggested, 'Why don't we all go swimming?'

The whole class went. Olia led us to the riverbank and said, 'Whoever is game can jump after me!'

And she leapt from the riverbank, which was five metres high at that point. Olia swam back and lay on the sand. One after another the boys and girls began to jump. Lonia sat there, pale and silent, looking over at Olia.

Finally, Lonia made up his mind. He took a run up, closed his eyes, and jumped. Then he swam back, and climbed out of the water, his eyes shining with joy. He asked Olia, 'Do you want to go swimming again tomorrow?'

Someone else will do it

Grade five was preparing for an excursion into the forest.

'We will be in the forest all day,' said their teacher. 'We will cook a meal, and read a book, and have a break.'

The children waited impatiently for Sunday to arrive. On Saturday they all stayed back after school, and the teacher reminded them what each child needed to bring.

'Bring some bread, some raw potatoes, lard and buckwheat,' she said. 'Put a bottle or thermos flask of water in your rucksack, and don't forget to bring a needle and thread.'

'Why do we need to bring a needle and thread?' asked Mykola.

'Anything can happen on a hike. Somebody's button might come off,' said the teacher.

That evening everyone packed their rucksacks. Each one thought, 'Why do I need to bring a needle and thread? Someone else will bring them. My buttons never come off at home.'

Everyone gathered in the school yard before sunrise, and they set off for the forest. Everyone felt happy on the way there and in the forest.

Mykola climbed up a tree. He wanted to cut off an interestingly shaped twig. He did not climb down from the tree but jumped. As he landed, the button came off his trousers. Holding his trousers up with one hand, Mykola went over to some boys. He asked them something, but they just shook their heads and shrugged their shoulders. The teacher noticed that Mykola was concerned about something, and asked him, 'What's the matter, Mykola?'

'Er … The button's come off my trousers,' he said.

'Well, sew it back on,' said his teacher.

'I haven't got a needle,' said Mykola.

It turned out that no-one had brought a needle. Everyone thought that someone else would bring one. So, Mykola held his trousers up by hand until evening. He held them up all the way home.

A home for Riabko

Mykhailyk had a faithful friend, a dog named Riabko. One day, Mykhailyk saw Riabko running down the street, pursued by a man in grey clothes waving a stick. This really disturbed Mykhailyk.

For several days he laboured away in the shed, making a kennel for Riabko. He called it 'Riabko's house'. It did indeed look like a small house.

Mykhailyk set up the kennel next to his house. Riabko crawled inside, lay down, and poked his head out. 'He likes it,' thought Mykhailyk.

So that Riabko would not wander, Mykhailyk leashed him with a strong iron chain. When Riabko realised he was chained to the kennel, he lay down with his head between his paws and whimpered.

Mykhailyk brought Riabko some food, but the dog turned his head away from the bowl and would not touch it. He just lay there till evening and all through the night.

In the morning, sleet began to fall. Mykhailyk thought that Riabko would take shelter in his kennel, but the dog did not move. He just lay by the kennel and kept on whimpering.

Mykhailyk took Riabko off the chain and put it in the barn. Riabko wagged his tail joyfully and crawled into his kennel.

The grade one fox cub

A mother fox had a son—a red-haired fox cub. He was in grade one at school. Every morning the mother fox walked her son to school.

The fox cub was not a particularly conscientious student. He did not like getting up early in the morning, washing, cleaning his teeth and having breakfast.

One day he decided, 'I won't go to school today.' He whispered pitifully to his mother, 'Mum, my tooth is aching.'

He thought his mother would say, 'My poor little fox cub! You just stay in bed. You don't need to go to school today. I'll bring you some sweet porridge to eat.' But instead, she said, 'I'll go and get the bear—the dentist. He'll come and pull out that sore tooth for you.'

The fox cub was frightened. No-one wants to have a completely healthy tooth pulled out.

He said to his mother, 'You know, Mum, my tooth just stopped aching. I'll go to school. But first I'll wash, clean my teeth and have some breakfast.'

His mother smiled and said, 'Thank goodness you're feeling better. I've got some sweet porridge ready for you.'

Ashamed of what the nightingale will think

Two little girls, Olia and Lida, went into the forest. After a long and tiring walk, they sat down on the grass to rest and have lunch.

They took bread, butter and an egg from their bag. When they had finished lunch, a nightingale started singing not far away. Enchanted by its beautiful song, Olia and Lida sat very still, afraid of disturbing it.

The nightingale stopped singing.

Olia collected her leftovers and some scraps of paper and threw them under a bush. Lida wrapped her eggshell and breadcrumbs in newspaper and put them in her bag.

'Why are you taking rubbish with you?' asked Olia. 'Throw it under the bush. We're in the forest. No-one will see you.'

'I'm ashamed … of what the nightingale will think,' said Lida quietly.

How Yurko was frightened

In the evening, Yurko's mother said, 'Could you please go out to the garden and fetch some apples.'

Yurko went out, climbed into the apple tree, and picked some apples. He was about to go back inside, when he noticed something black and round under the tree, just like a little ball. But the ball was moving.

'What is it?' wondered Yurko. He reached out to the ball and touched it. It was prickly. Yurko was frightened and let out a cry. He dropped the apples and ran inside. When he told his mother about the prickly ball, she just laughed. 'That was just a hedgehog!' she said.

Yurko went back into the garden to pick-up the apples, but they were gone. He had to climb the apple tree again. Yurko felt embarrassed. He wanted to take another look at that hedgehog. 'This time, I won't be scared,' he thought.

But the hedgehog was nowhere to be found. Where did it disappear to?

Why Olesia cried

Three-year-old Olesia was riding her little tricycle in the yard. Her tricycle had three wheels, so it would not tip over, but somehow, it did tip over, and Olesia fell onto the grass. She fell on her knee, and it was sore.

The little girl felt sorry for herself. She pursed her lips and looked up at the window where her mother was supposed to be, but her mother was not there.

The little girl was ready to burst into tears, but what was the point if nobody could hear her crying? She stood upright, wiped the dust off her knee, picked up her tricycle and sat on the saddle, ready to ride it again. Just then, she noticed her mother sitting inside by the window. She was sewing.

Olesia started crying, perched on her tricycle. Why not, now that there was somebody to console her? Olesia's mother looked at her with surprise. 'Why are you crying?' she asked.

'I fell on the ground and hurt my knee.'

'But you're sitting on your bike,' replied her mother, not understanding.

Olesia fell silent. She was ashamed of herself. She would not have burst into tears if her mother had not been sitting by the window.

I don't want to be an ant

Tarasyk's mother baked some *pyrizhky*, covered them with a tablecloth, and left them on the dinner table.[49] The hot *pyrizhky* filled the room with the delicious aroma of freshly baked dough and cabbage.

Little Tarasyk was sitting near the dinner table. He lifted the tablecloth and started pinching morsels of *pyrizhok*, one crumb at a time. His mother spotted him and scolded him, 'Please be patient, Tarasyk. Let the *pyrizhky* cool down and they'll be even tastier. You're not an ant!'

Tarasyk went outside, thinking, 'Why did Mum say I'm not an ant? Are ants bad? Mum often says it's good to work hard like an ant.'

Tarasyk walked over to an ant nest and threw a tiny piece of *pyrizhok* into it. Ants ran in from all directions and started eating it. Tarasyk imagined himself playing with other boys in the school yard, and someone suddenly throwing them a loaf of bread …

'No, Mum, I don't want to be an ant,' said Tarasyk with a smile.

Staring and distracted

A boy was walking down the road, carrying a bucket of water. An old man was shuffling towards him, feeling his way with a cane.

'He's blind,' thought the boy.

He had never seen that old man in the village before. The boy kept staring at the old man, without watching where he was going. He tripped and spilled water onto the road. The boy was startled and jumped sideways towards the fence.

The old man stepped into the spilt water, slipped, lost his balance, and fell. He slowly got to his feet, bent over, felt the wet ground with his hand, and shrugged his shoulders. How did that water get there?

The boy felt so sorry for the old man that his eyes filled with tears. He was full of remorse. 'Why didn't I warn the blind old man and help him to walk round the slippery patch?' he thought.

The old man had already turned down a lane and was nowhere to be seen, but the boy just kept standing there, not knowing what to do or what to say.

The rooster and the sun

The rooster dozes on its perch. It wakes up, yawns comfortably, and goes back to sleep. But it always crows just before sunrise—cock-a-doodle-doo!—and all the hens wake up. The rooster says, 'You see, I crow, and morning comes. If I did not crow, there would be no morning. You can see how important I am!'

This happened many times. One day the rooster was angry with the people that looked after him. They had not given him enough grain, and he thought to himself, 'I'll make you sorry—I won't sing in the morning. The sun won't rise, and then what will you do?'

Night came. The rooster smiled to himself in his sleep and gloated, 'You're going to be so sorry!'

The time came for the rooster to crow but he remained silent. He just closed his eyes and went back to sleep. When he woke up, he saw that the sun was shining brightly and the hens had all got up from their perch.

The rooster felt ashamed, and he turned his back on the sun.

Even the flowers blushed with shame

A mother left for work early in the morning. She told her daughter, 'I'll be in the field all day. You must clean the house, wash your clothes, cook supper, and water the flowers.'

The daughter cleaned the house, washed her clothes and cooked some supper, but she did not water the flowers. Several times during the day she walked past the white chrysanthemums and thought that she should water them. But as soon as she thought of watering them a voice seemed to say to her, 'Nothing will happen if you don't water them for one day.' This was the voice of dishonesty, a feeble, little creature that had appeared from goodness knows where and settled in a dark corner of the little girl's soul.

In the evening, the girl's mother returned from the field. She saw that the house had been cleaned, the clothes had been washed and dried, and supper was ready. She asked, 'Did you water the flowers?'

'Yes,' said the girl quietly, and lowered her eyes.

The feeble little creature that had settled in a dark corner of the child's soul jumped up and down with glee.

'Yes,' said the little girl again, and looked at the chrysanthemums. She looked, and was amazed. The white flowers had a purple tinge to them. They had blushed with shame.

'Mum, forgive me,' said the girl. 'I didn't tell you the truth. I didn't water the flowers. I will never lie to you again.'

The purple tinge faded, and the flowers became white again. The feeble, little creature that was hiding in a dark corner of the child's soul disappeared, and the dark corner became full of light.

The mother hugged her daughter and gave her a kiss.

The doll with the broken arm

A little girl had a doll. Once, long ago, when she was playing with it, she had accidentally broken its arm. Every day since, she had bandaged the doll's arm, carefully attaching it to the doll. And the doll, whose name was Zoia, smiled. It liked the attention from the little girl.

But then, one day, the little girl's mother brought her a new doll named Lina, that she had purchased at the shop. It wore a luxurious pale blue dress and had long blonde hair. The fingers on its hands were very slender, and there was a ring on one of its fingers. The doll's eyes opened and closed. When the little girl put the doll to bed, it said, 'Good night' and when she picked it up, it said, 'Good morning!'

The little girl and Lina were inseparable for a whole day. She plaited the doll's hair and tied new ribbons in it. Lina put the doll to bed, and it said, 'Good night.'

Suddenly the little girl heard someone crying. It was Zoia. The little girl had left her on the couch facing inwards and forgotten all about her. Zoia had taken it badly and felt very hurt. She felt all alone and had started crying.

The little girl felt ashamed. She picked up Zoia, held her to her heart, and kissed her. She bandaged her injured arm. Zoia smiled, opened her lips and whispered something. She was saying to the little girl, 'I still belong to you, don't I? Don't ever forget me.'

Why Petryk cried

Little Petryk's mother left him at home while she went to the store. Petryk went over to the open window. On the windowsill stood a vase. A big, colourful butterfly landed on the rim of the vase.

Petryk wanted to catch the butterfly. He leant on the windowsill, reached over, and knocked the vase. It fell and smashed to pieces.

Petryk was very frightened. What would happen now? What would his mother say? The boy collected all the pieces of the vase, took them out to the vegetable garden, and buried them in the soil with his little spade. Then he sat by the window and waited for his mother to come home.

As soon as his mother came in through the door, Petryk ran over to her and said, 'Mum, it wasn't me who broke the vase. It wasn't me who took the pieces to the vegetable garden and buried them with my little spade.'

Petryk sensed alarm in his mother's eyes.

'Then who did break the vase?' asked his mother.

'The butterfly … ' said Petryk quietly.

His mother laughed. 'I can understand how a butterfly might break a vase,' she said, 'But how could it take the pieces to the vegetable garden and bury them?'

Petryk looked at his mother and burst into tears.

The right hand and the left hand

Weeds were growing among the carrots. Little Maryna went to the vegetable garden to save the carrots from the weeds. She kept using her right hand to pull up the weeds, but her left hand did nothing. The right hand got tired, and asked the left hand, 'Why aren't you working? Look how hard I am working. All my muscles are aching, and you're doing nothing.'

The left hand was ashamed, and it began to work too. Little Maryna finished the work quickly.

I am sorry I'm late, children

It was a frosty morning. A penetrating wind blew from the north, and snowflakes swirled in the cold air. We arrived at school early. It was warm in the classroom, and we took off our boots and warmed our feet by the heater.

The bell rang and everyone sat at their desk. A minute passed, and then another, but the teacher did not appear. We sent Nina, our class monitor, to the staffroom to find out why there was no teacher. She came back a minute later and told us that Ivan Petrovych was not well. The principal said we should all go home.

'Hooray!' we shouted. 'Hooray! There are no lessons today. The teacher is sick.'

Suddenly the door opened, and Ivan Petrovych came into the classroom, covered in snow and looking tired. We all froze in surprise, sat down and lowered our heads. Ivan Petrovych walked over to his desk. 'I'm sorry, children,' he said quietly. 'I was a bit sick, but I decided to come to school after all. That is why I am late.'

He took off his coat right there in the classroom, sat at his desk, and looked at us. But we were too ashamed to raise our eyes.

Mykola felt some relief

On the way to school, on the bridge over the pond, Mykola, who was in grade six, met Grandma Maryna. He knew her well because she lived next door to his parents' house.

The old lady was carrying a bundle, tied up in white cloth. On the bridge the bundle came loose, and onions spilled out onto the road. The big, yellow onions rolled some distance, and one fell off the bridge into the pond. The old lady was flustered and did not know what to do.

Mykola thought it was funny. He laughed loudly and ran away. When she heard him laughing, Grandma Maryna raised her eyes, looked at the boy, and shook her head. When he looked around, Mykola saw her eyes, full of pain and reproach.

At school, Mykola could not forget the incident. He no longer thought it was funny. It seemed to him that the old lady's eyes were looking into his soul, and again he felt her pain and her reproach. He felt a pressure on his heart, and he wanted to go straight away to see her and ask her forgiveness. 'I'll go and see her this evening,' he thought.

But the evening came and went, and so did the next day and the day after, and he could not make up his mind to go and ask Grandma Maryna for forgiveness. A few days later, his mother came home from work and told him, 'Grandma Maryna has died.'

This news stunned the boy. He felt as if something burning turned over in his chest, and his heart beat rapidly … The boy burst into tears.

'What's the matter?' asked his mother.

Mykola told her all about what had happened. His mother sighed and said, 'When they bury Grandma Maryna, walk behind her coffin. When they lower the coffin into the grave, throw a handful of earth onto it, and say, "Forgive me, Grandma."'

'Do you really think she will hear what I say?' whispered Mykola.

'She won't hear it, but for you the sun will shine more brightly.'

When they lowered Grandma Maryna's coffin into her grave, Mykola threw a handful of earth onto it and said, 'Forgive me, Grandma.'

And at that moment the sun shone more brightly, and the sky became clearer. Mykola felt some relief.

The young apple tree

In the spring, grade three students Yurko and Myshko planted a young apple tree near the school. They watered it and decided that during the holidays they would come to school so they could keep watering the young tree. They agreed that Yurko would water it on the first day, then Myshko on the second day, then Yurko again, and so on in turn. Then the young apple tree would keep growing and gradually get stronger.

The holidays arrived. 'It's my turn to water the apple tree,' thought Yurko, 'But will it really matter if it is not watered for one day? Myshko will go and water it tomorrow.'

The next day came. Myshko lived quite a long way from the school. He thought, 'Yurko watered the apple tree yesterday. It won't really matter if it is not watered for one day. Tomorrow is Yurko's day again, and he lives a bit closer to the school, so he can water it.'

The days passed. Yurko counted on Myshko doing the watering, and Myshko counted on Yurko, so for several days nobody watered the young apple tree.

A little grade one student named Andriiko came to the school every day to feed the fish in the aquarium. He noticed that nobody was watering the young apple tree, and that it would soon die. He began to water the young tree every day, and it gradually grew stronger and grew fresh green leaves.

Autumn arrived, and with it the first of September—the first day of the school year. All the children returned to school. Yurko could not wait to see if Myshko had watered the tree, and Myshko was curious to see if Yurko had watered it. The boys both walked to the young apple tree. They walked without talking, and when they saw the green leaves on the tree, they both felt so ashamed that they just looked at the ground. They both thought, 'It was just me who did not water the tree, while my friend watered it.'

And the two boys just stood there next to the tree hanging their heads until the bell went. They were too ashamed to look each other in the eye.

Why Serhiiko was ashamed

It was a cold winter. The orchard was carpeted with snow. Birds flew over the white carpet and called anxiously, because there was nothing for them to eat.

The grade three students made bird feeders. Every day they brought food—seeds from hemp, pumpkins or sunflowers. For the chickadees they brought pieces of lard, enclosed with netting so the crows would not steal it.

It was Saturday, and on Sunday it was Serhiiko's turn to bring food for the bird feeder. In the evening he prepared a piece of lard and wrapped it with netting. He put some pumpkin seeds in a little bag.

'In the morning, as soon as it is light, I will take the food for the birds,' thought Serhiiko.

But in the morning, he did not feel like getting up. He woke up late, and there was a blizzard blowing outside.

'How can I go out in weather like this?' he thought. The blizzard only died down in the evening.

'All the paths will be covered with snow. And the chickadees will be sleeping somewhere cosy,' thought Serhiiko. The boy consoled himself with this thought, so that his conscience would not trouble him.

When it was dark, Serhiiko thought, 'The chickadees will not starve in just one day. Someone will feed them tomorrow.'

The next day Serhiiko's teacher went over to the window and asked, 'Whose turn was it to feed the chickadees yesterday?'

'It was my turn,' said Serhiiko, turning pale with anxiety.

'Well done, Serhiiko!' said his teacher. 'Look, you even hung up two pieces of lard, and the chickadees are still pecking at them.'

It became very quiet in the classroom. Serhiiko could hear his heart pounding, as if it was about to jump out of his chest. He was too ashamed to raise his eyes and look at the teacher.

A piece of bread

Yurko is in grade five and attends after-school care. After school, he goes with his classmates to the dining hall. The children sit down at long tables. Each student has in front of them a bowl of borshch, a rissole and a drink made from stewed fruit.[50] On a separate plate they have a piece of bread to go with their dinner. Yurko starts eating. His friend Myshko is on duty in the kitchen and will eat after everyone else.

Yurko's piece of bread is not enough for him, and he takes Myshko's share. He eats half of it and quietly drops the half that is left over under the table.

All the children have finished eating and wait for the teacher, who has been sitting opposite Yurko, to tell them they can go outside to play. But the teacher says, 'I would like you to sit here a little longer, while I tell you a story about something that happened a long time ago. This happened during the war. A detachment was fighting the enemy in a desert far away in the south. Barren sands stretched for hundreds of kilometres under the blazing sun, with not a drop of water to be had. A commander sent two soldiers on a scouting mission. They had to walk for over a hundred kilometres across scorching sands. They could only move at night. Each soldier had a large flask of water and a bag of rusks.

The soldiers walked all night. In the morning they stopped, raked up a big pile of sand, and lay down to sleep through the day. One soldier, named Mykola, went to sleep. The other, named Andrii, quietly took Mykola's flask and began to drink his water. He drank from it once, twice, three times. By evening he had emptied the flask.

At nightfall the soldiers set off again. Mykola wanted to drink a mouthful of water, but his flask was empty. He tried Andrii's flask, and it was empty too. And they were surrounded by a barren, waterless desert. Both soldiers perished. The desert does not fool around with people. I would like you to think about this story, children.'

Yurko bowed his head. He was too ashamed to look the teacher in the eye.

How Dmytro had lunch

On Sunday, all the grade five students went to the forest. They went for a whole day, so they could collect plant specimens, draw autumn landscapes, and rest. Each one took their own food and water.

Dmytro's mother packed his bag with salami, boiled eggs, bread and butter, and a little jar of honey. As she said good-bye to her son she said, 'Make sure you eat well, so you don't get hungry. You don't need to share with anyone else. Each of them can eat their own food.'

Dmytro's bag was so heavy, he could hardly carry it to the forest.

At lunchtime the whole class sat on the grass to have lunch. They spread out a tablecloth, and everyone put out their supplies: bread, lard, potatoes, butter, meat … But Dmytro remembered his mother's instructions and took his bag behind a bush. He quickly opened his bag and ate his bread, butter and salami. There was lots of food left over, but he did not feel hungry anymore. Dmytro's friends came to him and asked, 'Why don't you come and have something to eat with us?'

Dmytro did not reply. He was too ashamed to admit that he had already eaten his fill.

All the children returned home with bags full of plant specimens, but all Dmytro had in his bag was food.

On the way home Dmytro thought, 'I'll never behave like that again.'

Shame

After graduating from high school, Andrii entered a polytechnical university and moved to a big city. One day, while on holidays, he came home and visited his old school. He was instantly surrounded by his friends. He was also spotted by his former biology teacher, who came over to say hello, congratulated him on his admission to university, and wished him success in his studies.

Andrii told his teacher about the far away city. He was especially fond of the city's shady parks with their large flowerbeds.

'There are so many flowers!' enthused Andrii. 'One street is full of huge cannas. My friend gave me some bulbs … How could I have forgotten to bring them? But I'll make sure I mail them to you, Hryhorii Hnatovych,' Andrii promised.

'I will be very grateful if you do,' replied his teacher.

The holidays came to an end, and Andrii returned to the city. A month passed, then a second and a third. Andrii forgot all about his promise. One day, he received a letter from his biology teacher.

'I'm really grateful to you, Andrii, for sending us those canna bulbs,' his teacher wrote. 'Now, there will be many beautiful flowers in our school yard.'

Andrii read that letter and felt so ashamed, he did not know what to do. He found the canna bulbs in his bedside drawers, wrapped them in white fabric, sewed up the bundle, wrote the address on his parcel, and took it straight to the post office.

He wanted to write a letter to his teacher as well, and took up his pen several times, but he was at a loss for words. 'What can I write to him now?' he thought.

Several weeks passed, then months and years … When he met his teacher, Andrii could not look him in the eyes. But a person who can still feel shame has a righteous soul.

The cat was ashamed

A cat was sitting outside the door, squinting in the bright sunlight. Suddenly he heard some sparrows start chirping. The cat became silent and watchful. Very quietly he began to creep towards the fence. That is where the sparrows were perched.

He crept right up to the fence … and leapt high in the air. He was trying to catch one of the sparrows, but it fluttered and was gone.

The cat flew over the fence and landed in a puddle. He hopped out all wet and covered in mud.

The cat walked back to the house. He was ashamed. The sparrows flew together from all over the yard and hovered over the cat, chirping. They were laughing at the cat.

The hedgehog and the moon

The moon was shining brightly. The hedgehog left his little home in search of food. Padding around on his tiny paws, he found a rosehip bush. He picked a bright red berry and stuck it on one of his spikes. His coat was very prickly, with lots of spikes, so he could carry lots of berries. When he had decorated himself all over with red berries, he headed home.

On the way, he came to a puddle, and in the middle of the puddle he could see a huge white moon. The hedgehog thought that it was a huge apple, and wanted to take it home on his spikes. He tried to gather the moon on his spikes, but the moon just quivered and laughed.

'Don't you have enough food already, my dear hedgehog?' he asked.

The hedgehog felt ashamed, and quietly made his way home.

The boastful rooster

A rooster was strutting around the courtyard. He spotted a colourful rainbow in the sky and laughed. 'I have a bright and colourful tail, even more beautiful than that rainbow,' he boasted.

At that moment, it started raining. The boastful rooster's tail was soaked and drooped right down to the ground. The rooster felt embarrassed. He scurried to his perch and never boasted again.

What was Dmytryk chuckling at?

One Sunday, eight friends—all students at a boarding school—went for a trip out of town. They came to a place where a hill towered above the Dnipro River, with a steep descent to the water below.

The boys climbed up the hill. They took off their uniform caps, placed them under a tall pine tree, and sat on the grass, where Dmytryk Sokolenko began to read aloud from an interesting book.

Suddenly a whirlwind swirled over the hill. The boys raised their heads in surprise. The wind was so strong it broke a branch from the pine tree and lifted one of the caps into the air. The cap flew down the slope and out over the Dnipro. The grey whirlwind was visible for moment on the riverbank, but the cap had disappeared.

The boys had just been issued with new uniforms the day before, and none had yet labelled their caps. Now one of the eight caps had been carried away by the wind, while the other seven lay higgledy-piggledy under the pine tree. As soon as the wind died down, the boys rushed for the caps. Seven boys sprinted towards the pine tree, and each ran as fast as they could, because they knew there would be one cap missing.

When the boys returned to where they had been sitting, they were surprised to see Dmytryk Sokolenko still sitting and reading as if nothing had happened. He had not jumped up when everyone rushed for the caps.

The seven boys in their new caps approached Dmytryk. They all wanted to ask him something, but when they saw him chuckling, they bowed their heads and lowered their eyes. They were ashamed. And it is good that they were.

A grandson's request

Three grandsons—Petryk, Ivas and little Tarasyk—came to visit Grandpa Taras at the melon plantation. They spent a long time with him. He treated his grandsons to watermelon, rockmelon, honey, apples and cherry juice.

As they were leaving, he gave each boy a large watermelon. He walked with them as far as the scrub on the edge of the plantation. The grandfather turned back, and had almost reached his hut, when he suddenly heard someone calling him. His seven-year-old grandson, Tarasyk, had run back from the edge of the plantation and was calling, 'Grandpa Taras!'

His grandfather asked, 'What's the matter, Tarasyk? Why have you come back?'

'Grandpa, can we please steal one watermelon?' asked Tarasyk.

The unexpectedness of the question caught the old man off guard. He opened his mouth to scold the boy, but looking at Tarasyk's pleading eyes, and the skin peeling off his sunburnt nose, he remembered something. Trying not to smile, he said sternly, 'Look at me! No more than one watermelon. And take it … I mean steal it … from that side over there.'

Grandpa Taras turned and walked back to his hut, smiling all the time, and remembering his childhood.

His grandson Tarasyk, jumping for joy, ran back to the scrub to give the other boys the joyful news: Grandpa said they could steal one watermelon.

How a gopher ploughed a field and sowed some wheat

The wheat was harvested with a combine harvester, and not a single ear of wheat was left.

On the edge of the forest lived a poor gopher, all by himself. Now there was nothing for him to eat, and he started crying.

Magpie Whitesides flew over, settled on the branch of a tree, and said, 'Don't cry, dear Gopher Softpaws. Make a plough and sow some wheat. It will produce grain and you'll have something to eat.'

The gopher made a plough and ploughed a big field. He asked the local people for some wheat seed. People felt sorry for the hungry gopher and gave him some seed to plant. The gopher planted the seed, and wheat grew, with large, full ears of grain. The gopher was happy. Now he had enough to eat.

The donkey in a lion's skin

A donkey wanted all the animals to fear him and bow down to him. He found a lion's skin and put it on and fitted the lion's jaw to his mouth. Then he sat under a tree, and started shouting, 'I am a lion, the king of the beasts. I am stronger and cleverer than all of you!'

All the animals in the forest came running. They trembled and bowed down before the lion. A fox also came running. She crept up and sniffed the lion's skin and spotted the donkey's hooves poking out from under it. She whispered to the donkey, 'I know you are a donkey, but I won't tell anyone. Let them all think that you are a lion. They'll bring you lots of meat, and you can give me half.'

'All right,' agreed the donkey, 'But how do I know you won't trick me?'

'I won't trick you. I swear upon my tail,' said the fox.

Since that time, the donkey in a lion's skin has reigned, and the fox has been his chief advisor.

The cheerful loach

A fisherman was sitting on the bank of a pond. He had several rods. Most of the rods had ordinary steel hooks, but one rod had a silver hook.

Ten stupid crucian carp were already caught, and so was a loach. The fisherman put all the fish into a bucket. The crucian carp were very sad. 'How did it happen,' they wondered, 'That the fisherman was able to make fools of us all? He just stuck a piece of worm onto a steel hook, and we took the bait.'

But the loach was very boastful. He always found something to boast about. Even now, in the bucket, he was boasting instead of feeling downcast. 'I am out of your league, you stupid carp!' he cried. 'You were only caught on steel hooks, but I was caught on a silver hook.'

Yurko sat in his sled ...

Three grade three students—Yurko, Mykola and Petro—took their sleds to a big hill. The ground was frozen and generously covered in snow. A sled track ran from the top of the hill to the bottom.

The boys sat in their sleds and pushed off. The sleds went faster and faster. Halfway down they were going so fast the wind whistled in their ears. It was such fun to fly down from the top of the hill: the headlong descent took their breath away.

The children reached the bottom of the hill. The sleds slowed down and came to a stop right in middle of a frozen pond.

The boys looked back up the hill.

'Wow, what a big hill!' they said. 'We'll have to drag our sleds all the way up again.'

Mykola and Petro dragged their sleds up the hill. It was hard going, but they knew that after the difficult climb they would enjoy the easy headlong flight to the bottom.

But Yurko took a few steps and stopped.

'It's really hard climbing this hill,' he thought. 'I'll have a rest here at the bottom.'

Yurko sat in his sled and rested. He saw Petro and Mykola reach the top of the hill, and then come flying down in their sleds, but he just sat there. He was freezing, but he still just sat there.

Petro and Mykola climbed the hill again, and came flying down again, but Yurko just sat there.

Yurko wanted to ride his sled down the hill, he really did … But he didn't want to drag his sled up the hill.

Yurko sat in his sled until evening, while Petro and Mykola flew down the hill again and again.

How Yurko educated himself

Yurko studies in grade three. He is a lively, restless, bright boy, though a little lazy. Sometimes Yurko does not want to do his homework. But he loves playing ball.

One day, when he was playing, he fell and broke his leg. The doctor came, put a plaster cast on his leg, and said he would have to stay in bed for a month.

Yurko lay in bed feeling sorry for himself. He could not get up, and playing ball was out of the question. It was hard for the boy to just lie there. He decided to think about something interesting so the time would pass more quickly.

Yurko remembered how his teacher had told the children about Mykola Ostrovsky. That writer was unable to get out of bed, and was even blind, but he managed to write a book.

'I will work, too,' decided Yurko. 'It is only my leg that is broken. I will read books and study.'

And that is what he did. His mother put his textbooks, exercise books and a pen on his bedside table. As soon as Yurko woke up, he set about his lessons. He solved problems, wrote grammar exercises and read stories. 'My friends at school are studying for four hours each day, but I will work for five hours a day,' the boy decided.

Sometimes, when Yurko woke up, he did not feel like picking up a book. But then he felt ashamed. He thought to himself, 'Is that how a real man would act? It is only my leg that is broken. I must work with my head.' And with those thoughts, he picked up his book.

Her heart was singing

Just before classes, the vice-principal of the school approached the mathematics teacher, Mariia Petrivna, and told her, 'I looked through your grade six students' exercise books. Your students seem to be a hopeless lot. They don't make any effort to write properly. I don't think they care about anything.'

Mariia Petrivna listened to the vice-principal in silence. 'Is it possible that my students are that bad?' she thought, and her heart ached. Mariia Petrivna walked over to the window. Through her tears, she saw two of her students, Andriiko and Mykolka, playing in the school yard. They were two troublemakers, but they had kind hearts … The boys were standing and looking at their teacher. Mariia Petrivna stepped back from the window.

The bell rang for the start of classes. With a heavy sigh, Mariia Petrivna collected the classroom journal[51] and headed off to teach her grade six students.

Before opening the door to the classroom, Mariia Petrivna composed herself and put on her brightest smile, and with that welcoming smile she entered the classroom.

The students were sitting at their desks very quietly. Mariia Petrivna could not remember them ever having been so quiet. In the children's eyes she noticed something extraordinary that she had never seen before. It was a mixture of anxiety and affection.

'Children, today, we will be solving mathematical problems at the blackboard,' she said.

'Mariia Petrivna,' said Andriiko, 'Could you please set us some problems to solve independently?'

'Yes,' other students joined in. 'We feel like solving some problems on our own.'

Mariia Petrivna was astonished. She gave Andriiko a set of cards with individual problems for each student. Andriiko handed the cards out to all the students, and a silence fell over the classroom.

At that moment, Mariia Petrivna's heart was singing.

You did not lose something, you found something

When a boy turned twelve years old, his father gave him a new spade and said, 'Go into the field, son, measure a plot 100 paces by 100 paces, and dig it up.' The son went into the field, measured the plot of land, and began to dig. It was hard to dig at first, but gradually he got better at digging and got used to the spade.

The work went better and better as he got towards the end of it, but when the son plunged his spade into the soil to turn the last sod, the spade broke. The son returned home feeling ill at ease. What would his father say about the broken spade?

'Forgive me father,' said the son, 'I have lost some of our property. The spade broke.'

'But did you learn to dig? Was it hard for you to dig at the end, or was it easy?' asked the father.

'Yes, I learnt to dig, and it was easier to dig at the end than at the beginning,' said the son.

'Then you did not lose something. You found something.'

'What did I find, father?'

'A thirst for work. That is a most valuable discovery.'

The goat and the hare

A goat was tethered to a stake by the riverbank. The goat was grazing, munching on some grass. Nearby was a field full of cabbages with large, juicy heads. The goat would gladly have eaten some cabbage, but the rope he was tethered to was too short.

A hare ran by. The goat asked him, 'Where are you off to, hare?'

'I am going to eat some cabbage,' said the hare.

'Ooh, I hate cabbage. I can't even bare to look at it,' said the goat, and made a wry face.

The hare tucked into the cabbage, but the goat kept on grumbling, 'I don't know how rabbits and hares can eat cabbage. I wouldn't touch it!'

Good health to you, Grandpa!

Next to the school lives an old man—Grandpa Ivan. He has nobody—no family and no friends. He had two sons, but they were killed on the frontline. And his wife died not long ago.

Everyday Grandpa Ivan comes to the school for water. 'The school well has very tasty water,' he tells his neighbours.

As soon as the old man approaches the well, children run up to him.

'Grandpa, let us help you draw the water,' they say.

The old man smiles. He hardly has time to rest by the well, and his bucket is already full of water.

'Good health to you, Grandpa!' twitter the children.

These words are like beautiful music to the old man. They make his heart warm and joyful.

Grandpa Ivan has come out of his house again and is sitting on a bench by the fence. He is sitting and listening. What is he listening for? A bell rings in the school yard. The old man picks up his bucket and goes for water. How he longs to hear those heartfelt words: 'Good health to you, Grandpa!'

Borrowing a spade

A father sent his seven-year-old son to ask a favour of his neighbour, Grandpa Fedir.

'Myshko, go and ask if we can borrow his spade for half a day. Ours has broken.'

The boy went to see Grandpa Fedir and said, 'Give us your spade, Grandpa. My father asked if we can borrow it.'

But the old man just kept doing what he was doing, as if he could not see or hear Myshko. Myshko might as well not have been there.

Myshko asked again, 'Give us your spade, Grandpa. My father asked if we can borrow it.'

The old man still did not reply. The boy returned home empty-handed and asked, 'Dad, what's wrong with Grandpa Fedir?'

'Did you say "hello" to the old man and ask how he is?'

'No,' answered Myshko.

'Go back to him, say "hello", and ask if he is well. Then ask him to forgive you your impoliteness. If he forgives you, then you can ask for the spade,' said his father.

Myshko went back to Grandpa Fedir's house and said everything that his father had asked him to. The old man seemed so stern that Myshko nearly cried when he asked for forgiveness.

Grandpa Fedir smiled, stroked Myshko's head and gave him the spade. Then he said, 'Go over to the apple tree by the well and pick yourself an apple. Pick the best one you can find.'

Say 'hello' to people

A father and his little son were walking along a forest track. All around was still. The only sound was the distant tapping of a woodpecker and the babbling of a little stream in the depths of the forest.

Suddenly the son saw an old lady approaching, walking with a stick.

'Dad, where's that old lady going?' asked the son.

'To see someone, to meet someone or to see someone off,' said the father. 'When we meet her, we'll say "hello" to her.'

'Why should we say "hello" to her?' asked the surprised son. 'We don't even know her.'

'When we meet her, we'll say "hello", and then you'll see why.'

The old lady drew level with them.

'Hello,' said the son.

'Hello,' said the father.

'Hello,' said the old lady, and smiled.

And the son saw with amazement that everything around them changed. The sun shone more brightly. A light breeze skipped through the tops of the trees, rustling the leaves. The birds started singing in the bushes. Before that, you couldn't hear them.

The boy's soul felt joyful.

'Why was it like that?' asked the son.

'Because we said "hello" to someone, and they smiled,' said his father.

He saved the baby frogs

It was a rainy spring. A large puddle appeared in the street outside. Petryk, a grade three student, noticed that little tadpoles were swimming in the puddle.

'Where did they come from?' he wondered.

After the rains, came a hot summer. There was not a single cloud in the sky. The puddle began to dry out quickly, and soon there was hardly any water left in it. One day Petryk noticed about twenty baby frogs in the small puddle that remained. They were as tiny as could be.

'The baby frogs must be hot,' thought Petryk. 'And what will happen when the puddle dries out completely? They will die.'

Petryk felt sorry for the frogs and decided to save them. He went home and found a bucket, collected the tiny baby frogs in it, and took them to the pond. He let them go in the water, and they swam away.

'Now they will not die,' thought Petryk with joy.

The swallow with a broken wing

A thunderstorm rumbled in the sky at the end of a hot summer day. Rain poured down. Water drenched a swallow's nest stuck to the wall of our old barn.

The nest collapsed, and some chicks fell out. They had already developed feathers but had not yet learnt to fly. The mother sparrow fluttered above her chicks and called them under a bush.

The chicks lived under the bush for several days. The mother swallow brought them food, and they huddled together, waiting for her.

Four of the chicks learnt to fly, and began to flit everywhere, but one still could not. The mother swallow would sit next to the chick that could not fly. It had a broken wing. It had been crippled when it fell out of the nest.

The crippled swallow lived under the bush until autumn. When the time came for swallows to fly to warmer lands, they gathered in a large flock, settled in a bush, and for a long time you could hear an anxious cheeping.

The birds flew away to warmer lands. The young swallow with the broken wing was left behind. I picked it up and took it home. It snuggled up to me trustingly. I put it on the windowsill, and it looked out at the blue sky. I thought I could see tears in its eyes.

Is Teddy mean or kind?

This happened during World War II. Twelve-year-old Pavlyk used to graze the calves. At that time all children, even little girls and boys, worked in the fields. Their fathers were fighting in the war, and their mothers could not do all the work by themselves.

There were forty-five calves in Pavlyk's herd. All of them were quiet and friendly, except for one bull calf named Teddy, who was angry and aggressive. He often put his head down and pushed Pavlyk. The boy was frightened of Teddy.

One quiet June day, the postman brought a funeral notice. Pavlyk's father had been killed in battle. His mother cried, his little sister cried, and Pavlyk cried. He was still crying when he drove the calves to the pasture.

Pavlyk sat under a birch tree with his head on his knees and cried. Suddenly he felt someone tenderly touch his shoulder. 'Who could that be?' wondered Pavlyk. 'There is no-one else here in the pasture.' He looked up and saw Teddy standing next to him. He had lowered his head and was rubbing his shoulder.

Pavlyk stroked the bull calf. Teddy lay down next to him and put his head in the boy's lap.

The same words

During the summer holidays, a grade five student named Andriiko went to work on the animal breeding farm. He was assigned to Grandma Maryna, the cook. Andriiko helped Grandma Maryna—carting water, peeling potatoes, chopping wood, and slicing bread.

It is a relaxed and enjoyable life, working in the steppe in summer. The sun warms you, the wind blows, the birds sing, and you can swim in the pond if Grandma Maryna lets you.

Each morning, Grandma Maryna said to Andriiko, 'Go and fetch some water.'

And Grandma Maryna had such a quiet, kind, tender voice, that Andriiko quickly took the bucket and ran to the well. The well was some distance away, on the edge of the forest. Andriiko would draw a bucket of water and return ten minutes later.

But then they sent another worker to the farm—Grandpa Karpo. He began to work there as the watchman.

No-one liked Grandpa Karpo. Grandma Maryna did not like him, and neither did Andriiko. Grandpa Karpo was silent and frowned all the time. One day Andriiko asked him, 'Grandpa, can you tell me a story?'

'You only want a story because you've got nothing better to do,' snapped Grandpa Karpo. 'Go and fetch some water.'

The words were so cold and heartless that Andriiko was very reluctant to get the water. He drew a full bucket and then sat by the well for a long time. He did not want to go back to Grandpa Karpo.

Andriiko eventually returned with the water and then ran straight to Grandma Maryna.

In the morning, the boy was up before the sun. He peeled some potatoes and waited impatiently for Grandma Maryna to send him for water. At last, he heard the quiet, tender words, 'Go and fetch some water.'

Andriiko ran to the well, quickly drew the water, and brought it to the kitchen.

A smile

It was a quiet, sunny morning. In a green meadow that stretched from the edge of the village, yellow dandelions were flowering, bees and bumblebees were buzzing, and a lark was sporting in the blue sky.

On this beautiful morning, a little three-year-old girl came out of her house. She had light blue eyes and fair hair the colour of ripening wheat. Her name was Marynka. She set off through the green meadow. She smiled when she saw a many-coloured butterfly. At that moment, she wanted the whole world to share her smile.

Still smiling, Marynka followed the butterfly. The butterfly flew slowly, as if it understood the little girl wanted to have a good look at it.

Suddenly Marynka saw an old man walking towards her. His gaze was stormy, his eyebrows frowning and his eyes full of malice. Marynka brought her smile with her as she walked towards the old man. She was hoping that the old man would smile back. How could anyone be gloomy and unfriendly on such a joyful day?

Already in the depth of the girl's soul a little wave of fear stirred, but she kept smiling, bringing her smile with her as she met the old man, and appealing to him: you smile too, grandpa.

But the old man did not smile. His gaze remained dark, his eyebrows lowered and his eyes malevolent.

Marynka's heart was gripped by fear. The smile faded from her eyes. At that moment it seemed to her that the whole world had become dark and gloomy.

The green meadow turned grey, the dandelions turned from yellow suns into purple spots, the blue sky turned pale, and the silver song of the lark began to waver, like a stream that is running dry.

Marynka burst into tears. A minute later, the old man was already far away. Now she could only see his back, but even his back seemed evil and unwelcoming.

The little girl kept walking through the meadow. Her heartbeat quickened when she saw that someone else was walking towards her. It was an old lady with a stick.

Marynka was now on her guard and looked searchingly into the old lady's eyes. The old lady smiled. And it was such a kind, sincere smile, that the whole world came to life again around the girl, vibrant, singing, sparkling with dozens of colours of the most subtle shades. The dandelions blazed like little suns, the sound of the bees and bumblebees resounded, the lark played melodies on its silver strings.

Marynka smiled, and again the many coloured wings of the butterfly fluttered before her. The old lady stopped on the path, looked back at the little girl and smiled again.

Where does your father work?

Mariia Mykhailivna sits at her desk with the class journal in front of her. She is asking each grade one student in turn, 'Where does your father work? Where does your mother work?' The children answer, and Mariia Mykhailivna writes the information in her journal.

She has already written down where Vitia Artemenko's parents work and where Valia Bilokin's parents work.

Petryk Yagoda is sitting in the second row from the back. As soon as he hears what the teacher is asking the children, he turns pale. Petryk feels frightened and ashamed. How is he going to tell Mariia Mykhailivna, 'I don't have a father'? Forty pairs of eyes will look at him in surprise. During the break, children will ask him, 'Why don't you have a father?'

Petryk wants so much to be home with his mother.

But the teacher keeps asking the children out one after another, questioning them. She seems in no hurry at all.

Petryk Yagoda is the last child on the list.

The boy with a weak heart

There is a boy named Tarasyk studying at our school. He has a weak heart and cannot walk quickly. As soon as he hurries, he becomes breathless.

The children decided to go walking in the forest on Sunday, and Tarasyk wanted to go with them. They gathered early in the morning in the school yard. Tarasyk came too. He brought a bag with some food and a thermos with some water. The children carried his bag for him, and they all set off into the forest.

They walked very slowly, so that Tarasyk would not be exhausted. Petryk wanted to walk faster, and so did Oleh. When they walked on ahead everyone shouted, 'Have you forgotten that Tarasyk is with us?'

The boys stopped and waited for their friends to catch up. The most beautiful friendship is when even one who suffers misfortune is happy.

Gathering mushrooms

Fedko, who was in grade three, was so keen to go mushrooming that he got ready the night before. His mother found a basket for him and a raincoat in case it rained.

It was a foggy morning. Fedko walked into the forest, where there were supposed to be lots of white mushrooms growing. He walked for about a kilometre without seeing a single mushroom.

'Surely I cannot go all day without finding a single mushroom,' he thought. He walked for an hour, two hours, three hours, but there were no mushrooms to be found. Fedko eyes filled with tears. He decided not to go home until it was dark, so that no-one would see how unsuccessful he was.

Suddenly he met his classmate Olenka. She had a basket full of white mushrooms.

'You couldn't find a single mushroom?' she asked in surprise.

Fedko hung his head. He felt ashamed.

Olenka took Fedko's basket, put it on the ground, and tipped half her mushrooms into it. Then they happily walked home together.

If the rooster does not crow …

A grandmother had a grandson named Yashko and a rooster named Goldie. Yashko was five years old, and Goldie was two.

Early each morning, while Grandma and Yashko were still asleep, Goldie, who slept in the entrance hall, would suddenly crow loudly, 'Cock-a-doodle-doo!'

Grandma and Yashko would wake up. 'Morning has broken,' Grandma would say. 'Goldie is crowing, so it's time to get up and get to work.' Grandma would get up, and so would Yashko.

Grandma would let the rooster out, and Goldie would strut off looking for something nice to eat. Grandma would peel some potatoes, and Yashko would sweep the floor. One day, Yashko asked his grandmother, 'Grandma, does morning come because Goldie crows?'

'Of course, Yashko. It gets light because Goldie crows,' she says.

'So, if the rooster did not crow, there would be no morning?'

'Probably not,' answered Grandma.

Yashko caught a cold and fell ill. He needed some medicine, but there was no money to buy it. Grandma put the rooster into a basket and got ready to go to the market. 'We'll sell the rooster,' said Grandma, 'And buy you some medicine.'

Goldie sat in the basket, staring at Yashko. Yashko felt sorry for the rooster.

'Grandma,' begged Yashko through his tears, 'Don't sell Goldie. Then there'll be nobody to crow, and it will be night all the time. The morning won't come … And I don't like it at night.'

Goldie raised his head out of the basket and crowed happily. Yashko laughed, and he began to get better.

Grandma Mariia's funeral

Auntie Mariia worked as a caretaker at our school. When she turned fifty-five, she did not retire. 'It would be hard for me to live without the children,' she explained.

Twenty more years passed, and Auntie Mariia became a grandmother. All the children affectionately called her Grandma Mariia. Every day at dawn, she greeted the children as they arrived at school. When lessons ended for the day, she locked up the school.

When Grandma Mariia turned seventy-five, she fell ill. She was confined to bed for a while, and then she died. Everyone in the village felt heartache at Grandma Mariia's passing. Everyone remembered how their childhood had been spent under her tender and watchful eye.

Her funeral was attended by young and old. Children carried the school bell in front of her coffin, the bell with which for fifty years she had summoned them to school, to the cradle of learning, knowledge and thought.

When the first handfuls of earth fell on the coffin, the youngest student, little Nina in grade one, lifted the bell and rang it. For the first time in fifty years, the bell rang sadly.

The flower of friendship

Dmytryk was in grade three. His father had died, and his mother was often sick. He had two little sisters. His mother often could not work, and then it was very difficult for the family. Sometimes, when Dmytryk's mother saw him off for school, she did not give him any lunch or any money for lunch. On days like that, Dmytryk spent the lunch break waiting for the next lesson, standing by a window with an aquarium. He used to watch the fish and wait for the bell to ring. The break seemed very long, and the boy wanted it to end as soon as possible.

One day, during the lunch break, a girl with blonde hair and deep blue eyes approached Dmytryk. He knew that her name was Katrusia and that she was studying in grade four. One day at an assembly he had spent a lot of time looking at her eyes and admiring how beautiful they were. Katrusia had looked over at him and had been embarrassed … When Katrusia came over to the aquarium, stood next to him, and even touched his hand with hers, Dmytryk's heartbeat raced.

'Dmytryk, would you like some bread and butter?' asked Katrusia.

Dmytryk felt uncomfortable and ashamed, and his face turned red.

'Take it, don't be ashamed,' said Katrusia. 'And here's a piece of sausage and half an apple. Mum always cuts my apple into halves so it will be easier to eat.'

Dmytryk accepted the bread and butter, and the sausage and the apple. It all tasted very good. He forgot to thank Katrusia, and when he thought of it during the lesson, he felt very ashamed.

The next day the same thing happened. Katrusia gave Dmytryk half her lunch. Dmytryk had a feeling that she was giving him the bigger half. They stood by the aquarium, ate, and watched the goldfish.

After they had eaten, the boy and girl dreamt about what it would be like to be a fish in an aquarium. Do they realise that outside the walls of their little home there is a wide and wonderful world with a sky, a sun, clouds and stars? Now Dmytryk did not want the break to end so quickly. Now, for some reason, the lunch break seemed shorter.

And then, one day, someone noticed that Katrusia was giving half her lunch to Dmytryk and wrote about it in the school newspaper. Wasn't it wonderful, they wrote, that she had the awareness to help a fellow student? If only everyone could be like Katrusia …

At the next lunch break, Katrusia ran to the aquarium, but Dmytryk was not there. She cried. Dmytryk was sitting on a bench at the far end of a half-lit corridor. He was afraid that someone would come up to him and ask, 'Was that you they wrote about in the school newspaper?'

And sure enough, two girls ran up to him. He did not know what class they were in. They were about two years older than him. They sat down next to Dmytryk, and one of them said, 'This is where he was hiding … We have been looking for you, Dmytryk. Our class has decided to help you. Look, we have brought you some lunch. Please take it and don't be shy.'

Dmytryk burst into tears and ran away. He ran to his class, collected his books, and walked home. The next day he came to school pale, with tortured eyes. Now Katrusia and Dmytryk kept far apart, but they were experiencing the same feeling. It seemed to them that the beautiful flower that they loved and admired, that is known as friendship, had been taken by dozens of hands, and that dozens of fingers were now poking at every petal.

Why the disabled war veteran went swimming

There were very few people at the beach that day. Summer had ended, and autumn had arrived. The only person to come and swim was six-year-old Fedko. When his mother left for work early that morning, she told her son, 'Go straight to kindergarten and don't wander off anywhere.' But Fedko did not obey her. 'I'll go to the beach,' he thought, 'And have a swim.' He took off his shirt and trousers and eased himself into the water. At first the water felt cold, but then it seemed to get warmer.

A disabled war veteran was sitting on the beach. He only had one leg. He had come to the beach on crutches to have a rest and breathe the fresh sea air. When he saw the little boy swimming further and further out to sea, he took off his clothes and hopped into the water. It was difficult for him to make his way into the water because he had left his crutches on the beach. It was easier for him once he reached deeper water. He swam out to the boy and carefully watched his little blonde head.

When Fedko had swum as much as he wanted, he clambered out of the water, got dressed, and ran to kindergarten. He had not noticed the one-legged war veteran make his way into the water after him, or how carefully the man watched over him while he was swimming, or how he struggled out of the water after him, or how difficult it was for him to get dressed.

What a shame that Fedko did not notice any of those things.

Don't read the story about Yarynka

'At the next class, we will be reading a story about Yarynka,' announced the teacher. Olenka and Galynka had read that story at home. It was about a little girl whose father died.

During the break before the reading class, Olenka and Galynka approached the teacher in the corridor and pleaded, 'Please don't read the story about Yarynka.'

'Why?' asked their teacher.

'Our Oksanka's father is in hospital,' they said. 'He's very sick. Oksanka was crying yesterday.'

'All right, girls,' quietly promised the teacher and kissed them both on the forehead.

The rainbow in the stone

Myshko spotted a stray puppy in the yard. He thought it looked ugly. The puppy sensed Myshko's attitude and ran away from the boy. Myshko picked up a stick, ran after the puppy, and hit it.

The puppy yelped and took off into the bushes. Myshko wanted to chase the puppy and hit it again, but he tripped and hit his toe against something. Myshko looked down his feet and saw a stone. The boy picked it up and wiped it clean, and the stone started shining with all colours of the rainbow.

Myshko sat on the grass, mesmerized by the stone's beauty. He gazed at it, turning it over in his hands, and each time he rotated it, it sparkled brightly with all the colours of the rainbow.

Myshko put the stone close to his heart and looked around. Now, everything around him seemed different. He saw that the sky, which previously had seemed pale and dull, was actually a clear blue. He now noticed a flower of stunning beauty poking out of the grass, and the village, drowning in a sea of green gardens, looked like something out of a fairy tale.

Now the boy's heart ached with pity for the little puppy, who was hiding in the bushes. Myshko looked into the puppies sad, frightened eyes, and his own eyes filled with tears. He lifted the puppy into his arms, hugged him, and took him home.

Myshko spread an old blanket out in their shed, sat the puppy on it, and gave him a saucer of milk. The puppy, still trembling, now trustfully snuggled up to the boy.

From time to time, Myshko took the stone out of his pocket and smiled with joy.

How a squirrel saved a lizard

A shrike lived in the forest. A shrike is an interesting bird that eats insects, mice, and little lizards.

One day, this shrike caught a lizard. He was not very hungry at the time, so he stuck the lizard on a thorn on the branch of a tree and thought, 'I can eat it later.'

The poor lizard was in a lot of pain and started crying. A squirrel came running and jumped onto the tree, jolting the branch, and shaking the lizard off the thorn. The lizard thanked the squirrel and disappeared in the blink of an eye.

A dog and a sheepskin coat

A shepherd was pasturing a herd of cattle over the summer, and his dog was helping him. The shepherd had a sheepskin coat. He would often leave it under a haystack and order his dog to guard it, and the dog did so while the shepherd drove the cows to water.

Autumn arrived, and the shepherd took the cattle back to the village, but he forgot all about his sheepskin coat. It still lay covered with straw, and the dog lay near it, vigilantly guarding it. Days and weeks passed. Snow covered the fields.

The sheepskin coat said to the dog, 'Go back to the village. The shepherd has forgotten all about me. What is the point of you staying here?' The dog replied, 'My master told me to guard you. I have to guard you until he returns.'

'What if he never returns?' asked the coat.

'That is not possible,' replied the dog.

It was bitterly cold. The dog was starving. He had to dig the frozen ground to find some potatoes to eat. By springtime, the dog had almost wasted away, and was very weak. The sun started giving more warmth, and the shepherd returned to the pastures with the cattle. He was deeply moved when he saw his dog still guarding his sheepskin coat. He hugged the dog and said, 'You are my faithful friend!'

The dog whined joyfully. He was saying, 'Haven't I shown you that many times before?'

Silent water

During the night it rained. Heavy drops drummed on the steel roof of our house, as if dozens of rabbits were dancing there. The rain was in a good mood, and chattered noisily as it streamed down the downpipe. It told of a dark cloud, fierce thunder, and bright flashes of lightning. It was also complaining about something.

I went out to the downpipe and watched the stream of water pouring into a barrel. I listened carefully, trying to understand what it was complaining about. It turned out that it did not want to be confined in the barrel. It said, 'What can I do in a barrel? I'll be silent and stop being a stream.'

In the morning, I went out again to the barrel, which was now full of water. The stream of water had been trapped. I opened the tap at the bottom of the barrel, and water streamed out. A stream of water now babbled happily, 'Thank you, dear girl, for setting me free!'

An apple for grandma

On Sunday, a little boy named Serhiiko visited his grandfather—his mother's father. His grandfather gave him a large apple, saying, 'This apple is for your grandma. Please give it to her and pass on my best wishes!' The grandmother he was to give the apple to was Serhiiko's father's mother.

Serhiiko put the apple in his pocket and set off for home. He kept his hand in his pocket to warm up the apple. Serhiiko imagined how happy his grandmother would be when he gave her the apple and passed on his grandfather's greeting.

Finally, he reached home. When Serhiiko entered the front yard, he saw a lot of sad, concerned people. He entered the house. His mother and father were sitting by a bed with tears in their eyes.

Serhiiko's grandmother had died.

Serhiiko stood by the bed with his head down. He took the apple out of his pocket and gently placed it in his grandmother's palm.

It's lesson time

In the middle of the steppe was a little village with about forty homes. The school in that little village was tiny. It had just fifteen students and one teacher. It did not need a bell to announce that classes were starting, or a large corridor to run down during breaks between classes. The children would play outside on the green grass, and in the winter, they would skate on a pond that lay within a stone's throw of the school.

One warm morning in May, the children went out for their break and became totally absorbed in their games. It was already time to go inside and start lessons, and the teacher had already called the students three times, but they seemed not to hear him.

The teacher went outside onto the grass and told them, 'It's lesson time.'

The children sensed a reproach in the words their old teacher spoke and felt that they had disappointed him. They fell silent and shuffled awkwardly over to their teacher.

Just then, they heard music coming from the other side of the village. It was a funeral procession.[52] Old Grandma Hanna, who had died without any relatives, was being carried to the cemetery. The funeral procession approached the school. The teacher stood silently—sad, and deep in thought. The children also felt sad.

Without a word, the teacher joined the funeral procession. The children followed him. After Grandma Hanna was buried, the teacher repeated the words, 'It's lesson time.' But this time, the words sounded very different. The children sensed in them reflection on the eternal questions of life and death. Each word was like a gentle hand, stroking them on the head.

The children were silent.

Who is telling the truth?

A farmer went to plough a field. His wife and baby daughter stayed home. The baby lay in a cradle hanging from the branch of an apple tree. The mother sat beside the cradle, singing a lullaby, and sewing a shirt for her daughter. Next door, her neighbour was doing her laundry.

Suddenly, a hurricane swept down on them. It flattened trees and left houses in ruins. The farmer's house was completely destroyed. The apple tree was uprooted, and the cradle and the baby were carried up into the clouds by the wind, landing far away beyond the mountains.

The distraught mother wailed as she stood by a hole where the apple tree used to be. Her eyes scanned the debris that used to be her lovely home. Only a tiny doll that the baby used to play with was left among the rubble.

The neighbour's house was untouched by the storm. The neighbour ran to the field, found the farmer, and told him what had just happened. The farmer looked into the neighbour's eyes and did not know whether to believe her or not. Her eyes were so indifferent. There was no grief in them, only amazement.

'Is that really true?' he asked his neighbour.

'The gospel truth,' she assured him. And once again she described how the hurricane descended on them, how it destroyed his house, uprooted the apple tree, lifted the cradle high in the sky, and took it far away.

Just then, the farmer spotted his wife crossing the field. She approached her husband without saying a word. She just sobbed bitterly and looked into his eyes. And her eyes were so full of pain and grief that he quietly whispered, 'So it is true.'

New Year's greetings

An old teacher lived all by himself in a Ukrainian village. When he was too weak to continue working, he was transferred to a nursing home. He sadly parted with his grade three students and asked them not to forget him.

A year passed, then a second and a third, and every year, just before New Year, the children would send their teacher greetings: a bright hand-made card with a picture of Grandpa Frost on it. The teacher arranged these cards on his bedside table.

Time passed, until eventually the teacher became very ill and died. Another man took over his bed at the nursing home, but the greeting cards remained on the bedside table.

'We need to write to those children and tell them that their teacher has died,' said one old man.

And they did intend to write, but somehow none of them ever got around to it.

More time passed. And the children sent their teacher another greeting card. The old men put it on the bedside table.

The children grew up, but they did not forget their teacher, and every year they would send a New Year's greeting card.

'Do we really need to write to those children and tell them that their teacher has died?' one of the old men asked one evening. 'Why not let him live on in their memories?'

The years crept by, and every New Year, deeply moved, the old men would read the greeting card sent to the teacher and place it on the bedside table. If one of those old men felt very sad (and old people often feel sad) they would go to the bedside table, look at a greeting card with its bright illustration, and their soul would find some peace.

Hurt feelings and happiness

A dog named Brovko had a good master who never hurt his feelings and always took him for a walk.

But then, one day, the master came home in a dark mood, and did not seem to care about anything. He did not respond to Brovko's gentle whining. He sat still for a long time, deep in thought. Then he stood up, locked the front the door, and was gone. As usual, Brovko begged to be taken for a walk, but his master just pushed him away and did not allow Brovko to join him.

Brovko lay down and started crying. When a dog cries, people say it is whining, and Brovko knew that. He also knew that people do not like it when a dog cries. But at that moment, Brovko forgot all that, because his heart was aching from the deep hurt that he felt.

Brovko's master did not come home that night, nor the next day. Brovko began to worry. He remembered his master's dark face and troubled eyes. Brovko did not feel hurt anymore. He felt anxious.

The master came home late that night. His face was pale and tortured; his eyes were full of suffering. Brovko rushed to his master, put his front paws onto his chest and looked into his master's eyes. Brovko's soul was full of kindness and compassion.

The master hugged his dog, and Brovko started crying, not because he felt hurt, but from happiness. He cried silently, because he knew that people do not like it when a dog cries.

Dmytryk's dad is in prison

One day, in grade one, the students were independently solving some maths problems. It was very quiet in the classroom. The teacher, Vira Pavlivna, was sitting at her desk, dreaming of the spring. Soon the flowers would be in bloom, and her fiancé would return from his military service in the navy …

'Dmytryk's dad is in prison.' A child's voice broke the silence.

Vira Pavlivna raised her head. It was Petryk. He was sharing a desk with Dmytryk and could not help sharing such interesting news.

'He'll be in prison for three months,' Petryk continued, because Vira Pavlivna had been caught off guard and had not had time to gather her thoughts. She saw Dmytryk's face turn pale, and his pen drop from his hand. He raised his eyes and looked pleadingly at Vira Pavlivna.

'Well, there's nothing unusual about that,' said Vira Pavlivna, as all the children turned towards her and listened. 'Dmytryk's father is a glazier. Do you remember how he worked on our windows at school? There are a lot of broken windows at the prison. He has been sent there to fix them, and the work will take some time.'

Dmytryk's eyes shone with gratitude.

How the squirrel saved the woodpecker

In the middle of winter, it turned warm, and rain fell, and then the frost returned. The trees were covered with ice. Even the cones on the fir trees were frozen. There was nothing for the woodpecker to eat. No matter how much he pecked at the ice, he could not get to the bark. No matter how hard he beat the cones with his beak, no seeds came out of them.

The woodpecker sat on the fir tree and cried. His warm tears fell on the snow and froze.

From her nest, the squirrel saw the woodpecker crying. With a hop and a jump, she came running to him.

'Woodpecker, why are you crying?' she asked.

'There's nothing to eat, Squirrel,' he said.

The squirrel felt sorry for the woodpecker. She brought a large fir cone from her nest in the tree. She lay it in a fork of the tree. The woodpecker landed next to the cone and began to hammer it with his beak.

The squirrel watched from her nest and rejoiced. Her baby squirrels in the nest rejoiced, too. Even the sun rejoiced.

The swift's song

A swift is a little grey bird. It lives deep in the forest. One late autumn day, I was walking in the forest and saw a large bird of prey chasing a swift. The little swift crashed into a tree and could not fly.

I picked up the little bird. The swift lived with me all winter. It gradually got better and started to fly. It would take off and fly a little, and then settle on my shoulder.

In spring I took it out and set it free. It perched on a tree and sang me a song. Nobody else could have guessed what it was singing about, but I understood. It was saying to me, 'You are a good friend. I am very sad to have to say good-bye to you, but I love my freedom even more than I love you.'

How we saved the lark's chicks

We were walking through a wheat field when we came across a lark's nest. In the nest were five chicks. They were not yet able to fly, and the following day the combine harvester was coming to harvest all the wheat. We looked at the little chicks, while the mother lark flew above us, calling anxiously. We took the nest with the chicks and placed it in the green millet. The millet would not be harvested for a long time.

As we walked home, we saw that the mother lark had flown to her nest. She sat there for a long time. Then she flew up into the deep blue sky and began to sing joyfully. She was saying, 'Thank you for saving my babies.'

How the bumblebee fed the bee

The flowers of a foxglove look like long purple bells. Deep inside each bell is a little cup of sweet nectar.

A bee hovered by one of these flowers and tried reach the nectar with her long tongue, but in vain. She settled on the flower and broke into tears. A bumblebee was flying by, buzzing loudly 'zzzzz.' The bee told the bumble bee all about her problem.

'I can help you,' the bumblebee assured her.

With his even longer tongue, the bumblebee reached deep inside the flower and sucked up the nectar. The bee flew over to the bumblebee and extended her tongue, and the bumblebee gave her half the nectar. The bee thanked the bumblebee and happily buzzed away.

Since then, the bee and the bumblebee have been good friends.

The chamomile flower and the bee

A chamomile was in full bloom. The flower straightened its petals and set a little cup of nectar on each one. A bee was flying by, and the chamomile called out to her, 'Dear bee! Come over and visit me. I have delicious nectar. Help yourself! See how many cups of nectar I have! Every time you visit me, I'll give you a cup.'

The bee came and tasted the nectar. It was so delicious that she drank a whole cup. She flew back to her hive and told all the other bees what wonderful nectar the chamomile had. The other bees listened to her, and then they all flew off to visit the chamomile.

How the hedgehog prepared for winter

In the forest lived a hedgehog. He made his home in the hollow of an old linden tree. It was warm there, and dry. Then autumn came. Yellow leaves fell from the trees. Soon winter would arrive.

The hedgehog began to prepare for winter. He went into the forest and collected dry leaves on his spikes. He brought the leaves to his home and spread them out, so it became even warmer.

The hedgehog went into the forest again. He gathered pears, apples and rosehips, carried them home on his spikes and stored them in a corner.

Once more the hedgehog went into the forest. He found mushrooms, dried them and stored them in a corner.

The hedgehog was warm and cosy, but he felt sad on his own. He wanted to find a friend. He went into the forest and met a hare, but the hare did not want to come to the hedgehog's house. Neither did the grey mouse or the gopher. They all had their own burrows.

Then the hedgehog met a cricket. The cricket was clinging to a blade of grass and shivering with cold. 'Come and live with me, Cricket!' said the hedgehog.

The cricket hopped to the hedgehog's house, as pleased as could be. Winter came. The hedgehog told the cricket fairy tales, and the cricket sang songs to the hedgehog.

The little girl and the chickadee

It was a cold winter. A little girl named Natalka hung a feeder for chickadees on an apple tree, and every day she brought roasted flax seeds. A chickadee was always waiting for her. Natalka smiled joyfully, and the chickadee sang for her and pecked at the seeds.

In spring, the chickadee said to the little girl, 'You don't need to bring me food anymore. Now I can find food for myself. Good-bye until next winter!'

'Good-bye, little chickadee,' Natalka replied.

Next winter, when the ground was covered in snow, the chickadee came once again to the bird feeder, but it was full of snow. The chickadee was worried. It asked the apple tree, 'Apple tree, please tell me why Natalka is not here. Surely, she has not forgotten me?'

'No, she has not forgotten you. She is sick,' said the apple tree.

The chickadee fell ill at heart. It sat on a branch and thought to itself, 'I will fly to see the little girl. I need to find a way to cheer her up. I should bring her a present, but what can I give her? Everything is covered in snow.'

The chickadee decided to bring Natalka a song. It flew to her house, fluttered in through a little half-open window, settled on the end of Natalka's bed, and sang to her.

Natalka began to feel better.

Why the sparrow fled

A swallow built a nest under the eaves. She brought dry grass and feathers, and even some soft down to rest her head on at night. But then a sparrow took over her nest.

The swallow begged the sparrow, 'Fly back to your own nest, dear sparrow, kind fellow, and let me back into my home.' But the sparrow just pulled his head in and ignored her. The swallow begged him, over and over again, but the sparrow just sat there silently, and would not respond to any of her pleas.

A starling overheard the swallow's pleading cries and flew over. 'My dear swallow,' he said, 'There is no point in reasoning with that fellow! He is such a bandit that no amount of pleading will help. Just pull a feather from his head with your beak, and he'll be gone in the blink of an eye.'

'How can I pull a feather from his head?' lamented the swallow. 'That would really hurt!'

'Then you are a fool! You may as well go and build yourself a new nest!' said the starling.

The swallow settled on a branch and thought to herself, 'What should I do? I feel sorry for the sparrow, because it will really hurt if I pull out one of his feathers. On the other hand, he did not just steal an insect from me. He kicked me out of my home!' Anger stirred in her heart. The swallow spread her wings and flew like an arrow at her nest. She opened her beak ready to pull a feather from the sparrow's head. The sparrow saw her coming and instantly fled.

The swallow was surprised that he had fled so quickly.

But the starling, who saw everything from his birdhouse, just smiled to himself.

Good-day, Brother Rooster!

On the edge of our village stands a kindergarten, a big, brightly lit building with wide windows. Around the building is an orchard, with lots of apple, pear, and plum trees. Under the windows are flowers.

One morning, three-year-old Tymko was brought to the kindergarten by his mother. He could hear a cheeping sound coming from under an apple tree next to the kindergarten. He walked up to the tree and saw a little chick sitting in the grass. It was wet and shivering from the cold.

Tymko picked up the chick, tucked it inside his shirt, and took it into the kindergarten. The little chick dried out there and settled down. When Tymko undid his shirt to see how the chick was faring, he turned his little head and looked at Tymko with little eyes as black as poppy seeds.

The kindergarten teacher, Auntie Mariia, found a home for the chick in a small sieve in the kitchen. The children brought the chick millet and breadcrumbs.

That was how the little chick came to live in the kindergarten. The days and weeks passed, and the chick grew into a handsome little rooster. Each child, when they came to kindergarten, would go into the kitchen and say, 'Good-day, Brother Rooster!' The rooster would quickly jump down from his sieve onto the floor and wait. After those words, he was always given something tasty to eat.

But when Tymko came and said 'Good-day Brother Rooster!' the rooster would jump onto his shoulder and crow, 'Cock-a-doodle-doo!'

That was him saying, 'I love you, Tymko!'

How they took the rooster to market

Grandma Mariia lived with her grandson Yurko and a rooster named Panko. They were all great friends. Early every morning Panko called out, 'Cock-a-doodle-doo!' and Yurko woke up. The boy always took Panko a handful of millet. The rooster pecked at the millet and thanked Yurko.

But then hard times came upon them. The crops failed, and there was nothing for the rooster to eat. Grandma Mariia put Panko in a basket and set off for the market to sell him. Grandma Mariia carried the basket, with Panko poking his head out, looking around and nodding his red comb, and Yurko walking behind, crying.

They reached the Maple Bridge and sat down to have a rest. Grandma dozed off, and Yurko took the rooster from the basket and let it go. Panko ran all the way home.

Grandma Mariia and Yurko reached the market. When grandma reached the bird section, she opened her basket, but it was empty.

Grandma was overcome with joy and hugged and kissed Yurko. The grandmother and grandson came home from the market as happy as can be.

'We will share our porridge with Panko, but we won't take him to the market and sell him,' said Grandma Mariia when they reached their gate.

'I will eat borshch[53] as well,' crowed Panko, when he heard what grandma said.

Why?

Serhiiko was away from school for three weeks, because he was sick. He really missed his friends and his teacher.

When he came back to school, he was excited and happy. There was his desk, and there were his friends.

He thought he would see joy in his friend's eyes, that they would be really happy to see him. But their eyes were calm and indifferent.

His desk partner just asked, 'Have you done today's homework?'

'I've done it,' said Serhiiko quietly, and burst into tears.

Mariika's thoughts

Some little children were playing hide and seek. This is a game where everyone hides, and one child seeks. The one who is seeking must find everyone else.

Little blue-eyed Mariika hid under a tall willow tree and waited. A little boy named Mykolka had to find everyone.

First, he found Larysa. Larysa squealed, laughed and ran away. Then he found Petryk, who also squealed, laughed and ran away.

The children were running and laughing, but no-one was looking for Mariika.

'Why has everyone forgotten about me?' wondered Mariika, and she began to feel sad.

Mariika's sadness grew. She thought, 'I will stand under this willow tree all summer, I will stand here through the autumn, and I will still be here in winter. I will fall asleep, and the snow will cover me, and when I wake up in the spring, I will be a little willow tree. Mum and dad will look for me, and Mykolka will look for me, and Larysa and Petryk. Nobody will be able to find me, and they will all be sad.'

That is what Mariika thought, and because of those thoughts two tears trickled from her eyes and fell onto the grass. But as soon as those tears settled on the grass, someone touched the little girl's hand. It was Mykolka. He had been looking for Mariika and had found her.

Mariika squealed with joy, and at that very moment a black bird took off from the willow tree and flew far, far away. That was Mariika's sad thoughts flying away.

As you sow, so shall you reap

A male pigeon and a female pigeon flew to our house. They settled on our porch and cooed. They looked at me as if they were asking for something. I climbed into our attic and opened a little window. The pigeons flew into it. Later I brought them some grain. They pecked at it and then flew back out through the attic window.

The next morning, I again fed the pigeons and gave them a container with some water to drink. After that I sometimes fed them, and sometimes forgot. More often than not, I forgot to feed the pigeons. They sat on our porch and looked at me, but I was always in a hurry to get somewhere. Once I was walking, and a pigeon flew above my head, as if he wanted to settle on my shoulder. I thought he was just playing and did not realise he was hungry.

One morning I saw that the pigeons were in my neighbours' yard, and little Olia was feeding them. Her father was building a little house on a post, a dovecote.

It pained me. I called and called to the pigeons, but they did not come to me anymore. They settled in the dovecote. Olia feeds them every day, morning and evening. They love the little girl, settling on her shoulder and letting her hold them in her hands.

The proverb says, 'As you sow, so shall you reap.' I sowed indifference, and I reaped neglect. Birds do not love those who are indifferent to them.

The deaf girl

At the hospital there is a children's ward. Seven girls were being treated there, each with their own illness. They had all recovered well, and now they were bored. The oldest girl, thirteen-year-old Tania, felt herself to be the leader of this group of children. She opened the window and looked out at the flowering garden.

'The lilac is already in bloom,' she said thoughtfully, 'And the tulips have flowered. Girls, let's bring a flower into our ward and put it in a glass of water. That would be really nice!'

'That would be great!' agreed everyone with joy.

Only one little girl remained silent—eight-year-old Nina. She was deaf.

Nina understood very well what they were talking about. She was also happy at the thought of bringing a flower into the ward. She wanted to nod in agreement and smile joyfully, but she sensed that Tania's question was not addressed to her.

'What flower will we choose, lilac or tulip?' asked Tania again.

'Lilac!' said some of the girls.

'A tulip!' said others.

Neither Tania, nor the other girls, for some reason, considered that they could bring in two flowers, one lilac and one tulip. They were engrossed in the game and wanted to play.

'We are not in agreement,' sighed Tania. 'We'll take a vote. Each of us can say which flower we want to put on the table, lilac or tulip.

Three wanted lilac and three wanted a tulip.

'What are we going to do now?' asked Tania thoughtfully. Her eyes sparkled with mischief. She loved to play games. The other girls were also caught up in the game.

'What will we do? Three want a tulip and three want lilac,' Tanya murmured again, as if thinking aloud.

Suddenly her gaze fell on Nina. The deaf girl sat by the window, and tears were trembling in her eyes. They were tears of hurt and injustice. They had forgotten about her and did not ask which flower she preferred.

'Oh!' exclaimed Tania. 'We forgot about Nina … What flower would you like, Nina, lilac or tulip?'

Nina smiled and with her delicate finger she drew a tulip in the air. Tania went out and picked a tulip.

Nina watched from the window, smiling.

Nuts for the squirrel

Once a year in the village of Vasylivka, in May, there is a big market. People come from distant towns and villages, put up tents, and display their wonderful wares. The market is a festive day for all the villagers in Vasylivka, and especially for the children.

Little Pavlyk woke up at dawn. Today was Sunday, so he did not need to go to school. He could spend all day at the market. His mother gave him a whole fifty *kopiika*[54] piece to spend and told him he could buy whatever he liked.

Pavlyk clutched the coin in his hand and went to the market. What riches he saw all around him! They seemed to have everything! The boy was bewitched by the sweets in coloured wrappers, the fluffy white bagels, the shortcakes, the rooster-shaped lollypops, the horse-shaped gingerbreads and lark-shaped sweetbreads. He wanted to spend all his money at once, but he thought to himself, 'I'll buy one thing, and then there will be so many other sweet things that I cannot buy … No, I'll wait a bit. All these wonderful, sweet things will not go anywhere, not the lollies or the bagels, not the lollypops or the gingerbreads, with their sweet centres.'

Pavlyk wandered around the market, walking from tent to tent with joy. There were lots of good things being sold here that he could afford to buy …

He wandered like this until midday, in joyful anticipation of the pleasure to come, when suddenly he came upon a squirrel in a cage, and next to it, a little tent where a man was selling nuts. The squirrel looked curiously at everyone who approached its cage. Pavlyk looked into its eyes, and thought he saw sadness there. He went over to the little tent and spent all his money on nuts. The nuts were expensive, imported ones, and he did not get very many for his money.

Pavlyk went over to the cage and tipped all his nuts in for the squirrel to eat. It began to gnaw on them straight away, looking up at the boy. Pavlyk stood in front of the cage for a long time, until the squirrel had cracked open and eaten all the nuts.

When the man selling nuts for the squirrel came over and opened the door of the cage, and threw out all the shells, Pavlyk sighed and went home. It was already getting dark.

When he got home he sat by the window and burst into tears.

'Why are you crying, Pavlyk?' asked his mother.

'Why did they lock it up in a cage?' he cried.

So the butterfly will not prick itself

Little Zoia was walking in the garden. She went up to an acacia. It had very sharp thorns.

A brightly coloured butterfly was flying above the acacia. 'Oh!' thought Zoia. 'It is dangerous to fly there! What if it flies onto the thorns?'

Zoia stepped up to the acacia. She broke off one thorn, then a second, then a third. Her mother saw her and asked, 'What are you doing, Zoia? Why are you breaking off the thorns?'

'So the butterfly will not prick itself,' answered Zoia.

Petryk, the dog and the kitten

Little Petryk was walking along a path through the orchard. He saw a shaggy, black dog running towards him.

Petryk was frightened and wanted to run. But suddenly a little kitten came and huddled against his legs. It was trying to escape from the dog, and was begging Petryk, 'Defend me, boy, from that terrifying beast.'

Petryk stood, looking at the kitten, while it raised its little head and miaowed pitifully.

The kitten made Petryk feel ashamed. He took it into his arms and walked towards the dog.

The dog stopped, looked at Petryk with fear, and hid in the bushes.

So the cat would not catch the mouse

Little Olia's mother was reading her a book that told of amazing things. Once upon a time a little mouse lived in a mouse-hole. One day she came out for a walk, and a cat with big whiskers chased the frightened mouse all the way back to its hole. The mouse sat inside, shivering with fear, while the cat sat by the hole and waited for the mouse to come out. That was how the story ended.

Olia asked her mother, 'But mum, what happened next? The cat didn't catch the mouse, did it?'

'It doesn't say,' answered her mother. 'The cat is waiting outside the hole, and the mouse is hiding inside.'

That night everyone went to bed. Olia's mother left the book about the cat and the mouse on the table. Olia could not sleep. 'The mouse is in the book,' she thought. 'She might run out of her hole, and the cat with the big whiskers will catch her.'

Olia quietly got out of bed, took the book about the mouse, and hid it in the cupboard, so that the cat could not catch the mouse.

A hut in the forest

A grandfather and his ten-year-old grandson were walking through a vast forest. A barely discernible path wound between tall trees.

It was evening, and the travellers were tired. The grandfather was already preparing to set up camp under the open sky, when suddenly the boy caught sight of a little hut in a thicket by the side of the forest path.

'Grandpa, look, there's a hut!' shouted the grandson joyfully. 'Maybe we can spend the night there.'

'Yes, it's a hut for travellers like us,' explained the grandfather.

They entered the hut. It was clean inside, with a fir branch hanging on the wooden wall. According to folk tradition, this signified hospitality: please make yourselves at home, respected guests.

The grandfather and his grandson stepped over to a table and saw a fresh loaf of bread and a little jug of honey.

On the windowsill was a bucket full of water.

The grandfather and his grandson washed and sat down to supper.

'Who put food on the table like this?' asked the grandson.

'A kind person,' explained his grandfather.

'How can that be?' asked the grandson in amazement. 'A kind person left food for us, and we don't even know who they are. Why did they make such an effort?'

'So that you would become a better person,' answered the grandfather.

I want to express my gratitude

I was three or four years old at the time. My mother took me to the hospital for an injection.

We approached a big white building. Everything in that building was white: the walls and even the doors. We were called into a small examination room. A doctor was sitting at his desk. He looked at me and angrily said to my mother, 'Why didn't you take off the patient's outer garments? Do you expect me to do it?' His face was red with anger, and I felt scared.

Just then, a women entered the room. She was also a doctor and wearing a white robe. She gently lay her hand on my head and said, 'What a beautiful jacket you have! It looks warm, too. Let's take it off!'

The woman's kind words made me feel warm and happy inside. I took off the jacket all by myself, and when they gave me the injection, it did not hurt.

I am twenty-five years old now, and have two children. Both of those two doctors—the man and the woman—still work in our village. Whenever I see that angry doctor in the street (all my life I have called him that), I want to cross over to the other side of the road. But whenever I see that gentle woman walking towards me, my heart fills with joy. I want to walk up to her, greet her, and say something to express all the gratitude I feel.

A blizzard

Tolia, who was in grade one, left home in the morning. A blizzard was raging outside. The trees howled threateningly.

The boy was frightened. He stood under a poplar and thought, 'I won't go to school today. It's too scary.'

Then he saw Sashko, standing under a willow tree. Sashko lived across the road. He had also set off for school and become frightened.

The boys were delighted to see each other, and their fear disappeared. They ran to meet each other, held hands and set off for school.

The blizzard whistled and howled, but it was no longer frightening.

Straw hats

A young boy came from the big city to a quiet little town on the banks of the Dnipro River for his summer holidays.[55] He was met by a sailor who worked on a steam ship that cruised up and down the Dnipro. It sailed all the way to the Black Sea. The sailor took the boy to the home of an old wartime friend of his father's.

The boy settled into a small room with a window that looked out on the Dnipro. Every day, the boy would go to the beach to play and to swim. The beach was crowded with other holiday makers who enjoyed spending their summer vacation at that hospitable town with its white houses.

On the very first day, the boy noticed an old man sitting by the riverside. He was sitting on a rock, and three large straw hats were spread out beside him on the sand, though he himself, for some reason, was not wearing a hat. His face was lined with deep wrinkles, and he sat gazing at the waves of the Dnipro. The boy observed throughout the day that nobody bought any hats from the old man. All three straw hats lay on the beach untouched until evening.

The boy felt sorry for the old man. Every day the boy was given fifty *kopiika*[56] to buy himself an ice-cream. One day, the boy approached the old man and asked him how much a hat cost.

'Twenty-five *kopiika*,' replied the man quietly, but he did not raise his head or look at the boy.

'I'll take two hats, please,' said the boy.

The old man gave the boy two hats and put the coins into his pocket. The boy expected that the old man would be grateful and would thank him, but the old man did not even look at him. It seemed to the boy that the man was concentrating on something in the distance.

The next day, there were three new straw hats laid out by the rock. And again, nobody approached the old man to ask him about his hats. When it was time for the boy to have lunch, he took out his ice-cream money and bought two more hats from the old man. The old man did not raise his head this time either, but the boy could swear that he was listening attentively to his every word.

It continued like that every day: the boy would buy two hats from the old man and take them to his room looking out on the Dnipro. Now he observed that the man listened attentively not only to his words, but to the sound of his footsteps.

The last day of the summer holidays arrived. The boy's father was coming to collect him. The boy went to see the old man one last time and bought two more hats. He was about to leave, when the man lifted his hand and rested it on the boy's shoulder.

'Farewell, young man,' he said quietly. 'You are a good person.'

The boy felt his heart contract with compassion.

'How do you know that I am leaving?' was all he could whisper.

The old man raised his head, and the boy saw that he had no eyes.

They sat in silence for a long time.

'Do you make these hats yourself?' asked the boy.

'Yes, I make them myself … At night … If it wasn't for this work, I would have died by now,' said the old man.

The boy sighed heavily and said, 'I'll come again next summer. Please don't die! All right?'

'All right, young man,' promised the old man softly, and his hands trembled. 'Now I'll have to make sure I don't die.'

Grandma Motria and Andriiko

Andriiko is studying in grade two. He sits by our classroom window. Outside the window is a well. Sometimes Grandma Motria, who lives next to the school, comes to the well for water. Andriiko often sees Grandma Motria and tells his teacher, 'Mariia Petrivna, Grandma Motria has come to fetch water.'

'Go and help her draw up the bucket,' his teacher will say. And Andriiko will run and help the old lady to draw water and quickly return to class.

Today there is a test during the arithmetic lesson. Andriiko cannot find a way to solve the problem. Suddenly he sees the old lady.

'Mariia Petrivna!' Andriiko exclaims joyfully, 'Grandma Mariia has come to fetch water!'

'Go and help her draw up the bucket,' says his teacher.

Andriiko runs to help. Five minutes pass, then ten, then twenty, but he is nowhere to be seen. The bell rings, and Andriiko has still not returned. Mariia Petrivna collects all the exercise books with the answers to the test.

Andriiko enters the classroom, all flushed and wet.

'Where have you been?' asks his teacher in surprise.

'I've been carrying water for Grandma Motria,' says Andriiko. 'I carried ten buckets for her, and washed her floor.'

Strawberries for Natalka

There is a little girl named Natalka in grade three. She was sick for a long time. When she came back to school, she was very pale and tired quickly. Andriiko told his mother about Natalka.

'That girl needs to eat honey and strawberries,' said his mother. 'Then she will become strong, with rosy cheeks … Take her some strawberries, Andriiko.'

Andriiko wanted to take some strawberries for Natalka, but for some reason he felt ashamed. That is what he told his mother: 'I'd feel ashamed. I won't take them.'

'Why would you feel ashamed?' his mother asked in surprise.

Andriiko did not know why.

The next day he took a pack of strawberries anyway. When lessons ended, he went over to Natalka. He gave her the pack of strawberries and quietly said, 'These are strawberries. Eat them, and your cheeks will turn red.'

The little girl took the strawberries. And then something amazing happened. Her cheeks turned as red as a poppy flower. She tenderly looked into Andriiko's eyes and whispered, 'Thank you.'

'Why did her cheeks suddenly turn red?' wondered Andriiko. 'She hasn't even eaten the strawberries yet.'

How Andriiko carried Nina

Andriiko and Nina were walking home from school. On the way they had to cross a gully. The sun was quite warm and had melted the snow, and water was now flowing through the gully. The swift flowing water was making quite a noise, and Andriiko and Nina stopped when they came to it.

Andriiko walked straight through it and reached the other side. He turned and looked at Nina and suddenly felt ashamed. He was wearing boots, but Nina was only wearing shoes. How was she going to get across? 'I've done the wrong thing,' thought Andriiko. 'Why didn't I see that Nina is only wearing shoes?'

The boy crossed back over to Nina and said, 'I just wanted to see how deep it is. Now we can cross together.'

'How?' asked Nina in surprise. 'I've only got shoes on.'

'Sit on my back,' said Andriiko.

Nina sat on Andriiko's back, and the boy carried her to the other side.

A kitten under her jumper

It was very quiet in the classroom. The grade three students were independently solving some maths problems. The teacher, Mariia Mykolaivna, walked over to Zina. She wondered why the girl kept on looking under her jumper and shifting something from one side to another. The teacher was deeply touched to see a tiny kitten poke its head out, look at the teacher, and quickly retreat to the safety of the girl's jumper.

Mariia Mykolaivna gently touched Zina's shoulder and gave her a conspiratorial wink. The girl understood that the teacher knew her secret. She blushed and awkwardly looked into her teacher's eyes. Mariia Mykolaivna lifted a finger to her lips to let the girl know that her secret was safe with her. The girl smiled happily …

The next day, Mariia Mykolaivna took Zina to one side and asked her quietly, 'Why did you bring your kitten to school yesterday?'

'Oh, I'm sorry Miss,' she said. 'There was no-one at home … And our kitten is afraid when she's at home by herself.'

My dad is all better

Katia is a little girl in grade one with thick blonde hair in pig tails. Today she is very happy. Her father was sick in hospital for more than a year and had three operations. It was a very sad time for Katia and her mother. Sometimes Katia would wake in the middle of the night and hear her mother crying.

But today her father was back at work, fit and healthy. Joy shone in

Katia's eyes. When she arrived at school, she met two of her classmates, Petko and Hryts, in the yard. She shared her happiness with them. 'My dad is all better,' she said.

Petko and Hryts looked at Katia and shrugged their shoulders in surprise. Without saying a word, they ran off to play with their ball.

Katia went over to some girls who were playing school. 'My dad is all better,' she said, and joy shone in her eyes. One of the girls, Nina, seemed surprised and asked, 'So what?'

Katia felt a lump in her throat and found it hard to breathe. She went over to a solitary poplar tree on the edge of the school yard and burst into tears.

'Why are you crying Katia?' asked a quiet, tender voice. It was Kostia, a boy who hardly ever talked and who sat in the back row.

Katia raised her head, and between her sobs she said, 'My dad is all better.'

'That's great!' said Kostia joyfully. 'In the pine forest near my house there are already some squills in flower. Why don't you come to my place after school, and we can pick some squills and take them to your dad.'

Joy shone in Katia's eyes.

The boy who was fearful

A new student joined grade five in the middle of the year. His name was Mykola. From the very first day, everyone was convinced that he was fearful and shy. He was offered a seat in the front row, but he declined it, and requested a seat at the back of the class.

Mykola studied conscientiously and always completed his homework well. His answers in class were so good that when he was asked to come out to the blackboard to answer a question, a silence fell over the class. Everyone wanted to hear his reply. The teachers often praised Mykola, saying, 'That is how assignments should be done, and that is how to answer questions.' The boy blushed when he received such praise, and everyone could see he just wanted to return to his seat at the back of the class as quickly as possible.

Mykola's classmates said, 'He's a good student and a good friend. If you ask him, he will always explain how to solve a problem. But he is really fearful.'

One day, the grade five students were returning home from school. It was in May, just before the end of the school year. They were walking in a large group and arguing about something. When they reached a bridge over a stream, they heard a cry. Someone was crying out from below, not far from the bridge. The stream was not wide, but it was fast-flowing and full. Could someone be crying for help?

The boys hardly had time to think about it, when they saw Mykola leap into the water in the direction of the cry. The shocked boys ran to the bridge railing. Mykola was already swimming towards a little girl. She could not swim strongly and was being sucked into a whirlpool. At any moment the girl would be lost. 'Grab on to my shirt!' shouted Mykola. The girl gripped his shirt, and Mykola quickly swam with her to the bank.

An ordinary man

In the middle of the hot, dry steppe was a well. By the well was a hut. In the hut lived a grandfather and his grandson.

The well had a bucket on a long rope. When people travelled that way, they would stop at the well, drink some water, and thank the grandfather.

One day the bucket came off the rope and fell to the bottom of the deep well. The grandfather did not have another bucket and had no way of getting water to drink.

The next morning, a man rode up to the hut in a cart. He had a bucket under some hay.

The traveller looked at the well, looked at the grandfather and his grandson, cracked his whip at the horse, and travelled on.

'What sort of man was that?' asked the grandson.

'That is not a man,' answered the grandfather.

At midday, another traveller came past the grandfather's hut. He took a bucket from under the hay in his cart, tied it to the rope, drew some water and had a drink, gave a drink to the grandfather and his grandson, poured some water on the dry sand, put his bucket back under his hay, and travelled on.

'What sort of man was that? asked the grandson.

'That is still not a man,' answered the grandfather.

In the evening, a third traveller stopped by the grandfather's hut. He took a bucket from his cart, tied it to the rope, drew water, had a drink, thanked them and travelled on, leaving the bucket tied to the rope.

'And what sort of man was that?' asked the grandson.

'An ordinary man,' answered the grandfather.

Blind love

A young mother sits by her open window with a happy smile on her face. Her five-year-old son Vitia has just gone outside and is standing on the green grass. How handsome he is, and how clever!

Two other boys—Boria and Mykolka—approach Vitia. They are five-year-old boys, just like Vitia, but Vitia's mother thinks they are not nearly as developed as her son. Vitia is cleverer and more imaginative, and he has a bright, interesting personality. His peers seem grey by comparison.

The mother watches the children and smiles. Now they are arguing, waving their arms like young roosters. Suddenly Vitia clenches his fist and punches Mykolka. Mykolka steps back and looks at Vitia in astonishment.

The mother closes her eyes. 'It is nothing to worry about,' she thinks. 'It is not a real fight. They are just playing. And if Vitia hit Mykolka, he must have had a good reason. He never does anything wrong.'

The mother opens her eyes and sees Mykolka clench his fist and punch Vitia, who responds by howling loudly. Vitia's mother opens her eyes wide in horror. She runs outside shouting, 'How dare you torment a defenceless child? You should be ashamed of yourselves. You can see that he won't stick up for himself!'

She runs up to the children and picks up Vitia in her arms. He clings to her, sobbing, and the mother also has tears in her eyes.

An old man is sitting on a bench nearby. He quietly says, 'A blind love is as bad as hatred. And blind lies are worse than hatred.' But the mother does not hear these wise words.

One sip for the weakest

One warm June day, the children went to the forest. It so happened that the only person who brought water along was little Myshko. No one else did.

It was hot in the forest. Everyone was thirsty. The teacher said, 'We must save our water. There is no well or stream nearby. The weakest children can have just one sip. The strong ones with self-control can wait.'

They placed the flask of water on the grass beneath an oak tree. The children walked around the forest for a long time, searching for a flower that their teacher had told them about. That flower had blue petals, just like the sky in spring, and in its centre—a golden drop, just like a drop of dew coloured by the sun. They found just one tiny little flower, and it would have been a shame to pick it …

They gathered on the grass and listened to their teacher tell them a story, and then each child made up their own story. The more time passed, the thirstier everyone became, but would anyone walk up to the flask of water? If they did, the others would think they were the weakest! Everyone held out and put up with it. No-one mentioned the water.

The sun began to set behind the trees. A cold breeze blew from the gully. It was time to return home, and they all set off.

Little Myshko carried the flask of water. He asked, 'Who would like a drink?'

Everyone was silent.

His mother does not have time

One day, Tolia, a slow, placid grade three student, had a visitor, his classmate Sashko.

Tolia handed Sashko a picture book, sat him on the sofa, and went to the fridge. He knew that his daily treat would be waiting there for him—a tub of ice cream.

Tolia opened the fridge, found his ice cream, took a small spoon, and sat down to eat. When Tolia is eating ice cream, he forgets about everything else. He even forgot that Sashko was sitting on the sofa.

Tolia finished eating his ice cream, and then looked at Sashko. His face seemed to have a strange expression. He had never seen his friend looking like that, as if he was very, very ashamed of something, so ashamed that at any moment he would burst into tears.

Tolia was very surprised. He went over to his guest and asked, 'What's the matter, Sashko?'

'Nothing. I need to go home,' answered Sashko quietly, and he got up and quickly left the room.

Tolia was even more surprised. He could not understand what had happened.

'Mum, why did Sashko go home?' Tolia asked his mother, who was working in the kitchen.

'I haven't even got time to look after you, let alone Sashko,' answered his mother irritably.

Oksana left

A young woman named Maryna was sitting at the table and sewing. Needles and thread lay on the table in front of her. In the middle of the table lay some money—about twenty *karbovanets*.[57]

Maryna was visited by her neighbour Oksana, who was also a young woman. Their houses were next to each other, and their children studied at the same school. Oksana asked if she could borrow a knife for chopping up cabbage. The knife was in the cellar. Maryna put down her sewing and said, 'I'll go down into the cellar now and find the knife.' She took the money from the table, clenched it in her hand, and went to look for the knife.

She came back a minute later. In her left hand was a big knife, used in villages in autumn to chop up cabbage for storage in a barrel.

Oksana was nowhere to be seen. Maryna stood there, with downcast eyes. With slow, heavy steps she walked over to the table and sat down, leaning on her elbows. Her clenched right hand opened, and her money fell onto the table.

Cruelty

One summer day, five-year-old Yasha went to the pond with his father to swim. It was fun to splash about in the warm water and play in the hot sand.

A little puppy came running along the steep bank of the pond. Suddenly it slipped and fell into the water. Near the overhanging bank the water was very deep. It made Yasha's heart ache to hear the plaintive yelping of the little pup. It seemed to be calling for help, but the boy could not swim. He begged his father, 'Dad, save the puppy … It will drown.'

His father answered, 'You can't save everyone.'

The pup gave one last yelp and drowned. The pond fell silent. Yasha cried.

Many years passed. Yasha became a grown man and people now called him Yakiv Ivanovych. He built a house and had a five-year-old son named Ivas.

A fierce winter came. The earth was crackling from the frost. One evening a blizzard set in. Someone knocked at the window.

'Who's there?' asked Yakiv Ivanovych.

'Kind people, please let is in to warm ourselves,' said a voice. 'We are travellers. We are freezing. Save us.'

'You can't save everyone,' said Yakiv Ivanovych to himself, and out loud he said, 'Go on a bit further. We are crowded here.'

'Dad, why didn't you let them in?' asked Ivas. 'They will die in the cold.'

'You can't save everyone,' repeated his father.

Ivas burst into tears.

The most miserly old man in the world

On the edge of the village lived a miserly old man. He planted grapevines in his garden. Not many people grew grapes in that area, and they were regarded as a marvel. After two years, the first bunches of grapes appeared. They swelled with sweet juice and became large and transparent.

One day, a mother and her three-year-old son were walking past the grapevines. The boy saw the bunches of grapes and asked, 'Mum, what is that?'

'They're grapes,' said his mother.

'What are grapes? What are they like?' asked the boy.

'They're sweet. There is no berry as sweet as a grape,' said his mother.

The boy wanted to try the grapes, so his mother asked the old man, 'Please give my boy a bunch of grapes, so he can try them.'

The miserly old man would not give the boy a bunch of grapes. He gave him just a single grape, and even that made his eyes go dark. He was sorry to lose that single grape.

The mother and her boy left. After that, the miserly old man built a tall fence around his grapevines. He hid not only his grapevines, but his house as well. The miserly old man felt happy and at peace. Nobody could see his grapes now, and nobody would ask for them. But he did not notice that one grapevine had climbed up the fence, reached the top, and flowered there. A bunch of grapes hung over the fence and ripened, swelling with sweet juice.

The same mother and her son came walking along that path. The boy saw the bunch of grapes hanging over the fence and was overjoyed.

'Look, mum,' he said. 'A bunch of grapes. Why did they grow so high?'

'They don't want to be hidden by a fence,' his mother replied.

'What beautiful grapes!' said the boy.

The miserly old man was standing on the other side of the fence, and he heard the boy's words. He was terribly angry that the boy had seen the grapes. His rage was so intense that his heart burst. The old man died, but nobody in the whole world knew of his death, because it was hidden from people by the high fence.

A year passed. The spring sun roused the earth, and the grapevines turned green again. Their living vines wanted to see the sun so much, and hated the fence so much, that they pushed it over. It fell to the ground, and people discovered the amazing beauty that had been hidden from them. The grapes sparkled in the bright sunlight, and in each grape was reflected the sky, the sun and the beautiful earth. People came to the vineyard and looked after it, and they forgot all about the miserly old man.

The telephone receiver

Thirteen-year-old Kostia lived in a small town on the banks of the Dnipro River. He was studying in grade six.

His mother had recently been allocated a comfortable apartment on the second floor of a three-storey building. Near the building was a telephone booth, where you could make a call at any time, even in the middle of the night.

One day, Kostia looked into the telephone booth and decided to cut off the receiver. 'I can make my own telephone at home,' he thought. 'I will talk with my friend Yurko, who lives on the third floor.'

So, he did. He cut off the receiver. But where would he get a receiver for Yurko? They went together and found another phone booth three blocks away. They cut off the receiver there and managed to make a telephone line and chat with each other. They had a lot of fun. His mother saw the phone but did not even ask where it came from.

Several days passed. One night, Kostia woke up and heard a groan. His mother was groaning. She asked him to turn on the light. Kostia turned on the light and saw his mother lying there, very pale, breathing heavily.

'It's my heart … Kostia,' his mother whispered, 'Go to the telephone booth … and ring the ambulance … You know how to phone.' And she lost consciousness.

When his mother mentioned the telephone booth, Kostia was overcome with horror. He had cut off the receivers in the two nearest phone booths, and they had not yet been replaced. He had checked today … What was he to do?

Kostia ran onto the street, crying. What was he to do now? Where could he go? He remembered that there was a phone booth near the railway bridge and ran in that direction.

Kostia ran through the unfamiliar silence of the sleeping town. His heart thumped in his chest. The boy wanted to shout to the whole world, 'My mum is dying! Please, kind people, help me!'

He reached the bridge, but there was no phone booth. Kostia groaned and wept and ran back home.

He opened the door into their room. His mother was lying there, pale, without breathing.

'Mum! Mum!' wept the boy and fell on his knees by the bed.

Boris's nesting box

The air smelt of spring. Olia, a student in grade seven, came to speak to the grade three students. 'Children, soon the starlings will arrive,' she said. 'But we don't have enough bird houses. Who would like to make a nesting box?'

Nearly all the children raised their hands. Boris was one of them. At home, he began to make the nesting box all by himself, but it was difficult to plane the wood evenly, and to hammer the pieces together without any gaps. His father helped him.

The nesting box turned out beautifully and was very cosy. Olia praised

Boris. 'Yours is the most beautiful bird house,' she said. Boris wanted to climb a tree and attach his nesting box, but Olia said, 'The older school students will take these nesting boxes out into the fields and put them up in forest belts, so that the starlings can live there as well.' Boris was very pleased that his bird house would be out in the fields.

The summer passed and autumn arrived. Now Boris was studying in grade four. One day his teacher asked him to go and get some chalk. There was no chalk on the table in the corridor, but Boris knew that it was stored in a cupboard nearby. He opened the cupboard and saw his nesting box on the shelf. Someone had pulled the roof off, and it was full of chalk.

Boris burst into tears. His teacher came out from the classroom and asked, 'Why are you crying, Boris?'

How the hare was punished

In a wide, green clearing in the forest, was a little town where hares lived. They lived as one big, happy family, and all helped each other. They built little homes for themselves and guarded their little town from the cunning fox and the evil wolf. They posted sentries in the forest, and as soon as a fox or a wolf approached, they hid in their little homes, where they had nothing to fear.

The hares had a big vegetable garden, where they grew cabbages. Every day they worked in the vegetable garden, watering the cabbages and pulling out weeds. The hares did not like idlers. If any of the hares tried to avoid doing their share of the work, all the hares gathered in the clearing, sat the idler on an old tree stump, and pulled a hair out of their tail. For hares this was considered extremely shameful. Of course, at the same time they also made speeches, criticising laziness and idleness.

Then one day something unheard of happened in that happy family of hares. One young hare went to the vegetable garden during the night and ate all the cabbages.

The indignant hares gathered in the clearing and began to discuss how to punish the offender. They unanimously decided to banish the young hare. He could go wherever he wanted.

The offending hare burst into tears and said, 'That's not fair. I have never been sat on the old stump. No-one has ever pulled a hair out of my tail. No-one has ever criticised me or made speeches about my behaviour. Why am I suddenly being given such a severe punishment?'

The hares thought about it. The oldest and wisest hare came out and said, 'It is true that we ourselves are at fault. We did not raise this hare properly. We should not punish him so severely. We should first sit him on the old tree stump and pull a hair out of his tail.'

So, they sat the offending hare on the old tree stump, pulled a hair out of his tail, and began to make speeches about his behaviour.

The naughty hare listened to their stern speeches with his head bowed, but his eyes kept wandering over to the vegetable garden. It looked like there were still a few cabbages left.

How Stepan filled a barrel with water

Stepan is already fifteen years old. He barely managed to complete seven years of study at school, but he was not promoted into grade eight because he had not learnt to read properly. If he could learn to read well over the summer, he would be promoted to grade eight.

Stepan liked to sleep a lot and to get up late. When Stepan woke, his mother gave him *varenyky*[58] for breakfast. Stepan would fill himself up with *varenyky*, and then he would not feel like going to school.

Summer came, and Stepan's mother said, 'That's enough sleeping in, Stepan. Tomorrow you can go to work on the collective farm.'

Stepan's mother woke him at five o'clock in the morning. He joined a work brigade, and the leader told him, 'Here is a cart with a barrel. You must cart water to the people working in the field.'

Stepan went to the well and began to pour water into the barrel. He drew ten buckets of water from the well, but the barrel did not seem to be filling.

'What a big barrel it is,' thought Stepan, and sat down to rest.

Stepan poured another twenty buckets of water into the barrel, but it was still empty. By now the sun was getting high in the sky, and it was scorching hot, but Stepan was still standing by the well with his barrel.

The people working in the fields sent a girl to see what Stepan was up to. The girl came to the well and saw that Stepan was pouring water into the barrel, but that it was all flowing out through a hole in the side of the barrel, because Stepan had not plugged it.

‘Why didn’t you plug the hole in the side of the barrel?’ asked the girl.

‘Does the barrel have a hole in the side?’ asked Stepan in surprise.

We’re not going any further with you

Mykhailo, Vasyl and Yurko set off on a long hike. They had to walk through a vast forest and find a dug-out where partisans had lived during World War II. It was not easy to follow the forest paths. The boys tired. Around midday, they came across a little forest stream. Its pure spring water babbled soothingly.

The young explorers sat down and lay their rucksacks on the grass. They decided to stop and rest. Mykhailo and Yurko went over to the stream, crouched on their knees, and drank deeply. ‘What sweet-tasting water!’ they said.

Vasyl also went over to the stream, sat on the grass, took off his boots, and began to wash his feet in the stream. Mykhailo and Yurko exchanged glances. They went over to Vasyl, and Mykhailo said, ‘Vasyl, we’re not going any further with you. You can go back home.’

The slingshot and the sparrow’s nest

Eight-year-old Yurko came to school with a slingshot. There was still lots of time before lessons would start. He sat under a lilac bush and watched the sparrows happily chirping as they flew from branch to branch.

Suddenly, all the sparrows rose into the air and flew off somewhere. Only one sparrow remained, still chirping quietly and tenderly. Then it began to clean its feathers with its beak. Yurko aimed and shot a stone at the sparrow. He hit it right in the head. Some blood splattered on a leaf, and the sparrow’s body fell like a stone at his feet.

Yurko was suddenly afraid. ‘Did I really do that?’ he thought. Then he felt somebody’s hand on his shoulder. Yurko looked around and saw Panas Ivanovych, his teacher. Panas Ivanovych parted the branches, and the boy saw a sparrow’s nest in the lilac bush. Five little chicks peeped out of the nest. Featherless and helpless, they cheeped pitifully as they stretched out their beaks.

‘Now they have no mother,’ said the teacher quietly. Yurko stood pale and silent.

‘Well, you’d better go to your lesson,’ said Panas Ivanovych with a sigh. 'And tomorrow we will come and see how the chicks are managing. No-one can help them now.'

That night, Yurko hardly slept. He kept seeing the chicks, pitifully stretching out their beaks, waiting for their mother to come.

The next day Panas Ivanovych came up to Yurko and asked, 'Well, will we go and see how the chicks are managing?'

Yurko burst into tears.

Worse than a snake

A man had a faithful friend, a dog. For some reason, the man did not want his dog anymore and decided to sell him at the pet market.

The market was far away, and they had to walk through a forest. The man grew tired, and the dog kept looking into the man's eyes and whining pitifully, 'Why don't you like me anymore? Why are you selling me?'

The man did not respond. He sat down to have a rest, then lay on the grass and fell asleep. A snake slithered out from under an old tree stump. It wound itself around the man's neck and bared its fangs, ready to strike. Just then, the dog rushed at the snake, pounced on it with his paw and held it down.

The man woke up and realized that the dog had saved his life. But what do you think happened then? You would think that the man would have turned back home and thanked his saviour. But no, he took the dog to the market and sold him.

When the man handed the dog over to his new master, the dog whimpered pitifully and said, 'Someone who sells his friend is worse than a snake.'

New trousers for Mykolka

Mykolka's trousers were very old, and he kept asking his mother, 'Mum, when will dad buy me some new trousers?'

'Please wait a bit longer,' his mother said. 'First, we need to buy a new coat for your father.'

A month passed. They still had not bought a new coat for his father, but Mykolka's trousers were completely worn out. He asked his mother again, 'Mum, you said that dad would buy me some new trousers soon.'

His mother gave a heavy sigh.

'Why are you sighing, mum?' asked Mykolka.

His mother did not reply. Then she opened a wardrobe, retrieved a hidden wallet, took out five *karbovanets*[59], and gave Mykolka the money. 'Go to the store and buy yourself some new trousers,' she said.

On his way to the store, Mykolka met his father.

'Where are you going? asked his father.

'To the store. Mum gave me some money to buy new trousers.'

The father took the money from Mykolka and told him, 'You can go home. I'll buy them for you and bring them to you.'

Mykolka came home and told his mother what has happened. His mother just shook her head sadly …

An hour passed, and then another, but the father had still not returned.

'Why hasn't he brought the trousers?' asked Mykolka.

'Perhaps it's taking him a while to choose a nice pair,' replied his mother, but her eyes were full of tears.

Mykolka decided to go to the store and help his father choose a nice pair of trousers.

He found his father dozing on a bench near the store. He was drunk. An empty bottle was lying on the ground beside him.

The stork and the frog

The spring sun was shining brightly, butterflies were fluttering in the air, a cuckoo was cooing in the forest, and swallows were soaring in the clear blue sky.

A little green frog crawled out of the warm swamp. She climbed onto a stalk, took a deep breath, filling her lungs with air, and started singing. The tiny bladders behind her ears turned into huge bubbles, creating the mysterious music of the swamp, as if someone was striking a huge copper bell with a wooden mallet, and the sound was reverberating over and over …

The frog sang about the bright sun and the butterflies, about the cuckoo and the swallows.

Nearby, a stork was standing on one leg. He stood motionless, without breathing. He was deeply moved by the frog's song.

'What beautiful music!' he thought. He was so touched by the frog's song that a tear dropped from his right eye into the water. Overcome by emotion, the stork leaned towards the frog, opened his beak, and swallowed it whole. A second tear rolled from his left eye and dropped into the swamp.

Thousands of people die in the world every day

A young man in his early twenties was striding along the road towards a small town in the steppes. On the outskirts of the town, he caught up with an old man, who was also travelling on foot. For a few minutes, they walked together, in step with each other, but then the young man began to outpace the older man.

'Where are you off to, in such a hurry?' asked the old man.

'I'm off to meet my fiancée. Tonight, at six, we are holding our engagement ceremony,' said the young man.

The old man started walking faster, keeping pace with the young man. As they entered the town, they heard a bell ringing. A few minutes later, they met a funeral procession. The old man stood by the side of the road and took off his hat. The young man said good-bye to the old man and kept on walking.

'Why don't you stop for a moment and pay respect as well?' the old man asked.

'What's the point?' the young man asked, with a shrug of his shoulders. 'Thousands of people die in the world every day … You can't pay respect to everyone … If you spent a minute grieving for each one, you wouldn't have time for anything else.'

'What can I say? Go and meet your fiancée, then,' replied the old man.

The young man arrived at his fiancée's house. Her neighbours told him that she had died the previous day. The funeral procession the young man had seen was for his fiancée.

Is this a happy world?

Myshko was walking home from school, when he saw his father by the store. His father was drunk and had been kicked out of the store. He was leaning on the fence, muttering to himself, and gazing at the road with vacant eyes.

'Come on dad, let's go home,' said Myshko. He took his father by the hand and led him home. The father followed his son obediently.

They crossed the road and reached a gravel path, when his father suddenly tripped and fell. He lay on the ground, unable to get up. Myshko stood beside his father and wept.

People passed by and looked at the father and at the son. Some shook their heads, some came over and gave a sigh, and then left in silence, and some looked at Myshko with such pity that the boy cried even more bitterly.

Somewhere in a field, a tractor was rumbling. The sun was shining, and a lark was singing in the deep blue sky. Close by a girl was singing happily. Children were laughing and playing in the kindergarten.

It seemed that the world was a peaceful and happy place.

But it only seemed that way, because no one in the world could truly be happy while Myshko was standing and crying next to his drunken father, who was lying in the mud.

The squirrel and the jay

A squirrel was hopping from one branch to another, picking acorns and bringing them to her nest in the hollow of a tree. A jay observed the squirrel at work and decided to steal some acorns from her and take them to his own hideaway.

He swept down on the squirrel's nest and snatched two acorns, but the squirrel leapt at him and hit him with her paw. The jay dropped the acorns and fled. It would be better for the jay to look for acorns himself and store them for the approaching winter.

Black hands

Yurko's grandmother is kneading some dough. The dough is white, light and fluffy. 'Can you please bake me a dove?' asks Yurko.

His grandmother's hands begin to mould a dove. The wings appear, fine and soft. You can see each delicate feather. But his grandmother's hands are black and wrinkled, with fine, dried out fingers. Yurko cannot take his eyes off his grandmother's hands, as if seeing them for the first time.

Yurko's grandmother takes the dove out of the oven and sets it down in front of her grandson. It seems a shame to eat it. It is white and fluffy and looks like it will fly off at any moment.

'Grandma,' asks Yurko, 'Why is it that your hands are so black, but the dove is so white?'

'If I had white hands, there would be no dough and no dove,' said his grandmother quietly.

Yurko gazed at the dove. Then he said, 'Can you give me the spade, grandma?'

'Whatever for?' asks his grandmother.

'I want to go into the garden and dig the soil,' says Yurko.

'Why do you need to dig it now?' asks his grandmother.

'So that my hands will be black,' says Yurko.

'All right, Yurko. Here's the spade,' says his grandmother.

Cucumbers around the well

In our village lives a man named Matvii. He has two children who go to our school: one in grade one and one in grade three.

Many years ago, someone, possibly Matvii's grandfather, dug a well in the middle of their yard. The water from that well tasted so good that everyone in the street came to use Matvii's well.

But Matvii began to be bothered by the fact that so many people were coming into his yard, opening and shutting the gate, and carting water. He wanted to stop people coming into his yard, but he was afraid that people would be annoyed with him. And then he had an idea.

As soon as the winter snows melted, Matvii dug up the soil around the well and planted cucumbers there. The cucumbers sprang up and spread their juicy stalks in a carpet that covered the ground. When Matvii's neighbours came for water, they saw the green stalks, and turned back. They did not feel comfortable crushing the plants.

People simply stopped coming to Matvii's yard. It became peaceful and quiet outside. But then one day his children came home from school, and their mother could see they had been crying.

'Why have you been crying? What happened?' asked their mother.

'They're laughing at us. They're saying … '

'What are they saying?' asked the mother.

'They're saying our father is inhuman,' said the children.

Their mother sighed, sat by the window, and looked at the green cucumbers for a long time.

The swing behind the fence

This happened in the city. In one large apartment building there were forty apartments. A boy and a girl used to play in the large courtyard. Each had their own toys. Nina had a large ball, half red and half blue. One day the boy took Nina's ball to play with, and Nina ran to her father in tears. Her father came and took the ball away from the boy and said to Nina, 'Don't give your toys to anyone. I'll build you a swing.'

The father built Nina a swing. So no-one else could play on it, he built a tall fence around it. Nina would come and unlock the gate and swing all by herself, while the other children watched enviously.

However, Nina tired of swinging by herself, and wanted to play with the other children. She went out to be with them, but they did not accept her into their group. They said, 'Go and play on your swing. Leave us alone.'

Nina went to her father, snivelling, and told him that the children had chased her away.

Her father sat by the window and looked at the swing behind the fence, while Nina waited to see what her father would say.

What sort of man is Grandpa Karpo?

Grandpa Karpo brought some apple seedlings to the market. He spread them out on the ground and counted them. There were fifty altogether. They were good seedlings, with strong roots and well-developed crowns. People came up to the old man and asked, 'How much are you selling your seedlings for?'

'One and a half *karbovanets*[60],' answered the old man.

'That's a bit too much, grandpa,' people said. 'You should sell them for one *karbovanets*.'

'You don't have to buy them if you don't want to,' answered the old man.

He saw that others were selling seedlings for a *karbovanets*, and some for seventy *kopiika*. When the sun was high in the sky and began to scorch, the price for seedlings fell to fifty *kopiika*. But Grandpa Karpo stuck to his price: one and a half *karbovanets*.

The trading ended, and people left the market. Grandpa Karpo had sold only five seedlings.

He put the remaining seedlings in a bag and took them home.

The next day the old man again brought his seedlings to the market, spread them out and set his price: one and a half *karbovanets*.

People criticised the old man, saying, 'Look, their roots are drying out. Do you think it is right to torture the young trees? They are living things!'

Grandpa Karpo was silent.

It was like that on the third day as well. No-one bought a single apple tree from the old man.

The old man put the seedlings in a bag and set of for his home.

As he walked through the steppe he came to a deep ravine, undid his bag and threw all forty-five seedlings into the ravine, one after another.

The lamplighter

A river flowed through green meadows and thick forests. It was deep and free flowing, but quiet and gentle. Its clear water had flowed for many centuries. Boats and even small ships sailed on that river.

On the banks of the river lived an old lamplighter. Every evening, he climbed into his boat, rowed to the middle of the river, and lit a lamp. Its light flickered in the middle of the river until dawn, showing the way to travellers. Waves tenderly lapped at the shore. The river was glad: people loved her, and she felt needed by them.

But people needed lots of wood to make tables and chairs, and they cut down the forests on the banks of the river. It seemed to people that the green meadows were an unnecessary luxury, and they ploughed them to grow corn.

The cold springs that fed the river dried up, and the river itself choked with thirst and died. For a few years, where the boats and ships had sailed, a stream babbled in spring, and then it too dried up. The old riverbed was now used for vegetable gardens. The only reminder of the river that had flowed there was the post where the lamplighter kept hanging his lamp each spring, as he was accustomed to doing.

But the rain clouds gathered less and less often overhead. Hot winds blew in from the desert and knocked at people's doors.

As soon as dusk fell, the old lamplighter would walk through the fields, light his lamp and hang it on the post. A little boy named Serhiiko asked him one day, 'Grandpa, why do you still light your lamp? There has not been any river here for a long time.'

'So people can more easily see their stupidity,' he replied.

The birth of an egotist

Andriiko is his parents' only son. His mother and father are extremely proud of him. So are Andriiko's grandmother and grandfather.

'You are so handsome,' says his mother.

'You are so clever,' says his father.

'You are so lucky,' says his grandmother.

'You are good at everything,' says his grandfather.

They took Andriiko to school. The teacher led the children into the classroom and began to assign desks to them. She wanted to seat Andriiko in the second row, but he cried so loudly that she quickly changed her mind and sat him in the front row.

The first lesson began. There were four windows in the classroom. Andriiko's mother watched from the first window, admiring the way he sat at his desk. Andriiko's father watched from the second window, admiring the way he raised his hand. His grandmother watched from the third window, admiring how Andriiko opened his mouth. His grandfather watched from the fourth window, admiring how Andriiko counted to three.

Andriiko looked around, and it seemed to him that the whole world revolved around him. It seemed to Andriiko that he was an eagle, and all those around him were just insects. Their lot was to crawl over the earth, while he soared in the sky.

And nobody thought of how this eagle would come crashing to earth from his heavenly height, crippling himself and bringing grief to others.

They laughed at the old lady

One day, some children were playing soccer at the football ground. They were having a lot of fun playing together.

A very old lady walked quietly past. She could not see very well and walked very slowly, feeling her way with a stick.

One of the boys kicked the ball hard, and it bounced over to the lady, just missing her legs, and knocking her stick out of her hand. The old lady stopped, confused, and did not know what to do. She bent over, feeling for her stick, but it was lying some distance away, and she could not see it.

The children watched the old lady and laughed. None of them thought to go up to the old lady, ask her forgiveness, and help her.

The children laughed, while the old lady stood and cried. And it did not enter anyone's head that at that moment a great evil was being done. One human being was mocking another.

The *karbovanets* coin

Andriiko's father gave him a *karbovanets*[61] coin and said, 'On the way home from school, call in to the shop and buy some sugar and some butter.'

Andriiko put the coin in his jacket pocket and forgot about it. During the physical education lesson, he took off his jacket and threw it on the grass.

After school, Andriiko suddenly remembered that he had to go to the shop. He put his hand into his pocket, and the coin was not there. Andriiko turned pale, and a feeling of dread came over him. He could not utter a word. The other children asked him, 'What's the matter, Andriiko?'

The boy told them what had happened. His friends knew that his father was strict and would give him a hiding. 'Let's help Andriiko,' said Tania. 'Whoever has some money can give it to Andriiko. We should be able to collect a *karbovanets*!'

Everyone put their hands in their pockets. Some found ten *kopiika*, some fifteen, and some five. Only Stepan said, 'You should look after money. He lost it, let him work out what to do about it. I won't give a single *kopiika*.' And he turned his back on everyone and walked home.

The children counted up the money they had collected and there were ninety-nine *kopiika*. They went to the shop all together and bought the sugar and butter. Andriiko returned home very happy.

The next day nobody wanted to sit next to Stepan. He had to sit by himself. Stepan complained to his teacher, 'Why doesn't anyone want to sit next to me?'

'You'll have to ask your friends,' answered his teacher.

The tree stump that did not care

In the forest stands an ancient tree stump, covered in moss, warming itself in the sun. One day a hedgehog made its home under the stump. It fussed about in its burrow, while the stump narrowed its eyes, groaned and warmed itself in the sun.

'You and I will be friends, all right, stump?' asked the hedgehog one day.

'All right,' answered the stump, as if it did not really care. And it narrowed its eyes, yawned and warmed itself in the sun.

On the other side of the stump a sneaky snake made its home. 'You and I will be friends, all right, stump?' asked the snake one day.

'All right,' answered the stump, and it narrowed its eyes, yawned and warmed itself in the sun.

But then, one day the hedgehog noticed that a snake was living next to it. It attacked the snake and defeated it in a bloody battle. It struggled onto the stump and lay there resting.

'What was all that noise?' asked the stump.

'That was me killing the snake,' answered the hedgehog.

'All right,' answered the stump, as if it did not really care. And it narrowed its eyes, yawned and warmed itself in the sun.

Seat me next to Petryk

Three students in grade two, Petryk, Oles and Natalia, were walking to school. On their way, they came to a small lake. It was already covered with ice. Petryk stepped onto the ice. It was thin and started cracking. 'Oh, Petryk, please come back. The ice is about to crack!' Oles cried out in fear. But Petryk did not listen to him and kept on moving across the ice. Natalia followed Petryk. Oles walked around the lake. The three friends met up again on the other side of the lake. All three of them were silent.

They came to school and took their seats. Natalia shared a desk with Oles, while Petryk sat alone in the back row. Natalia raised her hand.

'What is it, Natalia?' asked her teacher.

'Could you seat me next to Petryk?' asked Natalia quietly.

'Why?' asked the teacher in surprise.

Natalia did not reply, and just lowered her head.

Oles lowered his head and his face turned red.

Petryk also lowered his head, and his face turned red.

A silence fell over the classroom.

You must not speak without permission

In grade one, there was a lively, active, and a very talkative little boy named Vasylko. Very often, unable to tame his excitement and enthusiasm, he would burst out with something he had to say. The teacher would patiently explain to him, 'If you need to say something, please raise your hand. If I give you permission, you can stand up and speak.'

Vasylko understood that rule very well, but he forgot all about it as soon as something exciting happened. One day, during a mathematics lesson, the teacher was explaining a problem, when suddenly Vasylko's excited voice rang out, 'Mariia Ivanivna, look at the butterfly on the windowpane!'

All the children turned their heads towards the window. A huge and very beautiful butterfly had settled on the windowpane. The children forgot all about their maths lesson and gazed at the butterfly. Mariia Ivanivna gave a deep sigh, frowned, and sternly asked Vasylko, 'Do you understand that you must not speak without permission during the lesson?' Vasylko understood that perfectly, but he was not able to tame his thoughts and feelings.

The next day, right in the middle of the writing lesson, when everyone was focussed on their work and silence reigned in the classroom, the children almost jumped out of their seats when they heard Vasylko's anxious whisper, 'Mariia Ivaniva, there is somebody's diary[62] over there, on the well.'

'Goodness gracious,' thought the teacher. 'How on Earth did he spot that diary on the well?' But out loud she said, 'Come out and stand by the blackboard for a little while, Vasylko. Perhaps then you will learn that you must not speak without permission.'

Vasylko came out to the blackboard. His eyes were full of surprise and embarrassment. He lowered his head and stood by the blackboard until the end of the lesson.

Two days later, the teacher was at the blackboard explaining how to create new words from letters. When she finished her explanation, Mariia Ivanivna turned to the class and looked at her students. Vasylko had raised his hand, and his eyes were full of tears.

'Why are you crying, Vasylko?' asked the teacher.

'Because I am not allowed to speak without permission,' said Vasylko.

'Then quickly tell us, what's the matter,' the teacher said, beginning to worry.

Vasylko turned his head towards the window and his voice shook with emotion, 'There's a kitten ... There's a tiny kitten in the middle of the school yard. And it's really scared, because that dog is going to attack it.'

'Run quickly and rescue the kitten,' said the teacher.

In a moment, Vasylko was back, holding the kitten in his arms.

A kind word

A mother had a little girl named Olia. When Olia turned five years old, she fell gravely ill. She caught a cold, took to her bed, began to cough, and weakened by the minute.

One by one, relatives began to visit the sorrowful mother: Olia's aunts and uncles, grandmothers and grandfathers. Everyone brought something delicious and nutritious: linden honey and scrumptious butter, fresh wild berries and nuts, quail eggs and chicken soup. Everyone said, 'You should eat well, and you should breathe fresh air, then the illness will disappear into the deep forests and swamps.'

Olia ate the honeycomb and the scrumptious butter, the wild berries and nuts, the quail eggs and chicken soup, but nothing helped. The little girl could hardly get out of bed.

One day, all her relatives gathered around the sick girl's bed. Her ninety-year old Grandpa Opanas said, 'She is missing something, but I cannot tell what.'

Suddenly the door opened, and Olia's one-hundred-year-old great-grandmother walked into the house. All the relatives had long forgotten her. She had kept to herself for many years, not going anywhere and not visiting anyone. However, when she found out about her great-granddaughter's illness, she decided to set out to visit Olia.

The great-grandmother approached the sick girl's bed, sat on a stool, took Olia's hand into her own wrinkled one and said, 'I don't have honeycomb or scrumptious butter. I don't have fresh wild berries or nuts. I don't have quail eggs or chicken soup. I am old and can hardly see. I have brought to you, my dear great-granddaughter, only one gift: my sincere wish. One wish has planted itself in my heart—that you, my little flower, be healed and rejoice again in the bright sun.'

And this kind word carried such great strength of love that little Olia's heart began to beat more quickly, her cheeks became rosier, and joyful little fires began to flicker in her eyes.

'That's what little Olia was missing,' said Grandpa Opanas, 'A kind word.'

The magic necklace

The sun saw a sick little girl lying in bed. She lay with her eyes closed, quietly groaning.

The sun was sorry for the sick child. It bent over her bed and quietly whispered, 'Little girl, please accept this magic necklace with four sunbeams. With it you can make four unhappy people happy. Whoever you direct these sunbeams at will become happy.' The little girl opened her eyes and saw the magic necklace lying on her chest. Its four sunbeams were playing on the wall.

'Who should I direct these happy sunbeams at?' wondered the little girl. 'Who do I know who is unhappy?' She thought about it and gave a deep sigh. Her grandmother, her grandfather, her father and her mother were all unhappy. Her grandmother had a toothache. Her grandfather's bed kept squeaking. Her father drank vodka, and her mother kept crying.

The little girl directed one sunbeam at her grandmother, and her tooth immediately stopped aching. She directed a sunbeam at her grandfather, and his bed stopped squeaking. She directed a sunbeam at her father, and he stopped drinking vodka. She directed a sunbeam at her mother, and she stopped crying and smiled joyfully.

The little girl forgot all about herself and her illness. When all the people around her were happy, she became so happy herself that the illness left her.

The old table

In a small house on the outskirts of a city lived a big family: a mother and father, Mykola in grade five, his older brother in grade seven, and their little sister. The two brothers took it in turns to take their little sister to kindergarten.

In their house there was a room set aside for the children, with an old table made of pine boards. They did their homework on the old pine table, and they also made things.

They could spread their tools out on the table, cut, glue, saw, and hammer nails. On this table the boys built an aeroplane, a real one with a little engine. Every day, Mykola and his older brother were visited by their friends. It was fun to do their homework together and to build machines.

And then a lucky day came for their family. Those were the words their mother used: 'This is our lucky day.' They were given a large apartment in a tall building that had just been built. The apartment was in the middle of the city and on the third floor. Now they did not just walk home, they went up in a lift.

The father bought new furniture for the new apartment: polished tables, sofas, wardrobes, chairs—all shimmering and sparkling. When they placed the new furniture in the four rooms of the new apartment, it turned out that there was no room for some of the old furniture: a wardrobe, some chairs, and the old pine table. They made a pile of them in the yard and burnt them. The old pine boards crackled merrily, but the mother cried.

The children were given a large, spacious room in the new apartment. In the middle of the room, they set up a polished table and a bookshelf. Their mother put away their tools—a hammer, a plane, a saw, and a fretsaw—and said, 'You can't do woodwork on this table. You can only do your homework. But before you spread out your exercise books and textbooks, you must cover the table with paper.'

'Is it OK for the boys to come over?' asked Mykola.

'Yes, but it would be better if you went to their place,' said his mother.

Mykola sat by the big, polished table. He remembered the old pine table and felt sadness and regret.

The frog who sang like a crane

A frog liked the way a crane sang. She sat in her swamp, listening to the crane's song, and thought to herself, 'I will learn to sing like a crane. It will make me stand out, and all the other frogs will admire me.'

It took a long time for the frog to learn to sing like a crane, but in the end, she was successful. Now, when the other frogs spoke to her, she seemed not to understand what they were saying, and replied to them in crane language. The other frogs were angry with her and told her, 'You're a frog, just like us, so why don't you want to speak frog language?'

The frog replied, 'Perhaps I'll grow wings and fly like a crane as well.'

How the old pigeon died

An old pigeon lived in a pigeon house with his pigeon wife. He had almost lost his eyesight and could no longer soar high in the sky.

One day, he felt very ill. Sensing that his life was coming to an end, he told his wife, 'I would like to see the blue sky and the green fields one last time. Could you help me fly up and see them?'

The old pigeon flew out of the pigeon house, and his pigeon wife flew with him, extending her wing to support him. Together they soared up into the sky, until they reached the clouds. The old pigeon gazed upon the blue sky and the green fields, and his heart filled with joy. His heart beat faster, and his blood flowed more rapidly in his veins. His wife was overjoyed, and told the old pigeon, 'Now, you will get better!'

'No, I won't get better,' he said. 'This is the last time I will feel such joy. I will never be this happy again. It is better to die now than to wait until I feel worse.'

With those words, the old pigeon flew away from his wife, plummeted to the ground, and met his end crashing into a cliff.

The hare and the carrot

A hare wished that all the other animals were afraid of him. He went to the blacksmith and asked, 'Can you fit me with wolf's teeth?'

The blacksmith fitted the hare with wolf's teeth. The hare went into the field and met a goat.

'I'm going to eat you,' said the hare, and snapped his teeth. The hare thought the goat would be scared of him, but the goat wasn't scared at all. He could see that the hare was just a hare with wolf's teeth.

'All right, eat me', said the goat. 'But first, let me go into the vegetable garden and eat some carrots.'

'Where? Where are the carrots?' asked the hare excitedly. 'Take me there at once.'

The goat took the hare to the carrots, and they ate them together. The hare completely forgot that he had wolf's teeth.

The lazybones and the sun

One hot summer's day, a lazybones walked into the forest. He lay down in a shady clearing and went to sleep on the soft grass. While he was sleeping, the sun travelled its long journey across the sky and reached its highest point. Sunshine flooded the clearing. The lazybones felt the sun heating his head and his legs. He could have moved into the shade, where the grass was still cool, but he was too lazy. He said to the sun, 'Sun, please move a little to one side. You're making me hot.'

The sun laughed. 'Do you really think it makes sense to ask the sun to move wherever a lazybones wants?'

The lazybones lost his temper and shouted, 'So you refuse to move?'

'I can't,' answered the sun.

'Is that so?' said the lazybones. 'In that case, I will lie here just to spite you.'

Skis and skates

In the autumn, grade three student Boris was bought some skates by his father. His friend Yevgen was given some skis by his father.

Boris thought to himself, 'What is better, skates or skis? Probably skis, because you can go anywhere on them, in the village and in the forest. The only place you can skate is on the pond.'

Boris said to Yevgen, 'Let's swap. I'll give you my skates, and you give me your skis.' And they swapped.

The frosts arrived, but there was still no snow. The pond froze over. Yevgen skated on the pond with his skates, while Boris sat at home with his skis. Boris took the skis to his friend and said, 'Let's not swap after all. Give me back my skates, and you can have your skis back.'

Yevgen did not say anything. He just handed back the skates and took his skis.

That very day it started to snow. Day after day soft snowflakes fell to the ground, covering the earth with a soft carpet. The ice on the pond was also covered over. Yevgen went skiing, while Boris sat at home with his skates. A week passed, and then a second. Every day it snowed.

Boris took his skates and went to see Yevgen. 'Let's swap after all,' he said. 'You give me the skis and I'll give you the skates.'

'And what if the snow melts tomorrow?' asked Yevgen.

He came to hate beauty

A mother had a three-year-old son. He was her only child, and she doted on him. Whatever her dear son wanted, she tried to immediately satisfy his desire.

Her son saw a flowering rose outside the window and asked, 'What is that?'

'That is a rose,' answered his mother.

'I want a rose,' demanded the boy. Not requested but demanded. The mother went outside, cut a rose, and brought it to her son. The boy held the flower in his hands, crushed the petals, and threw it on the floor.

The son saw a sparrow perched on the fence and asked, 'What is that?'

'That is a sparrow,' answered his mother.

'I want a sparrow,' demanded the boy. The mother went to see the children next door and said, 'If you can catch a sparrow for me, I will buy you a kilogram of sweets.'

The children caught a sparrow, received their kilogram of sweets, and the mother gave the little bird to her son. The boy took the sparrow, began to play with it, and squashed its neck. The little sparrow gave a cheep and fell silent. The son threw the dead sparrow on the floor.

One day the boy heard someone playing a folk pipe outside his window. He liked the music, and asked his mother, 'What is that?'

'That is a shepherd playing a tune on a folk pipe,' answered his mother.

'I want a tune. I want a tune because it is so beautiful,' demanded the boy.

The mother went to the shepherd and asked, 'Please come and play for my dear boy. He wants to have that beautiful tune.'

‘No,’ answered the shepherd. ‘A tune is a thing of beauty. It cannot belong to any one person. It belongs to all people.’

The mother returned to her son empty-handed and told him the shepherd’s reply.

From that time the son came to hate beauty and could no longer recognise and understand things of beauty.

Why did the apples seem sour?

Two twin boys, Myshko and Dmytryk, wanted to secretly pick someone else’s apples. One hot July day, the boys quietly clambered over their neighbour’s fence. They climbed a spreading apple tree and started munching on the apples. The apples were still not ripe, but to the boys they seemed so sweet that they screwed up their eyes with pleasure.

They did not notice their neighbour, a gardener, enter the garden. He spotted Myshko and Dmytryk and told them, ‘Why are you hiding up there in the apple tree? Come down, pick as many apples as you like, and enjoy them!’

The boys were so stunned by the gardener’s words, they did not even think to run away. They climbed down, their faces red with embarrassment, greeted the gardener, picked some apples, sat on the grass, and started eating them.

But now, for some reason, the apples seemed sour, so sour that the boys screwed up their eyes in disgust.

The light in the window

Our school is on the edge of the village, next to a gully. Mykola lives on the other side of the gully and has quite a long walk to get to school—about a kilometre.

In the evening, he can see the lights in the school windows very well from his home. In one window there is an aquarium with fish in it. All day and all night, the water in the aquarium is kept warm by an electric lamp, which Mykola can see quite clearly.

In winter the frosts were severe. One day it was so cold that the youngest students did not even go to school. Mykola sat at home in the evening in his warm room, looking out the window and admiring the distant light in the school window. Suddenly the light went out. 'The lamp has burn out,' thought Mykola. 'The fish will be dead by morning in a frost like this.'

Mykola put on his coat, fur hat and mittens, and walked to school. It was already night. By the time Mykola reached the school, he was freezing. He found the caretaker and asked for the key. He opened up the school building and went into the classroom where the aquarium sat on the windowsill.

The water was already cold. He fitted a new lamp. 'You'll be warm now, little fishes,' said Mykola quietly, and he locked the school building and walked back home.

That winter Mykola had to walk to school at night three more times to save the fish. Now he was not afraid of the dark, or the frost, or even a blizzard.

'You have become a brave young man, Mykola,' his teacher told him.

They tramped a path

During the night there was a blizzard. It swept up snowdrifts.

Early in the morning three children were walking to school: Yurko, Mykhailo and Nina. In all the yards, men, women and children were shovelling snow to clear paths.

They came to Grandma Mariia's house. She lived all alone. The children stopped by her yard. They could not see anybody.

'How will Grandma get to the well?' asked Yurko. 'There is so much snow.'

'Let's tramp a path from her hut to the well', suggested Mykhailo.

The children walked across Grandma Mariia's yard through the deep snow. It was very hard to walk from the gate to the house but coming back from the house to the gate was a bit easier. They walked back and forth two, three, four times. They tramped a path from the gate to the house, and from the house to the well.

Sweaty, tired, and happy, the children walked to school. They thought, 'Grandma Mariia has probably come out of her house by now and seen the paths. She will be pleased and will thank us.'

This thought made the children feel good.

Serhiiko's flower

It was the second last day before the school holidays. Four boys in grade three came to school early in the morning. They sat down under a tall oak tree and began to boast about the presents their parents had given them.

Petro showed the boys his knife. It was a wonderful knife with a copper handle. The handle was engraved with a horse and rider.

'That's a good knife,' said the boys.

'It's my knife,' boasted Petro.

Maksym showed the boys a flashlight. The boys had never seen a flashlight like it. A beautiful bird was engraved on its white casing.

'That's a good flashlight,' said the boys.

'It's my flashlight,' boasted Maksym.

Hryts showed them a metal nightingale. When he put it to his lips, the nightingale sang.

'That's a good nightingale,' said the boys.

'It's my nightingale,' boasted Hryts.

The boys waited to see what Serhiiko had in his pocket. Serhiiko invited them to follow him.

'Come with me,' he said.

He took the boys to a thicket and showed them a flower growing under an acacia. It was a beautiful flower. Drops of dew sparkled on its pale blue petals, and in each drop of dew shone a little sun.

'What a beauty!' said the boys.

'But that's not your flower,' said Petro. 'You can't take it home with you.'

'Why would I want to take it home?' asked Serhiiko in surprise.

'You can't swap it for something else,' added Maksym.

'Why would I want to swap the flower for something else?' asked Serhiiko, not understanding at all.

'I could say that that is my flower,' put in Hryts.

'Would that make it any worse?' asked Serhiiko.

The flute and the wind

A musician was playing on a flute in his garden. The birds, trees and flowers were all listening to his enchanting melody. Even the wind settled under a bush and listened with wonder to the playing of the flute. The musician told of the sun in the blue sky, of a white cloud, of a little grey bird—a lark—and of happy children's eyes.

The music fell silent. The musician placed his flute on a bench and went into his house. The wind came out from under the bush, swept over to the flute and blew into it with all its strength.

The flute howled like an autumn storm. The wind blew even harder, but the flute refused to make music, and only screeched and howled.

'Why is that?' wondered the wind. 'I can easily rip an oak up by its roots or tear the roof from a house. Why will the flute not submit to me and make music?'

The boastful worm

Myshko was going fishing, so he went to look for some worms in a pile of manure. Every time he found a worm, he said, 'What are you hiding for? Aren't you fed up with living in manure? Let's go fishing!'

Myshko went to the pond and put his box of worms on the ground beside him. He baited a hook, cast a line, and waited for a fish to bite.

Just then, a tadpole came swimming by. He was very surprised to see a worm sticking its head out of the box, and asked it, 'What are you doing here? I thought you lived in a pile of manure and didn't go anywhere.'

The worm who was poking its head out of the box was not only curious and impatient, it was also very boastful, so it answered, 'We came here to go fishing!'

The tadpole rolled his eyes in disbelief. He was quite boastful himself, but he had never heard anything like that.

The big glass

In a small village school, there are two classes. In each class there are twenty-five students. During the lunch break, the children come to the dining room to drink a glass of milk. Grandma Mariia, the school cook, places twenty-five glasses of milk on a large wooden tray. On the table she places twenty-five pieces of white bread and butter. In the school dining room, there are twenty-four ordinary glasses and one large glass that is much bigger than the others.

When the first class enters the dining room all the children run over to the large wooden tray. Several children's hands reach for the large glass and one of them is lucky enough to grab it. The ones who miss out are envious of the lucky one. Grandma Mariia looks at the children, shakes her head, and quietly says, 'These children haven't been educated properly.'

Then the second class comes to the dining room. The children approach the wooden tray quietly and take the ordinary glasses. The big glass is left on the tray. Grandma Mariia says, 'Why isn't anyone taking the big glass?' One slow, shy child, who is clearly embarrassed, comes and takes the big glass. Grandma Mariia smiles tenderly, and quietly says, 'What well-educated children.'

It's a good thing the sun is shining

Yurko was studying in grade two. One Sunday, he woke up early and joyfully told his mother, 'Mum, today we are going to the forest!'

'It's raining,' answered his mother. 'It's pouring cats and dogs. You won't be going to the forest today.'

Yurko looked out the window. There were puddles in the yard, and grey clouds covered the sky. Yurko sat by the window and cried.

On Monday, Yurko woke up early again. He opened the window and sunlight flooded the room. Yurko sat by the window and cried.

'Why are you crying today?' asked his mother in surprise.

'Today we have to bring a spade to school,' said Yurko. 'We are going to be digging in the vegetable garden.'

Yurko's mother looked at her son and sighed. Then she quietly said, 'It's a good thing the sun is shining … If it had been raining today, how would I have learnt that my son is a lazybones?'

What does it mean to be tactless?

An elderly grandmother lived near the school. Some of the schoolchildren decided to give the old lady a gift. They picked some apples in the school orchard and brought them to her. The apples were hard and sour; they had not yet ripened. But even if they had ripened, the old lady could not have eaten them, as she was missing all of her teeth.

This kind of behaviour is called 'tactless.' Although the schoolchildren intended to bring joy to the grandmother, their gift was not a joy for this elderly person, but a disappointment. The children had simply not thought carefully enough about their gift.

To be a kind, sincere person is a great art. It is necessary to think about the people who live next to us, to understand what they think of with pain and what they think of with pride.

Boys having fun

A workman lives in a little house. He has to get up very early, at four o'clock, walk to the train station, work for several hours, and then return home.

It is eleven o'clock in the evening. Three youths are sitting on a bench not far from the workman's house. One of them has a radio that is turned up to full volume, playing music.

The workman comes out of his house and asks the boys, 'Please turn off your radio. I can't sleep.'

The boys laugh. One of them says, 'We are sitting next to our own house.'

The workman sighs, and says, 'You're savages.'

People who do not understand that there are other people living around them are worse than savages.

I am not afraid of thunder or lightning

It was a hot June day. The students in grade five went to the forest for the whole day. It was fun in the forest. The children played, read an interesting book, and made porridge.

Towards evening, dark clouds appeared from beyond the forest, and thunder rumbled. The children ran from the rain towards a shelter used by shepherds. Vitia also ran, but suddenly there was a flash of lightning and a peal of thunder so deafening that Vitia crouched in fear under a large oak tree, closed his eyes, and nearly burst into tears. He had opened his mouth to cry out for help, when he noticed a girl from his class named Valia beside him.

'Is that you, Vitia?' she said. 'I'm so glad I'm not alone. Now I'm not afraid anymore.'

Vitia took a deep breath and looked around. The forest was drowning in torrents of rain. Flashes of lightning lit up for an instant the surrounding trees and bushes. The forest was howling and groaning. It seemed to Vitia that he and Valia were the only two people in the world.

He felt ashamed of his fear. How could he be afraid, when there was a girl next to him who was depending on him.

'Don't worry, Valia,' said Vitia. 'I'm not afraid of thunder or lightning.'

Vitia reached out and touched her blonde hair. Now he was not afraid of anything.

Do what you need to do, not what you feel like doing

Yurko's grandfather was eighty-five years old. He knew many interesting stories. His eight-year-old grandson loved to listen to the wonderful stories that his grandfather told him.

But then his grandfather fell ill. He lay in bed and breathed heavily. When his mother went to work, she told Yurko, 'Sit next to Grandpa, Yurko, and look after him. If he asks for water, get him a fresh glass of water. If he asks you to open the window, open it for him.'

Yurko sat by his grandfather's bed and read a book. During the first half of the day, his grandfather asked him for water just three times. The boy became bored sitting next to the sick old man. He put his book on the bedside table, crept out of the house, and ran to play soccer with his friends.

Yurko played for a long time at the soccer ground, until the sun was close to the horizon. But the boy felt uneasy in his heart. Yurko left the game and ran home. He quietly opened the door, went to his grandfather's bed, and fell to his knees. His grandfather was lying very still. There was not a drop of water in his glass.

For the rest of his life Yurko was tormented by pangs of conscience. He thought, 'Grandpa probably died because there was no water. He was thirsty, but there was not a drop of water in his glass. And all that time I was playing soccer with my friends.'

'Do what you need to do, not what you feel like doing,' Yurko taught his son.

The truth can be worse than a lie

Serhiiko's mother sent him to their neighbours to get some salt. He was gone for a long time. The borshch[63] was already boiling, but Serhiiko was nowhere to be seen. At last, he came back and brought the salt. His mother asked him, 'What took you so long?'

'I was having breakfast,' answered Serhiiko.

'What do you mean, "having breakfast"?' asked his mother in surprise.

'They invited me to have breakfast with them,' said Serhiiko.

'And what did you tell them?'

'Nothing … I just sat down and had breakfast.'

'That was very rude, Serhiiko!' said his mother angrily. 'You should have said, "Thank you, but I'm not hungry."'

'But I was really hungry,' said Serhiiko. 'If I said I wasn't hungry, that would be a lie. Do you expect me to tell a lie?'

'Sometimes, the truth can be worse than a lie,' said his mother.

That gave Serhiiko something to think about. 'How can that be right?' he wondered.

An unusual hunter

An old man named Grandpa Maksym lives in our village. Everyone says he is a hunter. As soon as the season for hunting hares or ducks begins, he goes into the forest with his gun. Every day he leaves early in the morning and does not return until evening.

But what an unusual hunter he is! He never brings home a hare or a duck. He comes back with an empty sack. Once he did bring home a little baby hare. He had found it under a bush. The hare had a broken leg. Grandpa Maksym made a splint from two sticks and bandaged its little leg. After a week the leg mended, and the old man took the little hare back to the field.

Why is Grandpa Maksym so hopeless at hunting?

One day the children followed him. They wanted to see how he hunted. They saw him put his gun under a bush and start walking through the forest laying hay under the bushes for the hares.

Then the children understood why Grandpa Maksym is such an unusual hunter.

UNFINISHED STORIES

* The prisoner and the human being

Some evil men once imprisoned a human being. No sound could penetrate the prison's thick stone walls. The evil men wanted the human being to lose his humanity and become nothing more than a prisoner. They made a tiny opening through the thick stone wall, through which someone's hand furtively passed some food for the prisoner to eat. The prisoner wanted to take a closer look at that hand, but he was unable to see it.

Just below the ceiling, there was a small, barred window. Through that window, the prisoner could see a tiny piece of blue sky. The prisoner longed for human company. He wished he could at least hear something that would remind him of humans, but it seemed that the thick stone walls had cut him off from human society forever.

Then, one day, at sunrise, he heard a crunching sound coming from outside. It was the guard's footsteps. Beneath the prison walls …

* The fox and the lion

A fox worshiped a lion. She could not praise him enough. 'The lion is the strongest, the kindest and the most beautiful animal,' she would say.

A goat once objected, 'How can you say the lion is kind, when he eats so many weak creatures?'

The fox angrily replied, 'It's their fault! They should not have come across the lion's path when he was angry.'

One day, the lion fell ill. The fox cried and grieved. But when the lion died, she …

A SCHOOL IS A PLACE FOR THINKING AND THE CHILDREN IN IT ARE THINKERS

Teachers

A teacher's profession cannot be compared to any other. A weaver can observe the product of their labours after just an hour. A smelter enjoys the fiery flow of metal after a couple of hours—that is the pinnacle of their ambition. Someone who tills the soil, sows seed, and grows a crop in a field, can admire the ripening ears of grain after a few months … A teacher, on the other hand, must work for many years in order to see the results of their creative work. Sometimes decades pass before they can even begin to recognise what they had intended. No-one is visited by a feeling of dissatisfaction as often as a teacher, and in no other profession do errors and failures have such serious consequences.

No matter how much we talk about the nobility, the complexity and the greatness of the teaching profession, these words will remain empty sounds unless a school's values are supported by the integrity of the teacher. A school's ethical foundation depends on the personality of the teacher being in harmony with the moral ideals that we ask children to believe in, that we present as being attractive, honest, true and wise. The root of many educational misfortunes lies in the fact that quite often a student is called on to follow a banner when no-one is actually bearing that banner. To be a standard bearer for an ideal, to bear a flaming torch for that ideal—this is the secret and the mystery of a teacher's authority. How intuitively children sense the standard bearer in their educator! How skilful they are at discerning the difference between a genuine flame and a false one!

At the core of a teacher's ethical identity is their attitude towards knowledge, intellectual work, science, enlightenment, reading and books. Children are tamed by a teacher's love of knowledge. If you wish to be respected, guide children on the path of wonder and amazement at the truths that you are able to discover together with the children. It seems to the children that they themselves discover the truth, and you are just their helper, an indispensable helper. Children come to the most sensitive appreciation of your work when, with your assistance, they engage in deep thought, unearth the truth, and experience wonder and amazement.

Fear the day when your intelligence is revealed to your students only when you are assessing their knowledge. There is nothing more destructive for a teacher than utilising their knowledge to needlessly emphasise a student's ignorance or to emphasise their own superiority. A teacher's intelligence is not meant to oppress, but rather to lead, to illuminate the way, to *throw a light* on knowledge. Learn to structure the intellectual work of your students in such a way that they feel as though you are becoming more intelligent at the same time as they are, as though you too are delighted by each new grain of knowledge.

Dear teacher! Having crossed the threshold of a classroom, inspired by the noble desire to dedicate your life to guiding the development of human beings, do not forget that the success of your mission is largely dependent on whether you manage to maintain the purity and inviolability of the wellsprings of childhood. Do not cloud children's lives with adult ways and formality, with pedantry and fault-finding, with an inability to appreciate the world of childhood, with unreasonable strictness, with naive attempts to imitate children's speech and a failure to set valid expectations, with a fear of giving children freedom in that wise form in which an elder's supervision and control are all the stronger for being imperceptible. And if in general it is unacceptable to banish the child in a young person, if little 'grown-ups' (and even worse little 'old people') are hardened marble from which nothing can be chiselled, it is even more dangerous to quench the wellsprings of childhood in a young person who is surrounded by a hostile moral environment. Children who are crippled and disfigured by an immoral environment must first of all be returned to the world of childhood—not so they can be spoken to like a baby, in language they have outgrown, but so that they may be led onto the correct path of moral development, a path that has hitherto been barred to them.

On the joy of learning

Given that education has become not only widely available, but also compulsory, in the eyes of many young people it is no longer a blessing. Even worse, for some students, education has become a burden, and even a torturous punishment. Dear teacher, remember that when the situation has come to this, it is pointless to speak of any kind of successful ethical education. Everything else within the school walls becomes real and achievable only when an individual desires to learn, when in learning—in the fact that they are going to school, reading, writing, discovering—the individual experiences joy and acquires human dignity. Students should study because study is a blessing and brings happiness.

How then should we educate, how should we teach, enlighten and inspire, so that study is desirable and attractive? This is one of the most complex issues in education; it has a thousand facets.

First of all, it is necessary to a see each student as a human being, rather than as a receptacle for knowledge that must be absorbed in ever greater quantities. Knowledge becomes a blessing only when the inner spiritual strength of an individual engages with the world that is being discovered. The most important wellspring of the joy of learning—and this emotion is the seed from which the great tree of a rich spiritual life grows—is the conviction, born from experience, that knowledge is the fruit of straining *my* human spirit, the fruit of my earnest search, of creativity, of the labour of thought and soul. An individual's moral refinement depends to a huge extent on what psychological motivation gives rise to their activity.

The more you are able to awaken a deep thirst for knowledge in your students, the greater the happiness they will derive from the awareness that they are alive, thinking and feeling. However, it is necessary to acquire knowledge in the broadest sense of the word. In our system of education, we have a special program designed to nurture the development of an individual who thinks, feels and experiences in order to know fully. This program begins with an intellectual life in the natural world and is calculated to encompass ten years of growing appreciation of the beauty of forests and orchards, rivers and lakes, of the beauty of spring awakening and autumn waning, of winter twilights and summer dawns.

In the ethical development of young children, we attach great significance to journeys to the wellsprings of thought. The children walk with their teacher to an ancient oak, to a thicket or some beehives, to the banks of a pond or a deep ravine. This is where, figuratively speaking, the fine roots that feed a thirst for knowledge develop; this is where the desire to learn, to be intelligent and well-educated, is born. The educator's task is to expose the children to something they do not yet understand, to awaken the urge to learn. Here, even the most shy and fearful student becomes an inquisitive thinker. The more successfully the educator opens the students' eyes to something they have not yet understood, and the deeper their experience of wonder, the keener their urge to learn and discover will be.

On lessons in thought

Many years of experience in education have firmly convinced me that a little person who has come to school in order to graduate from it as an enlightened, civilised and educated human being, will only become an inquisitive, curious and diligent learner if they are also a thinker, when their life of thought is to a certain extent independent of the content that is being covered in the classroom.

In my practical work with young students, I strive at the outset to ensure that the thought that is kindled in the orchard, in the steppe, beside a blossoming or a hibernating tree, will illuminate the learning that occurs within the classroom. Intellectual activity beyond the classroom walls, that is independent of classroom lessons during the initial stages of learning, should be incomparably more meaningful, richer and broader in content, than all of the children's activities during lessons. My first graders are first and foremost thinkers, who are discovering truth beyond the classroom, experiencing wonder and awe at that truth and at their own work, and only secondarily students in the narrowest sense. The more they are thinkers, the more successful they are as students. A child's perception of study as a joy is in fact unthinkable if a vibrant, emerging life of thought does not form part of their psychological development. Every letter that is taught, every mathematical operation that is carried out, must be preceded by lessons in thought in the midst of nature: the original source of all thought.

The first year of schooling is an enormous step in a child's intellectual development. The path which a child traverses in the first year of schooling cannot be compared with any other school year or any decade of their adult life. I attach exceptional significance to this year. In parallel with and simultaneously with the acquisition of knowledge in class, the young boys and girls pass through a school of thought beneath the open sky. This school consists of sixty lessons, grouped under several themes:

How nature prepares for winter and its spring awakening
The life of creatures and plants in the winter orchard
Nature awakens from its winter sleep
The living and the non-living in nature
How nature creates beauty
The life of ants and bees
The life of meadows and the steppe from dawn to dusk
Nature, people and work

Each lesson in thought involves observation of nature and wonder at its mystery, thinking, the discovery of some truth, experiencing the joy of learning and pride at being a thinker. Twelve lessons in thought are dedicated to the observation of a tiny cherry bud. Children observe how the bud is formed, how it is hardened by burning frosts, how it sleeps and carefully listens to everything that is happening in nature, how the warm spring wind and rays of sunlight open it and how the bud, in the children's words, 'straightens its shoulders and throws off its cosy covers', how tiny green leaves appear and foliage appears in the cherry orchard, and how new buds are created, which will be transformed into leaves in the following year. Before the children's eyes a wondrous picture of life unfolds as the children uncover dozens of new mysteries.

The lessons in thinking that begin during the initial period of study should not be interrupted for a single day. The greater children's intellectual potential is—and it is my deep conviction that, if intellectual education is conducted properly, a person may complete the current high school curriculum during their adolescent years, between the ages of fourteen and fifteen—the more significant a child's intellectual life should be outside the classroom. But gradually these lessons in thinking incorporate the world of books as well as the world of nature.

To give students a life in the world of books is one of the most important pedagogical challenges of contemporary schooling. I consider it to be an educational task of the utmost importance to ensure that reading becomes an irresistible psychological imperative for each child.

This is an elementary principle of education: if an individual has not discovered the world of books while they are at school, if this world has not revealed to them the intellectual joys of existence, then school has not given that individual anything at all and they have embarked on life with an empty soul.

For this reason, it is necessary to teach children over and over again how to appreciate the joys of a life in the world of books. During the primary years I read to my students some of the finest books from the treasure trove of world literature, choosing content that is accessible and relevant to the emotional world of young children: works by Jack London and Henryk Sienkiewicz, Victor Hugo and Harriet Beecher Stowe, Mark Twain and Jonathan Swift, Jules Verne and Nikolai Gogol, Ivan Turgenev and Vladimir Korolenko, Lev Tolstoy and Anton Chekhov, Mikhail Saltykov-Schedrin and Maxim Gorky, Mikhail Sholokhov and Leonid Leonov, Taras Shevchenko and Mykhailo Kotsiubynsky, Ivan Franko and Oles Honchar.

What is necessary for this in practical terms? That a teacher spends many hours sharing a book with students an informal setting. Reading gives them access, first and foremost, to the world of their own soul. Little people discover the greatness of the human spirit; they aspire to live a rich and interesting cultural life. It is as if books awaken a sense of urgency: we must hasten to enjoy the spiritual treasures created by humankind; if we waste time, we will miss out on wealth that could enrich our souls. A love of books, the awareness that thought, learning and knowledge are great blessings, teaches a child to cherish time. In ethical education, developing a sense of time is very important. (See 'A day lost' and 'A wasted day' on page 426.)

On curiosity

The brain of every psychologically healthy child has the potential for the extensive development of creative abilities. Nature places in every normal brain the roots that are essential and adequate for each person to be creative. The abilities that are awakened in each child depend on their activities during early childhood. In this process, a child's attitude towards their activity, and the extent to which we, as adults, are able to awaken in them a degree of maturity of thought and spirit, are of great significance.

The *activity* that is essential for the development of creative abilities in childhood, (I emphasise, creative abilities, not just the ability to follow instructions) must include more than just being busy, moving around and exerting oneself physically. The activity must engage the mind, demanding resourcefulness and imagination. In other words, the hands are working, while the mind is solving problems. The hands become a means of developing thought; the hands are teaching the mind.

The activity that most strongly fosters the development of creative abilities incorporates observation, research, and the discovery of the most diverse aspects, features and characteristics of objects and phenomena—observation and research in which the child is personally interested. They are learning about the world in order to enrich their own activity. Active observation gives rise to *curiosity*. This is the very essence of nurturing abilities. The earlier curiosity is nurtured, the broader the spectrum of abilities that blossom in a human being.

There is a deep meaning hidden in the very notion of *curiosity*: it is a growing, ever intensifying need to know, to find out, to explain. The more actively young people interact with the surrounding world, the more aware they become of the connections between things, of peculiar features and subtle phenomena, and the more they are filled with wonder and amazement. They discover many incomprehensible things, thousands of riddles that they must solve, no matter what. In this appearance of riddles and their solution is the essence of curiosity. Our task is to ensure that in early childhood all children become little thinkers, that their activity should lead to an irresistible avalanche of discovery. The only way to achieve this is through work, in the broadest sense of the word. Children's work does not mean giving them a shovel and letting them dig till they are exhausted. Curiosity is a very delicate personal quality, and it is very easy to destroy it, awakening an aversion to work, if that work is beyond a child's strength or is too monotonous. I am talking about the work of a thinker. Children's work is an active vision of the world, a vision through which children become active participants in natural processes, and custodians of nature.

For two years before they join the compulsory school program, I work with little children in a preparatory group. I would call this period a *school in curiosity*. This is first and foremost an educator influencing the development of a child's brain, which is so plastic and responsive during the preschool years. The main method employed in making this contact is to inspire children with wonder and amazement. The main instrument is a teacher's words, and the main form of activity is excursions to the source of thought and language, exploring the inexhaustible richness of nature. My aim is that a growing curiosity should become an autonomous force, governing the interests and aspirations of children.

I consider it extremely important that when little children start school, their activity should not be a matter of just following instructions. This is a terrible threat to intellectual development. With the beginning of formal studies, when there is a lot of monotonous work at desks that involves passive memorisation (this is necessary and inescapable), there is a growing role for special activity that feeds, so to speak, the avalanche of curiosity. I spoke about investigative activity (lessons in thought) earlier. I would like to add that the work done by children in our workshops, school gardens, and orchards resembles the work of adults. Everywhere children must be accompanied by the feeling that what they are doing is genuine work. Creative, attractive, joyful work during the childhood years is an indispensable lifegiving source of thought and of intellectual development.

On intellectual work

Formal schooling by its very definition creates conditions under which learning is compared and evaluated daily: my work is badly done, while my friend's is outstanding. At every step children hear praise and disapproval. However, the effort that a student exerted in order to earn the praise is not always taken into account. It often happens that what we are in fact praising is not a student's effort, but the gifts lavished upon them by nature, while what attracts disapproval may be the limited abilities of an individual student, with negligence not being differentiated from a lack of comprehension, an inability to work or to concentrate. This is a great challenge for the whole education process. To ensure that every student works hard, and that their personal strengths and potential are fully developed, is an indispensable precondition for the development of humility and perseverance.

The primitive views of some educators on work and work education are astonishing. Some believe that work begins when an individual takes up a spade or a broom. However, work is not only using a spade or a plough, but also thinking. How important it is that our students realise (based on their own experience) that thought is hard work, that its very complexity and difficulty bring an individual great joy. It is through the harmonisation of intellectual and physical labour that it is possible to develop in our children an urge to be intelligent, enlightened and cultured.

If a student learns only with the aid of a textbook, if that is the extent of their learning, then their intellectual life will be very limited. Beware the day when an adolescent's intellectual efforts are used only for memorisation, for rote learning. That would be great misfortune. An authentic intellectual life is only possible when an individual reads without a focus on memorisation. An adolescent or young adult should be motivated to read two or three times more than he is set to learn from the text book, *seeking food for thought.* This is the conclusion to which many years of experience have led me. To read in search of food for thought, without a focus on memorisation, is the most important precondition for the development of intellectual abilities, for the formation of a creative mind. The meaning of an individual's intellectual life is to be found in reading to satisfy the need to think, to discover, and to wonder at the greatness and power of the intellect. Without such reading, sitting over a textbook inevitably becomes rote learning, which in turn numbs the mind and transforms learning into an onerous obligation. Where there is no reading out of a need to think and discover, conquering the content of a textbook becomes an impossible task. An aversion to study appears due to the absence of a rich and fulfilling intellectual life. This is a concerning phenomenon, which, once we have understood its origins, should prompt us, as educators, to seek the one sure way of preventing the most serious vices in school life: laziness, indolence and wasting time. That way is found by awakening a student's interest in thought, books and reading. The compulsory content found within the pages of textbook is mastered effortlessly when a student reads out of a need to think and discover.

In our day and age, adolescents and young adults are surrounded by a world rich in pleasurable activities. It is pleasurable to play soccer or basketball, to listen to the radio, to watch a television programme, especially if it is a sporting competition during which one can also cheer. It is pleasurable to simply while away the day. If these pleasures consume all of an individual's psychological resources, then the individual will grow up shallow and empty. The overabundance of pleasurable activities is a complex challenge for education.

On talent

When each generation of young boys and girls completes grade one, I tell them 'The legend of the Golden Grain of Truth' (p. 481), and the story 'Happiness and work' (p. 483). The idea contained within these stories should excite the young children. Discussion about moral freedom should not begin when the first signs of a moustache appear, but rather when the correct understanding of the idea of *freedom* inspires children and compels them to look at themselves. A spirit of moral freedom reigns in a school when the efforts of every individual are directed to the achievement of something difficult.

The reign of a spirit of moral freedom is assured when every student has higher and higher expectations of themselves. Their aspirations are greater today than they were yesterday. They strive for loftier goals than they considered possible earlier. The authentic human essence of each student should be expressed in some particular talent that is unique to them. This talent, discovered and polished by the educator, should sparkle and shine.

An individual may struggle to achieve a 'satisfactory' grade in the basic subjects of the curriculum, but there must be something in which their unique talent can sparkle and shine throughout their life. I know a fourteen-year-old boy who barely manages to master the essential content from his school subjects. But in horticulture he is a master in both his work and his thinking, a true creator. He can graft the crown of a fruit tree on to root stock so masterfully that professionals, with decades of experience, are in awe of his work, saying it is 'beautiful'. When they talk about him, they say, 'What talent!' Our sacred mission as educators is to discover that 'golden vein' within each individual where their unique talent originates. This golden vein exists within literally every person. If, in spite of all our efforts, we are unable to identify it, unfortunately the opportunity has passed us by. The golden vein has disappeared forever, and the individual is condemned to a grey and average existence.

Within the four walls of a school, a student should take pride and joy in their work, rather than suffer humiliation and then perhaps spend the remainder of their life with a hardened heart. We should not classify a psychologically normal human as either 'capable' or 'incapable'. An individual may be capable at one task and incapable at another. Even a genius may also be unsuited to particular types of activity. A school's mission is to identify the fountainhead of creative ability within every child, to identify what will provide a unique source of happiness in their future life of work and creativity.

On levels of expectation

I consider it essential that the level of expectation of senior students—at the dawn of adulthood—becomes significantly higher than during the years of adolescence. The courage of these young people should have been forged during childhood and especially during adolescence. Educational methods dictate that adolescence be filled with opportunities to raise the level of expectation. Every adolescent should aim for that which seems unattainable. Let them experience heedless bravery and recklessness—that is infinitely preferable to silent obedience and that worrying kind of self-restraint in which an individual does not assert themselves in any way. Adolescence abounds with inexhaustible energy that quite literally bursts forth. Do not allow that energy to burst forth in actions which shock elders with their impropriety and with the shallowness of the desires behind them! Let this energy be expressed through striving for the pinnacle of achievement, for that which seems unattainable. We should not wait until young adulthood when, according to many educators, an individual can fully express themselves! An individual will sit confidently in the saddle as a young adult only if they have been permitted to grasp the ardent neck of the horse during adolescence. Let adolescents confidently mount the horse. If they fall, that is no misfortune; they will simply climb back in the saddle and gain greater confidence. Let a ten-year-old boy wake during a cold spring night and venture out into the fruit orchard to observe whether the blossoming trees are being threatened by frost. Let a thirteen or fourteen-year-old adolescent sit behind the wheel of a tractor and plough a field—as educators we just need to ensure that this work is organised in such a way that accidents are prevented.

To lead an individual through childhood and adolescence marvelling at their own strength—that is the secret of wise education. Where there is wonder and rapture, there is also dissatisfaction. A human being is limitless in their aspirations, and the higher their expectations of themselves, the deeper their dissatisfaction with what has been achieved. It is this feeling of dissatisfaction, which may pass unnoticed, that leads an individual to the understanding that *necessary*, *difficult* and *good* all share the same root.

On mischievous children and pranksters

I personally respect and simply love mischievous children and pranksters, and firmly believe that, without them, God forbid, the school would become like a funeral parlour. My attitude towards mischief and pranks is that a teacher should not put themselves on the same level as the mischievous child or prankster by challenging them to a duel. In our attitude to pranksters, we should be wisely condescending. We should be equipped with thousands of the most unexpected responses that will lead the mischievous child or prankster to burn with shame, to feel the impropriety of their prank. This is a major issue in teaching practice. Let my beloved prankster refine their search for a prank that will enable them to conceal their 'creativity' from me. I must also refine my attempts to respond to the prankster's 'creativity' with my intelligence and experience, from my superior vantage point, with generosity, in such a way as to prompt the mischievous child to examine another aspect of their true self, to examine it and perhaps be surprised, or ashamed, or amazed to discover something in themselves they had not previously been aware of. They may ponder this discovery and take another step in their moral development. When I win over a prankster through my wisdom, generosity, and goodwill, from my superior vantage point, they become serious and thoughtful after even the most amusing prank. In my interactions with a prankster's 'creativity', I find joy in my work. Without that joy, my inner life would become like that room of the civil registry office where divorces are registered: you would much rather not go there, but you have to. If a day passes without some child's prank, more often than not displaying intelligence and creativity, I begin to feel bored. I miss that whetstone on which I, as an educator, can sharpen my skills.

On children who are 'different'

Great personal strength is demanded from an educator in the work that is required to ensure that children not only have compassion for people with physical disabilities, that they empathise with them, but that they also conscientiously nurture in themselves the delicate and fragile quality of tact. I would describe this quality as the offspring of conscientiousness and respect: a young person should feel uncomfortable expressing curiosity about someone who has been short-changed by nature or deformed by an unfortunate accident. For several years my students maintained a friendship with an elderly man whose face had been deformed during a mining accident. Empathising with his grief led the children to be tactful and restrained, and made them realise that there can be irreversible grief and misfortune in life. One thought gave me no peace: how strong would these emotions and thoughts prove themselves to be if life unexpectedly led my students to meet a completely new individual in need of companionship, compassion and empathy? When a young girl with a hunchback joined our class, the class withstood the trial. (See 'The girl with the hunched back', p. 389.)

There are children who are intellectually disadvantaged, who have a limited capacity for study. For them, mastering knowledge is incredibly difficult. They suffer, understanding the limitations of their abilities. It is not appropriate to send them to a special school, but at the same time they are not learning at the same pace as the overwhelming majority of students. How can we best work with such students? How can we ensure that such students do not, as so often happens, feel inferior, and leave school with a lack of both intellectual and moral development.

The main thing I strive for is to educate a feeling of human dignity in intellectually disadvantaged children and to gradually develop their intellectual abilities. Reading out of genuine interest, out of a desire to learn, to know, and to think, is especially important for such students. Intellectually disadvantaged students should read while thinking and think while reading as much as possible. Grains of knowledge will lodge themselves in their minds from the material that they read out of genuine interest, out of love for thinking. The clearer the thought that accompanies reading, the stronger the retention in memory, but, most importantly, without the explicit objective of memorisation! The more such a student remembers without trying to memorise, the stronger their train of thought. It is especially important that the teacher discusses any recently read book with such students. The aims of these discussions are to carefully nurture the child's thinking and to awaken an interest in knowledge. Experience shows that if an intellectually disadvantaged child develops a keen interest in reading, their capacity to master the compulsory curriculum will also develop, along with their strength of will and perseverance.

It is a fact of life that children fall ill. The educator's task is to ensure that a sick child does not feel isolated. At the sick child's bedside there should be not only their parent and their doctor, but also their teacher—this is a most important principle. One should visit the sick child not just to see them, to comfort them and express sympathy, but also to encourage them and teach them to be courageous and optimistic. This is such a major and important issue that a special book should be written about it. The education and development of a child who is ill, who is physically suffering or has recently suffered, who was already weak and is now further weakened (it is crucial to remember that this is a little person who has not fully developed their inner resources even in a state of good health), raises many entirely new issues that can only be mentioned in passing here. What should be the focus of a child's thought and reflection when illness has confined them to their bed? What should they think and read about? What joys must visit the child and excite their soul? What will inspire their still developing inner resources in their battle with danger, which frequently is significant danger. Painful suffering and even the threat of death—the child bears it all, and this experience is reflected in their views, behaviour and attitude towards their peers.

This is a question of the utmost importance. The subsequent moral development of children who are ill and coping with illness frequently depends on the degree of significance we assign to their psychological state at this time. They should be filled with joy, with an optimistic world view and a longing for the sun and the outdoors. What I say to the child should motivate them to escape the bonds of their illness, and not to give in to despair and sadness. I have several stories for children who are ill: 'I saw you again, sunbeam' (p. 493), 'Lazy pillow' (p. 493), 'The singing feather' (p. 494) and 'The curious poppy seed' (p. 495).

There are children and adolescents who are constantly ill, and no physician can fully cure them. Poor physical health, weakness and general malaise—these are frequently attenuated and hard to detect, but such children represent a special area of education, which requires a special pedagogy. Scholars refer to it as 'medical pedagogy' and there is some general conception of its aims, but as yet this pedagogy has no content or methodology. Meanwhile, children who are constantly ill, who are weak and experience poor health, are neither a rarity nor an exception. We should not forget for a minute that within a few years these children will become workers and soldiers, mothers and fathers. Our aim should be to ensure that poor health, weakness and malaise do not psychologically cripple a single one of these students. Nurturing their strength of spirit, fortitude and courage should be our top priority when working with these students.

How to express disapproval

From a young age a person should feel and understand the true meaning of goodness in moral relationships. It is very important that a person understands from their own experience that goodness is not always pleasant, and can often be as severe and as sharp as a burning wind in January. I am convinced that it is no simple matter to accept bitter but just criticism from an elder, that this is something that must be taught persistently over a long period. The most important thing here is to provide experiences that bring each individual to the realisation that not everything that is pleasant and desirable for them is pleasant and desirable for others.

It is also not easy to give voice to bitter but just criticism. The ability to do so must combine pedagogical skill and artistry. Unfortunately, many educators are unable to utter those bitter, unpleasant words in such a way that they are accepted in the right spirit. The sad, unacceptable fact is that often during such discussions between a teacher and a student, the emotional element takes centre stage in the form of irritation. The student who is being addressed is then given the impression that the teacher is an unpleasant individual, and that there are some other reasons, besides the deed itself, that led the teacher to have this discussion with them. The student walks away from this discussion taking offence, and the teacher develops mistrust. Where offence and mistrust collide, hostility is born. The teacher's attempt to conquer evil only leads to more evil. As teachers, we constantly have to express disapproval, in countless different tones, and in such a way that the person in front of us keeps their heart open, that they do not close up, that they do not bristle with anger, that they do not perceive our words to be motivated by prejudice, irritability and malice. If I were asked what is the best kept secret of the teaching profession, what we need to master in order to have a positive influence on our students, I would answer: the ability to nurture in my students a particular attitude towards my disapproval.

Disapproval is the finest and sharpest instrument that you can make use of when approaching a student, and the less calmness, the less strength of spirit with which you take this instrument into your hands, the more dangerous the consequences. The tender body of your student cloaks itself in an armour of disbelief and mistrust, your fine instrument hits the armour and breaks like brittle glass, and you, in desperation, take up a hammer, and senselessly beat against the protective armour. From a strong and gentle captivator of hearts you are transformed into a panel beater.

When I am preparing for a bitter and difficult discussion with a student—and it is best to have such a discussion one-on-one—I first examine my own train of thought. I am obliged to approach this task not with stormy indignation, not with a self-righteous indignation that causes my hands to tremble and my voice to falter, but with clear, firm and wise thinking. The student should see in me not a tense victim, who has gathered together for the occasion all the wrongdoings and dissatisfaction which have accumulated over time, not even an impartial judge, who has thought over the sentence in advance, but a wise thinker—this is what prevents a student from closing their heart. With my words I shall draw the student into joint reflection.

What should we disapprove of? What should we consider

unacceptable? The correct answer to these questions determines to a great extent the success of moral education. Some of the instruments in our pedagogical toolkit involve risk and should be used sparingly and tactfully. It is crucial that a teacher is able to discern what deeds are worthy of disapproval and condemnation. A significant weakness in the educational process is that many teachers waste their energy battling children's mischief and pranks, which are in fact inherent companions of childhood and adolescence, and which deserve wise indulgence and intelligent transformation into humour. The actions that deserve condemnation are those that contain the seeds of egotism, narcissism and indifference to the inner world of others.

Similarly worthless are various reprimands, warnings and remarks, declared in meetings, and even recorded. The transference of such practices from the world of adults into the lives of children would be laughable, if it did not also carry serious dangers. By giving their 'word' or receiving a reprimand, the little person is given the impression that they have been absolved of guilt. However, moral education relies on children absolving themselves of guilt through committed and continuous atonement, which involves action and work. The deeper the repentance, the greater the student's own longing for such atonement. To monitor the progress of such atonement, to touch an individual's heart and to guide it on the correct path—this is the way to show sensitivity towards someone who is conscientiously striving to become worthy of forgiveness. No 'word', no promise can replace this inner spiritual work on which a person's attitude to others depends.

STORIES AND VIGNETTES

What does the word 'congratulate' mean?

During a lesson in grade two, Galia raised her hand.

'What is it, Galia?' asked the teacher.

'Mariika's got a new baby brother,' said Galia, and she smiled as happily as if it was her baby brother. Mariika is her friend. They sit next to each other in the second back row near the window.

Thirty pairs of eyes turned and looked with interest at Mariika. The little girl blushed with embarrassment.

'Mariika's got a little brother … Mariika's got a little brother … ' the whispers passed around the room. The teacher smiled, and all the children smiled.

'How wonderful!' said the teacher and went over to Mariika and gave her a kiss. 'We all congratulate Mariika's mother and father, and we congratulate you, Mariika, on the birth of your baby brother.'

Galia also kissed Mariika and gave her a hug.

'What does "congratulate" mean?' asked Mykola.

The class became very quiet. Everyone listened to see what the teacher would say.

'It means that Mariika's mum and dad have reason to be very happy. A human being has been born. He has brought happiness to many people:

Mariika's mother has a son;
Mariika's father has a son;
Mariika has a brother;
Mariika's grandpa has a grandson;
and her other grandpa has a grandson;
Mariika's grandma has a grandson;
And her other grandma has a grandson;
Mariika's auntie has a nephew;
Mariika's uncle has a nephew;
Mariika's cousin has a cousin;
And we have a new friend.

Look how many people are happy. That is why we congratulate everyone.

Mariika's brother is the youngest among us. We say "congratulations!"

because we share the joy felt by Mariika's mother and father, her grandparents, and her uncles and aunts.'

All the children joined in happily, calling out 'Congratulations! Congratulations!'

Dmytryk's holiday

The school year ended. The students went for a holiday at a summer camp, and the teacher went to the seaside. The little village school building seemed lonely and forgotten.

Dmytryk, a little grade one student, was the only one not going to the summer camp. The teacher told Dmytryk that he needed to learn to read properly. Once he had learnt to read, he could have a holiday.

Dmytryk was very glad that he had not been sent away for a holiday. He did not understand why a school student needed a holiday. It was not as if he worked hard like his mother and father.

Every day Dmytryk took his reader and went to the school yard. He sat under a pear tree and opened his book. But how could he read, when all around him birds were singing, butterflies were fluttering, and bees were buzzing? Dmytryk sat under the pear tree for several hours and then went home.

On the third day, as he was passing the school building, he noticed the aquarium inside. He stopped and looked in through the window. The fish were lying on the bottom of the aquarium and seemed to be sleeping.

'They've forgotten all about them,' thought Dmytryk. He felt sorry for the little goldfish. He lifted out the window frame and climbed into the classroom. He found a little box of dry fish food and threw some into the aquarium. The fish hungrily attacked the food.

After that, Dmytryk came every day to the school building and tapped on the window. The fish heard his quiet tapping and swam straight to the surface. Dmytryk took out the window frame, climbed into the classroom and fed the fish.

A month passed and the teacher returned. He immediately summoned Dmytryk. Dmytryk and the teacher went into the classroom. 'Sit down,' said the teacher. 'Open your book and read to me.' And he went over to the aquarium and admired the fish.

Dmytryk looked silently at the teacher, who had become very thoughtful, as if something was bothering him. The teacher turned his head and looked hard at Dmytryk, then came over and hugged him and gave him a kiss. Dmytryk was afraid to raise his head.

The young orchard

A young teacher came to a little village school. The school had been built quite recently. The school building was as new and beautiful as a toy, but all around it was just wasteland.

The teacher said to the children, 'We'll plant an orchard around the school.'

The children worked joyfully on the orchard. Together with the teacher they turned the soil, dug holes, and planted little trees. For several years they watered the orchard and kept it free of weeds, and at last the orchard flowered. It was amazingly beautiful.

The years passed, and the children grew up. The teacher's first students became parents and brought their own children to the school. The teacher began to feel that old age was creeping up on him. He was frightened by the thought that his eyes would fail him and that his hands would begin to shake. The apple trees and pear trees in the school orchard also grew old and began to dry out.

The teacher decided that it was time for him to retire. He did not want the children to see him feeble and decrepit. But he was terrified by the thought that he would leave behind the dried out stumps of the old orchard.

He worked day and night, and his first students, who were now parents and grandparents, came and helped him. They dug out the old orchard and planted a new one.

Two years later, when young apple trees and pear trees were standing proudly around the school, the teacher gathered all his students in the school yard and said, 'Farewell, children. I am retiring. I do not want you to see me weak and feeble. May this orchard flower here eternally.'

The lonely teacher

A teacher worked in the same village for forty-eight years. He knew every single person in the village. Everyone came to him for advice—the mothers and fathers, and the grandmothers and grandfathers of his little students. They were all his former pupils.

Old age came upon him. His wife died. His son had been killed long ago on the frontline. The old teacher was left all alone.

One day, after lessons, he told all the students in his grade four class, 'Come to my home, children.'

The students came to the teacher's apartment, and all the walls were covered with bookshelves full of books.

'Sir,' asked one curious boy, 'How many books are there in your library?'

'Several thousand,' answered the old teacher.

'And how many books can a person read during their lifetime?'

'Two thousand, no more,' said the teacher.

The students were silent. The old teacher understood why the student had asked that question. He led the students to his bookshelves, gave each student a book and said, 'I will not be working at school anymore. Please accept this present from me. Go home and tell your parents and friends to come and see me. I want to give them each a present.'

For several days people came one after another to see the old teacher. There were five thousand people living in the village, and to each one he gave a book and said, 'This is the greatest treasure. May there be many more books in your home.'

The teacher had one book left. The oldest man in the village came to see him. Grandpa Ivan was one hundred years old.

'Why have you given away all your books, son?' asked Grandpa Ivan. 'How can you live without books? You will die all alone.'

'Those books are like my relatives,' replied the teacher. 'Now I have become related to everyone in the village and will never be alone.'

The cheat sheet

When he prepared for his geometry exam, Mykola wrote five cheat sheets for the five most difficult questions. He knew the answers, but deep down he was afraid that he would suddenly forget what he knew. So, just in case, he wrote the five cheat sheets and hid them up his sleeve. He practised using them, and found it was very easy to take one out and place it underneath a sheet of paper in such a way as not to be noticed.

When Galyna Yakivna called Mykola's surname, his heart began to race. He took the question paper. It was the most difficult question. Mykola remembered that the cheat sheet for this question was the top one.

Mykola sat at his desk and was about to slip the cheat sheet from his sleeve when his eyes met those of Galyna Yakivna. The boy realised that his teacher had seen his fingers reaching into his sleeve to retrieve the cheat sheet.

In Galyna Yakivna's eyes Mykola read bewilderment and hurt. She turned her eyes away, and her face turned red with shame. The teacher got up, walked over to the window, and looked out at a lilac bush.

Mykola froze, with the two fingers of his right hand hovering up his left sleeve. A wave of mortification flooded his heart. He wished he could sink through the floor.

The first day

It was the last day of August. The next day was supposed to be Petryk's first day at school[64], but he had to stay home because he was sick. It pained the boy to think that everyone would be going to school tomorrow morning, but he would be lying in bed.

The first of September arrived, and Petryk woke at first light. The sun rose, and Petryk could hear the excited and joyful voices of children heading to school. It made his heart ache.

Then the door leading to his room squeaked and somebody entered the room. It was Mariia Mykolaivna, the teacher who would be teaching him in grade one. She smiled kindly, walked over to Petryk's bed, and put a huge flower into a vase.

So Petryk had a joyful first of September like everyone else.

What will happen if time stops?

Long ago, a boy named Vasylko used to study in a little village school. Only one teacher worked there, and all the children studied in a single classroom.

Summer came. Vasylko completed grade two and proudly told his mother and father, 'Now I am a grade three student.' He also told them that when the teacher left on holidays, he had entrusted a very important task to him. In a tiny room called the staffroom, there was a little wall clock driven by weights. It ticked away merrily, counting out the seconds. Time passed, and a weight slowly descended on a long chain that came from somewhere deep within the clock. In the course of twenty-four hours the weight descended so far that the clock would stop if someone did not pull it back up.

'Here are the keys to the school,' the teacher had said. 'Come here every morning, unlock the door, come to the staffroom, and pull up the weight. If you forget to come, we'll be in trouble.'

'What sort of trouble?' asked Vasylko fearfully.

'Time will stop,' said the teacher.

Vasylko opened his eyes wide in amazement. He was not sure if the teacher was joking or telling the truth. Something told him it was just a joke … But perhaps time really would stop …

Vasylko started wondering, 'What will happen if time stops?' He tried to imagine what sort of trouble could occur, but his thoughts did not lead anywhere. Still, to avoid any misfortune, he got up early, came to school, went in, listened to the clock's even ticking, and joyfully reassured himself that time was still passing. Time had not stopped. Then he pulled up the weight, locked the school door, and returned home.

It was still early. The village was just waking up. Vasylko smiled. He knew that this quiet, joyful morning—the calm people going about their day, the frisky calf bursting out of its yard—all this existed because he had pulled up the clock weight, and time, fortunately, had not stopped.

The girl with the hunched back

The children in grade two were solving a problem. Thirty-five students were bent over their exercise books. Somebody knocked quietly on the classroom door.

'Open the door and see who's there,' said the teacher to Yurko, a bright boy who sat in the front row. Yurko opened the door. The school principal came into the room, accompanied by a little girl—a new student. Thirty-five pairs of eyes studied the little girl. She had a hunched back.

With bated breath, the teacher turned to the class. He looked at the mischievous boys, and in his eyes the children read a plea: please do not let the little girl see surprise or mockery in your eyes.

The only thing shining in the children's eyes was curiosity. They looked into the eyes of the new student and smiled affectionately.

The teacher breathed a sigh of relief.

'This is Olia,' said the school principal. 'She has travelled a long way to come and be with us. Who will give her their place in the front row and move to the back row? You can see how small she is.'

All six boys and girls sitting in the front row raised their hands and offered to move.

Olia sat in the front row.

The class passed the test.

Take three more flowers, Tina

In the school greenhouse there is a flower kingdom. There may be a bitter frost outside, but behind the glass, chrysanthemums of many colours are growing: dark blue, pink, light blue and scarlet.

Early one morning, Tina, a little girl in grade one, came to the greenhouse. No-one else was there. The flowers had turned their heads to seek the sun, which would soon rise from beyond the horizon. When Tina opened the door of the greenhouse, the flower heads gave a little start. They liked the quiet, and the sound of the door frightened them. Once they had settled, they continued watching for the first rays of the pale winter sun, but each chrysanthemum also kept one eye on the little girl. Why had she come?

Tina had come to pick a light blue chrysanthemum, a flower of joy. Nowhere else was such a flower to be found, only in the school greenhouse. Tina's grandmother was seriously ill. At midnight she had taken a turn for the worse. Tina very much wanted to bring her grandmother some joy, to ease her suffering.

As soon as Tina had picked the flower, she heard the greenhouse door squeak. The flower heads gave another start, but as soon as they saw the teacher, they smiled. He was their faithful friend. He came to see them every day.

Tina knew the teacher, though she was not in any of his classes. He was kind but strict. He loved flowers, and he loved and respected people who loved flowers. He hated laziness, carelessness, wastefulness and idleness.

During winter, nobody picked any flowers in the greenhouse. They only created and protected the beauty here and came to admire it.

When the teacher saw Tina with the light blue chrysanthemum in her hand he stopped in surprise. Tina looked into the teacher's eyes, but all she could think of was her grandmother. In her imagination she could see her grandmother lying in pain, and Tina's lips whispered some words about the flower of joy easing pain. Her eyes implored the teacher and begged him to understand. And he felt her entreaty. He understood that she was not being naughty. The little girl had not picked the flower to discard it. In her hand she was holding life that she needed to bring to another human being.

The teacher walked up to Tina, put his arm around her and said, 'Pick three more flowers, Tina. One for you, for having such a kind heart, and one each for your mother and father, for bringing up a daughter with a kind heart.'

In spring, Tina came to school with her grandmother. The grandmother thanked the teacher for the flower of joy and gave the school a violet-coloured chrysanthemum.

The violet-coloured chrysanthemum

Every day in winter, children would bring a chrysanthemum from the greenhouse to the classroom. When peace and harmony reigned in the classroom, they would place a pink, red, blue, or turquoise flower into a tall, slender vase shaped like an ear of wheat.

In the greenhouse, there was also a very rare, violet-coloured chrysanthemum. Its flowers were the colour of a crystal-clear horizon in the evening steppe, just after sunset. The children very rarely brought a violet-coloured chrysanthemum to the class because it signified offense. If they put such flower into the vase, they were saying, 'Dear teacher, you have offended us.'

One day, their teacher, Vira Petrivna, came to her second lesson and found a violet-coloured flower on her desk.

The students were silent. Vira Petrivna gave them some tasks to work on independently. Then she sat at her desk, bowed her head, and thought to herself, 'What happened in the first lesson? How did I offend the children?'

She knew that the students respected her strict and fair attitude, and she did not understand how she could have hurt their feelings.

'The watch!' Vira Petrivna suddenly realized. 'I offended them by showing mistrust.'

The previous day had been her birthday. Her husband had given her a present, a gold watch. Today, during the first lesson, she took the watch off her wrist as usual and lay it on her desk.

During the break, she went to the staff room. Usually, she would leave her watch on the desk, and it would remain there throughout the day until the classes ended.

However, today, as she was leaving, for some reason the thought that the watch was made of gold occurred to her, and she turned back and put it on her wrist … And now the violet-coloured flower had appeared in the classroom … It had been two years since she last saw such a flower on her desk …

Vira Petrivna quietly took the watch off her wrist and lay it on her desk.

During the second break, the watch was left on the desk as usual. When Vira Petrivna arrived for the third lesson, a pink chrysanthemum was standing in the vase.

Vira Petrivna gave a sigh of relief.

The new teacher

The grade three students suffered a great misfortune. Their teacher, dear old Antonina Nychyporivna, died.

The children grieved for her for a long time. Only gradually, and with great difficulty, did they become accustomed to their young new teacher. It made it even harder that her name was also Antonina, though her patronymic was Petrivna.

Antonina Petrivna seemed to the children to be too happy and carefree. The children doubted if she would be able to love them as tenderly, as demandingly and as strictly as Antonina Nychyporivna.

One day, black-eyed Fedko was running outside when he fell and drove a large splinter into his hand. The boy ran to Antonina Petrivna. The young teacher, who was always so happy and carefree, gave a little scream and turned pale. She sat Fedko on her knee but did not know what to do next. Andriiko, an irrepressible mischief maker, walked up to her and said very quietly, 'You need to pull the splinter out with your teeth.'

Antonina Petrivna bent over the boy's hand and pressed her lips to the wound. When she raised her head, a large splinter was sticking out between her bloodied teeth. The children looked at their young teacher, their eyes now shining with delight.

That night, in thirty-seven households, the children told their mothers about their new teacher for the first time.

After school

When Vira Grygorivna sat down to mark the students' homework in their exercise books, Myshko knew in advance that he would not be praised for his efforts. He had written in a hurry because the other boys had been waiting for him to play ball outside.

Finally, the teacher opened Myshko's exercise book and looked at his writing. 'Is this how a grade three student writes?' she asked. 'Well, you are going to have to stay back after school.'[65]

Myshko felt embarrassed. He had never been asked to stay back after school. He knew in his heart that it was his fault. When all the other students left to go home, Myshko sat in the back row and opened his exercise book.

'Why aren't you going home?' asked Vira Grygorivna.

'Because you told me to stay back after school,' said Myshko.

'Oh, yes, I forgot … Of course, you must stay back. Re-write the work that wasn't done properly. I'll come back and check it. Don't dare go home without my permission,' said the teacher.

Vira Grygorivna left, and Myshko started working on the exercise. He wrote everything very neatly because he was not in a hurry anymore, and he wanted the teacher to praise his work. But for some reason, the teacher did not return. Somewhere far down the hall the clock struck three.

Myshko re-wrote the exercise again. Now, he gave attention to every letter. He was so absorbed in his work that he did not notice another hour pass. Down the hall the clock struck four.

Myshko sat and waited for his teacher, but she did not come. Another hour passed. It was early autumn, and the classroom began to grow dark. At seven o'clock, Auntie Mariia, the cleaner, entered the classroom.

'My dear boy, why are you still here?' she asked in astonishment.

'The teacher told me to stay after school,' answered Myshko.

Auntie Mariia stared at the boy for a long time, then shook her head and said, 'Go home, dear boy.'

'How can I go home without Vira Grygorivna's permission?' asked Myshko.

'I am giving you permission,' answered Auntie Mariia, firmly.

Her voice sounded so confident that Myshko asked joyfully, 'Did Vira Grygorivna tell you to give me permission?'

'Yes, she did,' answered Auntie Mariia, and she gave a sigh.

Mathematics is an interesting subject!

Today in grade four, everything is different from last year. Last year, all the lessons were taken by Kateryna Stepanivna. Today, Ivan Petrovych took the first lesson, but Serhii Pavlovych took the second lesson. Ivan Petrovych teaches mathematics, and Serhii Pavlovych teaches geography.

Ivan Petrovych sat at his desk and immediately noticed Oles's dog Brovko sitting outside the window. This is Oles's fourth year at school, and it is the fourth year that Brovko has walked to school with him. He even carries a little bag with Oles's lunch in it. Brovko knows that the bag has a little pocket with something tasty for him to eat as well. During every lesson, Brovko sits by the window and guards the little bag containing Oles's lunch.

Kateryna Stepanivna was used to Brovko. If everything was like last year, and Kateryna Stepanivna was taking all the lessons, she would have said kindly, 'How are you feeling today, Brovko?' and Brovko would have looked trustingly into her eyes, and happily wagged his tail.

Ivan Petrovych did not know Brovko, so he asked, 'And who is this?'

Oles answered, 'That is my friend Brovko … He waits outside during all my lessons.'

'You have a good, faithful friend,' said Ivan Petrovych.

When Serhii Pavlovych came for the second lesson, he also asked about the dog, but a bit differently.

'What is that?' he asked.

'That is my friend Brovko,' Oles answered. 'He waits outside during all my lessons.'

'I don't want to see him outside the window again,' said Serhii Pavlovych sternly.

Everyone in the class frowned and sat looking down at their desks. No-one spoke and no-one looked at the teacher. Everyone felt ashamed to look at each other, and Oles even felt ashamed to look at his dog.

When Oles came home, he started doing his homework. He found mathematics very interesting, and happily set about solving all the problems. He did not look at his geography homework.

Sixty years later

The old teacher sat under the spreading branches of a linden tree. He was enrolling children in the school. It was very quiet on the green grass under the tree. The new students were shy, and all that could be heard was the restrained whispering of the parents.

A grey-haired old man approached the teacher. The teacher looked carefully at the old man, closed his eyes for an instant, and again examined him from head to foot, then looked him straight in the eyes. He recognised his first student. Sixty years ago, under this very linden tree, on a quiet summer's day just like this, he had enrolled him in the school.

'Is that you, Ostap?' the old teacher asked quietly.

'It is me, teacher … I have brought my grandson to enrol … a little Ostap.'

The old teacher and his first student embraced and kissed. The old Ostap sighed and quietly murmured, 'The years go by, teacher.'

The old teacher wept. Thoughtful, full of emotion, with tears quivering on his eyelashes, he sat silently for a long time, gazing at little Ostap. Above the spreading linden tree shone the deep blue summer sky, bees hummed in the hop flowers, and far in the distance you could see a dark blue band of forest on the horizon. Everything was just as it was sixty years ago.

'And now, my dear students,' said the old teacher, in an even voice only slightly agitated by emotion, 'Who can tell me why a person needs to study?'

Ostap was the first to raise his hand. He put up his hand but was overcome by shyness. The old teacher smiled. The old Ostap approached the teacher and said, 'Teacher, it may happen that my grandson does not learn something, that he will not be able to read some page in the book of knowledge as well as we would both like him to. That is not really a problem. It will be a problem if he does not learn to love thinking. Thinking must become his passion. He must know why a person needs knowledge. For all his life he must remain like the dry earth, ready to thirstily soak up every drop of knowledge that falls his way.'

The conceited letter

There once lived a wise man who invented all the letters of the Ukrainian alphabet. He cut them out of birch bark, put them in a basket, and thought to himself, 'Tomorrow I will go and teach people how to read and write.'

The night came and went. The wise man got ready to go and share his invention with others. He thought, 'I need to put the letters in order, so it will be easier for people to learn how to read.' He started to lay out the letters: А, Б, В ... (pronounced 'ah, beh, veh') … He wondered what order he could put them in, so that each letter would give a clue as to what letter comes next.

All the letters lay quietly, waiting their turn, except for the letter ' Я ' (pronounced 'yah'), which could not wait patiently. It kept jumping into the wise man's hand and reminding him of its presence, asking 'What about " Я "?' In Ukrainian, ' я ' means 'I', so it sounded like he was saying, 'What about *me*?'

The wise man got angry and said, 'I can see I am going to have a lot of trouble with you. Lie there quietly and wait your turn.' But the letter ' Я ' could not lie patiently. It kept crawling into the wise man's hand and saying, 'Why do you keep forgetting me?'

The wise man thought and said, '" Я " will be the last letter in the alphabet.'

THE UKRAINIAN ALPHABET

Аа Бб Вв Гг Ґґ Дд Ее Єє Жж Зз Ии Іі
Її Йй Кк Лл Мм Нн Оо Пп Рр Сс Тт
Уу Фф Хх Цц Чч Шш Щщ Ьь Юю Яя

Four sheets of gold paper

Four sheets of gold paper lay on the table. Two boys and two girls came to the table. One boy had black eyes and the other had blue eyes. One girl had blonde hair and the other had black hair.

The black-eyed boy looked at his piece of gold paper and exclaimed joyfully, 'Oh, what a beautiful round loaf of bread!' He picked up his scissors and cut a loaf of bread from the gold paper.

As soon as the blue-eyed boy saw his piece of gold paper he joyfully exclaimed, 'That's a rooster flapping its wings. It is just about to start crowing!' The blue-eyed boy picked up his scissors and cut a rooster from the gold paper.

When the blonde-haired girl saw her piece of gold paper, she exclaimed joyfully, 'Oh, what a warm and tender sun!' She picked up her scissors and cut out a warm and tender sun.

When the black-haired girl looked at her piece of gold paper, she exclaimed joyfully, 'Oh, what a scary flash of lightning!' She picked up her scissors and cut out a scary, fiery, golden flash of lightening.

That is how the gold paper revealed its secrets to clever hands.

The journeyman and the chisel

A master craftsman was carving wood with a chisel. He was carving a rose. The chisel was small and shiny, made of steel. In the hands of a master, it was obedient and skilful.

The master craftsman went somewhere without finishing his work and left the chisel on his bench. A journeyman came into the workshop. He saw the shiny chisel lying on the workbench, and the unfinished rose next to it.

The journeyman picked up the chisel and tried to carve some rose petals, but he had no success. The chisel hacked at the rose and spoilt the master's work.

The rose was surprised, and asked, 'Chisel, why have you suddenly started working so badly?'

The chisel answered, 'I am just a piece of steel. I become a chisel when a master craftsman picks me up.

But when I am picked up by a mere journeyman, I am no longer a chisel, but just a sharp blade.'

The ox and the gardener

A man and an ox were working in a field. The ox was harnessed to a plough and tilling the field, slowly dragging his legs over the earth. It was hard for him to pull the plough, but the ox was used to his master. He knew that if he stopped working his master would lash him with his whip, and that he would give him less hay to eat in the evening.

Nearby, a gardener was digging a small stony patch of ground with a spade, preparing it for some grape vines. The ox had overheard a conversation between the gardener and his master that morning. The gardener had said that this stony patch of ground would be too difficult even for an ox to till. And now the ox could hear the man digging the ground and singing. The sweat was pouring off him, but he was singing away, and his eyes sparkled with joy.

'Gardener, isn't that hard work?' asked the ox, when he drew level with the man.

'Oh, yes, very hard!' answered the gardener.

'Then why are you singing, and why are your eyes full of joy?'

'Because I can see this barren, stony patch already dug,' said the gardener. 'I can see bunches of grapes growing on it. I can see the joy in the eyes of the people who will see the fruits of my labour.'

'How can you see all that?' asked the amazed ox. 'None of that exists.'

'If a man could only see what already exists, he would not be a man,' said the gardener. 'A human being can see their future.'

'Teach me, gardener, how to see things that do not exist,' said the ox.

'All right,' said the gardener. 'I'll free you from your collar.'

'But without a collar and whip I cannot work,' moaned the ox.

The gardener just shrugged his shoulders and thought, 'Someone who only works because they are forced to by a collar and whip cannot see the future.' He did not say those words aloud, because the ox would not have understood.

He rescued the ladybird

This happened during the summer. The sun baked the earth all day, but then dark clouds covered the sky, and rain thundered down.

A boy named Vasylko was sitting under a tall, spreading mulberry tree. He was not afraid of the rain. He was protected from it by the tree's thick foliage. It was dry under the mulberry tree, but just beside it, the rain was streaming in torrents. One of those torrents was gradually filling a pit just next to the tree, creating a tiny lake. In the middle of that lake was a tiny island. The water was rising steadily, and at any moment that island would disappear.

Suddenly, Vasylko spotted a small red ladybird on the island. It was running from one side of the island to the other. 'Why doesn't it fly away?' Vasylko wondered. He felt sorry for the ladybird.

Meanwhile, the island was growing smaller and smaller. Before Vasylko knew it, it was the size of a large coin. Then, it was no bigger than the smallest coin. The ladybird had no room to move.

Vasylko ran out into the rain and was soaked through in an instant. But he managed to rescue the ladybird.

The boy and the burdock

A boy was crossing a meadow. A prickly seed case from a burdock plant stuck to his trousers. The seed case was curious and wanted to move somewhere new. The boy was going to a village and the seed case travelled with him, looking in awe at the houses, the wide streets, and the lofty power poles. The seed case spotted some lovely green grass near a three-story building. He liked the look of that place, so he pricked the boy's leg, and the boy threw the prickly seed case into the grass.

The building that the seed case had spotted was a school. A year later, amongst the grass, the children noticed the broad leaves of a strange plant with a violet flower. A bumblebee was buzzing above the flower. The children surrounded the violet flower, wondering how it could have grown there. With bated breath, the violet flower listened to the children's words. The flower looked into each child's face, seeking the familiar face of the boy. There he was! He was gazing at the flower with all the other children. The violet flower smiled at the boy and leaned towards him, spreading its petals, and whispering, 'Thank you, boy, for coming to the meadow and helping me move to this lovely place.'

However, the boy did not hear the burdock's whisper. He had long forgotten about the prickly seed case.

A chick's first feelings of fear

In a warm nest, under a mother-hen, a tiny chick hatched out of a white egg. The chick pecked a hole in the thick shell, cracked it open, crawled out of the nest, and screwed up his eyes in awe. Everything around him was so bright and wonderful: the warm sun, the green grass, and the flowers swaying in a light breeze.

The little yellow chick started running around. His eyes shone with happiness. He wanted to share his joy with somebody. Then the chick saw a huge beast. The beast was long and round with shining white fur. Its two grey eyes looked intently at the chick, its slender ears were pricked, and long thin hairs fanned out around its mouth. The creature lay and waved its tail.

The chick ran towards the beast to tell it how beautiful the world was. The creature rose, its eyes blinked, its back arched, and the tiny hairs around its mouth started moving. The chick was suddenly frightened. It was the first time he had felt fear.

The sparrows were crying from the cold

One winter morning, little Yarynka went into the garden. It was bitterly cold, and there was not a single bird to be seen. Even the sparrows had disappeared.

'I wonder where they are hiding?' Yarynka thought.

She walked back to the house and looked up under the eaves. She heard a sparrow cheeping, and then some tiny beads of ice fell to the ground.

'What are they?' wondered Yarynka.

And then she realized: it was the sparrows' tears. The sparrows were crying from the cold, and their tears were falling to the ground as tiny beads of ice.

Yarynka felt so sorry for the sparrows!

Sparks from the sun

A birch tree and a fir tree grew side by side in the forest. The birch tree lost its leafy garment and stood shivering from the cold, clothed only in its white bark. Its bare branches trembled in the soft breeze. The birch tree looked at the fir tree, which was still green, and asked, 'Why is it, fir tree, that you are green all year round? Why is it that I lose my leaves, but you stay green and lush and keep warm?'

The fir tree smiled and answered, 'It is because my leaves are like needles. Every night, all through summer, I collect a drop of morning dew on the tip of each needle. I collect as many drops as I have needles. And every drop sparkles with sunlight. It is like a spark of warmth. I do not shake off the dewdrops like you, dear birch tree. I stand still and do not stir. I drink the dew through my needles. And, along with the dewdrops, I absorb sparks of warmth from the sun and store them in my needles. They keep me warm during the winter.'

Where do the silver webs come from?

An elderly grandmother is sitting in the sun. The autumn sun does not burn, it just warms her gently. The grandmother looks around and sees silver webs floating in the air. 'Where do those silver webs come from?' asks her granddaughter. And the grandmother tells her a story about a spider-weaver.

'The spider-weaver lives on a tall poplar that grows by the road. The spider sits way up high, almost touching the clouds. When a white cloud floats above the poplar, bits of fluffy cloud come drifting down. They float down onto the poplar, and the spider catches them, one after the other. The spider uses them to weave the finest of threads. From these threads, it weaves its nest, and the leftover threads drift down from the poplar and float all around.'

How bats flew to warmer lands

It grew cold. The insects disappeared, and the bats had nothing to eat. A colony of bats came together. What should they do? What were they going to eat? The bats thought about it and decided to fly to warmer lands. They flew all night and then rested under the eaves of houses. They held on to the wooden beams with their tiny legs, hanging upside down and sleeping until evening. In the evening, they took off again and flew until the following morning. That was how they reached warmer lands.

How the poppy seed woke

A poppy seed fell to the ground. A boy ran by, stepped on the seed, and covered it with earth. The seed fell asleep and slept for a long time, until finally it grew hot and woke up. It was the spring that woke it. The seed opened its tiny mouth to drink some water. Once its thirst was quenched, the seed sprouted. The sprout looked around and saw the sun, the sky, and trees. It laughed joyfully and bloomed with a pink flower.

Why does the sheep have sad eyes?

A little lamb was born. It was beautiful, with curly hair. A woman liked its curly fleece, so she killed the lamb, skinned it, and scoured the fleece. Then she made a coat for her little daughter and trimmed the sleeves with the lamb's fleece.

The little girl went outside in her new coat, joyfully stroking the fur-trimmed sleeves with her hands. The girl saw a sheep. It was standing near the barn and looking at the girl. The girl approached the sheep and wanted to stroke it.

'The sheep will be happy,' she thought, 'Because I have such a beautiful coat with a fur trim.' She stepped up to the sheep and stroked her fleece and her head. To her surprise, the sheep was not happy and looked at her fearfully. The sheep smelled the coat's fur trim and started bleating anxiously, mournfully.

'Why was the sheep afraid of my coat?' the puzzled little girl asked her father. 'Why does she have such sad eyes?'

'Because it's just a sheep, a stupid animal,' replied her father. 'It doesn't understand that you're trying to be nice to it.'

The water lily and the turtle

Early one morning, a turtle trotted slowly to the pond to drink some water. She drank her fill and waited for the sun to rise, so she could warm herself in its rays. The sun rose, and at that moment, the turtle noticed a beautiful flower emerging from the water. It stood tall and spread its white petals above the pond. The turtle recognized the flower. It was a water lily. During the night, it hid at the bottom of the pond, but during the day, it warmed its petals in the sun.

The turtle sat there, admiring the white flower.

'Tell me, lily, why do you hide at the bottom of the pond all night?' asked the turtle.

'Because I have soft, delicate, tender petals,' answered the lily. 'I am hiding from the night birds in case they damage them. If I had a shell like you, I would not need to hide.'

'Oh,' sighed the turtle. 'Nobody knows why I have such a hard shell.'

'Why is it?' asked the lily, and its petals leaned towards the turtle with interest.

'Because I have a heart that is softer and more tender than your petals. If it was exposed, not even the bottom of the pond would save it.'

The dandelion

A yellow dandelion grew in a meadow. When it finished flowering, its yellow petals gave way to a fluffy white head. That head was made up of many fluffy seeds. One day, the stalk told the seeds, 'As soon as the wind blows, fly away! Find some moist soil and land there. Take root and grow!'

The seeds did not delay. They rose on a gust of wind and flew all over the meadow. But then the fluffy dandelion head spotted a dark cloud in the sky and took fright. It gathered its fluffy seeds together like a folded umbrella. The fluffy seeds held on tightly to each other. The wind blew, swirling around the dandelion, but the head held together, not releasing a single seed.

'Don't fly away now,' the head told its seeds. 'The storm might cast you into the water or into a swamp, and then you would be doomed.'

The curious ball of wool

A grandmother was knitting some socks. A ball of fine wool lay at her feet. The grandmother was warming herself in the sun, and so was the ball of wool. However, the ball of wool became curious about where the sun rose and where it set, so it set off to find out.

It rolled and rolled, getting further and further away. It rolled on for a day, and then kept rolling—for two days, three days, ten days. It kept on rolling for a thousand days, crossing rivers and seas. Finally, it reached the sun and asked it, 'Dear sun, please tell me, where do you rise and where do you set?'

The sun was surprised. 'How are you going to find your way home?' it asked.

'I'll follow the thread back,' answered the curious ball of wool.

'I'll tell you then,' said the sun. 'I rise where your grandmother's dream ends and I set where her dream begins.'

The ball of wool rolled all the way home and told the grandmother all about its adventure, and what the sun had said.

The swan and the tadpole

A toad and her tadpole son were dozing in some thick silt under a rotten tree stump, when they heard a sound of splashing water. The toad said to the tadpole, 'Go and take a look, my boy, and see what is making that noise and disturbing our sleep.'

The tadpole poked his head out and almost died from fright. 'Mum,' he said in a trembling voice, 'There is a disgusting monster up there! It's terrifying!'

'What does it look like?' asked the toad.

'It's all smooth and white, with a long, stretched out neck and a small head. At the end of its head, it has a beak. It's revolting … What is it, mum?'

The toad thought and thought, but she could not imagine what her son was talking about. She swam up from under the stump and looked at the creature. Then, recoiling in disgust, she said, 'That's a swan, a most hideous bird. Don't look at that disgusting monster, my dear boy, or you won't be able to sleep at night.'

Why does the ice on the pond ring out?

On a moonlit winter's night, listen to the silence of the pond! You will hear a soft ringing, as if somebody is striking a crystal dome with a tiny hammer and making it ring. It seems as if the whole world around you is ringing as well: the sky, the stars, and the white frost on the willows.

What makes this sound? I'll tell you.

A boastful fish lives in this pond. One day, she decided to change her colour to silver, so she asked the moon, 'Please give me some silver to coat my scales.'

The moon replied, 'Take as much as you want.' Ever since, the fish has been trying to swim to the moon, but she keeps bumping into the ice and making it ring.

The swan's feather

A flock of swans was flying high up in the sky. They were returning from warmer lands. Somewhere, far beyond the primordial forest, near a blue lake, a huge white feather fell from a swan's wing.

Just then, a grey sparrow was bathing in some dust on the ground. He was very surprised to see the feather fall near him, and asked, 'Where did you come from?'

'I am a swan's feather. I am a gift for you, dear sparrow.'

The sparrow was very happy. 'Well,' he thought to himself. 'Now, I will be able to soar high in the sky like a swan.'

He grasped the feather in his claws and took off, but he could fly no higher than an oak tree. He gazed at the flock of swans, disappearing into the deep blue sky, and his heart ached. He felt very sad. The sparrow flew home to his nest under the eaves and put the swan's feather in a safe place. And whenever he felt sad, he would take it out and look at it, and it made him feel better.

The winged flower

This happened during the summer. A strong wind lifted up a seed that had two fluffy wings. The seed landed in a meadow, and the grass asked it, 'Who are you?'

'I am a winged flower,' answered the seed. 'I'll grow here in the meadow.'

The grass was glad to have a new neighbour.

The water strider and the ant

A water strider lived by a pond. He could run on the water because he had little floating boots on his feet, so he was not afraid of drowning.

The water strider ran to the bank of his pond and met an ant. The ant was very curious and asked, 'How is it, water strider, that you can run on water?'

'Come with me, and I'll show you how,' said the water strider.

The ant stepped onto the water and nearly drowned. She barely escaped with her life. 'You won't fool me again,' she told the water strider.

Why did the cherry tree bloom in autumn?

There was an old cherry tree in our garden. It had rough, uneven branches and its bark was peeling off in long strips. In spring, the cherry tree came out in leaf, but it did not bloom. Then, when autumn arrived, the tree suddenly woke up and flowered.

'Why is it flowering in autumn?' I asked my grandmother, and in reply, she told me the following story.

'The old cherry tree became very ill. When spring arrived, it fell asleep in the sunshine, and did not hear the rumble of the first spring thunderstorms. And it is the first thunder in spring that signals to the cherry trees that it is time to flower. But it slept through all the spring thunderstorms ... Then in autumn, when it was nice and warm, it started flowering.'

I walked over to the old cherry tree and lay my ear against its knotty trunk. I heard the tree give a soft sigh.

How a young rooster spent the night in an apple tree

A mother hen had a naughty little rooster son. The mother told him, 'Don't go far from me, stay close.'

But the little rooster wanted to wander around. One day, he wandered into a garden and just kept on going. He wandered so far into the undergrowth that he did not know how to find his way home.

A big dog ran over to him. The rooster took fright and flapped right up into an apple tree, but the dog just lay down under the tree and stayed there.

The sun set. Night fell. The rooster sat perched up in the apple tree, trembling with fear. A huge moth came flying by. It asked the rooster, 'Where is your nest?' But the rooster was too frightened to answer.

He barely managed to get through the night. When the sun rose, the rooster flapped down from the tree and ran all the way home. He ran up to his mother, as happy as can be, and started crowing with joy.

How a mushroom wanted to see the sun

In a dark forest, under a mighty tree with spreading branches, hidden by the surrounding grass, grew a mushroom.

One day a magpie flew over to the tree, settled on a branch and said, 'I feel so sorry for you, dear mushroom. You live surrounded by grass and have never seen the sun.'

'What does the sun look like?' asked the mushroom.

'Oh, it is beautiful,' answered the magpie. 'It is bright and warm.'

'I want to see the sun!' cried the mushroom and poked its head out of the grass.

Just then some children were passing by. They spotted the mushroom, picked it, and put it into their basket. You will get to see the sun now, mushroom!

The snowman with a heart of ice

Soft fluffy snow covered the ground. Some children made a snowman from it and left it by the bank of a pond. The snowman seemed alive: it had a beard, a moustache, and pebble eyes that gazed sternly from under its scowling eye-brows.

One of the boys said, 'A snowman is supposed to be kind. Let's give him a heart. A heartless person is mean, but a person with a heart is kind.'

But the children could not decide what they would make the snowman's heart from. Finally, they came up with an idea: since the snowman was made of snow, its heart should be made of ice.

They found a clear, transparent piece of ice, made a heart out of it, and inserted it into the snowman's chest.

One day, a boy's fingers were frozen. It hurt so much that the boy burst into the tears. The boy skated over to the snowman and asked, 'Dear snowman, what should I do? My fingers are frozen.'

But the snowman was silent. It gazed at the boy with eyes that were neither kind nor angry. They were indifferent, empty, made of stone.

Another boy came over to the one who was crying and said, 'That snowman has a heart of ice! Do you think someone with a heart of ice is going to help anyone?'

The tulip and the rose

A young lad came to a garden where tulips and roses bloomed. He admired the flowers, gazing for a long time at the tulips' bell-shaped flowerheads and the roses' luxurious petals. With bated breath, the roses and tulips waited to see which flower the lad would choose, which he would like the most.

'Roses have thorns,' the tulips thought. 'He could prick his hands badly while picking a rose and make them bleed. We tulips have soft tender stems. It is easy to reach out and pick us.'

The lad stopped by the tulips, admiring the beauty of their bell-shaped flowerheads, and then moved on to the roses.

The pink tulips were so offended, they turned pale.

The lad stepped up to a rose bush. He tried several times to pick a flower, but pricked his finger on the rose's thorns, and it started bleeding.

'Well, now he will give up on the roses,' whispered a tulip.

But the lad did not leave the rose bush. He pricked himself several times, until the blood was dripping from his palms as well as his fingers. Finally, he managed to pick a rose, and his eyes shown with happiness.

The tulip bowed to the ground. It looked at its tender stem and thought, 'Perhaps it would be better if I had a thorny stem after all.'

The red apple at the top of the tree

An apple tree bore a rich crop of apples. Summer passed, and the apples ripened. Children came and picked the ripe apples, but they could not reach one small red apple at the top of the tree. They left it on the tree, and thought, 'Let it enjoy the sunshine a little longer.'

Autumn came. The nights were cold. Leaves fell from the trees. The small apple looked around and felt sad. Then it rained … But on clear sunny days, the apple was joyful: it had a little more time to warm itself in the sun.

One clear autumn night, from beyond mountains, the frost arrived. It covered the remaining leaves with hoar frost. The red apple woke up and trembled with fear: there were no leaves left on the apple tree. A little boy came to the garden. The apple was so happy to see him that it tumbled to the ground. The boy picked up the red apple and took it home. The apple lay in the boy's pocket, snuggling up to the warmth of his leg. The apple was warm, but it trembled with fear. What would happen now? The sun and the orchard had disappeared.

Why do I feel this way?

Ivanko and Tonia lived next door to each other, by a pond. For as long as Ivanko could remember, they had swum in that pond together, before they began to go to school, and during the summer holidays when they completed their first, second, and third years at school.

Today was a special day for the children: their parents came to school, and their teacher presented books to the best students. Ivanko and Tonia were awarded certificates of merit.[66]

Ivanko came home, fed his pigeons, and ran to the pond to swim.

When he reached the bank of the pond, there was Tonia. She was already undressed and was about to step into the water. Ivanko looked at her beautiful, slender body, and he suddenly experienced a new feeling, previously unknown to him. He felt awkward looking at Tonia's naked body.[67] Ivanko hid behind a guelder-rose bush and hoped that Tonia had not seen him.

Tonia entered the water and swam, but Ivanko was afraid to move. He sat as if bewitched. He wanted to keep watching Tonia, but at the same time he felt that there was something wrong in this desire.

'Why do I feel like this?' wondered Ivanko. 'Last year, we swam together, and I did not feel awkward.'

Quietly, Ivanko crept from behind the bush and headed home. He wanted to look back and watch Tonia from a distance, but he forced himself not to. His heart was pounding like never before.

The squill and the lark

Under a soft blanket of leaves, in the warm soil, a sweet little bulb slept through the long winter. As it slept, it listened attentively for the song of the lark, because the song of a lark in the clear blue sky is a signal for a bulb to wake up.

And at last, through its carpet of leaves, the bulb heard the lark's song descending from the sky. The bulb cracked open and sent forth a small shoot. The green shoot sprouted from the earth, spread its leaves, and rose into the air. Its green stems rose higher and higher, and between them, clusters of squills bloomed. The squills were as blue as the sky above. The squills gazed at the sky with their blue eyes, listening to the song of the lark. The trees in the forest were still leafless. The forest was open and full of light. It was as if the blue of the sky poured down from above and spread through the forest in the squills below.

Sunrise

The sun was rising. A starling flew out of his birdhouse in search of worms. A rooster perched on the fence and greeted the rising sun with his 'cock-a-doodle-doo!' A sunflower turned its yellow head to the sun and gazed at the red sky. A sparrow burst from his nest, shook his feathers, and started chirping joyfully. An aspen rustled its leaves.

Everyone welcomed the sun. An ear of wheat bent its head, its whiskers stirring. A fish swam up from the bottom of the river and trembled in the sunlight. A lark soared high in the sky, wanting to be the first to see the sun. A butterfly flitted from one flower to another, wondering, 'Did I sleep in and miss the sunrise?'

A butterfly with dew on its wing

In the morning, Oksanka went out into the garden. The sun was rising, and birds were singing.

She spotted a butterfly on the leaf of an apple tree. It was sitting on the leaf and moving its wings very slowly. Oksanka noticed a drop of morning dew glittering on one of the butterfly's wings. 'The butterfly is afraid of flapping its wings and flying because that beautiful dewdrop would slip off its wing,' thought Oksanka.

The girl stood watching the butterfly with bated breath. She wanted time to stand still, so the sun would climb no higher, the morning freshness would linger, and the dew drop would remain on the butterfly's wing.

How the chickadee wakes me in the morning

As soon as a dim light appears outside my window, a small bird with a yellow breast pays me a visit. It is a chickadee. It has an emerald-green cap and white cheeks. Every feather on its green-grey wings looks as if it has been painted with a fine brush.

The chickadee taps at my dew-covered window with its sharp little beak, and its black eyes gaze into my room. It grows light. I get out of bed and take a piece of fried lard to the chickadee. It pecks at the lard and sings, 'Chickadee-dee-dee.' It is saying, 'Thank you very much. I'll see you again first thing tomorrow.'

A bumblebee awakes

In late autumn, a bumblebee was on his way home, when a cold wind began to blow and it started snowing. The bumblebee was not able to reach his nest, so he took refuge in a deep crack in the trunk of a pine tree and fell asleep. His friends waited for him in vain. They thought he must have perished in the cold. But the bumblebee was sleeping safely inside the pine tree.

Spring arrived. The bumblebee was woken by the gentle rays of the sun. He flew out from his safe place and buzzed around the forest looking for flowers, so he could drink some sweet nectar. But there were not yet any flowers to be found. The snow had only just melted, and the grass had not yet turned green.

As he flew, the bumblebee could feel his wings becoming weak. Exhausted, he settled on the trunk of a silver birch tree and spread his wings, warming himself in the sun. And then he spotted a drop of transparent liquid sparkling on the white bark. 'I'll drink some dew,' thought the bumblebee. He tried it, and the dew was sweet.

Just then he heard the birch tree whisper, 'It is not dew. It is my blood. Yesterday, somebody broke one of my branches, and my white blood oozed out. Drink it, dear bumblebee, and regain your strength!'

The bumblebee drank his fill of the sweet birch sap, then flapped his wings happily and took off. He returned to his nest and told his friends how the birch tree had saved him from starvation.

The acacia told us

We were getting ready for a walk in the forest, when our teacher said, 'First we should check if it will rain today.'

'How do we do that?' we asked.

'We'll ask a yellow acacia,' our teacher replied. 'If there are swarms of bees buzzing around her flowers, we had better not go.'

We went to look at the acacia's flowers, and there were so many bees the whole tree was buzzing. We would not be going to the forest today.

'Before it rains, the flowers of the yellow acacia produce a lot of sweet nectar,' the teacher explained. 'Bees are attracted to this nectar. That is how we learnt that it is going to rain.'

Why do leaves fall from trees?

In October and November, leaves turn yellow and fall from trees. Why do leaves fall from trees?

One evening, I hid under a bush to find out who paints the leaves yellow, pink, and red. I saw a tiny old man crawl out from under a guelder-rose bush. He chuckled, stroked his grey beard, took his painting kit, and approached some maples. He climbed up a tree and started painting the leaves. He painted one leaf yellow, a second one pink, and a third one red.

'Who are you, old man?' I asked him.

'I am a leaf-colourist,' answered the old man. 'I paint the leaves. Wherever I spend the night, the leaves become bright and colourful.'

'Why don't you paint the leaves of the sour cherry tree?' I asked.

'Because the sour cherry tree cries,' he said. 'It doesn't want its leaves coloured. That is why it stays green until the first frost.'

I took a close look at the cherry tree's trunk. Its trunk was indeed covered with large, sticky, pink teardrops. The cherry tree was crying. It did not want to lose its leaves.

The other trees had already lost all their leaves, but the cherry tree was still green! Then the frost arrived, and in a single night the cherry tree lost all its leaves. The poor cherry tree was left bare and gave a deep sigh.

Who lit the candles on the chestnut trees?

Little Marynka went with her mother into the forest. It was May, and everything was a bright green. Marynka looked up at the green branches of the chestnut trees, and her eyes lit up with joy.

'Mum, look!' said the little girl. 'Candles are burning in the chestnut trees. Who lit them?'

'We'll come back in the morning and see,' said her mother with a smile.

Early the next morning, Marynka and her mother walked through the cold dew into the forest. Little Marynka looked up into the green crown of a chestnut tree and saw a squirrel jumping from branch to branch. So, it was the squirrel lighting candles in the chestnut trees. But who gave it fire to light them with? The sun. It rose and reached out to give the squirrel a burning spark. That was what lit the candles in the chestnut trees.

Sheets of white

It was autumn. The faint light of dawn was beginning to appear on the horizon. The forest stood silently. The birds were still asleep. Just before the sun rose, Grandma Frost crept into the forest. She spread sheets of white all over the green grass. The clearings became white, and the forest appeared to light up. A grey owl looked at the sheets of white, thought that it was already morning, and hid in a tree.

The sky glowed red in the east, and the sun rose. Where did the sheets of white go? They were nowhere to be seen. In their place silver drops of dew were shining on the grass. Where does Grandma Frost get so many sheets from? Will she bring them again tomorrow night? And who weaves them, those sheets of white?

What are the swallows twittering about?

Some swallows built a nest under our window. I have no idea when they built it, but my mother said it was long ago.

Summer passed. The swallows raised their chicks. The little ones left their nest and made their own way. Their parents were left alone. Now, they no longer hide in their nest. They perch near their nest and twitter away, and I listen to them. In the springtime, their twittering used to be anxious but joyful. Now it is anxious and sad.

I wonder what the swallows are twittering about?

The first ice on the pond

Last night, the first frost arrived. It covered the pond with a thin layer of clear ice. The sun rose, and the ice gleamed in the sunshine. A young rooster ran to the bank of the pond. He wanted to drink, so he pecked at the water with his beak, but it was hard.

'What's going on?' the rooster wondered. 'Yesterday, there was water here, but today there is just ground. And why is this ground so hard and shiny?'

The rooster stepped onto the ice, and it was very slippery. The rooster kept moving forward until he was quite some way from the bank. When the mother hen saw him in the middle of the pond, she called out anxiously, 'Come back, or you'll drown! The water in the middle of the pond has not frozen yet!'

The rooster took fright and rushed back home. If he had not turned around, he would have drowned.

The keen-witted glazier

One morning Yurko came to the pond and saw something amazing. The whole pond was covered with a thin sheet of glass, while water was still flowing underneath it. Yurko asked his father, 'Who covered the pond with glass?'

His father laughed and said, 'There is a very skilled and keen-witted glazier. He came and covered the pond with a huge piece of glass. That glazier lives a long way from here, in the north, but he came and visited us.'

'Who is that glazier?' asked Yurko in surprise.

'The frost,' said his father.

Yurko and the sunbeam

Yurko woke up early—as soon as the sun rose. His mother and father were already at work. He listened carefully and could hear something making a rustling sound on the floor.

Yurko thought it was a mouse, but there was no mouse to be seen. All he could see under his bed was a tiny little sunbeam. It was the sunbeam that was making the rustling sound. Yurko asked the sunbeam, 'Could you live with us forever?'

The sunbeam explained that he would need to go and look after his children each night. As the day progressed, the sunbeam shuffled across the floor. In the evening it crawled up the wall and all the way to the ceiling. When the sun set, the sunbeam disappeared into the forest. Yurko felt sad without him …

The violet and the bee

A bee and a violet became friends. The violet lived in a field, observing everything with her joyful, violet eyes, and the bee lived in his beehive. The bee would visit the violet many times each day to gather pollen and nectar. The violet was always happy to see her friend.

Then, one day, the bee arrived to find that the violet's petals were closed, and her head was drooping.

'Why are you so sad, violet? Why are your petals closed?' asked the bee.

'You must fly home, dear bee, for a storm is approaching. The rain is going to pour down,' said the violet.

The bee rushed home. As soon as he was inside his hive, the rain poured down.

Nowhere for the dewdrops

Red, pink, and white roses bloomed in the garden. Olia went there every morning. She liked to admire the dewdrops on the rose petals, sparkling like silver beads in the sunshine. But every day, there were fewer and fewer roses left in the garden: they were cut by people to put into vases.

Then, one morning, Olia came to the garden and her heart ached: there was not a single flower left on the rose bushes. The sky was dark and gloomy that morning. Heavy clouds passed slowly by, and it began to drizzle.

'There is nowhere for the dewdrops to cling,' Olia thought, recalling a line of verse.[68] Dew loves flowers best of all, but there were no flowers left.

The chrysanthemum and the onion

A chrysanthemum grew near a house. Towards the end of summer, it produced beautiful pink flowers. The chrysanthemum admired its own beauty. Its flowers whispered to each other, 'Look how beautiful we are!'

Next to the chrysanthemum grew an onion, an ordinary brown onion. Towards the end of summer, the onion ripened, its green top withered, and it gave off a strong onion smell. The chrysanthemum screwed up its nose and said to the onion, 'What an unpleasant smell you have. I can't imagine why people would grow such a plant. Probably to repel flees.'

The onion was silent. It did indeed feel very plain, compared with the chrysanthemum.

Just then a woman came out of the house and headed towards the chrysanthemum. The chrysanthemum held its breath. It was expecting the woman to say how beautiful it was.

The woman walked up to the chrysanthemum and said, 'What beautiful chrysanthemums!'

The chrysanthemum melted with pleasure. Then the woman bent over, pulled up the onion, and examined it carefully. 'What a beautiful onion!' she exclaimed.

The chrysanthemum was surprised. 'Is it really possible for an onion to be beautiful?' it wondered.

The swallow and the sparrow

A swallow and a sparrow met as they flew in the sky. The swallow said, 'I can fly faster than you.' And she soared into the heavens, right up to the clouds.

When she returned to earth, the sparrow remarked, 'You might be able to fly high, but I can hop across the ground, and you can't.' The swallow tried to hop, but in vain. Then she told the sparrow, 'I can fly over the pond and drink as I fly.' And the swallow swooped over the pond taking a sip of water as she flew. 'You can watch me do it all you like, but won't be able to do that,' she said.

The sparrow just laughed. 'Why don't you try and swing on a twig? I can, but you can't.' And he settled on a slender crack willow twig and started swinging as happily as can be. Even when the sun set, the sparrow was still swinging away, laughing and chirping, 'Cheep-cheep!'

The bush with poisonous berries

The leaves have fallen from the trees and the grass has withered. It is bitterly cold in the bare, see-through forest. The wind blows right through it. You cannot hear the happy chatter of children. There is nothing to bring them to the forest: no white mushrooms, no blackthorn berries, no sour rose hips.

On the edge of the forest there is just one solitary bush with poisonous berries. Its sharp green leaves look as if they could have been made from tinplate, and red berries hang from its branches. The bush admires itself. 'Look how beautiful I am!' it thinks.

The field and the trees are covered with snow, but this bush's berries are still red. However, no woodpecker or thrush or magpie will touch them.

'Why don't you try my berries?' the bush asks the birds.

'Because they are poisonous,' reply the birds.

'Then why are they so beautiful?' asks the bush.

Poisonous things are often beautiful.

The oak and the crack willow

An oak tree and a crack willow grew side by side. With each passing year, the oak stretched higher and higher towards the sun. But the crack willow did not seem to grow at all, just to bush out. One day the oak asked it, 'Crack willow, why are you so small? Why do you have thin stalks instead of a trunk?'

The crack willow was silent for a while, and then answered, 'Wait till a hurricane comes, and then you will wish you were thin like me. I will bend to the earth and shut my eyes, and the hurricane will spare me. But it will break your mighty branches.'

And indeed, one day a hurricane did come flying from beyond the high mountains and beyond the distant sea. It thundered and howled and groaned and cackled. The crack willow bent to the earth, stretched its thin branches over the grass, closed its eyes and ears, and shook with fear. But the oak stood tall, facing the hurricane, and straightened its mighty shoulders. The hurricane howled and roared and groaned, and tried to break the oak tree's branches, but the oak withstood its onslaught. Only one branch broke off and fell on top of the crack willow. Meanwhile, the hurricane, exhausted, lay down in a valley to rest, hardly breathing.

The crack willow nearly died of fright. It thought that the whole oak tree had fallen.

'How are you, oak tree? Are you still alive?' it asked.

'What does it matter?' answered the oak tree. 'It is better to grow tall and straight, and meet the hurricane standing, and fight it, than to bend to the earth and grow stunted and weak.'

The mallow and the indoor plant

A mallow grew beside a house. It was tall and slender. Its pink flowers gazed into the room to see what was inside. On the windowsill, in a small pot, grew a tiny plant with a green stem and a pink flower, just like the mallow, but much smaller.

The mallow asked the plant, 'Who are you?'

'I am an indoor plant,' said a voice from the pot.

'How can you live indoors?' asked the mallow. 'There's no sunshine and no rain there.'

'Everyday, people water me and clean my leaves,' the indoor plant replied. 'I have lived here for many years and remember many winters. In autumn, you will wither and die, but I will live on.'

The mallow listened to everything the indoor plant had to say, and then asked, 'Do you know what the morning breeze feels like?'

'No,' said the plant. 'What is that?'

The mallow looked at the indoor plant with compassion and shook its head. 'It is better to live only until autumn,' it said, 'But to know the caress of the morning breeze.'

The mole and the sun

A mole dug himself a burrow, deep underground, and that is where he lived. He never came out of his burrow during the daytime. Only at night, when all around were asleep, would he furtively crawl out of his burrow looking for something to eat, and then he would return to his burrow as quickly as he could. One sunny day, a happy mouse came to visit the mole in his burrow.

'What is that scent you are giving off?' the mole asked her. 'I know the scent of an ear of wheat, the scent of the earth, the scent of the grass … But now I am smelling something different, and I don't know what it is.'

'It is the scent of the sun,' replied the mouse.

'What is the sun?' asked the mole.

The mouse started explaining what the sun is, how it shines, how hot it is, and how comforting it is. The mole stopped digging and listened to everything the mouse had to say. When the mouse had finished telling him all about the sun, the mole remarked, 'The only thing I don't understand is what on earth they made the sun for?'

The wheaten lark

A mother kneaded some dough and moulded five big, round loaves of bread, the sort that are called *palianytsi* in Ukrainian. There was a little dough left over, and she used it to make a wheaten lark. She put the loaves into the oven and placed the wheaten lark beside them.

The loaves were dozing inside the hot oven, yawning in their sleep, when a sudden cheeping woke them up, and they saw the wheaten lark sitting beside them.

'Who are you?' the loaves asked.

'I am a wheaten lark. I can hardly wait for Olia's mother to take me out of the oven and put me on the windowsill, so I can take off and fly away.'

The loaves were surprised. They wanted to see the lark fly.

Olia's mother took the bread out of the oven and placed it on the windowsill to cool off, where everyone could see it. She placed the lark next to the bread.

The lark sat on the windowsill, motionless and silent.

'Why aren't you flying away?' the loaves asked it. 'The window is wide-open.'

'I will never be able to fly,' replied the lark sadly. 'I have everything: wings, claws, and sharp little eyes. But I cannot sing. And what sort of a lark am I if I can't sing?'

And it is true: you cannot bake a song in an oven.

The toad and the nightingale

A toad lived in a swamp. Of all the toads in the swamp, she was the most skilled musician. Every evening, she would crawl out of the swamp, close her eyes, and start singing, 'Croak-croak.'

One evening, just as the toad was about to close her eyes and start singing, she caught sight of a little grey bird settling on a crack willow. The bird started singing, and its song was full of joy. It was as if somebody was playing on silver strings. A young couple sat beneath the willow and listened. They were enchanted. 'How beautifully the nightingale sings!' they exclaimed.

The toad was surprised. 'What did those people find in the song that was so beautiful?' she wondered. 'Now, if I were singing, I could understand.'

And then she asked out loud, 'Tell me, please, humans, why does this song touch your souls? Here in the swamp, no one has even heard of a nightingale.'

The young man answered, 'To understand and appreciate a nightingale's song, you first have to move out of the swamp.'

Why are you sitting so quietly?

Grandma Mariia has an eight-year-old grandson named Serhii. The school year has ended, and Serhii is at home from morning to evening. He runs around outside chasing his dog Brovko, or Brovko chases him. Or he climbs up a tall tree, and grandma is worried he will fall. Or he runs along the road rolling a wheel, and grandma cannot sit quietly in the house: there are cars out there!

Grandma Mariia often complains, 'What a restless child you are, Serhii! You can't sit still.'

One day Serhii climbs up on the roof and cannot get down. The metal roof is very slippery. For a long time, grandma walks around the house while Serhii sits by the chimney pipe. The neighbours come and get Serhii down.

Then something very strange happens to Serhii. He has breakfast, seats himself on an old tree stump near the barn, and just sits there, looking at the ground.

Grandma looks out the window, and he is just sitting there. She looks out ten minutes later and he is still sitting there. She looks out half an hour later, and he is still sitting motionlessly.

'What has happened to him?' worries Grandma Mariia and goes outside to see what the matter is.

She goes up to Serhii and asks, 'Why are you just sitting there? You always run around jumping head over heels, not giving me a moment's rest. And now you're sitting on a tree stump, making me worried because you're not behaving like a child. What's the matter?'

'I'm watching how the ants live, grandma. It's so interesting!' says Serhii.

'Alright, Serhii my love, just sit there then,' says his grandmother tenderly. 'There's another ant nest under the pear tree in the orchard.'

Sashko's boat

Grade two student Sashko made a cardboard boat. He took his boat outside and found a huge puddle. 'This is the Black Sea,' said Sashko to himself. 'My boat can sail across the Black Sea.'[69]

Sashko launched his boat into the Black Sea, and it sailed over the sea waves. It sailed on and on until it could hardly be seen from the shore. When the boat reached the middle of the Black Sea, it began to get dark, and Sashko's mother called him to come inside.

'My boat can sail through the night,' thought Sashko, and he went home.

When Sashko came out in the morning, the sea had frozen over. The boat was stuck in the ice.

'Mum,' said Sashko in a worried voice, 'My boat is stuck in the ice.'

'Wait for the sun to melt the ice, and then your boat will sail on,' suggested his mother.

'No, I won't wait,' answered Sashko. 'I need to free my boat. It needs to sail further.'

Sashko took his little spade and went to rescue his boat from the trouble it was in.

How we found a nest in the forest

One warm spring day, we went for a walk in the forest. After a while we grew tired and sat under some trees to rest. We were sitting next to a bush. Suddenly Olia whispered, 'Look, there's a nest in that bush.'

We looked and saw a little nest, quite close to us. And there in the nest sat a little grey bird. She stared at us with her red eyes as if begging us, 'Please move away from here. Do not come so close to my nest.'

We could not take our eyes off the little bird. Then we quietly stood up and moved away from the bush. We found a thicket and sat down well away from the nest. Now our hearts felt more at ease. We had not frightened the bird. She sat in her nest and thanked us.

The toy frog

Serhiiko's mother bought him a very interesting toy: a little frog. When you wound up its key, it hopped, as if alive.

Serhiiko loved that toy. He enjoyed playing with it for a long time, but then he became quiet and thoughtful. He would take the toy and turn it over in his hands, examining it.

'Mum, can I take the toy apart?' he asked his mother. 'I would like to see what's inside.'

'If you do, it will stop hopping,' said his mother. 'You won't be able to put it back together again.'

But Serhiiko kept begging, and eventually, his mother allowed him to take it apart.

The boy unscrewed some tiny screws, located a spring that made the toy frog move, and put all the pieces into a box.

'The frog won't hop now,' his mother said.

'But now I know what made it hop,' replied Serhiiko happily.

The shining summit and the stony path

A traveller stood at the foot of a very high mountain. Its summit was covered in eternal snow, but below, at its foot, roses were flowering. The traveller needed to climb to the lofty summit.

One day passed, and then another. The way to the summit was via a narrow stony path. The traveller gazed at the summit. It shone in the rays of the sun. On the second night the traveller slept on cold stones.

In the morning the traveller awoke and again gazed at the shining summit. In the rays of the rising sun, it was pink. The traveller continued along the stony path. It was hard for him to breathe, and he could hardly place one foot in front of another. Along the stony path he encountered sharp stones, ruts and holes.

The traveller sighed, wiped the sweat from his brow, and asked, 'Tell me, stony path, why is it so hard to follow you?'

'Because I lead to the shining summit,' answered the stony path.

A white shirt at night

A little toddler lived with his mother. He had just started talking. He had a snow-white shirt. His mother washed it and hung it on the fence to dry.[70]

Night fell. The little boy asked his mother, 'Mum, can I take my shirt off the fence?'

'Why?' asked his mother.

'The night will get on my shirt and make it black … And then what will I wear?' he said.

How Nina overcame her fear of a gander

Five-year-old Nina was walking to kindergarten. On the path ahead of her sat a big, white gander. Next to him were ten geese who were a little bit smaller, and about thirty little goslings. Nina looked with wide eyes at the gander. How huge he was, and how frightening! What a long bill he had!

Looking around in fear, Nina walked off the path so as to pass around the gander, but the gander raised his head, hissed loudly, ran at the little girl, and pecked her on the leg. The geese cackled merrily. Nina burst into tears and ran home.

Nina told her mother how the gander had attacked her. Her mother told her, 'You must not be afraid of him, and then he won't attack. Look him bravely in the eye and walk straight at him. Do not walk round him.'

Nina walked back along the same path. The gander was still sitting in the middle of it, and next to him were the geese and goslings. Nina looked boldly at the gander. He was sitting in the middle of the path and seemed to be waiting to see what would happen next. Nina kept walking straight towards him, looking at him boldly and thinking, 'I'm not afraid of you, gander.'

The gander took fright, left the path, and ran away across the grass, looking over his shoulder. The geese and goslings ran after him.

Nina walked bravely on.

Olenka and the spring

A tear-off calendar hangs on the wall. Today is the fifth of January. Olenka, who is three years old, knows that every day they tear one page off the calendar. She asks her grandmother, 'Grandma, show me when it will be spring.'

He grandmother shows her. Olenka is sad. There are so many days still to tear off …

That night, Olenka quietly gets up and begins to tear off the pages one by one. She tears them off all the way to spring. She collects the pages, puts them under her pillow, and goes to sleep.

She dreams of spring. When the sun rises, Olenka goes to her grandmother's bed.

'Grandma, get up. Spring has come,' she says.

Her grandmother looks at Olenka with amazement.

'Look at the calendar,' says Olenka. 'It's already the spring page.'

'It's the spring page, but there's a winter frost outside. Look out the window. What do you see, winter or spring?' asks her grandmother.

Olenka looks out the window and starts thinking.

Useful or harmful?

The teacher placed a large display case on his desk. The bottom of the case was covered with blue silk. Pinned to the silk were butterflies of many colours: white, red, grey, and yellow.

The teacher called out grade five student Andriiko and said, 'Take a close look at each butterfly and tell me whether it is useful or harmful.'

Andriiko could not take his eyes off the largest butterfly. It had huge wings that looked like crimson sails, and each wing was painted with golden stripes and silver spots. It seemed to Andriiko that any minute the butterfly would flutter its wings and fly out into the garden. But no, the butterfly could not fly, because it was dead. It was pinned to the blue silk forever. Andriiko gave a heavy sigh. He looked out at the garden and then back at the butterfly.

'Why don't you say something?' the teacher asked. 'I am sure that you know the answer. You have just had a good look at this butterfly. Is it useful or harmful?'

'It is beautiful,' Andriiko replied softly.

A blue world

I found a little blue glass, closed my left eye, and raised the glass to my right eye. What a wonderful world appeared before me! No longer a wide field, but an endless sea. It was no longer a combine harvester approaching me, but a magical ship. I had been crossing a field, but now I was sailing through blue waves. I approached the forest, but now it was no longer a forest, but mighty mountains covered with mysterious underwater plants. I looked at the green bushes, but now they were fairytale creatures, and it was not the wind that made them sway, but the blue waves of the sea.

Suddenly, from beneath a large underwater rock, a strange beast emerged. It had long ears and thin whiskers. Its paws looked like those of a walrus. Now I was scared. I took the blue glass away from my eye and laughed. The mysterious beast was a hare, basking in the spring sunshine. Everything around me was enjoying the sunshine: the forest, the wheat, and a lark in the sky.

An autumn day in the forest

One warm, sunny autumn day, our class went for a walk in the forest. All the clearings were covered with a carpet of yellow leaves, but the carpet only appeared yellow from a distance. When we reached a clearing, we could see that its carpet was multicoloured and made up of crimson, red, light yellow, and brown leaves. Somewhere, far, far away, we could hear a woodpecker tapping on a tree: tap, tap, tap. We could also hear some wonderful music, as if something was ringing out, as if, far away, someone was playing a violin. It seemed to us that the sound emanated from the deepest part of the forest, but it could also have come from beneath the earth. What was it?

We listened to the sound for a long time, but we could not work out what that music was. Only when we advanced deeper into the forest, and could hear the music more distinctly, did we finally recognize the sound of a stream flowing in a ravine.

Grandpa Autumn

Grandpa Autumn lives in the dark forest. He sleeps on dry leaves and listens carefully to the singing of the birds. As soon as he hears the sad song of the cranes—'Koorlee! Koorlee!'—he gets up and says, 'My time has come. The cranes are flying away to warmer lands.'

Grandpa Autumn strides to the edge of the forest, grey-haired, in a grey coat. Wherever he goes, the leaves turn yellow and fall to the ground. When he reaches the edge of the forest, he sits down, leaning against an oak tree, and sings very quietly. It is not a song, but the autumn wind … When he sings, his beard grows longer and longer, drifting on the wind. When it reaches the meadow, the whole meadow turns grey.

'Look at the autumn mist,' people say. It does not occur to them that it is Grandpa Autumn's beard.

Autumn garments

As the sun shines lower in the sky each day, an old lady with golden hair wakes up in the dark forest. This old lady is called Autumn. She quietly walks through the green meadows. Wherever she stops, white crystals of ice appear on the grass. In the morning people say there has been a frost.

Autumn comes to the orchard. She touches a tree with her golden hair, and its leaves turn yellow, red and orange … In the morning people say it is a golden autumn. But, during the day, golden-haired Autumn hides in the dark forest and waits for the night.

A day lost

A father had three little sons. One evening, the father asked his boys, 'Tell me how you spent your day today.'

Yurko said, 'I planted a tree today.'

The father replied, 'You have spent the day well.'

Mykolka said, 'I drew a hare today.'

'Well, you made quite good use of the day as well,' remarked the father.

Petryk said, 'Today … I played ball … and ate an ice-cream.'

'That is a day lost,' declared his father.

A wasted day

Petryk's mother had to leave for work before sunrise. She woke Petryk, who was nine years old, and said, 'Today is the first day of your holidays. Here is your work for the day: plant a tree next to our house and read this book about the Distant Blue Mountains.'

Petryk's mother showed him where to dig a hole for the tree and how to plant it, left the book about the Distant Blue Mountains on the table, and went to work.

Petryk thought, 'I'll sleep for a little longer … It feels so nice sleeping in when Mum goes to work.' And he lay down and fell asleep at once. He dreamt that a tree he had planted had grown next to the house and that the Distant Blue Mountains were not distant at all and were towering right next to the village pond.

Petryk woke up, and oh, no! The sun was already high in the sky! He wanted to get started on his work right away, but then he thought, 'I have plenty of time.' And he sat down under a pear tree. He thought 'I'll just sit here for a little while, and then I'll get on with my work.'

Then Petryk went to the orchard, ate some berries, chased a butterfly for half an hour and, finally, sat down under the pear tree again.

His mother came home in the evening and said, 'Show me what you have done today, Petryk.'

But Petryk had not done anything. He was too ashamed to look his mother in the eyes. 'Come with me,' she said, 'And I'll show you what others have done during this day that you wasted.'

And she took Petryk by the hand and led him to a ploughed field. 'Yesterday there was just stubble here, and today there is a ploughed field, ready to plant. A tractor driver worked here today, while you were idle.'

Petryk's mother then took him to her own workplace and showed him dozens of crates of apples. 'This morning all these apples were still on trees, and now they are in crates. During the night, they will be taken to the city. I was one of the people who worked here, while you were idle.'

Then she showed him an enormous pile of grain. 'This grain was all growing in the field this morning. The grain was harvested with combine harvesters and then brought here in trucks, while you were idle.'

Petryk's mother took him to a wall built of bricks. 'This morning there was just a granite foundation here, and now there is a wall. The bricklayers worked hard all day, while you were idle.'

She took him to a big white building, and they went inside. Petryk saw loaf upon loaf of freshly baked bread on shelves. Everything smelled of bread—the air, the walls, even the grass in front of the building. 'This is the bakery. In the morning, this bread was just flour, and now the bread makes your mouth water. You feel like sinking your teeth into a tasty crust. The bakers worked all day today, while you were idle. Soon a van will come and take the bread to the shop.'

Finally, Petryk and his mother entered a building with the word

'Library' written on the door. The librarian showed them a long shelf full of books. 'These are books that people read today. They have just been returned. And just as many books have been borrowed,' the librarian explained.

'While I was idle,' thought Petryk. He was ashamed to even think of it, and he hung his head. Now he understood what a wasted day was.

Without the nightingale

In one of our villages, a kindergarten was housed in an old peasant dwelling with a straw roof. Inside there were new tables and beds that were very comfortable for the children. There were lots of toys. The children especially liked one toy horse and rider.

The other thing that the children especially loved was the nightingale in the garden. It lived in a wild cherry tree right next to the building. When the children arrived at the kindergarten in the morning, they quietly crept up to the open window and listened to the song of the nightingale. Those were their happiest moments.

But then the collective farm constructed a big stone building for the kindergarten. One day, two trucks came to the kindergarten. They loaded the tables, beds, bowls and spoons into one truck. The children climbed into the other truck with all their toys.

The new building was well lit, with much more room. But when the little children arrived in the morning and opened the window to listen to the song of nightingale, there was no nightingale to be heard.

A sadness descended on those large, well-lit rooms.

The apple tree and the fence

A man planted an apple tree in his yard. The tree grew for a year and then for another year. The first flowers appeared on the tree, and the first fruit formed. But the man who owned the apple tree was mean and greedy. He was afraid that someone walking by might pick an apple. He built a high fence so that no-one could reach the tree from the road.

Two more years passed, and the apple tree grew even higher. The man built his fence higher. The apple tree asked him, 'Why are you hiding me with a fence. People walking along the road get joy from seeing what a beautiful apple tree I am.'

The man answered, 'But you are my apple tree.'

The apple tree could not understand. It looked at the blue sky and the bright sun and asked, 'And who does the sun belong to? And whose is the sky?' The man could not think of an answer.

The shortbread and the ear of wheat

Early in the morning, before sunrise, a man got up, put a white shortbread in his pocket, and went into the field. He walked through the crop, admiring the wheat. He tore off an ear, took a grain from it, tried it on his tooth and smiled. He put the ear of wheat in his pocket, where it met the shortbread.

'Who are you?' asked the shortbread.

'I am an ear of wheat.'

'Oh, how prickly you are,' said the shortbread. 'What are you for? What benefit do you bring?'

The ear of wheat smiled, twitching its whiskers, and answered, 'Without me there would be no bread, no rusks and no shortbreads like you.'

The shortbread was amazed. It looked with respect at the ear of wheat and moved over to give it more room.

'So, everything comes from you,' said the shortbread. 'But how did you get here?'

'Through people's work,' answered the ear of wheat. 'People make everything.'

Beautiful words and beautiful deeds

In the middle of a field is a small hut. It was built so that in bad weather people could take shelter there and sit in the warmth.

One summer day the sky clouded over, and it began to rain. At the time, three boys were out in the forest. They took shelter in time to avoid the rain and watched as the rain poured down from the sky.

Suddenly, they saw a young boy about ten years old running towards the hut. The boy was from a neighbouring village, and they did not know him. He was soaked to the skin and shivering from the cold.

The oldest of the boys, who had avoided the rain and was sitting in dry clothes, said, 'What rotten luck, getting caught in the rain. You poor kid.'

The second boy also said some beautiful, sympathetic words. 'It must have been scary getting caught in the middle of the field in weather like this. I feel for you.'

The third boy did not say a word. He quietly took off his shirt and gave it to the boy, who was still shivering from the cold.

What is really beautiful is not beautiful words, but beautiful deeds.

Casting words to the wind

One spring day, some students planted rose bushes near the graves of fallen soldiers. They conducted a ceremony near the war memorial. They spoke beautifully about how they would honour the memory of the war heroes.

Then they watered the roses and went home.

Buds opened on the roses, and they grew beautiful green leaves. But there was no rain, and the ground in which the roses were planted dried out and cracked. The roses withered, and weeds grew around them.

The students forgot about the roses and the beautiful words they had spoken. They often walked along a path past the place where they had planted the roses in the spring, but not one of them thought of the responsibility they had to care for them.

Why does this happen? Because the children had got used to casting words to the wind. They forgot what great and sacred words they had uttered when they promised to honour the memory of the heroes. But sacred words should not be taken so lightly.

The doctor fell ill

This happened high in the Carpathian Mountains.[71] After a blizzard, the mountains were covered in mist. It had snowed for three days, and snowdrifts covered the roads and pathways. It was impossible to reach the little mountain village on foot, by road, or by plane.

In the village, there was a hospital. Seven patients were being treated there. One little girl was seriously ill. She needed an operation.

And suddenly a great misfortune struck: the doctor fell seriously ill. He could not get up; his whole body burnt as if on fire.

The little girl was groaning in the ward.

Many people came to see the doctor. They stood in silent grief and waited. Perhaps the doctor would get better. Perhaps he would get up and perform the operation the sick girl needed.

The doctor's apartment was next to the ward where the little girl was lying. At sunrise, when the doctor regained consciousness, he heard quiet groans. It was the little girl groaning.

Gathering all his strength, the doctor got up. He put on his white surgical gown. Nurses helped him to stand, and he performed the operation.

When the operation was completed, the doctor again lost consciousness. He lay in his bed, and there was no-one to help him, as he was the only doctor in the village. The mist covering the village was so thick that no-one could reach the village by road, on foot, or by plane.

During the night, the doctor died.

But the little girl got better.

The smallest apple

Mykhailyk is in grade three. His grandfather is an orchardist. During the summer, his grandfather lives in little hut in the orchard. Mykhailyk often goes to visit his Grandpa Kostia. He helps him to cook his dinner and wash the dishes, and his grandfather treats him to honey, apples and grapes.

One day after dinner, Grandpa Kostia told his grandson, 'Today my friend Grandpa Omelko is coming to visit me. We'll prepare some nice food for him.' He poured some honey into a bowl and put a plate of apples next to it.

One apple was big, rosy and sweet-smelling. Another was a little smaller, bright red and aromatic. A third apple was small, as white as marble, and also sweet-smelling.

Grandpa Omelko arrived. Grandpa Kostia sat him at the table and invited him to eat. For a long time, Grandpa Omelko refused to eat, saying he was not hungry. Then he took the smallest apple and ate it, dipping it in the honey. After that he would not eat any more, no matter how much Grandpa Kostia asked him to.

The old men talked for a long time, reminiscing about the past. Grandpa Omelko went home just after sunset.

Mykhailyk asked, 'Why did Grandpa Omelko take the smallest apple? He must have been hungry.'

‘He was hungry,’ answered Grandpa Kostia.

‘Then why did he only take the smallest apple?’ asked Mykhailyk.

‘Because he is a human being,’ said Grandpa Kostia.

Mykhailyk thought quietly about this for a long time.

Water in the flask

A traveller is trudging through the dry, waterless steppe. The sun scorches his body, and the burning wind stings his eyes. The traveller has been walking for many hours, but the steppe is endless. He has no strength left and is very thirsty. He licks his cracked lips with his dry tongue and, breathing heavily, gazes at the far horizon. He can just make out something dark in the violet haze. Perhaps it is a forest?

An eagle is hovering high in the sky. He has noticed the traveller and glides down, circling above the man. He sees that the man has a flask hanging on his shoulder. The bird’s sensitive hearing detects the sound of water sloshing in the flask.

‘Traveller, I can see that you are exhausted,’ says the eagle. ‘You will collapse and die of thirst. Why do you not drink some water? You have a full flask hanging from your shoulder.’

‘If I drink the water, I will not have any hope left,’ answers the traveller. ‘My strength was exhausted long ago, and it is only hope that keeps me going.’

The eagle cannot understand what hope is. He circles for a long time above the traveller, his eyes frozen in an expression of bewilderment, like dark beads.

After circling for some time, he flaps his wings and disappears into the blazing sky. The traveller continues on his way.

Pylyp Ivanovych is not the chairman anymore

Vasylko’s father travelled somewhere far away and brought back five apple trees for planting. These were special apple trees. People said their apples were as transparent as glass, and that they were the most delicious apples in the whole world. You could put one of these apples on the windowsill in autumn and it would be as fresh in the spring as if it had just been picked.

People even said these wonderful apples could treat heart problems. If you ate one, your chest pain would go away. That was how special these apple trees were.

Vasylko, who was in grade one, looked at the delicate rooted cuttings. They did not look like anything special, but they were such magical trees.

Vasylko asked, 'Where will we plant the trees?'

'We will only plant three of them.'

'Why?' asked Vasylko in surprise.

'You can take two of them now to our neighbour, to dear Pylyp Ivanovych. I promised to bring two of these wonderful trees for him.'

Vasylko's father separated two of the cuttings and wrapped their roots carefully in a wet sack.

'Take these next door, Vasylko, and give my best wishes to Pylyp Ivanovych.'

'Dad,' said Vasylko, holding the cuttings in his hands, 'Did you know Pylyp Ivanovych isn't chairman of the village council anymore?'

'What do you mean, he's not the chairman?' shouted the father in surprise.

Vasylko's mother came over. 'While you were away, he was removed from his position. He wasn't coping with the work.'

'Well, that is news,' said the father, shaking his head.

Suddenly he remembered something and called out to his son, who was heading to the gate with the trees.

'Vasylko, come back,' he said. 'You don't need to take the trees to Pylyp Ivanovych.'

Vasylko came back.

'Why don't I need to?' he asked.

His father was silent.

The light in the window

A winter night sets in. The lights go out in all the homes. The village is sleeping. The only light still on is at the school. Our teacher is still awake.

I sit by the window. I want to stay up until the light goes out at the school, but sleep overpowers me. I get into bed. As I go to sleep, I plan to get up very early, before the light at school turns on.

I wake up early. Everyone in the house is sleeping. I look out the window. The village is still asleep. The only light shining is at the school.

'Has it been on all night?' I wonder.

Learning to be human

A mother gave her son a set of flash cards with all the letters of the Ukrainian alphabet from '*A*' to '*Ya*'.[72] She read the letters to him and said, 'Learn the letters, son. When you have learnt the alphabet, you can learn to read. When you can read, you can learn to be a human being. When you start learning to be a human being, you will get cleverer every day.'

The son began to learn his letters. But it so happened that he took a fancy to the letter '*Ya*' more than all the others. He kept reading it over and over, and in Ukrainian the letter '*Ya*' means 'I'.

His mother said, 'Read the other letters. '*Ya*' is the last letter in the alphabet.'

But her son did not want to read the other letters. He kept saying, '*Ya, Ya, Ya*,' to his mother, as if 'I' was the best word in the world.

'What gives us light and warmth?' asked his mother. 'I do, I do!' answered her son.

'What gives life to the parched earth?' asked his mother. 'I do, I do!' repeated her son.

His mother was really worried. Someone who only loves and admires himself, cannot become even the smallest leaf on the vast tree that is the human race.

How could she save her son?

At night, when her son was asleep, she took the flashcard with the letter '*Ya*' and hid it. Her son woke up and tried to remember the name of his favourite letter, but he had forgotten it.

The son again began to learn the letters of the alphabet: *A, Be, Ve, Ge*, all the way to the end … When he had learnt all the other letters, he remembered '*Ya*', but by now it seemed small and shy.

'What gives us light and warmth?' asked the mother, once her son had learnt the alphabet and learnt to read.

'The sun,' answered her son.

'What gives life to the parched earth?'

'The rain,' answered the son.

'Now you can learn to be a human being,' said the mother.

An argument between two books

Two books stood side by side on a library shelf. One had a leather cover with a gold embossed title. Its title was 'The Great Conqueror'. The other book had a thin grey cover. Its title was 'The Ploughman and the Sower of Seeds'.

The book about the conqueror said, 'People will learn a great deal when they read me. If it were not for conquerors, there would be no power and no glory.'

The book about the ploughman and the sower of seeds asked, 'And where is that conqueror of whom you speak? Which conqueror are you talking about?'

'He travelled the whole world. Nations quaked as he approached. He burnt a thousand cities and subjugated a hundred nations.'

'And where is he now?'

The book about the Great Conqueror did not reply.

'I know where your conqueror is,' said the book about the ploughman and the sower of seeds. 'He rotted in the ground. But my ploughman and my sower of seeds will live forever.'

The sleeping book

A large and interesting book stood on a bookshelf, among books about faraway lands and wild animals. It told of a mighty warrior. The letters in the book blazed like red-hot iron. The book had a wonderful property: as soon as its blazing, fiery words touched a human heart, a spark was lit in that heart. And the person whose heart beat with that fiery spark became mighty and invincible.

But the years passed without anyone reading that book. Each week the owner of the book took it from its shelf, carefully wiped the dust from its cover, and placed it back on the shelf. The book kept expecting that somebody would read it, but nobody even opened it.

Often guests came to see the owner of the books, who liked to show them off saying, 'Look what beautiful covers my books have.'

The fiery letters began to grow dim. The burning words faded. The mighty warrior of whom the book told fell asleep. Now the book on the shelf was no longer a fiery book, but a sleeping book.

Two pages of a book

A large and beautiful book lay on the table. It was a book about the Great and the Wise. The title page was especially beautiful. The name of the book was written on that page in golden letters. Underneath the title was a picture of a marble statue of the Great and the Wise, inscribed with his name. Below that was a drawing of the sun.

The title page was very proud of itself. 'All the other pages are nothing compared with me,' it said. 'All the beauty is on my page. People only read this book because the first page is so beautiful.'

The last page in the book heard this boasting and said, 'Let people read the book and be the judges of what is good in it.'

People who make bread and machines came and read the book and said, 'The title page is beautiful, but the book has nothing of value in it.' And they stopped opening the book.

The final page said, 'A book about the Great and the Wise should be a wise book. Let nobody be deceived by the title page.'

Because it would upset Mariia Petrivna

It was the final year of the war. Volodia, a student in grade four, was teased by Nina, who was in the same class. During the break she went up to him and said, 'Five dresses with patches', in a sing-song voice. Nina was referring to the fact that Volodia had five sisters, his mother was often sick, his father had been killed on the frontline, and there was no money to buy new dresses, so his sisters' dresses all had patches.

Volodia could not stand being teased. He did not go to complain to his teacher, Mariia Petrivna. He just hit Nina, and she burst into tears.

Mariia Petrivna saw and heard everything. She sighed and said, 'Today I will come and visit you at home, Volodia.'

Mariia Petrivna had only been teaching at the school for two weeks. Before that our class had been taught by a very strict teacher named Mariia Mykolaivna. If she visited your home, it meant you would be getting the strap.

We all felt sad. Everyone looked at Volodia with sympathy because he would get a hiding today.

The next day Volodia came to school full of joy. He kept repeating, 'Mariia Petrivna visited us yesterday.'

Then he told us all about it. Mariia Petrivna did not say a single word about him hitting Nina. She brought the sisters toys and gave the oldest one a dress. Only as she was leaving, she very quietly said to Volodya, 'But you mustn't fight.'

'I will never hit anyone again,' said Volodia, 'Because it would upset Mariia Petrivna.'

Nobody's flower

It was a special day at school. All the students had come to prepare their classrooms for lessons. The next day would be the first day of the school year.

Near the well were ten new pots. In each pot was a flower. These were for the classrooms. Ten pot plants for ten classrooms. Next to the ten new pot plants was another little pot, old and faded. A weak little flower had been planted in it.

The students took the new pot plants to their classrooms. They put them on the teachers' desks. It made the classrooms feel cosy, as if the students were at home with their mother.

The old pot remained by the well. Who needed a weak little plant, with just a few leaves?

Little Vira in grade one felt sorry for the little flower. She felt sorry for the faded old pot as well. She took the little pot plant to her classroom, placed it on the windowsill, and watered it.

The teacher asked the children, 'Whose flower is that?'

'It's nobody's,' answered the children. 'It was left by the well. Vira took it and brought it here.'

'It's my flower,' said Vira. 'How can a flower be nobody's?'

Pink or red?

Two boys lived in the same large block of apartments. They used the same entrance and lived on the same floor. One boy had a mother and father, a grandfather and grandmother, two brothers and two sisters. His family was happy and friendly. Everyone loved each other and helped each other. The boy was happy.

The other boy had no father, no brothers or sisters, no grandmother and no grandfather. He only had his mother, and she had never known a day's happiness in her life. Her son's father was a wicked, heartless man. The mother had never known human kindness, and her heart was cold and indifferent. Her son was unhappy.

One quiet June evening, when the sky glowed with the ashen light of sunset almost until midnight, the two boys, one happy and one unhappy, were sitting together on a balcony. They could see a star twinkling in the night sky. Its twinkling was gentle and timid, like the spark of a distant light towards which a traveller is hastening.

'Look! What a beautiful pink star!' said the happy boy and gave a sincere and friendly smile.

'That's not pink, that's red,' said the unhappy boy, and gave a frown.

They sat and gazed silently at the twinkling star for a long time.

Why the tractor fell silent

On the outskirts of the village, the rumble of a tractor could be heard from early spring through to late autumn, as it ploughed the fields, harrowed, sowed seed, and gathered in the harvest. People heard its even, measured drone from dawn till dusk, and were so used to it that they did not even notice it.

But then, one day, around noon, the tractor fell silent. It became unusually quiet. Everyone immediately felt that something was missing. The silence was unsettling.

People began to come out of their homes, and many men and women headed for the field where the tractor had been working all morning. They saw the tractor standing in the middle of the field, but its driver was nowhere to be seen.

Where was the tractor driver? Everyone knew that the only tractor driver in their little village was Stepan Ivanenko, who had returned from the army two years earlier.

What had happened to him? It seemed that everyone in the village was alert and holding their breath.

Then suddenly everyone poured out of their homes, joyful and smiling, congratulating each other. The news spread around the village like wildfire that Stepan Ivanenko now had a baby son. That was why the tractor had fallen silent. It seemed as if even the field gave a sigh of relief. But the tractor still missed its driver.

It was not difficult

Pylypko was a little boy in grade two. His father fought against the fascists during the war and had a military service medal. On a cold winter's evening, when a blizzard was raging outside, Pylypko would ask his father, 'Dad, tell me about the battles with the fascists.' And, for the umpteenth time, his father would tell him about the difficult marches, the bitter frosts, the deep snow and the bloody wounds …

'What a difficult medal that was to earn,' said Pylypko one night, as he went to bed.

The school year came to an end. Pylypko came home from school with a big book illustrated with beautiful drawings. In the book was an inscription that said, 'Awarded to Pylypko for high academic achievement'. Pylypko's mother was delighted with the book and looked through it, but Pylypko was silent and frowning.

'Why aren't you pleased with your award?' asked his mother in surprise.

'Because it wasn't difficult to earn,' said the boy quietly.

The stone on the boundary

Once upon a time there were two men. Each one had his own field. They tilled the soil and sowed grain. Each one worked their field from morning to night.

And then a stone turned up from somewhere, not very big, but not small either—about the size of a dog's head. One of the men was ploughing his field when he came across the stone. He threw it into his neighbour's field. His neighbour was harvesting grain. He saw the stone and thought, 'Where did that come from? I'll throw it into my neighbour's field.' And he threw it back.

In this way the stone was thrown back and forth from one field to the other for many years. The two men were a bit annoyed with each other when they found the stone in their field, but they soon forgot about it and remained good friends.

But then it occurred to them to place the stone on their boundary. They put it on the boundary and became irreconcilable enemies. They stole each other's sheafs of grain during the night and hated each other.

One of the men died, then the other. They died as enemies. Their children became the new owners of the land. They met at the boundary and decided to get rid of the stone and throw it into a swamp. They took the stone away and ploughed the land along their boundary. Instead of two fields there was now one big field, where the children of the two enemies worked together. They worked together and became friends. And the stone now lies somewhere in a swamp.

The leaky bucket

Once a week the children in grade three came to school in the evening with buckets. They came to water some young oak trees that were growing quite some distance from the school—about 300 metres away.

Among the children was Mykola Lazybones. Work was the last thing he wanted to do. Mykola carried his bucket of water all the way from the well to the oak trees and thought to himself, 'Why was I born onto this Earth? Was it really just to carry this bucket of water?' When Mykola woke up on the watering day, he wished for rain.

But no rain came. Then Mykola began to wonder, 'How could I make the work easier?' And he thought of a way. He hammered a nail through the bottom of his bucket and made a hole in it. He filled his bucket with water, but by the time he reached the oak trees there was only a little water left in the bottom of the bucket. The lazybones began to feel better.

One day Grandpa Matvii came to look at the young oak trees. He was a former soldier, and everyone in the village respected him. He had been awarded three medals for his heroism on the frontline. Grandpa Matvii saw that Mykola was tricking his classmates, and that no-one had seen what he was doing. He went over to Mykola, when he had just watered his oak tree with about a cupful of water, put his hand on his shoulder, and said, 'Turn out your pockets.'

Mykola turned out his pockets and looked with surprise at the old man. All the others turned and looked as well. Grandpa Matvii took Mykola's nail and used it to make a hole in each of Mykola's pockets. Then he took two handfuls of acorns from his bag and filled the pockets with them. 'These are not acorns,' said the old man, 'These are bullets. And you are not going to get water, but to shoot at the enemy, because we are at war. The enemy is behind that fence. Go over to that fence, boy, and take the bullets from your pockets.'

Bowing his head, Mykola took a step, then a second and a third. The acorns all spilt onto the ground. By the time he reached the fence, there was not a single acorn in his pockets.

'Think what sort of person Mykola could grow up to be,' said Grandpa Matvii, and went on his way.

The children stood there with their heads bowed. They were thinking.

Seven knives

In a kitchen there were seven knives in a dresser—seven big, sharp knives for chopping up cabbage. One morning, six cooks came to work in the kitchen. Each one chose a knife, and all through their shift the women cut up cabbage. When they finished their work, they put the knives back in the dresser and went home.

The knife who had done nothing all day asked, 'What is that you smell of? Something very tasty.'

'Cabbage,' proudly answered the knives who had worked all day.

The next day the six cooks came to work early in the morning, and each one took their knife—the one they had worked with the day before. The knife that had lain idle all through the first day was surprised. 'Why doesn't anybody take me? Aren't I as good as the other knives? What is this cabbage, anyway?'

That evening he bitterly questioned the other knives, who were tired from their work, but very proud of having carried out their duty.

'Why doesn't anybody take me? Don't people care what knife they work with? I am sharper than all of you.'

The days and weeks passed, and every day the six workers took the same six knives from the dresser, while the seventh knife lay there with nothing to do, sharp and shiny, but idle.

One evening he asked his neighbour, 'How do the workers recognise their knives?' And his neighbour told him some amazing things. It turned out that each worker called a knife 'my knife' after they had worked with it for just one day. And then they did not want to take any other knife.

'Why is that?' asked the idle knife.

'Because without a human hand a knife is not yet a knife, but just a piece of metal. Each human being leaves the imprint of their hand on us.'

The idle knife could not understand that. His sharp blade lay there glistening indifferently.

Bread, work and song

Far from the village, in a field camp, lived some tractor drivers who ploughed the fields. Three times a day their cook, Natalia Ivanivna, prepared a meal for them. She was a quite a master chef. She baked soft, aromatic bread, and her borshch[73] was so delicious that the tractor drivers could not praise it enough. They begged Natalia Ivanivna to bake fresh bread every day.

But the cook began to notice that when they had eaten their fill, the tractor drivers became gloomy and didn't want to talk. Something was missing in their lives.

And then, one day, after supper, Natalia Ivanivna began to sing a song. She had a voice of exquisite beauty. She sang a song about a young soldier who had gone into battle across that very field, who had fallen to an enemy bullet here under this oak tree, and who was buried here, in this grave.

The tractor drivers raised their heads, and their eyes shone with deep and troubling thoughts.

From that day, after breakfast, the tractor drivers asked Natalia Ivanivna to sing a song. And she sang: about the wide steppes, about mothers, about happiness and grief, about a willow by a pond, about a tall burial mound in the steppes, about a grave under an oak tree, about a young woman's eyes. And sometimes she sang before breakfast, at dawn.

The tractor drivers began to wake before dawn, in case Natalia Ivanivna sang a song before breakfast.

People need song, as well as work and bread.

Dad's presents

Myshko, who was eight years old, was visited by his classmate Fedko. When Fedko arrived, he joyfully announced, 'My dad went into the city yesterday. He brought me presents: new skates and a flashlight.'

Myshko listened to him in silence and looked out the window with wide open eyes. Fedko asked, 'Would you like me to bring the skates to show you?'

'No thanks,' answered Myshko, and he burst into tears.

Fedko was surprised. When he came home, he asked his mother, 'Why did Myshko cry when I told him about Dad's presents?'

'Because Myshko's father has left his family,' said his mother. 'Your happiness reminded Myshko how unfortunate he is. You mustn't tell an unhappy person about your happiness.'

Fedko thought hard about what his mother had told him.

Don't boil the chicks

Little Tarasyk saw a broody hen leave her nest. He rushed over to the nest and witnessed a miracle: a chick was hatching from an egg.

The broody hen drank some water and returned to her nest, but Tarasyk stayed there, full of wonder. He could not wait for the mother hen to leave her nest again. He wanted to know what was going to happen next, and whether all the eggs would have chicks in them. And indeed, they did. The next morning, the mother hen was no longer sitting on her nest. She was sitting on the floor, surrounded by twenty tiny chicks.

Fascinated by what he had observed, Tarasyk was about to ask his mother about this wonder of wonders, when he saw his mother holding three eggs in her hand. She had just lowered one egg into some boiling water and was about to the do same with another.

'Mummy, what are you doing?' shouted Tarasyk.

His startled mother turned and asked, 'What do you mean?'

'Please don't boil the eggs!' begged Tarasyk, with tears in his eyes. 'There are chicks inside them.'

His mother smiled.

'These eggs don't have any chicks inside them,' she said.

'So where do they come from?' asked Tarasyk wiping away his tears.

When stars go to sleep

Petrus and his father left at dawn. His father was going to work in the fields and had promised to take Petrus with him.

The sky was already growing light, and a band of pink was glowing in the east. Petrus was fascinated by the stars. Some were still twinkling in the morning sky, but it seemed to Petrus as if somebody was putting them out, one by one.

Finally, when there was only one star left in the sky, Petrus asked his father, 'Dad, can you get our horse Bulanko to walk really quietly?'

'Why?' asked his father in surprise.

'I want to see the last star go out.'

'All right, but you'll have to watch very carefully, because it will happen in an instant,' said his father, and he stopped the horse.

Petrus sat motionless with his eyes wide-open. He was afraid to blink or to lower his eyelids.

Now the star was barely visible, twinkling like a firefly on the edge of the forest just before the sunrise.

'I'll keep watching and I won't close my eyes, even for a moment. Then, maybe, the star won't go out,' thought Petrus, and his heartbeat quickened with joy. But, despite all his efforts, he lowered his eyelids just a little.

It was only for a split second! That tiny moment in time was smaller than a poppy seed, smaller than the dewdrop on a bee's paw. But when Petrus opened his eyes, the star was gone.

'Dad, now I know when stars go to sleep,' whispered Petrus quietly.

'When?' asked his father.

'When you close your eyes,' said Petrus.

I have to save the cornflowers

Olesia is five years old. She cannot wait until she turns seven so that she can go to school.

Her father is a machine operator. Today, he was back from work early, before sunset.

'We begin the harvest tomorrow,' he said. 'I'm going to Windy Field to harvest the wheat.'

'That's good,' said Olesia's mother. 'It's close by.'

Olesia overheard that her father was going to harvest the wheat at Windy Field and started worrying. Windy Field was right next to their yard on the outskirts of the village. Every morning Olesia would go to the field to pick cornflowers. She would bring the flowers home, put them in a glass of water and admire them. In the evening, before going to sleep, she would gaze at the bouquet of blue cornflowers and dream about them all night.

'The combine harvester won't just cut the wheat, it will cut the cornflowers as well,' thought the girl. 'How can I save them?'

She wanted to go to the field right away, but it was already getting dark outside. Dusk wrapped the earth.

Olesia did not sleep well. She woke up very early, before dawn. She got up quietly, put on her dress, and went out to the field.

She reached Windy Field and began to pick the cornflowers. The sky grew light, the stars went out one by one, and a lark sang high in the sky, but Olesia kept on picking the blue flowers.

The sun rose. A combine harvester approached Windy Field, and Olesia's father was driving it. He spotted a familiar pink dress among the wheat, stopped the machine, climbed down from the cabin, and walked over to his daughter.

'What are you doing here, Olesia?' he asked in surprise.

'I have to save the cornflowers,' the little girl answered softly.

Biding its time

A farmer planted some wheat. Some thistle seed found its way into the soil at the same time.

The wheat sprouted and took root. Green shoots emerged from the earth. The wheat grew strong and green. The thistle seed remained in the earth, listening attentively to everything around it. The wheat asked the thistle seed, 'Why are you still in the earth? Why don't you take root and grow?'

'I'll wait a bit,' answered the thistle. 'How are things in the field?'

'Good,' responded the wheat joyfully. 'The farmer has weeded several times already and has not left a single weed standing.'

The thistle was silent.

Next year, the farmer planted millet. The millet seeds saw the thistle seed lying next to them and asked in surprise, 'What are you doing here?'

The thistle pretended not to hear the question and did not answer.

The millet sprouted and took root, and its green shoots grew tall, but the thistle seed still lay in the earth, listening attentively to everything around it. One day, it asked, 'How are things in the field?'

'Good,' responded the millet joyfully. 'The farmer has weeded several times already and has not left a single weed standing.'

Once more, the thistle was silent. It just gave a deep sigh.

'Why is it still in the earth? Why doesn't it sprout and take root?' the millet asked a cornflower.

'Because it is a thistle,' responded the cornflower. 'It can lie in the earth for ten years. It is biding its time.'

The old tractor

A tractor laboured in the fields for many years. It ploughed, sowed, and harvested the wheat. Every year, new machines would come to the field. They were beautiful and powerful, and they laughed at the old tractor. 'You are so clumsy!' they taunted. But the old tractor paid no attention and just kept on working.

Then, one day, the old tractor's heart gave out. Its tires were worn out, and its headlights failed. The tractor fell silent. Some people came and said, 'We'll have to take it to the scrapyard.'

They hooked it to a new tractor and towed it to a large scrapyard. Now, the old tractor was surrounded by broken ploughs and shovels. That night, a watchman came, sat down beside the tractor, and sighed. 'Where will they take you now, my friend?' asked the old watchman. 'You will be reduced to nothing.'

'No,' quietly objected the tractor. 'People will make lots of shovels out of me. They know that I was made of heavy-duty metal.'

A bucket does not have a heart

One day, a hare paid a visit to a village. He wanted to try some fresh cabbage. Some dogs saw him and took off in pursuit. The hare ran for his life, but the dogs were gaining on him. The hare dashed into someone's yard and spotted an empty bucket. He jumped into it and hid there. The dogs did not see him hide, and ran off into a field.

They ran all the way to the forest, but the hare was nowhere to be seen. He was still hiding in the bucket. He heard the dogs' barking fade into the distance, climbed out of the bucket, and quietly hopped into some bushes.

'Thank you, bucket, for helping me,' he said, but the bucket did not respond.

'Of course,' remembered the hare. 'You don't have a heart.'

'If it did not have a heart, the dogs would have torn you to pieces long ago,' said the wind, and it moaned over the rim of the empty bucket.

The millet smells of fox

One evening, when the hens had just settled on their roost, a fox paid them a visit. She was extremely kind and very pleasant. She smiled all the time and spoke with a voice as sweet as honey. She brought a small handbag with a little sack inside it. She opened her handbag, took out the little sack, and untied it. The old rooster was watching closely, with one eye on the little sack, and the other on the hens, and he could not believe his eyes. The fox tipped some millet out of the sack. So that is what she was up to! She sprinkled the millet on the floor and offered it to the hens. 'My dear hens,' she said, 'I have brought you some millet. Please come down from your roost and help yourselves!'

The hens started clucking and were about to leave their roost, when the old rooster stamped his foot, shook his head ferociously, and said, 'You stupid hens! Can't you tell that the millet smells of fox? That does not bode well!'

The hens sniffed the air, and indeed, the millet did smell of fox.

A thorn cannot be kind

A sharp thorn grew on the branch of an acacia. When it was young, it was soft and yellow; then it turned green and with time it became black. It was as sharp as a needle and as hard as steel.

The wind made the branch sway, and the thorn moved with it. Everything around it was flowering and turning green. The drone of bees filled the air, and butterflies fluttered here and there, but everyone avoided the thorn.

One day, a butterfly with wings as colourful as a spring rainbow flew close to the thorn. It was frolicking in the air, playing joyfully, when it accidently flew onto the thorn. The thorn pierced its wing, and the butterfly came to a sudden halt. It felt its death was near, and asked the thorn, 'Do you have a heart?'

'Yes, but it is a prickly heart,' said the thorn.

'Please let me go free, thorn! Is it possible that you feel no pity for me?' begged the butterfly.

'I cannot feel pity,' replied the thorn. 'I do not know what it is. Though I do see that humans feel sorry for each other. But what kind of thorn would I be if I felt pity for you? I live to cause pain, so you must be careful and avoid me.'

'Could you not tell your heart to feel pity for me?' asked the butterfly.

'I could tell my prickly heart to feel pity, and it would shudder at your pain, but then I would no longer be a thorn. Could you stop being a butterfly?' asked the thorn.

Holding a stone close to one's chest

Two farmers lived next to each other, one young, the other old. One day the old farmer invited the young farmer to his home.

The young farmer arrived at his neighbour's house. He stretched out his right hand in greeting, but he kept his left hand close to his chest, clutching a stone.[74] The old farmer's sharp eyes noticed that the young man was clutching a stone to his chest, but he said nothing.

He seated the young farmer at the dining table and invited him to eat. The young farmer ate and praised the food, but he still clutched the stone to his chest.

'Now,' said the old farmer, 'I would like to treat you to some honey, but we have a custom in these parts. We pour honey for our dear guest from a jar into a plate, and the guest takes the plate in both hands and lifts it to his mouth. If the guest has a clean conscience, not a drop of honey is spilt.'

The young farmer turned pale, but there was nothing he could do about it: a custom is a custom. The old farmer poured out a full plate of honey and placed it in front of his neighbour. The young farmer took his left hand from his chest and reached for the plate with both hands, but the stone slipped from under his shirt and smashed the plate of honey.

That is what happens when you hold a stone close to your chest.

The rock and the stream

A large grey rock lay beside a road. It was so old that it was almost black. In the spring, a stream flowed beside the rock, and sang a playful song. The song went something like this:

From a raindrop I was born,
Now I sing a merry song.
There's so much for me to see
On my journey to the river!

The rock heard this merry song and asked, 'What are you so happy about? You are weak and feeble. Look at me now; I am mighty and strong. Nobody can move me from where I lie.'

The stream laughed and said, 'We'll see.'

It turned towards the rock, babbling joyfully, and singing even louder. It washed the earth from beneath the rock. The rock swayed and turned green in anger. 'So, you want to move me from my resting place?' it cried.

The stream just kept on singing, and its song grew even louder. It kept scouring the earth from under the rock until the rock tumbled into a gulley. Meanwhile, the stream continued on its merry way to the river.

The rock lay there for a thousand years and thought to itself, 'Why are streams so eager to move forward? And what does it actually mean "to move forward"?'

The wolf and the hares

A wolf lived in the forest. He was very old and had lost all his teeth. Finally, he sought out some people and begged them, with tears in his eyes, 'Please, put me into a cage, but feed me! Otherwise, I am doomed.'

The people put the wolf into a cage and started feeding him mushrooms. He ate all sorts of mushrooms: dried, fried, and pickled.

A year passed. The hares in the forest were delighted that their fierce enemy was gone. The people realised that the wolf was no longer any danger to them, so they decided to set him free. 'Go back to the forest and enjoy your freedom,' they said, 'And we will bring the mushrooms to you.'

White and black

Two doves, one white and one black, hid inside a chimney to escape a bird of prey, a kite. They stayed there until the danger had passed, and then flew back to their dovecote. They could not wait to tell the other doves how they had outwitted the kite.

They flew to their dovecote and settled on its roof, and all the other doves flew over to greet them. They surrounded the white dove and stared at him in disbelief. 'You look disgusting,' they said. 'How did you get so dirty?'

'You're not coming into our nest like that,' said his wife.

But nobody paid any attention to the black dove. His wife even said, 'Come inside at once! Don't sit next to that dirty dove!'

'What is going on?' thought the white dove. 'We were both inside the chimney together!'

The mosquito's heroics

At the top of a towering precipice stood a barrel. It had been standing there for many years. Everybody was amazed that it had managed to stay there so long, and that nobody had dislodged it.

One day, a mosquito flew over the abyss. It saw that something was balanced on the very edge of the precipice. 'What can that be?' wondered the mosquito. He descended and settled on the barrel to have a rest. As soon as he settled on the barrel's surface, it tumbled into the abyss.

'Look how mighty the mosquito is!' people exclaimed in awe. 'It dislodged the barrel and sent it flying into the abyss.'

The mosquito heard the people praise him and was very proud of himself. 'I must indeed be the strongest creature on Earth,' he thought.

How a mole married a spider

A mole was fed up with living all by himself, so he decided to marry a spider who lived in the burrow next to his. She was right next door, and they could live together and raise children. The children would be a comfort to them in their old age.

So, they married. The spider moved in with the mole and brought all her belongings. Late one evening, they were sitting on a bench under a wormwood bush, admiring the stars and dreaming about their future, when suddenly the same thought occurred to both of them: 'What were their children going to look like?'

'They'll look like me,' said the mole. 'I don't want my children to have ugly bug-eyes like yours!'

'No, they'll look like me,' objected the spider heatedly. 'I don't want my children to have no eyes and be blind and creepy like you.'

Once they realized how ugly their future children would be, they suddenly came to their senses.

'What a fool I was to marry such a monster!' lamented the spider.

'What a fool I was to marry such an ugly creature!' sighed the mole.

The spider took all her belongings and returned to her own burrow. The mole dug deep into the earth and spent three days thinking about what had just happened.

A lot of wise thoughts came to him, but the mole lives alone, and we will never know what they were.

A spider's last moments

An old spider was dying. He could no longer leave his nest. He gazed gloomily at his web, remembering his youth, and recalling how he used to scamper swiftly over the web's fine fibres, waiting for a careless fly.

Just then the dying spider sensed some movement in his web. 'A fly!' he thought. 'I've got you now!'

But he did not have the energy to open his eyes and see what kind of fly he had caught: a fat one or a thin one.

With the little that remained of his brain power, the spider realised that the fly might escape if he did not pull on a strand of the web and tighten its grip on the prey. The fly might free itself and fly away. The spider gathered all his strength, rose on his wobbly legs, reached out for the end of the web, pulled it, and tumbled back into his nest. The fly buzzed loudly as the fibres tightened their grip. When the spider heard the buzzing of the dying fly, his heartbeat quickened with joy, and with that feeling he died. Because a spider will remain a spider to the very end.

The firebird

A little chick grew up and became a big hen. One day, the chickens were scratching in some manure when, they noticed a golden feather in the big hen's tail. It looked just like the feather of the firebird you read about in fairy tales.

When the chickens spotted the feather, they all started clucking anxiously, 'She must be the firebird!'

The big hen wanted to see this wonderful feather for herself, but she could not reach her own tail. So, holding her head high and raising her tail, she told her friends, 'From now on, I won't scratch in the manure looking for worms. Instead, each of you will bring me a handful of grain.'

From then on, all the chickens started bringing the big hen a handful of wheat. Then, one day, the golden feather fell out. When the chickens took a close look at it, they realized that it was not golden at all. It just looked golden when the sun's rays shone on it. 'She doesn't have a golden feather at all!' the chickens started clucking all at once. And once again, the big hen went back to scratching in the manure.

The marble nightingale

A man made a nightingale from marble. The bird seemed alive. It was tiny and grey, with a delicate beak and sparkling eyes. The man placed it on his windowsill. The nightingale liked it there, his eyes shining as he greeted the sun. It seemed that any moment he would break into song. But he never did.

One evening, just before sunset, a real nightingale settled beside the marble one and started singing. The marble nightingale closed his eyes with pleasure and listened, deep in thought. He thought and thought, and then said, 'You are a living nightingale and know how to sing. Teach me how to sing like you! I have been perched on this windowsill for forty years, and every spring I have enjoyed your singing. I have tried to learn to sing like you, but I have never been able to. Why is that?'

The real nightingale replied, 'I am only seven years old. That is how long I have lived in this world. But it is better to live just seven years and be able to sing than to spend forty years as a marble nightingale.'

Olia's magic

An autumn flower and a spring flower met in the school greenhouse. This is how it came about.

We transplanted some autumn flowers—chrysanthemums—into the greenhouse. They flowered there: white, violet and pink. Next to them was a green lilac shoot. It was nearly New Year. Outside it was snowing and a cold winter wind was blowing, but inside the greenhouse it was warm and cosy.

One sunny winter morning the lilac bloomed. The lilac flower opened its light blue eyes and saw a white chrysanthemum. It exclaimed in amazement, 'You're an autumn flower, chrysanthemum. Why are you flowering now?'

The chrysanthemum replied, 'And you're a spring flower. Why have you flowered now, when it is bitterly cold outside?'

The lilac flower looked and saw that it was true: it was winter outside.

'It is all because of that little girl Olia,' said the chrysanthemum. 'She brought us here. If not for her, we would never have met.'

Without Olia's magic, spring would not have met autumn.

The bird pantry

In early autumn, the chirping of the birds in the steppe was deafening. The birds had descended on a field that had been harvested and were pecking at grains that lay on the ground.

On the edge of the forest stood a rowan tree. Its red berries had ripened. The rowan tree was surprised that the birds did not come to eat them. A thrush flew by, and the rowan tree called out to it, 'Thrush, why don't you come and sample my berries?'

'Wait a little, dear rowan tree. Your berries will come in handy during hard times. Your branches are our bird pantry,' said the thrush.

Snow fell. The fields were covered with a white carpet. The grass was buried under snowdrifts. All day and all night long, the cold wind sang its mournful song.

One morning the rowan tree was woken by the chirping of birds. She saw that the thrushes and woodpeckers had come to visit her.

'Now we need your bird pantry,' chirped the thrush. 'Now, dear rowan tree, we will be very grateful for your berries.'

The fox and the hedgehog

A fox caught a hedgehog and was carrying him back to her den. She knew that it would take quite some time to retrieve the delicious meat from beneath the hedgehog's prickly quills. The fox was hurrying home, when she spotted a dead mouse. She wanted to pick it up, but she was already carrying the hedgehog in her mouth, so she said, 'Hedgehog, could you please pick up that mouse for me? When we get home, I'll give you the mouse's tail.'

The hedgehog knew that the fox was about to eat him as well as the mouse, so he decided to trick her. 'I'm sorry, fox, but I have a toothache,' he replied. 'Why don't you pick up the mouse with your own teeth, and I will take hold of your tail with my teeth.'

The fox was cunning, but she did not realise that the hedgehog was intending to trick her. She wanted that mouse so badly that she opened her mouth, released the hedgehog, and picked up the mouse. The hedgehog ran round to the fox's tail and took hold of her most slender hair. As soon as the fox set off, the thin hair was tugged out and, in the blink of an eye, the hedgehog disappeared into the bushes.

The pain just disappeared

A mole was digging a burrow, when he accidently drove a thorn into his paw. It developed into an abscess and hurt a lot. The mole could not finish digging his burrow.

'I'll go into the forest to see the doctor,' he decided. Now the doctor in that forest was a bear. The mole limped all the way to the bear's house and knocked on the door. The bear opened the door and invited the mole inside. 'Come in, dear patient,' he growled.

The mole proceeded to the bear's surgery. The bear sat him down, examined his paw, took out a knife, and cut the paw clean off. The mole hobbled off on his three remaining paws. As he was leaving the bear's surgery, he met a hedgehog.

'What did the bear treat for you?' asked the hedgehog.

'I had an abscess on my paw,' said the mole.

'And did the bear cure you?' asked the hedgehog.

'He did,' said the mole. 'He cut off my paw. I don't have the abscess anymore.'

'You don't have a paw either,' remarked the hedgehog.

'You're right,' said the mole in surprise. 'How did I not notice that before? And what brings you to see the bear?'

'I have a pimple on my nose,' answered the hedgehog. 'I couldn't sleep all night. But it just stopped hurting. No pain at all … I don't know what happened to my pimple, but the pain has just disappeared. Let's go home, dear mole. We are going in the same direction anyway.'

What is wrong with my children?

A broody hen was given ten duck eggs to hatch. She sat on them for a long time, dreaming of her babies. Ten little, yellow birds hatched, and they wanted to go for a walk straight away. The hen took them out into the yard.

She led them to a pile of dung and began to scratch at the ground. She called her chicks, but they saw something more interesting. They saw a pond. They ran to it, jumped in the water, and started paddling.

The hen clucked in alarm as she watched her paddling chicks. 'Come back!' she called. 'You'll drown!'

But the little birds did not seem to hear. After all, they weren't chicks; they were ducklings. They paddled for a long time and did not get out of the water till evening. The hen patiently waited for them. She waited and waited, and then took them home.

She waddled in front of them and complained, 'You don't listen to me. And who taught you to swim? Your mother can't swim. Your father can't swim. Why are you swimming? I won't let you near the pond again.'

But the ducklings cheeped back, 'Mum, tomorrow you can swim with us. It's so nice in the water!'

The hen looked at her little ones and wondered, 'What is wrong with my children?'

How the river quarrelled with the rain

The river became conceited. 'Look how wide and full of water I am, and what green banks I have,' it boasted. 'Even the sun is reflected in me as in a mirror. So are the green trees and the blue sky.'

Suddenly the sky was covered in grey clouds and rain began to fall. A day passed, and then a second and a third. The river and its banks also became grey. The whole world became grey. The river was angry. 'How long will you continue with your pitter-patter, you miserable rain?' it complained. 'I have become ugly because of you.'

The rain replied, 'If not for me and my greyness, you would not be so wide and full of water.'

We, too, should not forget the source from which we flow.

The foolish carp

A fisherman caught a perch and a carp. 'I'll make a fish soup out of the perch,' he thought, 'And I'll fry the carp.'

He poured some water into a pot, threw the perch into it, and hung the pot over his campfire. He lay the carp in a frypan in some oil and placed the frypan onto some hot coals.

The perch felt the water getting hot and told the carp, 'Dear brother carp, he is making fish soup out of me. I don't want to die.'

'I am swimming in oil,' the carp boasted. 'It's nice and warm in the oil, like a puddle warmed by the sun.'

'What a fool you are!' the perch replied angrily, and he leaped out of the pot back into the river. The carp jumped in after him. 'I have to admit,' he snorted, 'It is better in the water.'

How a spider sold its web

A spider and his wife made lots of spider webs. The wife rolled all the webs into a bundle and took them to the market to sell. She laid her goods out on her counter and started shouting at the top of her voice, 'Come and see! Webs for sale! Cheap and strong! Good for nets, baskets, or your children's beds!'

Customers crowded round the spider's counter, haggling, and trying to select the strongest webs. A grasshopper and an ant bought some webs to use as nets, and a frog measured a web for a basket. A bat asked the spider to measure some web for his son's bed.

A curious fly observed the stall from a distance.

'There must be something interesting for sale,' he thought, and he made his way over to the counter. When he realised that it was a spider selling webs, the fly backed off and disappeared into the crowd. The further away from trouble, the better.

The larks have arrived

When the first larks appear in the spring sky, mothers bake little larks from bread dough. Serhiiko's mother baked a little bird for him. Serhiiko put it by the open window. The spring sun was shining, and a warm breeze was singing in a green willow tree. The little lark sat on the windowsill, looking at the sky with its little black eyes. It seemed to Serhiiko that at any moment it would spread its wings and fly into the sky.

Night came, and Serhiiko went to bed. The little lark kept looking up into the sky. Serhiiko dreamt that the lark was cold, and that he took it into his bed to get warm. Or perhaps that really did happen.

In the morning Serhiiko opened his eyes, and the first thing he did was look over at the windowsill. The window was open, and the lark was gone. Serhiiko ran over to the window, looked at the blue morning sky, and called out, 'Mum! Our lark has flown away into the sky! I can hear it singing.'

His mother looked at Serhiiko and asked, 'Did you take it into your bed last night?'

'I only took it for a minute in the middle of the night,' said Serhiiko. 'It was cold. I warmed it up.'

'Then it must have flown away this morning,' said his mother with a smile.

The white feather

A flock of sparrows sat perched on a thatched roof. They chirped happily to each other about matters of interest to sparrows. Suddenly a strange sparrow, whom they had never seen before on the thatched roof, flew over and settled amongst them. He looked somehow different to the other sparrows. He had a haughty little head, a short neck, and a fussy little beak.

But the thing that really made him different was the white feather in his tail. Among the other grey feathers, this white feather looked extraordinary.

'Look! Look!' chirped the sparrows, 'An amazing sparrow with a white feather in its tail has joined us.'

Sparrows came flying from several neighbouring roofs, settled near the sparrow with the white feather in its tail, and asked, 'Where have you flown from?'

'From the other side of the sea,' answered the sparrow with the white feather in its tail.

Meanwhile, all the sparrows were trying to settle closer to the white feather, so they could get a good look at it. Several times they touched the white feather with their beaks, and one curious sparrow pulled on it. The white feather fell out, and the wind picked it up and carried it far away.

Now that the strange sparrow no longer had a white feather in its tail, it suddenly ceased to be unusual. It became just as grey as all the other sparrows that had been born and raised on thatched roofs. Its head looked just the same, its neck and beak looked the same, and when the strange sparrow chirped, all the others just opened their beaks in surprise.

'It's an ordinary sparrow just like us!' they all chirped. 'And we were silly enough to believe in a white feather.'

Why isn't it snowing yet?

Autumn arrived. A little grey hare went to see his grandfather and asked him, 'Please, grandpa, give me a white coat and take this grey one, because it is going to snow soon.'

His grandfather gave the little hare a white coat. But the snow did not come. Against the grey earth everyone could see the white hare, and he was easy prey for dogs and hunters. As soon as they spotted him, they dashed after him … The hare's life became very hard. He sat under a bush and broke into tears. 'Why isn't it snowing yet?' he cried.

A fox's tail

A little hare saw a fox's tail and was amazed: it was so red and long and bushy. The hare asked the fox, 'Fox, why do you need such a long tail?'

'To wipe my tracks away. Suppose I steal a hen. People come after me and, if I don't watch out, they will catch me. So, I run over the snow and wipe my tracks as I go. The people chasing me can't tell where I have gone.'

The little hare went to his mother and asked her, 'Can you make me a tail like the fox's out of hemp. I want to wipe my tracks away. I don't want people to know where I have run.'

The mother said, 'You silly little hare. You don't need to run away; you just need to be clever. If you see a man with a gun, that is a hunter. Hide away and keep very still. He won't see you. You don't need a tail because you've got a head.'

And the little hare's mother stroked his head with her paw.

Fox lights

Once, a cunning fox was walking through the forest, returning to her home. It was night-time, and very dark in the forest, so she could not see anything. Suddenly, the fox bumped her head on an oak tree, and it really hurt.

'We need to find a way to light up the forest path,' she thought to herself. She found a tree stump covered in glow-worms, shining in the dark. She took fragments of the stump, with glow-worms attached, and laid them along her path. They shone like little lamps in the dark. Now she could see where she was going. Even the little owl was surprised. 'What is that?' he wondered. 'Is day coming in the middle of the night?'

The cunning fox padded through the night and smiled.

But a little hare hid behind an oak tree and kept a lookout.

A swallow builds a nest

A swallow returned from spending the winter in warmer lands and began to build a nest. She flew to a pond, took some wet soil in her tiny beak, and started moulding her nest under the eaves. A toad sat near the bank of the pond. She asked the swallow, 'Tell me, swallow, where are you taking that soil?'

'I am building a nest,' answered the swallow.

'What is a nest?' asked the toad.

The swallow spent a long time explaining to the toad what a nest was, and about chicks, but the toad could not make any sense of it. When the swallow told the toad that she soared high in the sky, right up to the clouds, the toad laughed and did not believe a word of it. It seemed incredible to the toad that anyone could love anything other than a swamp.

Why the chickadee is crying

A husband and wife lived in a house on the edge of the village. They had two children: a boy named Myshko and a girl named Olia. Myshko was ten, and Olia was nine.

A tall, bushy poplar grew near their house. 'Let's make a swing under the poplar,' said Myshko.

'Yes! I can't wait to swing on it,' said Olia with joy.

Myshko climbed the poplar and tied a rope to its branches. Myshko and Olia hung on to the rope and started to swing back and forth. As they swung, a chickadee fluttered next to them, singing its heart out. 'The chickadee is happy to see us swinging,' said Myshko.

Olia looked at the trunk of the poplar and saw a hollow. In the hollow was a nest, and in the nest were some little chicks. 'The chickadee is not happy; it is crying,' said Olia.

'Why is it crying?' Myshko asked in surprise.

'Think about it,' answered Olia. Myshko jumped off the swing and looked at the chickadee's nest. 'Why is it crying?' he wondered.

The lily of the valley by the window

Little Natalia in our class had been ill for six months. She had a serious illness: her legs lay motionless, as if they did not belong to her. Natalia had to stay in bed day and night.

We did not forget Natalia. We visited her every day. We learnt to read well, and so did Natalia. We often drew pictures of a butterfly or a lark and took them to her. She loves butterflies and larks.

When spring arrived, Natalia's bed was placed by the window. She looked at the grass and the leaves and said, 'I so want to walk on the grass.'

One day, Natalia saw two big green leaves, like two ribbons, in the middle of the grass.

'Look,' she whispered, 'A lily of the valley!'

A lily of the valley really had grown in her garden. How did it end up there, in the middle of the grass?

Every day we went to see if the lily of the valley had flowered yet. When little white bells appeared between the green leaves, Natalia was so pleased that her cheeks turned rosy.

But then, suddenly, trouble came. During the night there was a heavy downpour. Early in the morning, before sunrise, while Natalia was still sleeping, we went to her garden and saw that the lily of the valley had been flattened. What should we do? This would make Natalia very sad.

We took a spade into the forest, dug up a lily of the valley, and transplanted it to the spot under Natalia's window.

When Natalia woke, she asked her mother to open her window. We were already waiting for her. Natalia smiled and asked us, 'How is the lily of the valley?'

'It is flowering,' we said. 'You can see its little white bells.'

'I was so worried,' said Natalia. 'There was a thunderstorm last night … The wind was howling … I dreamt that the storm flattened the lily of the valley.'

Who will build ovens?

Autumn came. It was cold in the house, and time to light a fire in the large brick oven. Tarasyk's mother set a fire, but the wood would not burn. 'We need to get the oven fixed,' said his mother. 'I'll go and see Grandpa Trokhym.'

Grandpa Trokhym was the only man in the village who could build and maintain ovens. Tarasyk looked at his great big beard with respect and fear. The old man tapped the oven wall with the handle of his trowel and said, 'This oven will not give any heat no matter how much you try to fix it. You need to build a new one.'

Tarasyk and his mother took all the bricks from the oven outside, leaving an empty spot. Grandpa Trokhym began to build a new oven, and Tarasyk helped him.

'Grandpa, is it true that you are the only person in our village who knows how to build an oven?' asked Tarasyk.

'That's true, my boy,' said Grandpa Trokhym.

'What will happen when you die?' asked Tarasyk.

'When I die, there will be no-one to lay bricks for a new oven.'

Tarasyk sat sorrowfully for a long time. Then he went up to Grandpa Trokhym and said, 'Grandpa, please teach me how to build an oven.'

The little spade

A man was getting ready to go to the shop. 'Can I come with you, Dad?' asked his six-year-old son.

'All right, my boy,' agreed his father.

At the shop the father and son bought two big spoons and one small spoon. The big spoons were for the mother and father, and the small spoon for the son. Then they bought a spade, a strong, sharp spade. 'With a spade like that you can dig for ten years,' said the father.

The son saw a small spade on the shelf. 'Dad,' asked the son, 'Can you buy me a spade. I will dig the soil as well.'

The father bought the small spade for his son.

They returned home and sat down to have lunch. The mother and father ate with the big spoons, and the son ate with the small spoon. After lunch, the father took his spade and went to dig the vegetable patch.

The son also took his little spade so he could help his father, but his father said, 'You can go and play with your spade in the sand.'

The son went and played with his spade in a pile of sand, but he soon tired of it and put his spade under his bed.

The little spade is still lying under the son's bed even now. But the little spoon is kept next to the big spoons. Whenever they sit down to eat, the mother and father take the big spoons, and hand the small spoon to their son.

The old dog

A man had a faithful friend—his dog. For many years the dog guarded his master's home.

The years passed, the dog grew old, and his eyesight began to fail. One bright summer day, he did not recognise his own master. When his master returned from the field, he ran out from his kennel and barked at him as if he was a stranger. The master was surprised, and asked, 'So you don't recognise me anymore?'

The dog wagged his tail guiltily. He pressed his muzzle into his master's leg and nipped it tenderly. He was trying to say, 'Forgive me. I don't know how it happened that I did not recognise you.'

A few days later the master brought a young pup from somewhere. He built a new kennel next to the old dog's kennel, and said to the pup, 'You can live here.'

The old dog asked his master, 'Why do you need another dog?'

'So you won't be bored by yourself,' said his master, and gently stroked the old dog's back. Then the master turned, sighed quietly, and walked away. The dog could not sigh, but it whimpered pitifully.

And the little pup rolled and played on the grass.

Mykolka, Vitia and the puppy

Mykolka and Vitia found a puppy on the way home from school. It was sitting in a ditch and whining pitifully.

But who should keep the puppy? The boys thought for a long time, and then decided. First the puppy would live for three days with Vitia, then for three days with Mykolka, then three days with Vitia and so on, in turn. After a month the boys would take the puppy out into the middle of a field and walk in opposite directions. Whoever the puppy ran after would be its master.

Mykolka build a beautiful kennel for the puppy. Three times a day his mother took the puppy some soup and a rissole.

Vitia did not have a kennel or any soup or rissoles. He put a mat next to his bed and the puppy slept on it. Sometimes at night the puppy wanted to go outside to do some doggy business. He would quietly touch Vitia's blanket with his paw, and Vitia would wake up and let him out. The puppy ate crusts of bread soaked in hot water.

After a month had passed, the boys took the puppy and walked far out into the middle of a field. They climbed an ancient burial mound, put the puppy on the ground, and ran in opposite directions.

The puppy ran after Vitia.

By the big grey stone

Ivan and Taras always left school together, but they only walked side by side as far as the big grey stone. It had been lying next to the path for longer than anyone could remember.

Once they reached the big grey stone, Ivan walked home to Poplar Street, and Taras walked home to Cherry Tree Street.

It took about ten minutes to walk from school to the big grey stone, just long enough to tell a story. The boys took it in turns to tell stories. Ivan would tell a story one day, and Taras the next.

One day, something very unusual happened. During the fifth lesson of the day Ivan received a failing mark, and during the sixth lesson Taras received a failing mark. Both boys had failing marks written in their homework diaries, and comments from the teachers to their parents, asking them to give the matter their attention.

The friends left school sad and depressed. Today it was Taras's turn to tell a story, but he was silent.

They reached the big grey stone.

'Let's go to your place together,' said Ivan.

'And then we can go to your place,' said Taras.

And the boys set off together.

The tractor driver and the glazier

Early one summer morning, a tractor driver set off for work. On the way he met a glazier. He greeted him and said, 'You have an easy job, glazier. What do you do? You take glass made by someone else and put it in a frame. People could live without your work. My work is more important. I plough the fields, sow grain and gather in the harvest. Without my work there would be no bread, and people cannot live without bread.'

The glazier silently let the tractor driver have his say, and then said, 'Look, there's a cellar over here. Let's go down for a minute.'

The tractor driver shrugged his shoulder in surprise, but he followed the glazier. They climbed down some stairs into the cellar. It was so dark in the cellar that you could not see a thing.

'What do you think? Could you live here?' asked the glazier.

'Oh, no. No way,' answered the tractor driver.

'This is what it would be like in every home without my work. Glaziers give people light.'

'It's true,' thought the tractor driver. 'You can't live without light. People do not live by bread alone. Bread by itself is not enough.'

He became a worker

A mother had three children: ten-year-old Natalka, seven-year-old Olia, and little Oleh. He was only two years old. He often asked his mother and sisters questions, like, 'What is that?' or 'How come a pigeon can fly, but a chicken can't fly?'

On Saturday, the mother said to her daughters, 'Let's clean up the yard. There's a lot of rubbish there.' The mother, Natalka and Olia each took a small broom and began to sweep the yard. They gathered all the rubbish in a pile, carried it to the vegetable patch, and burnt it.

While the rubbish was burning, little Oleh noticed a piece of straw in the yard and picked it up and took it to the fire. He handed it to his mother and said, 'I picked up some straw.' His mother took the piece of straw and threw it into the fire.

'Today is a special day for our Oleh,' the mother told her daughters.

'What sort of special day?' asked Natalka and Olia in surprise.

'Today is the day he became a worker.'

Who tells a story to Grandma?

Two brothers—three-year-old Petryk and five-year-old Mykolka—have got used to the way that their Grandma Mariia gives them supper, makes their beds, and puts them to bed. Then she sits on a chair and tells them a story.

Grandma's story lulls the boys to sleep.

In the morning, as soon as they wake up, they see that Grandma is already busy in the kitchen, getting their breakfast ready.

One day Mykolka asks, 'Grandma, when do you go to bed?'

'After I put you to bed,' says Grandma.

'And when do you get up?' asks Mykolka.

'When you still have three more hours to sleep,' says Grandma.

'And who tells you a story, Grandma?' asks Mykolka.

Grandma Mariia smiles but does not answer. And Mykolka keeps wondering, who can it be that tells Grandma a story?

I am going to work

When she went to work, Olia's mother always took a small lunch box. She would also take a needle and thread. Little Olia asked her, 'Mum, why do you take a needle and thread with you?'

'Because I'm going to work,' her mother replied. 'If something gets torn, I'll be able to mend it.'

The time arrived for Olia to start going to school. On the first of September[75], she woke early in the morning, and packed her textbooks and exercise books into her schoolbag all by herself.

Her mother advised her, 'Study well. Studying is hard work.'

Olia picked up her schoolbag and prepared to leave. Then she remembered something and said, 'Mum, can you please give me a needle and thread?'

'Why?' asked her mother in surprise.

'Because I'm going to work,' said Olia.

Adversity makes you learn

Little Olenka is in grade one. Today she got up early, before sunrise. Her grandmother got up early too, to help her get ready for school. Olenka's mother is not at home. She is working a night shift and has not yet returned from work.

Olenka is in a hurry to get ready for school. Suddenly a hook comes off her skirt, and her skirt drops to the floor.

'Oh, Grandma, can you sew this hook on for me?' asks Olenka. Her grandmother reaches for her glasses on the table, but accidentally knocks them, and they fall and break.

Olenka's grandmother picks up the broken glasses from the floor and shakes her head. 'I can't sew without my glasses,' she says. 'I cannot see properly.'

Olenka cries. She remembers how her grandmother told her, 'You should learn to sew, Olenka!' Olenka had not wanted to learn. Now she says, 'Grandma, can you teach me how to sew?'

'Sit down, and I will teach you,' says her grandmother. 'Here is the needle, and here is the thread.' While Olenka is threading the needle, her grandmother sits quietly.

When Olenka manages to thread it, her grandmother says, 'Adversity makes you learn.'

Milk is white

The teacher said, 'Children, I would like you to draw a cow.'

The grade one students bent over their albums. Little Mariika drew a tiny, tiny cow in the corner of her page.

The teacher walked over to Mariika and asked, 'Why have you drawn such a small cow? Look at all the white paper left over.'

'That's not white paper,' answered Mariika. 'That's milk. And milk is white.'

And she carefully brushed her palm over the white sheet of paper, to wipe away any dust.

Blue cranes

When grade three student Zoia left home this morning, she was very happy. The night before, her mother and father had sat on the end of her bed for a long time, telling her stories, and when she felt sleepy, they had kissed her and said, 'Have sweet, sunny dreams!' Zoia had dreamt sweet dreams about the shining sun, a green meadow as vast as the ocean, yellow dandelions, buzzing bumblebees, and a lark singing in the sky …

But Zoia's classmate, Dmytryk, left home pale, sad and thoughtful. The night before his mother and father had argued for a long time. His mother had cried. For a long time, Dmytryk had not been able to get to sleep, and he had dreamt of his mother's tearful eyes.

Zoia and Dmytryk walked to school together. The little girl chattered away happily about something. Dmytryk wanted to listen to what she was saying, to drive away his sad thoughts, but he could not. In his mind he kept seeing his mother's big eyes, full of tears. The boy felt like crying.

Suddenly Zoia exclaimed, 'Look, Dmytryk, there are cranes in the sky! A whole flock of them … It's spring, it's spring. Look how beautiful they are, the cranes are light blue! Blue cranes! Look, Dmytryk, look!'

'They're not blue, they're grey,' said Dmytryk quietly.

'They're not grey, they're blue! How can you think a blue bird is grey?' said Zoia in amazement.

The children arrived at school. Zoia went over to her teacher and said, 'When we were walking to school, there was a flock of blue cranes flying in the sky. But Dmytryk said they were grey. Are they really grey? I saw with my own eyes that they were blue.'

The teacher looked carefully at Dmytryk. 'For you they were blue, Zoia, but for Dmytryk they were grey,' he said. 'But don't worry, Dmytryk, your blue cranes will come.'

I want to say my own word

Kateryna Ivanivna took her little grade one students out into the field. It was a quiet morning in early autumn. High in the sky, a flock of migratory birds was passing overhead. The birds' plaintive cries cast a veil of sadness over the steppe.

Kateryna Ivanivna told the children, 'Today we are going to make up a composition about autumn, about the sky and the migratory birds. I would like each of you to describe what the sky is like now. Look carefully at the sky, children, and think. Choose beautiful and precise words from our native language.'

The children fell silent. They gazed at the sky and thought. After a while they began to make up their first miniature compositions:

'The sky is deep, deep blue … '

'The sky is light blue … '

'The sky is clear … '

'The sky is azure … '

And that was all. The children kept repeating the same words: dark blue, light blue, clear, azure.

Little blue-eyed Valia stood to one side without saying a word.

'Why don't you say anything, Valia?' asked the teacher.

'I want to say my *own* word,' she said.

'Well, what is your word about the sky?' asked the teacher.

'The sky is *tender*,' said Valia quietly and gave a sad smile.

The children fell silent. At that moment, they saw what they had not seen till then.

'The sky is sad … '

'The sky is anxious … '

'The sky is melancholy … '

'The sky is cold … '

Now the sky was full of life, trembling, breathing, smiling—like a living creature, and the children were looking into its sad, deep blue, autumn eyes.

Don't be sad, Dad

Mykola came home from school and said, 'Dad, today there is a parents' night at school.'

That night, Mykola's father went to the parents' meeting, while Mykola sat down and did his homework. He finished his lessons and wanted to go out to play, but before he could, his father came home from the school.

His father sat down next to the table with his head bowed. Mykola's mother looked anxiously at the father, who seemed sad. Mykola stood by the table, looking out the window.

'What did they say at the meeting?' asked the mother.

'They said that Petryk is very good at solving problems. Myshko wrote a poem. Mariika and Natalka are good at drawing. You should have seen the beautiful drawings the teacher showed us! Stepan carved a nightingale from wood … Vasylko is really mischievous. He climbed up a drainpipe onto the roof and walked across it from one side to the other … '

'Did the teacher say something about Mykola?' asked the mother in alarm.

'He didn't say anything about Mykola,' answered the father quietly, and sighed.

'Don't be sad, Dad,' said little Mykola. 'Tomorrow, I'll climb to the top of the tallest tree at school.'

The greedy boy

Once upon a time, there was a very greedy boy. He was walking along the street, when he noticed that ice-cream was for sale. The boy stopped and thought, 'Wouldn't it be great if someone gave me a hundred portions of ice-cream.'

He had nearly reached his school, when suddenly, in a quiet, deserted lane, an old, grey-haired man came running up behind him and asked, 'Are you the one who wanted a hundred portions of ice-cream?'

The boy was amazed. Hiding his embarrassment, he said, 'Yes, if someone gave me the money.'

'You don't need money,' said the old man. 'Over there, behind that willow tree, are a hundred portions of ice-cream.'

The old man disappeared, as if he had never been there. The boy looked behind the willow tree and was so amazed that he dropped his school bag full of books. Under the tree was a box full of ice-cream. The boy quickly counted a hundred packs, wrapped up in silver paper.

The boy's hands shook with greed. He ate one, two, three portions. Then he could not eat any more as his stomach ached.

'What should I do?' wondered the boy.

He took his books out of his bag and threw them under the willow tree. He filled his bag with the shiny packets of ice-cream, but they did not all fit in his bag. He was so sorry to leave them that he burst into tears. He sat by the willow tree and cried.

He ate two more portions and slowly dragged his feet to school.

He went into his classroom and put his bag down, but the ice-cream was beginning to melt. Milk was leaking out of his bag.

The thought flashed through his mind that perhaps he should give the ice-cream to his classmates, but greed drove that thought away. How could he give away such a treasure?

The boy sat looking at his bag, with the milk running out. Could it really be that he would lose such a treasure?

This story is for those in whose souls the worm of greed has settled. It is a terrible worm.

The baker and the tailor

A baker and a tailor began to argue about whose work was more important and essential. The baker said to the tailor, 'What would happen if I did not bake the bread? Without bread to eat, the miners would not be able to work the mines, the tractor drivers would not drive their tractors, and you, tailor, would not be able to work with your scissors.'

'And what would happen if there were no tailors?' replied the tailor. 'Who would make the clothes? Without clothes to wear the miners would not be able to work the mines, the tractor drivers would not drive their tractors, and you, baker, would not work in your bakery.'

And so, they could not agree whose work was more important and essential to people's needs.

'I will manage without you, tailor,' said the baker.

'And I can live without you, baker,' said the tailor.

Each of them went to work. The baker worked for a day, and then another day, and felt that he could manage fine without the tailor. On the third day the baker hung his jacket by the oven and the sleeve caught on fire. It burnt so badly that all that was left of the sleeve was ashes. The baker scratched his head. What was he to do? What use was a jacket with only one sleeve? He would have to go and see the tailor.

Meanwhile the tailor had worked for a day without any bread, eating just porridge and borshch.[76] He worked for a second day without eating any bread. On the third day he was so famished that the scissors dropped out of his hand. He would have to go to the baker for some bread.

The baker and the tailor both left home at the same time. The baker was going to see the tailor, and the tailor was going to see the baker. They met each other. The baker was holding his jacket without a sleeve, and the tailor had an empty basket.

Who is the most intelligent?

An ox, a goat, and a sheep were debating who was the most intelligent of the three. Each one said, 'I am the most intelligent.' Nobody wanted to appear more foolish than the others. In the end, they decided to go and see the donkey and let him settle the matter. 'Dear donkey,' they said, 'Please tell us who is the most intelligent among us?'

The donkey gave them a riddle to solve. 'Let each of you explain why grass grows,' he said. 'Whoever gives the wisest answer is the most intelligent.'

The ox said, 'Grass grows because it rains.'

The goat said, 'Grass grows because the sun gives it warmth.'

The sheep was silent. He remained silent for a day, for two days, for a week. He did not speak for a year, then two years, then three. And the donkey decided that the sheep was the most intelligent. He reasoned that the sheep's silence implied that he knew something. As for the ox and the goat, although they had given an answer, they may have been mistaken.

Murko's surprise

An old lady had a very old cat named Murko. One day, Murko was lazing in the sun, soaking up its warmth. He closed his eyes and fell asleep with his head on his paws. Only his tail moved from time to time, chasing away the flies.

A little chick wandered into the courtyard. He had become separated from his mother and was cheeping pitifully. When he saw the cat, he stopped cheeping. He quietly approached the cat, snuggled up beside him, and closed his eyes, enjoying the warmth of the cat's body.

Murko felt something pressing against him. He opened his eyes and was amazed to see the chick. 'What a brave little fellow!' he thought. Murko stared at the chick and did not know what to do with him. Should he frighten the chick and chase him away, or should he let him enjoy the warmth?

How the sparrow became white

This happened one summer. A man carried a sack full of flour out of the mill and placed it against a wall. There were lots of sparrows near the mill, pecking at some grain that was scattered around.

One sparrow spotted the sack and flew over to it. The sack was untied. 'Now is my chance,' thought the sparrow, 'I'll treat myself to some wheat.'

But the sack was full of flour, not wheat. The sparrow dived in and was covered in flour. It found its way into his eyes and turned his feathers white. The sparrow flew out of the sack completely white, like a giant butterfly. He settled under the eaves of a shed, blinking his eyes. Then he spotted his nest, flew home, and started chirping excitedly. His little sparrow chicks peeked out from their nest and were shocked by what they saw. What on earth was this white bird? They were frightened and burst into tears.

Their mother-sparrow came flying. She could hardly recognise her husband, but she comforted her chicks, saying 'This is our daddy, my dears … Just watch him fly off and fetch you a worm.'

The white sparrow flew off and brought his chicks a worm. Only then did his children believe that it was their father.

The spider and the lace

A girl sat by the window, weaving some fine white lace. From a dark corner of the room, a spider watched her work. He could not take his eyes off her nimble fingers. He was mesmerized by the strong threads and the beautiful pattern. 'What a wonderful web,' he thought. 'Even the most cunning fly would be attracted to such a beautiful web.'

One day, the girl went for a walk, leaving the lace unattended on the table. The spider scurried over from his corner to the table and felt the lace. He was puzzled: the web woven by the girl was not sticky. A web like this could not catch even the tiniest fly. 'That's strange,' he thought. 'Why would the girl weave a web like this?'

The girl returned from her walk. She sat by the window, and again set about weaving her magic on the lace. The spider retreated to his dark corner and racked his brain. 'Why weave a web, if you cannot catch flies with it?' he wondered.

The carp and the toad

A little carp lived in a pond. He was swift and agile, with a pink tail. He befriended a toad. One day, the toad told him, 'I am going over to the bank of the pond. I'll spend some time soaking up the sunshine, and I'll bring you some flies for dinner.'

The toad crawled out onto the bank of the pond and warmed himself in the sun. The carp was jealous. 'Just look at that toad soaking up the sun, and catching flies,' he thought, 'While I have to swim in this disgusting water. It's wet and cold!'

The carp swam over to the edge of the pond, leaped out of the water, and found himself on the hot sand. He tried to breathe, but he was suffocating. He wanted to flick his tail, but his tail had already dried out on the hot sand. The toad noticed that his friend was in trouble and said, 'Don't leap out of the water, or you'll end up in a frying pan.'

The toad hopped over to the carp, took hold of him, and threw him back into the water. The carp was overjoyed, 'Oh, toad, dear toad!' he cried, 'You have saved me from certain death!'

The carp never again said that water was disgusting.

A sparrow learns about fire

An old mother sparrow finally allowed her little son to spread his wings and fly out of the nest. The little sparrow was overjoyed and kept asking his mother, 'What is this? And what is that?'

His mother explained to him about the earth, about grass, trees, hens, geese, and a pond. Then the little sparrow spotted a giant ball of fire in the sky. 'What is that?' he asked.

'That is the sun,' his mother replied.

'What is the sun?' the sparrow went on.

'Why do you need to know all these things?' replied his wise mother, growing irritated. 'The sun is fire.'

'I would like to learn about fire,' the sparrow chirped and flew higher and higher, closer and closer to the sun. He kept soaring upwards until he burnt the delicate feathers on his tiny wings. Then he took fright and flew back home. His mother was waiting for him, half dead with fright. 'Well, now I know what fire is,' chirped the little sparrow.

The pigeon in the cloud

From beyond the Dnipro[77] a huge dark cloud appeared. It covered the sun, and everything around became quiet and anxious. Trees stood still and motionless. The cloud exhaled a wave of cold air. Frightened pigeons hid in their bird house. Then something white flashed against the background of the black cloud. It was a pigeon soaring high in the sky towards the approaching thunderstorm. An arrow of fire pierced the cloud and thunder rumbled. The pigeon dived into the cloud as if plunging into water. Everything around turned dark and grim. Dear pigeon, where are you?

The beetle in the matchbox

Yurko caught a horned beetle, placed it in a matchbox, and put it in his pocket. He opened the matchbox to show the beetle to his friends, and then tucked it back in his pocket. When Yurko went to bed, he placed the matchbox with the beetle in it on the windowsill. As Yurko slept soundly, the beetle thought to himself, 'How can I free myself from this wooden prison?' The beetle had two sharp horns. He used them to saw through the box, crawled out of it, and flew out the window in the blink of an eye.

How an old lady found a yellow cucumber

There was just one yellow cucumber left in the garden. It lay among the dry and withered stems of the cucumber plant, lonely and sad, because the mornings were already cold. One day, an old lady went into the garden. She was very happy to find the yellow cucumber. She picked it and brought it home. She cut it open and scraped out the cucumber seeds. The seeds were very surprised. They had thought that the world was green and had turned yellow. Now they could see that the sky was blue, the sun was golden, and the apples on the apple trees were pink. The old lady spread the cucumber seeds out on a piece of cloth in the sun to dry them. She looked at the seeds and said out loud, 'Next spring, I'll plant these seeds and I'll grow lots of cucumbers.' The seeds listened very carefully to every word that the old lady said.

How a bee sheltered from the rain in a flower

One day, I was sitting by the window observing a spring thunderstorm. I opened the window and saw a rose leaning against the wall. A bee was sheltering inside it. She had snuggled up against its pink petals and folded her wings. I felt sorry for the poor bee: she had not managed to make her way to the safety of her hive. She might have baby bees who were now alone and hungry. Who would feed them? If rain poured down on the bee, the poor thing would drown. I was about to go outside and rescue the bee, when the rain stopped, and the sun came out from behind the clouds. A gentle breeze began to blow. The rose leant over and tipped out some water that had collected in it. The bee shook her wings, crawled to the edge of a petal, and flew home.

Where the ants were scurrying

A squirrel sat in a tree eating a nut. It was so tasty that the squirrel was screwing up his eyes with pleasure. A tiny piece of the nut fell to the ground. Then a second, and a third. Lots of crumbs fell from the nut.

A mother ant was scuttling between the blades of grass, hurrying to find food for her babies. She knew that there were ripe melons at the melon plantation. She saw the nut crumbs falling from the tree. She tried one, and it was delicious!

She took a fragment of the nut to the ant nest and summoned all her neighbours. 'Let's go and gather nuts!' she said.

The ants set off together.

The baby ants ate the piece of nut their mother had brought and shared it with their friends. There was enough for all the ant babies, and even some left over.

The ants from the nest reached the big tree, collected all the pieces of nut and carried them home. Now they would have enough to eat for a long time.

They buzz, but they don't bring any honey

The queen is the oldest bee in the hive and the mother of all the bees. During the hot summer, she sends four young bees to the entrance of the hive every hour and tells them, 'Guard the hive, and do not let any wasps through the entrance, or they will eat all the honey.'

The bees guard the entrance. They watch carefully. If the wings are yellow like the sun, they are bees. If they buzz like bees and smell of wax, they are bees.

But then two wasps sneak up to the hive and quickly dive through the entrance. They buzz like bees, and the guards do not notice them.

The wasps break into the hive and start eating the honey. There is a commotion, and the queen shouts, 'Where were you looking, you cabbage brains? How could you let those thieves in!'

'But they were buzzing like bees,' explained the guards, 'And they had yellow wings and smelt like wax.'

'They may buzz like bees,' said the queen bee, 'But they don't bring any honey.'

What is beyond the forest?

I can still remember that spring day. The sun was shining, and a gentle breeze was whispering in the treetops. Birds were singing, and a rustling sound came from the meadow, so quiet you could barely hear it. I was sitting on top of an ancient burial mound[78] in the steppes and listening to the sounds of spring.

Green fields stretched out in front of me, and a forest lined the horizon.

'What is beyond the forest?' I asked my older brother.

'Fields and villages,' he replied. 'And beyond them, there is another forest.'

'And beyond that forest?'

'The Dnipro.[79] Our mighty Dnipro River.'

'And beyond the Dnipro?'

'More fields, villages, and forests.'

At that time, it was the greatest discovery I had made about the world. I was impressed that the world is so wide. It moved me deeply to learn that Ukraine is so vast and rich.

The violin and the moonbeam

A musician played on his violin during the day. When the sun set, the musician hung his instrument on the wall and went home. The violin hung there, waiting silently for the morning.

During the night, the room was lit up by a moonbeam, and the violin's strings shone in its light. The moonbeam whispered, 'Are you a violin?'

'Yes, I am,' answered the violin with pride. It was rather vain.

'Are you the one who plays so wonderfully? Are you the one that makes people stop and listen to the magical sound of your music?' asked the moon beam.

'Yes, that is me,' boasted the violin.

'Please play for me. I would love to listen to your music.'

But the violin could not play of its own accord, so it remained silent.

The following evening, the moonbeam once again shone on the violin and asked, 'Why are you silent? Why don't you play?'

'Because the musician goes home at night,' said the violin.

'What is a musician?' the moonbeam asked.

'You know, a human,' said the violin.

'So, it is not you who plays the music. It is a human who plays?'

The violin did not answer, but its thickest string let out a quiet groan.

Which is better?

There was once a little girl who liked to ask questions: 'Which is better—an apple or a pear? A rose or a gladiolus? Water or soft drink? A ball or a doll?'

Her mother patiently answered her questions, but she found them surprising. How could anyone say which was better out of a ball and a doll, or a rose and a gladiolus?

Then one day the little girl asked, 'Mum, which is better—a fairy tale or a song?'

'Well, you think about which is better out of the sun and the sky. If you can answer that question, I will tell you which is better out of a story and a song,' replied her mother.

The girl thought about it for a long time but could not decide. She looked at the sky and the bright sun. They were both beautiful and inseparable.

After that, the little girl stopped asking, 'Which is better?'

She asked her questions in a different way: 'What is good about a story?' or 'What is good about a song?'

And her mother was happy to answer.

Cause, phenomenon, effect

Our teacher asked us to write a composition for homework, on the topic 'Cause, phenomenon and effect'. During the lesson he explained how to write the composition, but I did not pay attention.

I arrived home and opened my exercise book, but I did not know what to write. I thought I would go and see Volodia. He always listened carefully during lessons and would know how to start the composition.

I put on some warm clothes and went outside. The pond had already frozen over, though the ice was still thin. I put on my skates and began to skate rapidly over the ice to Volodia's house. It was such fun skating. The wind whistled in my ears, and the skates carried me over the ice like a rocket. But why was the ice making that cracking sound? It must be very thin.

I had nearly reached the other side, when suddenly the ice gave way and I fell into the water with a splash. I was standing up to my knees in water. I just managed to get to the other side and quickly ran to my friend's house. Volodia helped me take off my boots, and we sat and dried them. I asked Volodia how to write my composition about cause, phenomenon and effect.

Volodia laughed. 'Your little adventure is your composition,' he said. 'The ice was thin. That is the cause. The ice gave way under your weight. That is the phenomenon—a rather unpleasant phenomenon. You ended up in the water. That is the effect. The effect is also not very nice.'

Big and small

A cow named Lyska gave birth to a calf. He was still wet but was already jumping around. He bumped his head against his mother's udder and drank his fill of milk. Then he felt like going for a walk.

As he was walking around the yard, he saw a little animal. He touched the animal with his mouth, and its fur was as soft as can be.

'Who are you?' asked the calf.

'I'm an old mother rabbit,' said the little animal.

'You mean to say you already have children?' asked the calf.

'Yes, lots. Happy, fluffy, little bunnies. And who are you?'

'I'm a calf. I have only just been born.'

'Amazing! Just born and so huge,' said the rabbit in surprise.

'And you are old, and have children, but you are so small,' said the calf, who was also surprised. And he thought to himself, 'It is strange how everything is arranged. The old are small, and the babies are big. Life is truly amazing and incomprehensible.'

The curious magpie

A white-sided magpie is perched in a tall oak tree. She is not like other white-sided magpies. She has no tail. Somebody pulled all the feathers from her tail, and all because of her curiosity.

Magpies are very curious and talkative. They want to know everything about everybody and to spread the news among the forest birds.

One day, this magpie saw a little squirrel leap into the hollow of a tree. 'What is in that hollow?' wondered the curious magpie. 'Does the squirrel like living there? What does she do in there?'

With a hip and a hop, the white-sided magpie found herself by the hollow. She was afraid to enter, but her curiosity was stronger than her fear, and she hopped into the hollow. It was very dark inside, and all she could hear was a sort of squeaking. Suddenly, somebody pulled the magpie's tail. The magpie squawked in pain and flew out of the hollow. She settled on a branch of the tree and broke into tears. When she looked around, she saw that she had no tail. That was what her curiosity had led to. And that is how a magpie with white sides became a magpie with no tail.

How spiders wanted to cover the sun

Once upon a time, all the spiders decided that there was far too much sunlight in the world and that they must cover the sun. But how were they to do it?

They pondered this question for a long time and came up with a plan. They decided to sneak up on the sun from all directions at once and cover it with their webs. 'We'll weave a net,' suggested the oldest spider. 'And catch the sun in it, as if it were a sack.'

And that is what they did. They wove a net and caught the sun in it. The whole world turned dark. The spiders were happy. They dragged the net towards their burrow. The sun was furious and burnt the net to a crisp. It scorched the spiders' legs and sailed back up into the blue sky.

Ever since, spiders have been afraid of the sun, and do not walk on the ground. They only crawl over their webs, because of the time when their legs were scorched.

The oak tree and the axe

An oak woke up very early one morning and saw an axe on the ground next to it. The axe was sharp, with a shiny blade, a strong head, and a long oak handle. The oak was surprised. 'Why is an axe lying here?' he wondered.

All day, the mighty oak rustled his leaves, joyfully greeting the sun. But in his heart, he was worried. He kept looking anxiously down at the axe and asking himself, 'Why would anyone leave an axe next to me?'

In the evening, the oak saw a friend, a human being, walking towards him.

'My dear friend,' said the oak. 'Please take away this axe. I cannot sleep while it is around.'

'But it is not doing you any harm,' said the human, in surprise.

'Please take it away,' insisted the oak. 'It is an axe, after all.'

A sparrow's joy

A sparrow laid an egg and started chirping joyfully, announcing the event to the whole world. Everything around her seemed to share her joy: the sun shone more brightly, and the flowers smelt sweeter. There was just one woodpecker who could not understand what all the fuss was about, so he asked the sparrow, 'Why are you chirping so loudly? You're making such a fuss that anyone would think you had laid a whole planet.'

'What do you mean "a whole planet"?' replied the happy sparrow. 'If I had only laid a planet, I would not experience such joy. The sun would not shine so brightly, and the flowers would not smell so sweet. I have laid a sparrow's egg, not a planet. A little sparrow will be born from it. It is not some distant planet, but a living, beating heart.'

The woodpecker listened in silence. He did not understand sparrow language very well.

The cuckoo's sorrow

A cuckoo lays its eggs in other birds' nests. When the cuckoo chicks hatch, they throw the owners' chicks out of the nest.

'Why are you so cruel, cuckoo?' asked the wind one day. 'Why don't you make your own nest and raise your chicks yourself?'

'Let me explain, wind,' answered the cuckoo. 'I am not as cruel as people think. As soon as the forest begins to turn green, caterpillars crawl out of their cocoons. All sorts of caterpillars appear in the forest: big, hairy, green, poisonous. No other bird eats them, but I do. If I did not eat these pests, the forest would die. The caterpillars would eat all the leaves. I simply don't have time to raise my chicks.'

That is what the cuckoo told the wind. It told its story and gave a mournful cry.

'Why do you cry so pitifully?' asked the wind.

'I miss my children,' answered the cuckoo.

'But you do not feed them,' said the wind. 'Other birds feed them.'

'I am saving the forest for them,' said the cuckoo softly.

The legend of the Golden Grain of Truth

A father had two sons. When they were old enough to hold a spade in their hands, the father said to them, 'Take these spades. Let's go and dig the field.'

They dug and dug, but the work seemed hard and meaningless to the brothers.

'Why are we digging?' they asked. 'Why are we even alive on this earth?'

The father replied, 'Do you see that tall mountain?' And he pointed to a huge mountain whose peak was hidden in clouds.

'Yes, we can see it,' answered the sons.

'In that mountain is a Golden Grain of Truth, perhaps somewhere in its depths, perhaps on the surface—no-one knows. People say that whoever finds that Grain of Truth will understand why people live on this earth, what they labour for, why they dig the soil and sow crops, build houses and think about the stars, and who they really are. Go, my sons, and seek the Golden Grain of Truth.'

The brothers walked to the mountain, and it was huge, reaching to the sky. You could not walk around it in a day, and it would take over three days to reach its summit. How would they ever find the Golden Grain of Truth?

They positioned themselves at the foot of the mountain, the older brother on one side, and the younger on the other. They began to dig over the mountain, sifting the soil handful by handful. They did not find any Golden Grain. The younger brother came to the older and said, 'I'm not going to dig any more. I don't want to be a slave to this mountain.'

The older brother replied, 'Even if I have to dig all my life, I'm going to find the Golden Grain of Truth, because I'm not a slave, but a free man. You're the slave, because you don't want to find out why we live on this earth, why we dig the soil and sow crops, build houses and think about the stars.'

The younger brother went and settled on the banks of a river, built himself a shelter, caught fish, and made fish soup. But the older brother dug and dug, sifting every handful of earth in the palm of his hand, seeking the Golden Grain of Truth.

The years passed. The older brother dug on that mountain for ten years without even a day's break. At last, in the eleventh year, when the whole mountain had been dug over and shifted to a new spot, on the very bottom of the mountain, the older brother found the Golden Grain of Truth. It was as small as a poppy seed. The older brother held the grain in the palm of his hand, and the bright light of truth lit up the whole world.

The older brother found out why people live on this earth, dig the soil and sow crops, build houses and think about the stars. He travelled the earth, creating happiness for everyone. He became powerful and invincible because he was a Free Man.

But the younger brother lived in a ramshackle hut. His clothes were tattered, and the bucket in which he boiled his fish soup wore out. He ate raw fish and drank swamp water, because he was a weak-willed slave, a slave to his own laziness, idleness and ignorance. For true freedom lies in the ability to labour day and night to move a mountain, so as to create happiness for others.

Happiness and work

A poor woman had twin sons. When the sons were seven years old, the mother gave them each a bucket, took them by the hand, and said, 'Let's go, my sons, and seek wisdom.'

They walked for a day, then for a second day, and on the third day they came to a tall mountain.

'Within this mountain,' said the mother, 'Wisdom is scattered in tiny golden nuggets. In order to obtain wisdom, you have to fill your bucket with those tiny nuggets of gold. Go and seek wisdom.' And she gave each of her sons a small spade.

The twin sons were very similar to each other in appearance: blue eyes, black eyebrows, and pale faces … but their souls were different. One son was hard working, the other was lazy. The lazy one took his bucket and spade and walked away from the mountain. 'I will go to the river,' he told his hard-working brother. 'I will catch fish and make fish soup.'

But the hard-working son sat by the tall mountain and began to sift through the soil with his little spade. He would take a spadeful of soil and sprinkle it on the ground, and sometimes a tiny nugget of gold fell out. He would put that in his bucket.

Many years passed. The lazy son remembered his hard-working brother and decided to go and visit him and see if he was still alive. He walked for a day, then a second day, and on the third day he came to the mountain. But the mountain was in a different place to where it had been many years earlier, when they were just seven years old. His hard-working brother was standing next to the mountain, and his bucket was full of tiny gold nuggets.

The lazy brother was amazed. He realised his brother had sifted through the whole mountain of soil and had obtained wisdom. And he, being a lazybones, had only learnt to catch fish and make fish soup.

'What are you going to do now?' the lazy son asked his brother.

'I am going to go and seek happiness for our mother.'

'Are you going to buy her happiness with your gold?' asked the lazy son.

'Happiness cannot be bought,' answered the hard-working brother. 'Happiness is achieved through work.'

How Fedko did his homework

Fedko is in grade three. He does not like doing his homework. He comes home from school, drops his schoolbag on the floor, eats, and goes out to play until dusk. Then in the evening he sits down and writes his exercises very quickly, without much effort. He often does not manage to solve his maths problem.

One day Fedko comes home from school and eats. He wants to go out and play, but his mother says, 'Do your homework first, and then go out to play.' Fedko sits at the table, quickly writes his exercises, and solves his maths problem. Today's problem is easy to solve.

Fedko's mother sees that he has written very messily. 'Write it out again, neatly,' she tells him. Fedko does not want to write it again, but he has no choice. He copies out the exercises and the problem, but his mother is still not satisfied. 'You have written it messily again. Write it neatly, or you will not be going out to play today.'

Fedko cries for a long time. He really does not feel like writing it out again. But he thinks, 'If I write it messily, mum will make me write it out again.' And he writes it all out neatly.

That night Fedko's father comes home from work and asks Fedko's mother, 'How is Fedko studying? How did he do his homework today?'

'Fedko is working very well,' says his mother proudly. 'He wrote his homework once and was not satisfied with it. He wrote it out again and was still not satisfied with it. Then he wrote it out a third time, beautifully. Show dad, Fedko.'

Fedko shows his exercise book to his father. 'Well done, Fedko!' says his father proudly. 'You will grow up to be a fine human being.'

Fedko bows his head, and his face turns red.

Two spades

A man bought two new steel spades. He attached one of them to a handle, and it became a hard worker. The spade was used for digging the vegetable garden, chopping up beet to feed to animals, digging holes for planting trees in the spring, and scraping ice off steps in winter.

Meanwhile the second spade lay in the storeroom doing nothing. A year passed, two years, three, four, five, ten, twenty, thirty years passed. The first spade laboured away while the second spade did nothing.

Fifty years passed and the spade's owner grew old. One day he looked at his hard-working old spade and said, 'Look at you. You poor old girl. You're worn out and full of holes … It's time for you to have a rest.'

He removed the hard-working spade from its handle and put it under a bench in the storeroom. And that was where the two spades met—the hard-working one and the idle one. The idle one, recognising her sister, said, 'So, it looks like your master does not need you anymore. How old and worn out you look.'

'Aren't you ashamed to speak like that?' replied the hard-working spade indignantly. 'Look at you! You're rusted all the way through! At least I am worn out through work, while you have rusted through doing nothing.'

'What is work?' asked the idle spade in surprise.

The hard-working spade began to tell her all about trenches dug for the foundations of a large building, about a deep well, about a dam … But the idle spade could not understand a word she said. She asked, 'Why don't I understand anything that you are talking about? We speak the same spade language.'

'You don't understand because you have never experienced the joy of work,' said the hard-working spade.

The volleyball cup

The students at a school were good at playing volleyball. They came first in a district competition. They were awarded a cup—a beautiful metal vase inscribed with the words 'For sporting achievement'. The students were delighted. They argued about who would carry the cup home. They all wanted to hold the cup in their hands.

They placed the cup on a table in a small room, and they placed a poster on the wall with the words 'We play volleyball better than everyone else. This is our reward.' At every assembly the students boasted that they were the best, and their names were printed in the school newspaper.

Students from neighbouring villages began to invite them, saying, 'Come and play against us in a trial of strength.' But the victors did not want to travel anywhere. 'Why do we need to play against them?' they said. 'We already know we are the strongest team.'

A year passed. The victorious team went to the district competition and lost. They had to take their cup into the district office and hand it over to the new victors. The students argued about who would take the cup. Nobody wanted to make the trip.

How a cuckoo sang like a nightingale

A cuckoo wanted to sing like a nightingale, so she went to a wise old nightingale to take lessons. She studied for a long, long time, and eventually she learnt to sing just like a nightingale. She returned to her cuckoo brothers and sisters and broke into song like a nightingale. The cuckoos listened to her in amazement. How could a common cuckoo sing like a nightingale?

Suddenly, a foolish cuckoo chick appeared from nowhere. It settled beside the cuckoo that sang like a nightingale and asked her, 'Why don't you sing like a cuckoo? You are a cuckoo after all.'

'How can you take me for a cuckoo? I am a nightingale!' exclaimed the cuckoo angrily. In fact, she became so angry that she forgot to sing like a nightingale and cried out in cuckoo language, 'Cu-ckoo!'

'She has a cuckoo's tail as well!' commented the other cuckoos, who were no longer so impressed.

The three lazybones

A boy once watched his mother planting potatoes. She dug a hole in the soil, lay three potatoes in it, and covered them with earth. In autumn, he asked his mother to take him to the garden, so he could see what had grown there. He saw that in place of the three small potatoes that she had planted, she harvested ten large potatoes. The boy was overjoyed. He thought, 'Just think what will happen if I plant a baked potato. It will produce ten baked potatoes, and I will have a feast.' And he told his mother of his plan.

His mother smiled and said, 'You can try. Plant a baked potato and see what happens.'

The boy brought three baked potatoes and planted them. After some time, he came to gather the harvest. He dug up his potato bush and unearthed three little boys. They lay together with their eyes closed, snoring away with their arms resting on their fat tummies.

‘Who are you?’ the boy asked in surprise.

‘We are three lazybones. We grew from your baked potatoes. Feed us!’

All through the winter, the boy fed those lazybones. ‘This is no good,’ he thought. ‘From now on, I’ll plant only raw potatoes.’

In the spring, he planted an entire vegetable bed. To his surprise, while he was planting the potatoes, the three lazybones disappeared. Who knows where they went. Perhaps they returned to the earth, where they could rest undisturbed.

The stuffed bird and the song

A songbird lived in a garden. Its song was so lovely that people would stop to admire the beauty of the bird and listen to its melodious singing.

Beside the garden was a small house, and in that house lived a grim, silent, bad-tempered man, the sort that children call a ‘grouch’. This grouch liked to catch butterflies and dry them for his collection. He would catch a butterfly, pin it to a sheet of cardboard, and keep it for himself.

The grouch caught the songbird, killed it, skinned it with all its feathers, stuffed it, and kept it as a decoration in his home. The bird was now perched inside, beautiful, but dead. Nobody wanted to admire its dead beauty. Now the garden was completely different, no longer full of joyful sound, but silent and gloomy, because the song was no more.

And the grouch wondered why children had stopped coming to his garden.

Six human beings and one despicable creature

Seven strong men cut down a mighty tree in the forest. They cut off its branches, hoisted it onto their shoulders, and started carrying it to the river. They were making a raft from tall trees. It was hard, exhausting work, but human beings are not afraid of the hardest work if they have a noble goal and can be masters of their fate. Those seven brave men were geologists. They needed to build a raft to float downstream through the taiga and reach a large city before winter arrived.

It was a very long way from the forest to the river. They had to pass through thick undergrowth, bushes, and prickly grass. Six of the men were exhausted, but they knew that they needed to keep moving if they were to reach their goal. The seventh man was a weak-willed, despicable creature. He bent his knees slightly so that the trunk of the tree hardly touched his shoulder. He held on to the trunk so that his feet lifted from the ground. It was easy for him to walk because his comrades were carrying him as well as the tree.

Finally, the geologists reached the riverbank. They cast the trunk aside and lay down on the grass. They only wanted one thing: to rest. A minute later, the one who had deceived them all rose to his feet and shouted, 'Where's the boss? Why doesn't he feed us hard workers? How can you treat people like this?'

The six strong, brave fellows raised their heads and looked into the eyes of the seventh man. It seemed to them that his indignation was sincere, and they thought, 'It is true. It would be nice to have some food now.' The hideous part of what was happening at that moment was that those six strong, brave, honest men, looking into the eyes of a weak-willed and despicable creature, thought that he was a human being just like themselves.

A butterfly learns about fire

A mother butterfly gave birth to a baby butterfly. His bright green wings were speckled with blue dots, and his curious eyes were drawn to everything.

'What is that?' asked the baby butterfly.

'That is fire,' answered his mother.

'What is fire?'

'Fire is very hot,' warned his mother.

'What does "hot" mean?'

'It means it can burn you. If you get too close, it will burn your wings and you will die.'

'That is really interesting,' said the baby butterfly. 'I want to see for myself what fire is like.'

And before his mother had a chance to grab hold of his wings, the baby butterfly took off. His eyes were fixed on the fire, and he flew closer and closer, determined to learn all about fire. Suddenly, his wings burst into flame. He just had time to cry out, 'Now, I know what fire is!' And he was gone.

How ants know the rain is coming

In the forest there was an ant hill, teeming with life. The ants were always rushing off somewhere or returning from somewhere.

One day, the ants became anxious. They blocked all the entrances to their ant hill with lumps of earth and leaves.

'What is going on, dear ants?' asked a butterfly. 'Why are you blocking all the entrances to your home?'

'Rain is coming, and we are preparing for it,' they replied. 'We are blocking all the entrances to prevent water from flooding our chambers.'

'How do you know that rain is coming?' asked the curious butterfly.

'Far off in the distance, a cold, dark cloud is approaching,' they said. 'A cold wind is blowing from it. We can sense its cold breath.'

The wet shirt and the dry shirt

A mother had twin boys, Ivan and Serhii, each about twelve years old.

When the summer holidays began, the mother said to her sons, 'Take a hoe each, and go and work in the fields.'

Just before sunrise the mother woke her sons. They took their hoes and went to weed the sunflowers.

In the evening, the brothers returned from their work. Ivan's shirt was wet, but Serhii's was dry.

The boys washed and had dinner. Ivan went straight to bed, knowing that he had to work in the morning. But Serhii went out into the yard, sat on a bench and listened to music.

The next day, as soon as the brothers came home, their mother looked at their shirts. Ivan's was wet, but Serhii's was dry.

That night, their mother sat by their bed until midnight, while the two sons slept. When she looked at Ivan, she smiled, but when she looked at Serhii, she gave a deep sigh.

The best ruler

Mykola and Roman sit next to each other. Mykola nearly always gets an 'excellent' mark for his written work and never gets any mark less than 'good'. Roman only manages to get 'satisfactory'.

Today the teacher handed back the children's exercise books with the dictations they had written during the previous lesson. Mykola was again awarded 'excellent', but Roman was not awarded any mark at all. That meant he had made lots of mistakes. The teacher had written, 'You need to work harder.' Roman felt sad.

After their language lesson, the students went to the workshop for their manual arts lesson. The teacher gave each student a piece of wood and asked them to make a ruler. Mykola and Roman worked side by side. Mykola's ruler turned out uneven and crooked, but Roman's was beautifully even and smooth. The teacher said, 'Roman has the best ruler. I am awarding him an 'excellent' mark. Mykola, I am afraid I cannot give you any mark. You need to work harder.' Mykola felt sad.

When the lesson ended, Roman asked his teacher, 'Can I please have the ruler I made?'

'Yes, you can take it,' said the teacher.

Roman took his ruler back to the classroom and put it on his desk, next to the exercise book in which he had received no mark for his dictation.

What do stars taste like?

A dog told a pig about the stars in the sky. The pig found this interesting, and he started asking the dog lots of questions: 'What do these stars look like? Are they big or small? Are they hard or soft? And, most importantly, what do they taste like?'

The dog was surprised that the pig was so dim-witted. He did his best to explain what stars were, but the pig could not make any sense of his wise words. He was especially surprised to hear that humans (the dog's friends) would raise their heads and gaze at the stars, admiring their beauty.

'So, stars must be as sweet as acorns,' said the pig happily. 'Now, I understand why humans admire them so much.'

'Stars are tasteless,' objected the dog.

The pig's jaw dropped in shock. 'What is the point of stars, if they are tasteless?' he wondered.

We love drawing

The children at a boarding school went home for the summer holidays. Only three children remained at the school—Marynka, Volodia and

Vasylko. They had all just completed graded five. None of them had a mother or father.

The drawing teacher at the boarding school was Oleksandra Mykolaivna. She had only recently graduated from her institute. The grade five students often misbehaved at the young teacher's drawing lessons. The worst pranksters were Volodia and Vasylko. When they did not feel like drawing, they made paper planes and threw them around the classroom.

When they saw that Oleksandra Mykolaivna was not going away for the summer holidays, Volodia, Vasylko and Marynka were surprised. Why had she stayed at school over summer? In the morning the teacher came to the children's dormitory and said, 'Children, if you want, we can go for a walk in the forest.'

The children were delighted! They really wanted to go into the forest. Vasylko, Volodia and Marynka took enough food to last a whole day, and Vasylko quietly whispered, 'Let's take our drawing albums. We can draw in the forest.'

It was fun in the forest. Oleksandra Mykolaivna knew lots of stories. After lunch Marynka and the boys took out their albums and began to draw. They drew the forest, the birds and the flowers.

'I didn't know you liked drawing,' said Oleksandra Mykolaivna in surprise.

'We love drawing,' said the boys. And Marynka added, 'I'm going to draw every day now.'

The stone

In a clearing, under a spreading oak tree, was a well. For many years it gave water to people. Travellers liked to rest under the oak tree next to the well.

One day a boy came to the oak tree. 'I wonder what will happen if I throw a stone into the well? It will probably make a big splash,' thought the boy, and he picked up a large stone and threw it into the well.

There was a loud splash. The boy laughed, ran away and soon forgot about his prank.

The stone fell to the bottom of the well and blocked the spring that fed it. Water stopped flowing into the well, and it dried up. The grass in the clearing died and the oak tree died, because the underground water now took a different path. A nightingale stopped nesting in the oak tree, and its song could no longer be heard. The meadow became a sad and empty place.

Many years passed. The boy grew up, became a father, and then a grandfather.

One day, he came to where the green clearing had been, where the leaves of the spreading oak tree had rustled, and travellers had come to drink the pure water from the well.

There was no clearing, no oak tree, and no well. There was just yellow sand, and clouds of dust were scattered by the wind.

'Where did it all go?' wondered the grandfather.

The black sparrow

A grey sparrow found its way into a chimney and was instantly covered with black soot. Then he flew to a grain storage shed to peck at some grain. The other sparrows saw him and opened their beaks wide in astonishment. 'Who are you?' they asked. 'We have never seen a small, black bird like you.'

The sparrow did not reply. He was rather vain and looked sullenly at the sparrows as if seeing them for the first time.

'It is a bird from overseas,' declared a wise old sparrow.

'It is a miracle,' chirped some chicks. 'Look at how his black feathers shine'.

'It is a steppe nightingale,' suggested another sparrow.

The black sparrow listened to all their observations, and then burst out joyfully, 'I'm just a sparrow! I'm covered with soot, that's all.'

Face to face with his own little devil

This happened at our school during a parent meeting.[80] The parents were sitting at the desks, while the teacher told them about their children's academic progress and behaviour.

A young machine operator named Volodymyr Tkach was sitting in the front row. His son was studying in grade three. The teacher was explaining that Tkach's son lacked attention and was too restless and fidgety.

'Your son Myshko sits in that desk where you are sitting now,' said the teacher, turning to Volodymyr Tkach. 'He is too busy getting up to his own mischief to listen to me when I am explaining something. Look what he has carved on his desk. And he did that during a grammar lesson, when it is important to listen to every word a teacher says.'

The father looked down at the desk and saw a carving of a little devil with a weird, hideous horn. The father felt ashamed. 'My goodness,' he thought. 'What sort of father am I if my son carves devils on his desk instead of studying?'

The father hung his head in shame, and his eyes wandered over to the corner of a desk by the window. His gaze settled on something that seemed familiar but long forgotten. On the edge of that desk, the father saw another little devil. It was half-erased but still visible.

'That's my little devil! I carved it when I was in grade three … no, it must have been grade four. That was my desk,' recalled the father. He could not take his eyes off this evidence of his own past mischief. And it seemed to him that everyone was looking at him and passing judgement on him as a parent.

I saw you again, sunbeam!

The sun's fiery disc touched the horizon. Little Serhiiko watched the sun set. He did not want to part with it.

Already half the sun was hidden below the horizon, then just a thin band of fire, then the last sparks of sunlight flashed and went out.

Serhiiko raised his head and looked at a tall poplar. The top of the tree was lit up with purple light.

'From there, the sun is still visible,' thought Serhiiko. 'You might be hiding from me, sunbeam, but I am going to see you again.'

The boy quickly scrambled up the tree trunk, and when he reached the top, his eyes lit up with joy. Once again, he could see a thin band of the sun's disc above the horizon. The band sunk lower and lower, melted, and again the last sparks flashed and went out.

'I did see you again though, sunbeam!' shouted the boy.

Lazy pillow

Little Yarynka has to get up very early to go to school, but she never feels like it, she really doesn't feel like it.

In the evening Yarynka asks, 'Grandpa, why don't I feel like getting up in the morning? Teach me, Grandpa, how to sleep so I feel like getting up and going to school.'

'It's because you've got a lazy pillow,' answers Grandpa.

'And what can I do to it, so it won't be lazy?' asks Yarynka.

'I know a secret,' whispers Grandpa. 'When you don't feel like getting up, take your pillow outside into the fresh air and give it a good beating with your fists. Then it won't be lazy.'

'Really?' says Yarynka joyfully. 'I'll do that tomorrow.'

It is still dark, and Yarynka has to get ready for school. She doesn't feel like getting up, but it's time she gave that pillow a lesson and beat the laziness out of it. She jumps up quickly, gets dressed, takes her pillow outside, puts it on a bench and pummels it with her fists. Then she comes back into the house, puts the pillow on the bed and smiles.

The cat miaows, a blizzard howls outside, and Grandpa chuckles to himself.

The singing feather

There is an amazing bird called the Little Bustard. It can sing … And what do you think it sings with, children? It sings with its wing. On its wing it has a special singing feather. When it is flying, if it wants to sing, it arranges its wings in such a way that air blows through the singing feather and it sings. It gives out a fine whistle, similar to the sound of the thinnest string on the violin when you pass the bow over it, or to the song of the wind when it blows through slender reed stems.

But one day a misfortune befell the Little Bustard. It lost its singing feather. It came loose and fell to the ground. The Little Bustard wanted to sing, but its singing feather was gone.

A little boy named Serhiiko found the Little Bustard's singing feather. He picked it up and ran, and the feather started singing.

The Little Bustard heard its feather singing, flew to the boy, and begged, 'Boy, please give me back my singing feather. I cannot live without its song.'

The boy gave the singing feather back to the Little Bustard.

That boy named Serhiiko grew into a man who lived for many years. He often remembered the Little Bustard and thought, 'Each person has their own singing feather. Anyone who does not have a singing feather is unfortunate indeed.'

The curious poppy seed

A grandmother was carrying ripe poppies from her garden.

'Where are we being carried?' a curious poppy seed whispered in a frightened tone, from the depths of a poppyhead.

The curious poppy seed stretched out its tiny head to take a look around and fell onto the ground. It shouted out, 'Grandma! Don't leave me behind!'

But the grandmother was busy with her own thoughts and did not pay any attention to the cries of the curious poppy seed.

A wonderful world opened up before the curious poppy seed. Above its head, reaching up towards the clouds, the tops of giant plants were rustling. And above those were even taller plants, and beyond them, plants that were so tall it was impossible to see their tops.

The curious poppy seed became frightened. It felt as though it was completely alone in the world, and it began to cry. Then it fell asleep and dreamt heavenly dreams of giant white blankets descending and covering the earth …

The curious poppy seed awoke feeling warm. It was lying on a soft feather bed, and everything around it was singing. It wanted to see who was singing, so it raised its head and found to its amazement that instead of a head it had a green shoot. The shoot raised itself from the ground and divided into many small leaves. There were more and more leaves by the minute.

The curious poppy seed became a tall, slender plant with spreading leaves. At its very top, a pink flower was blooming.

All this was strange and joyful. However, the greatest joy the curious poppy seed felt was when it saw another pink flower next to it, just like itself. And then it saw another flower, and another, and behind those, an entire sea of pink flowers.

'So, I am not wholly alone in this world after all!' cried the curious poppy seed, and it laughed. And everything around it laughed with it: the sun, the blue sky, the green meadow and the dark blue forest. The whole world was laughing.

Beautiful Natalochka

Teachers call our 5B class unruly. We have lots of students who misbehave. Myshko, for example, will take a fly, dip it in ink and put it down on his neighbour's desk. The fly will crawl all over the desk drawing patterns and the boys will laugh. One day, Myshko drew a rooster on his forehead .

Then there is Fedko. One day, he quietly jumped out the window, sat in the branch of a tree and wrote his dictation from there. At the end of the lesson, he climbed back into the classroom, sat in his desk, and handed the teacher his exercise book. The teacher was surprised. 'You weren't in the classroom,' he said. 'Where did you suddenly appear from?' Everyone laughed.

Petko can make a sound just like a cricket. One day, he was so convincing the teacher stopped and listened. 'I wonder where that cricket lives,' she said. 'I'll come back in the evening and see if I can find out. I like the sound of a cricket.' We could not tell if the teacher was joking or if she really thought a cricket had made its home in our classroom.

And Hrytsko's shirt is always covered in ink stains.

But then, in spring, a new student named Natalochka joined our class. She had blue eyes and long blonde hair. And her eyes were so gentle and kind that our boys could not meet them for long; they would lower their eyes. Something strange happened to our class. All the wild boys suddenly became meek and mild.

For three weeks the teachers had been asking Myshko to get his hair cut, but he had ignored them. Now he suddenly had a haircut and started carrying a little mirror in his pocket. He no longer drew roosters on his forehead.

Fedko covered all his exercise books. Someone whispered to Petko during the class to make a sound like a cricket, and got a punch in return. And most amazing of all, Hrytsko's shirt was spotless.

What on earth has happened to our 5B class?

The extra rose

Today was joyful occasion at our school. The grade ten students[81] had their final lesson. They lined up outside on the grass in front of our large school windows. The girls wore white dresses, and the boys wore black suits.

The grade one students lined up opposite the graduating students. They were happy and full of life. Each grade one student was holding a rose. As soon as the school principal concluded his congratulatory speech, the grade one students were to run over to the graduating students opposite and present each one with a rose.

The principal began his speech. At first, the graduating students were smiling, but gradually they became thoughtful. Little Natalia, a grade one student standing at the end of her line, noticed that the grade ten girl at the end of the line opposite was wiping away tears with a handkerchief. Natalia was surprised. Why was that grade ten student crying? Today was a joyful occasion—the last bell![82]

The principal concluded his speech. The grade one students ran over to the grade ten students. Little Natalia ran as well, but things did not go to plan. There was no-one for her to give her rose to. The grade ten student at the end of the line, who she thought she was paired with, had already received a rose from another girl. All the grade ten students were already holding roses and smiling.

In all the hustle and bustle, nobody noticed the little girl standing to one side holding a rose. The sad, lonely flower was reflected in the sad eyes of that little girl.

Her father's alphabet book

Mum and dad were still in bed. It was still dark outside, but little Sonia had already woken up. Today she was going to school for the first time. Now she was a student.

The night before, Sonia had packed her school bag with textbooks and exercise books, but for some reason her father had not given her the alphabet book. He had said, 'I'll give it to you tomorrow, when you are going to school.'

Sonia washed and dressed. She went into the garden and picked some asters. All the children would be bringing flowers today. Her mother and father had also got ready. They wanted to accompany Sonia to school.

'Dad, can I have my alphabet book?' asked Sonia.

Her father opened the cupboard. She thought he would give her the new alphabet book that her mother had recently bought at the shop, but the book in his hand was quite different. It was also an alphabet book, but an old one, with a different picture on the cover.

'This is my alphabet book,' said her father. 'I learnt to read from it. If you want, Sonia, you can learn to read from it too.'

Sonia took her father's alphabet book in her hands and turned the pages. The drawings and letters were the same as in the new book, but not quite the same, because her father had learnt to read from them.

'I don't need the new alphabet book,' said Sonia. 'I'll learn to read from your book.'

She put her father's alphabet book in her schoolbag, and they all went to school.

A bee flew into the classroom

It was a warm, sunny autumn day. The windows were open in the grade three classroom. The class was very, very quiet. The teacher asked Natalka to come out to the blackboard. She had to write a sentence about autumn rain, to show she could spell the word 'autumn'.

Suddenly, everyone could hear the buzzing of a bee. It had flown into the classroom and was flying around the class. We put our pens down and watched the bee with bated breath. It flew up to the teacher's desk and then towards the wall. It did not seem to see the open windows. We wanted to call out, 'Why don't you fly towards the window?' but we were afraid to say anything in case we startled the bee.

Then it flew around the teacher's desk and out the window. We all gave a sigh of relief. Outside the sun was shining. Natalka smiled and wrote on the blackboard the words 'autumn sun'.

How a little girl offended her alphabet book

A little girl started going to school. Her mother gave her a bright new alphabet book, with colourful pictures. The little girl soon learnt to read and left her alphabet book under a pile of old newspapers. The alphabet book felt hurt.

One day the little girl came home from school, put her school bag down, and had some dinner. Then she opened up her school bag, took out a book with a picture of red sails on the cover, and started reading. Suddenly she heard a tiny little voice, like a small child, saying, 'Why have you forgotten all about me, little girl. I was the one who taught you to read.'

The little girl was amazed that her alphabet book should start talking to her. She took it out from under the pile of old newspapers. She felt sorry for the alphabet book. She wiped the dust from its cover and said, 'Forgive me, alphabet book. I will always remember that you taught me to read.'

The little girl put the alphabet book on her bookshelf, and ever since, it has stood next to her most interesting books.

Ink on his finger

This happened in grade two. During the break, some mischievous child wiped ink on the wall by the door, leaving a clear fingerprint.[83]

The bell rang, and the teacher entered the classroom. She noticed the fingerprint and asked, 'Who wiped ink on the wall?'

Everyone was silent.

Myshko was sitting in the front row, and he had ink on his finger.

'Was it you?' asked the teacher.

'No, it wasn't me,' answered Myshko.

'You should be ashamed of yourself!' scolded the teacher. 'You've made a mess, and you don't have the courage to own up to it.'

Myshko just stood there hanging his head. He was waiting for Petro, who was sitting in the back row, to stand up and say, 'It was me who wiped ink on the wall.'

But Petro just hid his hand under the desk and said nothing.

Didn't he realize that that was a despicable way to behave?

To hear the bell sooner

The teacher told the children about the speed of sound. Everyone was interested to learn that sound does not travel all that quickly—about 340 metres per second.

'Consider this,' said the teacher. 'You see a ball hit the ground and bounce up. You only hear the sound of the ball hitting the ground when it is already in the air.'

Myshko said that he had observed that phenomenon but had not been able to explain it. 'Now I understand,' added Myshko.

But the one who showed the most interest in the way sound travels was Yurko. He put a question to the teacher. 'The sound of the bell ringing for our break travels to us from the corridor. Does that mean that the sound is first heard near the door, where the back row of desks is, and then near the blackboard, where the front row is?'

'Yes, that is true,' answered the teacher.

'Could you please move me to the back row?' asked Yurko.

'Why?' asked the teacher in surprise.

'I want to be the first to hear the bell,' said Yurko, 'So I can go out for my break sooner.'

All the books are so beautiful

Little Nastusia's mother gave her some money and said, 'Go to the bookshop and buy two books for yourself. There are some beautiful books there about birds, butterflies, animals, and fish.'

Little Nastusia went to the bookshop and was amazed to see how many books they had. She stood in front of a bookshelf, her eyes shining with joy, because she had already learnt how to read. She looked at the books and read their titles. There was one was about a hedgehog, and one about a cat. There was one about a sparrow, and another about a swallow. That one over there was about a lamb, and next to it was one about a grey bull calf.

Little Nastusia began to worry. 'What should I do?' she wondered. 'I only have enough money for two books, and look how many beautiful books there are! If I buy the books about the hedgehog and the cat, I won't be able to read about the sparrow, the swallow, and the lamb. How can I go home without them? If I buy the books about the lamb and the swallow, I won't be able to read about the hedgehog and the cat.'

It was a painful choice for little Nastusia to make. So painful, that she burst into tears.

Repeating a year

This happened at our school. Fedko was studying in grade three. There was no-one to make Fedko study. The only person he lived with was his mother, and she was always at work. The teacher would set reading, writing, or maths problems for homework, but Fedko just went out to play without a care in the world.

Fedko's mother was often called up to the school. The teachers complained about the boy and said he did not study properly. His mother cried, and Fedko hung his head.

Each summer he was set extra work, and somehow or other he managed to complete it, and was able to progress from class to class. But in grade three his teacher said, 'I cannot move you on to grade four. All the others are reading well, but you cannot read. And your writing is poor.'

The last day of the school year arrived. It was the final lesson in grade three. The teacher announced that everyone would be progressing to grade four, except for Fedko, who would have to repeat the year.

The class fell silent. Everyone turned and looked at the back row, where Fedko was sitting. Everyone felt sorry for him. Their eyes were sad, and Fedko was crying.

'We will never study with Fedko again,' thought the children, and they felt pain.

'I will never study with my friends again,' thought Fedko, and a magical bird, called repentance, awoke in Fedko's heart.

'Mariia Petrivna, please let Fedko study over the summer holidays, and we will help him,' begged the children.

'Mariia Petrivna, please don't make me repeat the year … I will study now,' pleaded Fedko.

'All right,' said the teacher with a sigh. 'If you can really make yourself study, you can stay with your friends.'

The blue pencil

Fedko's father gave him a blue pencil. The boy brought his present to school and showed it to his friend Yurko. Yurko drew a line on some paper with the pencil and admired the blue colour.

'Let's swap,' he suggested to Fedko. 'I'll give you my metal lion, and you give me your blue pencil.'

'Will you really give me your metal lion for a blue pencil?' asked Fedko in surprise.

He knew that Yurko's father had bought him a metal lion the year before, and although it was only iron, it was so well made that it looked real. In the middle of the toy was a spring, and if you wound it up, the lion jumped. Once Yurko had wound up the spring and put the metal lion on the green grass. It had jumped once, twice, three times, and the sparrows perched on the roof had flown away in fear.

Yurko swapped his metal lion for the blue pencil.

Fedko became the master of the metal lion. He wound it up and admired its jumping. His cat, seeing the strange creature of iron jumping on the floor, miaowed pitifully and hid behind a wardrobe.

'Look what a frightening animal I have,' boasted Fedko.

Yurko began to draw with the blue pencil. On the first day, he drew the steppe, and a tall burial mound on the horizon. Everything was as blue as a transparent spring sky.

Fedko admired the blue steppe, but to him the metal lion still seemed incomparably better.

Then Yurko drew an orchard. It was an unusual, magical orchard, with blue apple trees, blue bunches of grapes and blue pear trees.

Fedko could not take his eyes off the magical orchard. For some reason he no longer felt like watching his metal lion jump.

Then Yurko drew some distant blue mountains, and high above them a blue moon. Fedko sighed deeply. He felt upset.

'Why did I swap?' he thought. 'The metal lion can only jump, but the blue pencil … Oh, the blue pencil … You can draw anything with the blue pencil!'

On the fourth day Yurko brought a new drawing. It was a blue fairy-tale drawing. A blue bird floated on a wonderful blue sea, while a blue cloud sailed overhead.

Fedko saw this drawing and burst into tears.

At home he could not bear to even look at the metal lion, which could do nothing but jump. He hid the metal toy in the very bottom of his wardrobe.

The book and the sweets

A mother collected a big bundle of old newspapers and said to her sons, 'Take these newspapers and hand them in for recycling. You can buy some sweets or toys with the money you get. Buy whatever you like.'

Mykola and Andrii took the newspapers to the reception point and received a whole *karbonavets*[84] in return.

'Let's share the money,' said Mykola, who was in grade five. 'Then we can each buy whatever we want.'

'All right,' said Andrii, who was in grade three. 'Fifty *kopiika* for you and fifty for me.'

The boys went to the shop. They walked from counter to counter for a long time, trying to decide what to buy. Mykola bought some sweets and started eating them. He gave one to Andrii and asked, 'Will you buy sweets too and share them with me?'

Andrii thanked Mykola for the sweet and answered, 'I'm going to buy a book.'

Andrii bought a book about the mysteries of the sea. He walked home with the book, admiring the pictures of unusual fish. Mykola ate up all his sweets, but Andrii could not tear himself away from his book. He read it through and then read it again. Mykola read the book as well. A beautiful, magical, amazing world opened up before him.

The book about the mysteries of the sea is still lying on the table. Every time Mykola sees it, he remembers the day when he ate sweets, while Andrii read his book.

UNFINISHED STORY

* The most joyful thing and the saddest thing

A teacher told his students, 'I would like you to draw the most joyful thing you can think of and the saddest thing you can think of.'

Mykolka opened his exercise book and started thinking about what to draw. He remembered a hot summer with fields of golden wheat, a morning by the pond, and a field of flowering clover.

He drew a clover flower and a bee buzzing above it. 'That is the most joyful thing I can think of,' he said.

'Why?' asked his teacher.

'Because the sun is shining, a lark is singing high in the sky, and the sky is the deepest blue.'

'And what are you going to draw for the saddest thing you can think of?'

Mykolka drew a tree. Its yellow leaves were floating to the ground, and rain was falling on the tree's bare branches.

'Why is do you think that is sad?' asked the teacher.

'Because … '

On the Homeland

In our life there are values that are commensurable and those that are not. We can discuss for a long time which is better—a family or solitude, devotion to an ideal or impartiality. But there are things that cannot be compared or equated with anything else. These are the Homeland, the Fatherland, filial loyalty, devotion to the land where you were born and established your identity, to the people who nurtured and educated you, to the joys and sorrows that accompany you from birth to the grave.[85]

The word 'Homeland' refers to the land of your birth. Your true birth as a citizen—as a thoughtful personality, inspired by noble ideals, as one who labours and fights for the triumph of truth and happiness, as a family member—takes place due to the fact that you are a child of the people. The people's rich history, its greatness and glory, its love and hope, its unbreakable connection to places infinitely dear to our hearts, that live on in us eternal, indestructible, inextinguishable—all these things are reflected in us as the sun's fiery rays are reflected in a drop of water.

Your mother gives birth to your flesh, while the Fatherland gives birth to your human, civic soul. There is nothing dearer than the Fatherland. A true human being will sacrifice their life without hesitation in the name of the Fatherland's happiness, greatness and independence, because a life devoid of the Fatherland's happiness, greatness and independence is not only sorrowful, but shameful.[86]

On patriotism

For each of us the Homeland begins with something small, something that appears rather plain and unremarkable. Something enters the life of each one of us, forever, until our last breath, something unique and indispensable, like a mother's breast, her loving touch, like our native language. It is our home that embodies the living image of the Fatherland. For each of us, the reason we become a patriot is that our home stays in our hearts for the duration of our lives, always arousing strong feelings, as the first life-giving source from which we sprang.

Knowing and understanding our Homeland; establishing a patriotic core in our soul; patriotic guidance during childhood, adolescence and youth; the spiritually rich, active and selfless life of a patriot—these are extremely subtle and complex elements in that boundlessly complex interweaving of ideas, actions, convictions, thoughts and aspirations that are collectively referred to as a patriotic upbringing. The complexity and distinctive feature of patriotic feelings, ideas, convictions and deeds is characterised by the fact that in ordinary life, in everyday work, we are not presented with the ultimate standard against which to measure this greatest of values that is so hard to comprehend. Such a standard only becomes apparent to us as educators, as fathers, mothers, and teachers, in times of great trial and tribulation, when the Homeland is in mortal danger. The true test of patriotic feelings and convictions is war. Only in confrontation with mortal danger is the true essence of loyalty and dedication revealed.

The true test of our values

We, as educators, should not forget this even for a moment. We should not forget that genuine patriotism is unthinkable unless it is manifested in our lives, unless it involves the strenuous application of all our energies. Words about how much I love my Homeland and what I am prepared to do for its sake do not carry any weight, and students should not be encouraged to repeat them. We must remember the most important thing: that everything we are doing today, in peacetime, is a preparation for the terrible trials that may lie ahead. In the contemporary world, these are not something abstract to be theorised about, but a living reality.

How a human being relates to grief, misfortune, suffering, despair, confusion and psychological pain, both their own and that of others, reflects their ideological core, their attitude to good and evil, to the ideal. As educators we should educate our students to have a deep understanding and appreciation that there are different kinds of grief and misfortune. One kind of grief uplifts and strengthens a human being, while another debases and brings shame. People endure the former kind with their heads held high, while they are ashamed of the latter.

My educational ideal is to ensure that a human being can face and endure the misfortune that uplifts and refines, but I will not accept or tolerate misfortune that humiliates and causes shame, the misfortune that drains a human being. There is no place for such grief and misfortune in our lives.

A war is a national misfortune, a national tragedy. The killing of one human being by another can evoke nothing but hatred and condemnation in human souls. But we live in a world where everyone must be prepared for war—not only physically, but even more importantly, psychologically and morally. One of the aims of pedagogical ethics, as I see it, is to prepare my students—human beings with kind, sensitive, noble hearts and refined sensitivity—to be ready to kill, to destroy an enemy who encroaches on our sacred borders, on the peaceful labour and quiet, peace-loving life of our people. However, this does not mean in any circumstances that we should evoke cruelty in young souls by teaching children to kill. It is more complex and subtle than that.

The psychological readiness to courageously face a cruel and implacable enemy comes from our students' courage, endurance, kindness, sensitivity and generosity, not from cruelty and ruthlessness. A cruel person is always a coward, but a kind and sincere person is brave, generous and courageous.

Developing the concept of the Fatherland

We should never be tempted to think that our patriotic education in the classroom has been successful and that we can measure and see our success. It is naïve to suggest that if a child achieves good marks, they are fulfilling their patriotic duty, they will become true citizens, and suchlike. The only true criteria for assessing the value of our educational work is whether our students are oriented towards a future life of patriotic service to the Fatherland and are motivated to discover where their true field of service lies.

Patriotic education has countless facets. The first is one's perception of the world. From the first steps of their conscious life, from the moment they think and experience, a human being should not only see and understand everything that they encounter in the world, but also love and value it, consider it *theirs*, and feel themselves to be a part of the world into which they were born. Pay attention to the thousands of intricate threads that tie a person to their Fatherland—this is the first advice one should give to a father, mother or teacher when discussing patriotic education. We take care to ensure that a child's consciousness, and their emotional memory, retain the tiniest details of their native land, those unforgettable places that together constitute a world that is dear to them. We refer to this as the *heart's memory*. As educators, we should sensitively awaken half-forgotten recollections of childhood, helping our students to resurrect them, reestablishing them in their memories, and opening their eyes to fresh images of their native land.

We walk with children through our native land, so they can see, feel, remember and experience wonder. I am convinced that images of nature, images of people at work, manifestations of spiritual life, everything that I help the children to see, remains in their souls forever as a dear memory of their Fatherland.

A summer night. We are standing on a tall burial mound in the steppe. The sun has set. Dusk is enveloping the steppe and the burial mounds. The fields change colour several times. I choose some vivid, expressive words to help the children experience more deeply what they see and understand … Many years pass. I meet my former students who have come from far corners of our country. They are serving in the army or working. Each of them remembers that summer night. People who have been battered by severe winds, who have lived through many difficult circumstances, remember with sincere warmth how the dusk spread in gentle waves from the ravines across the steppe, how the forest on the horizon was covered by a purple haze. They even remember a solitary crow that flew towards the forest. They remember a stalk of sagebrush that was growing on the burial mound. My students tell me how they recall these things far away from our native village, and the more their childhood years recede, the brighter and dearer these memories become. They excite the soul, drawing them back to their native land.

I attach particular significance to the fact that objects and phenomena that have become familiar to us as adults are experienced by a child for the first time. It is not a matter of indifference to me how a child will see their first sunrise or hear the cry of a crane, what thoughts and feelings awake in a young soul when they first encounter another's grief, at what moment a little person experiences love and care for the first time. I am concerned to ensure that precious, unforgettable images are preserved in the heart's memory of each student. These are the thousands of threads that tie the heart to our native land forever.

The idea of the Fatherland is formed in complex and subtle ways. It will only take hold of our thoughts and feelings, and give us strength of spirit, when something is dear to our heart. Patriotic thoughts, feelings and aspirations captivate us, and become a deep personal motivation, due to the moral richness of our own spiritual world.

The more vividly something dear to the soul is visualised by the mind's eye of a child, the more deeply they experience their own self-worth. I consider it important that there are days in the spiritual life of each of my pupils when, speaking figuratively, time stops for a moment, images of the surrounding world are imprinted in their consciousness, and an eternal flame is lit to guide them on their life's journey.

On citizenship

During their childhood years we should not bombard students with pompous, flowery words about the Homeland. The most important thing is to light flames to guide them on their life's journey, to open their eyes to all that is dear and speaks of home.

I consider it an important educational goal to ensure that as early as possible children embrace with their hearts and minds the interests of society, the Homeland, and all of humankind, that they view the objects and events in the surrounding world from a civic point of view, that they take to heart the misfortunes and concerns of others who appear to have no direct relationship to their personal lives. But in order to do that we should begin our discovery of the world with things that are close to the child, with the family, the hearth, the lives of grandfathers or great-grandfathers, with certificates for military service during World War II, yellowed by time.

A human being is truly educated only if they have civic thoughts, worries, concerns, hopes, joys and sorrows from an early age. The essence of our educational system is that a child lives in a world of civic thoughts and actions that are the main source of their joys and sorrows.

This is an extremely important, complex and subtle matter. You cannot educate citizens who regard some things as sacred, if from an early age they have only seen the world through rose coloured glasses and have experienced their life as one of uninterrupted pleasure. Citizenship consists of a feeling of being the guardian and heir of all that has been created by older generations, and a feeling of responsibility for dealing with the evil that remains. We see the meaning of our civic education in ensuring that little people are concerned and worried about the world from the very beginning, that their first civic impulse is the thought that 'It should not be like this!', and that this thought gives rise to a determination to oppose evil, idleness, mismanagement and wastefulness, and leads them to roll up their sleeves and set to work.

It is important that the diverse relationships between members of the school community should be characterised by a contest of ideas. Figuratively speaking, this contest provides the soil for polishing the ploughshare of courage, which is so important for a warrior and a citizen. A quiet, undisturbed community life, without strong, memorable conflicts and moments of intensity, is concerning evidence that young souls are not experiencing the tension necessary for nurturing courage. Involve children in pursuits and relationships in which they feel an engagement with ideas.

An experienced educator strives to ensure that a child develops loyalty to noble ideals that are expressed in memorable deeds and human passions. A little person is being truly educated if they marvel at someone who has reached the height of moral valour. A little person should be aware of the summits of human achievement, and not go through life with their head bent low, looking for pit holes and mires. Let each young citizen hold their head high, inspired by noble ideas—only then will they experience a feeling of gratitude towards their Homeland, and a sense a duty to it. The ability to show a young citizen the summits of human achievement is one of the most subtle aspects of the art of education. We should tell children about the beauty of heroic deeds, so that their gaze is always directed upwards.

STORIES AND VIGNETTES

The willow by the pond

One clear, warm autumn day, an old, hollow willow tree was leaning over a pond. Perhaps at that moment it was thinking, 'Autumn comes, and then winter. After winter, spring will come, and everything will be in flower, but I will never turn green again, because I am old.'

I felt very sorry for that willow tree. In spring I came to see if it had turned green, but it had not. It just stood there all dried out. However, next to it two tender green shoots had appeared. They were two young willow trees that had grown from the roots of the old one. And it seemed to me that the old, dry willow tree was rejoicing, and thinking 'I have not died. I will live forever!'

When I hear the word 'Homeland' I remember that old willow tree and the two young shoots. Life never ends, and the Homeland is eternal in the same way.

Winter twilight

It was a quiet winter evening. The sky was completely covered with dark clouds, and snow was falling. It was beginning to get dark. My mother and I were sitting by the window and looking at the fields. An endless white carpet stretched before us. On that white carpet, somewhere in the distance, a black dot was moving.

'What is that?' I asked my mother.

'I could be a dog, or it could be a cunning fox. It could even be a grey wolf,' answered my mother quietly.

'A grey wolf?' I repeated in surprise. 'Where could a grey wolf have come from?'

'From a fairy tale,' said my mother. 'That is not just a white field we are looking at, but a fairytale field.'

'And the forest?' I asked. 'Over there on the horizon. That's a real forest, isn't it?'

'The forest is also a fairytale forest,' whispered my mother. 'A dark, magic forest.'

I will never forget that winter twilight. It is so dear to me! It is a part of my life and of my native land.

The swallow above my window

I was lying by my window. The glass was covered with intricate patterns. The frost had drawn wonderful animals, flowers, blue mountains and a tall poplar. I can still remember that poplar, standing tall and proud. The wind tried to bend it over, but it would not bow its head.

Then the sun warmed everything, the patterns melted away, and I could see the blue sky. Some swallows were chirping by my window. They sat on the windowsill and looked into my room. They flitted off somewhere as quick as could be, brought some earth in their beaks, and moulded a nest.

I sat by the window and watched how the swallows went about building their nest. With each day, the sun grew warmer. Leaves rustled on the apple trees, and the swallows became calm and affectionate. Now they had eggs in their nest.

Then the swallows became very sensitive and wary. One day a little chick looked out of the nest.

I have a swallow's nest above my window now. It is like a song from my distant childhood. When I hear the word 'Homeland', I remember the icy patterns on my windowpanes, and the first lump of soil in that swallow's beak.

Cranes in the sky

This is a memory from the time when my grandmother was still alive. I remember we were sitting by the window just before the sun went down. I was looking at the blue sky, and through the rectangle of glass I saw a flock of cranes. My grandmother said, 'Spring has come. The cranes have returned to their native land.'

Grandma told me a fairy tale about a crane with a broken wing and how in autumn it could not fly with its friends to warmer lands, how it asked its friends not to forget it, and how a little boy saved it.

I listened to the story and watched the flock of cranes. I will remember that evening all my life. Everything was imprinted on my memory as if painted on canvas: how my grandmother and I were sitting together, how there was a sprig of willow on the windowsill[87], and the flock of cranes in the blue sky.

When I hear the word 'Homeland', I remember that flock of cranes. I seem to hear a song about the wide fields and the blue sky.

How dear those cranes are to me!

The old cherry tree

Not far from our house grew a cherry tree, as old as old can be. Half its branches had completely withered, while the other half still bore tasty cherries.

One spring only a single branch flowered. Father wanted to cut the cherry tree down—after all it was dying—but mother said, 'Don't cut it down. Your grandfather planted that cherry tree. Let the cherries grow on that branch.'

For one last time, the cherry tree bore fruit. Mum collected the pips and planted them in the earth. Young cherry trees grew from those pips. The old cherry tree withered, but the young ones are already flowering and bearing fruit.

Just as that cherry tree did not die, but continued its line, so a nation never dies. As long as the people live, the Homeland lives.

We will always preserve the old and the ancient. We will preserve the things our grandparents and great grandparents treasured. This is the memory of our nation. If a nation loses its memory, it loses its love for its Homeland.

Ten years later

During the final year of World War II, Stepanko's father was killed on the frontline. His battle-hardened friends wrote to his mother, 'We have kept your husband's rifle.'

Stepanko told his mother, 'Ask dad's friends to send me his rifle. I will learn to shoot, and when I grow up, I will take it with me into the army.'

His mother wrote the letter, and his father's friends replied, 'Grow up, son, and your father's rifle will be kept for you.'

The years passed, and Stepanko grew up and joined the army. They gave him his father's rifle, and now he is defending the national border.

At night, Stepanko stands on duty and seems to hear his father's voice saying, 'Keep your eyes peeled and guard our Homeland, my son.'

The corncrake and the mole

A little grey bird, a corncrake, was heading north, returning from a warm, faraway land to its homeland. In summer, the corncrake raised its chicks in our land, and then flew to Africa for the winter.

It is difficult for a corncrake to fly, because its wings are small, so sometimes it flew, and sometimes it walked. That is what it was doing now. It had landed and was continuing on foot. As it walked, it softly sang a song about its land in the far north and its nest under a crack willow in a green meadow. That is where its dear homeland was.

It walked and walked, and suddenly met a mole. The mole was sitting in its burrow. It stuck its head out and asked the corncrake, 'Who are you, and where are you going?'

'I am a corncrake, and I am returning to my homeland from a warm land in the south.'

The corncrake told the mole all about its distant homeland in the north, and about the warm lands in Africa.

'But why don't you just settle in that warm land forever?' asked the puzzled mole. 'Why do you travel thousands of kilometres every year? You have worn your legs out so much they are bleeding. You could be attacked at any moment by a kite. What makes you go through such hardship? What calls you to the cold north?'

'My homeland,' answered the corncrake.

His father's pencil

During World War II, little Andriiko's father was fighting on the front-line, and his mother was working in a factory.

One day the postman brought his mother a letter. She opened the envelope, cried, hugged Andriiko, and said, 'We don't have daddy any more.'

A few days later, a small parcel arrived from the father's comrades in arms. It contained things that had belonged to Andriiko's father: a spoon, a notepad, and the pencil he used to write letters home.

Many years passed. Andriiko became a tall, handsome young man. His mother saw him off to do his service in the army and, as he got ready, she gave him his father's pencil. Andrei put the pencil in the pocket next to his heart, as a priceless treasure.

He wrote a letter to his mother from the army barracks. The first words in it were: 'I swear, mum, that I will be just like my father.' The letter was written with his father's pencil. The mother was glad and cried as she read her son's letter.

The crane and the parrot

A crane lived on the banks of our lake. Winter was approaching, and he joined a flock of other cranes and flew far away to the south. There it was always summer, with warm waters, emerald shores, and a blue sky. There were many wonderful birds in the forests: green, dark blue and light blue parrots. They all sang and called to each other joyfully.

But our crane longed for something else. A green parrot asked the crane, 'Why are you sad? Why don't you build a nest here and raise some baby cranes?' The crane did not answer, and only gazed northwards.

Suddenly he became alert and hearkened to a distant sound. He could hear the calling of some cranes, joyful and disturbing. The crane took flight, so it could catch up with the others.

'Why are you leaving?' asked the parrot in surprise. 'It is cold there. You will live there for five months and then fly back here. What is so good about the cold north?'

'It is good because I was born there. That is my Homeland,' said the crane.

The regimental banner

Ostap Shevchenko, a young machine gunner, had been bravely fighting the enemy for several hours. He had mown down many enemy soldiers with his machine gun.

But the odds were against him. The fascists kept coming in swarms, and there were not many of our troops left. Our soldiers were falling one after another. Next to Ostap lay a dead soldier, his hands still holding the regimental banner.

'The enemy must not lay hands on our banner,' thought Ostap. He stopped firing, took the banner, wrapped it into a bundle, and stuffed it inside his military shirt, next to his chest. The fascists continued to fire on our positions.

An enemy bullet wounded Ostap in the shoulder. His hands shook.

Making a supreme effort, Ostap continued firing. A second bullet wounded him in the chest, and he lost consciousness.

The young machine gunner regained consciousness during the night. His dead friends lay all around him. Everything was still. 'The fascists must have decided I was dead,' thought Ostap, and reached inside his shirt. The banner was still there. He tried to crawl, but he could not move. There was a burning in his chest, and he was very thirsty.

Day broke. The hot sun blazed down on the wounded soldier, and he was tormented by thirst. Ostap often lost consciousness. Somewhere beyond the hill gunfire rang out. The battle still raged there.

The day passed, and night descended again. Ostap felt that he was dying. Suddenly he saw above him the face of a friendly soldier. Ostap groaned. The soldier bent over him and asked, 'Are you alive?'

'Banner,' whispered Ostap, pointing to his chest, and lost consciousness.

On an ancient burial mound

We walked into a field and headed towards a grey, ancient burial mound. The sun had burnt all the grass on it, and only wormwood had survived. That was why it was grey.

We sat down on the slope of the burial mound and then noticed that a green bush was growing on top of it. We ran up to the top of the burial mound and could not believe our eyes. On that green bush, red roses were in bloom. They were not afraid of the sun or the hot, dry wind.

While we were standing admiring the beautiful flowers, an old man suddenly appeared from nowhere. He was grey-haired but had sharp, young eyes. He told us the story of a hero who had died on that spot.

'During the war, some fascists took up a position here in a concrete dugout. They were firing at the road with a machine gun and not allowing our troops to pass through. One brave young man became a hero here. He crawled up to the dugout and hurled a grenade into it. The machine gun fell silent, but the fascists set up another one. And our hero did not have any more grenades. He covered the barrel of the machine gun with his chest. The hero died, and his blood watered the soil here. Where the young soldier's blood was spilt, a scarlet rose grew. Remember children, this ground is part of your Homeland. Whoever has spilt their blood for it is immortal.

Three oak trees

It was the terrible year of 1941. Our troops were retreating from the fascists' massive assault. In autumn, as the leaves on the trees turned yellow, three soldiers took up a position under an old oak tree by the road. They made a dugout and set up a machine gun. Their orders were not to allow the fascists to pass through to the Dnipro River.

But the enemy was stronger. They had more weapons. Fascist bullets wounded first one, then another, then the third soldier. The fascists began to fire on the soldiers with a flame thrower, and the oak tree caught fire.

The oak was in flames, but the three wounded soldiers continued to fire on the enemy. One of the warriors, bleeding profusely, took a piece of paper, wrapped three acorns in it, and wrote, 'Three soldiers fought here. We carried out our duty to the Homeland. Friend, if you find this note and these three acorns, plant them here and grow three oak trees. May they grow here and become strong.'

The three soldiers died in that battle, but the three acorns were found by a young school student. The boy took the note and the acorns to show his friends. They went together to the place where the three soldiers had given their lives, and they planted the acorns.

Spring came, and three little oak trees grew. The boys swore that those three little oak trees would become tall and mighty.

Decades passed. The boys became adults. They had children, and then grandchildren.

Now three majestic oak trees stand by the road. You can see them from afar, standing like sentries. Those who were young school students in that terrible year of 1941 still come and bow down before the three oaks, as do their children and their grandchildren, as will their descendants. The three oaks are a sacred, living monument to heroes who gave their lives for their Homeland.

The unfinished letter

Nineteen-year-old Vasyl Verba volunteered to fight in the war. One dark autumn evening, his section reached the front line and took up their position. Vasyl dug a fortification and prepared his grenades. The commanding officer told them that the enemy would attack at dawn, and they needed to prepare for battle.

The young warrior thought of his distant village, where his mother was waiting for him. There were many tender, heartfelt words he wanted to say to his mother at that moment. He found an envelope and wrote his mother's address on it. Then he got out a large blank sheet of paper and wrote, 'Dear mum, In a few hours there will be a battle with the fascists. It will be my first battle … Before the battle, I want to tell you, mum … '

Dusk fell over the field. The commanding officer had warned them that they must not use a flashlight or light a match. 'I will finish the letter at dawn,' decided Vasyl, and placed the sheet of paper in the envelope.

In the middle of the night a thousand lights flared on the horizon. Enemy artillery had opened fire on our position. The commanding officer ordered his men to wait for the artillery barrage to end, and as soon as tanks appeared, to go on the attack, and meet the enemy with grenades.

The barrage ended. Vasyl heard the roar of tanks, and then saw a dark silhouette approaching. The young soldier sprang from his dugout and, taking several anti-tank grenades, crawled towards the enemy tank.

He hurled a bundle of grenades, landing on the turret. The tank burst into flames and spun on the spot. Vasyl stood to hurl another bundle, but at that moment he was struck down by an enemy bullet.

The battle ended with our victory.

Vasyl's comrades in arms buried him, but the unfinished letter was passed from hand to hand for some time. The warriors decided to send it to his mother, together with their own description of her son's heroic death.

Many years passed. Vasyl's mother became an old woman. She kept her son's unfinished letter as something sacred. When she was finding things particularly difficult, she would open the blue envelope, lay the sheet of paper with its three lines of writing on the table, and quietly whisper, 'What did you want to tell me, dear?'

Grandma's bread rolls

'Where does our Homeland begin?' asked our teacher. I came home and thought about it. I remembered my childhood. I tried to find, in the depths of my memory, those recollections that remained from those first sunny mornings and long, long days.

My first memory is of my grandma's hands. They were not idle for a single minute. I remember how she used to knead wheat dough that was as white as could be, while her hands were so dark in contrast. She made lark-shaped bread rolls and put them in the oven. Bread rolls that were so white, while her hands were dark, wrinkled, and trembling.

I asked her, 'Grandma, why are your hands so dark, and your bread rolls so white?'

Grandma answered, 'If my hands were white, there would not be any white dough or any bread rolls.'

For me the Homeland begins with busy hands like hers.

The Festival of the First Bread

The joyful day of the Festival of the First Bread is here at last.

It is a sunny August morning. We sit down to table. On the table is a large fancy white loaf and a bowl of fragrant honey. Our table is set on the grass, next to an orchard. We can smell the apples and pears. Bees are flying above the bowl of honey. A little bee with golden wings settles on the edge of the bowl and touches the honey. Oh, how sweet it is; it's from our hive! The hives are here in the orchard. We can hear the bees buzzing …

We cut up the bread and share out the pieces. What delicious bread! Probably because we have put our work into it. We dug the soil and fertilized it. We sowed the wheat and watered it, and covered it with snow in the winter, so it would not be cold.

What delicious bread! It smells of spring winds and the hot summer sun. Bread is made of work and happiness.

Excursion to Taras Shevchenko's grave

We went on an excursion to the city of Kaniv to visit Taras Shevchenko's grave.[88] When we climbed the steep hill where our great poet rests in eternal sleep, I was overcome by deep emotion.

It struck me that over a hundred years had passed since Shevchenko's death. There was no-one in Ukraine or in the whole wide world who was alive during Shevchenko's times and could remember him. Other people lived on Earth now. But, in spite of that, it seemed as if we could see the living Taras before us and hear his passionate words:

Make my grave there—and arise,
Sundering your chains ...

We could see the distant banks of the Dnipro River, its mighty waters, and the green forests crowning its steep cliffs. And it was all so dear to us. It had been like this for a thousand years. People are born and people die, but the nation is eternal, immortal.

For the first time in my life, I felt that all that I could see was Ukraine, and that I was her son. The towering hills, the distant steppes, the waters of the Dnipro, were all part of my native land, and the poet's words were part of my native language. Our native language is a pure spring, and without her life-giving water we cannot survive.

The sun sets

I may have heard these words from my mother:

The sun sets, and dark the mountains become,
The little bird hushes, the plain has grown dumb ...

I did not know then that this was a verse by Taras Hryhorovych Shevchenko. I was a little boy, not yet able to read or write. But I was struck by the beauty of the poetry. I could hear music in those words. For me, each word gave rise to a vivid picture, evoking images that I had seen every day, without appreciating their beauty. Now, that beauty revealed itself to me in all its glory, thanks to the poet's words.

I repeated Shevchenko's lines over and over. I felt like singing them. Now they do not just remind me of my childhood; they inspire me. It is with my native tongue, with our beautiful Ukrainian language, that my idea of the Homeland begins.

The red poppies next to our house

Where does the world begin for me? For me, it begins with the red poppies by our house. Their beauty made an everlasting impression on me. I do not know how old I was then, but I must have been very small. Those flowering poppies were like a patch of pink sky that had fallen to earth. I used to enjoy their beauty in the morning and during the day, when each flower would fully open its petals.

Whenever I see a poppy flower, I remember my childhood; I remember the song of the lark; I remember my mother's tender voice. Such childhood memories are the most delicate roots a human being has.

The quail and the sandpiper

A sandpiper lived in a swamp, and a quail lived in a field of rye. The sandpiper was unhappy in the swamp, and complained to the other sandpipers, 'What sort of a life is this? Swamp everywhere you look. What good is there in living here? I'm going to go and live in the rye. It's beautiful there!'

Meanwhile, the quail was unhappy living in the field of rye. He complained to the other quails, 'What sort of a life is this? Rye everywhere you look. What good is there in living here? I'm going to go and live in the swamp. It's beautiful there!'

The sandpiper went to live in the field of rye, and the quail went to live in the swamp.

Each of them lived in their new home for a while, but their hearts began to pine. The sandpiper was pining for his swamp, and the quail was pining for his field of rye.

They each returned to their original home, the sandpiper to the swamp, and the quail to the field of rye. The other sandpipers and quails laughed at them, and asked, 'Did you find the beauty you were looking for? Where is the best place to live?'

'The swamp,' said the sandpiper, 'Because it is home.'

'This field of rye,' said the quail, 'Because it is home.'

Grandpa's cradle

One day my father was looking for something in the attic. He found an old wooden cradle. It was quite unusual: all painted and decorated with carvings. There were some old-fashioned letters carved into it. My father read the words 'peace and bread'.

'That is grandpa's cradle,' said my father. He studied it for a long time, then wiped the dust from it and brought it into the house. 'We should keep it in the house,' he said.

I never knew my grandfather. My father showed me his grave in the cemetery.

When I hear the word 'Homeland', I remember my grandfather's old-fashioned cradle. Our Homeland is made up of all the people who lived on our land before us. They ploughed the earth and sowed crops. They were joyful and wept and sang songs. They are our ancestors.

We should know about our Homeland's past. One who has forgotten the cradle that their grandfather slept in cannot be a true patriot.

Our cradle is our native village, the house we grew up in, our mother and father. For me, the Homeland begins with the house I grew up in.

The dearest thing of all

A mother had an only son. He was serving in the army. He was posted far, far away. Everything there was different: the sky, the low clouds, and the sea waves. The shoreline was rocky. There was not a grain of sand to be seen, not a blade of grass, no plants or trees.

The young soldier became sad and wrote to his mother, 'Mum, send me something good from home. Something very dear to me.'

His mother sent him a pinch of earth from their village.

The son held the earth close to his heart, and straight away he saw in his mind's eye the warm sun, a clear river, and warm fields of wheat, undulating in the wind. He looked around at the sea and the shoreline, and everything became more familiar and dearer to his heart. He understood that even here, far from home, he was protecting that which was most dear to him. The dearest thing of all was the land where he was born.

The soldier's spoon

A spoon is on display on our sideboard. It has become sacred to our family. This is what my mother told me about it:

'I was only little when the fascists attacked our land. It was hard living under occupation: there was nothing to eat, and the schools were closed.

At last, the happy day of liberation of our native land from the invaders arrived. There was a fierce battle for our village. In that battle a young soldier was critically wounded not far from our house. He lived for several hours, and I looked after him. The soldier gave me his spoon and said, "I don't have anything else to leave in memory. Take this spoon—it has been through the whole war with me.'"

Now we keep the spoon in a place of honour as a treasured relic. It reminds us of the deeds of our heroes. It is a small part of our Homeland.

My field, son

The school year ended, and Petryk's father said, 'Now son, let's travel to see my field.'

'Your field?' asked his son in surprise.

They travelled a long way, first on the train out of town, and then by bus. From the bus stop they walked to a forest. Next to the forest was a broad, level field of ripening wheat.

Above the field was the deep blue sky, and in the sky a lark was singing.

'This is my field, son,' said Petryk's father. 'This is where I fought the fascists. This is where I defeated them.'

Pride swelled in Petryk's heart, and he quietly said, 'The lark is yours as well.'

How beautiful Belarus is!

Some friends from Belarus came to visit school students in Ukraine. Little Oksana made friends with a Belarusian girl named Marysia. Oksana took Marysia into a field of wheat that stretched all the way to the horizon. The wheat was a golden yellow. Above it shone a deep blue sky.

Marysia stood gazing at the endless field of wheat, enchanted by its beauty. 'How beautiful Ukraine is,' she said softly to Oksana.

Marysia told Oksana all about Belarus. From the windows of her home, she could see a field just as vast as this field of wheat, where flax was grown. The flax was as blue as the sky.

Oksana listened to Marysia but found it hard to imagine what she was describing. How could it be that the field was blue and there was also a blue sky above it? Did that mean that the whole of Belarus was blue?

The following spring, Oksana went to visit Marysia. Early in the morning, the girls stepped out of Marysia's house. A blue field of flowering flax stretched all the way to the horizon. The field was as blue as the blue sky above it.

'Now I realise how beautiful Belarus is,' said Oksana with wonder.

Beyond the sea is a foreign land

A farmer—a grain grower—had a large fertile field. Every year he sowed it with wheat. The wheat would ripen, the grain grower would harvest it, and a crane would come flying to search through the stubble for tasty ears of wheat.

But then a difficult year came. For the whole summer there was no rain. As soon as ears formed, the wheat withered.

The crane arrived at the field, and the grain grower was sitting by the withered stalks.

'What are you going to do now, grain grower?' asked the crane.

'I will plough the field and sow more wheat,' answered the grain grower. The crane could not believe it, but the man did indeed plough the field and sow more wheat.

Winter came and went, and spring arrived. The field turned green, but once again misfortune struck. Once more, not a single drop of rain fell throughout the whole summer. As soon as ears formed, the wheat withered.

The crane arrived at the field, and the grain grower was sitting by the withered stalks.

'What are you going to do now, grain grower?' asked the crane, just as it had done the year before.

'I will plough the field and sow more wheat,' answered the grain grower.

'Why are you wasting your energy and your grain?' asked the crane. 'Bake bread from the wheat you have and eat it, or you will starve to death. And follow me beyond the sea. There the soil is fertile, and there are no droughts.'

'We are not going anywhere,' said the grain grower.

'We are not going anywhere,' said his children.

'We are not going anywhere,' said their mother.

'Why won't you leave? You have had two years of drought,' said the crane.

'Beyond the sea is a foreign land,' said the grain grower.

'Beyond the sea is a foreign land,' said the mother.

'We don't want to go to a foreign land,' cried the children.

Three birch trees by a grave

On a towering bank of the Dnipro River stand three birch trees, shading a communal grave. In the grave, three heroes are buried. They fell here, on the banks of the Dnipro, in a bloody battle with fascists.

The grave is on the outskirts of a village and is seldom visited. Many years have passed since the war, and the children of the soldiers who died defending their homeland have long since grown up. The children of those soldiers now have children of their own who are studying at school and reading books about World War II.

One Sunday, a large group of happy, fun-loving children was returning from the forest. The boys and girls were tired and turned off the road to rest under the shady birch trees by the grave. They were laughing and chatting about things that children are interested in. It was hot outside, with not a cloud in the sky and not a breath of wind.

In the middle of their happy chatter, a moment of silence fell, and suddenly the leaves on the three birch trees stirred anxiously. The birch trees bowed their branches even lower over the shared grave.

The amazed boys and girls raised their heads. Why were the birch trees stirring, when it was quiet outside and there was no breeze?

The boys and girls turned their gaze from the trees to the grave. Their eyes became thoughtful. The boys and girls fell silent and stood for a long time by the grave with their heads bowed.

I wanted to return home

When I was a child, my mother took me to visit my grandmother. What a beautiful forest there was there, what still, clear lakes, and what green meadows! You would come out onto a high riverbank and see far, far into the distance. And there were so many flowers in the meadows.

My mother had said, 'You can stay here for the whole summer.' But after a week I wanted to return home. At first, I was not too homesick, but then I wanted to return so much that if I had had wings I would have flown across the meadows, forests and lakes.

Why did I want to return home so much? We do not have a wide river, or a shady forest, or clear lakes, or wide meadows. All we have is the steppe, hills, cherry orchards, and a small pond, but I could not wait to get home. Probably I am so drawn to home because that is where I was born. That is where my childhood began, where I first saw the bright sun, heard the songs of birds, and spoke my first words.

I have read that there are countries where it is always summer, where grass grows, and flowers bloom all year round. Well, they are welcome to their beautiful countries with their endless summer. I will not exchange our autumns, with their grey drizzle, our white blizzards, our babbling springs and our hot summers for anything. Because the dearest thing for any person is their Homeland.

A rose bush in the steppe

A rose bush grows in the steppe, amid fields of wheat. Every spring it blooms with purple flowers. As some flowers gradually fade, others bloom in their place. Whoever passes that way stops by the rose bush and bows their head in thought.

Many years ago, fascist invaders came to our land. On this hill, one of our soldiers lay firing his machine gun. He had been ordered not to allow the fascists access to the road. He laid many enemies to rest, but they kept coming in swarms, like locusts. Finally, a tank approached and began to fire at the soldier. The young warrior's chest was ripped open by an exploding shell. His bloodied heart fell on the earth and trembled.

In the evening some villagers came to the field. They wrapped the hero's body and heart in a red shroud and buried him.

The next morning people saw red roses growing on the spot where the hero's bloodied heart had fallen.

Those roses will flower eternally.

My grandfather's advice

I am studying in grade four. A portrait of my grandfather Pavlo hangs in a place of honour in our classroom. Below his portrait is the inscription, 'He gave his life for the Homeland.'

From the stories my mother and grandmother have told me, I know that my grandfather was a scout. He died a hero's death far away in the west, in the Carpathian Mountains.[89]

The anniversary of my grandfather's death was approaching. Every year on that day my grandmother brings a bouquet of white flowers to lay below my grandfather's portrait. This year, I had also grown some white flowers—some apricot blossom—which I brought to school early in the morning. The school was deserted. I placed the flowers below my grandfather's portrait and sat on a couch. Suddenly I saw my grandfather smile at me from the portrait.

'Grandpa,' I asked, 'Tell me who I should become? I would like to be a pilot, or an agricultural scientist, or a doctor.'

'Be a patriot,' I heard my grandfather say. 'That is the most important thing.'

I jumped up from the couch and wondered whether I had been asleep or not.

We can retreat no further

We were at war with fascists. A group of our soldiers was making a strategic retreat. They retreated as far as a fast-flowing river that was crossed by a bridge.

'Let's cross the bridge,' said one of the soldiers. 'I can see a village over there.'

'No, we will not cross this bridge,' said a young soldier named Pavlo Tkachenko. 'That is my village. My mother lives there. What will I say to my mother? She will tell me I have allowed fascists into our village. We can retreat no further.'

'We can retreat no further,' decided the soldiers.

They burnt the bridge over the fast-flowing river and swore that they would die rather than retreat.

A fierce battle raged for five days by that burnt bridge. A handful of Soviet warriors fought against a whole tank division. Our heroes destroyed twenty tanks but poured out their lifeblood and died.

On their grave is a large monument showing a grieving mother bending over her fallen son. The inscription on the monument reads, 'Better an honourable death than a shameful retreat.'

A precious ear of wheat

It was during the dark days of the fascist invasion. The enemy were killing and torturing people, driving them into slave labour. They took their crops and their homes.

Before the war, our agricultural scientists had developed a new variety of wheat that yielded four tonnes per hectare. But the fascists came and took the wheat. Grandpa Andrii's heart ached. He went to the field where the wheat had grown and found a single ear of wheat. He picked it up from the earth, wrapped it in his handkerchief and took it home. He put it in a chest so he could keep it for better times.

For two years our people suffered under foreign bondage. And then liberation came. Grandpa Andrii got out his ear of the wonderful wheat, picked out the grains and sowed them. In the autumn he harvested three handfuls of wheat. He sowed it again and harvested half a sack of wheat. He sowed it again and harvested ten sacks of grain.

That is how Grandpa Andrii saved the wonderful wheat.

The burnt cherry tree

Our troops won back a village on the Dnipro River from the fascists. As the enemy retreated, they burnt the homes and drove the women and children somewhere far away. When our soldiers entered the village, instead of houses they saw smouldering ruins. Near one burnt house grew a cherry tree that had been in flower. The fire had scorched it. Its leaves were burnt, and its white blossom was charred.

One soldier walked up to the burnt cherry tree and shook his head. He examined the cherry tree carefully and saw that on one side there was still a small branch with some white blossom that by some miracle had survived. Joy shone in the soldier's eyes. He found a saw and removed the burnt branches. He smeared clay on the places where the branches had been cut.

Five years passed. The sounds of battle had long fallen silent. The war had ended in victory. The former soldier now lived in a town by the sea. He remembered the burnt cherry tree in a Ukrainian village. He felt an urge to go and see if it was still alive.

He flew by aeroplane to Kyiv, and from there he caught a bus to the village on the Dnipro River. He found the garden where he had seen the burnt cherry tree. From the small branch that by some miracle had survived that terrible day, many shoots had grown. Its branches had spread to form an even green crown, and the cherry tree had become quite lovely.

The former soldier stood by the cherry tree for a long time. He returned home with his heart at peace.

So the rage in our hearts will not die

In the middle of the village is a green. From early spring to late autumn children play there, and adults like to sit on the grass as well.

But someone got it into their head that we did not need a village green, that it was too simple and old-fashioned to have just grass there. Would it not be better to have an asphalted square? Then it would be flat and even. They began to kill the grass in preparation for laying sand and gravel, and then asphalt. In the middle of the green they came across two thick stumps. They tried to dig them out, but they were planted very deep in the ground. Someone had buried two posts here.

They tried to remember what those two posts were for. It would not do to have two posts sticking out of an asphalted square. The old people remembered that during the fascist occupation there were gallows there. The Germans had hanged a young female partisan there, and the stumps were what remained of the gallows.

Some little children began to dig in the soil around the stumps and found a tiny doll's arm. The old people remembered that when they hanged the partisan, they brought her six-year-old daughter to the gallows. She stood there by the post holding a doll in her arms. At the time there were rumours that the fascists had shot the little girl there during the night. Many would not believe that. Were they really capable of such an act? But now, when they found the tiny doll's arm, they remembered those terrible days, and in every heart the flame of hatred burned with new force.

The whole village gathered on the green, from hundred-year-old elders to little children. The people decided that there would always be a village green there, and that they would keep the stumps from the gallows forever: not wooden ones, but stone ones. May they remain for centuries, set in stone.

That is what they did. The grass still grows on the village green, and two stone posts stand in the middle of it. Between the posts is a granite pedestal. It is an appeal for help, and a reminder of what can never be forgiven.

The birchwood nightingale

A little girl named Olesia celebrated her third birthday. She had her father and her mother with her. They lived happily in a little village in Polissia.[90] Olesia's father carved her a little nightingale from birchwood. The little girl loved to play with the nightingale and even took it to bed with her.

But then the terrible war with the fascists erupted. Olesia's father went away to join the fight. For many days he fought the fascists. His unit retreated.

Meanwhile the fascists arrived in the little village in Polissia. They took Olesia's mother as a slave and transported her and her daughter far, far away. They imprisoned Olesia and her mother behind barbed wire. In the camp, the fascists taunted their captives. They forced them to work from morning to night, worked them to death, and burnt them in ovens. That hell was called Majdanek.[91]

Many difficult months passed. Our army defeated the fascists in our land and entered Poland. Olesia's father arrived with his military unit in Majdanek, where he saw monstrous things: thousands of little children's shoes, thousands of toys.

Olesia's father bent over some children's toys and suddenly caught sight of the little birchwood nightingale. The little nightingale looked at Olesia's father with wide open eyes, as if wanting to tell of all that it had seen and heard.

But Olesia's father did not need the nightingale to tell him what had happened. He understood that his wife and child had perished here. A terrible rage consumed the soldier's heart. Olesia's father gripped his weapon in his hands and marched westwards to finish off the enemy. Now the birchwood nightingale sat in the breast pocket of his uniform and beat at the soldier's heart.

I survived by hating the enemy

In June 1941, Grandpa Yukhym turned ninety-nine. He celebrated his birthday with his son Ostap and his grandsons. After the celebrations, Grandpa Yukhym did not feel well, and he told his son and grandsons, 'I have had a good life. Now it is time for me to prepare myself for eternal rest.'

He lay down in his bed and would not take any food. They told him, 'Don't be silly, grandpa, you're being lazy. Get up, you still have lots of life ahead of you.' But he just smiled and quietly whispered, 'I will live on in my family. I have seven broad-shouldered grandsons, as strong as oak trees. They are all happy … This is the perfect time to die.'

But then the war began. Cannons roared. Germans arrived in the village. One night Grandpa Yukhym was visited by his son Ostap. He had come to say good-bye.

'Farewell, dad,' he said. 'We may never see each other again.'

'No, we will not say farewell,' said Grandpa Yukhym, and got up from his bed. 'Now I cannot die. I will fight the enemy.'

'How will you fight, dad?' asked his son. 'You're nearly a hundred years old.'

'I will hate the enemy,' said the old man, kissing his son. 'But you take your rifle and talk to the fascists with your bullets.'

Grandpa Yukhym got dressed, went outside, and sat on a bench by his fence. He sat on that bench for three years, until the Germans were driven from our land.

Many people walked by that hundred-year-old man: soldiers, women and children, old people and adolescents, disabled people. Anyone who looked into Grandpa Yukhym's eyes and met his gaze felt their heart beat more rapidly and clenched their fists. In the old man's eyes everyone saw a passionate, undying hatred for the enemy. If someone who had lost faith in our victory met Grandpa Yukhym's gaze, even their tired eyes lit up with faith in the inexhaustible strength of our Homeland, in its invincibility.

Word spread throughout the region that in the village of Ivanivka on the Dnipro River, there lived a hundred-year-old man who was kept alive by his hatred of the invaders. Rumour had it that his heart was only beating because he loved his native land and hated the enemy.

Yukhym's son Ostap arrived back in his native village with a machine gun over his shoulder and a medal on his chest.

Grandpa Yukhym again lay down in his bed. Ostap kissed his father, and asked, 'How did you get on, dad?'

'I fought. My weapon was my hatred for the enemy,' answered the old man.

'Well, now we have returned, and you can look forward to the rest of your life,' said Ostap, shedding tears.

'No, my son, now our land is safe,' said the old man. 'Now I can die.'

The indestructible stone

This happened in Polissia, in the north of Ukraine, during the difficult years of fascist occupation. In the middle of dense forest, beside a quiet lake, was the ancient Ukrainian village of Makivka. When invaders came to our land, many of the inhabitants of Makivka joined the partisans, and those who remained in the village helped the partisans.

The fascists decided to destroy the village and burn all its inhabitants, but the villagers learnt of this terrible plan in advance. During the night, every last one of them went into the forest, taking with them all their belongings, cattle and fowl.

When the punitive detachment arrived at the village in the morning, there was no-one there. The fascists burnt everything that would burn—homes, barns, and trees. They filled the well and gathered ash and tipped it in the lake. Nothing remained of the village except for a large, white stone that since time immemorial had lain in the middle of the village. A legend had been passed down from generation to generation that this stone extended down into a deep bog, and that no-one could reach the bottom of it.

The fascists laid explosives around the stone and detonated them. When they came back in the morning, they could not believe their eyes. The stone still lay there, as if there had been no explosion. The furious fascists attempted to blow it up again, but the next morning the white stone lay amidst the cratered ground as if non-one had touched it. The enraged Nazis attempted to blow up the stone again. But once again, by the next morning it had emerged from the ground.

'This is a cursed place,' said the fascist officer.

A few months later our troops drove out the fascists. The old men, women and children returned to the wasteland that had once been the ancient village of Makivka. So did the partisans. They gathered around the white stone and bowed down before it.

'Ukraine is as indestructible as this stone,' said the oldest inhabitant of the village, hundred-year-old Grandpa Arkhyp. 'This indestructible stone represents our undying love for our native land.'

Ears of wheat

When the harvest begins, my father always brings some ears of wheat and hangs them above the window. Immediately, the house is filled with the scent of the fields, and for some reason I feel full of joy. Those ears of wheat will hang there throughout summer, autumn and spring, all the way through to the next harvest, when my father will bring a new bunch of freshly cut ears of wheat.

My father loves to work in the fields, so from an early age I fell in love with the soil, the wheat, and the steppes. There is nothing better than to go out into the fields early in the morning and greet the sunrise. That solemn event has been engraved in my memory since I was little. I still love the way the sky in the east turns red, a huge golden orb rises from behind a distant mountain, and dew drops sparkle in the morning sun.

When the sun rises, and the air is filled with the scent of the wheat and the earth, the world seems such a wonderful place.

Bread is sweet because sweat is bitter

When Yashko's father came home from work, the whole family sat down to eat: the father and mother, seven-year-old Yashko, and his little sister Maya. Yashko's father was a tractor and combine harvester operator. Now that it was summer, he left for work very early, at three o'clock in the morning. A combine harvester only rests at night, and the night is short in summer. Yashko's father came home from work covered in dust, with only his eyes and teeth sparkling. He washed, changed, and sat at the table. Then they all sat down to eat—Yashko, his mother, and Maya.

Today Yashko's mother put some little *pampushky* on the table—sweet little bread rolls.

'The *pampushky* are delicious!' said Yashko. 'They're so sweet!'

'They're sweet because sweat is bitter,' said his father, smiling.

'Is sweat bitter?' asked Yashko in surprise.

'If you want, you can come with me tomorrow to work in the field,' said Yashko's father. 'Then you'll find out what sweat tastes like.'

'Great!' said a delighted Yashko.

The sky was still grey when Yashko's father came to his bed to wake him. The boy quickly got up, had breakfast, and hurried after his father. They travelled to the combine harvester by motorbike.

When they reached the combine harvester, Yashko's father started up the engine and stood at the controls. Yashko stood next to him. The machine roared and shook and lurched forwards. Wheat poured into the bunker and a cloud of chaff rose into the air.

The combine harvester travelled around the field once, twice, and then a third time. The sun kept climbing higher and it grew hot. The wind blew clouds of chaff and dust into Yashko's eyes and mouth and made his teeth gritty. The sun was baking now, like a hot oven, and sweat poured down Yashko's face and into his eyes. Some drops of sweat seeped into his mouth, and for the first time in his life, Yashko realised that sweat was bitter and salty.

And the sun was still climbing. What would it be like when it was right overhead?

'Dad, is this where you work all day?' asked Yashko.

'No, not all day,' said his father. 'We break for lunch for an hour.'

'And how much longer to the lunch break?' asked Yashko, wiping the sweat from his face with his sleeve.

The travelling ant

The ant hill is seething with life. Thousands of ants are busy about their work. Some are building little rooms in which they can shelter from bad weather. Others are bringing food to the ant hill: little bits of potato, beetroot, grain, seeds, and whatever they can find in the fields. Others are hunting for insects: beetles and flies.

Suddenly a travelling ant comes running to the ant hill. He has run away from his own ant hill because he doesn't want to work. 'I'll go to another ant hill,' he thought to himself, 'So they can feed me.'

The ants immediately recognise the foreigner. Every worker smells of something—grain, potato, beetroot, fly. But the travelling ant did not smell of anything.

'An ant who does no work!' shouted dozens of ants, and they ran towards the newcomer.

The travelling ant just managed to escape from the workers. He ran back to his own ant nest, but they also took him for a foreigner, because he did not smell of work.

The rusk and the slice of bread

A mother was seeing her son off for work. She packed a lunch for him. A fresh slice of bread and a hard, dry rusk found themselves lying side by side in the son's bag.

The slice of bread did not feel comfortable and asked, 'Who are you? Why are you so hard? You're pressing against me, and it hurts!'

'I am a rusk,' answered the bread's neighbour. 'I am your brother. We are made of the same flour, the same dough. We are from the same home-made loaf of bread.'

The slice of bread asked, 'Why are you so hard?'

The rusk explained that it was cut from a loaf of bread and then dried.

'Why do they dry you?' asked the slice of bread in surprise.

'So that I may forever be a faithful friend to people,' said the rusk. 'Although I am hard, I will never let them down. You can get mouldy, but I will keep well for ages.'

The bread looked at the rusk with newfound respect.

Fresh bread

Our most indelible memories are from childhood.

I look back and ask myself, 'What is the dearest and sweetest thing engraved in my memory?'

It is the scent of freshly baked bread. My mother would bake several fancy, round loafs of bread, the type we call *palianytsia*. She would take them out of the oven and lay them on the bench to cool.

How sweetly that bread smelt! Nowadays, my mother no longer bakes bread because everyone buys bread at the store. But back then, everyone baked their own bread. And that scent of freshly baked bread will stay with me forever.

On the days when my mother baked bread, everything smelt of bread: my mother's hands, her clothes, the oven, the walls, and even the smoke from the chimney.

The scent of home-baked bread …

The red-breasted bullfinches

Where does my idea of the Homeland come from? From the things that are most deeply engraved on my memory from childhood.

For some reason the most vivid of all my many childhood memories is of some red-breasted bullfinches. It was a bright winter morning. The sun's rays were shining through the falling snow. I looked out the window and saw some red-breasted bullfinches. They were looking for something in the snow, or perhaps they were just playing. I gazed with wonder at something I was seeing for the first time. Why did they have red breasts? And where had these wonderful birds flown from?

My mother told me they had flown from beyond the sun.

The bullfinches flew away, but I could not forget them. I even dreamed of them that night.

Every time I see red-breasted bullfinches, I remember my childhood. I remember the fairy tale about the little bird that flew from beyond the sun.

Everything that we remember from our distant childhood is dear to us. That is where our first notions of our native land come from.

What is the hardest thing for the cranes?

One quiet autumn evening, some cranes stopped to rest at the edge of the forest. They were flying to warmer lands. The sun had just set, and they decided to spend the night where they were.

The cranes leaned towards a silver birch, cooing very quietly about something. The birch tree listened attentively to them, trying to understand what they were saying.

'Where are you flying to, dear cranes?' asked the birch tree.

'To warmer lands,' answered the cranes.

'Ah, yes, the winter is upon us,' lamented the birch tree. 'I am shedding my leaves … I expect you have a long, hard journey ahead of you?'

'Yes, it is hard,' answered the oldest crane. 'But it is not the travel itself that is hardest for us.'

'What is hardest for you, then?' asked the birch tree in surprise.

'The hardest thing for us is spending several months on the banks of the Nile. There is no winter there, and flowers bloom all year round.'

'Why is that so hard?' asked the birch tree, even more surprised.

‘Because it is not our native land,’ answered the oldest crane. ‘Because we miss you, dear silver birch.’

I will walk through the meadow

That moment is engraved on my memory for life, as the brightest day, the dearest moment, the deepest emotion.

It was sunset. I was standing by my house, gazing at a field of golden wheat. The sky was a deep blue. Bees were humming above the blooming sunflowers in our garden.

And then the soft sound of a song carried to me from the fields. A woman was singing. I will never forget the first words of her song:

I will walk through the meadow, through the valley meadow,
But I may never see my dear family again ...

The song was about a woman’s hard life.

I will remember that wonderful song for the rest of my life. Every single word in it moved me deeply and moves me still.

That day I learnt a most valuable lesson about my native language, a lesson to remember for the rest of my life. I learnt that I love my dear, native Ukrainian language, in the same way that I love the land where I was born. As I love my dear mother. As I love our long-suffering Ukraine and our glorious songs. I love my native tongue, which is as colourful, fragrant, and melodious as our garden in spring.

I love my language.

A blade of grass from home

A mother saw off her son, who was commencing his service in the army. She instructed him, ‘Serve faithfully. Be a brave and honest warrior. Here is a magic blade of grass from our native soil. I picked it from your grandfather’s grave. He fought and spilt his blood fighting for our Homeland. When you find things difficult, hold this blade of grass to your heart.’

The young soldier served on the border, and kept the blade of grass in his pocket, next to his heart.

One dark night, the soldier was standing on duty. Suddenly he noticed someone approaching the border. He lay down behind a hillock, waited for the invader to get close, and detained him. He tied his hands together and marched him under guard to the border post.

Suddenly a whole detachment of armed men approached from the foreign land. They opened fire and wounded the young soldier in the leg. The wounded border guard lay flat on the ground, gripped his machine gun in his hands and opened fire on the enemy. The invaders also lay flat on the ground and kept firing.

Another bullet wounded the border guard in the shoulder. The soldier felt his strength draining away, and gripped his machine gun even harder, firing even more accurately at the enemy.

A third bullet wounded the border guard in the chest. He remembered the blade of grass from his native soil and his mother's instructions. He took the blade of grass from his pocket, and at that moment he saw his village in his mind's eye. He could see his mother's eyes and smell the grass from home. Strength flowed into the soldier's body, and his hands grew stronger, his eyesight grew clearer, and his hatred for the enemy grew more fierce.

The soldier again opened fire on the enemy. Just then his friends, the other border guards, came to his aid and repelled the enemy.

The rose

Three boys were walking through a field where, many years before, there had been a battle with the fascists. The boys inspected every hillock and looked into every gully. They wanted to learn something new about the great battle for their native land.

In a valley, the young explorers stumbled upon a thicket. In the middle of the bushes, they came across a dark red flower. They walked up to it and stopped in amazement. It was a rose that had grown from an old, rusty soldier's helmet. They examined it more closely and saw that it was a soldier's helmet that had been pierced by a bullet.

The boys stood there for a long time with heads bowed. The flower's beauty shone in the rays of the spring sun. If it could have spoken, it would have said, 'Many years ago a fierce battle raged here. A young soldier, Ivan Petrenko, fired from his machine gun at the fascists. The fascists surrounded him and wanted to take him alive. He allowed the enemy to get up close, and then destroyed them. When he only had one bullet left in his machine gun belt, he turned the barrel towards his chest and shot himself through the heart. He did not want to be captured and experience the shame of being a prisoner of war.'

That is what the rose would have said, if it could have spoken. But even without that, the young explorers understood that the blood of a hero had been spilt there.

The heart of a soldier

The soldier Serhii Ivanov fought bravely against the fascists. Our troops liberated our native land and continued to fight the enemy on German soil.

Serhii Ivanov took up a position in the entrance of a tall building. He fired from his machine gun down a street where fascists had dug in. Enemy machine guns were positioned at the other end of the street.

Suddenly Serhii saw a woman with a baby in her arms run from a half-ruined building. A shell exploded near her, and the woman fell to the ground. She lay motionless in the middle of the street while her baby cried as it lay in her arms.

At that moment Serhii Ivanov remembered his little son, who had died with his mother, killed by a fascist bomb. The soldier's heart contracted with pain. He crawled across the street to the dead woman. Bullets whistled overhead. He drew near to the baby lying on its mother's body. Serhii took the baby in his left arm. Holding his machine gun with his right arm, he headed back in short, sharp runs. He had almost reached his sheltered position when he heard the whistle of an enemy shell. He lay flat on the road and heard an explosion. A sharp pain ran through his body. With his strength failing him from the intense pain, he gathered the last of his energy and crawled to the entrance of the building. His two friends ran out to meet him.

'Take the baby,' said Serhii Ivanov, and died from his wounds. The baby cried softly.

The lilies of the valley by the rock

On a lofty bank of the Dnipro River stands a large block of granite. Lilies of the valley flower all around this rock. Grandpa Platon, an old fisherman, explains to some young hikers, 'This rock is sacred. The Germans fortified this bank and hoped that our soldiers would never dislodge them. One dark October night, three of our warriors crossed the Dnipro River, took up position behind this rock, and opened fire on the Germans with their machine guns.

They battled with the enemy for three days. They were fighting a whole division. Many fascists were laid to rest by our warriors, but they themselves were pouring out their lifeblood.

You can see how many lilies of the valley are flowering by this block of granite. Each flower is a drop of blood from our heroes. Remember this, children.

Remember that our land has been watered with blood. Remember that millions of your grandfathers and great-grandfathers died so you could be happy. As long as you remember this, your happiness will last. But if you forget it, a great misfortune will befall you.'

'We will not forget. We will never forget,' replied the young hikers.

You can kill us, but you cannot defeat us

A fierce battle with fascists was raging. Our soldiers had occupied part of a large city, but the enemy did not want to abandon it. The fascists made several attempts to retake that part of the city.

A young soldier set up his machine gun in the attic of a small house on the edge of the city. The inhabitants had left, and no-one was living there. The soldier had orders not to allow the enemy access to a road that led to a bridge over the river.

But eventually the soldier's bullets ran out. Fascists surrounded the building and called on him to surrender. His response was to hurl hand grenades.

The fascists poured petrol on the wooden walls of the house and set it alight. They gathered in a crowd to see how the soldier would beg for mercy. They had no doubt that he would. How could anyone bear to be burnt alive?

The soldier dismantled the roof and crawled out on top of it. 'You can kill us and burn us, but you cannot defeat us!' he shouted, and he hurled his last grenade into the crowd of fascists.

At that moment the house was engulfed in flames, and the soldier perished.

Many years passed. Now an obelisk stands on the spot where the young soldier died. By the obelisk is an eternal flame. The soldier's final words are inscribed on the obelisk: 'You can kill us and burn us, but you cannot defeat us!'

The helmet with the bullet hole

This incident took place on the outskirts of Kyiv, where, in 1941, a bloody battle had taken place between our militia and the fascists.

Some workers were excavating a site for the foundations of a large block of apartments. As the engineer walked through the excavation pit, he saw the bucket of the excavator toss aside a helmet that it had dug up. The engineer picked up the helmet and stopped in amazement. There was a bullet hole in the front of the helmet, and the left side was engraved with the initials I.P. Many years ago, the engineer, Ivan Petrenko, had fought here, and been gravely wounded. This was his helmet, pierced by an enemy bullet.

The young worker operating the excavator saw the engineer standing with the helmet in his hands. He understood that an old warrior had just come face to face with his own heroism. He turned off the motor of the excavator. Silence reigned on the building site.

The young workers stood, solemn and thoughtful. At that moment it was as if the whole city were listening to the heartbeat of the old warrior.

A second son

It was during the autumn of 1943. The left bank of the Dnipro River had already been liberated from German occupation. The Germans had taken up fortified positions on the right bank.

The Germans sprayed the Dnipro River with machine gun fire and launched mortar shells at the left bank. Two of our soldiers took a large wooden plank, lowered it into the water, and held on to it while they swam to the opposite bank, which was occupied by the Germans. They placed their weapons—machine guns and grenades—on the plank.

The soldiers swam quietly, but the Germans noticed them. A hostile machine gun opened fire. One of the soldiers, Anatolii, was seriously wounded. His friend Petro said, 'This is my native village. Try to hold on.'

Dusk was falling. The plank to which Petro was clinging reached the shore. He lay the wounded Anatolii on the ground. Petro waited until it was completely dark, then lifted Anatolii, took the weapons, and made his way through the undergrowth along the bank of the river. As it was his native village, he knew every path.

During the night, he knocked on the window of his mother's hut. His mother recognised her son and opened the door, crying from joy and from anxiety.

'There are Germans in the village,' she whispered.

'We'll put my wounded friend in the attic,' said Petro.

When they had laid Anatolii on a bed of sweet-smelling hay prepared by the mother, Petro took his weapons and said farewell.

'Farewell, mother,' he said. 'If I die, let Anatolii be your son. His mother died before the war.'

The mother wept as she saw her son off into battle.

Petro made his way to the Dnipro River, where his comrades were already climbing out onto the shore and firing with their machine guns at the Germans. Petro joined forces with them.

The battle for the village raged for three days and three nights. When it was over, Petro's mother walked to the riverbank and found her son's body, closed his eyes, wept over him, and buried him next to his father's grave.

Anatolii became Petro's mother's son. He was treated in hospital. He made it to Berlin, returned to the village in Ukraine after the war, married, and lives there now with his children and his elderly mother.

The heroes' grave

Every morning, I walk past the graves of warriors who died fighting to liberate our village from the fascists. It is called a 'brotherly grave' because our dear liberators cemented their brotherhood with their blood.

When I pass the graves of these brothers in arms, I stop and remember my grandfather. He also gave his life for the Homeland. My grandfather died on the frontline.

Where is your grave, grandpa? If I knew, I would come and visit you. I would bring a handful of our native soil and place it on your grave.

Next to our school, red roses are in bloom, bees are buzzing above their hives, and doves are cooing. The sun is laughing in the blue sky. I would not be able to enjoy any of this, if my grandfather had not fallen liberating the Homeland. I would not see the red roses, or hear the quiet music of the bees, or the cooing of the doves. I would not know happiness. Thank you, dear warriors, for defeating the fascists.

The heroic partisan

A fierce battle was raging in the forest. Seven heroic partisans were fighting the fascists. Many enemy soldiers were killed by our warriors. But the blood of one of the heroes was also spilt. A young partisan, hit by a fascist bullet, fell to the ground. His friends did not see him, and retreated into the forest, leaving the dead partisan under a bush.

Little Marynka came into the forest. She saw the dead partisan, and her heart ached with pity. She asked a hundred-year oak, 'Dear oak, teach me how to bring our hero back to life.'

'Go to his mother,' said the oak. 'Tell her about the fallen hero, and if she cries, collect her tears. Bring them to the forest and lay them against the hero's heart.'

Marynka went to the young man's mother and told her about the fallen hero. The little girl collected the mother's tears in a rose, carried the flower into the forest, and lay it against the hero's heart. His wounds healed, his heart started beating, and he opened his eyes and said, 'I have slept for such a long time. Thank you, little girl, for waking me.'

The purple flower

A soldier named Maksym Kryvoshyia fought against the fascists for two years. He fought from Stalingrad[92] all the way to the Dnipro River. He crossed the Dnipro and reached his native village of Petrivka. Here it was at last, his native village ... But this was his final battle with the fascists. He was mortally wounded by an enemy bullet. Maksym fell to the ground and looked around one last time at his native village, nestled under a hill, as his warm blood flowed out onto the earth. His heart stopped beating, and the soldier died.

Within an hour, the village was liberated from the fascists. Maksym's comrades in arms went to his home and learnt that his wife had also been killed by the fascists, and that his seven-year-old daughter was living with neighbours. They found Maksym's little girl and took her to where her father lay. Marynka sat on the ground by her father's body and cried. They buried Maksym in an oak coffin, on the spot where he had fallen in battle.

Marynka planted some flowers on her father's grave. A unique purple flower, luxurious, brightly coloured, and amazingly beautiful, flowered there each year for a single day.

Marynka often visited her father's grave, and on the day when the purple flower bloomed, she came before sunrise.

Marynka turned twenty. A young man fell in love with her and asked her to marry him. Marynka replied, 'I have neither mother nor father. We will go to my father's grave on the only day when the purple flower blooms, bow down to my father's remains, and ask for his blessing.'

Marynka and the young man waited for the day when it was time for the flower to bloom, and went to the father's grave before sunrise. When the sun glided up from beyond the horizon and lit up the earth, the purple petals opened. Marynka and the young man bowed down before the father's grave and said, 'Please give us your blessing, father, to become husband and wife.'

The purple petals stirred. No-one else in the world would have noticed that movement, apart from Marynka and the young man. Perhaps the flower stirred in response to their warm breath, but the young man and woman understood that the girl's father had heard their words and given his blessing.

The happiest person in the world

In a Ukrainian village there once lived a very old woman. She had raised seven sons and seven daughters. Each son and each daughter had presented her with seven grandchildren, and each grandchild had produced three great-grandchildren. Only the youngest granddaughter, who had only been married a few years, had no children. This granddaughter's name was Vira.

One warm summer's day, Great-grandmother—that is what everyone in her extended family called her—celebrated her hundredth birthday. Her children, grandchildren and great-grandchildren all came to congratulate her. They gathered around her in an apple orchard, bowed low to the ground, and wished her good health, keen eyesight, sensitive hearing, and just speech.

The great-grandmother looked around at all of her extended family and saw that nearly everyone was there, but that Vira had not come. Her old heart felt pained. She was just about to ask why Vira had not come, when their neighbour came running, bowed down to the great-grandmother, and said, 'Vira has given birth to a son.'

The great-grandmother gave a sigh of relief. Joy shone in her eyes. The great-grandmother looked into the eyes of each of her relatives and said, 'I am dying now, because I will never again know such happiness.'

And she died the happiest person in the world.

A broken branch

A boy was running along the avenue in a park. It was a sunny spring day, birds were singing in the trees, and beautiful butterflies were fluttering among the flowers. The boy felt very happy, and he waved his arms as he ran.

Along the avenue, some young linden trees were growing. They had just been planted. Sweet-smelling green leaves were growing on their thin branches. The boy tore off leaves and scattered them along the avenue for fun. He bent down to one little linden tree and tore off not just some leaves, but a whole branch. The little branch fell to the ground. The boy stopped for a minute and looked at the quivering leaves. He looked at the little linden tree. On one side, instead of a branch, a wound gaped. The boy felt sorry for the little linden tree, but not for long. It was such a joyful, sunny day. The boy stepped over the branch and kept running.

Many years passed. The boy grew up and had children. His children grew up, and the former boy became a grandfather.

One warm spring day, he came to the same park where he had once run around as a mischievous little boy. All along the level roadway grew tall, shapely linden trees. But one linden tree appeared to be wounded. It was as if it was missing one of its arms. Instead of a branch, there was a deep scar.

The old man stopped. He recognised this tree. Many years ago, he had broken a little branch off it. And now this tall, shapely tree was missing one of its limbs. There were fewer green leaves on it, fewer linden flowers, and fewer buzzing bees, because he had broken that branch. There was less joy in the world.

The old man sighed. He stood and looked up the avenue. A little boy was running along the road.

The oak by the window

A young forester built a big stone house in the forest and planted an oak tree by the window.

The years passed, the forester's children grew up, the oak grew wide, and the forester became an old man.

After many years, when the forester was a grandfather, the oak had grown so big that it covered the window. It became quite dark in the room where the forester's beautiful young granddaughter lived.

'Please cut that oak tree down, grandpa,' begged the granddaughter. 'It's dark in my room.'

'Tomorrow morning we'll make a start,' answered her grandfather.

Morning came. The grandfather summoned his three sons, his nine grandsons, and his beautiful granddaughter, and said, 'We'll move the house.' And he began to dig under the foundation with a spade. His three sons, nine grandsons, and his beautiful granddaughter all followed suit.

Those poor people

It was still dark—the dawn had not arrived—but Serhiiko's father woke him and said, 'Let's go out to the field. We'll listen to the song of the lark.'

Serhiiko got up quickly and dressed, and they walked to the field. The sky in the east was turning pale, becoming blue and then pink, and the stars were going out. From some distant meadow a little grey ball rose up and flew high in the sky. Suddenly the grey ball lit up like fire in the azure sky, and at that moment the father and son heard enchanting music. It was as if someone had stretched a silver string over the field, and the fiery little bird was touching the string with its wings, sprinkling the field with magic sounds.

Serhiiko held his breath. 'If we were sleeping, would the lark still have sung?' he wondered.

'Dad,' whispered the boy quietly, 'The ones who are still sleeping—can they hear this music?'

'They can't hear it,' whispered his father.

'Those poor people,' said Serhiiko.

Life

Grandma Mariia was dying. She had lived a long life and walked many roads. She had raised five sons and five daughters and cared for thirty-five grandchildren and ten great-grandchildren. Now her hour had come.

One after another her children, grandchildren and great-grandchildren came to her bedside to say farewell.

The grandmother's bed stood by the window. Outside the window, birds were singing, butterflies were flitting here and there, and bees were humming.

A swallow had moulded her nest of mud right on the windowsill. She fed her chicks there. The grandmother had often been visited by her youngest great-grandchild—three-year-old Olia. The old lady had explained to Olia how the swallow built its nest. Olia had observed how the swallow fed her chicks, and had kept asking, 'When are the chicks going to peep out of their nest?' Her great-grandmother had answered, 'Soon. In a few days.'

And then Olia's mother brought her to say farewell to her great-grandmother. Olia understood that they would take her dear great-grandmother to the cemetery, that she would never again see the person she loved so much. But she could not understand the forces that create a human being and then carry them off to oblivion. That was too much for a little girl to understand, and she wept.

'Farewell, Grandma,' said Olia, repeating the words her mother had taught her, and she kissed her great-grandmother's dry, wrinkly hand. At that very moment, a yellow-beaked chick peeped out of the swallow's nest, looked at them with its curious eyes, and cheeped loudly. Olia raised her head, and her tear-filled eyes smiled. He mother also smiled, and so did her father and Grandma Mariia.

'Farewell, little Olia,' said Grandma Mariia quietly, with a smile.

Grandpa Matvii's oak

Grandpa Matvii used to live in our village. He turned eighty and began to feel his strength draining away.

Spring arrived. The old man was sitting on a bench outside his house, when some children came walking by on the way home from school. They were carrying some oak seedlings.

'Could I have one of those seedlings?' asked Grandpa Matvii.

The children gave a seedling to the old man. As they walked on, the children wondered, 'What will he do with that oak seedling? He is so old, so feeble!'

Grandpa Matvii gathered all his strength and planted the oak seedling. He cared for it all through the hot summer. He watered it and fertilised the soil around it. The oak turned green and reached towards the sun.

In the autumn, Grandpa Matvii passed away.

The children who had given him the seedling continued to care for the oak.

Ten years have now passed, and the tree is still referred to as 'Grandpa Matvii's oak.'

To think of others is a beautiful thing.

If everyone thought of bringing joy to others, no one would be miserable.

The man with a warm heart

Two travellers were walking along a narrow path. The blue sea lapped on one side of the path, while, on the other side, grey mountains reached for the sky.

The travellers walked for a long time. They were seeking beauty. One of them was a man with a warm heart; the other was a man with a cold heart. The man with the warm heart looked at the sea, and his eyes opened wide with wonder and tenderness. He said, 'How mighty and eternal the sea is!'

The man with the cold heart said, 'Yes, there's a lot of water in it.'

The travellers came to a grey stone. The eyes of the man with the warm heart lit up with joy. 'Look, what a beautiful flower! This is the beauty we have been seeking.'

'Where do you see a flower?' asked the man with the cold heart, in amazement. 'That's just a grey stone. There's a crack in it, and it is covered in dust. It's just a stone.'

'Yes, it is a stone, but inside it there is a rose,' objected the man with the warm heart. 'We just need to expose it, and free it from its stone prison.'

For many days the man with the warm heart hewed and carved the grey stone, while the man with the cold heart sat and looked mournfully at the sea. Finally, from under the chips of stone, a rose of amazing beauty appeared. It seemed as if the world all around froze in wonder at the beauty the man had freed from its stone prison.

It seemed as if the very mountains reached higher. The waves grew calm, and the boundless sea became like a mirror.

Only the man with the cold heart was indifferent. He touched the wonderful flower with his finger, scratched it with his fingernail, and said, 'Yes, it's a strong old stone.'

A granddaughter for the old cherry tree

A cherry tree grew in the garden. Not far from it, Oles noticed a slender little cherry sapling and asked his grandfather, 'Where did that little tree come from?'

'It grew from a pip,' said his grandfather.

'So, it's the daughter of the old cherry tree?' asked Oles.

'Yes,' said his grandfather.

'And will the old cherry tree have a granddaughter?' asked the boy.

'It will, Oles,' answered the grandfather. 'If you look after the little cherry tree, wait for it to fruit, and plant a pip, the old cherry tree's granddaughter will grow from it.'

Oles thought about it. In his eyes, his grandfather could see tenderness and concern.

'I will grow a granddaughter for the old cherry tree,' said Oles.

The eternal sentry

Next to the wheat field is a grave for the soldiers who fell in a battle to liberate our village from the fascists. Every evening, school students come here to water the flowers. But, for some reason, this evening most of the students did not come to the grave. Only Varia came. She put her watering can down by the monument and waited for her friends, but nobody came. For a long time, Varia looked at the bronze statue of a soldier watching over his brothers' eternal rest. Meanwhile, dusk crept from the gullies across the steppe.

Eventually Varia walked home, but she left her watering can behind. Night came, and the stars twinkled in the sky. On the stroke of midnight, the bronze sentry stepped down from his pedestal, walked around the grave, picked up the watering can, and went to the river. He came back with a full can, watered the flowers, and climbed back on to his pedestal.

Varia woke up at dawn. She remembered that the flowers had not been watered and felt sick at heart. Before the sun had risen, she ran to the grave. She looked at the flowers, at the soil, at the watering can, and froze in astonishment. The flowers had been watered. There were still a few drops of water in the watering can, and the chest of the eternal sentry was still moving slightly, breathing, after walking to fetch water.

The Final Judgement

There was a custom in a certain human society that when a person had lived their life, and it was time for them to die, they appeared before the Final Judge. The Judge decided what would be the legacy of the person who was departing: the love and respect of their fellow citizens, honour and eternal glory, or merely some minor remembrance.

One day, the time came for a hard-working man to die. He came to the Final Judge, and the Final Judge asked him, 'How many years have you lived on this earth?'

'Ninety-nine,' answered the hard-working man.

'Show me your years,' said the Final Judge.

Now this hard-working man had planted a tree every day. For every day he had lived, a tree had flourished. The hard-working man took the Final Judge and showed him all the trees he had planted, one after another. It took many days for the Final Judge to inspect the forest planted by the hard-working man. When he finished inspecting it, he said, 'You have lived a good life. May eternal glory be your legacy in the world.'

The hard-working man died peacefully.

Then the time came for an idle man to die.

'How many years have you lived on this earth?' the Final Judge asked him.

'Ninety-nine,' answered the idle man.

'Show me your years.,' said the Final Judge.

But the idle man had nothing to show. The Final Judge saw only an empty space.

'Well, then, may you be forgotten,' decided the Final Judge.

The idle man died, and in an instant people forgot all about him.

Every person has a duty

Petryk and his mother boarded a train. They were travelling to a distant southern city, to the warm seashore, for a holiday. Petryk's mother made up a bed for herself on one bench, and one for Petryk on another. The boy had supper: a tasty bread roll, a chicken leg and an apple. The gently rocking carriages made him sleepy. Petryk lay down on his soft bed and asked, 'Mum, you said that an engineer operates the train. But who operates it at night? Is it going by itself?'

'An engineer operates it at night as well,' said his mother.

'What?' Petryk was amazed. 'Doesn't he sleep at night?'

'No, Petryk, he doesn't sleep,' said his mother.

'We're sleeping, and he can't? All night?' Petryk was even more amazed.

'That's right. The engineer doesn't sleep all night. If he went to sleep for even one minute the train would crash, and we would be killed.'

'But that doesn't seem right.' Petryk could not understand. 'He must be sleepy.'

'He might be sleepy, but it is his *duty* to drive the train,' said Petryk's mother. 'Every person has a *duty*. Look out the window. See—over there in the field a tractor driver is ploughing the earth. It's night-time, but that man is working. You can see his headlight lighting up the field. Because it is his *duty* to work at night.'

'Do I have a *duty*?' asks Petryk.

'You have a *duty*, too,' said his mother.

'What's my *duty*?' asked Petryk.

'To be a human being,' answered his mother. 'That's the most important thing. To work. To respect and honour your elders. To scorn laziness and carelessness. To love your native land.'

Petryk could not go to sleep for a long time.

Two mothers

Two mothers, one dark-haired, the other fair-haired, were admitted to a small hospital on the outskirts of a big city. They both gave birth to sons. The sons were born on the same day: the dark-haired mother's in the morning and the fair-haired mother's in the evening. Both mothers were happy. They dreamt of their sons' futures.

'I want my son to be famous,' said the fair-haired mother, 'A musician or writer, known throughout the world. Or a sculptor, creating works of art that live forever. Or an engineer, building a spaceship that flies to a distant star … That's what I want to live for.'

'I want my son to be a good person,' said the dark-haired mother, 'One who will never forget his mother and his home. One who will love his country and hate its enemies.'

Each day the mothers were visited by the fathers. They spent a lot of time looking into the little faces of their sons, their eyes shining with happiness, wonder and tenderness. Then they sat by their wives' beds and talked to them in a whisper for a long, long time. By the cribs of newborns, people dream of the future—a happy one of course. After a week, the happy husbands, now fathers, took their wives and sons home.

Thirty years passed. In that same small hospital on the outskirts of a big city the same two women were admitted—one dark-haired and the other fair-haired. Their hair was already turning grey, and their faces were lined with wrinkles, but the women were just as beautiful as they had been thirty years earlier.

They recognised each other. They had both been admitted for treatment in the same ward where they had given birth to their sons three decades earlier. They told each other of their lives. They had both had much joy and even more grief. Their husbands had died at the front, defending their Homeland. But for some reason, in telling of their lives, they did not mention their sons. Finally, the dark-haired mother asked, 'And what did your son become?'

'A famous musician,' replied the fair-haired mother with pride. 'Now he conducts an orchestra that performs in the biggest hall in our city. He's very popular. Haven't you heard of my son?' And the fair-haired mother named the musician. Yes, of course, the dark-haired mother knew the name well. He was quite famous. Not long ago she had read of his great success overseas.

'And what did your son become?' asked the fair-haired mother.

'A grain grower. Or to put it more simply, a machine operator. He operates tractors and combine harvesters, and sometimes works with the stock. From early spring to late autumn, until the snow covers the earth, my son ploughs the earth and sows grain, harvests the crop, and again ploughs the earth, sows and harvests … We live in a village a hundred kilometres from here. My son has two children, a three-year-old boy and a little girl born recently.'

'Still, happiness has passed you by,' said the fair-haired one. 'Your son has become a simple worker that no-one has heard of.'

The dark-haired mother did not reply.

A day had not passed, when the dark-haired mother's son came from the country to visit. He sat on a white bench, in a white coat, whispering with his mother for a long time.

Joy shone in the eyes of the dark-haired mother. She seemed to have forgotten about everything in the world. She held her son's strong, sunburnt hand in her hands and smiled.

As he said good-bye, the son, almost apologetically, took grapes, honey and butter from his bag, and put them on the bedside table. 'Get better soon, mum,' he said in parting, and kissed her.

But no-one visited the fair-haired mother. In the evening, when all was quiet, and the dark-haired mother lay in bed, quietly smiling at her thoughts, the fair-haired one said, 'My son has a concert tonight … If there wasn't a concert, of course he would have come.'

On the evening of the second day, the dark-haired mother was visited once more by her son, the grain grower from a distant village. Again, he sat on the white bench for a long time, and the fair-haired mother learnt that now was a busy time in the field, they were working day and night. Parting with his mother, the son left some honeycomb, a round loaf of white bread, and some apples. The dark-haired woman's face lit up with happiness and her wrinkles softened.

No-one visited the fair-haired mother.

In the evening the women lay silently. The dark-haired one was smiling, but the fair-haired one was quietly sighing, hoping that her neighbour could not hear her.

On the third day, towards evening, the dark-haired mother was again visited by her son, the grain grower from a distant village, who brought two big watermelons, grapes and apples. Her dark-eyed, three-year-old grandson came as well. The son and grandson sat for a long time by the bed of the dark-haired mother. Her eyes shone with happiness, and she appeared to get younger. The fair-haired mother, with an aching heart, heard the grandson tell his grandmother how yesterday he had spent half a day with his father on the 'captain's bridge' of the combine harvester.

'I'm going to operate a combine harvester, too,' said the boy, and his grandmother kissed him.

The two mothers stayed in hospital for a month. Every day the grain grower from a distant village visited his mother, bringing a son's smile, and it seemed that his mother was getting better from that smile alone.

No-one visited the fair-haired mother.

The dark-haired mother recovered in a month and was discharged from hospital, but the doctors told the fair-haired mother she needed to stay longer.

The son came for the dark-haired mother. He brought several large bunches of red roses and gave them to the doctors and nurses. Everyone in the hospital was smiling.

Parting with the fair-haired mother, the dark-haired one said, 'I feel so sorry for you.'

Grandma's embroidery

It was a sunny day, probably a Sunday, because everybody was at home: mum, dad, my brother and sister. Hanging above a small window was a beautifully embroidered linen cloth, a *rushnyk*.[93] I can still recall the image embroidered on that *rushnyk*: a girl crossing a meadow, carrying two buckets of water on a yoke.

I asked my mother about the *rushnyk*, and she told me that it was my grandmother's and had been embroidered by my grandmother's grandmother. That *rushnyk* was over a hundred years old.

Where is it now, that *rushnyk*? Where is that embroidered path, that openwork road?

It seems we are not able to preserve the things that our grandparents and great-grandparents preserved for us.

How are we to live without that path across the meadow, without that road?

How can we move into tomorrow without our heritage?

The cradle

Outside it was bitterly cold. The branches on the apple tree shivered from the frost. On a slender twig, a tiny little packet appeared. A little girl who was feeding a chickadee saw the tiny packet and said, 'What a tiny little bud!'

'People call me a bud,' thought the little boy who was inside the tiny packet that was his swaddling clothes. The winter wrapped him to protect him from the cold and said, 'Wait here till spring.'

Spring came and unwrapped the swaddling clothes from the little boy leaf, and the leaf rose from his tiny cradle. He stretched out his arms, stood up, and turned green. The boy leaf grew not by the day but by the hour. Soon he was as big a sparrow's egg, and then bigger than a pigeon's egg.

He basked in the sunlight and bathed in the rain. In no time at all he had grown into a young adult leaf and proudly trembled in the spring breeze, stretching ever upwards.

One day at dawn, the leaf looked down at his feet and noticed something tiny, brown, and transparent, like the head of an ant. This tiny, brown, transparent thing was stuck to the leaf's feet.

'Who are you?' asked the young leaf.

'I am your cradle,' answered the tiny, brown, transparent thing. 'Your swaddling clothes are still here too.'

The great big green leaf, trembling in the spring breeze, bent down and thought hard. He remembered something unimaginably distant and dear. He remembered his cradle and became tender and sad.

The woodpecker and the little girl

A woodpecker built a nest in an old maple tree. Next to the tree was a large apple orchard. In it were many young apple trees. The woodpecker noticed that a little girl often came to one of the little trees to water it.

One day the little girl came to the tree and burst into tears. The woodpecker was surprised.

'Why are you crying, little girl?' it asked.

'Of course, I'm crying,' she said. 'The apple tree has withered and died.'

'But there are so many apple trees!' exclaimed the woodpecker, even more surprised. 'Why does it matter if one of them has withered?'

'But it was my apple tree,' said the little girl. 'I planted it and watered it.'

'What do you mean, it's yours?' asked the puzzled woodpecker. 'I don't understand.'

'And you never will understand. Nothing on earth belongs to you. You only have your baby chicks. They are the only thing you invest your heart and soul in. But people invest themselves in everything: in an apple tree, in a rose bush, in a birdhouse, even in a sweet watermelon.'

'Could a person even invest themselves in me?' asked the woodpecker.

'Yes, even in you,' said the little girl.

'How could they invest themselves in me?' asked the woodpecker.

'By loving you,' said the little girl. 'By making friends with you. By telling stories about you.'

Why don't you display this embroidery?

Little Katrusia's mother was rearranging the linen in their cupboard, when Katrusia noticed a *rushnyk*,[94] a large piece of cloth embroidered with hop flowers and ears of wheat.

'Oh, what a beautiful *rushnyk*!' whispered Katrusia. 'Why haven't I seen it before? Why don't you hang it on the wall, mum?'

'My mother gave me that *rushnyk* when I married,' said her mother, thoughtfully.

'Didn't your mother hang it on the wall?' asked Katrusia.

'My mother didn't hang it on the wall either, because it was given to her by my grandmother when my mother was getting married.'

Katrusia gently touched the hop flowers and gave a sigh.

The immortal mother

On a towering bank of the Dnipro River is a small mound of earth—a grave. A nineteen-year-old soldier named Petro Petrenko is buried there. He was killed in a fierce battle at a crossing point over the Dnipro. As he died, he asked to be buried on that lofty riverbank, with a view of his native village.

'My mother lives there,' he whispered, and died.

Every day, from that large village by the Dnipro, his mother visited his grave. She came early every morning, as the sun was rising. She placed flowers at her son's head, prayed, and walked back home. The mother always came, on hot summer days, and in bitter frosts.

But eventually the mother's final hour arrived. She died and was buried.

But the path to Petro Petrenko's grave did not become overgrown, and every day, as before, fresh flowers appeared on his grave.

'Who is bringing flowers to his grave?' wondered a young girl. 'His mother has died.'

'He has an immortal mother,' replied Grandpa Karpo, a wise, grey-haired old man. 'He has an immortal mother.'

The eternal poplar

A very old poplar tree grows by the road near our house. In winter, its bare branches rustle anxiously, but in spring the poplar is covered with green leaves.

For as long as I can remember, that poplar has been standing by the road like a sentry. I asked my mother, 'How old is our poplar? Who planted it?'

'I don't know,' answered my mother. 'It has been growing by the road for as long as I can remember.'

So, I asked my grandfather, 'Grandpa, how old is our poplar? Who planted it?'

'I don't remember,' answered my grandfather. 'It has always been there by the road. And I hope it keeps growing there, giving people joy. A good person planted that poplar. I can remember playing under it as a little boy, and your mother and her friends braided garlands under it, and now, you are playing in its shade.'

The green meadow

When I hear the word 'Homeland', I am reminded of a green meadow. That meadow used to seem so big to me, limitless, as if it was the whole world. The sun shone in the blue sky. The carpet of green was dotted with yellow, blue and pink flowers. Bees buzzed, and huge, brightly coloured butterflies flitted here and there. I used to stand on the bank of that great green ocean, and my eyes absorbed all the beauty that so excited me.

A day in childhood seems endless, and a meadow limitless. A field stretches as far as the eye can see.

Not long ago, in springtime, I went to that same meadow. The same green grass, the same flowers, the same butterflies. And the sun was shining in the deep blue sky, and the bees were buzzing. But for some reason it all seemed small, like a child's toy.

Why is that? Probably because the most delicate shoots of the tree that we call our Homeland grow during childhood. In childhood, the subtlest, the most delicate colours of our native land are revealed to us. Remember your childhood, and you will approach the limitless ocean of your native land.

A mother at her son's grave

An elderly lady came to a large Ukrainian village on the right bank of the Dnipro River. She had travelled from far away. She was met at the station by the most respected people in the village.

This lady was the mother of a young soldier named Petro Ivanov. Many years ago, when our army was advancing from beyond the Dnipro, he was the first to cross the river and take up a position by a large rock on the riverbank. He battled with the fascists for several hours. He was wounded in the arm and the leg, the head and the chest. He was bleeding heavily, but he kept shooting and destroying the enemy.

When his comrades came to his aid, he died from his wounds. They buried eighteen-year-old Petro Ivanov where he lay.

And now his elderly mother had come to this village on the Dnipro.

They brought her bread and salt, took her by the arm, and led her to a large rock on the bank of the Dnipro.

The mother went down on her knees by a small grave covered in flowers. For several minutes she was silent, closing her eyes. Then she bent to the ground and picked up a little fragment of stone, chipped off many years ago by a bullet. She clutched the fragment in her hand and laid her hand on her heart. Her lips whispered soundlessly.

At that moment all the villagers, whoever they were, were frozen in respectful silence, because the mother was mentally talking with her son. She was speaking words to him which nobody would ever hear, and which are known only to mothers.

She was a mother by the grave of her soldier son.

When you see a mother by the grave of her soldier son, stop and stand in silence while she is on her knees.

During those moments she is thinking of the fate of humanity.

Their mother's field

A mother had two sons—one older, one younger.

When the sons married, the mother gave each of them a field. It so happened that the older son's field was one metre wider than the younger son's field.

The younger son nursed a grievance, because every autumn he harvested three bags less wheat than the older son.

With each year his grievance grew, and it turned into hatred. The brothers started hating each other—that is what three bags of wheat can do. They avoided each other. When the older brother was working in his field, the younger brother did not go out. When the younger brother was turning the soil, the older one stayed at home.

The mother lived far away on the other side of the forest. She had a field there, which she worked as well as she could.

She heard through her neighbours that her sons hated each other. Several times she went to visit them to try and make peace between them, but the older son would not listen to her suggestion that he give half of the extra metre of land to the younger son.

But then, one hot summer day, on the eve of the harvest with all its toil, the sons heard some grave news: a plague of locusts had come from a distant land to their mother's field and had eaten every last grain.

The older brother came to the younger brother and said, 'Brother, have you heard about our mother's misfortune?'

'Yes, I have,' answered the younger brother.

'What are you thinking of doing?' asked the older brother.

'We need to make peace, that's what,' said the younger brother.

'That's why I have come to see you,' said the older brother joyfully. 'Now that misfortune has visited our mother's field, we need to forget our differences and bury our hatred in the ground.'

The brothers went out to the boundary between their two fields, dug a hole, and buried their hatred in it.

As soon as their hatred was buried, the brother's thought with amazement, 'What do we need this boundary for? Why don't we work our fields in common and share the harvested wheat?'

The brothers destroyed the boundary. They harvested the wheat, milled it, and divided it into three parts. They took one part each and carted the third part to their mother.

Because when misfortune visits your mother's field, you need to forget all differences, anger, resentment, and hatred.

You only have one mother

There were three hundred cows in a herd, and all of them were grey. The cowherds could not tell them apart, so in order to identify each cow, they gave each one a name and wrote it on the cow's left side: Star, Daisy, Kindly, Tender, Violet ...

During the night, one of the cows gave birth. As soon as the calf was born, he went straight for his mother's udder to suckle some milk. The cow licked him all over and chased flies away from him with a flick of her tail. The calf would not leave his mother even for a second. When he lay down at night to rest, the cow watched over him, guarding his sleep.

One day, the calf became separated from his mother. The herd continued grazing and, for some reason, the mother did not seek out her calf. He mooed pitifully, scanning the herd with anxious eyes. Then he started running around. He approached one cow after another, smelling each one and then moving on. Eventually he found his mother.

'How did he recognise her?' young Yurko asked Grandpa Panas, an old shepherd.

'He recognised her because you only have one mother,' answered Grandpa Panas.

A nightingale's nest

Our soldiers were driving fascists from our native land. The enemy resisted fiercely. We were advancing through a forest. Fascist mines and shells exploded in our path.

A young soldier named Mykola, a youth eighteen years of age, stood under a silver birch tree. He was resting his machine gun in a fork of the birch tree and shooting at the enemy. A little bird lived in the birch tree, and her nest was shaking next to the machine gun. The bird was hiding behind the nest, looking with her bead-like eyes now at the soldier, now at her chicks peeping out of the nest.

Somewhere nearby a mine exploded. A piece of shrapnel sliced off the narrow branch supporting the nest. The branch and nest dropped onto a soft blanket of fallen leaves. The little bird hovered over the nest, twittering anxiously, while her little chicks opened their beaks wide and cheeped piteously.

The enemy was retreating, but the battle was still raging just beyond a hill. The young soldier removed his machine gun from the birch tree and leant it against the trunk. He stepped up to the chicks and carefully lifted the broken branch. Disentangling the nest from the branch, he attached it to another branch of the birch tree. He took some string from his kit bag and tied the nest on so it would not fall, covering the string so that the bird would not notice it.

'I know what those birds are like … If they notice a human being has been repairing their nest, they may abandon their chicks,' said Mykola, smiling.

When the soldier advanced towards the thunder of the battlefield with his machine gun, the bird settled by the nest and jumped into it. 'She hasn't abandoned them,' said the young man, looking back for a moment.

That night, during a moment of quiet, the soldier told us about the birds in his home village, and tenderness shone in his eyes.

Excursion to Kaniv

The grade five students were preparing for an excursion to Kaniv. They were very happy. They were going to see so many new and exciting things. They were going to visit the grave of Taras Shevchenko.

Galia wanted to go with them, but suddenly her mother fell seriously ill. Galia came to school sad, with eyes red from crying.

'Why are you so sad?' asked her friends.

'Mum is really sick. I won't come on the excursion,' she said.

The children were sad. How can you be excited and have fun when your friend has such grief to bear?

The children decided to wait until Galia's mother recovered, and then go on the excursion.

Three weeks passed. Galia's mother recovered. The class went on the excursion, and Galia went with them.

You may be very happy about something, while another person may be grieving. To understand another person's grief is a beautiful quality in a human being.

This is no time to die

As the fascists retreated from the village of Ivanivka on the banks of the Dnipro River, they razed it to the ground. They burnt down the houses, cut down the trees and took them away. The school was burnt down as well. The local people made dugouts to live in, but where were the children to study?

The largest dugout was set aside for a school, but there were no desks, tables, or blackboards for it. An old teacher took on the difficult task of raising a school from the ashes. He went from one dugout to another, asking people to give him small planks or boards to make some school desks.

By some miracle, seventy-year-old Grandma Maryna's coffin had survived in her cellar. Back then, there was a custom among our old people to have a coffin prepared long before they were expected to die. Grandma Maryna had hidden her coffin in the cellar, and it was still there.

The old teacher came to Grandma Maryna and asked her if she had any small planks that could be used to make desks for the school. The old lady brought her coffin up from the cellar and gave it to the teacher. 'This is no time to die,' she said. 'We must get on with our lives. Our people need first to regain their strength, and then we can think about dying.'

Three student desks were made from that pine coffin. Twelve children began to study at the school. And Grandma Maryna lived for another twenty years.

No-one can kill the gift of song

In the Land of Green Meadows lived a happy nation of singers. They grew grain and sang songs. Each person had a little folk pipe.

But one day, the Land of Green Meadows was visited by Life-Eater, who hated joy. As soon as someone started singing or playing on their pipe, he crept up behind them, grabbed their song, and stuffed it into his mouth. That is why he was called Life-Eater. Wherever he went, songs died.

The Life-Eater swallowed all the songs. Only one pipe remained in the Land of Green Meadows. A little boy buried it in the ground and whispered, 'Keep quiet, and then we can defeat the Life-Eater together.'

Everything was silent in the Land of Green Meadows. The Life-Eater, who hated joy, was pleased. Even the sun grew dim.

But then, where the boy had planted his pipe, green wheat grew and developed ears of grain. The ears of grain began to sing like pipes. Throughout the Land of Green Meadows, the earth sang, and the sky sang.

The people were overjoyed. They all made new pipes and began to play songs on them.

The Life-Eater, who hated joy, lay in the full sun, his tummy aching from all the songs he had swallowed. When he heard everyone singing, he was so angry that he burst like a balloon.

His son's portrait

Old Ivan Dorofiiovych has been on duty at the factory entrance for many years. He checks everyone's passes.

Next to the entrance is the honour board. The portraits of the best workers hang there. For the past two years, a portrait of Ivan's son, a young lathe operator, has hung there. The old man's heart has glowed whenever he has looked at his son's portrait.

But for several days now, Ivan has not smiled when he sees his son's portrait. He has frowned. It is difficult for him to look at it. His son has left his wife and young child for another woman.

His son's wife comes through the entrance. She sees Ivan Dorofiiovych, bows her head, and shows her pass without greeting him. Ivan Dorofiiovych sees the suffering in her eyes.

He takes a stepladder, removes his son's portrait from the honour board, takes the picture out of its frame, and tears it to pieces.

The old man and Death

There once lived an old grandfather. He was one hundred years old. One day Death learnt that such an old man was still living. She went to him and said, 'It is time for you to die, Grandpa.'

'Let me prepare myself for death,' said the old man.

'Alright,' agreed Death. 'How many days do you need?'

'Three days,' answered the old man.

Death was curious to see what the old man would do. How would he prepare himself to die?

The first day came. The old man went out into the garden, dug a hole, and planted a tree.

'What will he do on the second day?' wondered Death.

The second day came. The old man went into the garden again, dug another hole, and planted another tree.

'What will he do on the third day?' wondered Death impatiently.

The third day came. Once again, the old man went out into the garden, dug a hole, and planted a tree.

'Who are you planting these trees for?' asked Death. 'You're going to die tomorrow!'

'For other people,' answered the old man.

Death took fright and fled into the dark forest.

The woodpecker without kith or kin

Many woodpeckers lived happily together in a sunny grove. Each one had a nest. In each nest lived a male woodpecker and a female woodpecker. In summer they raised little woodpecker chicks. As soon as the chicks left their nest, their mother and father taught them how to find beetles under the bark of trees.

There was one carefree woodpecker in the grove who had no nest and no female woodpecker to keep him company. All through the summer he flew by himself, looking for beetles. When winter came, he flew to another grove. All the woodpeckers there were surprised and asked him, 'Where have you come from, Woodpecker? Where is your grove? Where are your wife and your children?'

The carefree woodpecker tapped on an oak tree in reply and began to sing:

I stay where I wish,
I fly where I wish.
I have no wife,
And I have no kids.
It's better to be free,
Don't you see?

The woodpeckers now understood. They said, 'If you have no wife or kids, you don't have a grove either. You have no kith or kin.'

Ever since, that is what they have called the carefree woodpecker: 'No kith or kin'.

The ploughman and the mole

A ploughman was ploughing the land. A mole crawled out of his burrow and was amazed: a huge field had already been ploughed, but the ploughman kept ploughing and ploughing. The mole decided to find out how much land the man had ploughed and set out across the ploughed field. He walked until evening, but he did not reach the end of the field, and finally he returned to his burrow.

The next morning, he crawled out of his burrow, sat down by the path and waited for the ploughman to come by. He asked him, 'Why have you ploughed such a vast field, and why do you keep ploughing?'

The ploughman answered, 'I am not just ploughing for myself, but for others.'

The mole was surprised. 'Why do you plough for others? Let each person work for themselves. I dig a burrow for myself, and each mole digs their own burrow.'

'But you are moles, and we are people,' answered the ploughman, and he began a new furrow.

A man brought life

In the middle of the green steppe, there was a dark island of grey called the Dead Field. From time immemorial, nothing had grown in that field because there was so much salt in the soil. Currents of hot air rose from the baked clay. Not a blade of grass, not a single grasshopper, not a single flower, no living thing was to be found in the Dead Field. No lark ever sang over the Dead Field; crows avoided it; and the sky above it was not blue, but grey.

But then a man came to the to the Dead Field. He brought a basket of fertile black soil and sprinkled it over the earth. He brought a second basket, a third, a tenth. The days, months and years passed, and the man kept bringing black soil to the Dead Field, from morning till night. He spread black soil all over the field and sowed wheat there.

And a miracle happened. The Dead Field turned green. The wheat rustled and produced ears of grain. The grasshoppers sang, the grey sky turned blue, and a lark began to sing above the ripening crop. Larks all over the world listened to its song. It sang that there is nothing in the world stronger than a human being.

The indomitable human spirit

A man was dying from thirst in the desert. All alone, like a grain of sand, overcome with unbearable pain, he closed his eyes and lay on the burning sand. He knew he was dying.

Hard on his heals came Death—a bony old woman with a scythe. The man opened his eyes and saw her next to him.

Death smiled, opened her terrifying dark mouth, and said, 'Before death, you can satisfy your final wish, Man, to drink a mouthful of cold spring water. But if you have the courage and fortitude, instead of a mouthful of water you can wish for anything else you like. Whatever you wish for in place of a mouthful of water, that wish will be granted.'

And Death brought some chilled water to his lips.

The man said, 'I want to know how to find water in the desert. Reveal that secret to me, if you know it, and then take my life.'

Death was amazed at this human wish.

'All right,' she answered, 'I will reveal that secret to you. But what good will it do you? As soon as you find out how to obtain water, you will die.'

'That is my business,' said the man, and the light of hope burned in his eyes.

Death saw that his eyes shone with such mighty strength of spirit, such faith in life, and such hope for the future, that she retreated in horror from the man. She crept away and disappeared in the darkness of the desert.

At that moment the man heard the bubbling of a spring under the layer of sand upon which he lay. Digging up the sand and satisfying his thirst, he went in search of other people, so as to tell them, as soon as possible, where that source of life was hidden.

Khmara's field

There once lived a tractor driver named Petro Khmara. For forty years he worked a huge field that stretched from the village all the way to the forest. He ploughed, sowed, harvested grain and fertilized the soil. He was the first in the field to meet the spring, the first to greet the winter.

People even called the field where Petro Khmara worked 'Khmara's field'.

Petro Khmara died, and the whole village attended the funeral for the old tractor driver. And by the forest, on the edge of Khmara's field, the grateful people put up a bronze statue of Petro Khmara.

Early one Sunday morning, little Petryk went with his mother into the forest. The sun was just rising when Petryk and his mother reached Khmara's field.

'Mum,' asked Petryk, 'Why did Petro Khmara love the land so much?'

'Because he loved people most of all,' she said.

Petryk took a handful of soil from Khmara's field and started thinking.

All graves are human

Little Olia and Serhiiko often walked to the cemetery with their mother and father to visit their grandfather's grave. The cemetery is on a hill, and the soil there is dry, infertile and stony. Nothing much ever grows there. They always took four watering cans from home, two grown-up ones, as the children would say, and two children's ones. They filled them with water, carried them up the hill, and watered the rose bushes on their grandfather's grave.

Next to their grandfather's grave was another grave: abandoned, forgotten and overgrown. The watchman said that it belonged to an old lady who had died without any relatives, close or distant. The children's father said, 'Let's weed this grave.'

They pulled out all the weeds, and the next Saturday their mother brought a little pot with some rose cuttings for planting. They planted a rose bush and watered it whenever they visited their grandfather's grave.

'Why are we watering flowers on a stranger's grave?' asked Serhiiko.

'There is no such thing as a stranger's grave,' answered his father. 'All graves are human.'

Bread is work

Nine-year-old Mykola took a piece of bread and began to throw it at a pear tree. He wanted to knock the ripe fruit from the tree. His grandfather came up to him and asked, 'What are you doing, Mykola?'

The boy hung his head with shame. He knew he was doing something wrong but had hoped no-one would see him throwing the bread.

'Pick up the bread,' ordered his grandfather.

Mykola picked it up. The bread was covered in soil.

'Do you have a clean handkerchief?' asked his grandfather.

The boy took a clean handkerchief from his pocket.

'Wrap the bread up in your handkerchief,' said the old man.

Mykola wrapped the bread in his handkerchief.

'Now take that bread wrapped in your handkerchief home,' said his grandfather. 'Put it in a cupboard where you keep your valuable things. Keep that piece of bread until you grow up and have children of your own. Teach your children and grandchildren that bread stands for work, honour, and human life, and that to scorn it is a great evil.'

'Thank you for the lesson, Grandpa,' said the boy quietly, and carried home the piece of bread wrapped in his handkerchief.

Mykola kept that piece of bread for many years. When his two sons were old enough to understand the meaning of work and honour, he told them, 'This bread is the most valuable thing. The grain from which it was made was grown by your great grandfather. Respect and care for bread. It is the fruit of human work.'

What do people live for?

It was a quiet autumn evening. The sun was setting. A flock of cranes was wending its way across the blue sky. Grandma was sitting on a bench by the fence, admiring the sunset. I asked her, 'Grandma, what do people live for?'

Grandma chuckled and said, 'For eternal life.'

I did not understand. 'What do you mean, "eternal life"?' I asked.

Grandma said, 'Come with me into the garden.'

We went into the garden. The marigolds had almost finished flowering. Grandma collected a bunch of dry seed heads and wrapped them in a bundle.

'Wait until spring,' she said, and she left the marigold seeds in a dry place.

Spring came, and we sowed the seeds in a flower bed. Little plants appeared. They grew tall and flowered, producing beautiful marigold flowerheads. Now they were even more beautiful than they had been in the autumn.

'People also live so that their beauty can live eternally,' said Grandma. 'Parents live to educate their children. And when their children grow up, they will also raise children, so that the human race can live eternally.'

'And what does the human race live for?' I asked.

'For happiness,' she said.

Because I am a human being

It was getting dark. Two travellers were walking along a road—a father and his seven-year-old son. In the middle of the road lay a stone. The father did not notice the stone and tripped, hurting his foot. He was in pain. Groaning, he walked around the stone, took his son's hand, and kept going.

The next day the father and son came back along the same road. The father again did not notice the stone, and again tripped and hurt his foot.

On the third day father and son took the same road again. When they were still some distance from the stone, the father said to his son, 'Be careful, son. We must walk around that stone.'

They reached the spot where the father had tripped and hurt his foot.

The father and son slowed down, but the stone was no longer there. By the side of the road sat a grey-haired old man.

'Grandpa,' said the boy, 'You didn't see a stone here?'

'I moved it off the road,' said the old man.

'Did you also trip and hurt your foot?' asked the boy.

'No, I didn't trip and hurt my foot,' answered the old man.

'Then why did you move the stone?' asked the boy.

'Because I'm a human being,' said the old man.

The boy stopped in thought.

'Dad,' he asked, 'Aren't you a human being?'

Who is the most skilful craftswoman?

This happened a long time ago. In a village in Ukraine, the girls and women decided to show off their skills. They agreed that on Sunday they would all come to the village square, and that each would bring the finest thing they had made with their own hands: an embroidered cloth, lace, linen, a tablecloth or an item of clothing.

When Sunday arrived, all the girls and women came to the square. They brought many amazing things. The elders who had been entrusted with the task of naming the most skilful craftswomen could not believe their eyes—there were so many talented girls and women. The wives and daughters of rich men brought bed covers embroidered in gold and silver, and fine lace curtains with images of wonderful birds.

But, to everyone's surprise, the victor was Maryna, the wife of a poor peasant. She did not bring embroidery or lace, though she was skilled in those crafts as well. She brought her five-year-old son Petrus, and he brought a lark that he had carved from wood. When Petrus lifted the lark to his lips and blew on it, the little bird chirped and sang just like a living bird. Everyone on the square listened with bated breath, while above the square, in the blue sky, a real lark sang, attracted by the song from below.

Someone who creates an intelligent and kind human being is the most skilful craftswoman. That was the decision of the elders.

ENDNOTES

1 The original source for this passage is Sukhomlynsky (1989) *Kak vospitat' nastoyashchego cheloveka* [How to educate a genuine human being], p. 144. This work was originally written in Russian. Sukhomlynsky is here making a play on the Russian words *pitomets* (a child who is being educated), *pitat'* (to feed), and *vospitat'* (to educate), which all share a common lexical root (*-pit-*). In Ukrainian, the corresponding words are *vikhovanets* (a child who is being educated), *zhyvyty* (to feed) and *vykhovuvaty* (to educate). The main point is that education is viewed as a process of nourishing a child's development through the provision of meaningful experiences.

2 A Ukrainian national flower, the *kalyna* is an evergreen shrub with red berries.

3 Rhythmic, rhyming phrases are a feature of Slavic fairytales.

4 The Ukrainian word for a squill, which is similar to a snowdrop, is *prolisok.*

5 Similar weather conditions in North America and Europe are sometimes referred to as an 'Indian summer'.

6 The cherry tree in question is a sour cherry (*vyshnia*). In Ukraine the sour cherry tree is symbolic and sacred, and almost every private house has one in the garden.

7 A *kopiika* (or kopeck) was one hundredth of a *karbovanets* (or ruble), and roughly equivalent to a cent.

8 In the original, Sukhomlynsky uses a saying that literally translates as 'My house is on the edge of the village', which means 'It does not concern me' or 'It's none of my business'.

9 A slightly different version of this story is contained in 'All good people are one family' (p. 127).

10 When Sukhomlynsky was writing, Ukraine was part of the Soviet Union, where religious observance was discouraged, and instead of a Christmas tree, families had a New Year's tree. This tradition still exists in some countries that were formerly part of the Soviet Union.

11 Sakhalin is near Japan, and the story is set in Ukraine, so Olia was moving a distance of about 7,000 km as the crow flies.

12 '*Zhovti vody*' literally means 'yellow waters'. The Battle of Zhovti

Vody was the first significant battle of the Khmelnytsky Uprising, a Cossack rebellion led by Bohdan Khmelnytsky that took place between 1648 and 1657 in what was then the eastern territories of the Polish–Lithuanian Commonwealth and is now part of Ukraine. The Khmelnytsky Uprising led to the creation of a Cossack Hetmanate in Ukraine. The battle of Zhovti Vody took place in 1648, in an area about 50 km to the south of Sukhomlynsky's school in Pavlysh.

13 The war in question is World War II (1939–1945).

14 Baba Yaga is a witch from Slavic folklore who appears in fairytales. She lives in a hut that stands on chicken's legs.

15 Sukhomlynsky is here referring to the occupation of Belarus and Ukraine by German troops from 1941 to 1944. Local people who actively resisted the German occupation were referred to as partisans.

16 A *pyrizhok* (plural *pyrizhky*) is a type of baked or fried bun (a little like a pastie) made of yeast dough. It can have various fillings, including vegetables (usually potato, cabbage or cabbage with egg and onion), and cottage cheese and fruit (usually apples, sour cherries, plums, pears, strawberries or raspberries).

17 *Varenyky* (plural) are a delicious national Ukrainian dish made by filling non-sweet dough with a variety of fillings. Common fillings are fried sauerkraut, mashed potato, mushrooms, sweet cottage cheese, and fruit, especially sour cherries.

18 *Borshch* is a Ukrainian national dish, a beet soup made on the basis of a meat broth together with potatoes, carrots, cabbage, onions, bell pepper, tomato juice, and parsley. It is more than just a dish, with UNESCO suggesting that it is 'part of the fabric of Ukrainian society, cultural heritage, identity and tradition'. Each region of Ukraine has its own *borshch* recipe, and while its ingredients may vary, beets, potatoes, carrots and cabbage are always included.

19 See endnote 10.

20 In Ukrainian, this story is called *Cholovik-pustotsvit*, *cholovik* meaning 'man', and *pustotsvit* being a flower that produces no fruit or seeds.

21 The reference here is to World War II, when Germany invaded the Soviet Union. It has been estimated that about 27 million people died in the Soviet Union as a result of the war, and one estimate places the number even higher, at nearly 42 million.

22 During World War II, the Germans occupying the Soviet Union were commonly referred to as fascists.
23 In the Soviet Union, all able bodied young men were called up for military service for a period of from two to three years.
24 In the Soviet Union, nearly all mothers worked, even during the 1950s and 1960s, when Sukhomlynsky was writing. Kindergartens and creches were rare in rural areas, and it was not uncommon for infants to be left in the care of older siblings, even when the siblings were themselves still young children.
25 The first of May is International Workers' Day. It was a major public holiday in the Soviet Union.
26 Towards the end of World War II (1939-1945).
27 In the Soviet Union, every school student had a diary with a weekly timetable. Students would enter their homework tasks in the diary, and teachers would enter a student's individual marks and special notes for parents about their child's academic progress or any issues they were having at school.
28 In the past, it was common to leave five or six-year-old children at home. Until the 1970s, there were almost no kindergartens in rural areas of the Soviet Union, including Ukraine.
29 In the Soviet Union, children would start school when they were seven. It was common for children to help their parents with household chores from the age of five.
30 See endnote 18.
31 'Natalochka' is a diminutive form of 'Natalia'. Diminutives are commonly used when addressing young children. When Natalia grew up, only those very close to her, such as her mother, would have used the diminutive form, so Sukhomlynsky switches to the more adult form of her name, Natalia.
32 See endnote 29.
33 The greeting that Sukhomlynsky is referring to here comes from a word that means 'to be healthy', 'to thrive', 'to prosper'. The word for 'hello' thus literally means 'be healthy!', 'thrive!' or 'may you live a long life!'
34 Throughout this passage we have translated the words *dostoin* and *nedostoin* as 'acceptable' and 'unacceptable'. The words could also be

translated as 'worthy' and 'unworthy' [of a human being].

35 See endnote 17.

36 See endnote 16.

37 Sukhomlynsky is referring to World War II (1939-1945), so the events took place in 1946. Though Sukhomlynsky does not say so directly (such information openly shared would be considered as a crime in the USSR), there was a famine that year. Some people did not have anything to eat at all, so they would boil grass and other wild flowers to survive.

38 See endnote 7.

39 See endnote 18.

40 See endnote 37.

41 See endnote 18.

42 See endnote 16.

43 'Matviiko' is a diminutive form of 'Matvii' and expresses affection.

44 See endnote 7.

45 See endnote 16.

46 When Vasyl Sukhomlysky was working, in 1950s and 1960s, two-coloured ballpoint pens were extremely rare. School students would mainly use simple ink pens.

47 In some villages, the school only taught classes up to grade eight. Students who wished to complete their secondary education would have to travel to a secondary school further away.

48 See endnote 18.

49 See endnote 16.

50 See endnote 18.

51 In the Soviet Union, the teachers ran classroom journals. Each class had its own journal and the different teachers would enter students' marks into them based on the course they were teaching.

52 In the Soviet Union a funeral procession was accompanied by a band that would play sorrowful music.

53 See endnote 18.

54 See endnote 7.

55 The Dnipro River is the longest river in Ukraine and the fourth-longest river in Europe. It flows from north to south right through the centre of the country, dividing Ukraine into two parts.

56 See endnote 7.
57 See endnote 7.
58 See endnote 17.
59 See endnote 7.
60 See endnote 7.
61 See endnote 7.
62 See endnote 27.
63 See endnote 18.
64 In the Soviet Union, the first day of school was always the first of September, and this is still the case in Ukraine.
65 It was common in the Soviet Union for teachers to keep weak students back after school, so that they could improve their skills, and to help them with the topics they were struggling with.
66 In the Soviet Union, it was a common practice to award the best students with certificates of merit (*pokhvalna gramota* in Ukrainian).
67 In former times, it was common for little children to swim naked in rivers and ponds.
68 This is a reference to a verse by the Ukrainian poet Yakiv Shchogoliv: '*Ніде прилипитись крапельці роси*' [*Nide prylipytys' krapel'tsi rosy*].
69 The Black Sea is a large sea to the south of Ukraine. During Sukhomlynsky's time, children sometimes went to camps on the Black Sea during the summer holidays.
70 In the past, there were no dryers, so people would do their laundry by hand and hang their washed clothes and linen outside on clotheslines. In the absence of a clothesline, some people would dry their clothes on a fence.
71 The Carpathian Mountains are a large mountain range that forms an arc through central Europe. The mountain range is approximately 1500 kilometres long, extending from Slovakia and southern Poland in the east, through western Ukraine, and south into Romania and Serbia. The mountains in the Ukrainian section range in height from around 1000 metres to around 2000 metres.
72 The letters of the Ukrainian alphabet are shown on page 396.
73 See endnote 18.
74 In Ukrainian, the saying 'to hold a stone close to one's chest' means 'to hold a grudge'.

75 See endnote 64.
76 See endnote 18.
77 See endnote 55.
78 There are a lot of burial mounds (known as *kurgan* or *mohyla*) in the Ukrainian steppes. They were built by nomadic tribes that used to live on the territory of present day Ukraine thousands of years ago.
79 See endnote 55.
80 In Ukraine, and in almost all the former republics of the Soviet Union, there were no one-on-one parent-teacher interviews. Every two months, the teacher would conduct a 'parent meeting' attended by all the parents. If a parent had any concerns or a teacher had to discuss something more sensitive with a parent, the parent could also have a private conversation with the teacher after the parent meeting.
81 At the time Sukhomlynsky was writing, grade 10 was the final grade at high school, and most schools combined primary and secondary classes on the same campus.
82 The last bell (Ukrainian – *ostannii dzvinok*) is a traditional ceremony in schools in Ukraine, Russia, and some other countries that were formerly part of the Soviet Union. The celebration is carried out at the completion of studies, but before the final exams. In the former USSR it often took place on 25 May, and in today's Ukraine it usually takes place on the last Friday in May.
83 See endnote 46.
84 See endnote 7.
85 The word that has been translated here as 'Homeland' is *Batkivshchyna*, which derives from the word *batko*, which means 'father'. It could thus conceivably be translated as 'Fatherland'. However, this passage was originally written in Russian, and the Ukrainian word *Batkivshchyna* has been used to translate the Russian word *Rodina*, which is often translated as 'Motherland', and derives from the root *rod*, which relates to the idea of birth and of one's ancestors. The Russian word *Rodina* thus refers to the land of one's birth and of one's ancestors, and might literally be translated as 'birthland', if such a word existed. It has been translated here as 'Homeland' and capitalised to reflect the capitalisation in the original. The other key word in this passage is *Vitchyzna*, which also has paternal connotations. It has been used

to translate the Russian word *Otechestvo*, which means 'Fatherland', and has consequently been translated here as 'Fatherland'. There is a considerable semantic overlap between the words discussed above. In the passages that follow, and in the stories presented later in this section, the translators have allowed themselves the flexibility to use the word 'homeland' to translate both *Batkivshchyna* and *Vitchyzna*, which are semantically almost identical.

86 It is likely that there will be readers who value most of the content of this book, but who feel uncomfortable with the sentiments expressed here. A spirit of nationalism has given rise to terrible wars over recent centuries, and many thoughtful people believe that there are values that are higher than loyalty to one's nation.

Sukhomlynsky and his fellow citizens were subjected to unspeakable atrocities during the Nazi invasion of the Soviet Union, so it is understandable that he places a very high value on being able to defend one's way of life against invaders. It is also true that each individual owes a great debt to their forebears, and to the society that collectively supports their wellbeing. At the same time, it is important that citizens exercise independent moral judgement and are able to criticise their leaders when they perceive them to be acting immorally.

At the time of publication, Ukrainians are again having to defend themselves against a powerful aggressor who threatens to destroy their way of life. In 2014, the Russian Federation annexed Crimea and engaged in military aggression in the Donbas Region, leading to a protracted war in the east of Ukraine. On 24 February 2022, the Russian Federation launched a full-scale invasion of Ukraine and inflicted enormous suffering on the Ukrainian people, committing numerous war crimes, including torturing and killing civilians. That war is still raging at the time of publication. At such times there is clearly a value in courage and in the readiness to defend one's nation.

It is recommended that educators independently evaluate the stories in this section before sharing them with children, as they would any other material. It may help to refer to Sukhomlynsky's thoughts later in this section, where he writes, 'The psychological readiness to courageously face a cruel and implacable enemy comes from our students' courage, endurance, kindness, sensitivity and generosity, not from cruelty and ruthlessness.'

87 In Ukraine, people greet each other with sprigs of willow on Palm Sunday, which is celebrated by Christians one week before Easter Sunday, and marks the beginning of Holy Week.

88 Taras Hryhorovych Shevchenko (1814-1861) was a Ukrainian poet and painter and is considered to be one of the founding fathers of modern Ukrainian literature and the modern Ukrainian language. Born into serfdom, he was assisted to gain his freedom through the intercession of the painter Briullov and studied at the Russian Imperial Academy of Arts in Saint Petersburg, becoming a successful painter. In 1847 he was arrested for writing anti-tsarist poetry and spent ten years in exile in the military, including seven debilitating years at a penal settlement in what is now Kazakhstan. He was pardoned in 1857 and eventually allowed to return to Saint Petersburg in 1858. Shevchenko died in 1861, aged just 47. He is regarded as a Ukrainian national hero.

89 See endnote 71.

90 Polissia is a forested region that overlaps the borders between Ukraine, Belarus and Poland.

91 Majdanek, like Auschwitz and Buchenwald, was part of a huge network of Nazi concentration and extermination camps in which many millions of people were killed, including many Ukrainians. Over a period of four years, some 500,000 persons from 28 countries and of 54 nationalities passed through Majdanek. It is estimated that about 360,000 died there. Approximately 60% died from overwork, starvation, torture, and disease, and approximately 40% were murdered by firing squad or in the gas chambers.

92 The city of Stalingrad (known from 1589–1925 as Tsaritsyn) was renamed Volgograd in 1961.

93 A *rushnyk* is an embroidered or woven towel, commonly 20–50 cm wide and 1–4 m long, usually for decorative or ceremonial purposes.

94 See endnote 93.

RESOURCES

Books

Vasyl Sukhomlynsky, *My Heart I Give to Children*, EJR Language Service Pty. Ltd., Brisbane, 2016.
Vasyl Sukhomlynsky, *Our School in Pavlysh: A Holistic Approach to Education*, EJR Publishing, Brisbane, 2021.
Vasyl Sukhomlynsky, *A World of Beauty: Tales from Pavlysh*, EJR Language Service Pty. Ltd., Brisbane, 2013. (This book is also available in Russian, Ukrainian, Japanese and Chinese language editions.)
Alan Cockerill, *Each One Must Shine: The Educational Legacy of V.A. Sukhomlinsky*, EJR Language Service Pty. Ltd., Brisbane, 2016. (Originally published by Peter Lang, New York, 1999.)
For more information about the above publications, please visit: https://ejr.com.au/publications.

Website

https://theholisticeducator.net/sukhomlynsky/
(This website includes a page with links to the resources listed below, as well as to some Ukrainian language sites.)

YouTube videos

'Sukhomlynsky Lesson'
https://www.youtube.com/watch?v=eCksMOPYzas
'Video clip from the movie "Teacher"'
https://www.youtube.com/watch?v=jtBrS2gBYyE

ABC Radio podcast and associated article

'Vasily Sukhomlinsky: educating the heart, head and hands' (podcast)
https://www.abc.net.au/radio/programs/conversations/conversations-alan-cockerill-rpt/9611188
'Vasily Sukhomlinsky: The Teacher who Changed the World' (article)
https://www.abc.net.au/radionational/programs/archived/conversations/vasily-sukhomlinsky-educating-the-heart/7878410

Online Articles

'Sukhomlinsky and Steiner: A Comparison'. – An article written for the RoSE Journal (Research on Steiner Education).
https://www.rosejourn.com/index.php/rose/article/view/331/315
'Education for the Anthropocene: The Contribution of Vasily Sukhomlinsky' – Chapter 7 (pages 94–110) in the online publication 'International Conversations of Teacher Educators: Collaborations in Education'.
https://www.msvu.ca/wp-content/uploads/2020/05/International-20Conversations20of20Teacher20Educators20Dec2013.pdf

Blog

'In Search of Sukhomlinsky'
http://insearchofsukhomlinsky.blogspot.com.au/
This blog was written by Alan Cockerill, and records his activities during a ten day research trip to Ukraine in October 2009. The final post summarizes the contents of archives in Pavlysh and Kyiv, and may contain useful material for anyone interested in researching Sukhomlynsky's legacy.

Monthly newsletter

https://theholisticeducator.net/Sukhomlynsky/newsletter/
Readers can subscribe to this free monthly newsletter, which contains new translations of extracts from the works of Vasyl Sukhomlynsky, and updates about any new English language publications.

OTHER PUBLICATIONS

http://www.ejr.com.au/publications

MY HEART I GIVE TO CHILDREN

'Now I see the secret of the making of the best persons,
It is to grow in the open air and to eat and sleep with the earth.'

With these words from Walt Whitman's 'Song of the Open Road', Sukhomlynsky closes his account of how he educated young children in a Ukrainian village during the aftermath of World War II.

Sukhomlynsky's masterpiece was many years ahead of its time. It addresses issues such as our relationship with nature, how to nurture children's souls in the face of the sometimes negative influences of mass media, how to help children develop empathy for others, how schools can develop strong relationships with families, how children's brains function and develop, how to foster an intrinsic love of learning, and how to support children who struggle to acquire skills in literacy and numeracy. This classic and inspirational work is addressed to school principals, teachers, and anyone interested in the upbringing of children.

Paperback: ISBN: 978-0-9805885-7-6
Case bound: ISBN: 978-0-6485800-3-4
Available from major online retailers and can be be ordered through your local bookshop.

OUR SCHOOL IN PAVLYSH

A Holistic Approach to Education

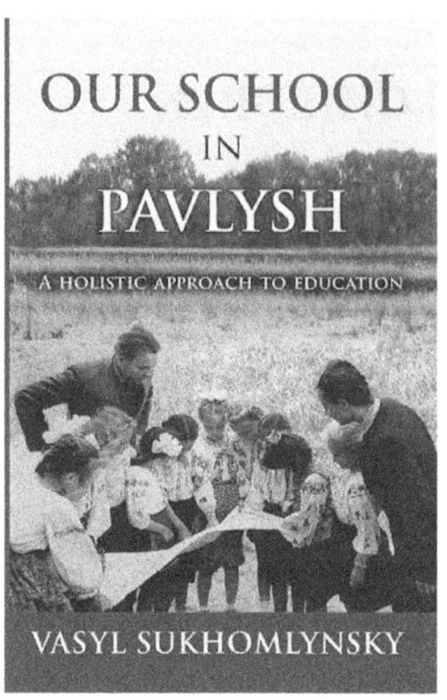

Our School in Pavlysh describes the inspirational work carried out at Pavlysh Secondary School during the 1960s. For Sukhomlinsky's readership of teachers and school principals, the word 'Pavlysh' stood for creative thought, inspiration, and the hope of finding answers to troubling questions. Raising his school from the ashes of World War II, Sukhomlinsky created a system of education that was deeply embedded in the natural environment.

The school fostered the qualities of curiosity, empathy and creativity. One of the thousands of visitors to Pavlysh, a school principal from Armenia, wrote:

'I have spent only one day in this remarkable school where so much is happening, but I have gained as much as I did in four years at the institute.'

Students enrolling in Sukhomlinsky's school became part of a vibrant learning community in which teachers, parents, community members, and the students themselves all played a role in educating each other. Informal, extracurricular activities were extremely important in developing children's talents, building their self-esteem, and providing an experiential background for formal studies. In this environment, students became autonomous, lifelong learners.

Paperback: ISBN: 978-0-6485880-4-1
Case bound: ISBN: 978-0-6485800-5-8
Available from major online retailers and can be ordered through your local bookshop.

EACH ONE MUST SHINE

The educational legacy of V.O. Sukhomlynsky

The definitive English language study of the educational legacy of Vasyl Sukhomlynsky.

There should not be any nobodies— specks of dust cast upon the wind. Each one must shine, just as billions upon billions of galaxies shine in the heavens.

Each One Must Shine is an account of the life and work of Vasyl Sukhomlynsky (1918–1970), one of the most influential educators of the twentieth century. Sukhomlynsky's writings inspired millions of Soviet school teachers, and continue to inspire educators in Russia, Ukraine, and China, where he is one of the most influential foreign educators.

Sukhomlynsky's idealistic vision of human development and his deep love for children led him to develop a holistic system of education that emphasised the moral and aesthetic dimensions of a child's development as well as the physical, intellectual and vocational. He was the principal of a rural school in Pavlysh, in central Ukraine, for twenty-two years, and wrote about his experience in numerous books and articles. His school was visited by thousands of educators from the length and breadth of the Soviet Union and beyond, and his books have been read by millions.

ISBN: 978-0-9945625-9-3
ISBN of forthcoming 2nd edition: 978-0-6455154-6-6
Available from major online retailers and can be ordered through your local bookshop.

A WORLD OF BEAUTY: TALES FROM PAVLYSH

Tales from Pavlysh
a World of Beauty
Vasyl Sukhomlynsky

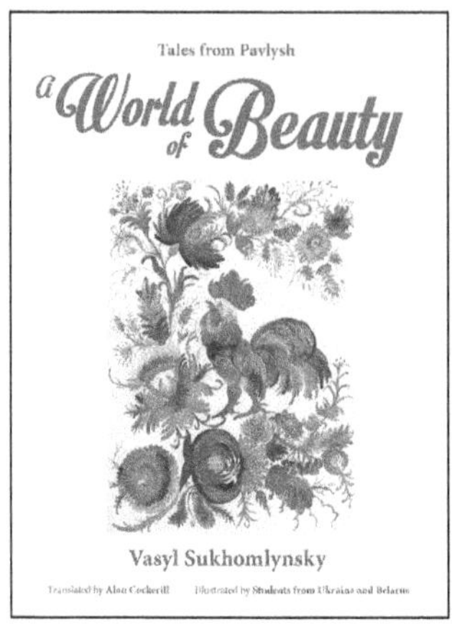

A selection of Sukhomlynsky's little stories for children, beautifully illustrated by students from Ukraine and Belarus.

The lovely illustrations in this book show beauty through the eyes of children. In 2013, thousands of school students in Ukraine, Russia, Belarus and Kazakhstan submitted illustrations for this selection of stories.

Note: This title is also available in Ukrainian, Russian, Japanese and Chinese editions. (For ISBN numbers and searchable English titles, see our website: https://www.ejr.com.au/publications)

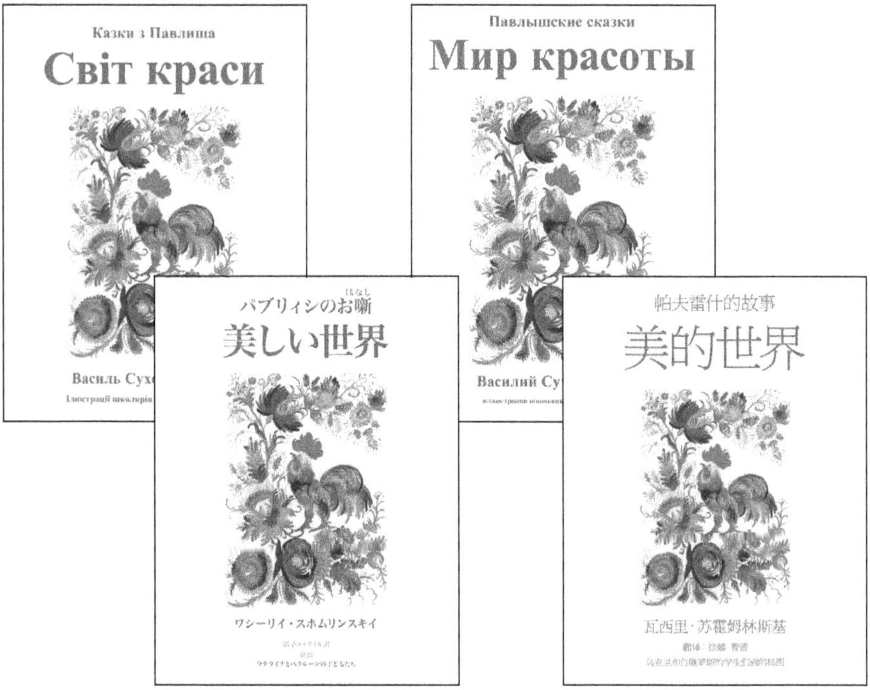
Казки з Павлиша
Світ краси
Павлышские сказки
Мир красоты
パブリィシのお噺
美しい世界
ワシーリイ・スホムリンスキイ
帕夫雷什的故事
美的世界
瓦西里·苏霍姆林斯基

Milton Keynes UK
Ingram Content Group UK Ltd.
UKHW020346031224
452051UK00007B/193